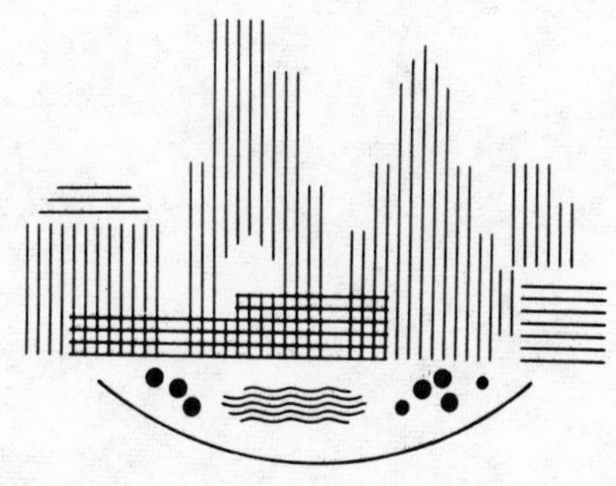

THE RISE OF URBAN AMERICA

THE TENEMENTS OF CHICAGO 1908-1935

Edith Abbott

ARNO PRESS
&
The New York Times

NEW YORK · 1970

Reprint Edition 1970 by Arno Press Inc.

Reprinted by permission of The University of Chicago Press

Reprinted from a copy in The University of Illinois Library

LC# 78-112535
ISBN 0-405-02431-2

The Rise of Urban America
ISBN for complete set 0-405-02430-4

Manufactured in the United States of America

THE TENEMENTS OF CHICAGO
1908–1935

Courtesy of the Chicago Daily News

A CHICAGO TENEMENT AREA

THE TENEMENTS OF CHICAGO

1908-1935

By EDITH ABBOTT

Assisted by

SOPHONISBA P. BRECKINRIDGE

And Other Associates

In the School of Social Service Administration of the University of Chicago

THE UNIVERSITY OF CHICAGO PRESS
CHICAGO ILLINOIS

COMPOSED AND PRINTED BY THE UNIVERSITY OF CHICAGO PRESS
CHICAGO, ILLINOIS, U.S.A.

In Memory of

JULIA CLIFFORD LATHROP

Early resident of Hull-House
Member of the Illinois State Board of Charities
First Chief of the United States Children's Bureau
Wise counselor and friend of the School of Social Service Administration

PREFACE

THIS volume on the history, development, and present condition of the tenement areas of Chicago is the result of a series of studies made over a period of approximately twenty-five years in different sections of the city by members of the faculty and groups of graduate students in the School of Social Service Administration.

These studies were first undertaken at the request of a former chief sanitary inspector (the late Charles B. Ball), who was one of Chicago's most distinguished civil servants, and who continued in office under various mayors and health commissioners of different political parties. Mr. Ball believed that a series of housing inquiries would help to secure support for better tenement-house laws as well as support for better enforcement of those laws.

These studies were also planned to give graduate students in a school of social service the opportunity of studying methods of social statistics and social research by sharing in a real study, undertaken at the request of a public department and carried on with the hope of improving social conditions. Since housing is one of the difficult problems with which social workers must learn to deal, these studies proved to be of great value for training purposes, and one group of students after another participated in them, year after year, with interest, and sometimes with enthusiasm.

There have been several housing reform movements in Chicago during its "century of progress," but very few improvements have come as a result of these efforts. Certainly no one political group can be charged with responsibility for the failure to find the way out of our tenement problems. The survey of the early Health Department at the close of the decade 1870–1880, the efforts of the new social settlements in the decade 1890–1900, the housing-reform enthusiasm that followed the World War, and the later plans that have come in the wake of the great depression, have all had some influence. But they have not yet brought about slum clearance, nor provided, on anything but a pitifully small scale, good homes that workingmen and workingwomen with low wages can afford to rent.

Even without a great program of slum clearance, there is much that the city of Chicago can do to mitigate housing evils: first, the housing code is inadequate; second, the Department of Health does not have, and has not had, a staff of inspectors large enough and competent enough to enforce such legislation as exists. The story of an untrained and inadequate staff of housing inspectors runs through the long history of attempted tenement-house reform in Chicago. The creation of a new tenement-house department has long been needed, but a greatly increased and well-trained staff for our present sanitary department is even more exigent. An attempt has been made in this volume to show the failure, over a long period of years, of the attempted enforcement of such tenement ordinances as we have had. During these studies, 151 city blocks in widely separated neighborhoods were covered by the method of house-to-house canvassing, and 18,225 apartments or one-family dwellings were visited. In every section of Chicago—north, west, south, southwest, northwest—are crowded tenement districts, with the same offensive and outlawed toilet accommodations, damp basements, dark and gloomy rooms, and, everywhere, wretched conditions of overcrowding. Many of the buildings in the districts investigated were old houses built before, sometimes long before, the tenement law of 1902, often overcrowded but not covered by the provisions relating to the construction of tenements. The same conditions, however, were also found in the buildings erected at a later date whose construction should have been regulated by the provisions of the code; but the results of one study after another showed how futile these provisions were and how frequently the law has been disregarded.

Immigration was at high tide when these studies were begun and since many housing reformers seemed to hold the immigrant responsible for tenement evils, special attention was given to the immigrant neighborhoods. The valuable co-operation of the Immigrants' Protective League is gratefully acknowledged, and especially the help of my sister and colleague, Grace Abbott, who was then a resident of Hull-House and director of the League. The immigrants have long been the most numerous of the tenement groups, and some emphasis has been laid in these studies upon the way in which the immigrant colonies developed in Chicago. The importance of the history of the immigrant parish churches is emphasized in the chapter dealing with the tenement districts, since these parochial histories provide some interesting and neglected source materials for the study of the social history of our American cities.

The limitations of this volume are clear. We have attempted some studies of tenement conditions in a great metropolitan area which has, almost within the memory of men now living, grown out of the swamps and the prairies. No attempt has been made here to deal with many important questions related to the problems of slum clearance and housing regulation, such as the problem of speculative landownership and development, city planning, or the planning of the newer integrated neighborhood housing units. Nor is any attempt made to prove that a large public expenditure for slum clearance and for new and better houses and gardens for the families living on low wages, or no wages, will in the long run be counterbalanced by smaller demands for hospitals, juvenile courts, reformatories, courts, and prisons. We have attempted only a study of tenement districts and their history.

It is difficult to express adequately the obligation for generous help of many kinds given over a long period of years. First and foremost, Professor Sophonisba Preston Breckinridge, my long-time colleague and friend, has been associated with these studies through the whole period during which they have been carried. Although it seemed necessary for one person finally to take charge of the organization and presentation of the material, Miss Breckinridge has helped at all times and at many points. These studies were first carried on from Hull-House, and Julia C. Lathrop, who was then living at Hull-House and who was a very active member of the Board of Trustees of the School of Social Service, was especially interested in this work in the early stages. Miss Addams was always interested in the housing problem, and not only welcomed with characteristic enthusiasm the planning of a new attack, but gave our investigators a place to work in and from. The students and social workers who have helped with these studies cannot all be enumerated. An attempt is made in the footnotes of the various chapters to give the names of student-investigators whose material was finally used in this volume, but if some are omitted that should be here, sincere apologies and belated acknowledgments would be extended if this were possible.

The names of some assistants should, however, be given special mention here. Helen Russell Wright, once a student and in recent years a valued colleague, has been a generously helpful consultant from year to year, as student groups have come and gone. Dr. Helen Rankin Jeter, who is now in charge of the registration of social statistics for the Social Security Board in Washington, and Mary Zahrobsky, research assistant, were responsible for the supervision of the very laborious work involved in the tabulation of material. Miss Zahrobsky has been responsible for recent recanvassing and checking of old returns, and in many cases for the final form of the tables. Leila Houghteling, whose untimely death has been a great loss to social work in Chicago, brought a new collection of valuable material on this subject in her study of *The Income and Standard of Living of Unskilled Laborers in Chicago*.

Among former students, many of them now well known in various lines of work, the following names should be listed: Elizabeth Hughes, Eleanor Goltz, Grace P. Norton, Alzada P. Comstock, William L. Chenery, Eunice W. Smith, Katherine F. Kiesling, Evelyn Heacox Wilson, Esther Crockett Quaintance, Alice Quan Rood, Alice Mae Miller, Mary Faith Adams, Berenice Davis, Joseph S. Perry, Milton B. Hunt, Natalie Walker, Helen L. Wilson, Frances Bruton, Nellie Foster, Marion Schaffner, Esther Ladewick, and Dr. F. M. Warner, now Commissioner of Public Welfare in Arizona.

The Russell Sage Foundation of New York made a generous grant to our early research department, which enabled us to undertake these studies and carry them on for the first five years. More recently the Social Science Research Committee of the University of Chicago made it possible for us to bring the material for the different sections of the city together, and to recanvass the areas that had been studied in the pre-war period. Mr. Newcomb and Mr. Lang, research assistants of the Social Science Committee, have been generous about giving the use of some of their maps, of which acknowledgment is made in the text. We are indebted to the Illinois Emergency Relief Commission for permitting the use of a recent relief map; and to the *Chicago Daily News* for allowing us to use several photographs which had appeared in that newspaper. The Index has been prepared by Maud E. Lavery, research assistant, School of Social Service Administration.

Finally, we are indebted for the publication of this volume, again, to the Social Science Research Committee, and also to one of the most generous friends of the School of Social Service, the late Julius Rosenwald, who gave help for our whole series of social service publications, including the present volume, at a time when help was very greatly needed.

EDITH ABBOTT

UNIVERSITY OF CHICAGO

TABLE OF CONTENTS

MAPS AND ILLUSTRATIONS

Queen of the West! by some enchanter taught
To lift the glory of Aladdin's court,
Then lose the spell that all that wonder wrought.

Like her own prairies by some chance seed sown,
Like her own prairies in one brief day grown,
Like her own prairies in one fierce night mown.

—BRET HARTE (1871)

CHAPTER I

THE GROWTH OF THE POPULATION AND TENEMENTS IN A PRAIRIE CITY, 1833–93

Population Growth in Chicago's First Decade; Early Expenses for "Poorhouse and Paupers"; Development of Slum Centers before the Great Fire; The Expanding City Limits; Population Growth through the Century; Homes of the Rich and Poor in 1871; Industrial Development, Immigration, and Overcrowding; The Early Hull-House Group and Housing Reform.

THE growth of the tenement districts of Chicago is, of course, a part of the history of the growth of the great city; and a brief review of the growth and distribution of Chicago's population over the period covering its first century of progress shows the steady development of housing and sanitation problems of many kinds, along with the astonishing growth of this relatively new western metropolis of the nineteenth century. For with a rapidly expanding population in a great industrial center, a tenement-house problem has, in the past, almost inevitably developed.

POPULATION GROWTH IN CHICAGO'S FIRST DECADE

The village of Chicago in 1833 was a small settlement on the western shore of Lake Michigan, at the mouth of the Chicago River. Estimates of the population at that time, before the first official enumeration, range from 100 to 250 inhabitants. When a city charter was obtained and the first local census was taken in July, 1837, returns showed a population of 4,066 people.[1] There were more than twice as many men as women, with only 1,800 white men and only 845 white women over twenty-one years old counted at that time, for women were safer in settled communities. There were, all told, about 450 buildings in the city, and 398 of these were dwellings. But these buildings were, for the most part, cheap frame structures referred to by visitors as "mere shanties."

[1] See Weston A. Goodspeed and Daniel D. Healy, *History of Cook County, Illinois* (1909), I, 135, and see also Everett Chamberlin, *Chicago and Its Suburbs* (1874).

In the first decade of her existence (1833–43), various factors were responsible for the growth of the new city. The "Indian War" of 1832 had brought General Winfield Scott and his soldiers west, and had awakened an interest in western development. The "western fever" had become epidemic in the eastern part of the United States and also in Canada, and was responsible for bringing thousands of settlers to Illinois and to the Chicago region. One early result was that opportunities for speculation were created by the "eastern invasion" and attracted adventurers of all kinds. A "speculation mania" was said to exist.

Two great "internal improvements" that were confidently expected to promote the commercial development of Chicago were a further attraction to prospective migrants. These improvements were, first, an expected harbor appropriation; and, second, the construction of the Illinois and Michigan Canal,[2] which had been decided upon by the two state legislatures. "Canal lots" were offered at a public sale in 1830. A similar sale in 1836 caused great excitement and brought people from distant places. The ceremony of breaking the first ground on the canal took place in the presence of a large group of spectators at Bridgeport, which was then called Canalport, and was a portion of the town of Lake. The names of Bridgeport and Canalport have continued to be important street names in the tenement areas of the city, and Canal Street also remains as a land-

[2] A brief history of the canal was given in the *Chicago Directory*, described as the *General Directory and Business Advertising of the City of Chicago for the Year 1844*, by J. Wellington Norris. In the "Historical Sketch" the following statement is made regarding the canal: "The history of this great work, which was contemplated from the first settlement of the State, and has been the subject of legislation for more than twenty years, presents a remarkable instance of the obstacles which frequently oppose the accomplishment of the greatest undertakings. The first survey of the canal was made in 1823. In 1825, a bill was passed to incorporate the Illinois and Michigan Canal Company; but no stock being taken under the charter, it was repealed at the next special session. In 1827, Act of March 2, Congress appropriated each alternate section of land within five miles of the prepared line. In 1829, a board of commissioners was organized, with power to determine upon the route, and to discharge other duties connected with the work. Chicago, Ottawa and other towns on the line were laid out by the board, and sales of lots effected. The work was commenced in the year 1836 and was suspended in 1842. Present appearances seem clearly to indicate the canal will be finished in about three years. . . . . Already has the prospect of the completion . . . . caused emigration to set strongly in this direction. . . . ."

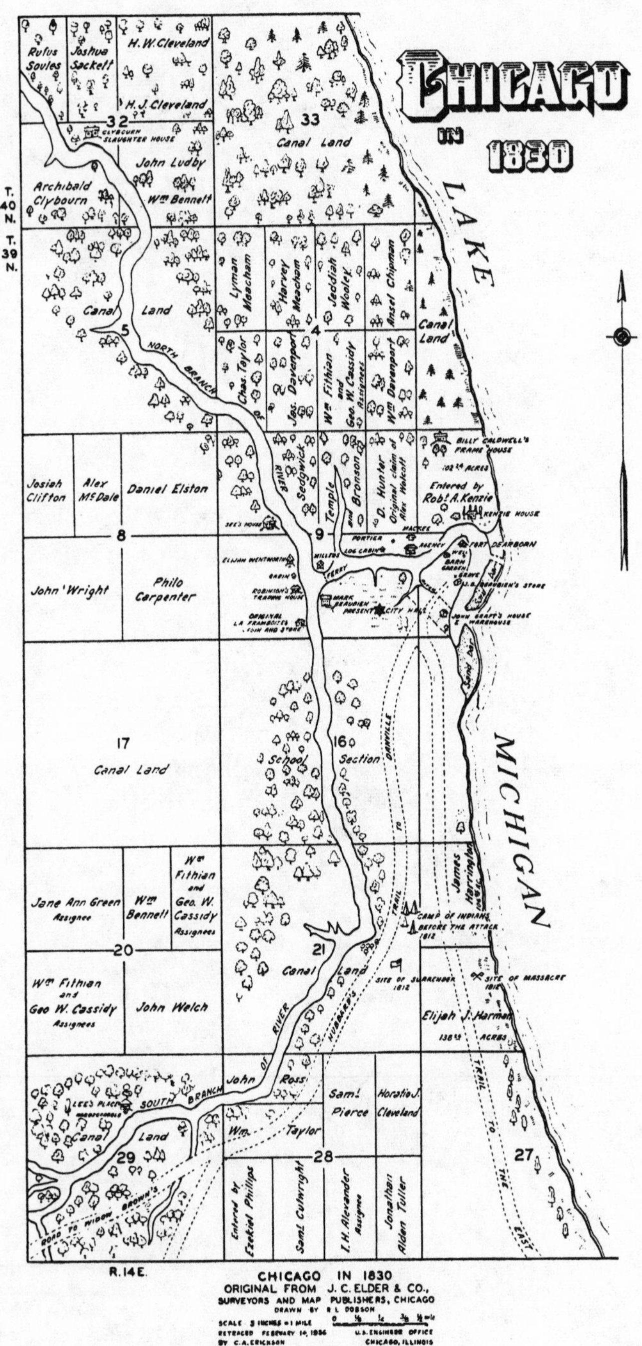

Courtesy of the U.S. Engineer Office, Chicago Illinois

THE EARLY CHICAGO CANAL REGION

mark. Colonel Archer, whose name has become famous in "Archer Avenue," better known at one time as Mr. Dooley's famous "Archey Road," broke the ground for the canal and threw the first shovelful of earth on the Fourth of July, 1836. It was not until twelve years later (April 10, 1848) that the new canal was opened and the first boat passed through.

An interesting description of the Chicago of 1836 told of the hotels which were "boisterous with swaggering adventurers buying and selling lots at imaginary rates amounting to hundreds of thousands." "The homeless prairie sportsman divided the proceeds of his wolf-scalps and coon-skins between ammunition and the conveyance fee of a corner lot 'on time'; and the dream of every resident was to sell at the top of a haply realizing market, pocket his riches and 'go home,' whence he had come." It was a community of men laborers, adventurers, and far-seeing pioneers who dreamed dreams of the great West.

An early account of the new city described "the scrubby timber which lined the east side of the south branch" as unbroken in many places; and where, a few decades later, great bridges swung open for the lake steamers and ore boats, and closed again for the traffic lines and the passing crowds, "for the throng of people and of vessels all day long," the solitary citizen of those early days "pushed through the bushes, untied his canoe and crossed the slough alone to count up with his partner, on the West Side, the illusory profits of the day's speculations, to discuss General Jackson's war on the National Bank, or how they might help each other to a clearer understanding of the novel and magnificent railway schemes with which the country was teeming. On the North Side, for the most part, the timber, though small, was thickly grown, much of it pine, a solitary tree of unusual height standing till long afterwards near the lake at the foot of Randolph Street."

In 1837, when Chicago became an incorporated city, it was divided into six wards. The first and second wards, divided by Clark Street, were bounded by the south branch of the river and by the lake—the first ward lying east and the second west of Clark Street. The third and fourth wards, which were divided by West Randolph Street, were on the west side of the river's north and south branches.

The fifth and sixth wards were bounded by the north branch of the river and the lake, and were divided by North Clark Street.

A level prairie, low and marshy, stretching west toward the almost unknown frontier country of the great plains, and a sandy beach along the great lake, made the site of the city, which was, until 1860, much smaller than the older cities of the Middle West. In 1840, when the federal census first reported Chicago as an incorporated place, the new city had, in round numbers, a population[3] of 5,000; while Cincinnati had 46,000, Pittsburgh, 21,000; Louisville, 21,000; and St. Louis, 16,000. Detroit had a population of 9,000 at this time, and Cleveland, Columbus, and Dayton—with 6,000 each— outranked Chicago. At this time New York had a population of 312,000; and Baltimore and New Orleans, 102,000 each; and Boston and Philadelphia, 93,000 each. In 1850 Chicago ranked twenty-fifth in population among cities of the United States; in 1890, and in all succeeding census returns, as second only to New York. Since 1890 Chicago's rate of population growth[4] has been greater than that of New York.

The list of the Cook County precincts and their population for 1845 as given in the old directory of the period is still of interest.

An historical sketch of the city written in 1843 called attention to

[3] *Sixth Census of the United States, 1840: Compendium*, p. 86. The United States census (1840) showed the following population data for Chicago:

		Whites	Negro
Males	2,431 (34 Negro)	Under 20— 906	Under 24—14
Females	2,039 (19 Negro)	Under 20— 988	Under 24— 9
Total	4,470 (53 Negro)	Under 20—1,894	Under 24—23
Males	20 or over (Negroes 24 or over) 1,511		
Females	20 or over (Negroes 24 or over) 1,042		

Listed as employed in "navigation of canals, lakes, and rivers"—44.

[4] "The growth of Chicago in the nineteenth century has been paralleled by that of no other great city of a million population or over in either ancient or modern times" (Maurice Halbwachs, "Chicago, experiénce ethnique," *Annales d'histoire économique et sociale*, IV, 10–11, quoted in Homer Hoyt's very interesting study, *One Hundred Years of Land Values in Chicago* [1933], p. 279). Dr. Hoyt pictures the "century of progress" during which the population of Chicago "increased from 50 to 3,376,438. It compressed within a single century the population growth of Paris for twenty centuries. From 1840 to 1890, the rapidity of its development outstripped that of every other city in the world. An insignificant town in 1840, Chicago forged ahead of its older rivals in the Middle West before 1880 . . . and by 1890 it was the second city in point of numbers in the United States. In 1930 only London, New York, and Berlin—all much older—contained more people."

the "great influx of immigration" that had been coming to Chicago even at that early day, and to the fact that the new immigrants were unskilled laborers so necessary for the building of a great industrial and commercial center. The immigrants destined for Chicago, and

POPULATION OF THE CITY OF CHICAGO, AND THE SEVERAL PRECINCTS IN COOK COUNTY, IN 1845*

Cook County Precincts†	Population
Chicago City	12,088
Chicago	575
Athens (Lemont)	593
Blue Island	234
York	346
Monroe	786
Lake	699
Lyons	554
Summit	619
Desplaines	999
Gross Point	738
Hanover	710
Barrington	594
Bridgeport	449
Thornton	546
Salt Lake	1,073

* J. W. Norris, *Business Directory and Statistics* (1846). Revised and corrected in "Fergus Historical Series," No. 25 (1883), p. 9.

† An account of the area of some of these precincts is interesting. For example, Chicago embraced all in the old precinct of Chicago outside of the corporate limits, except Bridgeport; Blue Island embraced Worth, Calumet, Hyde Park, and a part of what later became Lake; York included Palos, Orland, and all the south part of Cook County not embraced in Lyons, Athens, Blue Island, and Thornton; Monroe included Leyden, Cicero, Proviso, and Maine; Lake included Niles and Jefferson; Desplaines included Wheeling and Northfield; Gross Point included Lake View, Evanston, and New Trier; Bridgeport included the present section of that name and a portion of the present town of Lake; Salt Lake included Elk Grove, Schaumburg, and Palatine.

the supplies which came from abroad, were probably responsible for much of the western travel which "gave employment to a considerable amount of shipping." Steamboats and schooners were said "to ply regularly between this port and Buffalo." And along with this growing population came all the problems of poverty and destitution, including the problem of decent shelter, which is still unsolved after a century of progress.

EARLY EXPENSES FOR "POORHOUSE AND PAUPERS"

In the earliest lists of expenditures for Cook County, beginning with 1831, "pauper expenses" appeared regularly, year after year. The large increase in pauper expenses from 1834 to 1835, and again from 1836 to 1837, undoubtedly is due to the early influx of canal workers and the first depression of which Chicago felt the consequences. The burden of supporting the poor was said to be extremely heavy for Cook County[5] to carry when there were "swarms of destitute persons coming in through the Canal"; and applicants for relief seemed to come principally from the canal at this time. A strike on the canal in 1837 and the financial crisis of that year made a bad situation worse. All the activity in the new city temporarily came to an end. Immigration stopped almost automatically without quota laws or restrictive legislation of any kind.

"Pauper expenses" listed as $369 in 1834 became $3,421 in 1837; and in 1838, approximately $5,000, when Cook County had a population of less than 10,000 people.[6] A little later, "Poorhouse Expenses" are added to "Pauper Expenses." As early as 1836, a county poorhouse was standing on Chicago's public square. By 1852 the purchase of a tract of eighty acres for a new poor farm showed that the problem of poverty was increasing along with the population.[7] The expense of caring for the county poor which had been $18,352 during the decade from 1831 to 1841 had increased to $41,278 in the nine years from 1840 to 1849;[8] and in the single year 1863–64 the

[5] Goodspeed and Healy, *op. cit.*, I, 515. "In early times the greatest item of county expense was in behalf of the poor" (p. 530).

[6] *Chicago American*, September 28, 1839; see Goodspeed and Healy, *op. cit.*, I, 513, 521. The population was 10,201 in 1840, according to the U.S. Census.

[7] Discussions about the moving from the old South Side poorhouse to a new poor farm were the occasion of a good deal of discussion in 1850–51. "By November, 1854, the new Cook county poorhouse, located nine miles northwest of Chicago, was nearly finished. The building was of brick, three stories and basement high, cost about $25,000, and was located in the town of Jefferson. Upon the opening of this poorhouse the ladies of that vicinity thought best to give a house warming, on which occasion feasting and dancing were enjoyed. This act was regarded as very odd and was laughed at by the county newspapers. Connected with the poorhouse was a two-story wing and basement for the insane poor. The old poorhouse was situated about four miles south of the city" (*ibid.*, p. 541).

[8] *Ibid.*, pp. 525, 534.

county expenses for "Poorhouse and Paupers" had grown to $42,899. That is, poor people were here to be cared for by the taxpayers of Chicago from the very earliest days, and where there are poor people there is always a housing problem.

Irish immigration to the Chicago region had at first been stimulated by the building of the Illinois and Michigan Canal, to which reference has already been made. The contractors sent circulars to every seaport in the United States and to the Canadian ports as well, offering inducements to immigrants to come out as canal laborers. As one of the desirable features it was also advertised that land might be purchased at a nominal cost. A large proportion of those who responded were Irish, and the founding of the early Irish Catholic churches in the Chicago region shows the increase in Irish immigration to the new city. St. Mary's, one of the very old South Side churches, later the Church of the Paulist Fathers, was established in 1833 in response to a petition signed by Catholics who were already living in the Chicago district. The Bishop of St. Louis sent a priest to St. Mary's in 1836, and this became one of the well-known churches of the Chicago area, a church which at a later period was said to be "the patriotic rallying place" for the Irish soldiers during the war for the Union and especially for the famous "Irish Brigade."

The first parish organized to care for the Irish immigrants on the West Side was St. Patrick's, founded in 1846.[9] Some lots were purchased for the new West Side church from the Canal Commissioners for $3,000 and a frame church was soon built on Desplaines Street near Washington and Randolph, not far from the river.

[9] This is one of the historic Chicago parishes. During the Civil War the Irish Legion (the Ninetieth Illinois Infantry) went forth from St. Patrick's to join the armies of the Union, under the command of Colonel Timothy O'Meara, who died gallantly in battle. This regiment carried the green flag of Ireland along with the Stars and Stripes through Vicksburg, on Missionary Ridge, on the "March to the Sea," and in a long series of other engagements; and at the close of the war the Irish Legion was "welcomed home" not by the West Side only but by the governor of Illinois and the citizens of Chicago. See the *Diamond Jubilee of the Archdiocese of Chicago* for an interesting account of this parish.

In 1854 foundations for a new brick-and-stone church were laid at the corner of Desplaines and Adams streets, but in the cholera epidemic of that year the priest of St. Patrick's died and the plans for the new church were delayed for a time. St. Patrick's corner has for more than fifty years been a well-known landmark in the heart of the West Side tenement district.

The Chicago of this early day has been described as "still a country town with cows browsing in pastures a mile from the city hall, and occasionally roaming through the main business street. Hogs recently had run wild in the center of town, and wolves had been seen at Wabash and Adams streets."[10]

DEVELOPMENT OF "SLUM CENTERS" BEFORE THE GREAT FIRE

At this time, from 1848 to 1857, when Chicago was building its brick business blocks on Lake Street, it was also "building thousands of frame cottages on the near South, North, and West sides";[11] and many of these old frame cottages are still found in the slums of the present day. Some of them have been made into two- and even three-story buildings by motley additions of frame and brick; but, in one shape or another, many of the old frame cottages of the middle of the last century are still standing in these areas of deterioration.

The West Side was, at this time, "growing fast as a manufacturing center." The *Gem of the Prairie* in 1848 said that the West Side near the south branch of the canal drew "houses, stores, machine shops, planing mills toward it as a magnet draws iron filings."[12]

Industrial and commercial development went forward rapidly: Wagon factories, iron foundries and planing mills; and along the north bank of the river "several large industries, including the McCormick reaper works near the mouth of the river. Large grain elevators were along the river near the railway terminals as far south as Roosevelt Road; there were a great many lumber yards on the west bank of the south branch stretching as far south as Twenty-second Street." But the Union Stock Yards were yet to be built. In 1848 there were the earlier Stock Yards at what were called the "Bull's Head" yards at Madison and Ashland Avenue; and "there were other important yards at Eighteenth Street and the south branch, and at Cottage Grove and Twenty-ninth streets." There were the Galena Railroad car-repair shops and "the shops of the American Car Company at Twenty-sixth Street and the lake which furnished employment for many men and gave rise to workingmen's homes and boarding-houses in their vicinity."

[10] Hoyt, *op. cit.*, p. 51.

[11] *Ibid.*, p. 65.

[12] *Chicago Tribune*, July 10, 1887, quoted in *ibid.*, p. 50.

A recent authority accepts the statement of earlier chroniclers that "of all the sections of the city, the West Side grew fastest in this period from 1848 to 1857."[13] He points out the areas of vice that were added to the slum areas along the river—to the old Kilgubbin, with a notoriously disorderly population of two thousand in 1858, to the equally notorious and disorderly "Sands" north of the river near Lake Michigan, which was raided and burned down by Mayor Wentworth in 1857,[14] and to the sailors' resorts on Wells and the streets west of Wells south of Washington—to these miserable slum centers "were now added such new patches as the forty or fifty acres of shanties on the West Side near Halsted and Twenty-second Street on the south branch; twenty acres of shacks near Halsted, Desplaines and Harrison [a few blocks from what was later the Hull-House corner]; the Milwaukee and Union Avenue section; the slums on Clark and State near Roosevelt Road and on North Rucker and Kinzie[15] settlements. . . . . The floating population brought in by the railroads contributed to the growth of these areas, which were often located near railroad shops and yards."

A new fear of the consequences of insanitary conditions when cholera and smallpox epidemics were again threatening in 1867 led to an early Chicago Board of Health Survey, which was completed in April, 1868, and which showed that 38,128 out of the 40,854 buildings were of wooden construction and that 31,702 were used as dwellings.[16]

It is interesting that an early letter to the *Chicago Tribune*[17] in 1872 attributed the bad results of the prevalence of intemperance chiefly "to the pressing want of decent and good homes, in which the people generally may be housed in accordance with the requirements of correct and just sanitary conditions." The writer thought that lack of good housing conditions contributed largely to the apparently low physical and moral level of Chicago's inhabitants. He thought

[13] *Ibid.*, p. 66, refers to Goodspeed and Healy, *op. cit.*, I, 221.

[14] See also Frederick Francis Cook, *Bygone Days in Chicago*, pp. 156 ff.

[15] Goodspeed and Healy, *op. cit.*, I, 190–91, quoted in Hoyt, *op. cit.*, p. 66.

[16] See the following chapter, "Tenement House Legislation in Chicago," pp. 42–44, for an account of early attempts to struggle with the sanitary problem of this area.

[17] By Ogden Whitlock. The author of the letter was apparently keenly interested in housing reform (see *Chicago Tribune*, Friday, October 11, 1872).

that perhaps 300,000 of the people of Chicago were then living "in wooden houses, with small rooms and poor ventilation; the larger portion at inconvenient distances from the business center, and too often situated in muddy and unimproved districts on the prairie." This early reformer suggested that the bodily discomforts and general degradation of living conditions led to drinking.

In the land-boom period that preceded the Great Fire of 1871, there were "on the South Side west of State Street some 40,000 frame houses of an average value of $1,000 each that were occupied by the population of over 200,000 persons."[18] Dr. Hoyt thinks the rapid increase in the volume of manufacturing which employed 60,000 workers by 1873 "had quadrupled the population of the West Side from 1862 to 1872 (57,000–214,000), doubled the population of the North Side from 1862 to 1870 (35,000–70,000), and almost doubled the population of the South Side from 1862 to 1872 (45,500–88,500)."[19]

This explanation shows why the great slum areas grew up in all sections of the West Side. "The majority of this increased mass of people were workers who crowded into frame cottages, some built on both the front and the rear of lots, near the factories along the river, on streets that had few sewers and practically no pavements." In the congested district of the lower West Side lying south of Harrison Street, one of the early plague spots was Maxwell Street near Halsted Street, which later came to be known as the Russian Jewish Ghetto, and which at this early day was said to be "singled out of a thousand by the peculiar, intensive stench that arises from pools of thick and inky compound which in many cases is several feet deep and occasionally expands to the width of a small lake."[20]

Other slum sections included the vice area of that day which "was then in that part of the downtown section that lies south of Washington Street and runs west of LaSalle Street to the south branch of the river, with the center of corruption in the notorious Conley's patch at Wells and Monroe streets." In another very miserable district, the Negro population of the city were living "chiefly in the section west of State Street just south of Harrison Street until the fire of

[18] Hoyt, *op. cit.*, p. 96. [19] See Chamberlin, *op. cit.*, p. 279.

[20] *Chicago Tribune*, June 19, 1873, quoted in Hoyt, *op. cit.*, p. 97.

1874 (this fire of 1874 is not to be confused with the Great Fire of October 9, 1871) forced their removal." The Negroes then moved farther south into the area that was the beginning of the Black Belt of the present day.[21]

THE EXPANDING CITY LIMITS

The *Chicago Directory* of 1844 gave a pleasant description of the growing city as occupying "a level prairie, on both sides of the main stream and the North and South Branches of the Chicago River" and covering "an area of about three and a half miles in length North and South, and two and a half in breadth, East and West." An area of about a mile and a half square was described as "already regularly built upon, and the streets opened and graded." The streets were also said to be "regularly laid out, wide and spacious, parallel and at right angles to the Lake." That part of the city which lay for several miles along the lake shore was sandy and dry, while "the portion removed from the Lake partakes of the character of all level prairie, being, in the spring and fall, wet and muddy." But the site of the City, "being a plain," was said not to afford "a very interesting field of vision," either from the Lake or the surrounding country.

The area of the new city, as incorporated in 1837 and as reported by the United States Census in 1840, embraced about ten square miles, an area of more than 6,000 acres, bounded on the south by Twenty-second Street, on the north by North Avenue, on the west by Wood Street, and on the east by the lake. The boundaries of this small city and its later annexations are shown in Map I.

The physical boundaries of the city did not change greatly between the date of its incorporation and the close of its third decade of growth, that is, from 1833 to the Civil War. Toward the southwest, the canal territory with the lumber yards and the canal slips had been promptly brought within the city limits; but except for the area along the South Branch of the river the entire section between Archer and Blue Island avenues was "largely unsettled marsh land

[21] See *ibid.*, p. 97. The Irish were said to have had "a stronghold at Bridgeport, the Swedes and Norwegians were thickly settled west of Wells near Chicago Avenue, and the Germans west of Wells near North Avenue. Other families in the lower-income groups lived over stores in the downtown area or along the secondary business streets."

MAP I

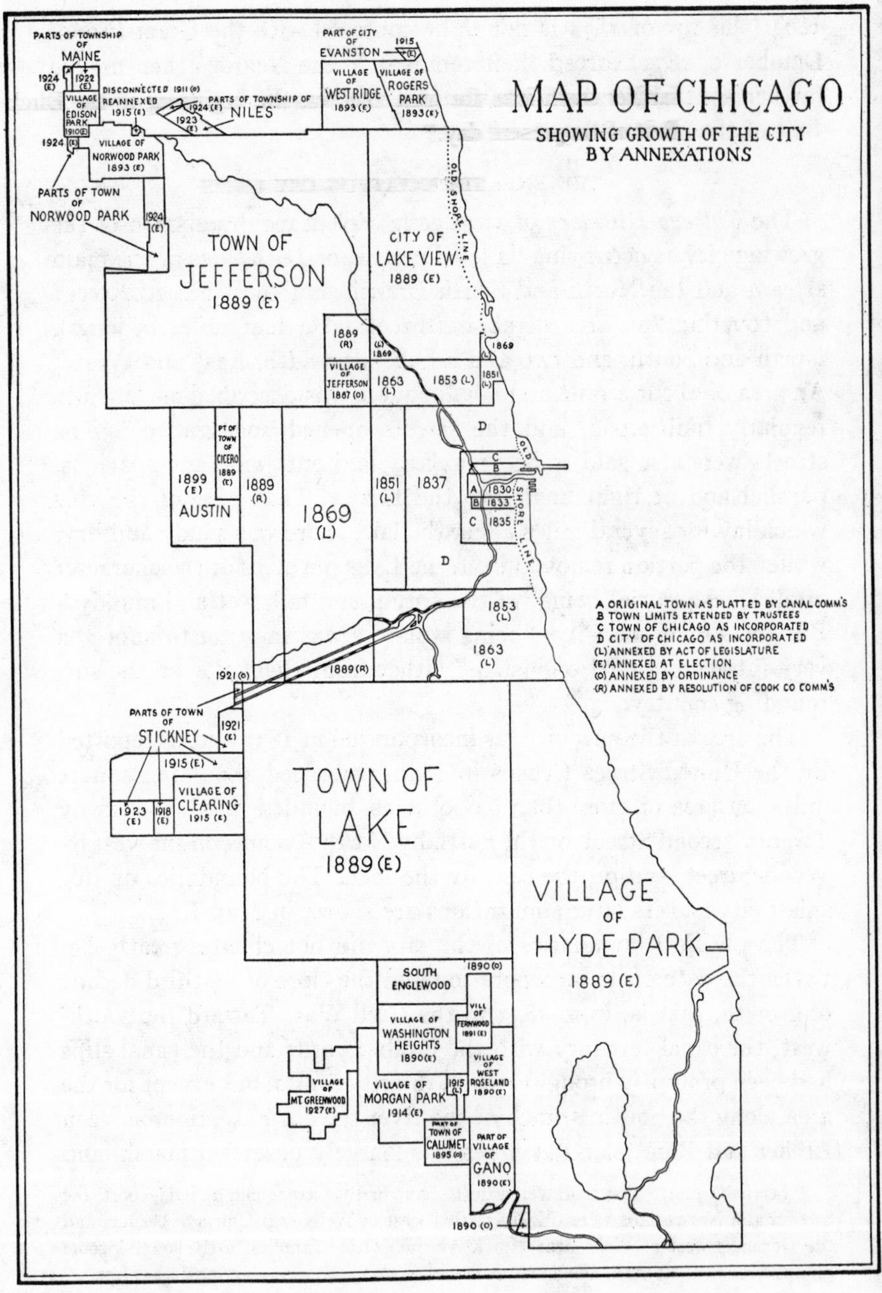
MAP OF CHICAGO
SHOWING GROWTH OF THE CITY
BY ANNEXATIONS
PARTS OF TOWNSHIP OF MAINE
1924 (E)
1922 (E)
VILLAGE OF EDISON PARK 1910 (E)
DISCONNECTED 1911 (O) REANNEXED 1915 (E)
PARTS OF TOWNSHIP OF NILES
1924 (E)
1923 (E)
1924 (R)
VILLAGE OF NORWOOD PARK 1893 (E)
PARTS OF TOWN OF NORWOOD PARK
1924 (E)
PART OF CITY OF EVANSTON
1915 (E)
VILLAGE OF WEST RIDGE 1893 (E)
VILLAGE OF ROGERS PARK 1893 (E)
OLD SHORE LINE
TOWN OF JEFFERSON 1889 (E)
CITY OF LAKE VIEW 1889 (E)
1889 (R)
(L) 1869
1869
VILLAGE OF JEFFERSON 1887 (O)
1863 (L)
1853 (L)
1851 (L)
D
PT OF TOWN OF CICERO 1889 (E)
1899 (E)
AUSTIN
1889 (R)
1869 (L)
1851 (L)
1837
C
B
A 1830
B 1833
C 1835
D
1853 (L)
1863 (L)
1889 (R)
1921 (O)
A ORIGINAL TOWN AS PLATTED BY CANAL COMM'S
B TOWN LIMITS EXTENDED BY TRUSTEES
C TOWN OF CHICAGO AS INCORPORATED
D CITY OF CHICAGO AS INCORPORATED
(L) ANNEXED BY ACT OF LEGISLATURE
(E) ANNEXED AT ELECTION
(O) ANNEXED BY ORDINANCE
(R) ANNEXED BY RESOLUTION OF COOK CO COMM'S
PARTS OF TOWN OF STICKNEY
1921 (E)
1915 (E)
1923 (E)
1918 (E)
VILLAGE OF CLEARING 1915 (E)
TOWN OF LAKE 1889 (E)
VILLAGE OF HYDE PARK 1889 (E)
SOUTH ENGLEWOOD
1890 (O)
VILLAGE OF WASHINGTON HEIGHTS 1890 (E)
VILL OF FERNWOOD 1891 (E)
VILLAGE OF MT GREENWOOD 1927 (E)
VILLAGE OF MORGAN PARK 1914 (E)
1915 (L)
VILLAGE OF WEST ROSELAND 1890 (E)
PART OF TOWN OF CALUMET 1895 (O)
PART OF VILLAGE OF GANO 1890 (E)
1890 (O)

in part known to old settlers as Hard Scrabble." The eastern boundaries had been extended considerably along the lake by two additions on the South Side, one in 1853 and the other in 1863 when Camp Douglas, which had become so famous during the Civil War as a concentration camp for the Union soldiers of the Middle West, was included in the city limits. Two small extensions on the North Side in 1853 and 1863 made the city boundaries like the three sides of a rectangle with the sandy and irregular shore of Lake Michigan serving as the fourth boundary. Successive additions of territory have extended the boundaries of the city to include an area of more than two hundred square miles. Formerly independent villages, towns, and smaller cities like Hyde Park, Jefferson, Lake, Lake View, Washington Heights, Rogers Park, West Ridge, Norwood Park, and many others have sacrificed their local autonomy and have been drawn into the Chicago city limits although they retain, even today, some of their local characteristics and are frequently called by their old town and village names.

After the close of the Civil War a wide strip to the west was added in 1869; but from that time, for a period of two decades, there were no changes of importance in the city boundary lines. Following the end of the first half-century of progress, there were in the single year 1889 a series of great annexations. The small suburban cities of Lake View to the north and Hyde Park to the south were added as were also the town of Jefferson toward the northwest and toward the southwest the town of Lake, where the Union Stock Yards had been located. Before the opening of the World's Fair in 1893 there had been added another little chain of outlying city communities, South Englewood in 1890, the Village of Fernwood in 1891, West Roseland in 1890, and in the same year the adjoining part of the village of Gano and the village of Washington Heights in the truck-garden area. Five years later, part of the town of Calumet came in, leaving the boundary of the southwest corner of the city jagged and unfinished. Toward the north and northwest the boundary was also extended irregularly. The large village of Norwood Park adjoining the extreme northwest corner was annexed in 1893, and to the northeast the villages of West Ridge and Rogers Park came in during the same year.

Municipal annexations do not present a satisfactory picture of population growth, for political factors have much to do with the extension of a city's corporate limits. On the west, for example, the village of Oak Park is just as much a part of the city as Austin, Stickney, and Clearing; but Oak Park has preferred to maintain a status of aristocratic independence. In the same way Evanston, to the north, is, as far as population distribution is concerned, as much a part of Chicago as are Niles, West Ridge, and Rogers Park. Population has stretched out along the lake toward the more fashionable suburbs of the north and at the same time toward the vast industrial area of the Calumet region on the south where the great industries follow one another in swift succession beyond the city limits into the adjoining states.

Along the old arterial roads to the southwest and the northwest, many of which were transformed from plank roads over the prairie and swampland to become city thoroughfares of a later day, along streets like Archer, Blue Island, Ogden, Milwaukee, and Clybourn avenues, there were population increases because of the convenient transportation arrangements that were made available. Diagrams of city growth show the population clustering along these lines which lie the map on like outstretched fingers from a giant hand.[22]

POPULATION GROWTH THROUGH THE CENTURY

Within the two decades that followed the crisis of 1837, the Chicago population had increased more than sixfold, with the census of 1850 showing 29,963 people. It was said that the growth would have been much greater had it not been for the fearful cholera epidemics of 1849 and 1850.[23] This terrible disease was believed to have been brought up the river from New Orleans in an emigrant boat. The first case was noticed on April 29, 1849, and the disease spread rapidly. One theory of the spread of the disease was that immigrants arriving from various parts of Europe where the cholera was epidemic were bringing in new cases. Probably about 1,000 persons suffered from the disease, and 314 deaths were reported between July 25 and August 28, 1849. In a period of twelve months there were 678 chol-

[22] See, e.g., Helen R. Jeter, *Trends of Population in the Region of Chicago* (1927).

[23] See below, chap. ii, "Tenement-House Legislation," p. 39.

era deaths, 1 out of every 36 of the population.[24] As with other epidemics, it was the poorer people, those who lived in the most insanitary neighborhoods of the city, huddled in the miserable shanty cottages that were so common in that day, who suffered most heavily. Few Americans were victims, and among the foreign-born it was the newly arrived immigrants who suffered most severely.[25] The greatest mortality occurred in a Norwegian neighborhood in the "North Division," where there were some three hundred people, principally Norwegians, "and scarcely one of the whole number escaped the infection. It was remarked as singular at that time that the ground in that locality was high and sandy, but the secret was afterward discovered that all had used water from the same well into which the drainings of an outhouse had found their way."[26]

The growth of the city was rapid during the decade 1850–60, and reached and passed the 100,000 mark on the eve of the Civil War. The United States Census of 1860 showed 109,260 inhabitants, and this number more than doubled in the following decade. In 1870, the year before the Great Fire, Chicago had become a great city with a population of nearly 300,000; and, like all great cities, it had a well-developed housing problem and well-defined slum areas.

The population of Chicago by decennial periods, the growing area of urbanization, and the average density per acre which will be found in Table I show the unparalleled development of the city over the first century of its history. It is interesting that the average number of inhabitants per acre for the city as a whole which had been 22 in

[24] Other large cities suffered proportionately. "In the same year Cincinnati lost 4,450, or one in 23; St. Louis lost 4,297, or one in 21; New Orleans 4,000, or one in 37; New York 5,122, or one in 79. The prevalence of the disease was such that it spread to nearly every cluster of dwellings in the Northwest, and for a time communication between Chicago and the interior was almost entirely suspended" (see Elias Colbert and Everett Chamberlin, *Chicago and the Great Conflagration* [1871], pp. 68 and 69).

The disease appeared again in July, 1850, but in a less severe form, though the aggregate mortality was again very great. From the middle of July to the first of September 416 persons died of cholera, and the total mortality was at the rate of one to 64 of the inhabitants. The disease reappeared in 1851 and 1852, but in a milder form. It was more severe in 1854, but the last visitation in 1866 was comparatively slight.

[25] *Colbert's Chicago: Historical and Statistical Sketch of the Garden City* (1868). "It is worthy of remark that the disease was chiefly confined to immigrants, of whom large numbers were attacked and died almost immediately on reaching the city" (pp. 18–19).

[26] *Ibid.*, p. 18.

1880 had actually fallen to 10 by the close of the decade. That is, the number of people per acre was about the same as it had been, three decades earlier, in the year 1860. This was of course due to the annexation of sparsely settled districts to the city area which left the number of people per acre about the same even in 1900 as it had been in 1860. In 1930 the Federal Census reported the Chicago population to be 3,376,438, an average of 25 people per acre.[27] Fifty years earlier in 1880 when the population was only 503,185, the average

TABLE 1

POPULATION, AREA, AND AVERAGE DENSITY OF POPULATION IN CHICAGO IN CENSUS YEARS 1840–1930

Census Year	Population*	Area in Acres†	Number of Persons per Acre
1840	4,470	6,806	1
1850	29,963	6,246	5
1860	109,260	11,519	9
1870	298,977	22,884	13
1880	503,185	22,884	22
1890	1,099,850	108,695	10
1900	1,698,575	122,008	14
1910	2,185,283	122,008	18
1920	2,701,705	127,598	21
1930	3,376,438	134,793	25

* Population given in decennial reports of the United States Census Bureau, 1840–1930 inclusive.

† Area in acres computed from area in square miles given by *Daily News Almanac* (1931), p. 803.

number of persons per acre had been 22. In one decade between 1880 and 1890 the area of the city had increased by annexation to approximately five times its size at the beginning of the decade. The population in 1890 was thus very unevenly distributed. The city was already divided into thirty-four wards. In the West Side ward, in which Hull-House had just been established, there were 92 persons per acre; in an adjoining West Side ward, 115 people per acre; while in five of the recently annexed wards on the edge of the city the "average population" showed only 1 or 2 persons per acre. Since 1890, although annexations have continued, the areas annexed have been relatively small and the growth in population has resulted primarily from increases in density rather than increases in territory.

[27] *Fifteenth Census, 1930*, Vol. I: *Population*, p. 8.

HOMES OF THE RICH AND POOR IN 1871

The chronicles of the Great Fire of 1871 have left us some valuable pictures of the distribution of population and residential areas at that time. The areas of poverty, as poverty was then concentrated, are closely related to the swift spread of the Great Fire. The site of the O'Leary home,[28] where the fire began, is marked today by a historical tablet in a congested area near Halsted Street, a few blocks south of Hull-House. At the time of the fire the city limits to the west were not far away and beyond stretched the apparently endless prairie.[28a] The district between Halsted Street and the river was built up largely of workingmen's four-room cottages, and the O'Learys, who kept three cows in their barn, had a four-room house.

Across the river in the older "south division" and south of the business center, the streets between State Street and the lake were largely occupied by residences of the wealthy and fashionable. But west of State to the river, and then farther and farther

[28] An account published by the *Chicago Tribune*, October 20, 1927, gives the recollections of a Chicago woman, who was thirteen years old and a near neighbor of the O'Leary family at the time of the great catastrophe. Our interest in her narrative lies in the fact that she gives an account of the neighborhood just east of Halsted at that time. She said: "Every evening I used to go through the alley to the O'Leary barn to get our milk. The O'Learys owned three cows and had a four-room house. Like nearly every one else in those days, they took in roomers. There was a couple living in the O'Leary home with a new baby.

"The three cows were housed in a little shed, and the middle cow was hard to manage. . . . .

"Well, my mother and father were going to bed that night about nine o'clock. As Mother looked out of the window, she saw a fire down the alley. She called to me and I ran out to the fire. As I came near, I saw flames coming out from between the boards of the O'Leary barn. There was no one about, no one in the barn. I ran to the house and tapped on the window. 'The barn's on fire,' I cried, then ran back to watch the fire. I was not interested in anything else. It had been a hot day, and the wind was blowing hard from the northwest. In a few minutes the barn was in flames.

"There was not a fire-engine in sight. The flames began to spread to the adjoining barns and the people began to save things from their houses. One woman tried to throw a feather-bed tick from an upper window. A spark caught it. That was the second big blaze.

"In three hours the fire had jumped the river and our neighborhood was a mass of blazing ruins. Coal piles were burning in every yard.

"People were hunting for O'Leary. They thought he had started the fire by going into the barn at night with a lantern. . . . ."

[28a] See the very interesting description of the early West Side in Carter Harrison's recently published *Stormy Years*, chap. i, pp. 18–20, 26–31.

west toward the city's changing boundary line, the great industries were building and around them large numbers of working people were congregating. A history of the Great Fire[29] pictures the well-to-do sections of the city as occupying the "land all along the lake shore, from $\frac{1}{4}$ to $\frac{3}{8}$ of a mile wide, and 11 miles long," which, it was said, included "the more aristocratic residence portions of the city and its outlying suburbs—Lake View and Hyde Park." Nearly the whole of this section was said to be "covered with the most costly buildings," and the lake-shore section of the "North Division" extending one mile from the harbor was said to have been "originally the most exclusive portion, being largely held by the oldest residents or their families." Later the Michigan Avenue section, lying near the lake shore in the South Division, began to compete with it. "Then Wabash Avenue next to the westward, with the cross-streets and courts, was filled up by the wealthier classes, the line of improvements gradually spreading southward, and covering the avenues that run in to the east of Michigan as the lake recedes from that thoroughfare in the southern part of the city."

On the other side of the picture, the same writers describe the early river wards where the homes of the working people had been established even at this early day along the river and its branches where the great lumber yards were located and where "seventeen elevators were dotted along the banks." Toward the north were distilleries, slaughter-houses, and shipyards; and toward the south "a host of packing-houses."

Not far from the junction of the two branches, "spreading over an area of nearly half a mile square, was what was known as the great machine-shop district." Here were the foundries and the establishments where "agricultural implements by the thousand were turned out annually."[30]

[29] Colbert and Chamberlin, *op. cit.*, pp. 174–77.

[30] It was noted that there was in the southwest part of the North Division a similar, but less important, district, bounded on two sides by the docks on the river. "A grand exodus had begun in the spring of 1871, to the south and southwest, where several important workshops had previously existed. Some of the largest manufactories were in process of transference to these new quarters at the time of the fire, and new ones were springing up on every hand. . . . . Near the middle of the southern limit of the city was the great Union Stock Yards, a town in itself; and the whole was surrounded by the

Take, for example, the account of the suburbs of 1874 by Everett Chamberlin, the journalist of the "great conflagration." Chamberlin wrote that on all the business streets of Chicago more or less manufacturing was to be found, "as a matter of course." "But," he added, "the heavier work naturally gathers along the North and South branches of the river, and on the north side of the main stream near its mouth, the south side being taken up by railroad warehouses and yards, by steamboat docks, and by heavy merchandizing warehouses."[31]

Chamberlin pointed out the tendency to growth along the river, North and South Branch alike, and along the canals. Of the manufacturing district of the South Branch he wrote in 1874, "The district which has become well known under this name lies on the west fork of the South Branch, west of Ashland Avenue and south of Twenty-second Street. . . . . It has been rapidly improved with special reference to the wants of heavy manufacturing establishments, and has already been occupied by half a dozen of the largest concerns in the West. . . . ."[32]

The housing situation became very exigent as a result of the Great Fire. Faced with the problem of providing shelter for large numbers of homeless people when "the most inclement season of the year" was rapidly approaching, the Citizens' Aid Committee at first erected some rude barracks.[33] But the Committee knew that forty or fifty thousand people could not be expected to use these temporary shelters for homes through the winter season. The inevitable results,

---

magnificent system of parks and boulevards which, when completed, would have made Chicago as much of a wonder in this respect as she had already become by virtue of her commercial importance" (*ibid.*, p. 176).

[31] Chamberlin, *op. cit.*, p. 138.

[32] *Ibid.* Chamberlin thought the growth of this district should be "almost exclusively" attributed to "the enterprise of Mr. Samuel J. Walker," who had purchased a mile and a half of the South Branch river front west of Ashland Avenue and south of Twenty-second Street. The purchased area of approximately 1,500 acres was developed for a manufacturing center. "Directly after the fire, he commenced dredging out slips and providing dock frontage and private railway tracks, with a view of attracting manufactures to that locality" (p. 138).

[33] This account of the care of the homeless is based on the *Report of the Chicago Relief and Aid Society of Disbursement of Contributions for the Sufferers by the Chicago Fire, 1874*, chap, xi ("Shelter"), pp. 183–95.

the Committee thought, of bringing such large numbers of people into "promiscuous and involuntary association" over the long winter months would be to "engender disease and promote idleness, disorder and vice." Moreover, such structures could be erected "only by sufferance" upon land from which the actual owners would sooner or later evict them. As the Committee saw it, therefore, "barracks for the homeless" meant only the postponement for a few months of the solution of an important public responsibility. There was also apprehension lest Chicago be left "with a large class of permanent poor still without homes, and demoralized by a winter of dependence and evil communications." The Committee were especially concerned about the immigrant workers who had owned their cottage or shanty homes and who, according to the Committee report, "made much the larger proportion of those who were sufferers by the fire." The Committee pointed out that these were "mechanics and the better class of laboring people, thrifty, domestic, and respectable, whose skill and labor were indispensable in rebuilding the city, and most of whom had accumulated enough to become the owners of their own homesteads either as proprietors or lessees of the lots." If these people could be restored to their homes they would be lifted, the Committee thought, "from depression and anxiety, if not despair, to hope, renewed energy, and comparative prosperity."[34]

The provision of "small but comfortable homes" for all the homeless except a minimum number who were to be put in barracks was the decision of the Shelter Committee of the Citizens' Aid Committee who were responsible for the expenditure of the large relief funds which had been raised in different parts of the country for the stricken city of Chicago. The Committee, as they later looked back upon their work, thought that "the result of their labors was even more successful and encouraging than the most sanguine had anticipated." But with all their good intentions, they had erected great numbers of "jerry-built" frame cottages again with no provision for

[34] The Committee's report said that these people would then have "all the incentives to industry left them, and with the conscious pride and independence of still living under their own roof-tree, they would thus settle for themselves, and in the best way, the question of title to land, and restore value to their real estate by proving it to be as desirable for occupation as before the fire."

more permanent structures to take their place. Long rows of these old frame houses are still to be seen, still constituting a part of the housing problem of Chicago, which is everyone's responsibility and yet seems to be no one's responsibility.

The journalists who became the historians[35] of the fire locate very clearly some of the poor sections of the city in 1871. The West Side at that time was a neighborhood already largely devoted to the homes of the poor. The area near De Koven and Jefferson streets, near the starting-point of the fire, is described as a "poor purlieu," and in this district there was said to be a "forest of shanties thrice as combustible as the pine woods of the North."

In this contemporary account there is a valuable description of the progress of the fire that preserves for us a picture of the misery of the West Side river wards in 1871. "The fire had already advanced . . . . through the frame buildings that covered the ground thickly north of De Koven Street and east of Jefferson Street—if those miserable alleys shall be dignified by being denominated streets. That neighborhood had always been a *terra incognita* to respectable Chicagoans, and during a residence of three years in the city I had never visited it. The land was thickly studded with one-story frame dwellings, cow-stables, pig-sties, corn-cribs, sheds innumerable; every wretched building within four feet of its neighbor, and everything of wood—not a brick or a stone in the whole area."

In the same account of the "great conflagration" there is a description of Gilpin Place, now one of the boundary streets of the Hull-House block, which was pictured as "quite a thoroughfare for that region." Described as being "a mere alley," it was said to be "somewhat broader than the surrounding lanes," with "elevated board sidewalks" and "passable for teams in dry weather." On the night of the Great Fire, a few blocks nearer the river than the Hull-House corner, Gilpin Place was "crowded with people pouring out of the thickly-settled locality between Jefferson Street and the river." A panic began here. "The wretched people were rushing out almost naked, imploring spectators to help them on with their burdens of bed-quilts, cane-bottomed chairs, iron kettles."

[35] Colbert and Chamberlin, *op. cit.*, p. 205.

Attention should perhaps be called at this point to the fact that these early accounts of the growth of Chicago do not confirm the rather popular theory of city growth which portrays different population groups lying in a series of concentric circles around the business district. The theory that population density is greatest in a semicircle around the business district in Chicago, and that it regularly decreases through a graded series of semicircles to certain outlying points; or the theory that the poor districts of a city are to be found in one circle, or, in Chicago, in a semicircle at a certain distance from the center of the city, are theories that seem to be purely theoretical and not realistic. A great city like Chicago has been made up of various smaller towns and villages, each of which had a business center and a center of population density. That is, Chicago was surrounded by "satellite cities," towns, and villages, and the small cities and towns stretched out to their boundary limits slowly, and were, finally, legally made part of the city of Chicago. There was a center of poor housing and of population density, for example, alike in Lake View, in Englewood, in Hyde Park, in Morgan Park, and in other once suburban areas. In Chicago proper there were well-to-do districts near the lake, and poor districts in parallel streets toward the less salubrious areas, near the river. It is clear that early accounts of Chicago do not show the poor in one semi-circle about the center of the business district but rather clinging to the irregular line of the river and living in parallel streets, rich and poor together, extending in lines south and north along the lake with the well-to-do streets near the lake and the poor streets to the west along the railroad lines that entered the city. At the time of the fire, the business quarter proper, "containing practically all the wholesale mercantile establishments, fine retail stores, public buildings and hotels, the newspaper offices, the two grand union railroad depots, and other institutions," usually to be found in the central portion of a town, was then located in the South Division of Chicago, north of Harrison Street.

The early chroniclers tell us further that to the south of "this precious tract" (approximately what is now "the Loop") were "the residences of the wealthy and of the poor, divided by State Street," a straight north-and-south street. On the north side also the homes of the rich and poor stretched out in lines almost parallel with the lake. In the North Division, La Salle Street, another north-and-south street, was the dividing line between the well-to-do and the poor and less well-to-do classes. The earlier accounts describe the Lower North Side at the time of the Great Fire as "occupied near the river and along Clark Street by stores and factories, the rest mainly by residences. The homes of the humble lie mostly west of La Salle Street, though toward the north the residences of the more luxurious classes, which had formerly been confined to select tracts in the southeast quarter section of this [North] Division, —the 'old Chicago,' substantial and elegant, ... had been of late seriously crowding the frugal Germans and improvident Irish out of their former haunts, and studding the country about Lincoln Park with mansions of the most elegant design and finish."[36] It is clear that the well-to-do in the North and South divisions occupied the streets and avenues near to and paralleling the lake; and west of them toward the river and the railroads lay the districts

[36] But it was in the poorer sections of the North Division that the fatalities of the Great Fire were said to have been "the most numerous and shocking." On the North Side, especially in "the quarter adjoining the river and north of Chicago Avenue, which was thickly covered with the cottages of the poor, the flames ran along as fast as a man could walk, and, what was worse, were constantly leaping to new points, both due forward and laterally, and propagating itself faster than its victims could possibly flee before it, even if they had not attempted to save any of their goods. It was in this way that the monster devoured hundreds with his fiery breath." Near Townsend Street and Chicago Avenue, "on an area of not more than forty acres, there were found the bodies of forty-five poor creatures, none of which were recognizable, but which were undoubtedly the German and Scandinavian people inhabiting that quarter." There were, of course, many explanations of the disastrous loss of life in this section. "There was a general hegira across all of the bridges leading to the West Side, and Chicago Avenue was the best of the thoroughfares tending in this direction—through this the people poured like the mountain torrent through its narrow gorge. All at once when the fiercest blasts of the monster furnace had begun to sweep through this section with heat which threatened death to thousands, it was discovered that the bridge was for the time impassable. . . . . They were forced to turn to the northward and attempt to escape through the burning streets to North Avenue, half a mile farther north, where there was another bridge. . . . .

"This exceptional case of great mortality, caused by people being pent up in 'no thoroughfares,' serves to illustrate how lives were saved in other cases by the fact that nearly every street in Chicago is . . . . straight and level; and that bridges occur at frequent intervals" (*ibid.*, pp. 273–75).

of the poor.[37] That is, the tendency has been, in general, in Chicago, for the well-to-do housing area to be located not in a semicircle with the business district as a center but in long parallel lines along the lake shore. In earlier periods there were also well-to-do areas in straight right-angled lines on the west, such as Washington Boulevard and Ashland Boulevard.

The early manufacturing enterprises were located not so much after a radial method of expansion with the city as a center, but, on the contrary, along the river and with the heart of the West Division as the radius, with the bend of the river and its branches as a boundary line. Along the river and the canals in a close semicircle were the factories and homes of the working people clustered closely from an early day.

Off to the southwest, stretching over the prairie, was the town of Lake, which became a part of Chicago only in 1889.

To the southwest also were the new McCormick works;[38] balanced by the Deering Harvester works to the northwest, and around each grew the usual clustering group of workingmen's homes. Far off to the south end were the Calumet industries, extending from the Great Harbor to Lake Calumet.

Not only the areas of poverty but the areas of vice were well

[37] Dr. Homer Hoyt (*op. cit.*, p. 311) describes the growth of the poorer areas as follows: "Workingmen's cottages tended to grow up in all sections of the city between the belts of fashionable land and the industries and factories along the Chicago River. They filled in the spaces not wanted for industries or for high-grade residences. The tracts they occupied were close to the noise and dust of factories but not directly contiguous to water or rail transportation. Such sites were poorly provided with street improvements and with surface-car transportation. The people who remained in such neighborhoods were in the lowest economic status, intelligence, and ambition since the more progressive elements tended to move to better neighborhoods as soon as possible. Located often near railroad yards or terminals, they suffered from proximity to the vagrant population of tramps and homeless men."

[38] "Our old manufacturers are not content to repose on their laurels, but keep pegging away and winning new ones. The McCormick brothers, for instance. A year ago the tract of twenty-three acres on the South Branch, now occupied by the works of this concern, had on it nothing except a thrifty crop of corn and cabbages. Now, not only has that ground been covered with a factory costing, with its machinery, half a million dollars, but that factory has already turned out 11,000 completed reapers and mowers, all of which have been marketed. This number is 2,000 greater than had been reached in any whole year previous to the fire. These works support a population of 4,000" (from an editorial in the *Sunday Times* quoted in Chamberlin, *op. cit.*, p. 142).

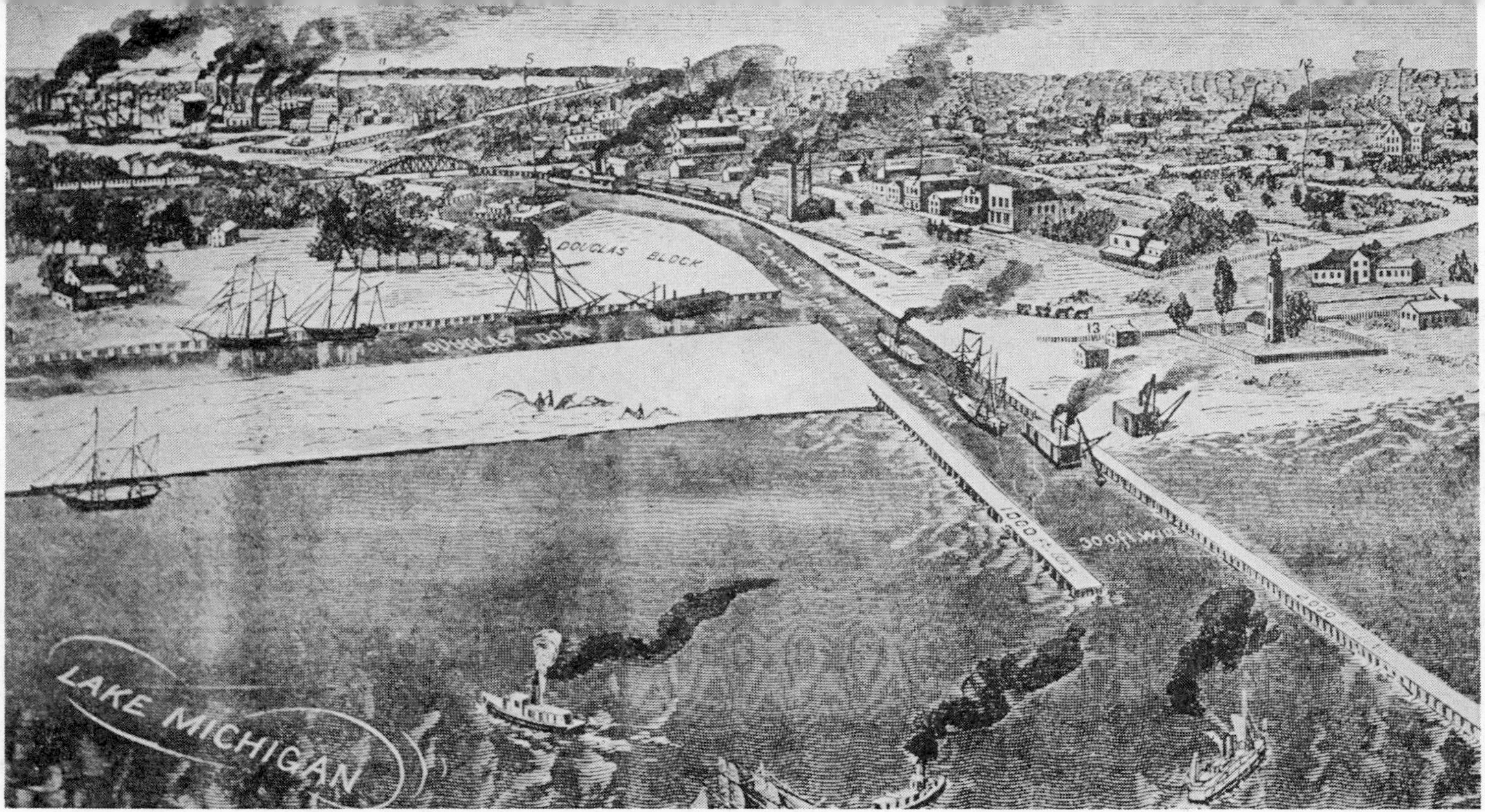

Courtesy of the Chicago Historical Society

THE CALUMET RIVER, 1871

known at the time of the fire; and there is a description of the scenes witnessed on the streets known as Fourth Avenue and Griswold Street of that day, which had "emptied their denizens into the throng. Ill-omened and obscence birds of night were they . . . . pinched with misery . . . . men who fatten on the wages of shame. . . . . Women, hollow-eyed and brazen-faced, with foul drapery tied over their heads, their dresses half-torn . . . . and their feet thrust into trodden-down slippers, moved here and there, stealing, scolding shrilly, and laughing with one another."[39] A contrast between the Chicago of that day and this is also seen in the great number of animals on the sands—animals which had fled or been taken from their stables, but which threatened to trample down the women and children, and greatly increased the terror of the helpless people.

Descriptions of the Great Fire lead us too far afield. It is clear from contemporary accounts that Chicago had some clearly defined areas of poverty, bad housing, and vice. But journalists do not always see the social problems of their own day, and it is not surprising that two of the men who wrote most vividly of the fire and of the poor districts it swept took them all as a matter of course. They saw no public health problem and no housing problem, although their book pictures both vividly for those who read it today with modern standards in mind.

Chicago they described almost complacently as "a healthy city." "The previously low and marshy site," they wrote, "had been raised sufficiently to permit of good drainage, but not high enough to allow any of the double-cellar style of life so common in New York; and

[39] Colbert and Chamberlin, *op. cit.*, pp. 216–17, quoting various eyewitnesses.

"The most natural resort of the people of this quarter, however, was said to have been the sandy beach of the lake, where there were but few houses and those were shanties. This strip of shore, known as 'the Sands,' was famous, or, rather, infamous, in years gone, as the *locale* of numerous low brothels, to which 'Long John' Wentworth, when Mayor of the city, gave the *coup de grace* by *allowing* them to burn up. Their place had never been fully occupied, and to this bleak, narrow area thus afforded, the terrified population shrank for refuge from the pursuing monster. Such an assemblage as there congregated Chicago never witnessed before, and probably never will witness again. It was a scene at the 'basin' repeated, with more diversity. The extremes of wealth and squalor had been dwelling within a stone's throw of each other in this section of the city, which had emptied itself upon this narrow skirt of sand. These inequalities of societies were now leveled off as smooth as the beach itself" (*ibid.*, p. 223).

the broad prairies furnished so much room for lateral expansion that there was much less of crowding than in other cities." It is also interesting that they thought that "the sickly tenement system" was almost unknown in Chicago and that it was "very rare to see one residence at the back of another, on the same lot."[40]

INDUSTRIAL DEVELOPMENT, IMMIGRATION, AND OVERCROWDING

Chicago was one of the first centers to be affected by that great development in the field of industry and manufacturing, of transportation and methods of communication, that followed the Civil War. Resident manufacturers of Chicago were responsible alike for the new output of agricultural machinery and for Pullman palace cars. Lumber yards were along the river north of Eighteenth Street, and there were also some great elevators on the river bank. In the decade 1860–70 Chicago had become the "foremost grain mart, lumber market, and packing center in the world."

Chicago's population increased fivefold from 1860 to 1880, and then increased again by 100 per cent before the census of 1890 was taken.[41] The revolutionary industrial and commercial changes, the great expansion of manufacturing, brought new waves of immigration into a metropolitan area that had no plan or policy for protecting these new, and often non-English speaking, workingmen from exploitation.

The immigrants constituted at an early date a problem for the charitable and, of course, a housing problem. The Relief and Aid Society, founded in 1857, dealt from the beginning largely with the foreign-born. "There are many strangers, frequently whole fami-

[40] *Ibid.*, p. 176.

[41] Dr. Homer Hoyt (*op. cit.*, p. 281), in discussing the almost miraculous development of this metropolitan area, asks: "Where did the people come from? . . . . And how were they brought to a spot which a century ago was a dismal swamp far removed from the path of settlement?" He puts immigration first as one of the "three main factors" which explain "so prodigious a rate of growth," and adds this comment: "Only a succession of improved transportation devices, combined with the stimulation of the flow of migration, settled so many people upon this prairie site in so short a time. Lake steamers and prairie schooners brought the advance guard of the thirties and forties, but combined ocean steamers and the newly completed railroads poured in the great stream of Irish and German immigrants of the fifties, sixties, and seventies, and the same agencies of transportation opened up the floodgates of southern European immigration beginning in the eighties."

lies, from foreign lands, as well as from remote parts of our own, with but little money and no friends, who arrive in this city and, through failure to find work, immediately are thrown upon this or similar charities for support or otherwise become public mendicants."[42] Out of 1,559 persons assisted in 1869, only 362 were Americans, either white or colored. The following data from an old report show the distribution of nationalities receiving aid in the year of the Great Fire and immediately afterward (1871–73): German, 14,816; Irish, 11,623; American, 4,823; Scandinavian, 3,624, and British, 1,967. The 2,389 others included Bohemians, Italians, Poles, and various other groups.

An official report of the health commissioner in 1877 describes the population of Chicago as increasing at what was, for that day, a very astonishing rate. The immigrant arrivals from abroad were said to consist of "picked men and women" in the hardy ages of life. Business men and skilled workmen were said to be "daily opening new shops and stores," and the commissioner thought that factories were "being removed from all parts of the United States to this commercial center. As a labor market," he said, "Chicago is fast becoming one of the most important points in the country," and he called attention to the fact that already there were "distinct settlements of Poles, Bohemians, Scandinavians, Germans, Irish, French, Belgians, and Dutch."[43]

In 1881 the city health commissioner again issued a report telling of the "great and rapid influx of population," which was said to have caused "a dangerous overcrowding in all the poorer districts." Overcrowding, he said, was becoming general "on account of an actual scarcity of houses within the city limits." Describing the great numbers of people coming to Chicago to find employment, he said they were not able to build and own their homes, and "the building of tenements on speculation" had become "a regular and profitable means of investing capital."[44]

[42] "Relief and Aid Report," *op. cit.*, p. 122.

[43] *Chicago Department of Health Report, 1877–78*, p. 15.

[44] He cited the federal census of 1880, which showed a population of 607,524 in Cook County—365,109 native-born and 242,415 foreign-born. "Amongst the natives are included the children of foreign-born parents, so that in actual numbers no more than one-half of the whole population are *native* Americans and their children" (*ibid., 1881–82*, pp. 47–50).

The number of occupants of tenement houses, he thought, was "about equal to the foreign population, not because of their nationality, but because it is the wage-workers of *all* nationalities who are compelled to occupy tenement houses." Most of the immigrant groups, gathered in foreign colonies, were living under unsatisfactory conditions, "as a rule," living "in close quarters on unimproved streets," and he thought it would require "thousands of new tenement buildings to accommodate properly those families who are now compelled to crowd together in houses too small for them." There were, he said, "a great many old buildings in this city which are unfit for habitation by civilized people; yet they are inhabited, and generally by Italians, Poles, Bohemians, and others, who, in their trans-Atlantic homes, have been accustomed to live in crowded quarters, in close proximity to their domestic animals, which in this city are not allowed to be kept within the premises used for human habitation." "Several thousands of Italians," he reported, were living "in a manner to require constant watching; several families living huddled together in one large room, with mere boards and curtains for partitions between their scanty household goods. Bohemians and Poles," he said, "would average one family to each room in many houses, while the mass of the Bohemian, Polish, Canadian, Irish, Scandinavian and Russian unskilled laboring classes certainly occupy no more than two rooms to a family, with perhaps a small closet for an extra bedroom." The danger of overcrowding, he wrote, was "largely increased by the below grade, imperfectly sewered character of these neighborhoods. Thousands of small houses and cottages arranged for one family are now packed with a family in each room, while the tenement houses—houses sheltering three or more families keeping house independently—are equally dense in population."[45]

[45] *Ibid.*, pp. 28–31. Discussing the nationality of the population of 600,000, which included 130,000 Germans, 120,000 Irish, 50,000 Scandinavians, 40,000 "Bohemians and Poles," and large numbers of others, the health commissioner was full of the kind of sweeping generalities that are still used in describing the foreign groups. He described the different nationalities as "quite distinct and separate in their hereditary peculiarities of home life and business habits. The Bohemians are compactly gathered in the southwestern section; the Scandinavians occupy both sides of the north branch of the Chicago River, the Irish live in the 5th, 6th, 7th, 8th and 17th Wards, while the Germans have colonized whole tracts in the north and west divisions, and the Americans cling to the

Certainly there was a serious housing problem in Chicago in 1880.

The commissioner described the results of a canvass in one of the West Side wards (the fourteenth ward of that day) which showed increasing congestion. The results of the very rude survey showed the small houses of the period used as multiple dwellings for many families. One house had twelve families; 2 houses had ten families each; 8 houses had nine families each; 5 houses, eight families; 15 houses, seven families; 64 houses, six families; 78 houses, five families; 443 houses, four families; and 491 houses, three families. On the Southwest Side the commissioner described the new Bohemian immigrant settlement where, he said, "the Bohemians are building up an extensive settlement where hundreds of families occupy a single room, and more than 1,000 families, swarming with children of all ages, average but two rooms to the family."[46]

Overcrowding and sanitary conditions, which had long been serious, were greatly aggravated during this period, and the homes of the workers were increasingly congested. These problems of lack of sanitation and of wretched housing conditions continued to become much worse as the industrial development proceeded. The decade from 1880 to 1890 was one of great expansion in the number of industries and the number of manufacturing establishments. Chicago had

---

lake shore, north and south, and on the west to the 9th, 10th, 11th, 12th and 13th Wards. The Negro and Italian find themselves homes in the second Ward."

Even more hasty conclusions were drawn as to employment, when the commissioner made these observations regarding the distribution of the newest and poorest inhabitants of this period: "By occupation the Italians are rag and junk gatherers, and fruit peddlers. The Poles and Bohemians perform common manual labor in rag shops, glue works, fertilizing establishments, tobacco factories, lumber yards, tanneries, and the women are largely employed in small tailor shops for manufacture of ready-made clothing. The Irish are teamsters, railroad laborers, moulders and iron-workers. The Germans are small shop-keepers and skilled artisans in all standard trades; the Scandinavians are also well represented in all skilled trades and occupations, and in small commercial pursuits. The Americans are chiefly in the professions and the several branches of commercial, distributive and speculative business."

[46] *Ibid.* The commissioner found the objectionable saloons of that day "frequent and well patronized in these localities; and he explained this as due chiefly to the fact that the fathers and older boys found that their own homes—"kitchen, dining room, sitting-room, and sleeping apartment all in one"—did not "afford even standing room for them until the smaller children are packed away in the corners after the evening meal."

become in 1890 the second city in the United States, not only in population but also the second manufacturing city in the country, after New York. The growth during this period[47] is shown by the statistics from the federal census given in the accompanying table, indicates the remarkable industrial development of the metropolis of the West. At the close of the decade 1880–90, the great expansion in

Year	Number of Industries Reported	Number of Establishments Reported	Capital	Hands Employed	Wages Paid	Cost of Materials	Value of Product
1880......	189	3,519	$ 68,836,885	79,414	$ 34,653,462	$179,209,610	$249,022,948
1890......	255	9,959	292,477,038	203,108	119,146,357	386,814,848	632,184,140

the industry led to an even greater expansion in the influx of immigrant workingmen, with the corresponding increase in congestion in the West Side. "Congestion of immigrants in large cities," wrote one of the leading investigators for the United States Immigration Commission, "has long been considered one of the most unfavorable features of the modern problem of immigration."[48]

THE EARLY HULL-HOUSE GROUP AND HOUSING REFORM

One of the early federal investigations, a report of the new United States Commissioner of Labor, described the tenement-house system of this decade as "largely engrafted on the life of Chicago." While the sanitary condition of houses and streets was said to be "bad," the commissioner took an optimistic view of the situation when he suggested that these evils were "being remedied by the vigorous action of the Health Department." The new federal bureau was perhaps too cautious in dealing with the evils of local communities in these pioneer social studies. It was considered a favorable aspect of the Chicago situation that Chicago houses were rarely found "in long blocks," and therefore they seldom contained more than six families. He did not take note of the fact that most of these Chicago houses were frame cottages and two-story dwellings built for one family. "Two or three families living in a separate house" was the general rule, he thought, and there were still many families occupying single

[47] See Moses and Kirkland, *History of Chicago*, I, 240.

[48] *Reports of the U.S. Immigration Commission*, Vol. I: *Abstracts*, p. 727. This was the federal investigating commission appointed by the first President Roosevelt.

dwellings. Rents were said to be high, "the markets inconvenient, and the cost of living greater than in any other western city."[49]

This was the now historic decade when Jane Addams, in 1889, established the first American social settlement in Chicago, and when she wisely chose as the place for her new experiment one of the congested river wards of the West Side. The influence of Hull-House soon brought a new and vigorous influence to bear upon the problems of housing and sanitation. Two other early reports of the commissioner of labor contained data regarding this section of the city. These reports were *The Slums of Great Cities* (1894) and *The Italians in Chicago* (1897). The investigation of city slums included New York, Chicago, Philadelphia, and Baltimore; and a resident of Hull-House, Mrs. Florence Kelley, who later became one of the leaders of the social-reform movement in America, was the Chicago investigator for this study. The area selected for the house-to-house inquiry was, appropriately enough, the area directly east of Hull-House, stretching straight across the river into the "bad lands" of that day, the disreputable area of vice and disorder that lay along the irregular western edge of the business district. A slum was defined for purposes of the federal investigation as an "area of dirty back streets, especially when inhabited by a squalid and criminal population," and the slum population of Chicago was estimated at 162,000. In the area studied, the saloons, instead of numbering 1 to 212 people, as in the city at large, were 1 to 127; the number of persons to a dwelling 15.5 instead of 8.6, as through the city as a whole.

Outside sanitary conditions were reported to be worse in Chicago than in the other three cities investigated. The conditions regarding sanitation and plumbing were bad in all the cities, according to any proper standard. In Chicago there were in the small area studied 811

[49] *Working Women in Large Cities* (*Fourth Annual Report, 1888, U.S. Commissioner of Labor*), pp. 6–17. There was said to be "a large foreign element in Chicago" with what was described as "a rough class of girls sometimes unfamiliar with the English language and again speaking it fairly." A further indication of the wretched conditions of the poorer districts was the report on the number of prostitutes, said to be "far below" the actual number. In Chicago, there were reported to be at the time of this federal investigation, "302 houses of ill-fame, assignation houses, and 'rooming' houses, known to the police, containing 1,097 inmates. This investigation involved 557 of this number." In certain other cities—e.g., Philadelphia and Brooklyn—the proportion of prostitutes interviewed was said not to be so large as in Chicago.

sleeping-rooms without any outside windows; only 2.8 per cent of the families in the slum area had bathrooms; and 73.5 per cent of the families were living on premises with insanitary privy vaults. With regard to congestion, the report showed that 5.9 per cent of the slum families were living in one-room tenements; 19.1 per cent in two-room tenements; and 26.6 per cent in three-room tenements. Thus more than one-half of the families included in the canvass were living in tenements that had fewer than four rooms, although approximately 60 per cent were immigrant families with many children. Of the 19,654 individuals in the 3,881 families covered by the investigation, 3,826 had less than 200 cubic feet of air per person; 4,426 between 200 and 300 cubic feet of air; 4,426 between 200 and 300 cubic feet; 3,584 between 300 and 400 cubic feet; and 2,558 between 400 and 500 cubic feet.[50] In 1893 the legislature passed the "anti-sweatshop law"[51] and created the State Factory Inspection Department, and this new agency became one of the vigorous forces in the attack on tenement conditions in Chicago. Mrs. Florence Kelley, who was appointed chief factory inspector, continued to live at Hull-House, and for four years she went in and out of tenement workshops and vigorously condemned in her official reports the conditions that she found on the West Side.

Mrs. Kelley's early factory inspector's reports (1893–95) give a vivid picture of life in the Chicago tenements during her long strug-

[50] The facts about wages and hours partly explained the miserable housing conditions, for it was found that, except for a small number classed as professional, the weekly earnings of the men ranged from $4.05 to $11.79, while the women earned between $3.05 and $5.97 a week. The theory that Chicago was too new a city for a housing problem to have developed is illustrated in a series of magazine articles, later published in book form under the title "The Poor in Great Cities" (1895). In the section dealing with Chicago a not very intelligent observer says the "tenement house evil, as it is known in New York and London, shows almost no trace in the new spacious mart on the edge of the Grand Prairie." However, although the writer saw no "tall, huge rookeries" like New York's, he found "The Dive," then occupied by Italians below the Twelfth Street viaduct, full of "squalor, filth, crowding."

[51] Smith-Hurd, *Revised Statutes of Illinois,* c. 48, secs. 40–46. This statute was one of the early achievements of the Hull-House residents and the labor group, and was called "An Act to regulate the manufacture of clothing, wearing apparel and other articles in this State, and to provide for the appointment of State inspectors to enforce the same, and to make an appropriation therefor, June 17, 1893," *Laws of the State of Illinois* (1893), p. 99.

gle to secure some public control over tenement-house sweatshops. The basement rooms she described as "low-ceilinged, ill-lighted, unventilated rooms, below the street level, damp and cold in winter, hot and close in summer; foul at all times by reason of adjacent vaults or defective sewer connections."[52]

By way of summary it may be said that at the time of the first World's Fair there were great cities of the poor gathered in different parts of the city of Chicago.[53] In these cities of the poor, covering many acres of the metropolitan area, were miserable tenements stretching along poorly paved, cheerless, and often filthy streets and alleys. The various attempts to regulate insanitary conditions and to improve tenement construction will be described in the following chapter which deals with the long struggle for tenement-house ordinances and efficient methods of inspection. A successful outcome still lies in the future.

[52] *Third Annual Report of Factory Inspector of Illinois, Ending December 15, 1895*, p. 54. Mrs. Kelley also described the "shops over sheds or stables" where "the operatives receive from below the stench from the vaults or the accumulated stable refuse; from the rear, the effluvia of the garbage boxes and manure bins in the filthy, unpaved alleys; and from the front, the varied stenches of the tenement house yard, the dumping ground for all the families residing on the premises." She also described the lack of proper ventilation; the upper floors which were "reached by narrow and filthy halls, and unlighted wooden stairways"; which were "cold in winter unless all fresh air is shut out, and hot in summer." In old houses, she noted there were "no sanitary arrangements beyond the vaults used by all tenants; if in modern tenements the drains are out of order, water for the closets does not rise to the upper floors, and poisonous gases fill the shops. This defective water supply, the absence of fire escapes, and the presence of the pressers' stove greatly aggravate the danger of death by fire."

All Mrs. Kelley's official reports are interesting and readable human documents. See E. Abbott and S. P. Breckinridge, *Truancy and Non-attendance in the Chicago Schools*, pp. 72–84, 299, 402, for a further statement about Mrs. Kelley's work in Chicago.

[53] Further accounts of the historical development of the tenement areas which were canvassed will be found below in chap. iii, which describes the tenement districts which were studied.

CHAPTER II

TENEMENT-HOUSE LEGISLATION IN CHICAGO[1]

The Health Department and Early Public Health Conditions; The Period of the Epidemics, 1833–71; Chicago's First Tenement-House Ordinance, 1874; Beginning of Tenement and Workshop Inspection, 1879–81; New Public Interest in Housing Reform; The Building Department; The City Homes Association; The Struggle To Establish a True Tenement-House Authority, 1903–7; The Sanitary Bureau, 1907–22; Reorganization of the Department.

AN ATTEMPT to outline the more important features of that body of legislation, whether enacted by the legislature or under statutory authority by the City Council, which is generally referred to as the "housing" or "tenement" law is not a simple task. In the first place, the law has been administered both by the Building Department of the city and by the Health Department formerly through its Sanitary Bureau; and now through a Bureau of Sanitary Engineering, which will be more fully described below; and duties are assigned to the Fire, Police, and Public Works departments as well. In the second place, while the portion of the law administered by the Building Department relates to efforts on the part of the city authorities to prevent fire and collapse, and so becomes very technical in regard to such subjects as materials and strain, the portion administered by the Health Department relates to primitive attempts to abate nuisances, and should include more elaborate discussion of the modern disposal of waste through plumbing and drainage than is possible here. It is important, however, that some attention be given to the earlier phases in the development of administrative machinery for dealing with those conditions antedating the "tenement problem."

This chapter will therefore consider five periods or divisions in the development of a housing authority:[2] (1) the early measures provid-

[1] By Sophonisba P. Breckinridge.

[2] The material for this discussion is drawn, with few exceptions, from public documents, the statutes, ordinances, and reports of the Health Department. The excep-

ing for a health authority in relation to what may be called outside insanitary conditions (prior to 1903); (2) a brief discussion of early building regulations and the more recent organization of the Building Department in relation to the administration of the housing code; (3) the development of a true tenement-law authority, 1903–7; (4) the Sanitary Bureau, 1907–22; (5) the abolition of the Sanitary Bureau and the distribution of functions among other bureaus in the Department.

THE HEALTH DEPARTMENT AND EARLY PUBLIC HEALTH CONDITIONS

The Health Department, like the Building Department, is under the duty of approving the plans of new buildings before building operations may be begun. In 1881 the approval of such plans in the case of "any projected tenement lodging-house or other place of

---

tions are the writings of the Hull-House residents and the report of the early City Homes Association on Tenement Conditions in Chicago.

A word should be said about the reports available. The Building Department has issued no reports since 1910.

The sanitary history of the city from 1833 to 1867 was fortunately reviewed by the Board of Health created in 1867, and is thus available in their first report. From that time until 1905, with the exception of a break in 1870, later accounted for in the report of 1874, the reports of the Health Department are continuous, and while often flat, without originality or vigor, they contain certain valuable data.

Between 1905 and 1910 nothing appeared. When in 1910 the reports for 1907, 1908, 1909, and 1910 appeared in one volume, the only recommendation bearing on housing conditions was that a housing census should be taken (see p. 212). From 1910 to 1918 nothing appeared; and again nothing was published in 1919 and 1920, so that the last seventeen years are covered by four documents, the *Reports* for 1907–10, 1910–18, 1918–21, and 1922. Again, the three years 1923–25 are covered by one report; and the five years 1926–30 are also covered in a single volume. No report was issued in 1931, while plans for reorganization were being developed. For the years 1932 and 1933 again small separate volumes are available. At the time of writing (January, 1936), the *Report* for 1934 has not been published.

If the Chicago reports are compared with the reports of the New York Tenement House Department, one great source of weakness of the movement for housing reform in Chicago may be easily discovered. There has been no tenement-house department in Chicago solely concerned with the housing problem, with regularly published reports of work done, courageously made, with the honest purpose of discovering the weak spots and the sources of failure. This basis for housing reform has been wholly lacking in the Chicago movement.

habitation"[3] in relation to "the ventilation of rooms, light and air shafts, windows, ventilation of water closets, drainage and plumbing" was laid on the "health commissioner or health commissioners."

But the duty of this Department includes likewise a continuing supervision over the use of "tenement houses," whether old or new, for the purpose of securing to the occupants at least a minimum of light, air, cleanliness, and freedom from nuisances.

This Department, like the Building Department, constituted one of the major divisions of the city's executive from 1879 to 1932; it had a similar organization under a commissioner, and a physician appointed by the mayor and Council. Until 1932 it was organized into the following bureaus:[4] medical inspection, hospital, baths and lodging-houses, vital statistics, food inspection, a laboratory bureau, and a bureau of sanitary inspection, which for a long time included five divisions of work: plumbing and new buildings; heating and ventilation; housing and sanitation; smoke abatement; and office and records. Tenement-house inspection has, therefore, been one of a varied assortment of departmental duties. Before discussing more at length the organization of the Bureau, it will be well to trace the legislation administered by this division of the city government.

As the Building Department control relates itself to the early attempts to secure protection against fire and against such dishonest building as led to collapse and physical danger, so the work of the Health Department is related in its earlier phases to the attempts to deal with the spread of epidemics, such as cholera, and with nui-

[3] In any incorporated city of fifty thousand inhabitants (*Illinois Laws, 1881*, p. 61, sec. 1).

[4] See *Report of Department of Health* (1922), pp. 227 ff. In 1915 the commissioner of health requested the efficiency division of the Chicago Civil Service Commission to make a critical study of the organization and work of the Department, and at that time the services of Dr. J. C. Perry, senior surgeon of the U.S. Public Health Service, were secured (see *U.S. Public Health Reports*, XXX Part II, 2422, 2536, 2850).

In 1924 the divisions of community and industrial sanitation replaced the divisions of housing and sanitation. This organization was continued until the reorganization of 1932, described below.

On January 1, 1935, the Bureau of Sanitation became the Bureau of Sanitary Engineering. This Bureau includes six divisions. One of these, the division of plumbing and new buildings, succeeded to the responsibility of examining plans for new buildings, inspecting plumbing on new buildings, and installations in old buildings.

sances. The problem of disposing of waste in a community in which numbers increase far more rapidly than living accommodations and sanitary conveniences can be provided, is one still confronting the city authorities.

THE PERIOD OF THE EPIDEMICS

The period at which the governmental organization of the city was being established was the period when the scourge of cholera was sweeping over various sections of the country and threatening all centers of population. When Chicago was incorporated as a town on August 5, 1833, among the first ordinances passed was one appointing a fire warden and another prohibiting throwing dead animals into the river.[5] Whenever cholera, or later, smallpox, seemed imminent and so long as the consciousness of danger was lively, emergency action of this kind was usually taken. In August, 1834, for example, during one of these visitations a board of health was created to provide a hospital, "to prescribe for all persons attacked with cholera" and to give such instruction to the town supervisor as would "promote the health of the town."

The following summer, June 19, 1835, a Board of Health was created, with seven members, and on them was laid the duty of examining "streets and alleys and dwelling houses," of causing owners to "remove all the predisposing causes of disease," and of abating "all nuisances of whatever kind."[6] The necessity of a safe water sup-

[5] Chamberlin, *Chicago and Its Suburbs*, p. 36; *Chicago Board of Health Report, 1867–1869; and A Sanitary History of Chicago, 1833–1870*, p. 10.

[6] *Ibid.*, p. 12: "June 19, 1835. At a Special Meeting of the President and Trustees of the town of Chicago, there were present John H. Kinzie, President; John K. Boyer, G. S. Hubbard, E. Goodrich and John S. C. Hogan."

The ordinance provided that the duties of the new Board of Health include the examining of all the streets, alleys, and other highways and "the condition of each and every lot, dwelling-house, cellar, out-house or other building of whatsoever description," and that the owners or occupiers be required "to remove all of the predisposing causes of disease, abate all nuisances of whatever kind"; and in case any owner or occupier should "refuse or neglect, for twenty-four hours after being required by any member of the Board of Health, or the Supervisor, so to do, to remove such cause of disease, or abate such nuisance," it was the duty of the Board of Health or Supervisor "to remove the same, at the expense of the person so neglecting or refusing." In addition, a fine of five dollars was to be paid.

At the first meeting of the Board, which was held on June 23, 1835, "Messrs. Hubbard and King presented their Report of inspection of that part of town near the front

ply was also faced, and the Chicago Hydraulic Company was organized in 1836 to sell water to the citizens of Chicago for a period of nearly two decades. On March 4, 1837, Chicago secured a city charter, and among other grants of power was that of electing sextons and scavengers as well as that of exercising various powers over the conditions affecting public health.[7] The charter likewise authorized the annual appointment of a Board of Health of three and the appointment of a city health officer, whose duty would be to visit persons suspected of being ill with infectious diseases and to board vessels on which any pestilential disease might be found.

During the following decade, population increased rapidly and a number of offensive trades developed. The slaughtering business was established in 1848, when Archibald Clybourn established a slaughtering business on the east side of the North Branch and Gordon Hubbard brought in about three hundred hogs and started a packing business, sending products East as well as selling in the local market; and the manufacture of by-products, candles, hides, and soap took on considerable proportion. Ordinances dealing not only with the condition of the streets and alleys but with other nuisances as well were necessary.

In 1846, for example, a plan for a weekly clean-up of the business district was embodied in an order that the Board of Health should make an examination of the lots, alleys, and sewers, "so that measures to preserve the health of the city might be adopted." At the same time it was ordered that the owners or occupants of lots on the streets in the business portion of the city be required "to collect into heaps, every Saturday morning, vegetables or other matter liable to decomposition, in front of their houses; and that the street Com-

---

end, west of the North Branch of the Chicago river . . . . ; Messrs. J. S. C. Hogan, Boyer and Alanson Sweet made their Report of inspection and of nuisances, etc. . . . . , Messrs. Fullerton and J. H. Kinzie made their Report of nuisances"; on motion of G. S. Hubbard, "it was further ordained that the Street Supervisor be authorized and directed to re-examine the several premises reported as having nuisances thereon, as reported by the above Committees, and that if they find the said nuisances not removed, or in progress of removal, forthwith to furnish the attorney of the corporation with the names of the delinquents, that prosecution may be commenced forthwith against such delinquents."

[7] *Ibid.*, p. 14; *Laws of Illinois*, *1836–37*, p. 50.

missioner provide scavengers to remove the same."[8] In the following year, owners of offensive businesses were required to move to outlying areas,[9] and power was secured[10] to establish and maintain a sewer system.

The year 1849 was again a cholera year, and there were vigorous cleaning-up efforts. The Board of Health was given increased resources in the shape of a number of assistant health officers, so that an officer could be assigned to each block in the city.[11] And under the pressure of the epidemic that summer the erection of slaughter houses in the city was prohibited (July 30) and a resolution to build sewers was adopted by the City Council (August 13).

The mortality of 1849 and 1850 from cholera in the localities where well water was used and the inability of the Chicago Hydraulic Company to supply more than a small proportion of the inhabitants with lake water led in 1851 to the inauguration of the present system of supplying water, when the legislature incorporated the Chicago City Hydraulic Company and appointed a board of three water commissioners designated in the act.[12]

The evidence already accumulated and the experience of 1852, when the cholera was again virulent, went to show the imperative need of an adequate supply of lake water to replace both the well water often relied on and the services of the private water company and the importance of a better drainage system, and during the next few years the city was visited not only by smallpox (in 1854 and 1855) but by typhoid and typhus fever, scarlet fever, and diptheria,

[8] *Board of Health Report, 1867–69*, p. 18.

[9] E.g., Mr. Cleaver, a soap and candle manufacturer, moved from a site in the business district and established a factory at Cleaverville between Thirty-seventh and Thirty-ninth streets and between State and Lake streets. See his account in *Reminiscences of Chicago*, republished by the Chicago Historical Society (*Reminiscences of Chicago during the Forties and Fifties*, p. 62). For account of the early packing industry, see pp. 69 ff.

[10] February 16, 1847 (*Private Laws, 1847*, p. 87, sec. 12).

[11] Forty-five were appointed, 28 on April 2 and 17 on April 23 (see *Board of Health Report, 1867–1869*, p. 22).

[12] February 15, 1851 (*Private Laws, 1851*, p. 213). The city charter had been reenacted in brief form, leaving the organization and powers of the Board of Health as under the earlier act (see p. 132).

and in 1856 a comprehensive sewer system was finally designed and approved, and construction was begun.

The warm approval of the Chicago Board of Health was given to this plan for sewer development. In the account given in a later report they point out that under the earlier act "an intelligent Board of Sewerage Commissioners" had been elected, and E. S. Chesborough had been "fortunately" appointed engineer of the Board. The Board of Health reported that Chicago was "mainly indebted" to him for its system of sewerage. The Chesborough report on the sewerage plan was approved by the Commissioners, was later adopted by the mayor and the City Council, and finally inaugurated "this most important sanitary measure."

From their later experience the Board reported with satisfaction that the Chesborough system was a great success. "To secure drainage, the filling and raising up of a large portion of the city was an absolute necessity, and, what [had] already been accomplished in this direction, [was] regarded as one of the greatest achievements of the age; and many localities that, several years ago, [had been] low, wet, and at certain seasons impassable, [were then] dry and solid ground."[13]

A still later comment of the Board pointed out that within a period of less than two decades 4,000 acres had been "raised to a grade of 3 to 5 feet above the bottomless quagmire which formerly bordered this shore of Lake Michigan. A system of water supply projected in 1861 [had] been completed, capable of furnishing 100,000,000 of gallons every twenty-four hours, drawn through a tunnel which [extended] under the lake two miles from shore."[14]

[13] "In this way not alone has dryness of the soil been obtained, but the prompt removal of the solid and fluid excreta of men and animals—one of the greatest sanitary necessities of our populous cities—in addition to the waste water and filth incident to domestic life" (*Board of Health Report, 1867–1869*, pp. 258–59).

[14] "There are 416 miles of water-mains laid and in use at this date. A plan of sewerage was prepared and its execution commenced in 1856, which has been faithfully and energetically followed. The difficulties overcome and success already attained is abundant testimony to the great ability of the gentlemen engaged in the work. The low level of the populous part of the city has been raised as before indicated; the current of the Chicago river has been reversed in its course by the deepening of the Illinois and Michigan canal, at a cost of $5,000,000, and the river now carries from our midst and away from the lake the sewage received from 266 miles of mains. There are 128 miles of streets improved by graveling, macadamizing and wooden block pavement, with 673 miles of sidewalk" (*ibid., 1879–1880*, p. 6).

The filling-up process not only provided drainage but "raised houses from the wet and mud—a frequent cause of sickness in damp localities." The Board pointed out that "the great sanitary necessity of all densely populated localities" was some provision for draining off the water as rapidly as possible, "thus keeping the soil dry, preventing dampness, and, at certain seasons of the year, the escape of noxious emanations." It was said that two-thirds of the mortality of Chicago in this post–Civil-War period occurred "in low, wet, damp and illy drained localities," and in times of epidemics the two-thirds increased to three-fourths. The lot-owners were charged with failing in many cases to make drainage facilities available. The Board of Public Works had constructed in sewered streets 19,803 house drains, but only 15,571 dwellings were connected with the sewers. In some cases this was because many houses were built upon leased property, the lease in many cases being renewed from year to year, and the lessees were "too poor to make the necessary connections, although by law they [were] compelled to do so; and in this way, to a great extent, [was] lost the sanitary benefit to the district." There were said to be streets with property owned by the wealthiest men in the city, where connections had not been made.[15]

In 1860, after a brief interval of four years when the city had not been visited either by cholera or by smallpox, the ordinance creating the Board of Health and office of health officer was repealed, and their duties were transferred to the Police Department under the direction of the mayor. The following year, however, in the act which replaced the City Hydraulic Company created in 1851 and the Board of Sewerage Commissioners created in 1855 by the Board of Public Works, a Board of Health and health officer were listed among the city officials without provision being made for their appointment or election. However, the City Council in the following year (August 25, 1862), after an investigation by a committee of its members, passed an ordinance creating a so-called Committee of Health, appointed by the mayor and made up of a representative from each division of the city. This Committee was to exist for a

[15] "An effort was made at the last Legislature by the Board to have the law changed so that owners of property should make the connections. In some cases, the connections being imperfectly made, the desired result is not attained" *ibid., 1867–1869*, p. 260).

year, and was to recommend to the Council ordinances which would in their judgment provide for the suppression of all nuisances that endangered the health of the city. The office of city physician was also created during the summer of 1862 to deal with the smallpox epidemic, and new negotiations were undertaken with the authorities of the canal looking toward the flushing of the river by drawing through its course the water from the canal. In 1863 this Committee of Health was abolished, and their powers were transferred to the police,[16] where they remained for the next four years.

During these years the condition of the Chicago River constantly received the attention of the authorities. In 1869 the Board was especially concerned about the sluggishness of the North Branch and what they regarded as a lack of public apprehension over the situation. Referring to the early ordinance for preventing the "carcasses of dead animals" from being thrown into the river, the Board pointed out that "with the increase of population, and of slaughtering, packing, distilling and manufacturing on its banks," laws and ordinances on this subject had been "made more stringent," but that these were still "all more or less temporary in their character." The Board therefore thought that the time had come when "more efficient means must be taken to prevent pestiferous and nauseous exhalations from this stream, at certain seasons of the year."[17]

The city as a whole was, in fact, deeply concerned; and engineers, the Board of Trade, and other groups devised various schemes for draining the river into the Des Plaines or for connecting it with the lake. Public meetings were held, a Committee of Thirty was formed to secure legislation, there was agitation and public education, ordinances were drafted, some of which were passed by the Council and

[16] *Private Laws, 1863*, p. 119; see also *ibid., 1865*, p. 591.

[17] "A large amount of noxious material was allowed to run into the river from 1861 to 1865. Since then, the laws passed in 1865 have been enforced as rigidly as possible, but they can not be strictly observed, without the total prohibition of certain branches of trade that are carried on on its banks. Should this even be accomplished with the increased quantity of sewerage that annually flows into the river, the means that are now provided for its purification, at certain seasons, are wholly inadequate, and, as far as the North Branch is concerned, practically of no use or effect. While I do not anticipate much trouble this season, judging by the experience of the past, unless something of more than ordinary character occurs, I am well satisfied that steps must be taken to introduce water into the North Branch" (*Board of Health Report, 1867–1869*, p. 6).

vetoed by the mayor; but, except for a greatly enlarged appropriation to the police authorities for health work and for a consequently greatly increased staff, owing to the fear of "Asiatic cholera," nothing effective was done to create permanent administrative machinery for dealing with nuisances or for protecting the public health.

Finally, another cholera and another smallpox epidemic strengthened the influence of those who had been for several years agitating continuously for reform, and in 1867 the legislature authorized the creation of a Board of Health of seven persons, the mayor, and six others to be designated by the judges of the Superior Court of Cook County to serve in rotation for periods of six years.[18] The history of the health authority in Chicago has, then, been continuous from 1867, when the first Board was appointed, down to the present time. And that authority retained the form of a board of seven as then constituted until 1879, when the Board was abolished and a commissioner was substituted as head of the Department.[19]

The creation of this Board led to an elaborate "Sanitary Survey" of the city, by wards, covering among other subjects the general features of the district, the grade and pavement, the drainage, the water supply, and the buildings.[20]

During the following ten years the reports of the secretary of the Board and of the health officer had to do with "outside insanitary conditions, filthy areas and alleys, full privies, cesspools, defective drains, gutters in yards, streets, and alleys"; "nuisances abated"; "loads of ashes removed"; "number of miles of gutter disinfected"—or with such inside nuisances as grow out of inadequate or defective plumbing.[21]

The City Council had been greatly concerned about the abate-

[18] See *Private Laws, Illinois, 1867*, I, 754 at 763.

[19] However, in the revision in 1872 of the Cities and Villages Act, the legislature had authorized the appointment of a Board of Health (*Smith-Hurd, Illinois Revised Statutes, 1933*, c. 24, sec. 65:75); and in 1923 the Supreme Court held that the commissioner was simply a ministerial officer and that many powers vested in him were beyond the authority of the Council, and the Board was therefore shortly thereafter restored (see *People* v. *Robertson*, 302 Ill. 422 [1923]).

[20] *Department of Health Report, 1867–1869*, p. 198.

[21] See, e.g., *Report for 1870*, p. 225; also *ibid.*, *1871–1873*, pp. 20, 21, 154, 160; *ibid.*, *1874–1875*, pp. 65–66.

ment of nuisances. But in October of 1871 came the unforeseen but dreaded conflagration, and, in the months and years immediately following, the question of crowding also presented itself, while the old question of the polluted condition of the river in both branches remained always present.[22]

CHICAGO'S FIRST TENEMENT-HOUSE ORDINANCE, 1874

In 1874 a tenement-house ordinance was submitted to the City Council, and a brief statement of its importance brought the discussion for the first time into the report of the health authority; but the ordinance was finally not passed. The tenement- and lodging-house problem is, however, for a number of years treated chiefly as a factor in the spread of disease rather than as a means of providing minimum housing standards. It was reported,[23] for example, that there were few tenement houses in the north division of the city, and those were "in the area of North Avenue and west of Sedgwick Street and occupied entirely by a foreign population—mostly Swedes and Norwegians—not overcrowded and in fair condition." And in his report for 1875, the sanitary inspector responsible for the South Side[24] re-

[22] "During the past few years the North Branch of the Chicago River has been in an extremely foul condition. The water remaining standing with the yearly accretions is, during the hot months, converted into a cesspool, seething, boiling and reeking with filth, which fills the north wards of the city with mephitic gases. That this has an influence on mortality in the district lying east of the river, where the prevailing winds give them the full effect of those gases, there can be no doubt. Take the mortality of the 15th and 16th wards during the hot months. The 15th, lying west of the river, has a flat clay soil, and the local conditions are such as would indicate a high death rate at all times; in the 16th, lying east of the river, the local conditions are more favorable to a low death rate, the soil being sandy and dry. But, as before stated, in the course of the west wind, as it sweeps over the river in this section, during the hot months, the mortality is increased, and with cold weather, when the water falls to a temperature at which it does not give off poisonous gases, the mortality of this ward falls below that of the 15th. I cannot too strongly urge the early commencement of the work of cleansing this stream.

"The south fork of the South Branch is in a condition that demands the immediate attention of the city authorities. This stream is now in a condition fully as foul as the North Branch, and with the immense packing business growing up at the stock yards, which must discharge its sewerage into this stream, it will each year become more and more foul. Steps should be taken by which the water in this stream could be changed. If it is not done at an early day the stream will become a source of disease" (*Board of Health Report 1870–1873*, pp. 13, 14.)

[23] *Ibid.*, *1874–1875*, pp. 21, 138.

[24] I.e., Wards 1, 2, 3, 4, 5, 6 (*ibid.*, pp. 71–72; see also p. 92).

ported that "the policy of the Board of Health in examining tenement and lodging houses and following up and vaccinating persons who had been exposed to smallpox" had been carried out in that district "with good results." But even as a factor in the spread of disease, the influence of congested living was regarded as less harmful than was the lack of a proper water supply and an adequate drainage system.

During this period, in fact, evidence was accumulating as to the connection between the spread of disease, "zymotic diseases," and lack of drainage facilities, so that lack of sewers rather than crowding seemed the source of disaster,[25] although the foci of infection were frequently said to be "tenement houses."[26] And in the report for 1878 the commissioner claimed authority under the act of 1867 to protect the health of the city. The facts with reference to this character of dwellings were stated at length and further legislation was urged. It was pointed out that there were "nearly 100 per cent more deaths from the filth diseases" in wards of the city not yet provided with sewerage. Chicago, he thought, furnished "striking illustrations of the influence of proper sewerage upon the death-rate." "Wherever sewers are placed," he reported, "privy vaults are abolished, slops and kitchen wash are kept from the gutters, and the 'below grade' character and habits of the population in matters of personal and domestic cleanliness are at once raised to a higher level. It is very true that good sewers do not supply the sum total of necessities for good living and healthy life, but in large cities they are the most important factor."[27]

At this time the tenement house was arbitrarily defined to include only dwellings occupied by three or more families. The commissioner said that "the improvement of these homes of the poorer or dependent classes" had constantly occupied his attention since his appointment as commissioner of health, and, he thought, "means to improve their character and condition" had been vigorously pressed. The term "tenement house," he said, was applied to "dwellings that

[25] See *ibid.*, *1876–77*, p. 11.

[26] See *ibid.*, p. 26; e.g., August 11: "Smallpox appeared in a tenement house on Milwaukee Avenue near Noble. Twenty cases arose from this source."

[27] *Ibid.*, *1877*, p. 11. A table is not cited for lack of space.

present the widest differences; the only feature which they necessarily possess in common is their occupancy by more than three families keeping house independently."

At this time there were 4,896 tenement houses in the city occupied by 17,768 families. However, in the absence of any tenement-house law giving him authority "to order the vacation of uninhabitable buildings and to refuse to let them be again occupied until placed in proper sanitary condition," the commissioner said that he had decided to act under the authority of the statute of 1867, which provided that when "the sanitary condition of the city should be of such character as to warrant it," it should be the duty of the commissioner of health to adopt any measures "for the preservation of the public health," which he "in good faith" should declare to be necessary for "the public safety and health."

The commissioner pointed out that while it was true that the Board of Health Act of 1867 had been drawn to meet the emergencies presented by epidemics, nevertheless he thought that it was also true that Chicago tenements, "without the energetic and vigilant attention of the sanitary authority," became "nurseries of every form of contagious disease, and of perpetual epidemics," and remained "a great menace to the public safety and health." The commissioner therefore announced that he planned to present to the Council in the following year the draft of a tenement-house law which would "give the Department of Health a direct and full control of the sanitary arrangements and condition of these homes of the laboring classes."

At this time he laid down three conditions which he said were necessary "for the sanitary well-being of any tenement house." These were: (1) a proper construction of the house itself; (2) a constant supervision of the house by the owner or agent; (3) a disposition on the part of the tenant to aid in the preservation of good sanitary condition of the premises.[28]

[28] The commissioner added: "The records of the Department show that 11,630 formal notices have been served during the year on owners, agents or tenants, to abate nuisances connected with this class of sanitary work, and 301 suits brought where formal notice to remedy or abate has not been promptly observed. More than 70,000 verbal explanations and importunities have been made by the sanitary officers which have caused the removal of the defect complained of without the necessity of formal notice" (*ibid., 1878*, pp. 10–11).

BEGINNING OF TENEMENT AND WORKSHOP INSPECTION, 1879–81

Beginning with the year 1880, the tenement and workshop inspection act, based on an ordinance of 1879 and re-enacted in improved form on September 13, 1880, was reported on by the Health Department. This ordinance[29] required employers to provide work-places that were not too crowded, that had proper and adequate ventilation, in cleanly condition, with suitable and adequate toilet accommodations, and also required a monthly inspection of such places with an annual report on them during the first quarter of the year.[30]

After three months' operation under the ordinance, the commissioner of health reported that a foundation had been laid "for broader and more efficient sanitary work" than had ever before been undertaken by the Health Department, and he added that when this service should include in its supervision "the sanitary inspection of the tenement-houses—the homes of the wage-earners"—it would be engaged in work "so definite, so comprehensive, and so thorough as to embody the very spirit and fulfill the best intention of sanitary effort." The commissioner announced that the inspection of tenement houses by his force would be undertaken early in the coming year, and that it was "confidently expected" that a new statute, the

[29] *City Council Proceedings, 1880–1881*, p. 157. This ordinance, "for the regulation and inspection of factories, workshops, stores, warehouses, yards, and all other places of employment," provided that such rooms or places of employment should "have a ventilator or ventilators, or other appliances sufficiently large to carry off all foul or impure air and to reduce the air of such room or place of employment to the standard of fresh air, and there shall be allowed to each person in a work room at least five hundred [500] cubic feet air space." The act also provided that the commissioner of public health should visit, or send an officer to visit, every month all "such places of employment or service in the city," in order to see that the provisions of the ordinance were complied with, and to have necessary arrangements made "for the safety and health of the employes." The act also provided for "full and detailed statistical reports of the work of the inspectors" not only violations of the ordinance, but also the "general and special sanitary condition of all people in labor or service in factories, workshops, stores, warehouses, elevators, yards, and domestic workrooms"; and the "number and kind of dangerous and unhealthy employments, and diseases of the several trades and occupations."

[30] One important feature of this ordinance was that it prohibited the work of children under fifteen at night in any place where machinery was used for more than eight hours in any day at any trade or employment and then only between 7:00 A.M. and 6:00 P.M. (*Municipal Code, 1881*, sec. 1357).

draft of which was said to be already prepared, would place the construction of house-plumbing, sewers, and ventilation of tenement houses under the immediate control of his Department.[31]

In 1881 the state legislature enacted the law, to which reference has already been made, which required in cities of fifty thousand inhabitants the preliminary examination of plans of "tenement lodging houses or other places of habitation." This act required that building plans be submitted in advance showing the proposed arrangements for ventilation, light, and plumbing.[32] Following the passage of this act, the commissioner of health announced that he had established general rules "to be observed for the ventilation of rooms, placing of light and air shafts, ventilation of water closets, placing and construction of drainage and plumbing fixtures, etc., etc., in all dwellings to be erected."

The commissioner also reported that the operation of the law had led to a "vast improvement in the sanitary character of the dwellings erected in this city," and he thought that few persons would "rent a room or a domicile who have not first visited the Health Department to inspect the plans and the sanitary history of the premises." The new plans for "tenement and work shop inspection" contemplated "the sanitary supervision of the wage-workers in shop and domicile." The commissioner reported concerning this statute of 1881[33] that relatively little was accomplished during the first few months after its passage, "because of the small number of officers employed for its

[31] *Board of Health Report, 1879–1880*, pp. 14–15. The commissioner's report also contained the following statement: "The execution of the law has been conducted with much judgment by the officers charged with the duty. The attempt to supervise in a sanitary sense by municipal ordinance 14,000 places of business and trade, comprising 350 distinct occupations, and directly interesting more than 125,000 people, is a delicate task, and especially so when the attempt is an innovation on the established custom, in our neighborhood, of trade regulating its own conditions. The difficulties have generally been met in an excellent spirit by all parties, and employers now regard the law with satisfaction, particularly when required improvements are once well made; indeed, many large manufacturers have expressed surprise that this care had not been exercised before."

[32] The act required plumbers to obtain certificates of instruction from the Department before beginning work and also required inspection of all plumbing before the fixtures could be covered and the work completed (*Laws of Illinois, 1881*, p. 61).

[33] *Board of Health Report, 1881–1882*, p. 50.

enforcement, and also because the public was not aware of such a law existing, or its requirement." When this law was passed, he said, "it was the exception when plans for proposed buildings were not defective in some of their important sanitary arrangements, and suggestions for needed changes were invariably met with opposition, interested persons seeming to think that the law should leave them to construct buildings entirely to their own ideas, and with no attention being paid to the sanitary conditions of said buildings."

Of the several hundred plans submitted the first year, according to the commissioner, none was "permitted to be carried out without complying with the law." Such opposition as came from owners or architects of proposed new buildings during the first few months of the new law "almost entirely disappeared before the close of the first year, and a very noticeable improvement was effected in the general sanitary conditions in all places of habitation then being erected, as compared with the same class of buildings erected during the first half of the year."[34]

The commissioner was undoubtedly too optimistic regarding his administration of the new act when he reported that "in two years' time" the new law had already been shown to include "the real and most important of all sanitary work; a complete control of the construction (manner, position, and material) of all sanitary conditions existing *within all* buildings wherein people are to live."[35] He also

[34] The commissioner was very hopeful about the progress made under the new law and later reported as follows: "No complaints [specials] are made to this department from the tenants of the new buildings erected during the past two years under the jurisdiction of the state law, whereas [as this report shows] more than fourteen hundred examinations have been made during the last year, pursuant to written complaints made from tenants living in houses built in the old manner, without regard to necessary sanitary requirements. During the year 1882, permits were issued for the erection of 2,484 places of habitation, which were submitted to this office for approval, so far as relates to light, ventilation, drainage, plumbing, and in fact *all* sanitary arrangements to be placed in the proposed buildings, and copies of 765 of said plans were properly filed for future reference, and included every class of house building, from the simple small cottage to be used as the home of the laboring Pole to the residence of the millionaire, and the complicated, palatial six-story 'French' flat buildings on some of our fashionable streets" (*ibid.*, p. 51).

[35] He thought that great progress had been made with new houses. However, he also thought that the old houses had been improved, and reported that after notices had been served upon the agents "of many unsafe and dilapidated buildings," these buildings had

reported with great satisfaction that much had "been accomplished without carrying the matter into the courts," and that no part of the tenement-house ordinance had "been contested as yet, notwithstanding its sweeping provisions."

NEW PUBLIC INTEREST IN HOUSING REFORM

The decade from 1880 to 1890 was a period when there was a great awakening with regard to the importance of the "housing question." In England the Royal Commission on the Housing of the Working Classes had been actively at work collecting evidence and preparing a report on the homes of the people; and the country was stirred by the various attempts to picture the miseries of "darkest England." In London, Walter Besant was portraying the lot of *All Sorts and Conditions of Men;* and Mr. Charles Booth and his able staff were studying the "Life and Labour of the People" and were reporting both with great skill and with honest sympathy on the wretched conditions under which great masses of people lived in the world's metropolis. At the same time Jacob Riis in New York was attempting to describe to the comfortable classes "how the other half lives"—everywhere the evils of neglected housing conditions with schemes of reform were being given wide publicity.

The new interest in housing was shared by the residents of Chicago. The health authorities continued to report on the insanitary conditions in the dwellings inspected, and as a result recommended more effective legislation. For example, in 1887 the commissioner of health reported that he had attempted to secure an amendment to

---

been placed "in a safe and sanitary condition," often at a great expense, and the dwellings had been made "as good as new in respect to parts which had been condemned."

The commissioner recommended the amendment of the ordinance regarding living-rooms in basements entirely below the street. These, he thought, "should not be permitted under any circumstances to be used for such purposes, the ground air alone being deleterious to health, to say nothing of dampness, insufficient light, etc." He also recommended that the ordinance should specify "the number, location, and kind [material] of fireproof stairways and escapes to be placed on certain specified kinds of tenement houses."

"House sanitation," he said, "is the latest demand made by the people on its local government, and from the reading of the revised ordinance, many people will expect a sort of radical revolution in sanitary matters, ignoring the fact that masses move very slowly, especially when every improvement requires an outlay of money and an acknowledgment of former delinquency."

the law relating to tenement-house inspection service but had failed and would try again at the next session of the legislature. In this same year, 31,171 inspections[36] had been made in occupied dwellings, containing 262,882 rooms and occupied by 60,855 families composed of 269,316 persons. Of these dwellings fully 85 per cent, he said, were seriously defective in plumbing, drainage, or ventilating arrangements.

The complaint regarding the law was to the effect that it was much too general and it was urged that the administration of the law would be facilitated by a greater rigidity in its requirements.[37] During all these years, too, attention was repeatedly drawn to the continued and obnoxious presence of the privy vault. In 1886 the Commissioner estimated that more than one-third of the population of the city were dependent on this form of sanitary provision. In 1889 and 1890[38] an ordinance was drafted declaring the privy vault a public nuisance on any street on which there was a public sewer, but the City Council was urged without effect to pass this ordinance.

Reference has already been made to the fact that the year 1889 brought a new and important agency for education and agitation when Miss Addams went to live in Hull-House in the tenement area of the West Side.[39] Describing the neighborhood of Polk and Halsted streets as it was at that time, she wrote in her first *Twenty Years at Hull-House* regarding the administration of the health and housing regulations that "the policy of the public authorities of never

[36] *Report for 1887*, p. 8. "These inspections were made on the request of the owner in person or writing, never on the request of the tenant until after the owner had refused or neglected to comply with a request that defects be remedied within a reasonable time" (p. 56).

In this year 2,557 new buildings, containing 16,813 rooms arranged for 5,356 families, were examined while in process of construction (p. 56). See p. 61 for the terms of the act the commissioner tried to have passed.

[37] Suggestions were made regarding the requiring of more specific qualifications on the part of inspectors and particularly in fixing a minimum for the number of "practical plumbers" in proportion to the whole number of inspectors employed. The suggestion seemed to indicate a protective interest in plumbers' jobs rather than in the tenements.

[38] *Annual Report, 1889*, p. 56; and *ibid., 1890*, p. 121. The commissioner speaks of the "sinks of filth that menace the health of the citizens." In the 1889 report (p. 64) the appointment of five "lady inspectors" is noted.

[39] See the preceding chapter, p. 31.

taking an initiative, and always waiting to be urged to do their duty," was "obviously fatal" in a neighborhood where there is little initiative among the citizens. "The idea underlying our self-government," she wrote, "breaks down in such a ward. The streets are inexpressibly dirty, the number of schools inadequate, sanitary legislation unenforced, the street lighting bad, the paving miserable and altogether lacking in the alleys and smaller streets, and the stables foul beyond description. Hundreds of houses are unconnected with the street sewer. The older and richer inhabitants seem anxious to move away as rapidly as they can afford it. They make room for newly arrived immigrants who are densely ignorant of civic duties. This substitution of the older inhabitants is accomplished industrially also, in the south and east quarters of the ward. The Jews and Italians do the finishing for the great clothing manufacturers, formerly done by Americans, Irish and Germans, who refuse to submit to the extremely low prices to which the sweating system has reduced their successors. As the design of the sweating system is the elimination of rent from the manufacture of clothing, the 'outside work' is begun after the clothing leaves the cutter. An unscrupulous contractor regards no basement as too dark, no stable loft too foul, no rear shanty too provisional, no tenement room too small for his workroom, as these conditions imply low rental. Hence these shops abound in the worst of the foreign districts where the sweater easily finds his cheap basement and his home finishers."

During the year 1891, it was estimated that new buildings equaling a frontage of fifty-three miles were erected, among them many large flat buildings and apartment houses;[40] and during that year the City Council passed an elaborate ordinance with reference to the conditions under which plumbing should be installed in new buildings or in old buildings undergoing repair.[41]

[40] *Board of Health Report, 1891*, p. 7.

[41] *Council Proceedings, 1891*, p. 1092. This ordinance provided that where water closets were placed outside of buildings the chief inspector should be notified before the work was started; that water closets should never be placed in an unventilated room or compartment but ventilated by an opening to the outer air or by an airduct or airshaft; that when water closets were placed in the yard, they should be separately trapped and conveniently and adequately flushed, the pipes and traps protected from freezing, and the compartment ventilated by slotted openings in doors and roof; that yards and areas

In 1893 an inspection of lodging-houses was inaugurated because of the great increase in the population of the over-crowded wards resulting from the World's Fair and from the business depression of that year.[42] In this inspection "many cases of overcrowding were found, especially in the Italian quarters." On the basis of this inspection it was recommended that all places used as lodging houses should be licensed after inspection, stating the number allowed. But, on the whole, the Health Department was satisfied with its work. Because the United States Bureau of Labor investigators[43] found only fifteen families to a dwelling in the Chicago "slum" tenement, while more than twice that number were found in the New York "slum" dwelling, the Department felt that the Chicago situation was not too discouraging.

In 1897 the City Council passed an ordinance designed to give the health commissioner full power to abate such nuisances as noisome privy vaults. This ordinance provided that "any building which, by reason of its insanitary conditions of its being infected with disease, was unfit for human habitation, or which from any other cause was a source of sickness among the inhabitants of this city, or otherwise endangered health, was declared a public nuisance," and the commissioner of health was given the right to serve notice upon the owner or agent, and if the building was not put in sanitary condition in sixty days, he might order its demolition. The same year saw the appointment of a Building Commissioner and in the following year a new and improved Building Code[44] was reported.

Up to this time, in spite of the studies to which reference has been made, the opinion had generally prevailed that Chicago had no real

---

should be properly graded, paved, and drained; that cellar and foundation walls shall, "where possible," be rendered impervious to dampness; that the general privy accommodations of a tenement house should not be permitted in the cellar, basement, or under sidewalks; that panclosets should not be allowed in any building, and that no privy vault should be allowed on premises where there is a main sewer in the street. For violation of any provision of this ordinance a fine of not less than $25 per day for each day the violation was allowed to continue was prescribed.

[42] *Board of Health Report, 1893*, p. 85.

[43] See preceding chapter, pp. 31–32, and see also the *Health Department Report, 1896*, p. xx.

[44] See the following pages for a discussion of the Building Department.

tenement problem, because there were so many small frame houses throughout the poorer districts and there were relatively few large buildings and "dumbbell" tenements such as made New York's housing problem so appalling. Moreover, it was difficult to arouse public sentiment when houses in the poorer districts were not infrequently owned, not by landlords with large holdings, but by working people who often lived in them as resident landlords.[45] The political influence of these small owners, living in the same tenement buildings with their tenants and influencing local politics, was thought by Miss Addams to be not inconsiderable at this time. But the new social welfare group at Hull-House, united with other public-spirited citizens, notable among whom was Mrs. Emmons Blaine, a daughter of the first Cyrus McCormick, in the formation of a new tenement-house improvement organization which was called the Chicago City Homes Association. Before considering the work of this important organization for housing reform, it is necessary to outline briefly the growth of the Building Department and its work.

THE BUILDING DEPARTMENT

Reference was made in the tenement-house ordinance, which has been summarized, to the part played by the Building Department in the administration of that ordinance. This department had been created in 1875 as one of the main executive divisions of the city government. The head of the Department was then an inspector of buildings, whose duty it was to grant permits for the erection and removal of buildings and who had a staff of ten fire wardens to serve as inspectors. During the period between this date and the enactment of the tenement-house ordinance in 1903, various ordinances were passed looking toward physical safety and protection from fire and from collapse. In the early years of the city's history, when the construction of buildings was dealt with in the city ordinances, the important considerations were those growing out of the danger of fire. A fire warden was one of the first officials appointed when the city was organized; and in 1849 certain "fire limits" had been fixed, and within the territory indicated no wooden or frame buildings were allowed, the construction of all buildings was regulated, it was re-

[45] See *Annals, American Academy of Political and Social Science*, XX, 99.

quired that all buildings be of fireproof materials, and the Fire Department was authorized to examine all buildings.[46]

Not only was a Department of Buildings created in 1875, but in the same year an elaborate building code was adopted requiring the submission of plans and specifications to the superintendent of buildings, who must, in turn, issue a permit before building operations could begin. This ordinance contained mainly provisions with reference to the materials of which foundations, walls, and roofs might be constructed, the thickness of walls, and required among other precautions the erection of fire escapes on dwellings of four or more stories.[47]

Nearly twenty-five years later, in 1897,[48] the Council authorized the appointment of a commission to compile and revise the building ordinances, and in the following year a building code presented to the Council by this commission was adopted. This act[49] conferred upon the Department of Buildings, consisting of a commissioner of buildings, a deputy commissioner, a secretary, civil engineers, and other salaried officers, the power to tear down a building constructed in violation of the law and to stop the construction of buildings being illegally erected. At that time buildings were classified in eight classes; and tenement houses, defined as buildings used as residences by three or more families, were placed in Class VI. Relating to this class were provisions regarding construction, protection against fire, and provision securing air and ventilation. The construction of shafts, columns, and joists was also regulated. Stairs were to be adapted in number and width to the area, height, and uses of the building. Many of the provisions of this ordinance are found taken over into the ordinance of 1902, which will be discussed later.[50]

[46] Strange irregularities and inconsistencies appear in the drawing of these limits, which can sometimes be explained in view of the ownership of property in certain areas (*Charter and Ordinances*, p. 65). In 1873 the Fire Department was authorized to require changes when conditions seemed perilous.

[47] *Chicago Council Proceedings, 1874–75*, pp. 363–65.

[48] *Ibid., 1897*, p. 438.

[49] *Ibid., 1903*, pp. 1517 ff.; *1898*, p. 1898; *1909*, p. 2449; *1921*, pp. 1248, 1643.

[50] At least two flight of stairs were required for buildings containing 2,000 square feet in ground area. Tenements 100 feet or more in height were required to be of fireproof construction, and buildings between 60 and 100 feet high of slow-burning or mill con-

In the intervening years the Building Department has retained a form not very different from that under which it was created. The chief authority has been for many years a commissioner of buildings, appointed by the mayor and Council, who must be a person with ten years' experience in the building trades, as architect, engineer, contractor, or efficient building mechanic. The duties of the Department have been of a broad and comprehensive character, and its power for good or evil was said to exceed that of any other department of municipal government except the Department of Police[51] when the Chicago Civil Service Commission in 1912, at the request of the commissioner, made an inquiry "into the conditions, methods, and systems in use and the organization within the department."

The important legislation administered by the Department dates from the adoption on March 28, 1898, of the building code first mentioned. This act was substantially replaced by the ordinance enacted in December of 1902, was revised in 1910, and again in 1920.

These acts, as has been pointed out, confer power both on the Building and on the Health departments. After the amendments of 1910, the Civil Service Commission in its Efficiency Division classified the activities and functions of the Department in the following three "great natural divisions" as follows: (1) actual field-inspection work;[52] (2) examinations of plans, drawings, and specifications of all

---

struction. Partition walls between apartments were required to be fireproof in all tenements. Fire escapes were required on tenements of more than four stories. Regarding air and ventilation, it was provided that in each habitable room there should be at least one window having an area of one-tenth of the floor area and opening into the outside air. Airshafts were required to be at least 36 square feet in area in a four-story building, increasing 10 square feet for each story. The definition of a basement was in this ordinance changed to a story having a floor two and not more than eleven feet below the level of the sidewalk. Finally, any building found to be dangerous, defective, or unsafe or unfit for human occupation, or in violation of the building ordinances, might be torn down, altered, repaired, or rebuilt (*Council Proceedings, 1898*, pp. 2041, 2053, 2068).

[51] Chicago Civil Service Commission, Efficiency Division, *Report on the Department of Buildings, City of Chicago: Inquiry December 28, 1911—May 6, 1912*, p. 5.

[52] This could be subdivided into (*a*) inspection of all buildings under construction or alteration; (*b*) inspection of fire escapes; (*c*) inspection of new elevators and the regular inspection of old elevators within the buildings in the city; (*d*) inspection of construction and upkeep of billboards and illuminating roof signs; (*e*) annual inspection of structures in the city.

new buildings and alterations for old buildings; (3) department records and clerical work.

The Department has been and is, to quote further, primarily a building-inspection organization for the city. Its chief function has been that of enforcing the ordinances which have to do with the construction, alteration, repair, removal, and safety of all buildings within the city. The number of new buildings erected each year during the years between 1906 and 1912 was about eleven thousand, with an average valuation of approximately $100,000,000. Attention will be called somewhat later to the conditions arising after the war. It is necessary to return now to the important developments which led to a new tenement-house code.

No attempt has been made in this chapter to discuss the question whether or not standards of efficiency and integrity have characterized the work of the Building Department. A superficial reading of the ordinances will show the very difficult position in which are placed public employees or officials who are not highly paid, who work often alone, and whose work may be—indeed, has been—most inadequately supervised and sometimes corruptly dealt with by those whose responsibility it was to safeguard it. In this chapter nothing has been attempted but a review of the development of this legislation as the conditions of the city swiftly changed from those of a small prairie settlement of a few families to a great metropolitan area.

It has been pointed out that the provisions of the building code so far as they are intended to prevent fire and collapse are highly technical, and their administration therefore lays the inspector open to many temptations. The builder or contractor and the "materials men" are under pressure to expand the dimensions of the building and to scrimp in the quality and quantity of the building materials. It is so easy for the inspector who approves the plans to make apparently slight concessions, or for the inspector who is observing the building in course of construction not to visit the site at the moment when the violation is apparent, that the organization and maintenance of the Department's work on a basis of honesty and efficiency have been often very difficult. In 1910 a committee of the City Council found the administration of this Department the weakest spot in the city administration, and in 1912 an investigation by the Bureau of Public Efficiency found the morale eaten into by corruption as well as by ineffective methods of supervision and of administration.

It is clear, then, that the protection of the city against dishonest and dangerous building lies in the efficient organization of the Department for all those tasks preliminary[53] to the granting of the permit authorizing the building operations to begin, the supervision of those operations while the building is in progress, while protection from fire depends to a very considerable extent upon the thorough and comprehensive periodic inspection of buildings in use.

The ordinances of Chicago to which reference has been made have been highly commended.[54]

THE CITY HOMES ASSOCIATION

The plans of the new City Homes Association, which have already been outlined, included as a first undertaking the investigation of housing conditions in three crowded districts on the West Side.[55] The investigators found all the bad effects of congestion—lack of light and air, whole lots being covered by one building, or by two, or sometimes by three buildings on the same lot. They found 39 per cent of all the lots investigated to be covered more than 65 per cent, 17 per cent covered more than 80 per cent, and 18 per cent covered 90–100 per cent. The only previous regulation regarding space covered was an ordinance requiring that 10 feet be left uncovered at the rear of the lot. Contrary to public opinion, large tenement houses were found to exist in Chicago with serious conditions as to lack of light and ventilation, and overcrowding within the buildings. Of 1,901 rooms examined and measured, approximately one-half were reported to be dark or gloomy. Three-fourths of the occupants of these rooms had less than the 400 cubic feet of air per person required by ordinance in the sleeping-rooms of lodging-houses; 4,845 persons were living in the 101 cellars and 820 basements found

[53] The commissioner must receive application, secure architect's certificate of compliance with the law, etc. (sec. 446).

[54] See *Report, Efficiency Division, Civil Service Commission, 1912*, p. 6; see also reference below to Surgeon-General Perry's summary, p. 36, n. 4.

[55] See below, p. 75.

among 9,858 apartments. Most of these cellar and basement occupants had insufficient light, poor ventilation, dampness, and bad odors from defective plumbing. The investigators found that 17 per cent of the houses investigated were badly dilapidated or in such poor repair as to be unfit for habitation, the rear houses showing the worst conditions. The plumbing was found to be defective; there were 1,581 privy vaults, as well as other types of insanitary provisions, and great dearth of bathing facilities. There were badly paved and unclean streets and alleys; dangerous sidewalks; filthy vacant lots, yards, courts, and passages; offensive stables and manure boxes. Neglect of garbage was prevalent.

After the publication of this report in 1901 showing the prevalence of ill-lighted, ill-ventilated, and insanitary tenements, built without regard to protection from fire, the Association turned to the framing of a proper tenement ordinance. After a period of public educational work, a new ordinance in general accord with their recommendations was passed by the City Council in December, 1902, by a vote of 47 to 7. This was a very great victory for the new association.[56]

The new ordinance embodied definitions and provisions (1) for protection against fire, (2) for sufficient light and air, (3) for proper sanitary regulations, and (4) for enforcement. A tenement house was defined as "any house or building or portion thereof which is intended or designed to be occupied or leased for occupation as a home or residence of two[57] or more families, living in separate apartments, and included all apartment houses, flat buildings, and residential hotels." The term "new tenement house" applied to every such building thereafter erected, converted, or altered to such use. Other terms connected with tenement houses were defined here for the first time.[58]

[56] See the *Survey*, IX, 617.

[57] The general assumption had been that the number of families should be three, though no definition had been formulated, and, in fact, often a rented house was spoken of as though included in the category without regard to the number of families.

[58] An apartment was defined as a room or suite of rooms to be occupied as a family domicile. The definition of a basement was changed to a story not more than one-half below the level of the sidewalk. Such terms as "inner courts," "lot-line courts," "exterior and interior shafts," "ventilating shafts," and many other technical terms are carefully defined.

In the same way detailed provisions undertook to secure better protection against fire.[59]

The provisions for light and ventilation were based on regulations as to the amount of the lot to be covered.[60]

The space and ventilation of rooms were also considered in detail.[61] The minimum widths and areas of inner courts were specified. The minimum floor space as well as the minimum height of all rooms in new tenements was provided for.[62] There were likewise specifications of dimensions for old tenements.

A provision of which much was heard later was to the effect that no room in any apartment might be occupied in which there was less than 400 cubic feet of air-space for each person over twelve years of age, and 200 cubic feet for each person twelve years or under. No cellar rooms were to be occupied and basement occupancy was regulated.[63]

[59] It was now required that new tenement houses, a basement and five stories in height, must be fireproof, that tenements varying from basement and three stories to basement and five stories in height must be either of slow-burning or fireproof material, and that the cellar or basement, and the floor of the first story, should be fireproof; that in frame tenement houses each suite must be separated from the next by a wall of incombustible material; that apartments of four or more stories should be provided with fire escapes with a metal railing between balconies; and that each apartment should have direct access to at least one fire escape or to two separate flights of stairs.

[60] No new tenement house was to occupy more than 85 per cent of a corner lot, nor more than 90 per cent of a corner lot bounded on three sides by streets or alleys, nor more than 75 per cent of the area of any other lot, provided space occupied by fire escapes not more than 4 feet wide be deemed unoccupied.

[61] No room was considered habitable unless it had at least one window of an area equal to one-tenth the area of the room, and leading to the outer air, i.e., opening on an area of at least 36 square feet for a three-story building, and increasing 10 square feet for each additional story. In new tenements every habitable room except water-closet compartments and bathrooms were to have at least one window opening directly upon a street, alley, yard, or court; the total area of such windows were to be at least one-tenth of the floor area.

[62] The floor space must be at least 70 square feet, and there was to be one room in each apartment containing at least 120 square feet and each room was to be at least 8½ feet high, except attic rooms which were to be 8½ feet in at least one-half their area. Basement apartments, unless to be occupied by the janitor only, must be not less than 8 feet high. Water-closet compartments and bathrooms were excepted from that requirement.

[63] No basement rooms were to be occupied unless the story was 4 feet above the street grade, and unless the room was 8½ feet high, except when it was to be occupied by the janitor, and unless there was a toilet provided as required in the ordinance.

With regard to plumbing, it was required that in new tenements there should be at least one sink on each floor, and that this sink must be accessible without passing through another apartment. It was also provided that in new tenements there should be separate toilet facilities within each apartment, except that where apartments consisted of one or two rooms there might be such provision for every two apartments; and each compartment was to have a window opening on a street, alley, yard, court, or vent shaft.[64]

The hygiene of the premises was prescribed. For example, the walls and ceiling of every tenement house were to be whitewashed or painted a light color every year, and the walls of courts, unless bounded on one side by a street or alley, were to be whitewashed once in three years, or painted a light color once in five years. There were, of course, provisions for repair and cleanliness.

For enforcement of the ordinance it was provided that the approval of plans and specifications, on written application from the owner, and a building permit from the Building Department were necessary for building a tenement house; no tenement house was to be occupied until the Board of Health had issued a certificate that the house conformed to the requirements of the ordinance. Tenement houses were to be inspected at any time by the Health Department, and an order made upon the owner; and a tenement house not conforming to the requirements of the ordinance was declared to be a public nuisance.

THE STRUGGLE TO ESTABLISH A TRUE TENEMENT-LAW AUTHORITY, 1903–7

The passage of the ordinance of 1902 was a victory in a struggle to establish a true administrative authority for tenement-house legislation. It was a struggle into which went great effort and in which no final victory has even been won. Eight years later the commissioner of health said that "the most important activity of the Bureau of Sanitation, the investigation and improvement of housing conditions in congested and neglected neighborhoods of the city," had not at that time "been dignified by organization into a separate division"; and the "greatest need" of that time was said to be a housing survey

[64] Privy vaults must be replaced by water closets, at least one being required for every two apartments in old houses. These might be in the yard, and, if so, long hopper closets were permitted.

which should "afford a basis of public action to better conditions."[65] That separate division has never been created, and the supervision of housing conditions constituted a less conspicuous group of activities in the work of the two departments in 1935 than in 1903.

In his report for 1922 the inspector-in-charge of the division of housing and sanitation, created in 1912, urged an "investigation of overcrowding in tenements." In other words, the Department had not yet obtained that "basis in fact" that would make possible a comprehensive treatment of existing dwellings; and this lack of a comprehensive housing census has served to justify the failure to act vigorously in the improvement of tenement-house regulation.

It is true that the problem has been, and still remains, very complicated and difficult. There were the old buildings and the question of their use.[66] The expectation of change made standards of repair difficult to enforce. The shoestring lot[67] invited the inefficient use of land so divided as to render wise planning very difficult. And the ordinance of 1902, while most carefully framed, was very elaborate and had to be subjected to the test of actual enforcement. But to secure even the gains sought by that ordinance had been by no means a simple task. When an attempt at enforcement was made, the new ordinance was at once attacked in what should have been the house of its friends, the City Council itself.

Before the following April 4, 1903, twenty-eight orders had in fact been issued by the Council exempting builders from the new requirements.[68] There were, too, weaknesses in the ordinance that could only be learned by attempts at administration. One of these was

[65] *Department of Health Report, 1907–1910*, p. 212.

[66] About them, Miss Addams said in explaining the situation to the American Academy of Social and Political Science in 1902: "The property in the river wards is kept because of the expected invasion of business and industry. Repairs are therefore not made, great dilapidation results, and rents are asked only sufficient to pay taxes and keep up a minimum of repair (*Annals*, XX, 99).

[67] See also Mr. Ball in the *Survey*, XVII, 90. New buildings were rarely on cleared areas but in outlying regions.

[68] *Ibid.*, X, 322. This was justified on the ground that building operations had begun before the ordinance was passed. This practice had been allowed under the earlier ordinance. The exemptions, however, permitted violations not only of the new but of the old ordinance.

lack of provision for adequate control over the moving of tenements from one site to another. Owing to this weakness, the very effort to bring breathing and play spaces into some neighborhoods not infrequently meant greater congestion in neighboring areas.[69]

But the great weakness was failure on the part of the authorities to make any genuine effort to enforce the new ordinance. In the case of some provisions no attempt at enforcement was made.[70] Although the ordinance required much more rigorous inspection than had been made before, no reorganization of the Health Department took place, and the following summer Chicago experienced a typhoid epidemic especially virulent in the crowded neighborhoods.[71] The mortality in the Hull-House Ward (then the Nineteenth) was very heavy, and the Hull-House residents undertook to study the situation and if possible to locate the responsibility. Their important conclusions were two: (1) that the uncovered privy vault, supposedly outlawed in 1897, was the source of the malady, the infection being carried by the common housefly; and (2) that the Health Department was either criminally inefficient or actually corrupt.[72]

As a result of this investigation, the Chicago Civil Service Commission ordered an investigation into the work of the Department, with the result that the Commission severely censured the head of

[69] *Ibid.*, XVIII, 413. In the case of one clearing in the Seventeenth Ward in 1907, the building commissioner refused his consent to the removal of seventeen tenements, to be removed from an area to be cleared for a park on the ground that they were unfit for human habitation. In such instances, when the removal was authorized, the house on the front of the lot to which removal was desired would be moved to the rear and the house from the cleared area would be put down on the front of the lot thus vacated. Congestion was increased in this way as the result of neighborhood improvements in various areas.

[70] Later Mr. Ball said that no attention had ever been paid to the provision requiring that cellars or basements below the grade of surrounding area should be damp-proofed (*ibid.*, XVII, 90).

[71] The number of deaths from typhoid fever rose from 212 during the summer of 1901 to 402 from the same cause in the summer of 1902. The deaths from typhoid were 2.08 per cent of deaths from all causes in 1901; they were 3.03 per cent in 1902, and fell to 2.03 per cent in 1903 (*ibid.*, X, 587; see *Report of Department of Health, 1899–1903: Vital Statistics*, p. 126).

[72] The Department had for years stated that, because of its limited staff, inspections were made only on complaint. Out of 2,002 houses, 220 were found to have privy vaults with sewer connection and 240 privy vaults with no connection.

the Department, preferred charges of bribery against the inspection service, and secured the indictment of five inspectors, including the head of the Sanitary Bureau.[73]

In 1905, when the areas investigated in 1900 were revisited, it was found that conditions had changed very little. There had been improvements in some streets because of paving, the disappearance of most yard vaults, and some change for the better in the frequency of garbage collection; but conditions remained much the same with regard to dilapidation, rear tenements, dark rooms and halls, basements and cellars, and fire hazards.[74]

The influence of the ordinance on the old tenement was, then, relatively slight. On the construction of new buildings, however, there was a marked improvement. One unexpected effect was on the height of new buildings. The fact that tenements of more than three stories were required to be built of the more fire-resisting material than the tenements of three stories, or fewer than three, led to the wide adoption of the three-story and basement plan.

The building ordinance inevitably became subject to change and was the object of constant attack and frequent amendment; but ex-

[73] *Survey*, XI, 353. Five were charged with accepting bribes in the performance of their duty, four others with inefficiency.

An able and experienced administrator, Charles B. Ball, then became chief sanitary inspector—a post which he held for nearly a quarter of a century. Those interested in housing reform had realized the importance of raising the standards in the administration of the law, and had induced Mr. Ball, who had had experience in Washington and had later been chief inspector in the New York Tenement House Department, to come to Chicago and qualify for the position of chief sanitary inspector. He was a civil engineer, who had been surveyor for the Union Pacific Railway Co., an examiner for the Patent Office in Washington, chief plumbing inspector there, and chief inspector in the New York Tenement House Department, where he was associated with Robert de Forest and Lawrence Veiller. Mr. Ball secured a position at the head of the eligible list. He was, however, enjoined from acting on the ground of nonresidence; and only in 1907, when the issue had been taken to the Appellate Court and to the Supreme Court, was he able to assume the duties of the office (*ibid.*, XIII [1905], 963; also XVII, 226). He died at his desk, October 17, 1928, and the health commissioner paid a tribute in the following words: "To Mr. Charles B. Ball, whose end came quietly during the performance of his duties, we are indebted for our present knowledge of and the strides which we have made in securing better housing in the City of Chicago. The value of his work will be realized when humanitarian considerations for those who are existing under poor housing conditions are acted upon" (*Department of Health Report 1926–1930*, p. 9).

[74] *Survey*, XV, 455.

cept for an important amendment to the plumbing law in 1905, no very serious change was made in the building code before 1910, when an elaborate revision occurred. This plumbing code of 1905 was framed in greater detail than any previous law and remained substantially unchanged until June of 1930, when a considerable revision was made to which reference will be made[75] at a later point.

THE SANITARY BUREAU, 1907–1922

With the advent of Mr. Ball to the position for which he had so ably qualified himself, technically and legally, the work took on a new aspect. One section of the law, for example, authorized the creation of a Board of Survey, composed of a medical inspector, a sanitary inspector, and a building inspector "to inspect any building alleged to be a public nuisance," and such a board was created on September 27, 1908, and was soon actively at work. Before the end of 1910, 125 buildings had been examined, 62 demolished, 36 repaired, and all of this was accomplished without court action.[76] The number of inspectors was increased.[77] In 1907 there were eighteen sanitary inspectors; in 1908 the number was increased to forty-five, and the appropriations for the work were increased from $70,799 to approximately $112,000. As the experience with the ordinance developed, even to a limited extent, it became clear that amendments were necessary, as well as a far ampler provision for enforcement.

In 1908 the commissioner of buildings proposed a complete revision of the ordinance and suggested that "architects, engineers, and representatives of all the various branches of the building industry" should be called before the Council, "with a view of perfecting our ordinances." There was at the time wide interest in the matter. The City Club appointed a committee to study the situation in other cities of the state; the architects and other housing experts actively co-operated, and the result embodied substantial gains in better definitions, more intelligent arrangement, and provision for clearer

[75] *Department of Health Report, 1911–18*, p. 604.

[76] *Ibid., 1907–10*, p. 215.

[77] *Ibid., 1911–1918*, p. 605. The number of inspectors during these years varied from 35 to 55. The appropriations gradually increased to $772,000 in 1916, then fell to $124,208 in 1918.

records. All new buildings were now to be inspected before occupancy, the percentage of the lot area that could be covered was reduced, the size and height of rooms and of light and airshafts were increased, and a new chapter on ventilation was added. The work of the Sanitary Bureau was considerably increased as a result of this enactment, and a new Division of Ventilation was created.

As the ordinance took on a more definite form, two results appeared. One was that possibility of enforcement was increased by greater exactness and the consequently diminished range for difference of opinion between the builder and the Department. On the other hand, efforts to evade likewise increased both in number and in vigor. One important section of the 1910 law provided for a certificate by the commissioner of health to the effect that all the requirements of the law had been met before occupancy was allowed. As a matter of fact, however, this section, like that in the law of 1902 requiring, under certain circumstances, damp-proofing of cellars and basements, has never been enforced. In the report for 1911–18, figures are given showing that "during the years 1913–1916, upwards of 6,000 tenement houses were constructed each year," and during that period only ninety-one such permits were issued. In 1915 the subject of basement apartments again engaged the attention of the City Council, and reliance was first placed on the old definition of "habitable room," which should have a window on the street, alley, or yard, with a glass area of not less than ten square feet, the top not less than seven feet, so that its upper half could be opened, a floor-space not less than eighty square feet, and a ceiling height of eight and one-half feet. However, the Building Code was amended in that year, with the support of both the Department of Building and the Department of Health, to make new provisions regarding the number of feet which this story might be below the grade and above the grade.

During the period of the war there was very little new building. Where plans for between eleven and twelve thousand new buildings had been annually approved during the years 1909–14, and the numbers increased to more than 14,500 for 1915 and 1916, there was a very marked reduction in building activity during the years from 1917 to 1920, when the corresponding figures averaged about 5,000 annually. Only in 1921 did the number rise again to more than 10,000. But in 1922 it remounted beyond pre-war heights and reached 18,171. This was the largest number of building plans that had been approved in any year in the history of the Department, and this increase continued through the next two years but declined in 1925. The Department developed a theory that the period from 1913 through 1916 was a "normal" period, that from 1917 through 1920 was subnormal, while the period from 1920 through 1925 was a period of reconstruction.

During these years there was little agitation for a change in the law,[78] but in 1920 proposals were made for some amendments, and in the following year a revision of various items[79] in the building code occurred. Concerning the effectiveness of these later changes in the law it is difficult to speak. Other problems seemed to absorb the energies of the Bureau, such as the increased effort to secure adequate heating for tenants growing out of the influenza experiences, the problems growing out of the housing shortage and the consequent profiteering which led to constant friction between the landlord and tenant.[80] The chief of the Bureau wrote that because of lack of staff it was "impossible to give any attention to housing conditions or other methodical special canvasses such as were made in former years, of places of employment, privy vaults, manure accumulations, yard and alley clean-up," and other similar work, including control of dumps and scavengers. The suspension of building activity during the war, according to the annual report, "produced a housing famine which was accentuated by the rapid return of discharged soldiers and the employees of war industries." The commissioner thought that the overcrowding evil was becoming serious and that retrenchment was an ill-advised policy at such a time. He further recommended that "the activities directed toward health con-

[78] Zoning activities were developing at this time but need not be discussed here.

[79] Some of these had to do with house drains, some with the design and erection of tenements, and much attention was devoted to the plumbing ordinance.

In the discussions concerning these changes, echoes were heard of the war experiences of the U.S. Housing Corporation. For later amendments to the Plumbing Code see *City Council Proceedings* (April 27, 1934), p. 2118. These have especially to do with water connections.

[80] See *Report, 1919–1921*, p. 247.

servation during the period of reconstruction should be conducted on a more efficient plane rather than relaxed, and those preventable agencies that undermine the health of the community should be watched and warded with extreme vigilance."

During this period an attempt was made to secure a revision of the Plumbing Code, which dated from the 1905 ordinance; and a committee was appointed with some representatives from the engineering groups to draft a new code. The report of that committee pointed to the possibility of simplifying the fixtures to be required, but this was not accomplished until 1930.[81]

The story of halting attempts at the enforcement of the housing regulations continued from one *Report* to another. In 1922 the inspector-in-charge of the Division of Housing and Sanitation reported[82] that his inspection staff had been no more adequate in numbers than the year before, and that the inspection and enforcement procedure had been practically the same as in 1921. Among his recommendations at this time were: (1) an investigation of overcrowding in tenements; (2) the adoption of an ordinance regulating the keeping of domestic animals in tenement houses; and (3) an ordinance regulating the construction of privy vaults!—all recommendations that recalled the legislation of 1881 and of 1897, and served notice that the efforts of the preceding quarter of a century had not been supported by efficient administrative agencies for the protection of the residents of crowded quarters.

[81] Many questions of departmental authority were raised during this same period. Attention is called below to the effect of the judicial decision in 1922 where the nature of the organization of the Health Department was said to jeopardize its authority (see *People v. Robertson*, 302 Ill. 422). In 1927 the plumbing division was transferred to the Department of Buildings, but because this is spoken of in the statutes as a Health Department function, the exercise of authority was restricted. (This goes back to the statute of 1881 [see above, p. 48].) At the end of 1928 the plumbing division was restored to the Health Department, which had been reorganized in structure. In 1930 a revised plumbing code was adopted, based upon a set of *Minimum Requirements for Plumbing in Dwellings and Similar Buildings*, issued by the U.S. Department of Commerce (*Report of Health Department, 1926–30*, p. 362), which was known as the "Hoover Code." The new Chicago Code of 1930, therefore, was a merger of the so-called Hoover Code and the earlier Chicago Code. In 1934 there were further amendments with reference to the water connections and methods and devices for flushing. After the reorganization of the Department, to which reference has been made, little space is devoted to the subject.

[82] *Annual Report, 1922*, p. 232.

REORGANIZATION OF THE DEPARTMENT

The legislature in 1872 in the *Cities and Villages Act* conferred upon the City Council among other powers that of appointing a Board of Health and prescribing its powers and duties.[83] In 1879, however, the Council had created a Department of Health, under a commissioner who was to be "a medical man of specified qualifications," appointed by the mayor and Council. This form of departmental structure remained for approximately a quarter of a century, when a Board of Health, first of three members and later of five, was substituted for the commissioner, and the president of the Board became the executive of the newly constituted department.[84] Under these conditions the staff of the Department is divided into two sections: one of four bureaus concerned with medical services and one of four technical bureaus and the research activities.[85] The section of public health engineering is the one responsible for the tenement and other housing inspection.

The division of community sanitation was to be concerned principally with the investigation of complaints of unhealthful and unsanitary conditions. The great majority of the complaints were the result of violations of the Sanitary Code and included the insanitary housing conditions with which Chicago has been so long familiar, such as defective plumbing and drainage equipment, lack of proper toilet facilities, accumulation of garbage and refuse in buildings,

[83] An Act To Provide for the Incorporation of Cities and Villages, *Illinois Laws, 1871–72*, p. 218. The section relating to the appointment of a board of health appears in Art. V, sec. 1, and reads as follows: "The city council in cities, and president and the board of trustees in villages, shall have the following powers: . . . . To appoint a board of health, and prescribe its powers and duties" (p. 233). Conveniently available also in *Smith-Hurd, Illinois Revised Statutes, 1935*, ch. 24, sec. 65:75.

[84] This development is described in the opening paragraphs of the *Report* for 1932. It is interesting to note that the Supreme Court had in 1922 declared that the Council was powerless to create a department of which the executive was an individual instead of a board (see *People v. Robertson*, 302 Ill. 422 [1922]), and evidently the validity of the Department's orders was frequently questioned. On December 16, 1931, therefore, an emergency ordinance was enacted and a comprehensive ordinance became effective May 4, 1932 (*Report, 1932*, p. 3; see *Council Proceedings* [December 16, 1931; May 4, 1932].)

[85] Each section is in charge of a "director," responsible to the Board but reporting to the president.

yards, and on vacant lots, insufficient light and ventilation, overcrowded living quarters, vermin-infested premises, and the prevalence of rats.

In the years 1932 and 1933 problems of destitution created by the years of the depression were facing all public authorities. In 1932 there had been such a decrease in the number of new buildings that more old buildings were altered than new buildings constructed. In 1933 there was reported to be little call for the services of the Department in connection either with new or with old buildings. The number of permits for new buildings increased from 115 in 1933 to 130 in 1934, but the number of old buildings repaired remained greater in both years.[86] The Department reported that special attention had been given "to proper housing, especially of the destitute, owing to the doubling up of families in limited quarters and to the use of previously abandoned buildings by squatters." There had been an increasing number of cases of "shutting off of water, gas and electricity, as a means of evicting tenants who are behind in payment of their rent." Going beyond the immediate question involved, the report called attention to "the menace to the health of small children," which resulted from these methods of eviction which "had been growing steadily as the business depression became prolonged, and a considerable amount of time and effort had been expended during the past year to correct such conditions."[87]

The problem of lodging-houses was again presented to the Department as another depression difficulty. The Department reported that "the overcrowding of the lodging houses provided for the destitute unemployed, made it necessary to direct special attention to the general sanitary conditions and method of conducting these establishments."[88] But in the reconstructed Health Department, as

[86] However, in 1935 a change seems to have taken place, and whereas in seven months 162 permits have been granted for repairs, 172 permits have been granted for new buildings.

[87] *Board of Health Report, 1932*, p. 8; see also below, chaps. xiv and xv, which deal with the effect of the depression on the housing problem in Chicago.

[88] It was reported that "methods of caring for the sick, isolation and quarantine facilities, and provision of needed medical service were also included in these inspections. A total of 170 inspections was made of these establishments during 1932. The inspec-

in the older organization, housing activities remain only one among many sets of activities, and the need of a separate department for housing inspection and regulation continues to be demanded by all those concerned for the provision of that minimum of decency, safety, and comfort required by an American standard of living in the new order.

---

tions were made at night to observe the actual conditions existing when the occupants were asleep. This activity was carried on in co-operation with the Department of Lodging House Inspection of the State of Illinois. Considerable improvement in certain lodging houses had been brought about during 1930 and 1931, which, together with the Health educational work of 1932, kept violations of sanitary regulations at a minimum during 1932" (*ibid.*, p. 62).

CHAPTER III

THE TENEMENT AREAS AND THE PEOPLE OF THE TENEMENTS

THE DISTRICTS CANVASSED: SCOPE AND METHOD[1]

Choice of Districts; Chicago's Deteriorated Areas; The West Side Revisited; The Old Lumber Yards District; The Bohemian Tenements of Pilsen; The Old "Ghetto"; Hull-House and Her Neighbors; The Polish Tenements of St. Stanislaus; The Lower North Side Tenements; The Old Plymouth Court Area; A Near South Side Colony—a Croatian and Italian Settlement; The Expanding Negro Housing Problem; A Lithuanian District; "Back of the Yards"; The Industrial South End: South Chicago—at the Gates of the Steel Mills; Burnside; Torrence Avenue (South Deering); Pullman; Hegewisch; The Chicago Tenement; Areas Selected for Intensive Canvass.

IN PLANNING a series of housing studies emphasis was laid on the possibility of controlling insanitary conditions and bad housing by means of tenement-house ordinances. How far, for example, had the Chicago ordinances been enforced? How far had they proved unenforcible—at least by any city government which Chicago had been able to achieve?

The building of new houses is very important in every city where there are extensive deteriorated areas. But dishousing and rehousing, important as they are, will protect only a very small percentage of the population from the evils of bad housing. Probably not more than 5 or 10 per cent of the tenement population can possibly be provided for in this way in any reasonably near future. For the remaining 90 or 95 per cent, adequate tenement-house legislation, together with vigorous enforcement of the tenement-house ordinances, is needed.

In social legislation it has been well said that "the life of a law lies in its enforcement." Housing standards as laid down in tenement-house codes may seem to be reasonably high, but are they enforced? Certainly when one turns from the printed ordinances to look at the houses in which the poor are actually living in Chicago, it is clear

[1] With Mary Zahrobsky, research assistant, School of Social Service Administration.

that the standards of housing tolerated and the standards of housing as set forth in the letter of the law are very different.

In order to collect certain facts with regard to the enforcement of the various provisions of the tenement-house code, the first of what proved to be a long series of house-to-house canvasses in certain of the deteriorated areas of the city was first undertaken as long ago as the winter of 1908–9, at the request of the chief sanitary inspector of the city of Chicago. These surveys had been continued winter after winter until a very considerable body of material had been collected bearing upon the subject of tenement-house conditions in Chicago and the enforcement—or lack of enforcement—of tenement-house legislation. During the war these surveys had been temporarily given up, and then resumed again as the housing problem became more serious in Chicago as in other parts of the country as a result of the suspension of building activities during the war years. The studies had been again given up before the onset of the depression, when the housing problem became more exigent than at any earlier period in Chicago's history since the Great Fire. It seemed worth while, therefore, to try to review the situation once more and to assemble the various studies that had been made since the first survey of 1908–9 and to make a recanvass of the old districts as far as the limited funds at our disposal allowed. It was believed that the results of the old and the new studies, when brought together, would be useful as a general resurvey of the tenement-house problem of Chicago.[2]

CHOICE OF DISTRICTS

The selection of the particular areas chosen for investigation was determined by a number of factors. Areas in different parts of the city were canvassed in order to include houses of all types in the various tenement districts. It was hoped that a sufficient number of districts could be so canvassed as to secure a representative sample of the houses in the deteriorated areas of the city. The districts canvassed were widely scattered in order to make certain of the inclusion in the sample of the various types of housing and to avoid concen-

[2] An early report of the City Homes Association, which was written by Robert Hunter, had been called *Tenement Conditions in Chicago* (Chicago: City Homes Association, 1901). See chap. ii, above, pp. 58–61.

tration on any single area of deterioration. A single block in a neighborhood was rarely investigated, for the plan was not to pick out the worst blocks here and there, district by district, but to select larger areas which would be a more representative sample than a selection of single blocks. Instead of single blocks, groups of blocks were, therefore, usually chosen, the number of blocks in a neighborhood varying from 4 to 22. It is believed that the 151 blocks finally canvassed may be called a fair sample of the tenement sections of the city where the great mass of Chicago citizens have their homes.

The canvass of the 151 blocks covered 6,294 buildings and 18,225 different apartments or households. The 6,197 buildings in the districts recanvassed and newly visited in the last decade included 4,324 houses used only for residence purposes, 1,426 buildings for residence and business purposes, 27 for residence and other purposes, 338 buildings used only for business, and 82 other buildings.

The method of house-to-house canvassing in selected areas having been decided upon, some preliminary field surveys were undertaken to determine the final selection of districts where these studies should be made. For although the areas of bad housing in Chicago were known to be very numerous, only a relatively small number could be included in the canvass.

CHICAGO'S DETERIORATED AREAS

The sections where bad housing was concentrated were of three general types: (1) The deteriorated areas like the old river wards of the West Side and the Lower North Side, parts of which were "jerry built" after the Great Fire. These districts had long been areas of poverty, where dilapidation and congestion were found together and where the encroachment of commercial and industrial establishments encouraged the property-owner to place a speculatively fictitious value on the land as a possible site of future business enterprise and made the improvement of housing conditions seem, to the landlord, a very poor investment. (2) The neighborhoods near the great industrial centers, such as the steel mills or stock yards, where great numbers of wage-earners, many of them irregularly employed and poorly paid, created a constant demand for the cheapest kind of homes with the lowest possible rentals. (3) And the different districts of the city in which the poor Negroes were segregated were almost invariably found to be deteriorated areas where all the signs of destitution and neglect were only too apparent.

When the present inquiry into tenement-house conditions in Chicago was planned, it seemed important to revisit the three districts which had been canvassed by the old City Homes Association in 1901,[3] in order to ascertain how far conditions might have changed since that time. The three areas investigated in the City Homes inquiry were all located on the West Side of the city and included, first, the Polish district to the northwest, known familiarly as the St. Stanislaus district because of the great Polish church which had long been a landmark there; next, the large district between Halsted Street and the river, in the Hull-House area, an area which included the "old Ghetto" and which was the best known of the districts canvassed by the City Homes investigators; and the third district was the tenement area of ten blocks in the Bohemian colony in one of the southwest wards, better known as Pilsen.

Although we began with the old City Homes districts, other West Side areas were canvassed, and then recanvassed as our work continued in the post-war decade. In the Greek-Italian district in the area both west and east of Halsted, for example, sixteen blocks were included, both in our first house-to-house canvass and in our later recanvass, because this area, especially the section to the west, was so neglected and had been so completely overlooked by earlier investigators. Later, a smaller area farther west on Polk Street was selected for canvass. We also studied the Slovak district on the West Side near the Lumber Yards—a district which was also in one of the worst of the river wards. Some other areas on the Northwest in addition to the Polish district which had been included in the City Homes recanvass were also selected for study—a Polish and Ruthenian district[4] on Division Street and a small district toward the northwest best designated by the name of one of its little streets, "Ancona," in the triangle between Milwaukee and Chicago avenues.

[3] For earlier discussions of this important organization see the preceding chapter, "Tenement House Legislation in Chicago," pp. 58–61.

[4] This district is predominantly Polish, but although the people usually called themselves "Poles," experienced workers in the Immigrants' Protective League were quite certain these families were Ruthenian and not Polish. The League workers thought they called themselves Poles because they found the name so much more familiar in this country.

Some blocks were also selected in the area of deterioration on the Lower North Side which, in the old days, was a great Italian colony; and two other districts, Upper North and Olivet, were also included in the canvass.

On the South Side four districts were selected for study, one in a very deteriorated section on the edge of the downtown area or "Loop"; a Lithuanian district on Halsted Street near Mark White Square; an area on the Near South Side which was Croatian and Italian; and another area which included two separate groups of blocks in the tenement districts near the Stock Yards in an area which was chiefly Polish and Lithuanian. In the Calumet region in the South End of the city four areas were selected, including a South Chicago district, largely Slovak but with other Slavic groups; an area in Burnside, a Magyar district; South Deering, largely Jugo-Slav; and Pullman, largely Slavic, but of mixed nationalities. Finally, four districts in the Negro areas on the South and West sides were selected at different times as the canvass proceeded.

In addition to the house-to-house canvassing, some special studies were also undertaken: (1) of the housing arrangements of the "non-family groups" of immigrant men found all about Hull-House and in certain other sections, and well known to the vigilant workers of the Immigrants' Protective League; and (2) of the families living, not in tenement apartments, but in "furnished rooms," many of whom were well known as Hull-House neighbors and as clients in the district offices of the relief agencies; (3) a special study of eviction policies during the depression; (4) a special study of the housing of dependent families under the care of one of the welfare agencies.[5]

[5] This study, by Eleanor D. Goltz, deals with families under the care of the United Charities, see chap. xiii, below. A study of evictions was published in the *Social Service Review*, IX (1935), 34–57, "Evictions during the Chicago Rent Moratorium Established by the Relief Agencies, 1931–33," by Edith Abbott and Katherine F. Kiesling. Other theses presented for the Master's degree, unpublished, in the University of Chicago Library, include the following: "Housing Conditions in the Stock Yards District," by Alice M. Miller; "Housing Conditions in the District of Burnside," by Berenice Davis; "A Study of Housing Conditions in One of the Negro Districts in Chicago," by Alice Quan Rood; "Rents and Housing Conditions among the Lithuanians in Chicago," by Joseph S. Perry; "Rents and Housing Conditions in the Italian District of the Lower North Side," by Mrs. Quaintance; "Housing Conditions in South Chicago, South Deering, and Pullman," by Mary Faith Adams; "The Slovaks in Chicago," by Mary Zahrobsky. Earlier reports of these studies, sometimes written by our students, were published in the *American Journal of Sociology* as follows: (1) XVI, 145, "Housing of

THE WEST SIDE REVISITED

Twenty-five years ago, when our intimate acquaintance with it first began, the old West Side was a much more picturesque area than the more business-like West Side of today. Immigrant tides then swept along and across Halsted Street, one overtaking the other in rapid succession. The West Side "river wards" were the poorest and most crowded sections, where the newest immigrants so often came to live, grew prosperous, and moved to pleasanter streets farther west. But whether they prospered and went on to more thriving neighborhoods or not—at any rate they moved. For the old West Side was all movement. Everyone had just come—from somewhere, usually from across the ocean—and all the world was going—somewhere else. Here were the most foreign of all the foreign newspapers, the foreign banks, the steamship companies—Italian in one section, Greek in another—all seeking immigrant patronage. Here were the private employment offices, recruiting (and exploiting) the newly arrived immigrants, the churches representing various nationalistic groups, that made these areas not unlike a series of foreign cities brought together within the metropolitan area.

To get a picture of a cross-section of the West Side, it is easy to follow one of the north and south streets and go from the bridge over the river's "south branch" straight ahead to the bridge over the "north branch." Cross the south branch of the river, for example, at Halsted Street, and follow this great thoroughfare under the railroad tracks between the canal slips, across Lumber Street, and then Twenty-second, which is a busy cross-street with street-car lines and bustling activity of various kinds.

THE OLD LUMBER YARDS DISTRICT

To the east of Halsted the Slovak district in the Lumber Yards area was selected for a first canvass as long ago as the last pre-war winter, and then was recanvassed before the depression with other

Non-family Groups of Men," by Milton B. Hunt; (2) XVI, 289, "Families in Furnished Rooms"; (3) XVI, 433, "Housing Conditions Back of the Yards"; (4) XVII, 1, "The West Side Revisited"; (5) XVII, 145, "South Chicago at the Gates of the Steel Mills"; (6) XVIII, 241, "The Problem of the Negro," by Alzada P. Comstock; (7) XVIII, 509, "Two Italian Districts," by Grace P. Norton; (8) XX, 145, "Housing Conditions among the Slovaks in the Twentieth Ward," by Helen L. Wilson and Eunice W. Smith; (9) XX, 289, "The Lithuanians in the Fouth Ward," by Elizabeth Hughes; (10) XXI, 285, "Greeks and Italians in the Hull-House Neighborhood," by Natalie Walker.

districts that had been visited in the earlier studies. An area of four blocks investigated in this district included the very shabby blocks between Sixteenth and Eighteenth streets in one of the most dilapidated of the river wards. The Slovak area here extended roughly from Halsted Street east to Burlington and Seward streets, where factories, and what was then a great brewing plant, cut the district off from the river. It stretched along from the freight houses running along Sixteenth Street, south to Twentieth Place, where factories and lumber yards again cut it off from the river, which turns west at this point.

This has never been what is called a "residential neighborhood." A low and swampy area in Chicago's earliest days[5a]—as late as the eve of the Civil War there were only a dozen houses east of Halsted Street near the point where Eighteenth Street is now located. At the beginning of the eighties, when the streets were first graded up to the present level and paved, the modern commercial expansion had called for the settling-up of the vacant spaces. Before the regrading, roads had been built by standing wooden horses across the proposed highway and nailing boards upon them lengthwise of the road. Old inhabitants, who were still living in the district at the time when our investigators first canvassed it, remembered falling through these roadways into the swamp, sometimes with a team of horses; and they also told of the difficulties of driving home a flock of geese. At the time of the regrading, the area was an Irish and German colony, with a group of Bohemians between Sixteenth and Eighteenth streets, and between Jefferson Street and the river. At the time of our recanvass, a few members of these earlier groups who were so provident, or so improvident, as to buy their homes were stranded among the newer immigrants, the Slovaks or other Slavs, who had begun settling there at the close of the last century.

Our pre-war house-to-house canvass showed that one-third of the 854 households in the area selected here were Slovak, nearly one-fifth Lithuanian, and one-sixth Bohemian. The Poles formed slightly more, and the Germans slightly less, than one-tenth, while all the other nationalities, including Irish and American, were less than a tenth of the total number of households. In one part of the area the

[5a] The study by Helen Wilson and Eunice Smith, *op. cit.*, is used here.

LOOKING WEST OVER THE SLOVAK TENEMENTS

settlement was predominantly Polish, with a few Russians, Letts, and Slovaks. In a block of dilapidated houses east of the old brewery and overlooking an expanse of tracks was a Lithuanian group.

Slovak immigrants began to arrive in Chicago as early as the middle eighties, but it was not until the nineties that they began coming in in any great numbers. The first settlers came chiefly from the two provinces of Nitra and Trencin, and settled in the vicinity of Bunker and Halsted streets, near the old Czech "colony" south of the Hull-House neighborhood. Gradually, with the increase in Slovak immigration, other little colonies developed—one important group "back of the Yards," another to the north,[6] and another a little farther south.

As to religion, the Slovaks are predominantly Catholic, and the important Slovak church of St. Joseph's[7] is located in the area we canvassed. But there is a large group of Lutherans and a much smaller group belonging to the Greek Uniat church. Like the Czechs, the Slovaks also have a group of Freethinkers, but it is proportionately much smaller.

The people of all nationalities who lived in the old Lumber Yards area were generally occupied at the more poorly paid and unskilled work. The men often worked as common laborers; about the freight houses, in car shops, or on steam or street railroads; they were factory workers of many sorts, metal workers, and expressmen, teamsters and draymen, scrubbers and cleaners. There were small shopkeepers and tradesmen, and at the time of the first canvass there were twenty saloonkeepers. Other workers in the district were scattered in a great variety of employments, ranging from the old man who owned a soda-water factory to the old woman who lived by "picking things up on the tracks."

The houses in this area were, for the most part, "old law" tene-

[6] The Slovaks who chose the northern section of the city lived in a community in the neighborhood of Chicago Avenue and Noble Street but gradually spread out to the adjacent streets. This group was reported to be made up chiefly of Protestants.

[7] The Roman Catholic Slovak parishes and the dates of their organization are as follows: St. Michael Archangel, 1898, in the Stock Yards area; St. Joseph's, 1903, near the Lumber Yards; SS. Cyril and Methodius, 1914, North West Side; Assumption of the Blessed Virgin, 1903, West Side; Sacred Heart, 1918, North Side; St. John the Baptist, 1909, South Chicago; Holy Rosary, 1907, Roseland.

ments—the first generation in the district, built before 1902, sometimes moved back to accommodate a new building on the front of the lot, which in its turn had become increasingly weather-beaten and dilapidated. And this condition of dilapidation extended beyond the area canvassed, especially to the south and west, where some of the old houses were really in tumble-down condition. Not only were the houses old and built before the days of tenement standards, but they were largely of frame construction.

Dilapidation was everywhere. The cellars, even the first floors, were damp because of the grading up of streets and alleys from three to seven feet above the level of the yards. The walls of the cellars and the floors of the first stories were often decayed and musty, with the water draining down about the foundations. Floors were warped and uncertain, plumbing generally precarious—defective sinks with soaking plaster in the ceiling below (one long-suffering Lithuanian showed our investigator the water dripping down on his bed), windowpanes broken or entirely gone, doors loose and broken, plaster cracked and grimy, woodwork splintered and long unvarnished. Yards, areaways, and passages were cluttered and untidy with accumulated rubbish and the keeping of fowls in unsuitable quarters—and other nuisances, such as the smoking of meat carried on in the rear of one lot.

There was a marked change when we moved across Halsted Street almost at right angles and went due west to the old City Homes area in the Bohemian district (Pilsen) that was also included in our canvass. Here the houses were well-built, substantial brick tenements, and good repair was as universal as dilapidation had been nearer the river where old wooden cottages and sagging frame tenements were the common type.

THE BOHEMIAN TENEMENTS OF PILSEN

The Pilsen district, although it is several blocks west of Halsted Street, is closely related in its history to the other district studied by the City Homes Association on the east of Halsted. The early Bohemian immigrants who had come during the period between the Civil War and the Great Fire[8] had settled largely in the district east

[8] The earliest Bohemian settlement in Chicago was probably on the North Side in the vicinity of North Avenue and Clark Street, but this was apparently a small settle-

of Halsted, and east and south of Hull-House. Certainly it was long before the founding of Hull-House that the district around De Koven Street was known as "Prague" because the Bohemian immigrants were so congested there.[9] After the fire the Bohemians moved farther west. There were various reasons for this. Toward what was then the western frontier of the city and even beyond it there were new opportunities for the purchase of homes in the semirural sections that were being "laid out" in the form of city lots and blocks. The account of the Bohemian settlement in *Hull-House Maps and Papers* tells us that the move from "Prague," their old settlement east of Halsted, to the new colony less than a mile west of Halsted, which they called "Pilsen" after their second largest city in Bohemia and which has long been a very congested area of high tenements, was made by the Bohemians because they loved "nature, pure air, and gardens." The early description of this neighborhood says that the original immigrants sold their property in the crowded area east of Halsted and moved to the new region, which was west and south, so that they might invest in more land and thus afford the luxury of a garden. The movement once started, it was not long before the whole community changed its location, and soon there grew up a large colony, "a city within a city," spreading from Halsted to Ashland and from Sixteenth to Twentieth street, and numbering not less than forty-five thousand Bohemians.[10]

As early as 1863 the Bohemians in the Prague colony had organized their first parish. Although the first Bohemian immigrants were very poor, they held a meeting and decided to buy the property on De Koven and Des Plaines streets for the erection of the first Roman Catholic Bohemian parish church, which was named St. Wenceslaus.

---

ment that scarcely attained the dignity of a Bohemian "colony." Bohemian life in Chicago certainly centered on the West Side almost from the beginning of Bohemian immigration.

[9] See the early volume, *Hull-House Maps and Papers,* chap. vi, "The Bohemian People in Chicago," by Josefa Humpal Zeman. The district extending from Canal to Halsted Street is described as "the largest and best settlement of Bohemians in the city" before the great fire of 1871.

[10] The increase in Bohemian immigration in the early eighties and the ease with which these intelligent and ambitious people acquired a competence soon made it possible for them to extend their settlement farther west and south, or rather to establish a new settlement toward the pleasant Douglas Park region.

"Eighty-five families subscribed as parishioners and promised to help build the church and support the parish."[11]

Bohemian immigrants began coming in while the Irish and Germans still lived in the district, which soon became, in common with the other "river wards" of the old West Side, a neighborhood struggling between the encroachments of business on all sides from the river district on the east, where business pushed its way in across Canal Street, and from the great thoroughfares like Halsted Street and Roosevelt Road. This is now only a gaunt remnant of a tenement area, a few scattered groups of houses largely in poor repair, jostled by factories, warehouses, freight depots, and business property of all kinds. As the neighborhood has changed physically, it has also changed in other ways. The Bohemians have followed the earlier German and Irish settlers and sought new homes,[12] while

[11] The account in the *Diamond Jubilee of the Archdiocese of Chicago* which tells of the efforts to establish the first Bohemian parish says: "On account of the scarcity of Bohemian priests in America and the fewness and poverty of the first Bohemian immigrants, they had no priests who could attend to their spiritual wants nor a place of their own where they could worship. They attended St. Peter's Church on Polk and Clark Streets, and St. Francis Church on Clinton and Mather Streets" (p. 355). The new frame building which was finished in 1866 included a church, parochial school, and living quarters for a priest; but when the new parish asked the bishop to send them a Bohemian priest, there was none to send. The Jesuit Fathers from the great "Holy Family" Church on Twelfth Street came to say mass every Sunday, but they could not hear confessions since they did not understand the Czech language. In 1869 more property, including an old Baptist church, was bought. The Baptist church was made over into a Bohemian parochial school, which was put in charge of the Franciscan Sisters. Later, the old church was enlarged and remodeled, a brick school building was erected, and a brick rectory which was later used as a convent.

This first Bohemian parish now appears to be largely Polish. In the list of twenty-four students graduated in 1934 from the parochial school, the names of all but one were Polish.

An interesting placard on the east side of the church reads as follows:

St. Wenceslaus Catholic Church
Shrine spared by the Great Chicago Fire of 1871
This original church was built in spring 1865 on opposite corner of present location and moved in spring 1932.
Conflagration started one block east
Interior is in its original form portraying architectural design of our forefathers
Visit this quiet and peaceful historical shrine

[12] Faithful Bohemian Catholics still attend the services at old St. Wenceslaus, but they come rather from the districts far to the southwest than from the St. Wenceslaus

their places have been rapidly taken by the Russian Jews, Italians, and Greeks. In the recent period between the World War and the depression, Mexicans, and even Negroes, have been crowding in.

The move to the so-called "Pilsen" district was marked by the founding of the third Bohemian parish[13] of Chicago, which was destined to be a much more flourishing one—this was the parish of St. Procopius, organized in 1875. An old Bohemian settler, in describing the growth of the Pilsen district after the Great Fire, said that such a "flood of families moved in that the growth of the colony was like that of mushrooms following a summer rain." Many of these families came from the older parishes like St. Wenceslaus, but there was also a "flood" of Bohemian immigrants from across the seas. Most of these were from the districts around the city of Pilsen, which explains why this colony came to be familiarly called by that name.

In the years 1905 to 1910 the Bohemians were practically the only people living in the Pilsen neighborhood. They had their own business houses, schools, and theaters. When our first canvass was made here, the neighborhood was a Bohemian city. Today, however, only 40 per cent of the people are of this nationality, so many of them have moved farther west within the city limits and into the suburbs of Berwyn and Cicero, where there are more open spaces, better homes, and fewer factories. In place of the Bohemians have come Slovaks and Croatians, who adjust well to the community because they are also Slavic. The Bohemians remain influential in a business way, and several of the large Bohemian banks, real estate offices, publishing houses, and newspapers are located here. Many of the

---

neighborhood. As a result of the increase in the Polish population in the neighborhood of St. Wenceslaus, a mission in Polish was conducted in 1907. After this "the Poles attended the services in the church regularly and were inscribed as parishioners" (*Diamond Jubilee Volume*, p. 357).

[13] Three lots on the corner of Allport and Eighteenth streets were purchased, and a deserted Methodist church on Halsted near Twentieth Street was bought and moved to the church property. The old church was remodeled into a combination church and school, but the parish "grew by leaps and bounds" and a new church was built in 1883. The one-room school at first had an enrolment of forty children, who were taught only Bohemian by a man teacher. In 1876, however, two additional classrooms were opened, and English was taught by two Sisters; and in 1889 a large new school was opened. As the work of the parish became so enlarged it was turned over to a group of Bohemian Benedictine Fathers from St. Vincent's Abbey, Pennsylvania.

professional men—doctors, dentists, and lawyers—still maintain their offices here. A national theater is at Eighteenth and Allport; Pilsen Auditorium is on Blue Island near Eighteenth; there is Pilsen Sokol Hall on South Ashland near Eighteenth; *Denní Hlasatel* and *Národ*, two Bohemian daily papers, are still published in this neighborhood; "Little Bohemia," an old and well-known restaurant, is at Eighteenth and Loomis. Everywhere there are signs that the Bohemians have prospered in the United States and have done especially well in Chicago, which ranks (after Prague, the capital city of the Czecho-Slovak state) as the second Bohemian city in the world.

Although this area had been included in our canvass because it was one of the "City Homes" districts, it seemed less important for our purposes because the housing conditions had changed so little that the recanvass of more than a selected block seemed unnecessary.[14] In our later recanvass we found very few outside changes in this district; the population, however, had decreased by about 25 per cent, probably because with so few new Czech immigrants, there was not the same pressure for housing space. This district showed no deterioration in the twenty years between our first canvass and our recanvass. It still had a foreign look, but the rather well-built Czech tenements had weathered the years, and industry had made slight encroachments there.

To the north and a little east of the Bohemian district as we went back toward Halsted beyond the railway tracks was "The Valley"—that journalistic name for a vaguely defined area to which authors of unsolved crimes could always be, and are still, assigned. "The Valley" was the name first applied to a little place on old Catherine Street—later Fifteenth Street—between Morgan Street and the tiny street only two blocks long, known as Solon Street, when one of the railroads in elevating its tracks demolished a row of wooden shanties on the south side of the street to make way for a steep embankment. On the opposite side the remaining small frame houses—shanties if you like—were to all appearances huddled in a valley off the main thoroughfare; and this small area, which was cleared in 1925 to make way for the new

[14] In the Bohemian neighborhood (Pilsen) the sample selected for recanvass was the neighborhood of Twentieth and Loomis streets.

South Water Street Produce Market, was for many years known as "The Valley"[15] to the changing groups of foreign immigrants who came, worked, and struggled there.

"The Valley" was the name finally adopted to describe a rather extensive area and in popular journalistic descriptions was applied rather generally to some of the West Side streets north of the railroad embankment.

THE OLD GHETTO[16]

Returning to the busy Halsted Street thoroughfare, one came to the large area studied by the City Homes Association, which included the Russian Jewish section, the greater part of which lay between Halsted Street and the river. Here, beginning approximately at Fourteenth Street, was the oldest Jewish colony of the West Side, which, at the time of our first canvass, extended both east and west across Halsted Street. But although the old Ghetto was still there with its picturesque market on Maxwell Street, it was gradually moving west; and before our post-war recanvass, it had become clear that the old section was rapidly disappearing.

In the pre-war period when immigration was at its height, this was one of the poorest and most congested sections of Chicago, where

[15] A typical newspaper account of "The Valley" is this story of a much-reported Chicago bandit in 1926 by the name of Durkin. This newspaper account of the rise of Durkin is typical of the stories of "The Valley":

"Durkin started from scratch. But no one ever heard him complain that the world was against him. He was born in a house on Rebecca Street, a thoroughfare long since transmuted into Fifteenth Place. It lay between Morgan and Center streets. Center has since become Racine Avenue. Thus, the locality was in the heart of what was known as 'The Valley.' When a railroad condemned a portion of the neighborhood, the Durkins moved to Henry Street, a little nearer the heart of things in 'The Valley,' if that were possible.

"There were no silver spoons in 'The Valley.' Durkin went early to find the one that had missed his mouth when he was born. John Kelley, the dean of Chicago police reporters, recalled yesterday that his first glimpse of Jimmy Durkin was in 1889.

" 'He must have been about nine years old,' said Mr. Kelley. 'He had come out into the world and was a member of the community known as the Waifs' Mission . . . . in State Street north of Randolph Street. . . . .' "

[16] The account of this section is based in part on a recent report of the Ghetto which was made by Mary Zahrobsky and an early study of the Russian Jewish colony which was made by Esther Ladewick (A.M., 1928), formerly a social-service research assistant. See also *The History of the Jews of Chicago*, by Hyman L. Meites, and *The Ghetto*, by Louis Wirth.

housing conditions in the old frame tenements were at their worst, marked by extreme dilapidation, bad plumbing, and great overcrowding. Even the streets were filthy, miserably paved, and, for Chicago, narrow and crowded. This Russian Jewish colony was one of the early settlements of the so-called "new immigration" and had been established before the Great Fire. As early as 1870 a Russian Jewish congregation built a synagogue on Canal and Liberty streets, which was not destroyed by the fire in 1871 and which soon became a center, or haven, for the Russian Jewish immigrants, who in the following decade came into Chicago in such large numbers.

In the ten-year period 1870–80, Jews from Russian Poland who, unlike the immigrants of the next decades, had not been the victims of any special persecution, were coming into this general district. These earlier settlers were drawn here by opportunities for trade in the rapidly growing city. The district around the synagogue at Canal and Liberty grew into a distinctly orthodox Jewish community, because these new immigrants came from one of the larger Russian cities from which Jews were then emigrating in large numbers. The earlier arrivals among the Jews from Russian Poland and from Russia made their living by peddling from push carts among the earlier immigrant groups—the Irish, Germans, and Bohemians, who were then still numerous in this section. For example, one of the oldest West Side merchants who had been an immigrant from Russian Poland said that he came to Chicago in 1876 and started out with a push cart, peddling among the Bohemians and the Germans in the district west of Canal Street along Roosevelt Road, then called Twelfth Street. Canal Street was at that time the main West Side business street, and the Jewish peddlers worked out from there into various immigrant neighborhoods.

Not until after 1882 and the passage of the restrictive laws against the Jews in Russia did the West Side Jewish colony begin to resemble the Russian pale. The increase in the Russian Jewish population on the West Side followed the waves of immigration that were the direct result of the various restrictive laws and other manifestations of hostility to the Jews in Russia—the May laws of 1882, the pogroms, and the further repressive laws of 1886–87, the persecutions of 1892, the Kishneff Massacre in 1903—all led to a great increase in Russian

Jewish immigration; and these successive waves of immigrants almost uniformly found homes at first in the most crowded part of the old Ghetto—the miserably deteriorated and congested section between Halsted Street and the river. Here the newcomers sought help and safety among their co-religionists who had preceded them in the exodus from the country of oppression.

Although there have been several other well-defined Jewish areas in Chicago,[17] the term "Ghetto" was used only for this early Russian settlement west of Canal Street. To many Chicago people the Ghetto meant the great West Side street market and the junk-shop district. A Ghetto in the old Russian sense could not, of course, exist in any American city and, in Chicago, the term "Ghetto" merely designated a place where the Russian Jews had voluntarily segregated themselves. The character of the immigration of the period 1880–1900 probably explains the segregation tendency. The editor of one of the Yiddish newspapers, who had collected stories of the efforts of the earlier immigrants in the Ghetto to help make some provision for the destitute refugees who came later, described this flight of the persecuted as a "volcanic eruption."

The general characteristics of the movement have long been known—the poverty and misery of the immigrants, the flight of whole families together, bringing aged dependents with them because there was no time for one member of a family to come in advance of the others to prepare a new home and to secure a business foothold. Relatives here were miserably poor, too, but it was customary for a man who found he could earn some kind of livelihood in the junk business, or with a push cart, to send back to Russia for an unhappy relative or friend with whom he was ready to share his business, and even his home. Most of these immigrant families found homes just west of the river, as the first immigrants of so many other nationalities had done before, because the neighborhood had long

[17] See the history by Meites, *op. cit.* The history of the Jewish people in Chicago goes back to the early forties, when a number of Jewish families driven from Germany by persecution were sent out to Cook County by the Jewish Colonization society of New York. These earliest settlers were from Southern Germany, Bavaria, and the Rhenish Palatinate. See an article, "Jews and Judaism in Early Chicago Days," in *Chicago Journal*, November 14, 1899, by Mr. Leopold Mayer, for many years a leader and teacher in the early Jewish community.

been an undesirable one and here were the oldest and poorest tenements. The Irish, German, and Bohemian immigrants of the earlier period were moving away.[18] The fact that there were two Russian Jewish synagogues in the neighborhood of Canal Street was one reason for the growth of the colony. The clannishness of the orthodox Jews from Russia which kept them so long in segregated, congested settlements was due in part to the fact that the refugee family first of all sought protection in semi-seclusion near the synagogue and the kosher markets—in a congregation of people "from home." In the earlier days when transportation was more difficult, this meant that housing conditions which were already very bad became much worse and an already congested area became more congested. People with a common history of persecution were huddled together in spite of widely differing traditions and habits. No one who saw men and women buying and selling unfamiliar foods in the crowded street stalls, or bargaining for cast-off clothing, could understand that back of all this there was an idealism which maintained the traditions of family life, education, and religion under the most difficult conditions.

The first Jewish street market seems to have been on Jefferson Street, and as early as 1893 the World's Fair guidebooks for Chicago described the Jewish market on Jefferson Street as one of the interesting sights of the city. Apparently many of the features of the later markets were then clearly visible. The chief market began on Jefferson Street at Roosevelt Road and then was extended around into Maxwell Street. But about the time of the war, because of the crowding along the street-car track, stalls were all moved gradually around to Maxwell Street.[19] The chief market was for a time between

[18] The old settlers of these earlier immigrant races used to tell about how they were "pushed out of the section by the Jews." The Bohemians said that they had been "forced" to leave one colony after another by Jewish invasion of their province. First they were on Franklin Street east of the river, then on Harrison Street, then on old Twelfth Street (Roosevelt Road), until a Jewish group of newer immigrants seemed to come crowding into every available space. The feeling was that an "invasion" of this kind led to an aggravated condition of overcrowding. This was, of course, only the usual crowding of newer immigrants into low-rent areas. See below, pp. 93, 128, 147. More recently, however, the Bohemians in Lawndale complained of the encroachments of the Jewish colony there.

[19] The dealers along Jefferson Street said that their trade had been severely injured by the moving of the market, and the owners of buildings on Jefferson at the time of our

Jefferson and Halsted on Maxwell; but stalls began gradually moving over to the west of Halsted as far as Newberry Street, and wagons and push carts began taking up temporary stations even farther west, where property-owners protested against this extension of the market.

At the time of our first housing studies, Friday was the great market day for the Ghetto trade, and buying the Sabbath food was an important activity of the orthodox Jewish housewives. Saturday was a very quiet day at that time when the Ghetto was all Jewish and orthodox and when the business was still in the hands of the older immigrants. Later, however, as the Jewish population continued to move west, the market began to depend upon the trade of the other nationalities who lived in the district. On Sunday the market became a fair, with peddlers of all sorts thronging into the streets at sunrise, and dealers buying stocks from rag-pickers and hucksters, and opening up their storerooms to select the articles which were to be sold in the stalls. Later in the day, customers and visitors swarmed in and out. The clothing business was then at its height, and stall after stall was piled with strange garments supplied from dark basement storerooms back of the sidewalk. The junk business, which for years centered in the district east of Halsted, gradually moved on farther west.

There was a great deal of confused moving about among the early residents of the Jewish West Side colony as among other new immigrant groups; but this was, at first, almost a continuous expansion—from the eastern quarter of the Ghetto directly west along Roosevelt Road and the parallel streets for several blocks south. There was also a gradual movement of those who secured economic independence from the West Side Colony and who went into the more prosperous Jewish districts farther west, on the Northwest Side and out to

---

canvass spoke with bitterness of the excessive rents realized from the old buildings—"mere rat holes"—along Maxwell, and of their own vacant rooms. Jefferson Street was still a distinctively Jewish business street at that time. Although there were no stalls, the wares exhibited in windows and hung outside the doors were not unlike those on the Maxwell Street Market, and salesmen were as hard to escape. On Maxwell Street east of Jefferson and on Jefferson south of Maxwell there was a junk business connected with the Maxwell Street stalls where old clothing, hardware, dishes, carpets, and bedding are piled in abandoned houses. Here much bargaining was going on between men with great "gunny-sack packs" and the dealers.

the South Side.[20] Until after the World War, however, this movement had little appreciable effect upon the Jewish neighborhood, for as the old settlers prospered and moved away their places were filled by later Russian Jewish immigrants. But after the war the old colony was changed—first, because the suspension of all European immigration in 1914 made a great change in the old district east of Halsted Street; and, second, because of the industrial and commercial development of the area between Halsted Street and the river. These changes together contributed to the gradual disappearance of the old West Side Jewish quarter.

Our canvass and recanvass in the old Ghetto were made during the period of transition. As the population changed, housing conditions changed only by growing steadily worse. At the time of the recanvass two decades later the houses had become disgracefully dilapidated both within and without. The great majority of the houses were old frame buildings not more than two stories high, and the problem of overcrowding was quite obviously not overcrowding on the block but a problem of overcrowding within the house and within the room.

When our canvass of this area was begun in a block on Liberty Street, the whole area was seething with newly arrived immigrants. Overcrowding within the houses had apparently become worse since the earlier City Homes Association inquiry, for the block population had increased in the ten years following the City Homes investigation, although there were fewer houses. One of our student investigators reported a case which illustrated the tragedies of that area and that time. A young Jewish immigrant was found apparently dying of tuberculosis in a crowded flat in a crowded tenement there on Liberty Street. He told of the sacrifices and courage needed to break the old home ties in Russia and make the long journey to America and Chicago. But he had been urged on by a friend from his village who had come to Chicago and who was living on Liberty Street. The name "Liberty Street" had fired the imagination of the Russian youth. He thought "Liberty Street" would be a wide and beautiful avenue; he dreamed of a parkway with a great statue like the "Lib-

[20] See Louis Wirth, *The Ghetto*, for an account of the westward Jewish expansion.

erty" he had seen pictured, "enlightening the world," welcoming poor immigrants to the Land of Promise! He then told of his bitter disappointments, the small, mean street, the miserable houses, the vermin, the dirt, the sky dark with smoke, no park, nothing but defeat and despair.[21]

Even before the war, at the time of our first canvass, the change in the colony had already begun, but it was not until 1916 that there was a general exodus of Jewish families that was almost a flight from the vanishing Ghetto. The restriction of immigration and the rapid change in the character of the neighborhood so altered the section east of Halsted Street between Taylor and Fourteenth that streets formerly occupied exclusively by Jewish families were given over to Poles, Russians, Lithuanians, Italians, and Negroes. Many houses had also been vacated before our last recanvass. Some were on property which had been bought for industrial sites and some had been condemned.[22]

A survey of Jewish community life in the old area made by one of the social agencies in 1919 showed that the district east of Halsted was being largely given over to factories and that very few Jews were left even in the section that extended west of Halsted for half a mile to Racine. The Italians, Greeks, and Poles were said to have been "crowding the Jews out for years," and only a few isolated Jewish families were to be found in their own homes.

[21] The extent of tuberculosis in the most congested part of this district had been pointed out in some early studies by the great Jewish physician, Dr. Theodore B. Sachs, the founder of the Chicago Municipal Tuberculosis Sanitarium, whose fine maps showed a dreadful concentration of black spots, indicating cases of tuberculosis under care in the blocks of the old Ghetto ("Tuberculosis in the Jewish District of Chicago," *Journal of the American Medical Association*, August 6, 1904).

[22] When the old Liberty Street area was canvassed twenty years after our first study, it had become almost depopulated. There were, in fact, only twenty houses still used for residence purposes. Some of the old houses, we were told, had "simply fallen down." There were still several very old buildings which looked as though they might "fall down" at some unexpected moment and these were occupied by poor Negroes. There were many abandoned buildings, empty shells of old tenements, piles of refuse where buildings had once stood, and remains of buildings which had been torn down or burned. In spite of the general deterioration, more than two hundred people were still living in the block. This was, of course, a great decline from the more than a thousand whom we found at the time of our first canvass, but there were still men, women, and children living in houses that could only be described as "unfit for human habitation."

One interesting group of newcomers who appeared here and followed the Jews were the White Russians who were employed in various large industries and who lived in the vicinity of Jefferson Street and Maxwell and other streets of the old Ghetto area. Practically the whole of the White Russian colony could be found within the rectangle formed by Taylor and Eighteenth, Clinton and Racine. It consisted largely of non-family groups of men living in old houses and basement apartments.

Returning to Halsted Street and going along to the north, the investigator finally comes to Hull-House and her immediate neighbors—swarming masses of Italians and Greeks.

HULL-HOUSE AND HER NEIGHBORS

In 1889, when Hull-House was opened, the Near West Side of Chicago had already become a crowded, immigrant neighborhood. In the earlier days when the family of Charles Hull lived in the old mansion that became the world's most famous settlement, they were near the city limits with only a few scattered groups of cottages to the west of them; and Mr. Hull from his little office[23] on the first floor of the house could look out on the market gardens that stretched along down what is now the confusion of South Halsted Street. The market gardens have, of course, long since vanished with the memories of those early days; but the famous old highway, Blue Island Avenue, still slopes diagonally across the West Side as it did in the day when it was only an old plank road. Later this section of the West Side had been a fashionable neighborhood, and twenty-five years ago, when the West Side was new to us as social investigators, there were still many of the old West Side mansions to be found in the streets between Hull-House and the old "Haymarket." Many of these we had visited from time to time in trying to help the families who came to Hull-House to ask for assistance of many kinds. And

[23] This little octagon office is still used by the residents of Hull-House as a general office for settlement purposes. The first Juvenile Court studies and other early social research undertakings of our School of Social Service, then the Chicago School of Civics and Philanthropy, were carried on in the Octagon of Hull-House, which still has in the wall the old safe of Mr. Charles Hull, and the long windows from which he saw the almost rural appearance of the West Side of his day. For an interesting account of the early West Side see also Carter Harrison's *Stormy Years*, pp. 18–20, 26–31.

when we were investigating "furnished rooms" or visiting persons in need of help, we often found that the old mansions had fallen easily into that stage of decrepitude marked by the presence of relief families. Some of these once spacious homes were quite well-known landmarks at the time of our first canvass, but they have disappeared along with more recent tenements under the pressure of the advancing business and commercial interests.

After the Great Fire of 1871 the change in the character of the neighborhood and the corresponding change in the inhabitants went on rapidly; the Americans largely gave place to the Irish and the Germans, who in turn receded before advancing hosts of Russian Jews and Italians, who still later gave way before the Greeks and Bulgarians, who are now in turn being superseded by Mexicans and Negroes. The Jews gradually became localized in the district south of Taylor Street, where, since the war, the Negroes and the Mexicans have been crowding in while the Jews have moved west. North of Taylor the Italians, in ever increasing numbers, crept into the ramshackle tenements both east and west of Halsted; and the Greeks made Blue Island Avenue and the "three points," where Blue Island, Halsted, and Harrison meet, their chief center of activity.

In the early days of the new Hull-House settlement, Halsted Street was already lined with saloons, restaurants, clothing stores, all kinds of shops and cheap lodging-houses, and had become the backbone of the congested district that had grown up between the north and south branches of the river. The whole district was a region of flimsy wooden dwellings and dilapidated sheds, of poorly paved and unpaved streets, and filthy alleys. Twenty-five years ago when we began our journeyings around the West Side, the streets were as dilapidated as the houses. Many of them had old cedar block pavements which had a fashion of sinking in certain sections so that they had deep holes and pools of water after a heavy rain. One of the old residents of Hull-House remembers that when she once told a class the story of Noah's Ark and described the flood, an eager child said quickly, "Oh, I know, just like Des Plaines Street!" For Des Plaines Street between Halsted and the river was one of the many West Side streets that after a rain was like a small lake.

Just when the Italians began to settle in the Lower West Side no one knows exactly. When our housing studies began, the largest group of Italians in Chicago was settled in this area and the colony ranking next in size was known as "Little Italy" on the Lower North Side. The Grand Avenue colony, near the Chicago Commons, was of growing importance and various other areas of the city had large groups of Italian residents. The Italians were certainly established along Halsted Street when Hull-House opened its doors in 1889; and in 1892, when the United States Bureau of Labor was making the investigation called *The Slums of Great Cities*,[24] there were large numbers of Italians in this district.

The federal census reported only 552 Italians in Chicago in 1870; 1,357 in 1880; 5,685 in 1890; 16,008 in 1900; 45,169 in 1910; 59,215 in 1920; and 73,960 in 1930. These figures give a very good picture of the great foreign colonies of this nationality in Chicago.

It was not, however, until the late 1890's that an Italian Roman Catholic church was founded in this neighborhood. This was the present Guardian Angel Church founded in the district which was originally inhabited by the earlier Irish immigrants who belonged to the famous old Holy Family Church of the Jesuit Fathers at May Street and Roosevelt Road, which was then Twelfth Street. In its infancy the little colony of Italians was wedged in between the Slavs on the south and the Irish on the west,[25] and they were cared for by the Church of the Holy Family and the Bohemian Church of St. Wenceslaus if they found the way too long to the Italian Church of the Assumption on the North Side. It was not until 1899 that the Guardian Angel Church was founded, and so rapidly did the Italian population increase during the great period of Italian immigration in the decade 1900–1910 that they overflowed the old boundaries of the Italian colony near Hull-House, which had been located at first chiefly in the territory east of Halsted Street. As they moved west across Halsted and took over the territory between Halsted and

[24] *Report, U.S. Commissioner of Labor, 1894*, p. 48. See also above, chap. i, pp. 31–32.

[25] A "second generation" Italian gave an interesting account of that period: "In those primitive, heroic days, stoning brigades would advance across Twelfth Street and drive the Italian boys back to Taylor Street. And if 'immigrant kids,' as the most recent arrivals were designated, cared to penetrate west to play ball in Vernon Park, they had to cut their way through fierce shock troops of young hooligans. But numbers brought independence, and the youthful, inter-gang battles passed into history."

Racine, the old Guardian Angel parish[26] was divided, and the district west of Morgan was formed into a new parish, picturesquely called Our Lady of Pompeii.[27] So rapidly had the Italian colony increased that the faithful were unable to crowd into the older church on Sunday and were compelled to hear mass from the street or the church yard.

At the time of a recanvass ten years ago the Italian colony on the West Side included the two large Italian parishes and extended from

[26] This is one of the great foreign parishes reflecting the growth of an immigrant colony. Before the founding of the Guardian Angel Church, one of the Jesuit Fathers who came to the West Side was an Italian, and he immediately founded a parochial school for the Italian children of the neighborhood. This was the Guardian Angel School on Forquer Street, just a block west of Hull-House and in the center of the rapidly increasing Italian settlement. Later, Italian priests of the North Side church came over to say mass on Sundays in a large hall.

[27] The original church of Our Lady of Pompeii was dedicated in 1911, twelve years after the founding of the Guardian Angel Church. This was a combined church and school on Macalister Place with the lower part of the building used for the church and the upper part for the school. The new church was in a residence district near Vernon Park that had been rather fine in its day, and where older Irish families lingered on after the Italian invasion had begun; but in 1924 the present church was built because of the growth of the Italian colony on the west side of Halsted Street.

One of the local workers, in discussing the growth of the Italian colony which led to the founding of the two Italian churches near Hull-House, said that the Italians came into this part of the city for two reasons: (1) rents were low and (2) countrymen from their own districts were already living there. These immigrants were almost entirely South Italians and unskilled workers. They have been employed as laborers, although in the "old country" the men were often farmers, masons, bricklayers, or followed some other skilled occupation. Here they have lived cheaply and tried to save, and they have been ambitious chiefly for their children and have wanted them to be educated. When they have saved enough money, they move out farther west and purchase small houses and bungalows. Some years ago, when the first rumor spread that the Burlington Railroad was going to buy the property along Des Plaines Street, the houses were allowed to get into a miserably dilapidated condition; and this hastened the movement out of the parish to the west.

Another factor in the westward movement has been the fact that when the younger generation, these Americans of Italian parentage, have married, they do not remain in the old neighborhood, but are anxious to move out "among the Americans." From whatever cause, the Italian population of the district has certainly been dwindling since the war, the ties with the mother-country are gradually being broken. Few of the older people are returning to Italy now. The young people know almost nothing about the "mother-country." The older generation has become naturalized, and, as far as is possible, Americanized. Their interests are here, and with the falling-off in Italian immigration, there has been much less direct connection with the Old World.

the Chicago River west to Paulina Street and from Van Buren Street south almost one mile to Roosevelt Road. "It contained, perhaps, half the total Italian population of the city. They came from all parts of Italy, chiefly South Italians from Apulia, Basilicata, Campania and the Abruzzi, but there are also small groups of Tuscans, Lombards, Romans and Venetians. The district has been heterogeneous in character, not obviously Sicilian or Calabrian like the North Side colony. Certain of the blocks, however, were almost solidly from one Italian countryside; Forquer Street, for example, between Halsted and DesPlaines streets, was distinctly Neapolitan. It was said that a few oxen teams would complete the illusion of an inland Campanian village."[28] This area is really "Little Italy," with the omnipresent church, the popular Italian newspapers—*L'Italia* and *Il progresso* offered for sale—and the Italian-American National Union (once the Unione Siciliana), which has local councils in other parishes, and other Italian societies, fraternities of men who have come from the same village or town in Italy, are located in this section of the city, and there are also parochial societies connected with the church. In addition, not less than sixteen Italian benevolent societies and six courts of the Catholic Order of Foresters celebrate their religious festivities here.

The neighborhood of Our Lady of Pompeii is a more prosperous-looking one than that of the Guardian Angel. Many of the old houses built by the early families are still standing and are in very good condition. However, the newer parish also feels the movement of the people "to the west." When they have saved enough to buy a home,

[28] Much of the information about the Italian colonies was furnished by John Valentine, who was at one time a visitor for the Immigrants' Protective League. He pointed out that "these immigrants did not come from Naples, itself, but from the rural districts. Inhabitants of Naples prefer life in the 'city of gay poverty,' on any terms, to expatriation and hard work in the New World." One of the most prominent groups at this time came from the province of Basilicata. Because their own homeland was the poorest in Italy, they were among the very first to migrate to America; and their history illustrates that the downtrodden need not remain so. Being pioneers gave them many advantages over their successors. They became to the later immigrants what the Irish were to all Italians. Many of them were the first bankers, doctors, and merchants. The second generation has been ahead of others, becoming the professional and business leaders in the colony; lawyers, dentists, real estate dealers, and saloonkeepers.

THE ITALIAN-GREEK NEIGHBORHOOD NEAR HULL-HOUSE

these Italians also move out toward Columbus Park and Oak Park.[29]

Farther north and west was a small French settlement. The French Catholic Church of Notre Dame, with its large dome visible from all parts of the neighborhood, is still there; but most of its French parishioners have gone and return only for ceremonial occasions.[30]

In the last three decades the Greeks have become very conspicuous in this neighborhood and have gradually made the district south of Harrison and west of Halsted streets their own.[31] In 1894 there were fewer than one hundred Greeks in the Hull-House Ward; in 1908 the number had increased to more than five hundred; and to nearly two thousand in 1914[32] when the area had become the largest Greek colony in Chicago and one of the largest in the country. In general, the Greeks settled in the better-class tenements on the more important streets of the district, on Blue Island Avenue, once a leading highway to the city from the surrounding prairie towns and for a long time the main thoroughfare of the Greek colony. Along Blue Island and Halsted are lines of stores with Greek letters on their windows. Here are the offices of the Greek newspapers, the Greek grocery stores, the Greek coffee-houses and poolrooms, and the Greek labor agencies. Here are the Pantheon Restaurant, the Crete Coffee Shop, the Atlas Shipping Agency, and other business places with romantic names. Not far away are St. Basil's Church and the

[29] Hundreds of the new generation here moved farther west. In some cases they have persuaded or forced the old people to go with them. But more often the parents have refused to leave the shadow of the Italian church and their circle of old village cronies. "The conflict of ideals between the two generations often comes to a crisis on the issue of moving. The young Americans are unwilling to remain behind in what they scornfully call 'Little Italy'; they want to live in a 'civilized neighborhood.' But the first generation of immigrants are very firm; it is as if they had had enough of moving by their coming to the United States."

[30] The French priests are still there, and the school is conducted by French Canadian Sisters. It is interesting, however, that many of the Italian children attend the "French School," and that they are said to feel a little superior to the children who attend the "Italian School" just a few blocks away.

[31] See Grace Abbott, "A Study of the Greeks in Chicago," *American Journal of Sociology*, XV, 379–93.

[32] I.e., the old Nineteenth Ward. For the number of Greeks see *School Census of Chicago, 1894*, p. 6; *ibid., 1908*, pp. 12–19; *ibid., 1914*, pp. 17 ff.

Socrates School. As it is on Blue Island Avenue, so it is on Halsted Street from Harrison Street south to Polk Street—everywhere there are Greek names and Greek faces. The Bulgarians, who often held meetings at Hull-House,[33] clung to Halsted Street and were found farther along toward Van Buren Street, as the famous Greek restaurants began to disappear.

In those days a "vice area" troubled the honest tenement-house neighbors of the West Side—a segregated district that hovered on the edge of the "furnished room" district.[34] A few blocks north of Hull-House, east of Halsted, we drifted into this less respectable neighborhood. When you called at a quiet "furnished rooming-house" in the evening, the rush of a police patrol might give notice of a "raid" on a nearby dwelling, and groups of children, and occasionally their elders, waited to see what haul might be brought forth.

This part of the West Side has long had an unenviable reputation for every kind of overcrowding and congestion. Reference has already been made to the early survey of the Chicago Department of Health in 1894, when this area was said to have the highest death-rate in the city. The first house-to-house investigation ever made by the Health Department was apparently begun at this time when the high mortality was said to be due chiefly to the filthy and unpaved streets and alleys, to the dampness of the houses on the many lots that were below street level, and to the overcrowding in the insanitary frame houses.[35]

One of the Hull-House residents, writing in 1895, just after the United States Bureau of Labor had completed a survey of the region south of Polk Street, described the rear tenements and alleys as conspicuous evidence of the dilapidation and disorder that characterized the whole district. In the rear, wrote this early observer, the worst congestion was always found and the most poverty-stricken were gathered—"the densest crowds of the most wretched and destitute congregate." She described "the filthy and rotten tenements, the dingy courts and tumble-down sheds, the foul stables and dilapi-

[33] See Grace Abbott, "The Bulgarians of Chicago," *Survey*, XXI, 653–60.

[34] See the map originally published in our article on furnished rooms where the vice areas of that time are located. See *American Journal of Sociology*, XVI, 433.

[35] *Report of Chicago Department of Health, 1895–96*, p. 64.

dated outhouses, the broken sewer pipes, and the piles of garbage."[36]

Again in 1901, when the City Homes Association[37] was working for an improved housing law, forty-four blocks were chosen for the house-to-house canvass, which extended from the Italian and Greek colonies at the Harrison Street end of the district to what has already been described as the Russian-Jewish colony called "the Ghetto," at the southern end of the large area which reached to Fourteenth Street. These blocks were selected not because this was the worst district in the city, but because it was believed to be representative of widespread conditions of neglect and overcrowding. The condition of overcrowding in this neighborhood had been especially serious because there were few large tenements, and there was, therefore, a great deal of overcrowding within the houses. Few of the tenements here were more than three stories high, and the typical house was the two-story frame cottage, containing from two to four small apartments, with overcrowding of the worst kind. A walk through some of these streets on one of the hot nights of a hot midsummer day found the streets not only full of people but full of disorderly rubbish of every kind; children sleeping on the steps and on the porches, hurdy-gurdys everywhere and anywhere, and the whole area with the appearance of a crowded and noisy amusement park instead of a quiet place of rest and sleep.

The Hull-House neighborhood has long been one of the great areas of deterioration awaiting the final business invasion, where industry and commerce have already pushed across the river and where the neighborhood is changing very rapidly from a tenement to a business district. A study of housing conditions seemed less important here because of the rapidly diminishing population, but we finally recanvassed a selected sample of nineteen blocks in different parts of the district. There had been many changes in the decade between the time when the City Homes investigators went over the territory and the time of our first canvass. But the changes in the two decades between our first and our last canvass were so striking that the whole of the Lower West Side was like a new district. Factories and business houses had been moving across Canal Street and into the heart of the district.

[36] *Hull-House Maps and Papers*, p. 5.

[37] See above, pp. 58, 73, n. 2.

Although some improvements have taken place in the district as a whole, there have been few improvements in the houses themselves. Unfortunately, the clearing of areas has not always meant the destruction of the old frame houses which occupied them. These have been in most instances sold for a very low price, and the enterprising neighborhood landlords who bought them moved their old houses to the rear and placed the new ones in the front spaces which had been made available. The result was an even greater congestion on the portions of the blocks still occupied for residential purposes.

Returning to the great West Side thoroughfare, the journey along Halsted continues directly north to the West Madison Street area. All along the streets that lie between, and parallel with, Harrison and Madison are tenements that still survive the business encroachments. But they are tenements doomed to go, and although they are now dilapidated, and generally unfit, no careful study was made here because of the certain disappearance in the not too distant future of all dwellings in this area. In the meantime, people of all nationalities come and go here. The large majority of the storekeepers seem to be Jewish, many of whom have become so prosperous that they have moved west with their families and now rent the rooms above their shops to Greeks and Italians. Just back of Halsted Street, at the time when we made our recanvass, there was a small colony of Turks, there were two blocks largely occupied by Bulgarians, and a block of Serbians near by; and all along east of Halsted great numbers of Italians, living in very crowded quarters, an occasional group of Gypsies, and a few representatives of almost every other nationality —that is Halsted Street as it crosses into the Madison Street area.

Madison Street is an important business street, but it is, like Halsted Street, unique, in a class by itself, but not a community by itself, for it is not a community at all. Madison is a great through street, but social workers think of it as a street long associated with the "down and out." This area was at the time of our first canvass, and is still, associated with the "homeless men," who drifted about then, as they do today, haunting the employment offices on Canal Street, and spending the nights in the numerous "flops" in the neighborhood; or, as a last resort, in the early days, they sought the Municipal Lodging House that gave service in Union Street for more than a quarter of a century, and, in the recent years, relief "shelters" have served a larger group of men of the same friendless type.

Here one found clothing stores, barber shops, low-priced eating places, and large furniture shops. In among them were the cheap hotels and lodging-houses, rooms at "five and ten" for the night, and up. There were rescue missions, between dingy saloons and more dingy employment offices. The old state employment offices were, in normal times, the worst part of the street—their windows placarded and walls chalked with the number of men wanted as ice-cutters in Wisconsin, as loggers in northern Michigan, or, in another season, for the wheat fields of Kansas, for construction work with one railroad or another—for even in prosperous times, when work was plentiful, there was always an impatient queue of men waiting at each office for a chance at an unskilled job. In hard times, even before the great depression period, it was impossible to get along the street because it was so crowded with men desperately eager for work. Later in the day, when the signs had been rubbed from the office windows and the unemployed had lost that chance to sell their labor for that day, they shuffled listlessly up and down, often without even enough to buy a newspaper and devour the "Men Wanted" advertisements, or even enough to get a night's lodging in the dreary rooms of the cheap hotels, or in the flops. Our first winter in this area was one of the "unemployed winters" before the war when the bread lines formed on the snowy evenings, and one of the student investigators also helped the Immigrants' Protective League in a study of the private employment offices scattered through the area, which were violating the law and exploiting the friendless immigrants of those days.

Beyond Madison Street, one comes to Washington Boulevard, which scarcely more than a generation ago was one of the fashionable residence streets of the city. Here at the time of our first canvass there were still many of the imposing houses with brownstone fronts, which might have a delicatessen in the English basement, or rooms furnished for light housekeeping to rent by the day or week. There was the occasional church struggling along, or, occasionally, a church turned into a warehouse or a mission hall.

On to the north, through and beyond the Haymarket, where toward the west an early Negro settlement was included in our first series of studies, there was another important Italian colony near the Chicago Commons, and here at Chicago Avenue was the end, at the Halsted Street line, of the "West Division"; for at this point the river turns around Goose Island toward the northwest, so that the West Division becomes wider, and one follows Milwaukee Avenue, which leads to the northwest, as Blue Island and Archer avenues go to the southwest.

Here, the Italian settlement, near the corner of Halsted Street and Grand Avenue, is, in a way, a continuation of the Lower North Side colony, where we also made an early canvass. The North Side Italian colony is connected with this one by the Grand Avenue bridge; and Italian families, moving out of "Lower North" as the recent Negro migrants came in, often went across the river to find homes somewhere in the Italian colony on the other side. The two colonies, Lower North and Grand Avenue, are separated by the factories and railroad tracks that extend along the river. From Halsted, however, for a full two miles to Western Avenue, scattered chiefly along Grand Avenue, is a great Italian community, bounded on the south by the right-of-way of the Northwestern Railroad. The northern boundary is not so easily defined, but may be said to lie near Division Street.

The Grand Avenue quarter has been made up of recruits from different parts of Italy; thousands of Apulians, especially immigrants from Bari and Modugno; others from Campobasso; later arrivals from the Abruzzi Hills; and Romans, Florentines, Marchesans; citizens of Bologna, Ancona, Ferrara, Modena, Parma; and smaller numbers of Piedmontese and Lombards. But Sancta Maria Addolorata is a Sicilian church,[38] and the members of the congregation are

[38] This church and parish have an interesting history. The Italians were preceded here by the Scandinavians, who had, in turn, been preceded by the Irish. Two of the oldest of the Roman Catholic churches of Chicago are in this neighborhood: St. Columbkille's, founded in 1859, and St. Stephen's Church, which was founded in 1869. St. Stephen's parish had finally dwindled until in 1916 it included only forty families. In order to preserve the church as an "old landmark of Catholicity" (see the large volume already referred to, *The Diamond Jubilee of the Archdiocese of Chicago*, p. 409) it was finally decided to form a mixed parish. So many Polish families had settled in the vicinity that a Polish priest was put in charge and it was made a mixed Polish and English

POLISH TENEMENTS NEAR ST. STANISLAUS

said to be for the most part Sicilians and people from Southern Italy.

Since earlier studies had been planned in other Italian colonies, no house-to-house canvass was made here in the Grand Avenue area; and the journey to the northwest continued from the point where Halsted crosses Milwaukee Avenue.

THE POLISH TENEMENTS OF ST. STANISLAUS

On beyond this great Italian colony to the point where Ogden and Milwaukee meet and cross lies the great Polish colony of Chicago. Here is the oldest of the Polish parishes, St. Stanislaus Kostka, which was founded in 1867.[39] There were then about 150 Polish families in the neighborhood in the prairie settlement on the north branch of the Chicago River—a settlement that has remained Polish down to the

---

parish. The old church buildings were restored; and a combination church, parish hall, and school was erected.

The church which became Sancta Maria Addolorata was actually built on the corner of West Grand Avenue and Peoria Street by the earlier Swedish colony in 1862, and was built entirely of brick at a time when many of the Chicago churches were frame buildings. It is said to have been the only building in this section of the city that escaped the "Great Fire" in 1871, and it became the refuge of hundreds of homeless families driven out by the fire (*ibid.*, p. 601). In 1903 it was bought by the Italian Catholics of the neighborhood, rechristened "Sancta Maria Addolorata," moved a little to the northwest, and dedicated to the uses of an older religion and newer generation of immigrants.

[39] We have laid stress before on the significance of the dates of the founding of the Roman Catholic parishes among the different foreign groups as indicating the dates of the founding of the different foreign "colonies." That this is particularly true of the Polish settlements has been pointed out by Miss Balch in her interesting Slavic-American investigation (Emily G. Balch, *Our Slavic Fellow Citizens*, p. 230): "The fact that practically all Poles are Roman Catholics and zealous ones, and that a Polish group is likely to found a church as soon as it is at all numerous, make the chronology of the founding of their churches to all intents and purposes an outline of the dates and locations of their settlements."

In Chicago, three of the Polish parishes were founded before 1880—St. Stanislaus Kostka in 1867, Holy Trinity and St. Adalbert's, both in 1873. An early chronicle, in speaking of the efforts to found a parish, said: "It is a well-known and certain thing that . . . . wherever there is a priest, a church, wherever a parish is being created, there Polish life grows vigorously, there our number multiplies, for from all sides people come willingly, feeling better among their own and with their own, feeling safer under the protective wings of the parish and with their own shepherd, who here in a foreign land is not only a representative of his brothers before the altar of the Lord, but leads and represents them in all worldly affairs . . . . is, in the whole sense of this word, a social and national worker." See document published in Thomas and Znaniecki, *The Polish Peasant*, V, 68.

present day. For nearly three-quarters of a century the St. Stanislaus district, as it is usually called, has been the center of Polish life in Chicago. The new colony grew rapidly. The first Polish association, the Society of Fraternal Help, with St. Stanislaus Kostka as its patron saint, was formed in 1864. The society was short-lived, but in the same year a Polish missionary priest came to Chicago, where he was "welcomed with open arms and willing hearts"[40] by the early Polish settlers. The Society of St. Stanislaus was formed in 1866, and in 1867 the colony secured from the Irish Catholic bishop, Thomas Foley, permission to found a parish. The first Polish church building was started in 1869—an unpretentious frame building with a parochial school and a hall for meetings on the first floor, with the church above. In 1877 the great church was opened—a building "in the form of a Roman basilica, 200 feet long and 80 feet wide. The height of the towers from the level of the street is 200 feet. Between these two towers can be seen a giant statue of St. Stanislaus, 17 feet tall."[41] This important church, which stands as a striking symbol of a dominating influence among the Poles in Chicago, gives to the Polish colony a dwarfed appearance, with the tenements huddled about the towering church like the houses in a European cathedral town.

There are really three important Polish churches in this area, St. Stanislaus, Holy Trinity, also an old parish founded in 1873, and St. John Cantius, eastward toward the river. Less than a mile away in the Division Street area is another important Polish parish church—the Holy Innocents—where we also made a house-to-house canvass. Near the center where the great lines of traffic converge, where Ashland Avenue, Division Street, and Milwaukee Avenue meet, the Polish settlement is most congested, and from this point the Poles have pushed out along Milwaukee Avenue, farther and farther to the north and west.

In the original Polish parish of St. Stanislaus Kostka the earliest Polish settlers came from German Silesia. It was in this congested

[40] *Diamond Jubilee Volume*, *op. cit.*, p. 379.

[41] Near the church are not only the rectory and school, but a convent, a great parish hall, and a gymnasium. The parochial school has had at times in the neighborhood of four thousand children in regular attendance, but the number has been declining.

Polish neighborhood that we began the field work for this inquiry. We found that it was in every sense a Polish community, and it remains a Polish community today, where even "chain-stores" have advertisements in Polish pasted on the windows. On Division Street, Ashland Avenue, and Milwaukee Avenue are the national headquarters of several important organizations, including the Polish National Alliance, which also maintains a library, the Polish Roman Catholic Union, and the Polish Women's Alliance. Farther eastward on Division Street are St. Stanislaus College, Holy Family Academy and High School, Holy Trinity High School, the Polish *Daily Zgoda*, and the *Polish Daily News*. Around on Ashland Avenue is the fine new building of the Polish Women's Alliance and a large Sokol Hall. Near by also is a well-known Polish restaurant where national dishes are served, and adjoining the restaurant is a picturesque Polish bazaar. The offices of professional men—doctors, dentists, and lawyers—apparently center at this point.

A recent careful review of the district showed that housing conditions have remained almost unchanged during the period of a quarter of a century since our first housing studies were made here. Evidences of congestion are still to be seen on every side. There are very few vacant lots, and vacant apartments or houses are very scarce. Along one street after another there are rows of tall and narrow brick tenements, usually three stories high, some four stories, built on twenty-five-foot lots. Looking down the narrow passageways, numerous frame shacks are to be seen on the rear of the lots. Wooden cottages on the front lots are occasionally found. These are in somewhat better shape than the frame dwellings in the rear, but even these front cottages show their age much more than do the brick structures. Many of the rear shacks can only be described as miserable fire traps that should be torn down. They are dirty, ill kept, and reported by one investigator to be "overrun with bugs and rats."

These tenements are all very similar in their arrangement. A narrow, dark entrance at the side of the buildings divides the front and rear flats. The toilets are usually in these halls, one on each floor, under the front sidewalk, or in a rear shed. Many streets in this area are above the level of the lot, which means a basement apartment in almost every house. At the time of the recent visit most of these appeared to be occupied. There is no doubt but that many of these basement rooms are dark, and probably damp also.

Leaving St. Stanislaus, we canvassed two other minor districts in this area. One of them we called "Division" and the other "Ancona." The Division Street area, within walking distance of St. Stanislaus, has more of the large tenements which are found in that area but fewer basement rooms. The houses here are level with the street. The alleys in the district, however, are even filthier than are those near St. Stanislaus.

Jutting off from the Division Street area is the little section which we called Ancona. For squalor this little district may be compared with the old Ghetto. The wretched, dilapidated frame cottages are in such a state of dilapidation that they look as though they might fall over at any moment. Yet most of these poor places are occupied.

Although the years have brought little improvement in housing conditions in this very crowded area, one change that must be recorded is that one of the most congested blocks has now been cleared and has become Pulaski Park—"one of the most complete and charming of the small parks, with a field house containing a most beautiful auditorium, besides swimming pool and gymnasium, and with its play-spaces and flower-beds lying pleasantly under the great towers of St. Stanislaus Church."

THE LOWER NORTH SIDE TENEMENTS

Leaving the St. Stanislaus district by way of Milwaukee Avenue, it is easy to cross the Chicago Avenue bridge into what was once the very congested Italian colony on the Lower North Side. Since the early days bad housing conditions have existed in this Italian section, which was known for many years as "Little Sicily," and not infrequently referred to in more vivid journalistic language as "Little Hell." The latter name is said to have been in use ever since the days of the Great Fire. Immediately after the fire, destitute and homeless families moved back into the district and built small wooden cottages in spite of the ordinance defining the fire limits.[42] This area

[42] The situation regarding the building of small frame houses after the Great Fire is described above in chap. i, pp. 19–21.

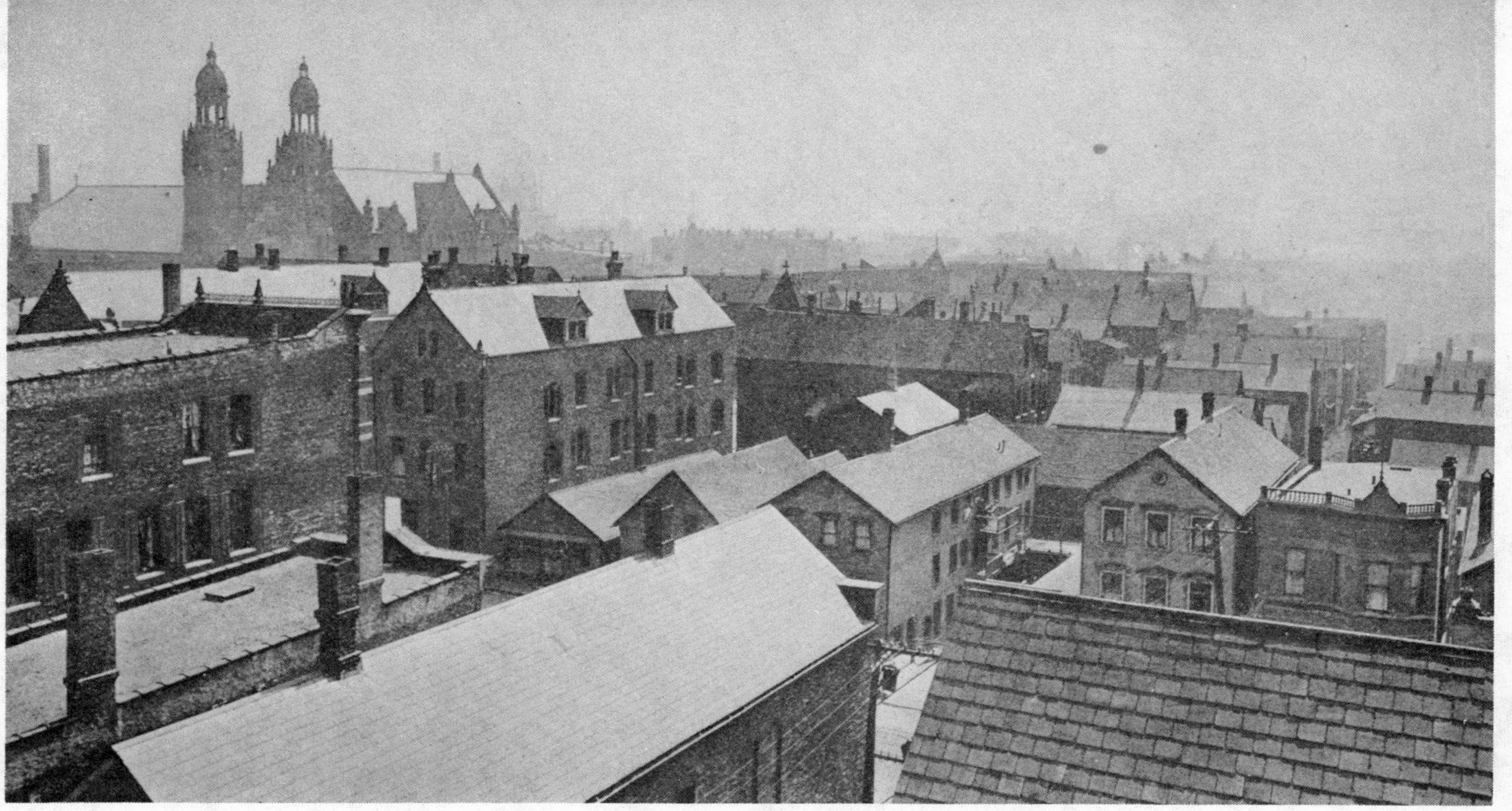

ANOTHER VIEW OF THE POLISH TENEMENTS

also enjoyed a great deal of newspaper notoriety for many years as the reputed home of what were said to be "black-hand" crimes. Undoubtedly there have been a disproportionate number of murder and manslaughter cases in the "Lower North" Italian Colony and many of them at a certain corner on Milton Avenue which newspaper reporters liked to call "Death Corner." But these were probably due much more to certain vice conditions and inadequate policing than to any "black-hand" organization. And it is only fair to emphasize the fact that although the so-called "black-hand" crimes may explain the survival of the name, the district was known as "Little Hell" before the Italians settled there, owing to the lawlessness of its residents in the years immediately following the fire.

Before the Great Fire the section lying between North Clark Street and the North Branch of the river was a network of narrow and unimproved roads crowded with poor cottages. This district, which was then chiefly German and Irish, lay in the fire's devastating course and suffered severely at that time. In the very blocks chosen for our house-to-house canvass the fire is said to have found its greatest number of victims. Almost immediately following the fire, people crowded into the frame cottages that were erected between the river and North Clark Street, either before the establishment of the fire limits (within which only brick and stone buildings were allowed) or in open defiance of them. As life became normal, the more substantial German and Irish residents began to move into cleaner streets and more solidly built homes. Room was thus provided for Danish and Swedish immigrants, and a little later as the Scandinavians became prosperous and "moved on" they made way for the Italians, who were beginning to find their way to Chicago. There were still a considerable number of Scandinavians in Lower North when we made our first housing canvass there.

In the decade 1920–30 many changes took place in this section. Business establishments increased, the Italian families as they became more prosperous were moving away, and the Negro migrants of the post-war period were crowding into the dwellings that were vacated. In our study of the neighborhood it appeared that the majority of the Negro families came directly to this district from the southern states; although an occasional family had lived for a few months in the poorer sections of the Negro area on the South Side before moving to their present location. At present there are only a comparatively small number of Italian families living in the old parish of the Church of the Assumption,[43] and the character of the Italian colony has radically changed. As the parishioners of the Church of the Assumption have been moving north and northwest, it has seemed to outsiders only a question of time when the old church will be sold.

[43] The history of the founding of this church, the oldest of the Italian parish churches of Chicago, is interesting. On July 1, 1870, three Italian priests are said to have left Italy to undertake missionary work in the United States. They are reported to have first presented themselves to the Roman Catholic bishop of Green Bay, Wisconsin, who had asked for missionaries in his diocese, but they soon decided to undertake work with the Italians in Chicago with the hope of ultimately forming an Italian parish here.

The Roman Catholic bishop welcomed them in Chicago, and an Italian mission was organized in the basement of St. Patrick's Church on the West Side. The founding of an Italian parish, however, progressed slowly, and in the meantime the Italian priests were given charge of the district lying west of Western Avenue, described as "nothing more than a wild stretch of prairie with a few straggling cottages here and there." But they were farsighted enough to buy land on Jackson Boulevard and what is now Albany Avenue, and the parish church of Our Lady of Sorrows began to rise in the midst of a cornfield, where they built not only a parish church but a monastery of the Servite order. It was not until 1878 that one of the Servite Fathers was asked to "unite the Italians of Chicago and care for their spiritual wants." This first Italian church, the Church of the Assumption, was founded in the Italian colony of the Lower North Side and opened in 1881. The first church building was only a temporary structure, but the permanent church on Illinois Street was opened in 1886. Originally there was quite a large congregation of Italians from Central Italy, Rome, Genoa, Umbria, Tuscany, and other Italian provinces, and these people sometimes still look upon the Assumption as their church; and even when they have moved as far north as Evanston they are said to return sometimes for great occasions like weddings, baptisms, and funerals, and for the services on Christmas and Easter. There have been many wealthy Italians in this parish.

A second Italian church in the North Side colony is the sister-church, St. Philip Benizi, also under the Servite Fathers, organized in 1904, not only because of the growth of the Italian colony but also because the newer Italian immigrants were largely Sicilians and Southern Italians.

On the Lower North Side the Italians have also invaded the parish of St. Dominic's, where earlier residents have been driven farther north not only by the waves of Italian immigration but by the business invasion as well. "Thus," says the parish history, "while in the beginning this parish could count nearly one thousand families as members, today the number of families has dwindled down to less than two hundred and fifty." The Italians enjoy the religious festival of St. Dominic's in August, which is celebrated with fireworks, chestnut booths, street concerts, paper flowers, and a procession quite in the fashion of Southern Italy (see the *Diamond Jubilee of the Chicago Archdiocese*, p. 621).

The parishioners of St. Philip Benizi have also been on the wing, and "Little Sicily" has been breaking up—the process hastened here as in other foreign colonies by the suspension of European immigration and the Negro migration from the South. Some of those who have saved money to buy a home go out to such districts as Craigin or Jefferson Park, but those who have purchased the old frame houses and even the flat buildings in which they are living, have found it hard to move, and reluctantly linger on among the incoming Negroes as the older Irish, German, and Swedish home-owners lingered on after the Italian invasion.

During the present investigation a house-to-house canvass of five blocks was made on the Lower North Side in a district lying north of Chicago Avenue, including the area once called Gault Court, now Cambridge Street. The investigation was extended to the downtown district, because of the different type of tenement house in which the Italians were living there. For this reason a canvass was also made of a part of the rather long block on Plymouth Court between Polk and Taylor streets, now taken over for business purposes.

In that section of the Lower North area where we made the house-to-house canvass, the narrow streets were graded up from three to six feet above the lot level. Few of the lots were filled in to a level with the street, and the ground-floor apartments are therefore often classified as basement or cellar apartments because although they are not below the lot level they are several feet below the street level. These apartments are often damp, especially during the winter and spring months. The streets and alleys have been greatly neglected and the alleys are used for garbage and rubbish of all sorts, which is allowed to accumulate in large quantities before being disposed of.

As in the other Italian and Greek sections of the city where peddlers were not infrequent, the substitution of motor vehicles for the old horse-drawn wagons had worked a noticeable change between the time of our first pre-war canvass and the later recanvass. Reference has already been made to another marked change found at the time of the second canvass—the large increase in the number of Negro families. Although the Negroes constituted less than 1 per cent of the fourteen hundred families who were found in these five blocks in the first canvass, this racial group had increased to nearly one-fourth of the block population when the recanvass was made more than a decade later. The Italians were still there at the time of the recanvass, constituting more than one-half of the population in the selected area of five blocks, but there had been a marked decrease in the number of German, Swedish, and Irish families in this district. The increase in the Negro population was, of course, due to the great Negro migration from the South into the northern industrial areas after the suspension of immigration caused by the World War.

In this area at the time of the first canvass and the recanvass, there was not only overcrowding in the number of buildings on the lots but also overcrowding within the apartments. A marked decline in the density of population per acre was found at the time of the recanvass.

THE OLD PLYMOUTH COURT AREA

Another Italian section that was included in our early pre-war housing studies but not in our later recanvassing was the group of Italian tenements in the "downtown" area on Plymouth Court near Polk Street. Southern Italians and Sicilians were found here as they were in Lower North. These old Plymouth Court tenements were in many respects the worst of all of the insanitary and crowded dwellings that we canvassed at any time. But these miserable tenements were gone before we undertook our first recanvass some ten years ago, and a brief statement is all that is needed here to record the fact that some of the worst houses and areas gradually disappear. In the earlier days the Dearborn Street Railroad Station marked the southern frontier of an Italian settlement lying just south of the Loop. This early Italian settlement, which grew up in the late sixties, on South Clark Street between the Polk Street and the Grand Central Railroad stations, belonged to the period of the padrone system. But now this old section is almost depopulated. At the time of our last post-war visit it still had an Italian grocery store and a steamship agency—the nucleus and the last outposts of any Italian settlement in this area. But large printing and tailoring establishments have crowded out its inhabitants. And St. Peter's Church, though still maintained, has lost its parish.

Almost up to the time when the World War suspended immigration, large numbers of Italians were in the district immediately south of the Loop, from State Street to the river. A district of segregated vice had once centered in what is now Sherman Street—a narrow thoroughfare once known as "Custom House Place"—and this small street was renamed Sherman Street when the vice-lords and their victims were moved farther south; and gradually both Sherman Street and Plymouth Court and the whole surrounding area became crowded and overcrowded with decent, hard-working Italian families. At the time when our investigators were making the house-to-house canvass in the larger Italian colony of Lower North, it was decided to make an intensive study of the tenements on Plymouth Court facing the railway yards of the Polk Street Terminal. Here fifteen premises covered with large tenements were canvassed, facing Plymouth Court, and backing on the alley between Plymouth Court and State Street. Opposite was the baggage department of the Dearborn Street Station, into which at that time came more than two-thirds of the large numbers of immigrants arriving in Chicago. Both the street and the sidewalk are very narrow.

In this block the nationality returns showed that 99 per cent of the families were Italians. A single Negro family lived then in a house which faced on Taylor Street, and was in the rear of one of the Plymouth Court premises. No block in any of the other Italian districts was so exclusively Italian as this Plymouth Court block. The neighborhood, as a whole, was, however, a polyglot territory. Just east of Plymouth Court on State Street were many Negroes; to the north were Chinese; at the old Jones School on Harrison Street, which these Italian children attended, probably more nationalities were represented than in any other school in Chicago at that time.

In the streets of this neighborhood, along between Dearborn and the river, there were still standing at the time of our canvass some of the fine old houses originally designed for the well-to-do residents of Chicago, but which had fallen into the days and ways of poverty, and were used as tenements for large numbers of very destitute families. Other buildings were put up as cheap lodging-houses of questionable character, poorly adapted for the use of the families who now lived in them. To this group belonged the Plymouth Court buildings canvassed. There were also larger and more recently built tenements.

It was at this time, in the pre-war days, that the railroad authorities offered to give the use of one of the tenements to the Immigrants' Protective League as a distributing center to care for the large numbers of immigrants who poured out of the immigrant trains that arrived almost daily.[44] The tenement, of course, was solidly Italian, and when notice was given to the Italian families to vacate the house, the order was received as a calamitous blow. Great excitement followed, and the little street was full of gesticulating people bewailing their fate. How and where could they move? They complained that they had "nowhere to go," and it was true that housing accommodations in this particular area were limited because of the continuous encroachment and the constantly increasing demands of business. Most of the families had had no contact with the other Italian colonies in other parts of the city. The evicted families finally refused to move, and the railroad authorities gave orders that their household goods were to be carried out and put on the sidewalk. This was actually done, and the confusion of the noisy street, with women and children crying, and sympathetic neighbors trying to offer consolation, was a scene of great disorder. It was strange to find people so attached to homes that were so lacking in all the attributes of comfort and decency. Even the cleanliness of running water was lacking, for two-thirds of the apartments in the blocks were even without sinks, and the water supply was carried in from a central outside tap. Some of the houses had once been houses of assignation, and were built with numerous small rooms, like large hotels converted later into makeshift tenements. The worst feature of the situation was that there were two hundred fifty children living in this block—"street Arabs" in the most realistic sense of those words. It was possible to find tenements for the evicted families in the West Side Italian colony, but they looked upon the journey one mile west and across the river as a journey into a far country, and felt that they were being harshly dealt with because they were compelled to leave.

A NEAR SOUTH SIDE COLONY—CROATIAN AND ITALIAN

On the way to the industrial areas toward the south and along the river we stopped for a survey of a very crowded neighborhood just below Twenty-second Street which was composed largely of two dif-

[44] See E. Abbott, *Immigration: Select Documents and Case Records*, pp. 468, 608 ff.

ferent national groups—Croatians and Italians. This is the fourth of the Italian communities lying not far from the "Loop"—a settlement in the congested district south and east of Twenty-second Street viaduct which crosses the river and the railroad tracks. The Italians, largely Neapolitans and Sicilians, began crowding down into this region as they were driven out of the area immediately south of the Loop district. From the whole area south of Seventh Street the Italians slowly moved farther south as their old tenements between Wabash and Dearborn were gradually taken over for business purposes. They came into the Twenty-second Street district because it was near the city, and many of the men in the early days supported their families by downtown news stands.

Originally this part of the city was occupied by Germans, Czechs, Swedes, and Irish; but it was predominantly German and Czech. At the time of our study most of the representatives of the older nationalities had left, and the tenements were crowded with Italians, Croatians, Chinese, Mexicans, and Negroes. North of Twenty-third Street the last three racial groups were the predominant ones. There has been a "farther south" movement in the Croatian colony away from the Twenty-second Street area, partly because they prefer a better residence neighborhood as soon as they can afford it but also because many of them object to the presence of other racial colonies.[45]

The Croatian colony here has ranked second in importance after the Croatian colony which is located near Throop Street, on the West Side. This Wentworth Avenue colony, as it is often called, is practically all Dalmatian, and centers about St. Jerome's Croatian Church on Princeton Avenue, very near the district canvassed. St. Jerome's is looked upon as the Dalmatian church by all those who have come from that province, even though living in towns outside of

45 The Englewood Croatian community, for example, which had grown slowly but steadily, included for the most part the Croatians who had been in the United States for many years and who were prosperous and progressive representatives of their national group. A new immigrant, except one who had been "imported by relatives," was rare in this section. Many of the Englewood Croatians moved in from the Throop Street and Wentworth Avenue colonies. Although many were peasants in the old country, a very considerable number of these immigrants very quickly and successfully adapted themselves to Chicago life.

Chicago.[46] The first church, a small wooden building on West Twenty-fifth Street, was formerly used as a Lutheran church and was a relic of the earlier German settlement in this district; the new church of brick was opened in 1922.[47]

The first Croatians began coming to this section about five years before the suspension of European immigration. Recruited largely from Dalmatia, the recruits were seamen and fishermen, shepherds and farmers, in the Old World. Here in Chicago the men have worked most frequently as laborers for the surface lines, in the building trades, and a few have worked in the Stock Yards, and found more skilled work. The Croatians are strong and vigorous men, and are said to do the very hard work wherever they are employed. They are also said to be good Union members and most of them are reported to be members of their various trade-unions. Sermons in St. Jerome's Church were still in Croatian, when we were working there, and the parochial school provided some instruction daily in the Croatian language, although the regular school sessions were conducted in English.

The majority of the Dalmatian immigrants were single men before the war; and since the limitations of the quota made it so difficult for them to bring over the Dalmatian girls they had hoped to marry, they gradually married other Slavs, not infrequently Czecho-Slovaks. There were still a good many unmarried men living as lodgers in Croatian families when our investigators were there, but there were usually only two or three in one family, while before the war from four to ten in one family was common. There were also a good many groups of these men who rented flats alone and lived in nonfamily groups of from four to seven men, where one of the men often did the housework.[48]

[46] There are said to be from 5,000 to 7,000 Dalmatians in the Chicago region; and, of these, 4,000 to 5,000 are said to be members of St. Jerome's parish. These estimates, of course, include the native-born children of Croatian parents.

[47] An old resident explained that at the close of the war there were no Croatians living south of Twenty-sixth Street. Until 1922 they lived farther north on Archer, Twenty-first to Twenty-sixth streets, and west to Princeton Avenue.

[48] There were said to be numerous benefit societies in the parish, but the exact number was difficult to ascertain. There are probably from twenty to thirty since it is cus-

In material ways the Croatians realize that they are far better off than they were in Europe; they have more money and can have better food and clothing, more comfortable houses and greater advantages than would ever have been possible there, but before the war many of them were homesick and dissatisfied and wanted to go back. Life in Chicago, they said, was only work and "hurry up about it." One of the old Croatian group said, "When two people meet on the street here they say, 'Got a good job?—How much do you get? Who's the foreman?' In Europe if the same men met they would have said, 'What are you going to do on Sunday?' Here they do not know what to do on Sunday—there is no form of recreation that appeals to them. In Croatia they might have gone to a fête in a village at some distance or on an excursion into the country. Here they do not feel free in the parks, they do not know how to reach the country."

A Croatian living near St. Jerome's Church contrasted bitterly the life of the Croatians here and at home. There is "many a man," he said, who has lived for years in this neighborhood who has been out in the "real America" not more than twice in all the time he has been here—once perhaps to Lincoln park on a hot July day and once perhaps to Washington Park. The contrast between the easy-going life of the Dalmatian peasant at home and the hard work and cheerless surroundings in a foreign colony make them homesick and discontented even when they know they are "doing well" here, earning "big wages," and with the hope of a foreman's job and higher wages ahead.

In all the Jugo-Slav groups the "lodger" evil has been serious. The Croatian and Serbian women complained that the system of keeping roomers, together with the insanitary housing conditions, overcrowding, and lack of light and air, made life very hard for them.

---

tomary for each group of immigrants who come from the same Dalmatian village or district to form a society of their own.

The benefit society, and especially the sickness-and-accident feature, makes a strong appeal to immigrants who are just getting "a start." At home in their native villages the care of the unfortunate was a neighborhood affair, the poor cared for the poor, or they just suffered together; here the same custom is kept up to some extent; if there is a needy family, a collection is made among people in the neighborhood. But they consider the benefit organization an American institution which is a wonderful help to immigrants.

The lodgers were mostly relatives—endless numbers of cousins and brothers-in-law—eager to earn enough to bring over their families. "Every Croatian family has three or four boarders" was a statement made even after the war when immigration had long been suspended.

The Italians also have been slowly moving out of the area in recent years, but there seems to have been no marked decline in the population, and there are said to have been few vacant houses in the neighborhood. The Italians in this neighborhood are reported to have come from the regions to the south of Naples. Approximately 60 per cent are said to be Sicilians and many of the others Calabresians. A local worker calls attention to the fact that, in spite of the great number of people of different nationalities, the neighborhood is quiet and enjoys a good reputation. "There is no trouble and the Italians get along very peaceably with all peoples, probably because they 'mind their own business.' There are never any 'fights,' he said, 'such as take place on the West Side.' "

The Italian parish of Sancta Maria Incoronata had its beginnings in St. John's School at Eighteenth and Clark streets in 1899. The Italians of this district then purchased the old Protestant church of St. Clemens and converted it into a Catholic church. A few years later the parish was large and prosperous enough to lay the cornerstone for a new church, which is said to be "the most elegant building that the Italians have in Chicago. Its style is Romanesque, the inside has three naves and a very artistic ceiling, supported by slender pilasters."[49] It is said that not many of this neighborhood return to Italy, and the younger generation know almost nothing about Italy and have no desire to go there. Their one ambition is to become Americans. About 90 per cent of the men are naturalized, for local workers say the Italians "are very easy to Americanize." While they read the usual Italian papers, *Il progresso* and *L'Italia*, they also read the Chicago daily papers. There are still various Italian societies here that hold their "festas" as they do elsewhere. Most of the people here are renters and not home-owners. When they have saved enough to buy a home, they move into more comfortable sections.

The foreign aspects of this Near South Side colony were very inter-

[49] *Diamond Jubilee Volume, op. cit.*, p. 580.

THE FEDERAL STREET AREA: SOME BACK YARDS AND REAR TENEMENTS

esting to our investigators at a time when immigration from Southern and Eastern Europe had practically come to an end—first, because of the war, and then as a result of the post-war immigration legislation. But, after all, we were chiefly concerned to learn about housing conditions rather than immigration, and we followed the method of house-to-house canvass in six blocks south of Twenty-second Street. It was a less crowded section than Lower North, or than most of the districts studied on the West or the Northwest Side. But it was much more congested than the Negro areas farther south. There were, for example, much larger numbers of rear houses here than there were in any of the Negro districts we studied. There were fewer ramshackle frame houses and more and larger brick tenements than in the areas farther south.

Other housing studies on the South Side were made, some before and some after the study of the "Wentworth Avenue colony." Most of them lay in the industrial area and were chiefly in Slavic neighborhoods, but immediately south of the Croatian and Italian area we stopped for a series of studies of housing conditions in the Negro areas.

THE EXPANDING NEGRO HOUSING PROBLEM

When the first housing studies were made before the war, six areas of the city were located where the Negroes were concentrated, and some house-to-house canvasses were made in three of these areas. After the war, however, the great Negro migration set in from the South to the industrial sections of the North; and large numbers of Negro migrants, who hoped to be able to secure the "jobs" once filled by new immigrants, crowded into Chicago. The quasi-segregated areas already occupied by Negroes expanded rapidly to care for the newcomers, and gradually other sections were called on to provide for the increasing numbers of migrants. But the finding of housing accommodations was very difficult because the Negro migrants confronted a solid wall of prejudice and labored under great disadvantages in these attempts to find new homes. The areas they have occupied have unfortunately become "segregated" areas,[50]

[50] The segregation in northern cities is, of course, extra-legal, but it is segregation none the less. For a discussion of segregation see the President's Conference on Home Building and Home Ownership, the volume on *Negro Housing*, chap. ii.

avoided whenever possible by all white tenants, who make a great effort to find any other place in which they can afford to live.

The color line, as it appears in the housing problem of Chicago and of every other northern city, is too important to be overlooked. The difficulty which the Negro experiences in finding decent housing accommodations for his family is, to be sure, only one of the many serious problems which he has always faced and which confront him anew as he leaves the South for new industrial areas. In the face of continued manifestations of race prejudice, the Negro has come to acquiesce silently as various civil rights are withheld from him in the old "free North," which was once the Mecca of his race. He rarely protests, for example, when he is refused entertainment at a restaurant or hotel, or when he is virtually excluded from places of public entertainment, public places of recreation, and even the better shopping centers. There are three points, however, on which he cannot yield, even "to keep the peace." He must claim a fair chance to find work for a living wage, good schools for his children, and a decent home for his family in a respectable neighborhood and at a reasonable rental.

It is the last of these three claims with which we are now concerned, and no attempt can be made here to discuss the general problem of race discrimination in this country. But it seemed important to collect and to present certain facts relating to housing conditions in the Negro districts of Chicago.

The Negro population of Chicago, as reported by the United States Census Bureau, was 44,103 in 1910; 109,594 in 1920; and 233,903 in 1930. Negroes constituted 2 per cent of the city's total population in 1910, 4.1 per cent in 1920, and 6.9 per cent in 1930. The Chicago Commission on Race Relations in 1922 reported that the increase in Negro population between 1910 and 1920 did not bring into existence any new large colonies, but resulted in the expansion and increased density of areas in which Negroes already lived in 1910.[51] But before the census of 1930 was taken, the continued northward exodus had definitely increased the number of Negro communities.

Looking at the map showing the distribution of the Negro popula-

[51] *The Negro in Chicago* (University of Chicago Press), p. 106.

MAP II

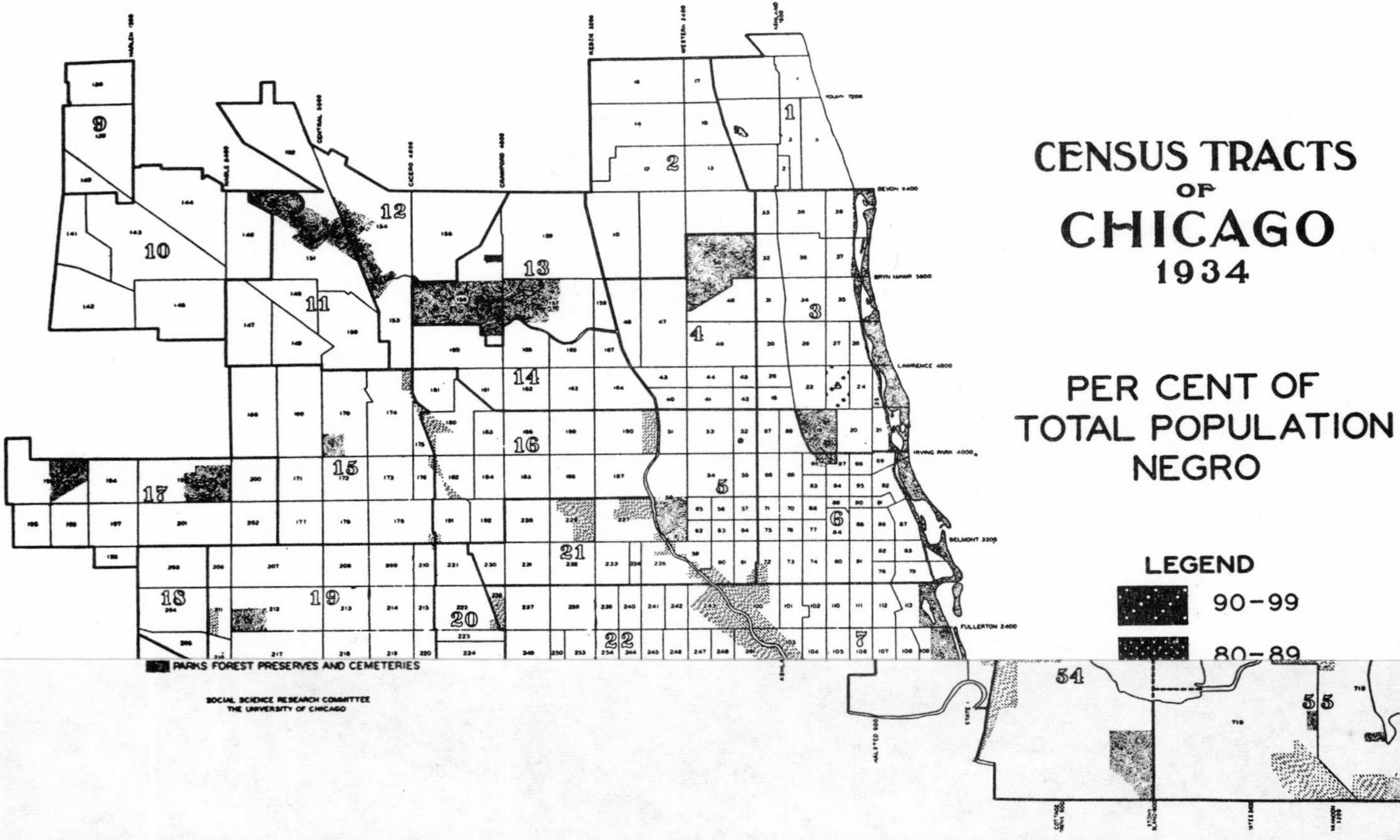

CENSUS TRACTS
OF
CHICAGO
1934
PER CENT OF
TOTAL POPULATION
NEGRO
LEGEND
90-99
80-89
PARKS FOREST PRESERVES AND CEMETERIES
SOCIAL SCIENCE RESEARCH COMMITTEE
THE UNIVERSITY OF CHICAGO
DEVON 6400
BRYN MAWR 5600
LAWRENCE 4800
IRVING PARK 4000
BELMONT 3200
FULLERTON 2400
127 STREET
135 STREET

tion on the basis of the 1930 census returns for Chicago, the relatively well-defined areas that were found at the time of our first study[52] are seen to be very greatly expanded, and more than twice as many new Negro areas had developed. At the time of the pre-war study, as well as at the time of the last census, by far the largest of these areas was the section on the South Side known as the "black belt." While the boundaries of this section have never been definitely fixed, they had clearly been extended on all sides by the new migrations from the southern states. The "black belt," particularly since the expansion, has come to include what was recently a very well-to-do residence section as well as some of the most miserable housing in the city.

The second largest Negro district in pre-war days was to be found on the West Side. This district, still an important Negro area, has always been much less densely populated with Negroes than the "black belt" on the South Side. It has been a poor district scattered along in the general area between Western Avenue and Ashland near Lake Street and a few of the neighboring east and west streets.

The smaller districts which were to be found on the South Side, such as the Englewood district, a small residence area near Ashland Avenue and Sixty-third Street; the Lake Park area, in the vicinity of Fifty-third Street and Lake Park Avenue; and a small area lying near Sixty-third Street and South Park Avenue, had all increased. An old North Side district, nearly as large as the Englewood colony, between Chicago Avenue and North Avenue, near Larrabee Street and State Street, was also enlarged.

The census returns of 1930 showed that the most important of the new districts were, first, the old Russian-Jewish Ghetto area south of Roosevelt Road, on the near West Side, extending from the river over a wide area east of Ashland. The second largest new area was in the southwest corner of the city between Halsted and Western and south of One Hundred and Seventh Street. Another large area had developed near State and Ninetieth Street, still another and less densely populated area between Halsted and Ashland south of Sixty-third Street. There was also the invasion of Lower North,

[52] The report on this early study was written and the earlier map prepared by Dr. Alzada P. Comstock, of Mount Holyoke College, then one of the social service research students. See p. 76, n. 5; see also the Chicago Commission on Race Relations. A later study of the South Side Negro area which we have used was made by Alice Quan Rood.

to which reference has already been made, and one minor area to the Northwest and one straight north near Lawrence Avenue and Halsted Street. There are also two areas to the Southwest along the canal.[53]

In our study of housing conditions, four areas that were predominantly Negro in population were selected for the more recent house-to-house canvass. These were the districts indicated in the tables as "Dearborn," "La Salle," "Upper Federal," and "Walnut." The first three are all in the old "black belt" of the South Side, the fourth in the secondary Negro area on the West Side. Dearborn and Walnut had been among the first districts studied in our earlier inquiries. Thus the data presented regarding the housing conditions among Negroes in Chicago are based on studies of the relatively stable prewar period, of the chaotic war period which caused a sudden increase in Negro migration, and of the post-war reconstruction period when Negroes continued to enter the large industries in increased numbers. The blocks chosen for investigation on the South Side in the so-called Dearborn area were above Thirty-second Street, in the poorer section close to the railroad tracks.[54] The second South Side district, La Salle, was an irregularly shaped district of five blocks farther south, lying below Thirty-fourth Street. This same area was first canvassed at the close of the war and then recanvassed more

[53] The map facing p. 119 gives the general location of these Negro districts; but care must be taken in examining the map since the information is given by census tracts, and if the tracts are large, the Negro population may be confined to one section of the tract although the map will give the rather misleading impression that the Negroes are scattered over the whole tract area.

[54] At the time of the first study the district of segregated vice was still tolerated on the South Side by the city government, but our block canvass was south of this district. However, it is hardly possible that the residents of these blocks could escape its influences. The report of the vice commission of Chicago (1911) emphasized this fact: "The history of the social evil in Chicago is intimately connected with the colored population. Invariably the larger vice districts have been created within or near the settlements of colored people. In the past history of the city, nearly every time a new vice district was created down town or on the South Side, the colored families were in the district, moving in just ahead of the prostitutes. The situation along State Street from Sixteenth Street south is an illustration. . . . . Any effort to improve conditions in Chicago should provide more wholesome surroundings for the families of its colored citizens who now live in communities of colored people" (see *The Social Evil in Chicago*, pp. 38, 39).

recently. The third South Side district, Upper Federal, lay along Federal Street to the north of Fifty-third Street. Everywhere, for block after block, the streets and sidewalks are in need of repair. Rubbish is allowed to accumulate, giving the neighborhood a most neglected and untidy appearance.

These South Side neighborhoods had greatly deteriorated between the time of our first and second studies, and a very recent study of the blocks included in the earlier canvass showed housing conditions here to be so wretched as to be unfit for Chicago homes in the twentieth century; and this district will probably continue to deteriorate steadily with the passage of time. Federal Street is poorly paved and inadequately cleaned. The investigators, in order to enter rear buildings, frequently had to walk along alleys that were almost impassable with mud and filth. Along some of the alleys there were ashes, refuse and garbage, and, in most cases, the accumulation was of long standing. So serious was the accumulation of rubbish that ice wagons, trucks, and other large vehicles were hardly able to find space for passage. In some places the odor from decaying garbage, and sometimes dead rats, was almost insufferable, and there was general evidence of neglect by the proper city departments.

The condition of the streets is the more objectionable, since this district has very small resources in the way of municipal playgrounds. The nearest approach to Washington Park, for example, is a long way off from some of the poorest streets. There is a public park at Princeton Avenue and Forty-fifth Street, but it is away from the poorest territory, shut off by the elevated railroad tracks. The playgrounds of the two public schools offer the only safe recreational facilities for the children of the neighborhood. The streets and alleys swarm with children who have no other place to go. In general, it may be said that no attempt has been made to keep these tenements in any sort of repair. For the most part they are frame houses, unpainted and grimy. Numerous windows have been broken and not replaced. The only noticeable change in the appearance of the district since 1924 was the large coal yard built at the southeast corner of Forty-seventh and Federal streets. The old shacks which once stood here have been torn down and replaced by a brick office building and a large storage yard.

It is difficult to exaggerate the wretchedness of the housing accommodations which the poor Negroes endure in this area. Housing conditions along Federal Street are much worse than along La Salle or Wentworth. The street is narrow and numerous houses unsightly. Even the children playing on the street seem to have ragged and tattered clothing and scuffed-up shoes. La Salle Street, which backs against the elevated railroad tracks, as does Federal, is wider, in better repair, and less depressing in appearance. The poverty of the people, however, is apparent from the "rundown" condition of the dwellings.

The Negro area investigated on the West Side lay in the neighborhood of Fulton and Paulina streets, Carroll Avenue, and Robey Street (now Damen Avenue). These streets lie in a neighborhood where there were a large number of old houses whose owners and agents, awaiting the inroads of the manufacturing district, had declined to make necessary repairs; and white and Negro tenants alike had been making use of houses ill suited either for lodging-houses or for small flats.

There are fewer large tenements in the Negro areas. The houses are small, usually of two stories, and some of them, with their boarded-up porches and shaky board walks, resemble the Negro cottages in small villages. Some of them were built as two-family houses, but others were plainly built for single dwellings and have been converted into two-flat houses, regardless of the fact that they are often not suitable for more than one family. A large number of them are "front" houses, that is, open directly upon the street. In the recent recanvass of the four Negro districts, 61 rear buildings, 1 middle building, and 718 front buildings were found. The few alley houses probably have been moved back from the street when new houses were built in their places. The rooms in these rear houses are usually poorly lighted and ventilated; the houses are much more dilapidated than the front houses; sanitary provisions are often inadequate; and the alley and the yard around the house are usually disorderly with rubbish and refuse.

On the whole, there is a considerable amount of vacant space in the lots which occasionally have fairly large back yards, sometimes with grass and shrubs growing in them, but more frequently disfigured by shacks and rubbish heaps.

Many lots have stables in the rear; there are also numerous shacks. There are many instances of a few goats, and an occasional pig kept in the small and cluttered areas. Litters of filth, garbage, and ashes were found in every block. A great many junk-dealers live in the region, and many of the shacks and yards are used for the heaps of old iron, old glass, old bottles, old papers, rags, and similar "cast-offs" of many kinds. The investigators found yards so heaped with rubbish that in some cases accurate measurements were difficult.

The streets in this district seem to be lined with old frame structures and endless rows of dingy wooden buildings. The count showed that approximately 85 per cent of the buildings are of frame construction, and another 5 per cent are old frame houses raised on lower stories of brick, or similarly made over. The old buildings are usually only one or two stories, with one "through" apartment on each floor. The buildings which contain more than two apartments to a floor need a word of explanation. Many of these apartments have only one or two rooms, sometimes sublet by the tenants of a larger apartment, and are occupied by one or two persons. Sometimes the landlord has rented these rooms separately. The buildings apparently have not been planned for a larger number of small apartments.

The dilapidation of the buildings is noticeable everywhere. Outside stairways and porches seem to be almost falling apart. The house-to-house canvass also showed the houses to be in conspicuously poor repair in other respects. Inside and out, they compare unfavorably with those in the other districts. The percentage of houses reported in "good repair," for example, was 71 per cent in the St. Stanislaus district, and 57 per cent in Pilsen, while the South Side Negro districts had only 26 per cent of the buildings in good repair. On the West Side, while 35 per cent were said to be in good repair, 31 per cent were absolutely dilapidated—a state of disrepair greater than in any district investigated except the old Ghetto. Broken doors and doorways, unsteady flooring, and general dilapidation were met by the investigators on every side. Windowpanes were out, doors hanging on single hinges or entirely fallen off, and roofs rotting and leaking. Negro tenants reported that they found it impossible to persuade their landlords either to make the necessary repairs or to release them from their contracts; and that it was so hard to find better places in which to live that they were forced either to make the repairs themselves, which they could rarely afford to do, or to endure the conditions as best they might.

On many of our schedule cards there are references to dangerous back stairs, bad toilets, and plastering in bad condition. One flat is reported as having no glass in the windows, and a kitchen floor constantly wet from a leaking pipe. On another card the following note appears: "Water has not been running in toilet since last winter, back stairs in very dangerous condition, can see daylight through outer walls." This general lack of repair is found throughout the neighborhood; and the danger of fire, which might gain headway in this region of crowded and dilapidated frame buildings, should not be overlooked.

Although the data on the erection of buildings are not entirely accurate, since the majority of residents had been there too short a time to know anything about the subject, nevertheless it seems to be clear that between 90 and 95 per cent of the dwellings are old-law buildings, that is, erected before 1902. The sanitary provisions in these districts are very inadequate, but there were marked improvements between the time of our first canvass and the most recent recanvasses. Old privy vaults have disappeared, but yard and basement toilets, which are still legal in old-law houses, were found in many of those old buildings.

One of the most acute housing problems that the Negro must face is the problem of high rents. Our studies confirmed the general impression that the rent paid by Negroes was appreciably higher than that paid by people of any other group.[55] Cases were found of the actual doubling of rents when a building was given over to Negro tenants. Since the apartment most frequently found in the Negro sections visited contained two or three more rooms than the ordinary apartment in five other districts investigated, it was found, as was to

[55] See also the very useful study submitted by one of our research students, Leila Houghteling, as a doctoral dissertation, *The Income and Standard of Living of Unskilled Laborers in Chicago*, for some very interesting data regarding the relatively high Negro rents. This study showed that "more than 80 per cent of the colored families of unskilled laborers spent 20 per cent or more of the earnings of the chief wage-earners for rent, while among the white families only 30 per cent paid that large a proportion" (p. 113).

A YARD AND AN ALLEY IN THE SOUTH SIDE NEGRO DISTRICT

be expected, that the rents in these two districts had a higher range. Moreover, it was found that the rents for even the four-room apartments were conspicuously higher than the rents for the four-room apartments in the other districts. The rents in the South Side Negro district were conspicuously the highest of all districts visited. Those on the West Side are nearly the same as the old Ghetto, but had a wider range. Moreover, as we have seen, the houses in which the Negro people live are in poorer repair. That is, a larger proportion of the Negro worker's wages goes for rent, with disproportionately small return to him; the immigrant, for a smaller amount of money, may live in a better house than the Negro.

Home-ownership among the Negroes is less frequent than in immigrant neighborhoods, with the proportion of owners in the Negro districts considerably below the average for all districts canvassed.

In any study of general housing conditions in Chicago, the problem of the Negro will be found to be quite different from that of the immigrant groups. With the Negro, the housing problem has long been an acute problem not only among the poor, as in the case of the Polish, the Jewish, or the Italian immigrant, but also among the well-to-do of the same racial group. The poor man in any national group finds the problem of dilapidated, insanitary dwellings. But for every man who is Negro, rich or poor, there is also a problem of excessively high rents. The results are far reaching. The prejudice among the white people against having Negroes living on what they regard jealously as their residence streets and their unwillingness to have Negro children attending schools with white children confine the opportunities for residence open to Negroes of all positions in life to relatively small and well-defined areas. Consequently the demand for houses and apartments within these areas is comparatively steady, and since the landlord is reasonably certain that the house or apartment can be filled at any time, as long as it is in any way tenantable, he takes advantage of his opportunities to raise rents and to postpone repairs.

The general demoralization caused by the non-payment of rents by the public and private relief agencies in 1932–33 greatly aggravated the neglected conditions of the Negro areas. The whole of the "black belt" seemed to be seething with misery during the terrible winters of 1931–32 and 1932–33.[56] Condemned houses that could be used rent-free were eagerly sought after. One family crowded in with another. Families lived without light, without heat, and sometimes without water. The misery of housing conditions at this time can scarcely be exaggerated. The deteriorated housing area of the South Side became constantly more dilapidated and the hope of better housing seemed to grow more remote.

A LITHUANIAN DISTRICT[57]

Among the South Side neighborhoods which were canvassed, the one nearest to the tenement areas of the West Side was the Lithuanian neighborhood near Halsted and Thirty-second streets.

Returning to Halsted Street, the great West Side thoroughfare, you leave the West Side and cross the river into the South Division. If one crosses the south branch of the river, along Halsted Street, the route lies through the great area of workingmen's homes that, less than two generations ago, was marshy prairie stretching south and southwest to the open farming country, beyond Canalport—an important diagonal street with a name reminiscent, like Blue Island Avenue, of Chicago's earliest days and plank roads, and beyond the "Archer Road" and other reminders of the great days of the canal-building era.[57a]

If one turned here to the southwest, the tenements were old and poor. The slanting streets that identify the old Bridgeport colony were interesting as one of the early settlements connected with the canal, but this was clearly not one of the most congested areas and no house-to-house canvass was attempted. The general objective here was the Stock Yards; but before reaching "the yards," there was the important settlement near the great Lithuanian church of St. George, not in the immediate Stock Yards area. The influence of "the yards" as a factor in living and working conditions was clearly felt in the Near Southwest region. Here, in the district

[56] See below, chap. xv, "The Rent Moratorium of the Chicago Relief Agencies and Housing Deterioration," below, p. 441, and for an account of "The Angelus" building in the South Side Negro area, pp. 468–70.

[57] The first report of this district was prepared by Elizabeth Hughes and the later report by Samuel Joseph Perry. Acknowledgments are made to both of these former research assistants. See above, pp. 76–77, n. 5.

[57a] See chap. i, pp. 2–3.

where St. George's impressive Lithuanian church with its parochial school dominates the neighborhood, ten blocks were selected for a house-to-house canvass.

This Lithuanian district seemed a typical tenement neighborhood, a region dominated by no one industry, for, although Stock Yards workers were more numerous than any other group of employees, there were also found iron and steel workers, street laborers, city railway employees, carpenters, bricklayers, contractors, janitors, tailors, and a rather large number of small business men of one sort or another.

The background of this district was interesting as the outgrowth of a prairie village called Hamburg. Until its admission as a part of Chicago in 1863, Hamburg was a prairie settlement, east of the fork of the south branch of the Chicago River, made up of recent German and Irish immigrants, together with earlier immigrants of these same nationalities who had immigrated at a still earlier period and had moved across the river. Even after 1863, when the prairie village of Hamburg had been brought into the city limits, the village life continued. More than one old house in the neighborhood began its existence here as a one-room shack moved by a struggling team of horses down the highway that is now Halsted Street. At the time of our inquiries there were still living in these houses old settlers who remembered the time when their only water supply came from a neighborhood well and they had to journey a considerable distance to the general neighborhood store for their purchases. These same people had, in the autumn of 1871, an uninterrupted view from their doorsteps of the burning city of Chicago across the low flat land that stretched between the village and the southern boundary of the city.

After the transition from village to metropolis by annexation to the city of Chicago, houses of every kind survived that belonged to the old life and the new. About forty or fifty years ago a prosperous firm of contractors built a uniform row of small brick cottages on Lime Street, but everywhere else a wide variety in age, architecture, and type of building is found. There are still numerous vacant lots on which rubbish of all sorts accumulates. As in the river wards of the West Side, there are small frame cottages, originally workingmen's homes, still occupied by one family, other old dwellings (originally cottages) made over into apartment houses, modern brick tenements belonging to the urban area, rows of tall, narrow buildings with steep gables that show a foreign influence.

This is one of the many tenement districts in Chicago where the changing tides of immigration have come and gone. First, German and Irish were driven across the south branch by the incoming Poles, and later the Poles crowded into the newer settlement, only to be displaced themselves in turn by a still newer immigrant group—the Lithuanians. The oldest residents in the area are, of course, the Germans, Irish, or Poles, who preceded the Lithuanians. These earlier residents have stayed on after they have been isolated among strange neighbors with a strange language and strange customs, either because their holding of property demanded it, or because, as one old German woman who had been in the district fifty years said, they "wouldn't feel at home anywhere else."

As early as 1886 the Lithuanians, with the help of a Lithuanian priest from the Holy Cross congregation of South Bend, Indiana, had organized St. Casimir's Society. The number of Lithuanian immigrants increased, and the first Lithuanian Catholic parish (St. George) was organized in this district in 1886. In 1891 twelve lots were bought on Thirty-third Street and Auburn Avenue (now Lituanica Street), in the center of the district selected for the housing canvass, just one block west of the great Halsted Street thoroughfare. It is an interesting commentary on the changing waves of immigration that this parish actually bought a little old wooden church from a vanishing German congregation.[58] Here, in our house-to-house canvass which covered ten blocks, we found that more than two-thirds of the people in the area were Lithuanians, and 16 per cent Polish, with only a few scattered Irish or German families left. The Poles were found largely in the blocks near the river, while in four of the eastern blocks over 75 per cent of the people were found to be Lithuanian.

The buildings in this district were of many different types. The

[58] See the *Diamond Jubilee* volume, *op. cit.*, p. 519. As the Lithuanian colony rapidly increased, a parochial school was established and two more lots were bought for a rectory. In 1896 a very handsome Gothic church with a seating capacity of twelve hundred people was built. In 1908, a three-story brick school building was erected.

one- or two-story frame cottage, the earliest erected, remained the most common type of house, and 44 per cent of all the houses were of the one-story type; an additional 42 per cent only two stories. But though so large a percentage of all the buildings were one-story frame cottages, nearly 75 per cent contained more than one apartment. Here, as elsewhere in Chicago, the old dwelling intended for one family had been requisitioned for two or three families in buildings that were old, more or less run down, with old-fashioned windows small and hard to open; and inadequate toilet arrangements. Basements, cellars, and attics were used as apartments.

By contrast the modern tenements scattered throughout the district, although provided with their own quota of building-code violations, seemed very desirable. These new buildings were brick, in much better condition as to repair, and with more modern plumbing.

At the time of our first canvass the problems of adult lodgers, immigrant workingmen and workingwomen, overcrowding, and other unfavorable conditions connected with the lodger evil were very acute in this area. More than one-half of the families had lodgers at that time; 28 per cent of all the people in the ten blocks were lodgers, a larger proportion of lodgers than was found in any other foreign district. The region "back of the Yards" and the Polish district of South Chicago, on the one side, showed a slightly lower percentage, while the Slovak district, on the other side, showed a proportion less than half as great. Overcrowding and other unfavorable conditions incident to the lodger evil were common. Sometimes every available bit of space in the house was occupied, as, for example, at the time of our first canvass, when what was originally intended for a clothes closet was turned into the windowless bedroom of a girl lodger, or in another house a pantry was used as a sleeping-place. Often not only the privacy of a lodger but also that of the members of a family had to be sacrificed. As a result, in a large number of houses lodgers were found sleeping with members of the family.

The density of population in this area was not high for any one of the ten blocks canvassed, probably because many of the lots were still vacant. But in spite of this there were the same overcrowded premises, houses occupying over 90 per cent of the lot and with only a narrow court three feet wide between adjoining houses.

"BACK OF THE YARDS"

Leaving the Lithuanian colony, a journey was made around to the back of the great Stock Yards area—around from Halsted Street one mile west to Ashland Avenue and a few blocks south—the area usually referred to as "back of the Yards," where very congested and insanitary conditions are still to be found.

In 1901, when the City Homes Committee made their housing inquiry, the Stock Yards district was one of those selected for investigation.[59] The appearance of the district showed it to be so neglected, and conditions in this area were, on the whole, supposed to be so far from typical that it was at that time regarded as unsuitable for purposes of intensive study. On this account little attention was given to conditions prevailing within the homes, and only a superficial examination of these conditions was made. The unpaved streets, lack of sidewalks, indescribable accumulations of filth and rubbish, together with the absence of sewerage, were said to make the so-called "outside insanitary conditions as bad as any in the world."[60]

[59] References to this report on *Tenement Conditions in Chicago* have already been made, above, pp. 58–61, 73.

[60] *Ibid.*, pp. 12 and 182. The comments on the district were as follows: "If the purpose had been merely to select the worst houses and blocks that the city can show, portions of the North and South Sides would have been chosen. The Stockyards district and portions of South Chicago show outside insanitary conditions as bad as any in the world. Indescribable accumulations of filth and rubbish, together with the absence of sewerage, makes the surroundings of every dilapidated frame cottage abominably insanitary. These evils do not extend over a large area. They are in their worst forms extraordinary and not typical of conditions elsewhere in Chicago. In the Stockyards district there is no large area, such as the one in South Chicago, where the conditions seem to be uniformly bad. On Avenue ——— there are some old rookeries and some new little brick boxes raised on stilts, which will probably be sold on some instalment plan to the working people in that vicinity. Many working people have bought, or have tried to buy, these houses, but before they paid up the instalments the houses were in very bad repair and wretchedly dilapidated. Very often workmen have tried to buy them on the instalment plan and have lost them again and again. There is a long row of houses on ——— Avenue where the conditions are about the same as stated above. Very few of the houses in this locality are deficient in provision for light and ventilation, and none of them seem to be overcrowded. The worst features are the external conditions which surround the dwellings. In many parts of the district there are no sewers and the sewage from the houses stands in stagnant pools. The south branch of the Chicago River is really a ditch which accumulates a great deal of sewage from the Stockyards, and fills the air with poisonous odors. The stench from the Stockyards is also present. The district is overshadowed by heavy clouds of smoke from 'the Yards.' "

The whole area, however, had been very greatly improved even by the time our first canvass was made, in the period before the great war-time expansion in the packing industry. The unpaved streets had been paved, permanent sidewalks had been laid, the sewer system had been extended, Bubbly Creek had been enlarged and made less offensive. Between the time of our first pre-war canvass and the more recent recanvass, still greater improvements in what are called "outside insanitary conditions" had taken place. Most of the stables were gone, the offensive "dumps," which had still been used for city refuse at the time of our first canvass, are now removed, and the old dump areas are largely filled in and grown over with grass and weeds;[61] the numerous saloons had largely disappeared in the early

[61] A brief statement here of what the city "dumps" meant to this neighborhood at the time of our first canvass when an excellent report on this subject was prepared by Mr. William L. Chenery, now editor of *Colliers Weekly*, is necessary to complete this record. In an open tract lying between Forty-seventh and Forty-second streets and near one of the railroad lines, he found four great holes from which the clay had been dug out for the neighboring brickyards. These holes were partly filled in with deposits of garbage and other waste material, but the clay was still being removed so the area was being enlarged and one of the great holes was partly filled with water. These holes were not only used for the dumping of city garbage but they were also used by private scavengers. One of the dumps was used by the Stock Yards and, as their waste was largely burned, there was always a smoldering fire here, separated by a pool of water from the inflammable material on the city dump.

The material "dumped" included such things as ashes suitable for filling in and probably useful for no other purpose; cans, bottles, old junk, wooden boxes, and other articles which could be used again; old mattresses, worn garments, and articles of personal use from all sorts of homes in all sorts of places which in the interests of public health should have been destroyed; and, finally, waste food, which came from many places, including South Water Street. Chance articles of real value tempted people to explore the dumps. On two dumps there were the professional dump-pickers who paid a regular stipend for the privilege of following their business of "picking" (a former alderman in the ward was said to farm out for an annual payment the right to pick on dump No. 2 to a colored man who employed some helpers). The bones went to one company; the metal of various kinds to a junk-dealer on Maxwell Street, near Canal; bottles other than those belonging to the large milk companies to another junk-dealer. One man who employed five helpers paid fifteen dollars a week for the picking on one dump. After these commercial pickers had taken their goods, the women and children, who had watched the wagon unload and the picking take place, were allowed to hunt for the wood they wanted for kindling, the old mattresses which might serve on the beds at home, and the fragments of still edible food. Of course the prospective find was most uncertain, but for both the women and the children there was the excitement of exploration and the hope of a bit of silver or some other article of value such as a lucky neighbor was rumored to have found. Although this was an obviously unfit place for

prohibition days; new brick buildings had taken the place of some old tenements; but in general the old houses remained and had become older and more dilapidated, and insanitary conditions within the houses have often become more insanitary as the years go by.

Since 1864 the packing industry has been identified with this territory which is now a vast "city wilderness" of congested tenements. Before the close of the Civil War, 320 acres of land "in the Town of Lake" were bought from the Honorable John Wentworth for $100,000 as a site for the Union Stock Yards which were then planned. These "yards" were opened in December of the following year[62] and the expansion of the industry since that time has been continuous and remarkable. But although the packing industry was very successful as a business undertaking, the physical conditions of the yards were for a long period of time offensive and insanitary and a public investigation was called for in 1906.[63] When this region was selected

children, from ten to twenty women and from forty to sixty children seemed a fair estimate of the number commonly found there.

This statement regarding the city dumps is made because housing conditions in this neighborhood were unquestionably influenced by this great stretch of territory, once, like "the Yards," a remote rural tract, then surrounded by dwellings, and yet devoted in part to the disposal of decaying refuse. Women and children were tempted to wander here in the hope of supplementing their meager supply of furniture and fuel. The whole neighborhood grew accustomed to insanitary conditions by their long association with them. For recent experiences with garbage dumps during the present Depression period see *Social Service Review*, VI (1932), 637–42.

[62] The packing industry in Chicago is, of course, much older than the Union Stock Yards. It is, in fact, almost as old as Chicago itself. Pork packing was carried on in 1827 south of the north branch of the river on Clybourn Avenue. In 1832 slaughtering and packing were industries located on what was then an open prairie near Michigan and Madison streets. Later, various other packing centers were established at Lake and La Salle streets, at Rush and Kinzie, on South Water between Clark and La Salle, at State and North Water, at Franklin and South Water. In 1848 the "Bull's Head" Yards on Madison and Ashland became the center of trade in live stock, but later some other large yards were opened. In 1856 the Sherman Yards were established on Cottage Grove Avenue, and in 1858 the Michigan Southern and Fort Wayne Yards were opened on State and Twenty-second streets.

[63] The early novel of Upton Sinclair called *The Jungle* (1905) and the Congressional inquiry of the following year, the famous Neill-Reynolds report, submitted June 4, 1906 (*House Doc. No. 873* [59th Cong.]), called attention to the insanitary conditions then prevailing in the Stock Yards, the use of paving materials which could not be properly cleansed and "were slimy and malodorous when wet, yielding clouds of ill-smelling dust when dry"; the neglected condition of the pens in which the animals were confined, and of the viaducts over which the animals passed; the unclean, dark, ill-ventilated rooms in

DISORDERLY STREETS AND ALLEYS IN THE STOCK YARDS AND WEST SIDE DISTRI[CTS]

for the location of the Union Stock Yards, it was a suitable place for what was destined to be an offensive business for a considerable period of time. The whole territory was then a reedy, undrained marsh, remote from the residential and business sections of the city. To this comfortably distant area the business of slaughtering seemed to be suitably relegated. For much the same reasons the brick yards and the city dumps were located here; and this western prairie region was appropriated to these unpleasant and malodorous uses. Later, as working people crowded into the area year after year, and decade after decade, they found themselves in a blighted region, with the city dumps, brick yards, and "Bubbly Creek" on one side, and the greatest slaughter-houses in the world on the other. Two groups of blocks, one Lithuanian and one Polish, were selected for the first house-to-house canvass in our study of housing conditions here. An attempt was made to select blocks which contained not the poorest but the typical homes of this neighborhood. A line of houses along Ashland Avenue, known in pre-Prohibition days as "Whiskey Row," was also canvassed because of the numerous groups of immigrant men and women lodging here.

The homes in this district have always been workmen's homes. Small frame cottages have gradually been displaced or outnumbered by tenements built for two or more families; but the area has continued to be almost solidly occupied by those who depend upon "the Yards" for work, and upon whose work the industry, in turn, remains dependent.

In this district, as might be expected, were found representatives of the various nationalities upon whom the packing industry had from time to time depended. In the earlier days the workers in the Yards and the dwellers in the neighborhood were almost exclusively Irish; but as they gradually found their way into higher-grade work, they were succeeded first by the Germans and later by the Slavs, who, in the decade before the war, were immigrating in increasingly large numbers.

---

which the slaughtering was done, "vaults in which the air was rarely changed; windows clouded by dirt, walls and ceilings so dark and dingy that natural light penetrated only 20 or 30 feet"; the lack of sanitary arrangements, with the consequent odors and fumes, and the failure to provide the ordinary decencies in the way of toilet accommodations for the workers.

The house-to-house canvass, which included the homes of more than 1,500 families in this area, of whom nearly 85 per cent belonged to different Slavic groups, showed how largely Slavic the population "back of the Yards" was in the pre-war days. It was found that the Poles and Lithuanians in those days tended to segregate. The blocks which contained the largest number of Poles contained relatively few Lithuanians, while the blocks which were predominantly Lithuanian had very few Poles. In the immediate neighborhood were important Polish and Lithuanian churches—St. Joseph's Polish Church, which had been founded in 1887,[64] and the Holy Cross Lithuanian Church, which was located in the district canvassed by our investigators, had been established in 1904.[65]

Next to the Poles and Lithuanians, the Slovaks were the most important group in this section; and the large church of St. Michael Archangel, which was built in 1898 not far from the blocks canvassed, is apparently the oldest and one of the best known of the

[64] The "mother-church" of the South Side Polish Catholic parishes was St. Adalbert's, which was founded as early as 1873 under the guidance of the Czech pastor of St. Wenceslaus Bohemian Church (see above, p. 82, n. 11). St. Adalbert's was the mother-church of St. Mary's of Perpetual Help in Bridgeport, of St. Joseph's in the Town of Lake (1887), and of St. Peter and Paul (1895), also near the Yards. These early Polish churches were described as founded by "hard-working people who had but recently emigrated from their native soil; poor in purse, but strong in the Faith of their Fathers and in their devotion to the Church and the best traditions of their native land." During the first years after its organization, St. Joseph's Polish Church was only a mission in charge of a priest from the Polish Church of St. Mary of Perpetual Help, in Bridgeport. But the parish grew rapidly in the period of increasing Polish immigration before the war. In 1914 a new church was built, and in 1922 the parish claimed 1,500 families, and the St. Joseph's Parochial School had 1,800 children. All parts of Poland are said to be represented in this parish. Other Polish parishes in this area included St. John of God, near Sherman Park, a Polish church founded in 1906; and the Sacred Heart of Jesus, another Polish parish farther west.

[65] At the time when the Holy Cross Lithuanian Church was founded, there was already a large Lithuanian colony here. There were said to be nearly five hundred Lithuanian families west of the Stock Yards at that time, and they had either to make the long journey to their first church, St. George's (see above, pp. 126–28), or attend the nearby Polish church of St. Joseph or the church of some other national group. The result was the purchase of ten lots and a temporary building combining church and school. But the Lithuanian colony "back of the Yards" increased rapidly during this period of great immigration, and the present church with a seating capacity of 1,500 was completed in 1915 (see *op. cit.*, pp. 609–10).

Slovak parish churches in Chicago.[66] The Slovaks began coming into this district in the middle eighties to work in the Yards. They came from almost every province in Slovakia. In the early days they settled in groups according to the section from which they had come. Later, as they became more at home in Chicago, and especially when they began buying their own homes, they became less closely confined to the Slovak colony. Although nearly a generation has passed since the first Slovaks settled "back of the Yards," many of them are still employed in the Stock Yards; however, the majority of those who are here have found their way into skilled work or have established themselves in business and a few have entered the professions. In the earlier days they relied upon the Bohemians for professional services. Out of 1,562 families visited, only 19 American families were found during the canvass in this area.

Here, as in other parts of Chicago, the problem of the newly arrived immigrant has been very closely connected with the housing problem. Here, as elsewhere, the families who had most recently arrived were most exploited in the matter of their housing situation. They have paid the highest rents for the poorest apartments, and have seemed quite unable to understand that they had a right to in-

[66] See above, p. 79, n. 7. St. Michael's was originally a mission founded by the Slovak Catholic Society with the help of the First Catholic Slovak Union. There were few parishioners, and they were only able in the beginning to secure the services of a visiting priest who came from a Slovak parish in Whiting, Ind. In 1905 "the burden of conducting this mission was entrusted to the Benedictines." St. Michael's Mission was only a frame building at 4920 South Paulina Street, but a new church was built in 1900 at Forty-eighth and Winchester. The parish grew so rapidly with the increasing Slovak immigration of this period that a new combination church and school was built in 1908. The parochial school, which was opened in the basement of the old church, with 82 pupils in attendance in its first year, grew rapidly; and the new school, which was opened in 1909 under the direction of thirteen Sisters of the Bohemian Order of Saints Cyril and Methodius, had "twelve large classrooms, with a regular eighth grade course and a capacity of 1,175 children" (*ibid.*, pp. 575–76).

There are numerous parochial societies, and the men of the parish have organized a Citizens' Club for the purpose of teaching members of their group and of helping them to get their second papers. Classes are held regularly once a week, the pastor often taking part in the conduct of the classes.

Because the parish is so large, most of the Slovak newspapers and magazines are in circulation, but the paper having the largest number of subscribers is *Jednota*, no doubt owing to the fact that so many of the Slovaks belong to the First Catholic Union, of which this paper is the official bulletin.

sist on needed repairs or a decent standard of cleanliness. If a roof leaked, or the plumbing was out of order, they had no idea how to set about getting the landlord to attend to it.

After the end of the great period of European immigration which came at the time of the packing industry's war-expansion period, increasingly large numbers of Mexicans and Negroes began coming into this as into other expanding industries. The Mexicans we found in our later recanvass "back of the Yards," but the Negroes live to the east and north and come into the area only during working hours.

A great deal of neighborhood hostility was felt toward this Mexican migration into the community, and older nationalities made every effort to keep the Mexicans away from the area. It became very difficult, therefore, for the Mexican workers to obtain satisfactory living accommodations at any reasonable rental, and the dwellings or apartments finally secured were seriously overcrowded.

In one case there were seventeen lodgers living with a Mexican family of two in a six-room rear flat, found before the beginning of the depression, in one of the most dilapidated houses in the block. All the lodgers and the head of the family were working in the daytime, and as the kitchen was not used as a bedroom, nineteen adults slept in five small rooms. This apartment rented for twenty-seven dollars a month to the Mexican group. The corresponding flat on the second floor, of the same building, identical in every way, was occupied by an Irish family and rented for twenty dollars.

In a very old frame cottage in which the plaster was falling from the walls and ceiling and the windowpanes were broken, fourteen Mexicans were living in five rooms. The rent for this place was eighteen dollars a month. In an old cottage of six rooms the Mexican tenants paid twenty-one dollars rent. A similar nearby cottage, in better condition, was occupied by a Polish family who paid ten dollars rent.

In all these houses which were occupied by Mexicans, conditions were found to be deplorable. Stairways were worn to the point of being dangerous, and the inadequate plumbing was and is a serious health hazard for the tenants.

In most cases the rooms occupied by Mexicans were cleaner than many of those in which various other national groups were living. In the few cases where there were beds, they were nicely spread with clean covers. But furniture was for the most part scarce. In a great many of these Mexican homes there were no chairs at all. The members of the family sat on the floor, or in some cases old boxes had been obtained from some source and used as chairs. In none of the apartments occupied by Mexicans was there gas, and in all of them coal stoves were used for cooking.

Some of the Mexican families lived in indescribably miserable conditions. A social worker, for example, came in contact with two Mexican families consisting of eleven members, living in a three-room apartment, very filthy, foul smelling, and generally insanitary. The garbage, which was hauled away once every two or three weeks, became piled up just opposite the door of this house before it was hauled away, and the family complained that the refuse blew in the house when the door was open. Only one window in the house could be opened, and this window and the door were the only means of ventilation.

The house was as bad as the surroundings. There was a partition about six feet high through the living-room, which divided off two small rooms, one used as a pantry and the other as the toilet. This toilet was also used by a family living in the front part of the house. One window served for both rooms, and the partition was placed so that half the window was in the pantry and the other half in the toilet. The window could not be opened, and the lower half was a board instead of a glass pane. The wet clothes were hung in the kitchen to dry. In the house, which was heated by a small coal stove, there were a few conveniences, gas and electric light and one cold-water faucet. Each bedroom had one window. The guest family occupied one bedroom and paid two dollars and fifty cents for this room and for gas and light. The four members of the guest family had all been sleeping in one bed. The other family had also only one bed, and a mattress on the floor for the children. During the time that the mother was confined, the father and all the children slept on the floor. It is significant that the social worker found that both the woman who had been allowed to come in as a quasi-guest and her daughter were suffering from active tuberculosis, and they were immediately removed for hospital care.

The houses here usually occupy only a small percentage of the lot, but they are almost uniformly frame buildings not more than two stories high. In this district, therefore, a relatively high density per acre was found together with a relatively small percentage of the lot covered; and this percentage was covered by small low houses. Nearly half the premises were not covered more than 50 per cent, and a considerable number were entirely vacant. The condition is well recognized as typical of many districts in Chicago, where the small houses and vacant lots, so unlike the crowded areas of the tenement districts in New York, give the impression that there is no serious problem of congestion here. The impression however, is a very misleading one in this area where there is a high degree of crowding within the houses. Not only was the number of occupants per room found to be high in this district, but sleeping-rooms especially were crowded far beyond the legal limit. This overcrowding within the house is often a source of much greater danger and demoralization than the more obvious overcrowding in some eastern cities.

The alley tenement, which has been a conspicuous feature of Chicago's housing problem, was not so prevalent "back of the Yards" as in some other districts. On a few premises there were three houses on a single lot, that is, not only front and rear, but middle dwellings as well. The alley houses, therefore, are almost uniformly old houses with defective sanitary provisions; but these alley houses were usually light and sunny, because in this neighborhood, with a large proportion of the lots having a vacant space in the rear, a rear house was likely to have more chance for light and air than the front house with only a narrow passage on either side.

There seem to be stores everywhere in this neighborhood, sometimes more than one in a building; but marked improvements resulting from the abolition of the saloons and stables occurred in all the neighborhoods after the war. At the time of the first canvass, the corner lot was usually occupied by a saloon[67] and, of course, saloons are now found everywhere again. One corner building contained a

[67] The saloons were usually the property not of the saloonkeeper but of the brewery, which often owned other property near by. The saloonkeeper was nevertheless a person of influence, and the hall in the rear of a saloon was often a social center in which weddings and other festivities took place.

saloon, a butcher shop, a milk depot, a bakery, a stable at the rear, and apartments for nine families.

At the time of our first canvass, the degree of congestion in the district was greatly increased by the large number of lodgers in the Polish and Lithuanian families. At that time, out of a total block population of 8,731, there were 2,383 lodgers; and so large a proportion of lodgers almost invariably meant, from house to house, a violation of the law against overcrowding. A marked decrease in the number of lodgers was found at the time a recanvass was made just before the beginning of the depression. This seemed to be explained, in part, at least, by the fact that a larger proportion of the women were working outside of their homes and supplementing the family income in this way, rather than by the earlier method of keeping lodgers.

Although this is a relatively new section of the city, the great majority of the houses, nearly 80 per cent, were built under the old tenement law, that is, prior to 1902. Some blocks, of course, contained a much larger proportion of old houses than others. In those more recently built up, less than half are old-law houses. Frame-houses are still common in this district, and although some of them are in good repair, many of them are old and dilapidated, the plumbing out of order, and the houses dirty. Rooms were dark, crowded, and ill ventilated—and in many cases yard toilets were still found.

Although the district "back of the Yards" now shows marked signs of improvement on the business streets, the dingy old frame houses are still there, overcrowding still continues, alleys are still filthy, and the neighborhood seems a vast expanse of drab and insanitary housing.

From the "Yards" we moved on to other industrial areas, and to some of the other centers of bad housing that are scattered over different sections of the "South End."

THE INDUSTRIAL SOUTH END

The large area familiarly called South Chicago, which formerly belonged to the village of Hyde Park, was the next point of intensive canvass. Most important of all of Chicago's satellite communities[68]

[68] See Graham R. Taylor, *Satellite Cities: A Study of Industrial Suburbs* (1915).

are these industrial centers in the South End, many of them now included within the city limits. Great open spaces and some of the world's greatest industries lie together along Lake Calumet and along the Calumet River and its branches, the Grand Calumet and the Little Calumet.

Our house-to-house canvass in the South End was made first in South Chicago at the gates of the steel mills, before the war, and more recently the seven blocks were recanvassed there; next, thirty blocks were also studied in Burnside, a relatively isolated region that grew up with the Illinois Central shops (however, eight of the blocks were hardly built on, so that the canvass really covered only twenty-two blocks); later, four blocks were canvassed in South Deering, in a section along Torrence Avenue, one of the busy South End thoroughfares; and, finally, different types of houses in certain blocks in Pullman were included in this South End canvass. Housing conditions are different in these four areas, which are among the oldest settlements in the region. They are all industrial districts which have grown up to meet the needs of some large industry or transportation unit. South Chicago's history covers the period of growth of the Illinois Steel Company; Burnside was developed when the Illinois Central shops were located there; South Deering exists primarily because of the Wisconsin Steel Mills and the By-Products Coke Corporation; Pullman was established by the president of the Pullman Palace Car Company, a village carefully planned to house the Pullman employees. These four districts were selected as representing different types of housing in the Calumet region, and as communities which have grown up because the workmen needed to live near their work.

The Calumet region[69] is the rather inclusive term used to describe the great industrial area that is sometimes called "Illiana," because it is almost a continuous industrial section extending over the Illinois boundary into the adjoining industrial region of Indiana. Lying within the city limits of the city of Chicago and to the north, east, and south of Lake Calumet are such industrial districts as Grand

[69] In this account of the South End, acknowledgments should be made to my colleague, Dr. Helen Russell Wright, who allowed me to use an unpublished plan she had drawn up for a study of the Calumet region.

Crossing, Burnside, South End, South Deering, Riverdale, and Hegewisch; west of Lake Calumet are such districts as Pullman, Kensington, West Pullman, Roseland, and Washington Heights. Beyond the city limits, to the south and east lie Burnham and West Hammond, Hammond, Whiting, East Chicago, Indiana Harbor, Michigan City, and Gary; Dolton, Harvey, and Blue Island lie to the south and west.

The entire district of Calumet changed in a comparatively few years from a famous hunting and fishing ground to one of the leading railroad and industrial centers of the world. Zealous friends of the region have pointed out that it has probably not been "by mere chance or coincidence" that the "greatest railroad interests of the United States, the greatest car works, the greatest paint works, the greatest coke works, the greatest grain elevators in the world, the greatest steel works (and more than fourscore of them) and hundreds of other plants have clustered about this location at the end of Lake Michigan." The pioneers who formed a settlement at the mouth of the Calumet River in 1830, seven years before Chicago received its first charter, had eager hopes of its industrial possibilities and believed they had found an ideal place for a great city on the great inland lake. The first bridge over the Calumet River, at the foot of what is now Ninety-second Street, was built in 1839; but the little settlement on the Calumet was soon outdistanced by its vigorous competitor on the Chicago River.

The old stagecoach road from Michigan City to Chicago ran through this region, following the old "horse and buggy route" along what is now Seventy-fifth Street and down through Woodlawn. In 1848 the Lake Shore and Michigan Southern Railroad built the first railroad tracks through the great area that was destined to become so important a factor in railroad development; and 1850 saw the beginnings of the station of Ainsworth, now known as South Chicago.[70] No evidence of permanent development appeared until after 1856, when some real estate dealers had sufficient confidence in the future

[70] Perhaps the first industry to be established in this area was the Northwestern Fertilizing Company plant, built there in 1867 but destroyed by fire six years later. See Henry W. Lee, "A General Résumé of the Industrial Development of the Calumet Region," *Calumet Record*, XXVI.

to lay out a considerable district; and the speculative character of this venture is evidenced by the fact that three-fourths of the lots were bought up by a single purchaser.

The development of the industrial South End really began after the Civil War, with the opening of a harbor at the mouth of the Calumet River.[71] At the time of the war the present site of the By-Products Coke Corporation was a "bottomless slough," and to the northwest was the heavily wooded section later known as Calumet Heights. But it was impossible to get to the timber because of the swamps, and for more than a decade after the close of the Civil War the country was still wild and beautiful.

In 1869 the founders of the Calumet and Chicago Canal and Dock Company were anxious to develop the district along both residential and industrial lines, and therefore allowed for wide streets and spacious avenues, and also undertook the work of draining the river and constructing docks.[72] The same community, however, was not destined to be equally successful both as an industrial and as a residential suburb, and the unforeseen success in so promptly attracting some of the world's greatest industries led to a corresponding failure in attracting fashionable homes. On the whole, the activity of the promoting company led to a very encouraging development in the region that might almost be described as a boom, except that it was quite permanent.

In 1876, when the first cargo of iron ore was landed, South Chicago had both a hotel and a macadamized road, the latter leading from the town to the Calumet River.[73] At that time the Illinois Steam Forge Works, the Chicago Iron and Steel Works, and the Silicon Steel Works were already established plants; and the South Chicago Rolling Mills, from which the great Illinois Steel Company descended, were established at the mouth of the Calumet River in 1880,[74]

[71] See J. S. Currey, *Chicago: Its History and Builders*, III, 338.

[72] The Calumet and Chicago Canal and Dock Co. served an important purpose in the industrial development of South Chicago, and was influential in the progress of the Calumet region as a whole. This company "sold a site to the North Chicago Rolling Mills on Lake Michigan north of the Calumet River" (see Lee, *op. cit.*, p. 9).

[73] Everett Chamberlin, *Chicago and Its Suburbs*, p. 362.

[74] A. T. Andreas, *History of Cook County*, p. 577.

in the district now known as South Chicago. Four blast furnaces, a Bessemer steel department, and a steel-rail mill were here in 1882.

Lying to the south of the Chicago Iron and Steel Works of 1874, south of the Illinois Steam Forge Works, south of the Silicon Steel Rolling Mills, between the Calumet River with its slips and docks and Indiana Boulevard, south of what is now One Hundred and Third Street, was the "Iron Workers' Addition to South Chicago." This was an early subdivision, planned to include twelve blocks in the neighborhood of the Rolling Mills. This area was described in 1874 as an "addition," bounded on the west by the wharfing lots on the Calumet River and on the east by Lake Michigan and the prospective manufacturing city of the future. The west half was described as "a high gravel ridge covered with a dense growth of forest trees." This was divided from a second timbered belt by a narrow prairie, and east of this belt a second prairie extended more than a mile to the south, from which, "by a barely perceptible ascent, one reached the timbered table lands along its line."

Until late in the summer of 1873, the "Iron Workers' Addition" was "in a state of nature, broken only by a single wagon road." There was a rich farm upon the southeastern portion, and after the Silicon Steel Company had purchased the northwestern corner for their rolling mills, it became evident that nearly a thousand homes would be needed within six months to provide for the workmen in the great factories soon to rise in the area. The work of surveying and opening the streets had begun before the financial crisis came in that year, and the building of workers' homes was not stopped. The Steel Company was under a contract to open their rolling mills by spring, and homes for the workingmen in a settlement which was then remote from the center of Chicago were needed immediately. In the midst of the financial depression a successful auction sale of home sites was finally held in the late autumn of 1873, and more than a hundred lots were sold at a time when "the bidders were actually driven from the field by the cold and the heavy snow-storm, through which the trains returned." The "Iron Workers' Addition" was to be "immediately connected with every railroad entering Chicago," and success was almost in the air.

On the west shores of Lake Calumet, also in 1880, that important year of industrial beginnings, the Pullman Palace Car Company began to build their plant and the model town of Pullman, where the employees of the company were to be housed. The first families moved into Pullman in 1881. And in the same decade, 1880–90, other important industries were founded, including the Iroquois Iron Company. Around these early establishments grew up the various tenement areas included in the region. In 1889 South Chicago, as a part of the village of Hyde Park, was annexed to Chicago.

How many of the people who live in the South End work there, and how many of those who work in the region also live there, no one knows. But the groups of residents and workers are certainly not identical. Some sections are largely occupied by "white collar" workers who are employed in the downtown area. Even in the districts outside the city limits there are residents who are commuters employed in Chicago; but apparently they are not numerous enough to be significant. On the other hand, many of the members of the managerial force of the steel mills of South and East Chicago, even down to the foremen, are said to live outside the district. There are some indications that not even all the wage-earners live in the district. In the Ford Plant area—in what was once part of Hegewisch, for example—the workers are said to come from all over the city, even from the North and West sides.

On the whole, the population of the district is made up, rather more than the population of most industrial cities, of members of the wage-earning group. Many of the lower-paid workers live in districts directly adjacent to the plant in which they work—districts in which are found all the characteristics of the city "slum," and especially housing conditions that are very objectionable.

SOUTH CHICAGO—AT THE GATES OF THE STEEL MILLS

The first intensive canvass in the South End was made in South Chicago, an area where the great steel mills are omnipresent, and where, during "good times," the day is gray with smoke and the night is bright with the glare of the furnaces. This South Chicago district lies in the very heart of the Calumet region, and the recurring vacant lots and numerous frame tenements show how recently it has developed. An area of six blocks was selected for a house-to-house

TENEMENTS NEAR THE GATES OF THE STEEL MILLS, SOUTH CHICAGO

canvass in the section known as "The Bush," which is surrounded by the railroad tracks and the mills on three sides. On the north the great Polish Catholic Church of St. Michael and the adjoining parochial school bear witness to the prevailing religious faith of the people.[75] Blocks were selected for canvass that seemed to be typical of the workers' section of South Chicago. Care was taken to avoid the streets, such as "The Strand," with an undesirable reputation, since the purpose of the whole inquiry has been to study housing conditions in neighborhoods in which the workers and their families live. A seventh block beyond "The Bush" and across the railroad tracks was added to the group because it was reported that conditions there might be different. No essential differences were found, however, and therefore no other blocks in the neighborhood were canvassed.

Half a century ago in this area of "The Bush" there was nothing but a strip of beach, a sand hill, and some shrubbery. In 1885 a large six-story pavilion was built there, "the biggest thing of its kind in the surrounding country," where amusements of all kinds were provided in anticipation of the boats that landed there. This pavilion was opened with much festivity, including colored lanterns, balloons, and speeches, but the new enterprise did not pay and was gradually allowed to deteriorate. When the pavilion and the boat-landing were later partially destroyed by fire, the steel company then bought up part of the land. The tenement section covered by our canvass now occupies the remaining portion of "The Bush."

This area has never been a place of residence for the well-to-do or for any leisure-class group. The land is low and swampy, the great industries have brought clouds of smoke, and there have been other reasons that made the region unattractive for so-called residential purposes to those able to afford much choice in the selection of their

[75] That Polish workingmen came into the region in the early days of its industrial development is indicated by the founding of the earlier Polish Catholic church of the Immaculate Conception at Eighty-seventh Street and Commercial Avenue in 1882. The more important Polish church of St. Michael was founded in 1892 where the South Shore Drive ends and the country of the steel mills begins; and another Polish Catholic church, St. Mary Magdalene's, was built in 1910 at Eighty-fourth and Saginaw streets. These great churches bear witness to the growth of the Polish population in the South Chicago tenement areas. There are other Polish Catholic churches in the South End, e.g., St. Florian's in Hegewisch, and St. Salomea's in Kensington. See above, p. 103, n. 39.

homes. An early commentator described the water supply as "even more polluted than that of Chicago by the sewage which the towns of Calumet dump into the lake, or allow the great industries along the lake front to empty there." But a population little short of half a million has been drawn there by the demand for labor.[76]

A description of the district in 1895 reported that the site of South Chicago was "low and flat," and "subject to overflow and impossible of drainage until treated as the site of the old city of Chicago [had] been, namely, by raising the grade to at least eight feet above the city datum." Pools of stagnant water were said to be everywhere, "open ditches clogged with silt, garbage and refuse; privy vaults and cesspools overflow the surrounding ground after every rainfall, decomposing animal and vegetable matter, from kitchen waste to dead animals, litter yards, alleys, roadways and vacant lots"; and this early report finally added that, in this area, "clearly, healthy living is impossible."[77]

In 1901 the investigating committee of the City Homes Association discovered in South Chicago "the most abominable outside sanitary conditions," but no attempt was then made to ascertain conditions within the houses. When the present study was planned, there-

[76] That the history of what is now a great industrial area and crowded tenement district is almost a present-day memory is shown by an interesting case that went to the Illinois Supreme Court in 1895.

This case of *Zirngibl* v. *Calumet and Chicago Canal and Dock Company*, 157 Ill. 430, shows that a German named Zirngibl came to this country about 1850, and first followed his occupation of fishing on the lake near Milwaukee. He then moved down near to what is now South Chicago, living with his family just across the Indiana boundary line. He found it difficult to do his fishing with his home so far away, and (it is claimed) bought the land in question and put up a fisherman's shack on it. Two months after he bought the land he died and was buried there. The little plot is fenced in and a cross marks the grave, with an inscription in German. The court decided that the man had not bought the land, but that because a burial ground had been established there, the descendants should have access to the grave. The Illinois Steel Company built along the shores of the lake on the left side of the river, and the Iroquois Iron Company first at Ninety-fifth Street and the river, and now an addition on Lake Michigan from the river to about Ninety-sixth Street. There is a valuable vacant space between the river and about Ninety-third Street, Ewing Avenue, and the Iroquois Plant on the lake; but the court decision in the Zirngibl case prevented the sale of that land to any industry because the decree allowed the heirs of a man buried there access to the grave, and no one wanted to buy the land because of the difficulty of providing for such access.

[77] See *Health Department Report for 1895–96*, p. 59.

fore, it was believed that a detailed inquiry into housing conditions in a selected group of blocks near the mills should be an important part of the new investigation.

Throughout the district the streets are wide and the blocks are divided by 20-foot alleys. Here, as in most of the other sections of the city, the shoestring lot is found, 25 feet wide and 140 feet deep; and, as later tables will show, here, as in other districts, the long, narrow lot has meant narrow passageways between the houses, and dark, ill-ventilated rooms. But there are still vacant lots in the neighborhood, and even in the case of those which have been built over, the buildings cover a relatively small percentage of the lot, and there is often a large space unoccupied. In the blocks visited, it was found that in 61 per cent of the premises less than half the lot was covered; and only 14 per cent of the entire number of lots measured were covered 70 per cent or more.

For a period of more than half a century a great industrial community has been growing up in South Chicago. It would perhaps be more correct to say that several communities have grown up there and passed on—for few of the men who live there today were there twenty years ago. The tides of immigration have ebbed and flowed before the gates of the steel mills; the workers of the "old immigration" have come and gone, and the Pole, who was there a dominating force on the eve of the World War, was giving place to the Magyar, the Croatian, the Serb, and the Bulgarian at that time; and these newer immigrants were only the vanguard of the army, including Negroes and Mexicans, who were camping there on the eve of the great depression.[78]

The first immigrants were English speaking—English, Welsh, and Irish, with the Irish predominating—some of whom helped to build the mills and then stayed on as foremen and skilled workers. The Dutch, Germans, and Scandinavians soon followed, and, later, various groups of Southern and Eastern Europeans. The great industrial development after 1900, the increase in the number of factories, and

[78] Mexicans are largely south of Eighty-sixth Street and across the railroad tracks. It is here, at the corner of Ninety-first and Brandon, that they built their large brick church, Our Lady of Guadalupe, in 1928. The Negroes seem to be found in the section east of Buffalo and south of Eighty-sixth. Conditions here are even more deplorable than in the Polish neighborhood, where our canvass was carried on.

the adoption of methods of large-scale production created a great demand for labor of all kinds, especially unskilled labor. To meet this demand a steady influx of immigrants came from the countries of Southeastern Europe. Many of the early German and Swedish settlers and their descendants still live in the Calumet region, where they are usually skilled laborers, or foremen, or heads of shops. But the Irish, who constitute so great a percentage of the Chicago population, are no more numerous in the South End than the British or the Dutch. The larger portion of these older immigrant workers who still live there own their homes. In the present century the Slavic groups, Poles, Slovaks, Serbians, Croatians, Slovenians, and Russians, and other members of the newer immigration, like the Italians, and now the Mexicans, have become the most important groups in the population. After the enactment of the federal "quota law," immigration from Southeastern Europe decreased and industry began to draw its labor supply from the south; Negroes and Mexicans in the years after the war were the new migrants to the Calumet region.

Another foreign colony of importance is found a little farther south of the district we studied and across the Calumet River, in the section known as the East Side. We became interested in this section because of the Jugo-Slav settlement there, but the housing conditions did not seem sufficiently different to justify a further house-to-house canvass. One of the important Slovenian settlements of Chicago was located around Ninety-sixth Street and Ewing Avenue, and St. George's Slovenian Church was built here. Estimates made by local leaders vary widely as to the number of Slovenes in South Chicago, one authority claiming as many as four thousand persons and another not more than twelve hundred. The smaller number would seem to be nearer the truth.

The Slovenians have been described as a small and ancient race of vigorous stock and clerical leanings. They have come largely from what in pre-war days was the old Austrian province of Carniola, a beautiful mountainous region where the snow-covered Alps look down upon the peasants' ancestral fields and vineyards. The contrast between their white stucco villages in the midst of the eternal hills and the rows of drab streets and tenements of their new homes in South Chicago will explain the homesickness with which they were at first afflicted.[79]

Farther south and to the west, the tenement district is also Jugo-Slav, but the group is not Slovene but Serbian. The South Chicago Serbian colony is one of the old settlements[80] of this national group in Chicago. The first Serbs came into this region of tenements about thirty-seven years ago, but the mass immigration occurred here in the five years before the World War. About ten years ago the Serbian Orthodox Church of St. Michael the Archangel was founded on East Ninety-eighth Street, at the corner of Commercial Avenue. At the time of our recanvass there were said to be two hundred Serb families in this South Chicago parish, and about fifteen hundred unmarried men in the colony. The parish covers a large territory extending approximately from Sixty-third Street south to South Deering. Some of the Serbian workers lived in the blocks we canvassed between Mackinaw and Green Bay avenues, and some lived in other steel communities—in Hegewisch, Pullman, West Pullman, and Roseland. Very few of these Serbs in the South Chicago colony are recent immigrants. Nearly all the colony came before the war[81] and

[79] In the pre-war days they often yielded to the longing to go back to their homes, but, like other "returned emigrants," they usually came back again to the good wages and to the better educational opportunities which America offered to their children. Miss Balch tells an interesting story (see *Our Slavic Fellow Citizens*, p. 155) of a Slovene immigrant who returned to Carniola, but stayed there only six weeks. He had planned to stay much longer, but he said that he saw so much poverty he simply could not stand it. He had given away at least 500 gulden ($200) during the six weeks he was there; and, if he had stayed longer, he would have given away everything that he had. He also said that, if he had never come to America, he too would have been a beggar in Carniola all his life.

Various reasons are given to explain the emigration movement in Carniola. Slovenians apparently emigrated as individuals at an early day, but the mass movement did not begin until about 1890. In 1893 remittances sent home by emigrants had grown so large that the governor of Carniola ordered an investigation.

[80] This colony is as old, and perhaps older, than the important Clybourn Avenue settlement near Fullerton Avenue.

[81] The Serbian colonies in Chicago were decimated by the tragedy of the Balkan wars and the World War that followed. Hundreds of Serbs returned to Europe from Chicago during the Balkan wars. A large proportion of the survivors returned to the United States, only to be recalled again to fight in the World War. Large numbers of Serbians, married as well as single men, returned to Serbia during the World War and fought on the Macedonian front. Many of these volunteers also returned, but large

have been here for nearly twenty-five years, and some for a longer time. Some of them have sons and daughters born in this country and now married. Many of the Serbs were peasants at home and began life in Chicago as laborers, but about 50 per cent were doing skilled work in the prosperous times when there was still work to do.

There is also a Slovak group here and a Slovak church on Burley Avenue between Ninety-first and Ninety-second streets.

When recently visited, the area covered by the house-to-house canvass was the same drab tenement neighborhood with dilapidation in full swing everywhere. Rear houses, some of them in a very wretched state of disrepair, are still being used for living purposes. Dirty shacks and rotten sheds are numerous, and undoubtedly many of these are used for the fowls which were seen running about in some of the back yards. The long, dark passageway which must be used in order to gain entrance to many of the houses is more objectionable than ever, because the walk is often broken and the stairway leading to the side entrance has become rickety from age and use. Basement apartments and basement rooms are still being used.

The streets are paved now, but they are generally untidy, and ruts and mud holes are common. Although a few are paved, the alleys are usually trenches of filth (decaying food, dead animals, ashes, and mud).

There are still vacant spaces here and there, but these are usually overrun with weeds and littered with rubbish. Some are used as parking spaces for the cars of steel-mill workers. A vegetable or flower garden is rare; the yards are unkept, bare of grass, and sometimes grown up with weeds. Saloons have been returning and are now very numerous. Along Green Bay Avenue, near the gates of the steel mills, nine were counted in one block.

The presence of animals, justified perhaps by the adjoining open

---

numbers of others were not able to get back because of the limitations placed on the emigration of men of military age by the new Jugo-Slav state. Their more fortunate friends and relatives here speak with regret of these men who returned to Europe voluntarily to serve their stricken country, but who are held there dissatisfied and unhappy, prisoners of poverty and war, homesick for the good wages and the greater promise of the American life which they once shared for too brief a time.

spaces, is one of the factors in the housing problem in South Chicago—for the occasional goat, pig, ducks, chickens, geese, pigeons, and rabbits may be a constant nuisance in a tenement district. This problem seems to be due, in part. to the presence of grain elevators and railroads in the immediate vicinity. Sending the children out to bring back the gleanings for the poultry was for a time a well-established custom.

In spite of the improved transportation of recent years, a large part of South Chicago remains a separate, industrial area that is apart from the main stream of Chicago life.

BURNSIDE

The district known as Burnside, which is a railroad rather than a steel-mill center, was included in our series of housing studies as an area that has perhaps an unusual degree of isolation and an area that also belongs industrially to the great manufacturing and commercial region of the South End of the city. A house-to-house canvass[82] was made in the so-called "Burnside triangle," a section comprising about thirty blocks. Nearly a fourth of these blocks were only "laid out," and at the time of this housing study they had never been built on. This district is literally a triangle, shut in on three sides by railroads and railroad shops, with the tracks crossing diagonally at one end. Thus it is bounded on the north by Eighty-ninth Street, on the south by the Belt Railway, and on the east and west, respectively, by the Nickel Plate and Illinois Central lines. Burnside was brought within the city limits of Chicago in 1889 as a part of Hyde Park. The site of the present Illinois Central shops was acquired in July, 1852, and in this year the main line of the Illinois Central was extended to the then suburban settlement of Kensington. Ten years later the station of Burnside was opened, named in honor of General Ambrose E. Burnside, who was then cashier of the land department of the Illinois Central Railroad, and later treasurer of the company. It seems to have had for its object the establishment of a settlement to aid in the

[82] See *Housing Conditions in the District of Burnside*, pp. 1–13, an unpublished Master's thesis, University of Chicago Libraries, by Berenice Davida Davis, a graduate social service student, whose study has been used here.

development of the surrounding territory. But during the next thirty years this object was realized only to a very limited extent.

In the first year of the Civil War, owing to the general financial stringency, many of the farmers who had purchased land from the Illinois Central Railroad were unable to make payments as their notes became due and the company agreed to receive corn instead of cash. Ten miles of corn cribs were built at this point, and the corn received by the land department was shipped here for storage. In 1911, when excavations for the Ninety-fifth Street subway of the Cottage Grove Avenue surface-car lines were in progress, a section of drain about three feet square, built of two-inch oak timber in a state of excellent preservation, was uncovered. This drain, according to old settlers in the community, had been constructed for the purpose of draining the land around these corn cribs and keeping it dry. All this land was part of the great "State Street Swamp," which extended from Englewood to South Chicago. The Indians had called it Lake Winnemac, and the farmers on the Michigan Avenue ridge, who lost their live stock in it, knew it as "Hogs' Swamp." In the seventies a main ditch was constructed along State Street which extended to the east, and included what is now "the triangle" and the surrounding region. This drainage system was not adequate, however, and the land continued to be a rather dismal swamp.

About this time a settlement of ten or twelve Dutch families located at Burnside and carried on truck-gardening operations. Some of the land so used is still being worked for garden purposes each summer by employees of the Burnside shops.[83] Conditions at Burnside in 1892 were, therefore, almost pastoral when this period of industrial development began.

Maps indicate that in April, 1890, the Calumet and Chicago Canal and Dock Company, and certain men associated with this enterprise, acquired land in the territory known as the "triangle," and subdivided it. This appears to have been the first definite attempt to develop this area.

The modern district of Burnside may be said to have had its be-

[83] Another somewhat larger Dutch settlement had been made at Roseland near West Pullman, where the immigrant settlers engaged in hay growing and curing. Edna Ferber's novel, *So Big*, describes the Roseland district.

ginnings in 1892, when the old Illinois Central shops at Weldon were discontinued to make room for the construction of the present Illinois Central Station. Since the company owned land at Burnside which was suitable for shop purposes, convenient to existing yard facilities, and with a suburban service which had been established as far south as Kensington at an early day, it was decided to locate the new shops at Burnside, where the necessary transportation for labor was available. Since that time the area has expanded along with the development of the Illinois Central system, and Burnside has grown as the shops have enlarged their force and as labor settled in the neighborhood.

From 1862, when the station at Burnside was first established, to the year 1892, when the shops were transferred there, the history of the area was uneventful. At the time of the World's Fair in 1893 there was a good deal of speculation in this section. Operators are reported to have sold the land to nonresidents for eight thousand dollars a block. After a heavy rain, however, it was necessary for a prospective buyer to go to see this "fine, high, and dry land" in a raft or rowboat.

The period from 1852, when the tracks were opened between Chicago and Kensington, to 1892, was also the period of the Northern European immigration, and the Irish, Germans, Swedish, and Dutch, who were coming to Chicago, furnished the laborers, with the Irish predominating, who laid the tracks and built the shops. But by 1900 the last of these races, the Dutch, had practically disappeared from the unskilled-labor group in this area. They were followed by the Italian laborers, who were superseded, in turn, by the rising tide of Slavic and other immigration from Eastern and Southeastern Europe. Hungarians, Russians, Lithuanians, Poles, and the races from the Balkans became the laborers in this area, until the Negroes began to come in from the South.

The workers living in the "triangle" have most of them been employed in the Illinois Central and the Nickel Plate shops and yards, in the Burnside Steel Company (established there in 1916), in the car barns of the surface lines, and in the various industrial plants in the vicinity. Among the Americans, who are only a small percentage of the population, are many railroad men doing skilled work. But while many of the workers employed in the Burnside area have lived in the "triangle," others have found homes elsewhere, and some were even said to "go home" to Pullman. There has been said to be some tendency to collect in racial groups near different stations on the Illinois Central. Many Polish and Lithuanian laborers are living in South Chicago and in Blue Island; some Italian laborers are said to be employed in Burnside and to live in Grand Crossing and Kensington. Roseland is still the home center for many of the Dutch, regardless of where they are employed, but workers of this nationality are not now found as unskilled laborers. The Negroes employed in Burnside live in the Negro area of the South Side, but some anxiety was expressed at the time of our canvass about an increasing number of Negro laborers being employed.

At the time of our house-to-house canvass, there were twenty-two different national groups living in the "triangle," with the Magyars constituting approximately 40 per cent of the whole number. Our Lady of Hungary, is an important Hungarian church in the "triangle," serving the Hungarians over a large area in the South End. The Ukrainians are the group next in importance to the Magyars, and there has been an active Ukrainian club in this district; and a large church belongs to the Greek Uniat denomination, St. Peter and Paul, where the priest is a Ukrainian. The Italians, who are also important in the picture, are reported not to have been enthusiastically welcomed by some of the Slavic representatives of the "triangle."

The Italians are said to have come into this district about thirty-five years ago, in the old days of the padrone system. They came to work as section hands and laborers on the different railroads in the Grand Crossing territory, and they wanted to live near their work. They purchased the small frame houses that had been built at the time of the World's Fair and had been previously occupied by Irish. There seem to be a good many Irish-Americans left in the neighborhood, and there are also Bohemians and Swedes, as well as Italians. On three blocks where there are Italians from Calabria and Sicily, nearly all the families own their homes. While the older men are still employed as laborers on the railroads and the padrone system is still used, some of the older men like to have little stores, of

A CROATIAN SETTLEMENT IN SOUTH CHICAGO (*above*)
SIDE DISTRICT WITH MAGYAR AND UKRAINIAN CHURCHES IN THE DISTANCE (*below*)

which there are quite a number in this little community. The young men, who are usually employed as barbers, chauffeurs, peddlers, and workmen in factories in the neighborhood, have the reputation of being quiet and industrious.

The "triangle" is unique among the districts canvassed because of its semi-rural aspect. A long stretch of vacant land called the "prairie" lies just south of Ninety-third Street, and there are several large vacant spaces elsewhere within this area. Some blocks are entirely vacant, while many have only two or three houses on them. Even in those sections of the "triangle" which are the most built over, there is ample room for yards and gardens. Here and there an occasional family keeps chickens, ducks, or geese. Next to the small sheds where the poultry is kept, or where fuel is stored, are sometimes seen dovecotes and pigeonhouses. In strange contrast to such a scene are the railroad tracks, shops, and factories which hem in these village homes.

There has been no problem of overcrowding in the "triangle," where almost 95 per cent of the lots were less than 50 per cent covered. In only eight cases were there two houses on a lot. Most of the houses have been built either on the front or on the rear of the lot, so that another house may at some time be added, if and when conditions in the congested parts of Chicago are reproduced here. Nearly three-fourths of the houses are frame, and more than one-half of them are one-story, of the frame-cottage type, although more recently some brick bungalows have been built. There were only five houses of three stories at the time of the canvass, and none with more than three stories. A very recent re-survey showed that the houses are, on the whole, in good repair and look relatively new. Only 9 per cent of the houses were built before 1902, and nearly half have been built since 1910.

Perhaps because of the long depression, a newly painted house is so unusual as to attract attention, but, despite the lack of paint, the houses in general do not have a look of neglect. A high percentage of home-ownership perhaps explains the care which the people give to their yards. Near an empty lot, covered with weeds and piles of rubbish, will be found a front yard that is very neat and well cared for. On the whole, it is a small town with a great city as its background.

TORRENCE AVENUE (SOUTH DEERING)

Another careful study[84] was made along the important street called Torrence Avenue, named after a sturdy pioneer, Joseph Thatcher Torrence, who was interested in Joseph H. Brown's "city rolling mills" built in 1875 at One Hundred and Ninth Street and the Calumet River, and opened with ceremony as the first factory[85] in the section which later developed into the town of Irondale, and was called South Deering when the International Harvester works were located there.

The new settlement prospered and grew rapidly, and "Brown's Mill," the Brown Iron and Steel Company, became part of the Calumet Iron and Steel Company, which in turn was taken over by the Wisconsin Steel Company, a part of the International Harvester Company. In 1902 the By-Products Coke Corporation established its works at One Hundred and Twelfth Street and Torrence Avenue, and a few years later the Federal Furnace Company began to operate its plant at One Hundred and Eighth Street and the river.

The industrial development of the district created a continuous demand for labor and in the days before the restriction of immigration the employees were, for the most part, Irish, English, and Welsh, especially the skilled workmen who were employed in the nail factory. Germans and Swedes later came into the industries, and still later Poles, Croatians, Serbians, and Italians; but some of the older settlers have continued to live in South Deering, frequently employed as foremen and as skilled workers, while unskilled labor was drawn from the new immigrant groups. In South Deering, as in South Chicago, the new immigration laws have changed the labor situation, and Mexicans have come into this section in large numbers and live chiefly as lodgers and non-family groups along Torrence Avenue, where their presence is made known in the little Mexican stores and cafés.

In the area studied, the Croatians, Serbians, Italians, and Mexicans together form approximately three-fourths of the population—

[84] A detailed report of this study and of the Pullman study (see pp. 158–62) was prepared by one of the graduate social service students, Mary Faith Adams, and is available as an unpublished Master of Arts thesis in the University of Chicago Libraries.

[85] See Henry W. Lee, in *Calumet Record*, XXVI, 7.

approximately one-fourth is Croatian, nearly the same proportion is Serbian, and a smaller percentage Italian and Mexican. Other nationalities include only a few scattered families or non-family groups of men boarding themselves. The Croatian families predominated in two of the blocks studied, and all but two of the Italian families were concentrated in two other blocks. Almost all the men living in this district are employed either in the steel mills or in the coke furnaces. When the data for the housing study were gathered, the number of Mexican households in these blocks ranked fourth in the nationality classification, following very closely the number of Italian families of a somewhat older migration. Changes in nationality groups in the population are also reflected in the types of churches in the neighborhood. The first church established in South Deering was Methodist Episcopal; and the South Deering Methodist Church is on one corner and St. Kevin's Church is near by, both close to the canvassed area. The center of the Jugo-Slav community is a little to the northeast, where the Croatian Church of the Sacred Heart and the Serbian Orthodox Church of St. Michael the Archangel are located.

The four blocks canvassed in the Torrence Avenue district are shut in by industrial plants, but they are less monotonous in appearance than the blocks canvassed in South Chicago. Here, too, the smoke and dirt of manufacturing processes are everywhere. The land in nearby open spaces is low and marshy and not free from rubbish heaps, but there is more variety in the type of dwelling found here. The two blocks along Torrence Avenue have a row of little stores and shops, before which groups of men stand and talk in the summer evenings.

But when one turns the corner off Torrence Avenue, there is a rural picture like the South End of half a century ago. Here one may sometimes see sheep grazing in a vacant lot or a flock of geese wandering about. Many of the small frame houses have gardens in which the members of the family work in the evenings. The majority of these dwellings are old, but often they are less dingy than those at the gates of the steel mills. Housing conditions here, however, are also very unsatisfactory.

The inhabitants of the blocks studied had vegetable gardens and kept chickens, pigs, geese, and other fowls and animals, giving the neighborhood a small-town appearance. The gardens are, for the most part, well cared for and attractive, offering some outdoor occupation to their owners, and perhaps a little saving in expenditure for food; but the keeping of animals is not infrequently a nuisance. One family said they had complained to the Health Department because a neighbor kept a horse on the rear of a vacant lot which he owned next door, but the Department said the neighbor could not be made to take the horse away. Attention has already been called to the unpleasant results—the filth and disagreeable odors that go with the keeping of animals in a tenement neighborhood. How far the keeping of animals or fowls is a nuisance depends, of course, upon the available land and upon the provision made for their care. One house with a very large side yard had chickens kept in the rear of the yard, which was very clean and well cared for. But there were complaints from neighbors about two pigs in a back yard, about a cow in another yard, about chickens and geese in the rear of another house.

PULLMAN

The history of the region called Pullman is too well known to be re-told here.[86] Work began in the spring of 1880 on what was to be an "employees' Utopia," the plant of the Pullman Palace Car Company and the town that was to house its workmen. In 1893 the town of Pullman was described as "a restful oasis in the wearying brick-and-mortar waste of an enormous city." A park with gardens and a band stand, the Green Stone Church, the Florence Hotel, the school building, and the Arcade, with its stores, theater, library, and bank, have often been described. The growing discord between the Pullman Company and the Pullman employees, the great strike of 1894, and the Illinois Supreme Court decision of 1898,[87] which held that the Pullman Company could not own the town of Pullman, need not be reviewed here.[88]

[86] See Graham R. Taylor, *Satellite Cities*, p. 28.

[87] *The People* v. *Pullman Car Co.*, 175 Ill. 125.

[88] The Pullman Land Association, composed chiefly of company executives, was organized to arrange for the disposition of the property, and sold the houses to the Pullman employees according to a plan that was considered very fair. Opportunity to purchase a house was first offered the tenant who had been living in it for the longest period of time; if he did not wish to purchase it, and there were other tenants in the same dwell-

The few scattered Pullman residents of 1880 had increased to a population of more than 8,500 in 1885. The 1890 census showed a population of more than 10,000 of whom about one-third were American born, approximately one-fourth Scandinavian and another one-fourth German and Dutch, leaving 13 per cent British and about 6 per cent Irish. In addition, there were a few representatives of various other nationalities, especially of the so-called new immigration destined to increase rapidly in the following decade. Immigrants were attracted by the opportunities of employment not only in the Pullman works but in the other large industries which had followed the Pullman Car Company in establishing plants in or near Pullman, including the Sherwin-Williams Paint Company, the Griffin Car Company, and, in West Pullman, a plant of the International Harvester Company.

The present-day representatives of the older immigration who are still living in Pullman are chiefly Swedish, but some German, English, Scotch, and a few Irish are found. Most of these nationalities live in the better types of dwellings, and many of them own their homes. But the proportion of Northwestern Europeans had dwindled during the years of heavy Southeastern European immigration, and the newer immigrant groups—Poles, Slovaks, Serbians, Greeks, and Italians—became the chief workers in the Pullman Company and in other nearby industries. At the time of our canvass, Poles, Slovaks, and Italians in the order named were the immigrants represented in the largest numbers; but native-born Americans of foreign parentage now constitute the largest single population group.

In making a preliminary canvass to determine what would be a representative area for a housing canvass, it was found that there are three types of dwellings in the older portion of Pullman, aside from the residences built for the employees of the company in the higher-salary group. Most of the houses are built in long rows adjoining one another and architecturally similar, and a small sample of three

---

ing, they were given a chance to acquire it; and if none of the tenants wanted to buy the house, it was put on the market. More than half the houses were bought by the people living in them. Many of the families have still been paying for their houses, during the last decade, and social workers report that some families, who have not been able to meet their payments regularly because of some misfortune, have been allowed to go on for several years without making any payments on their property.

blocks of different types seemed adequate for the house-to-house canvass. West of the Illinois Central tracks in the area not included in the old town of Pullman a number of modern brick apartment buildings have been erected. In the original Pullman, however, there had been little change. The houses built by the company were sufficiently well constructed and have been kept in such good repair that they have not become dilapidated as have so many other tenement districts.

The Pullman houses usually have five rooms, occasionally six. It is not easy to tell where one building ends and the next begins; two and sometimes three of these single-family residences are apparently included in one building, although on the inside the part belonging to each family is entirely separated from its neighbors. Some of these houses have been converted by their purchasers into two flats, a three-room flat downstairs, and a separate one of two rooms upstairs. The objection to this change is that the family living upstairs must either use an outside stairway in the rear or pass through the downstairs apartment when going in and out.

These rows of houses, all much alike, are on the whole neat, if somewhat monotonous, and are built on broad streets sheltered with trees. Most of the residents are also owners and therefore take pride in the care of their homes, with the front yards usually well kept, with shrubs and plants. They have the appearance of substantially built, neat, but not pretentious, dwellings.

Near the Pullman yards some of the so-called "block houses" are found. The block houses are very large tenements having from twenty-three to forty-eight apartments. There are three of these so-called block houses in a block, with the house in the middle of the block usually placed farther back from the street line than the two end houses. These houses have a rather desolate and unsightly appearance with old iron fire escapes in the front, and with the open spaces in front and on the side of the buildings littered with rubbish. The rear of the houses is back against the fences that inclose the switching tracks and yards belonging to the Pullman Company.

A third type of house is found in what is known as "foremen's row," in the block from Fourteenth Street to Fifteenth Street on Stephenson Avenue, extending down both sides of the street.

Why the foremen should have lived in these houses, if they ever did, is not easy to understand. The houses are certainly inferior in every way to the rows of one-family dwellings, although they are better than the block houses on Langley Avenue. These "foremen's row" houses are buildings with four apartments, three three-room apartments and one four-room apartment, including a room with a bay window. These apartments have no bath or toilet in them; the toilets are located in the front entrance hall, under the steps on the first floor. There is no crowding on the lot in the case of the row houses. While there is some yard space around the block houses, when the number of families living in them is considered, this yard space does not provide the children with adequate playground. All the houses in the blocks studied are located on the front of the lot. No basement or cellar apartments were found, so that the apartments of the Pullman Company workers are superior to those of the steel-mills districts in this respect.

On the whole, housing in Pullman is very much less deteriorated and presents a more substantial appearance than the smoke-dyed frame houses of the South Chicago area near the mills. The Pullman houses are brick, or occasionally brick and stone. The row houses visited by our investigators were reported in good repair. These are substantially built houses, erected at a time when construction costs for good material were not so high. During the time they were owned by the Pullman Company they were kept in good repair, and since that time they have been occupied by owners and have been well cared for. The block houses were also well built, although some of them were in a poor state of repair; but even the block houses in poor repair make much better homes to live in than the frame tenements of South Chicago.[89]

[89] See Taylor, *op. cit.*, p. 38, in the comment that "the substantial original construction of brick and the architectural scheme still give the houses of Pullman a distinct stamp in contrast with the stretches of dingy frame houses characteristic of Chicago's poorer sections." However, Miss Faith Adams (Mrs. Perry), who prepared our report on Pullman, criticized the dark hallways, "dark even in the daytime," and the bad plumbing. She pointed out that although each apartment in the block houses had a separate toilet, the toilet was not located within the apartment. "These houses are divided into two sides and there are usually three apartments on each floor on each side. All three toilets and the only sink on each floor are grouped together at the end of

HEGEWISCH

One of the areas considered for house-to-house study was the remote and little-known district of Hegewisch. The intensive canvass was decided against, but a word may be said here about what was, for a long time, a quite unique area in the South End. Very unusual housing conditions were found in this community, which lies at the extreme southeastern edge of the city limits. Hegewisch is a steel town in a very real way, although it has been unvisited, remote, inconspicuous, out of the way, and overshadowed by the great steel community of South Chicago on the one side, and, on the other, by the more recent development in Gary. When we made our South Chicago canvass, it was nearly three-quarters of an hour by through express train from the center of Chicago to the extreme southern boundary of One Hundred and Thirty-eighth Street, where the Indiana line served as the far boundary of the community of Hegewisch. Before the days of street-car service to this area, this was not only a journey to another state but almost a journey to a far country, from the skyscrapers of the city to the semi-rural area as isolated as was this community of workers. Hegewisch was named after a man who was given free land on condition that he start a factory there, and, as much of the land was a swampy waste, the houses for the workers were sometimes built on stilts. Some of the residents were said to catch fish for dinner from their back porches! The main industries include the Ryan Car Company, the Western Steel Car and

---

the public entrance hall. . . . . . Enough has been said of the evils of the semi-public type of toilet but when the number of apartments in the house is greatly increased, the evil of the toilet placed in a location without privacy is intensified proportionately."

"In addition to having all the toilets out in the ends of the halls, there is only one sink on a floor, and this also is in the partitioned-off space in the hall in which the toilets are found. This means that there is no sewerage connection, no plumbing at all, in the apartments of the block houses. All the water for cooking, for scrubbing and cleaning, and for doing the family washing, must be carried from this hall sink. And the effort involved in taking a bath, since there are no bathtubs at all in these houses, must preclude any save Saturday night ablutions for the tired worker in the Pullman Shops. This utter lack of necessary conveniences, typical of conveniences fifty years ago, should certainly have been supplied in all these years in houses sheltering so many people." She added, finally, that "there is one small block house made up of twelve apartments in Block I, in which sinks have been installed in each apartment. This house is also the only one of the three in the block that has electricity."

Foundry Company, the Interstate Iron and Steel Company, and the great Ford Plant, which was begun in 1923 near Hegewisch in what is now Ford City.

Hegewisch is roughly a mile square. The open country lies on three sides, while the steel mills and the car-works border it on the west. Two railroads lie along the east and west, meeting in a crossing to the south, so that the district is somewhat triangular in shape To the north and northeast lie Hyde Lake and Wolf Lake, small bodies of water about one-quarter of a mile apart and approximately half a mile from Hegewisch—a half-mile of open meadowland sloping gradually up to the town where there are shade trees, bits of "lawn," "flower beds," and many gardens.

Something like two-thirds of the homes are on single lots, with the other third occupying double lots or even larger areas of ground. In general, less than 50–60 per cent of the lot is covered by the houses and outbuildings. The region is marked by an absence of crowding on the lot, marked also by general cleanliness, and good repair of the streets and alleys. The buildings are almost uniformly of frame construction.

There are no "rear" buildings in the literal sense of the term, for a few yards of open ground always intervene between the back of the structure and the alley. There are, in a few instances, two-story dwellings which have been converted into apartments by the erection of outside stairways and porches on the lot line, and which come under the classification of "front, rear, middle" apartments—houses overcrowded with families. But light and fresh air are always available. There are rooms in Hegewisch that may be called "gloomy" perhaps but probably none that are dark like those in the crowded areas.

In spite of the open spaces, many of the houses and apartments are greatly overcrowded when industry is at the peak. Every room in every house was used for sleeping purposes by night—sometimes by day as well, at the time of our recanvass in the South End. Boarders literally swarmed on certain streets. For example, in a little four-room cottage, so tiny that it seemed scarcely large enough for two people, were four boarders in addition to the proprietor, his wife, and child. A huge boarding establishment on another street had turned into bedrooms a whole first floor formerly occupied by a store, by dividing the room by a low curtain. The part of the room along the inner wall behind the curtain was very dark, and the beds, floor mattresses and baggage, and the general heaviness of the air and odor, blankets washed only at long intervals, linen infrequently changed, made it seem unfit for human habitation. In scarcely a single boarding-house were conditions in any way satisfactory. All were overcrowded, all were cheerless, all were badly ventilated. The beds were not clean, and very often were occupied by relays of men, the day shift and the night shift, the bedding scarcely becoming cold after one occupant had left it before his successor tumbled in. This is known as the "hot bed"—an unpleasantly suggestive name. The beds were usually left unmade, a higher rental being charged if the boarding-housekeeper attended to their making. Men coming in heavily fatigued after their day's labor in the mills are not too particular where they sleep. Their one object is rest.

The country lying about Hegewisch, and other South End industrial centers, is pleasant and rural; the winds blow over the water, meadow grass, and trees. But the river is an iron-and-steel river, with giant industries along the banks, and the great industries are gradually expanding over the still open country areas that are in, but not of, the city of Chicago.

THE CHICAGO TENEMENT

Attention has been called in the preceding chapter to the fact that in the Chicago Building Code a "tenement" is defined as a dwelling occupied by two or more families living in separate apartments.[90]

Legally a fashionable apartment building is a tenement under the Chicago code. But the word "tenement" has an invidious meaning. As distinguished from an apartment, the tenement carries with it the idea of extreme deterioration and poverty. People in the tenements are for the most part people of very small incomes, and destitute people of all nationalities and races, frequently immigrants and Negroes. The names used in the tenement districts—the Ghetto, Little Sicily, Little Italy, Pilsen, and similar names—show how pub-

[90] *Revised Chicago Code, 1931,* chap. xxiv, art. ii, sec. 1200: "In Class VI shall be included every tenement and apartment house; that is to say, any house or building or portion thereof which is used as a home or residence for two or more families living in separate apartments."

lic opinion looks upon these neglected areas. Everywhere in the tenement districts are houses that are not tenements—for the most part very old cottages that were built in the early days when the Chicago slums of today were peaceful stretches of market gardens, farms, and open prairie. Some of these old cottages have had "additions" of various kinds that have made them over into multiple-family dwellings, but some remain single-family homes and not tenements. Every dwelling, whether tenement or single-family home, of every kind in every block canvassed was included in our investigation. But the standards prescribed in the code for tenements, or Class VI houses, are very much higher than regulations laid down for single-family houses, or Class III dwellings—on the theory that there is not the same need of regulation for conditions in the more independent one-family home.

It should, however, be emphasized that insanitary conditions are just as bad for the family living alone as for the family that occupies a flat. For this reason it has seemed best in the tables given to include all houses visited, whether tenements, which are required to conform to the standards for Class VI houses, or dwellings governed by the minor restrictions prescribed for Class III houses. If in some cases the law is not violated because the houses are occupied by a single family, the condition, even if legal, is not the less insanitary and objectionable. Children sleeping with two adults in a room not having enough cubic air space for one person will suffer just as much if there is only one family in the house as they will if they are occupying one flat in a large tenement.

One question that immediately arose in the first house-to-house canvass undertaken was the question whether to undertake to reform the various objectionable conditions which were found and which were so obviously in need of improvement. From the beginning, all our investigators were graduate students preparing for some form of social work. Unlike professional investigators or the students in a social science department in a university who are accustomed to "observation with the idle curiosity of the scientist," our investigators were accustomed to see "what could be done about it." Every effort was made to bring about an immediate improvement in any bad condition that seemed remediable. A prompt report was made to the supervising investigator who, in turn, reported to the proper authorities and undertook to have the illegal situation corrected—this meant, of course, reporting a leaking roof, plumbing out of repair that had been reported in vain by the tenant, the use of an illegal

TABLE 2

NUMBER OF HEADS OF HOUSEHOLDS OF SPECIFIED NATIONALITY

Nationality	Heads of Households*	
	Number	Per Cent Distribution
Total all nationalities	15,115	100.0
American:		
White	890	5.9
Negro	1,828	12.1
Foreign:	*12,397*	*82.0*
Bohemian	389	2.6
British	40	0.3
French	28	0.2
German	498	3.3
Greek	382	2.5
Irish	197	1.3
Italian	2,926	19.4
Jugo-Slav (Serb, Croat, Slovene)	241	1.6
Lithuanian	1,341	8.9
Magyar	247	1.6
Mexican	375	2.5
Polish	4,591	30.3
Russian (including Jewish)	186	1.2
Scandinavian	138	0.9
Slovak	407	2.7
Ukrainian	106	0.7
Other foreign	305	2.0

* Including non-family groups.

windowless room for sleeping purposes, serious overcrowding, and other conditions calling for an immediate remedy.[91]

AREAS SELECTED

As the inquiry was prolonged, data were accumulated for a large number of districts and many different national groups were included

[91] Reports of structural defects and reports regarding overcrowding were deferred until after the investigators had finished their work in the area, because of the fear that such reports would make it difficult to secure accurate data. The question regarding "number of occupants" was always disturbing in areas where lodgers were a source of income (see below, p. 343).

in the sample. In all, twenty-four different districts were finally canvassed. One of these had been entirely taken over for business purposes at the time of the recanvass, and the recent material, therefore,

TABLE 3

THE DISTRICTS CANVASSED, PREDOMINANT NATIONALITY, NUMBER OF BLOCKS, BUILDINGS, AND APARTMENTS

Location	Original Canvass			
	Predominant Nationality	Number of Blocks* Canvassed	Number of Buildings†	Number of Apartments†
Total for all districts		151	6,294	18,225
West Side:				
Old Ghetto	Jewish	1	65	200
Pilsen	Bohemian	1	71	295
Lumber Yards	Slovak	4	262	869
Hull-House	Greek and Italian	16	655	2,169
Polk Street	Italian	2	120	370
St. Stanislaus	Polish	10	743	2,785
Division Street	Polish and Ruthenian	12	424	1,465
Ancona	Polish	2	135	493
North Side:				
Lower North	Italian	5	404	1,462
Upper North	German and Italian	4	165	395
Olivet	German and Italian	7	223	530
South Side:				
Downtown	Italian	1	23	123
Near South Side	Croatian and Italian	6	337	1,027
Back of the Yards	Polish and Lithuanian	13	619	1,616
Stock Yards, South	Polish	2	93	289
Southwest	Lithuanian	10	412	1,031
Negro districts:				
Dearborn	Negro	4	209	458
La Salle	Negro	5	182	427
Upper Federal	Negro	7	297	558
Walnut (West Side)	Negro	3	131	254
South End:				
Burnside	Magyar	22	305	413
South Chicago (East Side)	Slovak	7	263	545
South Deering	Croatian, Serbian, Italian, Mexican	4	119	206
Pullman	Polish, Italian, American	3	37	245

* All of these have been recanvassed, and the dates are not therefore given for each district; and all areas have been revisited during the past autumn (1935).

† These are numbers at time of the original canvass. At the date of recanvass certain changes had taken place which will be discussed in later chapters.

MAP III

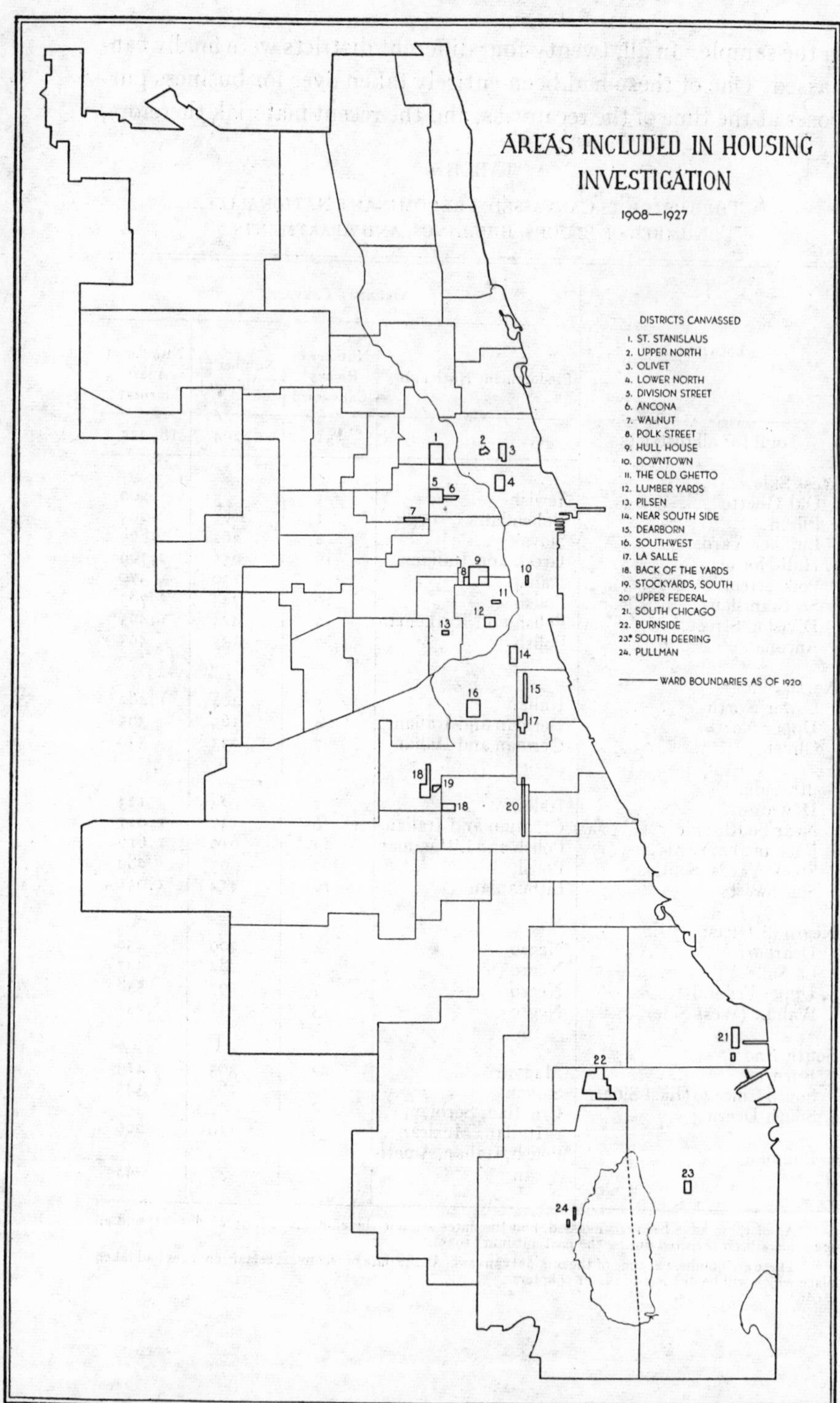
AREAS INCLUDED IN HOUSING INVESTIGATION
1908—1927
DISTRICTS CANVASSED
1. ST. STANISLAUS
2. UPPER NORTH
3. OLIVET
4. LOWER NORTH
5. DIVISION STREET
6. ANCONA
7. WALNUT
8. POLK STREET
9. HULL HOUSE
10. DOWNTOWN
11. THE OLD GHETTO
12. LUMBER YARDS
13. PILSEN
14. NEAR SOUTH SIDE
15. DEARBORN
16. SOUTHWEST
17. LA SALLE
18. BACK OF THE YARDS
19. STOCKYARDS, SOUTH
20. UPPER FEDERAL
21. SOUTH CHICAGO
22. BURNSIDE
23.* SOUTH DEERING
24. PULLMAN
WARD BOUNDARIES AS OF 1920

covers twenty-three districts in fifteen different wards. The distribution of the population by nationalities in these 151 blocks canvassed is indicated in Table 2.

In the past decade all the districts investigated before 1920 have been recanvassed in order to collect certain data regarding the changes in housing conditions during this period. In the recanvass a very simple schedule was used calling only for facts about number of residents, rents, number of rooms, and sanitary conditions. These data are presented along with the original material under the appropriate subject headings.

On a few points, notably rent, the districts that were canvassed for the first time during the post-war period represent conditions so different from the conditions indicated by the statistics secured in the districts of the pre-war canvass that, for some purposes, separate tabulations have been made of the pre-war and post-war schedules. The tables presented, therefore, fall into four different groups, which are referred to as follows: (1) data from recent recanvass and recent new canvass; (2) data from original canvass for all districts; (3) data from pre-war canvass; and (4) data from post-war canvass.

The general location of the groups of blocks canvassed is shown on the accompanying Map (Map III).

The making of schedules underwent numerous changes, but these changes were in the direction of "sloughing off" the items or questions that were found to yield results that did not justify the time consumed in securing the returns. As in so many inquiries it was possible to make a really satisfactory schedule only after much of the work was done. Fortunately, a long series of similar studies made possible a remaking of the schedule on the basis of experience. The schedule of 1919, which was used to the end of the work, was on the whole simple and easy to tabulate.[92]

[92] This proved to be a good working schedule for training research students in securing data in a field requiring accuracy of observation and careful recording. The general policy was to have two students work together and then to change members of the working pairs so that all the investigators worked with the same understanding of the standards covered in the instruction. See below, p. 253, n. 13.

CHAPTER IV

CHICAGO TENEMENT TYPES

Expansion Possible in a Prairie City; Development of the Gridiron Plan; Lot Overcrowding; Contrast with New York; "Old" and "New Law" Houses; Tenements Antedating the Tenement-House Law.

THE shambling, dilapidated tenement houses of Chicago, strangely varying not only from block to block but in some areas almost from house to house, are in striking contrast to the closely built, tall brick buildings that extend in deadly uniformity, row upon row and street after street, in New York's poverty areas.

EXPANSION POSSIBLE IN A PRAIRIE CITY

For the differences between the New York and Chicago tenement districts two important explanations may be offered. In the first place, Chicago is a new city, the metropolis of the recent prairie wilderness, a vast commercial and industrial center built where, less than a century ago, wild onions and willows grew over the low, swampy shoreland of an inland lake. In the second place, the new city had possibilities of almost limitless expansion in every direction except where Lake Michigan formed the permanent "city limits."

Everywhere else expansion was possible, and the city grew straggling and struggling. Being built on the edge of an almost limitless prairie, an irregular and scattered collection of settlements developed, finally grew together, and gradually became the present metropolitan area. The part of this metropolitan area included within the corporate limits of Chicago, and the boundaries of separate villages and towns which have joined together to form it, are shown in Map I. The limits of Manhattan Island and the land scarcity of New York were not reproduced in the prairie metropolis. Here the distant horizon offered the only limits to city growth, and expansion to the west, to the north, and to the south has been easily possible. Even state lines have not been impossible barriers, and the metropolitan area has outgrown its boundaries and now extends into the adjoining states of Wisconsin and Indiana. Only on Chicago's East Side has the lake prohibited the reaching-out for new land for city development; and even here the future is difficult to forecast, for in recent years Chicago has learned how to build parks in its lake and other uses of "filled in" areas are entirely possible.

DEVELOPMENT OF THE GRIDIRON PLAN

In spite of its magnificent distances Chicago has become a city of cramped lots. As in most modern cities, the gridiron plan has been followed and the city blocks have been divided into lots of 25 by 100 or 125 feet.[1] Chicago has become a city of respectable street frontages and neglected back-alley or service streets.

With many houses of varying heights and sizes crowded into a small area, one sees very clearly what has been called the "essential unrighteousness of the 25-foot lot." This lot, often referred to as the "shoe-string lot"—a piece of land 25 feet wide by 100 or 125 feet in length from the street to the alley—is typical of Chicago. It is inevitable that buildings erected upon such strips of land should extend to the very limits of the lot, and thus deprive each other of light

[1] In 1922, when the acting chief of the Bureau of Sanitation reported that the use of lots 25 feet in width was "not popular for homes and tenement buildings," a trend toward some improvement in regard to new buildings was indicated. The report said: "It is practically impossible to erect a house or tenement building on so narrow a lot because of the rather stringent requirements of the building ordinances pertaining to light and ventilation. The total number of plans approved for lots 25 feet in width or less was 95, and for lots over that and less than 35 feet in width, 3,226. In nearly all of the newly opened subdivisions lots are from 30 to 35 feet in width. This affords a building site which allows for the erection of a dwelling with ample space all around for the free lighting of all living rooms" (*Health Department Report*, pp.. 227–28). However, the difference between the 25- and 30- or 35-foot lot is a difference in degree and does not greatly alter the old "shoe-string" difficulty. Of course, the hopeful trend is toward a new planning for residential areas. See on this point any one of the many excellent volumes on neighborhood planning which describe the new developments, especially Henry Wright, *Rehousing Urban America* (1935); Thomas Adams, *The Design of Residential Areas: Basic Considerations, Principles and Methods* (1934); various volumes issued by the Committee on the New York Regional Plan; *Planning for Residentiai Districts* (President's Conference on Home Building and Home Ownership), Vol. I (1932); Louis H. Pink, *The New Day in Housing* (1928); Edith Elmer Wood, *Recent Trends in American Housing* (1932); Catherine Bauer, *Modern Housing* (1934) (a most excellent book), see especially for this point Part IV, "Elements of Modern Housing;" chap. iv, "Layout and Building Arrangements."

and air. Furthermore, they must be fairly deep (in which case there are difficulties of construction hard to overcome), or else a very considerable percentage of the lot space will be unused, and, for profit-seeking purposes, wasted. Modern apartments of the "Garden City" type, which are extensive enough to allow the vacating of the alley and the development of a small "housing area," can overcome this difficulty for the large "housing project." But for the great proportion of small builders, co-operative action has not in the past been planned or possible.

LOT OVERCROWDING

Certainly in the tenement areas where the houses have "just growed," along rectangular lines, through "one hundred years of progress," the lot spaces are badly utilized. Light, sunlight, and plenty of air for decent and healthful living cannot be had except by regulating the open spaces on the lot; and the crowding of the lot with buildings means not only lack of light and air but also that the families live much on the street and that the children have a street for their playground.[1a]

There are marked variations in density of population in different sections of the city.[1b] The Chicago tenements were built before the days of high buildings, and population density in the tenement area is explained in two ways: by the crowding of buildings, especially tenements, on the lot and by the crowding within the dwellings; that is, lot overcrowding on the one hand and congestion within the apartment on the other.

The tenement-house code at an early date prescribed regulations limiting the percentage of the lot that could be built over. The law of

[1a] Mr. Henry Wright points out in his recent and very useful book, *Rehousing Urban America*, that in Chicago 376,000 families, nearly 40 per cent of the whole population, live in wasteful, detached two-family flats. "These deep, narrow buildings facing streets running north and south, are so related as to fill up the generous size lot and block most of the sunlight." Mr. Wright thinks that 50 per cent more two-family units may be arranged within the same space so that all rooms receive either morning or afternoon sunshine, "by merely substituting modern broad-front attached flats of approximately the same living capacity, in four rows per block, running north and south with the streets." See especially Mr. Wright's excellent discussion of "The Blighting Effect of the Narrow Lot," *ibid.*, pp. 20–25.

[1b] See below, chap. viii, "The Problem of Congestion."

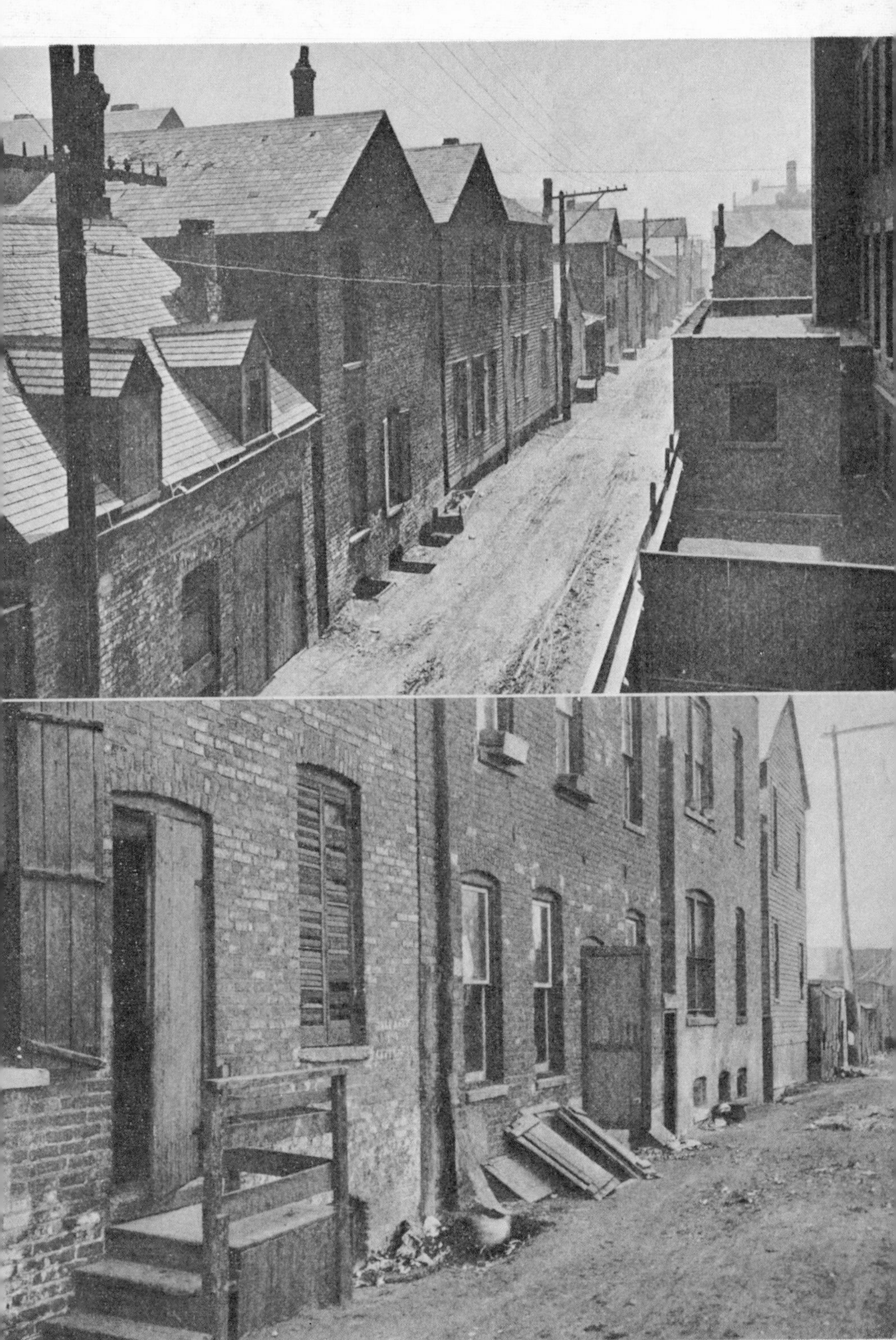

LOT OVERCROWDING: REAR TENEMENTS ON THE WEST SIDE

1910 provided that no existing house should be altered, or any new house constructed, so as to cover more than 90 per cent of a corner lot or more than 75 per cent of any lot.[2] And yet even among the comparatively small number of houses erected since this law went into effect, there are several instances in which the lot is entirely covered. It is generally understood that the standard prescribed by law is the minimum acceptable to the community; but in some neighborhoods nearly half of the lots are so covered as to fall below even this minimum legal standard.

The important question, of course, is whether the lot spaces are planned so as to give the greatest possible amount of light and air. With the law permitting the covering of 75 per cent of the area in the case of interior lots and 85 per cent in the case of corner lots,[3] it is evident that if all the rooms of the house are to be habitable the planning of the lot calls for as much care and ingenuity as the planning of the house itself. Many instances were found of houses too close to the lot line where the percentage of uncovered space was high enough, but courts were too narrow and wrongly placed. Such conditions call for a housing law that shall provide more adequate regulations and shall be thoroughly enforced. That enforcement especially needs emphasis is evident from the fact that in some cases houses built since the enactment of the tenement-house law of 1902 covered more than the legal percentage of the lot. The percentage of lot covered in twenty of the districts canvassed is shown in Table 4. For twenty tenement neighborhoods in different sections of the city, approximately one-third of the lots were covered less than 50 per cent and approximately one-tenth of the lots were covered from 90 to 100 per cent. Taking the numbers cumulatively, 21 per cent of the lots were covered 80 per cent or more and 36 per cent were covered 70 per cent or more.

The condition with regard to lot overcrowding varies, of course, from district to district. The percentage of the lot covered in the

[2] *Chicago Code, 1911*, chap. xvi, art. ix, sec. 440. Busch-Hornstein, *Revised Chicago Code, 1931*, sec. 1414.

[3] Above the first floor or under exceptional circumstances, 90 per cent. For example, 90 per cent "in the case of a fireproof building in which the windows of every habitable room open directly on a street."

districts for which this information was obtained is shown in Tables 5 and 6. Data on this point were not secured at the time of the recanvass, and the table is divided, therefore, into pre-war and post-war canvasses.

It should be noted, however, that on this point much more depends on the general neighborhood conditions than the year when the canvass was made. In the Stock Yards district the buildings are

TABLE 4

NUMBER AND PER CENT DISTRIBUTION OF LOTS*
COVERED A SPECIFIED PERCENTAGE OF AREA
(Original Canvass Data)

Percentage of Lot Covered	Occupied Lots	
	Number	Per Cent Distribution
Total reported	4,603	100.0
Less than 50	1,546	33.6
50 and less than 60	750	16.3
60 and less than 70	634	13.8
70 and less than 80	695	15.1
80 and less than 90	529	11.5
90 and less than 100	449	9.7

* In 20 districts. Pullman, Polk, Ancona, and Olivet excluded; downtown district included.

often small and cover a relatively small portion of the lot. There nearly half of the premises were not covered more than 50 per cent, and a considerable number were entirely vacant.

CONTRAST WITH NEW YORK

It is of further interest that the houses back of the Yards not only occupy a small percentage of the lot but are almost uniformly frame buildings not more than two stories high. In this district a relatively high density per acre is found along with a relatively small percentage of the lot covered by small low houses. The condition is especially interesting because typical of so many districts in Chicago. The small houses and vacant lots, so unlike the crowded areas of the tenement districts in New York, give the impression that there is no serious problem of congestion here. This impression, however, is a misleading one since a high degree of crowding exists within the

TABLE 5

EXTENT TO WHICH LOTS ARE COVERED BY BUILDINGS; NUMBER OF LOTS COVERED A SPECIFIED PERCENTAGE OF AREA; BY DISTRICTS
(Original Canvass Data)

District	Number of Lots Covered a Specified Percentage						
	Total Reported	Less than 50 Per Cent	50 Per Cent and Less than 60	60 Per Cent and Less than 70	70 Per Cent and Less than 80	80 Per Cent and Less than 90	90 Per Cent and Over
All districts	4,603	1,546	750	634	695	529	449
Pre-war, canvass	3,547	1,048	430	553	631	488	397
Back of the Yards	561	248†	65	92	75	56	25
Old Ghetto	47	2	5	......	12	6	22
Pilsen	43	4	......	13	6	6	14
St. Stanislaus	449	67	54	117	131	55	25
South Chicago (East Side)	205	134	12	28	15	12	4
Dearborn and Walnut*	293	164	35	34	23	17	20
Lower North	278	37	26	23	62	42	88
Downtown	15	2	......	......	5	5	3
Lumber Yards	207	44	22	38	42	48	13
Southwest	364	183	49	54	43	20	15
Hull-House	496	13	84	58	114	125	102
Division Street	310	96	38	48	55	41	32
Near South Side	279	54	40	48	48	55	34
Post-war canvass	1,056	498	320	81	64	41	52
Upper North	143	3	87	22	12	7	12
La Salle	170	2	131	12	12	5	8
Stock Yards, South	76	9	33	6	7	5	16
Burnside	296	283	5	2	3	2	1
Upper Federal	261	136	56	34	17	10	8
South Deering	110	65	8	5	13	12	7

* District includes two Negro districts on the West Side and South Side which were not separately tabulated on this point.

† Of these, 43 were vacant premises.

houses. Tables which will be given later, dealing with the number of occupants per room, show that in this district sleeping-rooms especially are crowded far beyond the legal limit, and this overcrowding within the house is often a source of much greater danger and demoralization than the more obvious overcrowding in the eastern cities.

In general, in the West Side districts there is a high percentage of

TABLE 6

EXTENT TO WHICH LOTS ARE COVERED BY BUILDINGS; PERCENTAGE* OF LOTS COVERED A SPECIFIED PERCENTAGE OF AREA; BY DISTRICTS
(Original Canvass Data)

District	Percentage of Lots Covered a Specified Percentage					
	Less than 50 Per Cent	50 Per Cent and Less than 60	60 Per Cent and Less than 70	70 Per Cent and Less than 80	80 Per Cent and Less than 90	90 Per Cent and Over
All districts	33.6	16.3	13.8	15.1	11.5	9.7
Pre-war canvass	29.5	12.1	15.6	17.8	13.8	11.2
Back of the Yards	44.2	11.6	16.4	13.4	10.0	4.4
Old Ghetto	......	......	......	......	......	......
Pilsen	......	......	......	......	......	......
St. Stanislaus	14.9	12.0	26.1	29.2	12.2	5.6
South Chicago	65.4	5.9	13.7	7.3	5.8	1.9
Dearborn and Walnut	56.0	12.0	11.6	7.8	5.8	6.8
Lower North	13.3	9.3	8.3	22.3	15.1	31.7
Lumber Yards	21.3	10.6	18.4	20.3	23.1	6.3
Southwest	50.3	13.5	14.8	11.8	5.5	4.1
Hull-House	2.6	16.9	11.7	23.0	25.2	20.6
Division Street	31.0	12.3	15.5	17.7	13.2	10.3
Near South Side	19.4	14.3	17.2	17.2	19.7	12.2
Post-war canvass	47.1	30.3	7.7	6.1	3.9	4.9
Upper North	2.1	60.8	15.4	8.4	4.9	8.4
La Salle	1.2	77.1	7.0	7.0	3.0	4.7
Stock Yards, South	......	......	......	......	......	......
Burnside	95.6	1.7	0.7	1.0	0.7	0.3
Upper Federal	52.1	21.5	13.0	6.5	3.8	3.1
South Deering	59.1	7.3	4.5	11.8	10.9	6.4

* The percentages in this table are based on the number reporting. Old Ghetto, Pilsen, and Stock Yards, South, omitted because total number is less than 100.

lot area covered by buildings. In the Hull-House district 46 per cent of the lots were covered 80 per cent or more. It is interesting to look back to the figures which were published by the City Homes Association in 1901. It was found that in the districts investigated on the West Side, 39 per cent of all the lots were covered more than 65 per cent, and that 17 per cent of the lots were covered more than 80 per cent.[4] In comparison with these percentages for the West Side, the figures show that in the territory back of the yards and in other South Side areas there is a relatively large amount of open space. The only exception is the Croatian and Italian district of the Near South Side where 32 per cent of the lots were covered 80 per cent or more. On the West Side, however, there is every kind and variety of overcrowding—overcrowding on the lot, overcrowding within the house, and overcrowding within the rooms.

The circumstances of lot overcrowding vary from one lot to the next and from one district to another. Sometimes, of course, it is a gaunt and ungainly tenement that covers the premises. Sometimes, a group of three houses, front, middle, and rear huddled together, and sometimes the overcrowding is caused in part by the ramshackle ugly sheds, ancient stables, coal bins, and clutter of every sort. While this clutter does not always shut out light and air, it does deprive the children who swarm in these neighborhoods of anything in the way of a place to play.

Even in areas in which the general condition is not especially bad, exceptionally bad spots are not infrequently to be found. In the Lithuanian district on the South West Side fifteen lots, seven of which were interior lots, were more than 90 per cent covered. In one case the only space on two adjoining premises not actually occupied by the houses was a covered stairway and hall 3½ feet wide. Another house, in which eight children were living, had no vacant space adjoining save a long 3-foot passage more than half roofed over. On the corner of one block was a three-story house occupying over 90 per cent of the lot. Here lived seven families, with thirteen children under twelve years of age. The only open space for another house, containing four families, was a court 3 feet wide by 14 feet long. In spite of many such instances, however, it is evident that so far as lot overcrowding is concerned, better conditions exist in this particular district than in many other parts of the city. For example, in the Italian district of the Lower North Side, only 13 per cent of the lots were less than half covered and again in the Lower North district 47

[4] Robert Hunter, *Tenement Conditions in Chicago*, p. 32.

per cent had 80 per cent or more of the lot covered in contrast to 10 per cent in the Lithuanian district.

On the South Side in the "Black Belt" there is a considerable amount of vacant-lot space. One-half of the lots in two of the Negro districts, Dearborn and Upper Federal, had less than 50 per cent of the lot space covered, and three-fourths of the lots in La Salle district were less than 60 per cent covered. Instead of the small irregular courts, usually paved, such as one frequently sees in the Polish section on the Northwest Side, these houses often have fairly large back yards, sometimes with grass and shrubs growing in them. The yards are almost always dirty and disfigured by rubbish, but at least they afford light and air which would not be available if they were crowded with buildings. In all of the foreign districts except those in the "south end"—and these industrial areas are, of course, of more recent development—the buildings are crowded more thickly upon the lots; in the Negro districts, as in other old and deteriorated areas, the property-owners are not making improvements, or utilizing the land space either by extending old buildings or by building new ones. However, the recanvass showed an increase in the number of buildings in LaSalle district—206 as compared with 182.

The colored people in these districts do not to any great extent live in large tenement houses. The houses are small, and some of them, with their boarded-up porches and shaky board walks, resemble small-town cottages. Here, too, the windows are sometimes filled with plants, and sometimes a straggling vine has been trained over a porch. It must be confessed that any attempt to utilize the unoccupied portions of the lot for garden plots is extremely difficult. Trees, shrubbery, grass, and flowers are not seen in the tenement districts, although there are occasional attempts at vegetable gardens in front or back yards.[5] Living things do not grow in the hard spaces between front, middle, and rear houses. The men and women, too, work hard and have little money to spend on the things that are beautiful but not necessary. Ducks, chickens, and goats are frequently kept in the tiny yards, but they serve a utilitarian purpose

[5] See, e.g., the picture of a back yard in the Lithuanian district (southwest) in Elizabeth Hughes, "Housing Conditions among the Lithuanians," *American Journal of Sociology*, XX, No. 3 (November, 1914), 299.

NEGRO HOMES ON THE SOUTH SIDE

and are raised with less trouble and expense than flowers, perhaps because they are less damaged by the pall of smoke in which the tenement districts are so often submerged.

"OLD" AND "NEW LAW" HOUSES

In Chicago the frame tenement has lingered on and is still the predominant type. Many of these frame tenements were originally frame cottages of the prairie period and were expanded into tenements to provide cheaper housing facilities for the increasing population. The old cottage was raised up, new stories added above and below, and further additions built, not infrequently, both front and rear. In many cases the cottage has not only been raised but moved back to the rear of the lot, and a new house erected in front. Sometimes the new front house is itself finally moved back to the middle of the lot and a third house is built in front. In one respect the tenement districts of Chicago are like the homes of the poor all over the world—the houses are old and in bad repair, business and factory buildings make the districts unsightly, and they are properly described as "deteriorated areas."

In collecting the data assembled in the course of our inquiry, an attempt was made to determine in each case whether the house visited was erected before or after the passage of the first tenement-house law, that of 1902, whether built between 1902 and 1910 or after the latter year. This inquiry appeared only on the original schedules and no further data on this point were secured during the recanvass. The provisions of the tenement-house code fall chiefly into two classes: (1) those applying to old as well as new buildings, such as the plumbing regulations and the provisions concerning occupancy of dwellings; (2) those applying to the structural conditions of the houses, such as the requirements as to size of rooms, the relation of window space to floor space, and windowless rooms, which apply only to "new buildings."

Our canvass in district after district showed that the provisions of the code which dealt only with new buildings would not in the lifetime of a generation affect the houses in the so-called "congested districts." Table 7 shows how large a proportion of the tenements canvassed were built before the passage of the first tenement-house law. Eighty-seven per cent of the buildings in the twenty districts canvassed were built before 1902. The percentage varied, of course, from district to district, as Table 8 shows.

TENEMENTS ANTEDATING THE TENEMENT-HOUSE LAW

According to Table 8 in all except two of the districts investigated the percentage of houses built before the enactment of the first tenement-house law in 1902 ranged from 74 per cent (in one of

TABLE 7

DATE OF ERECTION OF BUILDINGS CANVASSED IN TWENTY DISTRICTS*

(Original Canvass Data)

Date Erected	Buildings Canvassed	
	Number	Per Cent Distribution
Total	5,779	100.0
Before 1902	4,974	87.4
1902–10	478	8.4
After 1910	238	4.2
Date not reported	89	†

* This information was not secured for Pullman, Polk St., Ancona, and Olivet districts.

† Percentages based on known cases.

the Stock Yards districts) to 100 per cent in two of the West Side districts—Pilsen and the so-called old "Ghetto"—and in the "Down Town district." The two districts with less than 74 per cent of the houses built before 1902 were both relatively new industrial areas on the South Side of the city, the Burnside triangle, where only a tenth, and the South Deering district, where 61 per cent of the buildings antedated 1902.

The first house-to-house canvasses were undertaken in the winter of 1908–9, approximately seven years after the first tenement-house law was passed. Our canvass in three districts that winter showed that the enactment of the ordinance of 1902 had had no effect on the housing situation which had been exposed by the City Homes investigation in 1901. Similarly, our later canvasses have shown that only 8 per cent of the houses in these neighborhoods could have been affected by the 1902 law and that the newer ordinance of 1910 and its

TABLE 8

DATE OF ERECTION OF BUILDINGS CANVASSED; BY DISTRICTS

(Original Canvass Data)

District	Total	Buildings Erected					
		Before 1902		1902–10		After 1910	
		Number	Percentage of Total	Number	Percentage of Total	Number	Percentage of Total
All districts	5,690*	4,974	87.4	478	8.4	238	4.2
Pre-war canvass	4,551	4,200	92.3	285	6.3	66	1.4
Back of the Yards	587	488	83.1	99	16.9	‡	......
Old Ghetto	65	65	100.0	......	......	‡	......
Pilsen	71	71	100.0	......	......	‡	......
St. Stanislaus	736	717	97.4	19	2.6	‡	......
South Chicago	261	245	93.9	16	6.1	‡	......
Dearborn†	340	334	98.2	6	1.8	‡	......
Lower North	388	381	98.2	7	1.8	‡	......
Downtown	23	23	100.0	......	......	‡	......
Lumber Yards	258	253	98.1	4	1.5	1	0.4
Southwest	406	334	82.3	44	10.8	28	6.9
Hull-House	655	584	89.2	41	6.2	30	4.6
Division Street	424	394	92.9	26	6.1	4	1.0
Near South Side	337	311	92.3	23	6.8	3	0.9
Post-war canvass	1,139	774	68.0	193	16.9	172	15.1
Upper North	162	160	98.8	2	1.2	......	......
La Salle	181	168	92.8	12	6.6	1	0.6
Stock Yards, South	93	69	74.2	18	19.4	6	6.4
Burnside	288	29	10.1	117	40.6	142	49.3
Upper Federal	297	276	92.9	17	5.7	4	1.4
South Deering	118	72	61.0	27	22.9	19	16.1

* This total does not include 89 buildings for which the data were not reported.

† Includes Walnut district, a Negro district on the West Side.

‡ Original canvass was before 1910.

amendments have had no effect on the deteriorated areas where housing conditions are worst, since only 4 per cent of the houses in the districts have been erected since 1910.

How far are the new ordinances applicable to buildings erected before the passage of the ordinance and how far should they be applicable? There is, of course, the difficulty that landlords object to what they call *ex post facto* housing legislation. Houses once built outlast a generation or two, or even longer, but without constant expenditures do not remain decent and sanitary.

These areas are already overcrowded, and there is little room for new buildings. Moreover, as we have seen, many of these districts are awaiting the business invasion, and the deterioration is a result of the encroachments of business upon what may once have been a pleasant, or even a fine, residence district. The owners often have an exaggerated idea of land values. They consider the land in these areas as a speculative investment and think that if they hold it long enough it will be needed for skyscraper purposes. The houses have deteriorated, partly from age and the decrepitude of advancing years, partly because conditions in the district make even the repair of old houses an investment that will yield no returns. The reconditioning of these houses to meet the provisions of the new code will not be voluntarily undertaken. They become steadily more and more unfit for comfortable or even decent family life. The recent canvass of the districts first visited from ten to fifteen years ago showed that in the intervening years new buildings had rarely been erected except on a few business streets where combination "store" and flat buildings have been put up.

In the discussion that follows, attention will be frequently called to the differences in the housing standards laid down in the tenement-house ordinance and the standards actually tolerated in so many areas of the city during all this third of a century since the adoption of the first tenement-house ordinance.

CHAPTER V

THE SMALL TENEMENTS OF CHICAGO

Old Frame Tenements; Frame Tenements and Dilapidation; Rear Tenements; Tenement Alleys; Chicago's One- and Two-Story Tenements.

IN THE tenement districts, Chicago remains a city of one-family houses and small tenement buildings. Whatever the newer tendency may be toward the erection of vast apartments in the region of the Lake Shore and the South Shore drives, the old order still prevails in the deteriorated areas where new houses are rarely seen. Since Chicago's poorer homes are so largely in old buildings, it is not surprising that only 2 per cent of all the buildings canvassed were more than three stories high. And with more than one-half of the buildings having only two stories (Table 13), it is again not surprising that in approximately three-fourths of the buildings only one, two, or three apartments were found.

Attention should perhaps be called again to the fact that in the tenement districts a considerable number of the houses are not "tenements," for it has already been pointed out that one-family buildings are not "tenements" within the definition of the Chicago building code. Our house-to-house canvass in twenty-four widely separated and representative districts showed that one-fourth of all the houses were of this one-family type. These houses were subject not to the provisions of the building code relating to Class VI houses but to the minor restrictions relating to the so-called Class III houses.[1] But the houses used as dwellings for single families in the selected areas were all included in the house-to-house canvass.

[1] *Revised Chicago Code, 1931*, sec. 1200: "In Class VI shall be included every tenement and apartment house or building or portion thereof which is used . . . . as a home or residence for two or more families living in separate apartments." Class III includes every building used as a private residence (*ibid.*, sec. 1236).

OLD FRAME TENEMENTS

The contrast between Chicago and New York tenement buildings has already been discussed. A point of considerable importance is the continued existence of frame buildings in many Chicago areas in spite of the fire hazards involved. These old frame houses constantly remind the investigator of Chicago's wonderful youth. After all, our tenement districts are still new and in most of them some of the wooden shacks that have survived from the early prairie days are still being used. In some areas like the so-called Lower North Side many of the frame tenements were built hastily after the Great Fire of 1871,[1a] and the houses of that day, two-story frame buildings hurriedly constructed and poorly built, still remain after the hard usage of more than half a century. They are dilapidated, unpainted, dingy, and, in general, unfit for the kind of homes that twentieth-century standards of decent living demand.

The area in Chicago within which no frame buildings may be erected has been changed, of course, from time to time. In 1881 the fire limits of Chicago were coextensive with the corporate limits of the city. Tenement houses erected in Chicago after 1881 were to have circumscribing walls of brick, stone, or other incombustible material with proper foundations of masonry. If timber were used on which to rest the foundations, such timber had to be sunk below sewer drainage.[2]

By 1905, when the city ordinances were codified, the fire limits had been more definitely outlined. The fire limits no longer coincided with the city limits. Since that time there have always been certain areas which are excepted from the fire limits, and there are also territories known as provisional fire areas within which a person may erect a frame or wooden building, to be used for residence or mercantile purposes, if he receives permission from the commissioner of buildings. Under no circumstances is such a building to be of a height more than 45 feet above the sidewalk.[3] In 1905 seventeen

[1a] See above, pp. 19–20.

[2] *Municipal Code of Chicago, 1881*, secs. 1003, 1250. See also above, chap. ii, "Tenement House Legislation in Chicago," for a statement about the earliest fire limits and the provisions of the Tenement House Ordinance of 1902.

[3] *Revised Municipal Code of Chicago of 1905*, secs. 686–88; and see *Code, 1931*, sec. 1412.

FRAME DWELLINGS ON THE LOWER NORTH AND NORTHWEST SIDES

of the twenty-four areas which were included in this investigation were within the fire limits within which no exceptions could be made. The two Stock Yards districts, Upper Federal, South Chicago, Burnside, South Deering, and Pullman were either outside the fire limits or within the "excepted areas."

The question of building materials is determined by two sets of ordinances: (1) by the building-ordinance provisions regarding certain materials determined by the size and height of the building, and also (2) by the fire-ordinance requirements dealing with the location of the proposed structure. The present law, which states that every new tenement house of more than five stories and basement must be of fireproof construction, had been passed by 1905. All apartment and tenement houses of four or five stories must be of "slow burning" or "fireproof" construction.[4] Materials designated as fireproof are burnt brick, tiles of burnt clay, approved cement concrete, terra cotta, and approved cinder concrete. By "slow-burning" construction is meant buildings in which the joists are protected by incombustible materials. All stairs in buildings required to be of slow-burning construction must be of incombustible material.[5]

In all new frame tenement houses outside the fire limits of the city, each suite of apartments must be separated from the next suite in such buildings by a wall of incombustible material.

The fire limits have been extended many times, but it was in July of 1912 that the district south of the Stock Yards, South Chicago and Pullman, first came within these limits.[6] The district back of the Yards, Upper Federal, Burnside, and South Deering still lie outside the fire limits.

By 1881 provision had been made concerning requirements for fire escapes. All buildings in Chicago, with the exception of those used exclusively for private residences, of four or more stories in height were to be provided with one or more metallic ladders or metallic fire escapes.[7] Under the ordinance of 1905, however, these

[4] *Ibid., 1905*, sec. 390; *1931*, sec. 1424.

[5] *Ibid., 1905*, secs. 501, 556, 558; *1931*, secs. 1428, 2445(O)(P).

[6] National Board of Fire Underwriters Committee on Fire Prevention, *Report of the City of Chicago* (August, 1912), Map I.

[7] *Municipal Code of Chicago, 1881*, sec. 1063.

buildings, which are used exclusively for private residences, must have fire escapes unless they have two flights of stairs leading from the ground floor to the top floor of the building.[8] The law of 1911 required every building which was four or more stories high, except those used exclusively as one-family residences, to have at least one incombustible sliding or stairway fire escape. But if a building of Class III or VI which is not more than four stories in height has two flights of stairs leading from the top floor to the ground, a ladder fire escape may be used in place of a stairway fire escape.[9]

The proportion of frame dwellings is shown in Table 9. In the various districts canvassed, reports were made as to the material in 6,294 buildings. Table 9 shows that 60 per cent were frame and another 9 per cent were brick and frame, for the most part old frame cottages raised up above a brick first story or perhaps a brick front added to an old frame building.

TABLE 9

BUILDING MATERIALS: ALL BUILDINGS, BOTH PRE-WAR AND POST-WAR CANVASS

(Original Canvass Data)

Material	Buildings Canvassed	
	Number	Per Cent Distribution
All buildings	6,294	100.0
Brick and similar material	1,987	31.6
Frame	3,761	59.7
Brick and frame	546	8.7

The percentage of frame buildings varies from district to district, as indicated in Table 10. That a very large proportion of frame buildings can still be found in certain districts is shown in this table. That is, the frame buildings are not evenly distributed in the different sections of the city, but in eleven of the nineteen districts for which percentages were computed, more than 60 per cent of the

[8] *Revised Municipal Code of 1905*, sec. 675; *ibid.*, *1931*, sec. 1246.

[9] *Revised Municipal Code of 1911*, secs. 669, 671; *ibid.*, *1931*, secs. 1246 and 1428.

houses were frame. The proportion of frame buildings varied from 95 per cent in South Chicago and 93 per cent back of the Yards to 33

TABLE 10

NUMBER OF BUILDINGS OF SPECIFIED MATERIAL AND PERCENTAGE OF FRAME CONSTRUCTION; BY DISTRICT

(Original Canvass Data)

District	Buildings of Specified Material				
	Total	Brick and Similar Material	Frame		Brick and Frame
			Number	Percentage of Total*	
Total	6,294	1,987	3,761	59.7	546
West Side:					
The Old Ghetto	65	17	40	*	8
Pilsen	71	46	23	*	2
Lumber Yards	262	43	192	73.3	27
Hull-House	655	243	298	45.5	114
Polk Street	120	67	46	38.3	7
St. Stanislaus	743	341	337	45.4	65
Division Street	424	191	193	45.5	40
Ancona	135	55	65	48.1	15
South Side:					
Downtown	23	22	1	*	....
Near South Side	337	149	153	45.4	35
Back of the Yards	619	45	573	92.6	1
Stock Yards, South	93	16	69	*	8
Southwest	412	204	136	33.0	72
South End:					
Burnside	305	85	220	72.1	....
South Chicago (East Side)	263	13	249	94.7	1
South Deering	119	16	101	84.9	2
Pullman	37	37	....	....	....
North Side:					
Lower North	404	108	263	65.1	33
Upper North	165	30	115	69.7	20
Olivet	223	60	143	64.1	20
Negro districts:					
Dearborn	209	41	144	68.9	24
La Salle	182	90	69	37.9	23
Upper Federal	297	35	249	83.8	13
Walnut	131	33	82	62.6	16

* Percentage not shown where base is less than 100.

per cent in the Lithuanian district of the Southwest Side and 38 per cent in the Polk Street district west of Hull-House, and is to be explained in district after district by the history of the development in each area. In South Chicago, the blocks canvassed were almost at the gates of the steel mills and had been built as small workmen's dwellings as inexpensively as possible when the fire laws did not apply in that region. The situation was much the same back of the Yards. The Lithuanian section, on the other hand, lies a little north of the original Stock Yards tenements, and the houses were built after the fire laws had reached that district. In certain areas, however, although the proportion of frame buildings is not so large, the frame houses remaining are older and are fearfully dilapidated. Nationality, it should be said, clearly has nothing to do with this phase of the housing problem.[9a] The South Chicago tenements, with their high percentage of frame buildings, are largely inhabited by Poles, and so is the St. Stanislaus area, where more than half of the tenements are brick.

In the Hull-House neighborhood nearly one-half—46 per cent—of the houses are frame buildings, with an additional 17 per cent a combination of brick and frame, which means that the old frame cottage has been raised on to a brick foundation and made into a tenement. Only 37 per cent of the houses in the Hull-House area were brick and, in general, the houses in this area, whether brick or frame, have been slowly disintegrating for the period of more than a generation. Many of these houses were apparently intended to accommodate only one family, but they have long since been partitioned off to furnish quarters for three or four. The evil results of this change may easily be traced in the presence of dark and windowless rooms, inadequate plumbing in poor repair, insufficient ventilation, and generally insanitary conditions. When an attempt has been made to modernize some of the old frame dwellings by giving them a new front and an extra story of brick, from the street the hybrid buildings may appear fairly presentable; but from the alley or patch of yard it is easily seen that the improvement is only apparent and that the result is a hodgepodge with the old frame menace remaining.

The Great Fire of 1871 started only a few blocks south of this dis-

[9a] See E. Abbott, for discussion of housing statistics and nationality, in *Social Welfare and Professional Education*, pp. 152–56.

SOME SOUTH CHICAGO TENEMENTS

trict, at the corner of Jefferson and DeKoven streets, and the critical observer must see that a fire hazard still exists. Not only are the houses largely frame, but everywhere there are dilapidated wooden sheds; and patches of yard are littered with frame boxes and other combustible material. Less than 3 per cent of the houses are provided with fire escapes, for the law does not require buildings that are not four stories high to be thus equipped.[10] But it is clear that some of the larger three-story buildings, containing numerous apartments with very unsatisfactory means of exit, need fire escapes quite as much as the four-story tenements. A note, taken from one of the schedule cards, tells the story of many of the larger houses. The three-story building described in this schedule was reported to be a "conspicuous fire trap." There were twenty-four apartments on the second and third floors and no fire escapes on the building. There were only three narrow, winding, old wooden staircases at the rear for an exit to the ground in case of fire. If the doors of the livery barn in the rear should be locked, anyone trying to escape from the building by those rear stairs would be trapped between the building and the stable with no means of reaching the streets.

FRAME TENEMENTS AND DILAPIDATION

Along with frame buildings goes dilapidation. A large proportion of dwellings in bad repair were found in the Hull-House area. Wood, of course, does not survive the ravages of time, weather, and rough usage as do brick and mortar, and wooden houses are not built to endure long periods of neglect. Everywhere are rickety porches, stairs, and sheds, rotting clapboards and shingles, grimy, smoke covered, and dingy from lack of paint. The tenement areas have an air of general neglect—neglect by the landlord, neglect by the tenant, neglect by the city. Complaints are general here, as in many other tenement neighborhoods, about the great number of rats in the old frame buildings.[11] In the Hull-House neighborhood, some families slept with guns under the beds to shoot the rats in the night. In the St. Stanislaus district one woman told our investiga-

[10] *Revised Chicago Code, 1931*, sec. 1644.

[11] A very serious "rat menace" was recently found to exist when plans for demolition of condemned buildings was undertaken as a C.W.A. project and the clearing of other areas for new housing projects on federal funds was being planned. See below, p. 480.

tor that she could not leave her baby outdoors in the baby carriage because she was afraid of the large rats. Food, in more than one house where tin boxes were scarce, was hung from the ceiling by strings to protect it from the rats.

In many of these deteriorated areas the value of real estate is too often held speculatively, and the owners refuse to sell until they can secure exorbitant prices. In the meantime, the property remains unimproved—awaiting skyscraper prices, or the too long-deferred "business invasion," or some turn of fortune's wheel that will substantially increase land values.

There is also the problem of tenement ownership with the landlords, often foreigners themselves struggling hard for a foothold in this country, who are unwilling to expend even a small sum for the repair of a house which may very soon be displaced by a factory.

Our data as to whether buildings were in good repair or in fair or poor condition were only the personal estimates of a large number of different investigators, and their standards as to what constituted a building in bad repair varied, of course, and too much reliance is not placed on the returns on this point. However, it is worth noting that the condition of repair in which the buildings were found on the Near West Side, including what was once the old dilapidated Ghetto, was conspicuously bad and probably worse than in any other section except the Negro houses of the South Side. South Chicago was a close competitor. But everywhere the frame buildings were the worst of all the poor buildings. In the St. Stanislaus district, which is Polish, more than 70 per cent of the houses were reported as being in good repair. On the other hand, in South Chicago the number reported in good repair was only 28 per cent of the whole number, while 23 per cent were positively in bad condition. In contrast, the number of dilapidated buildings was relatively small in the Polish (St. Stanislaus) district, where only 5 per cent were reported in this class.

REAR TENEMENTS

In connection with lot overcrowding, there is in the poorer districts the problem of the rear tenement, for it is largely this crowding of two houses upon a lot which results in the covering of many lots

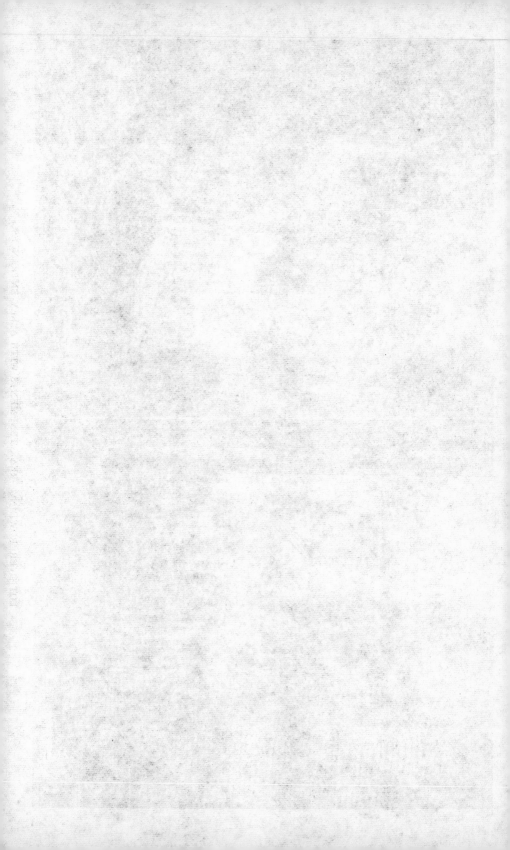

LOT OVERCROWDING—REAR TENEMENTS WITH ALLEY ENTRANCES

over a large percentage of their area. "Rear tenements" might also be called "alley tenements" since except for a very few "middle buildings"[12] they are on the alley, or very close to the alley, and one of their most objectionable features is their proximity to the insanitary conditions often found in the alleys in the tenement neighborhoods. In neighborhoods where the location of the house on the lot means merely that the bulk of the lawn will be in the front or in the rear or on the side, it is unimportant except as a question of landscape gardening. In the tenement districts, however, a house set on the rear of the lot means, invariably, not a garden in front, but one or two other houses on the same premises, and between the two houses a small court or yard, sometimes only the width of a narrow passage. This becomes, even more than the open yard, an abiding place for rubbish, even for scraps of rotting garbage. Water seeps down from the higher level of the street or alley and stands here often in stagnant pools. Rear houses are usually the small old houses—frame buildings, already far past their prime, that have been moved back to the rear lot line to make room on the front of the lot for a new and larger brick building. There are, of course, in the Bohemian and Polish district, as some of our illustrations (pp. 172 and 238) indicate, some very large new brick tenements on the rear as well as the front of the lot, but these were exceptional in other districts.

These rear houses are entered in some cases only through the alley; in other cases they are reached from the front street by the long, narrow passageway between two front tenements, a passageway usually gloomy, unpaved, or with broken paving, and too often cluttered with rubbish. The small yard or open court between the front, middle, and rear buildings, when it is not obstructed by sheds, is also frequently gloomy, and sometimes used as a dump. Rubbish of every sort, even decaying garbage, thrown there for want of any better place, fills this so-called yard, which may also serve as the home of various animals and as the playground for many little children. The problem of the rear house is important in the Chicago tenement districts, and approximately one-fifth of all the houses

[12] The schedules called for "front," "middle," and "rear" buildings, but at the time of the original canvass only forty-nine middle buildings were found, and those were tabulated along with the rear buildings.

visited in our canvass were rear or alley houses. Data showing the number of houses of different types visited in the original canvass and the number in the same area at the time of the recanvass will be found in Table 11.

This table shows that approximately 21 per cent of the houses visited were rear houses at the time of the original canvass. When the recanvass was made, it was found that the total number of buildings in these sixteen districts had fallen from 4,965 to 4,541, but the percentage of rear houses had changed very slightly from 21 per cent of the total to 20 per cent.

TABLE 11*

LOCATION OF BUILDINGS ON LOT (SIXTEEN DISTRICTS)

Location	Original Canvass		Recanvass	
	Number	Per Cent Distribution	Number	Per Cent Distribution
Total.....	4,965	100.0	4,541	100.0
Front........	3,927	79.1	3,651	80.4
Rear.........	1,038	20.9	890	19.6

* Italian downtown district is excluded, one block taken for a park in the Polish district before the recanvass is also excluded, and other districts not canvassed at both periods are omitted.

The number of houses of each type found in the twenty-three districts canvassed is shown in Table 12.[13] The figures in this table are the ones secured by the recanvass and by the new investigations, so that all the data presented here were secured after 1923.

That the percentage of rear houses varies in different sections of the city is shown in Table 12. In the Polish district on the Northwest Side and in the Bohemian district on the Southwest Side, approximately one-third of all the houses were rear houses; and, unfortunately, as has been said, rear tenements in some areas were

[13] The old downtown Italian district is not included since the old tenements have now been destroyed. There was a high percentage of rear tenements in the old district. When we canvassed it we found twenty-three buildings—fifteen front, one middle, seven rear. At a still earlier period this had been an old "segregated district," and the tenements that we found crowded with decent, hard-working Italian families had once been houses of prostitution. See *supra*, pp. 110–12.

often buildings of substantial size. In the Ruthenian district (Division St.), which is northwest, in the Italian district on the Lower North Side, and in the Jewish district on the West Side, the propor-

TABLE 12

NUMBER OF FRONT AND REAR BUILDINGS AND PERCENTAGE OF REAR BUILDINGS; BY DISTRICT

(Recanvass and Post-war Original Canvass Data)

District	Buildings with Specified Location on Lot			
	Total	Front	Rear	
		Number	Number	Percentage of Total*
Total	5,777†	4,767	1,010	17.5
West Side:				
Old Ghetto	20	14	6	*
Pilsen	67	47	20	*
Lumber Yards	237	196	41	17.3
Hull-House	517	429	88	17.0
Polk Street	120	103	17	14.2
St. Stanislaus	666	443	223	33.5
Division Street	410	318	92	22.4
Ancona	135	127	8	6.0
South Side:				
Near South Side	325	279	46	14.2
Back of the Yards	575	469	106	18.4
Stock Yards, South	93	70	23	*
Southwest	411	357	54	13.1
Burnside	305	276	29	9.5
South Chicago (East Side)	264	219	45	17.0
South Deering	119	110	9	7.6
Pullman	37	37	....	*
North Side:				
Lower North	340	255	85	25.0
Upper North	133	106	27	20.3
Olivet	223	194	29	13.0
Negro districts:				
Dearborn	190	175	15	7.9
La Salle	206	191	15	7.3
Upper Federal	297	269	28	9.4
Walnut Street	87	83	4	*

* Percentage not shown where base is less than 100.

† This is number of buildings used for residence; all other buildings excluded.

tion of rear houses varied from 22 to 30 per cent. On the other hand, there are some very deteriorated and ramshackle areas that have not been closely built up. This is particularly true, for example, of the Negro areas canvassed, and neither the West Side colored district (Walnut) nor any one of the three South Side colored districts had 10 per cent of rear houses. Toward the South End, where there were many open spaces, Burnside and the Torrence Avenue district had comparatively few rear houses and the Pullman area that was canvassed had none.

Rear houses are frequently occupied by the very low-income families who are obliged to look for the lowest possible rents—the families on the margin, or those who have already fallen into the dependent class. The housing of some families in one of the districts of a large relief society shows how antisocial the condition of the home is likely to be. A study of the housing of dependent families made by a graduate-student investigator in the Lower North district shows many rear buildings still being used as dwellings.[14] Some of these were three and others four stories high, and still others were one-family cottages, very old and poorly built frame dwellings often in a disreputable state of repair. The rear dwellings were usually in violation of the requirements of the present building code in regard to space between buildings—a provision[15] that did not exist, of course, when, for example, one family was found living on the fourth floor of a rear tenement which was reached by means of a narrow board-walk passageway between two four-story tenements, and by the wooden outside stairway of either the front or the rear building.

[14] See Eleanor D. Goltz, "The Housing of Dependent Families in Chicago," chap. xiii, p. 401.

[15] This provision of the building code is as follows: "At the rear of every lot containing a tenement house, there shall be a yard open and unobstructed from the earth to the sky, except by fire escapes not more than four feet wide, constructed and erected according to law, unless the rear of such lot abuts upon a public alley at least ten feet wide, in which case the rear line of such building shall be not less than 16 feet from the opposite side of such alley; every part of such yard shall be directly accessible from every other part thereof; such yard shall have an area of at least eight per centum of the superficial area of the lot on corner lots, except as otherwise provided in this section; and on other lots, such yards shall have an area of at least ten per centum of the superficial area of the lot. Every such yard shall be increased one per centum of the superficial area of the lot for every story above three stories in height of the tenement house situated thereon" (*Revised Chicago Code, 1931*, chap. xxv, art. vi, sec. 1415).

A wooden platform about five feet in width connected the two stairways at each floor, making the outlook for the apartments in the rear building a maze of grimy stairs rising from the deep shadows of the two relatively tall buildings.

In spite of the fact that the United Charities of Chicago did not encourage residence in rear buildings, approximately 10 per cent of the households visited in the Lower North district were in dwellings set between front and rear buildings on the lot. Two of these were one-family houses of a single floor.

One of them had four rooms, freshly painted over crumbling, partially patched plaster. This little old frame house with its dirty, dark exterior rented for sixteen dollars a month to a colored family of four. The home was as miserable within as it was without. There was a very old sink, an old-fashioned long-hopper toilet with its boxlike covering, and there was only a flickering lamplight, since the electricity had been turned off.

Another cottage had five rooms but was a dingy, sagging, and very cold building because of its loose construction. But it still brought twenty dollars a month to the landlord. A colored family was living here with nine people, five of them children under twelve. Dirty, cracking plaster, uneven slivering floors, cardboard-mended windows, an outworn iron sink, an evil-smelling toilet set in a dark closet off the kitchen which was "better now than it is in summer when it backs up on us," are a few details of the place. Here a sick father and a convalescent mother lived, using three of their rooms for bedrooms with two beds in two of the rooms. The building was located at two intersecting alleys.

Another rear building in this district that had two stories and was intended for two families was too dilapidated to attract any other tenants than the one dependent Negro family unable to pay more than the thirteen-dollars-a-month rent. This also was weather-beaten and dingy, crowded close to the building in front, and with the same story of rickety steps, doors which had long ceased to fit their casings, oil lamps, broken windows, and fallen plaster.

Still another shaky rear dwelling of four rooms was bright and sunny in spite of its dilapidation. The widow, a native-born American, who lived here with her five children paid for the repairing herself and by means of paint and calcimine had managed to make the place cheerful. The house was cold and the rooms very small, but there were windows and sunlight and air, and the rent was only fifteen dollars. The relief society had offered to help this woman find a new place, she said, but anywhere else might be darker. She led the way to the toilet, down her steep little outside stairway, across the littered court, through a damp entry into the first floor of the front building. Here one long-hopper toilet served five families in both front and rear buildings.

Other rear dwellings were three-story buildings, one of them for six families. One was backed up to the elevated tracks, and the family on the second floor had the elevated outside their windows.

A Mexican family with ten children (only two of them over twelve) lived in a five-room alley house, dark and sunless. A relative in misfortune came with his wife and two children to join the already illegally overcrowded quarters.

Sometimes the alley house had once been a stable or garage. A family reported by a school nurse as sick and in need of food and fuel was found by a social worker in 1928 living in a house that had been a garage. There were a loose board floor over the ground, an interior lining of beaver board, and a single partition across what had been the one-room garage. On a winter day, cold drafts came from both the floor and the unplastered walls. Although a fire burned briskly in the large heater, swirling drafts from all directions, and especially from the floor, made the rooms very cold. A third room just off the main garage section was too cold to use. This was separated from the other rooms by a cloth hung over the opening to close off as well as possible one room from the next. The same device was used as a door between the other two rooms in which the family lived. The toilet was in a small room or closet but not usable because the water was frozen. The father said they had been heating water to flush it. In this room the coal, sent that morning by the Cook County Bureau of Public Welfare, was stored. The sick man was lying in the one full-sized bed where the mother and some of the children slept at night. A cradle, constructed of a wooden box mounted on an old rocker, and a cot were the other beds.

An alley house recently reported to us was the home of a Mexican family. It was an uncomfortable home in many ways. Only one window in the house opened, and this window and the door were the only means of ventilation. The rooms were just $8\frac{1}{4}$ feet high. Flies and vermin were breeding in the garbage piles, making it very insanitary and unhealthful for the children who played in this alley. The house was bordered on the side and the back by a paved alley, 15 feet in width. The people from the surrounding tenements threw their garbage and tin cans in heaps along the alley, which made it very foul smelling and filthy. This garbage was hauled away once every two or three weeks, but just opposite the door to this house the garbage was piled up approximately 3 feet in height before it was cleared away. The Mexican family could not have their door open to get air in the house because the refuse blew in.

There are many objections to the rear tenement as a home. The outlook in the front is toward the unsightly rear porch and "back yard" of the front tenement. The outlook on the other side is over the alley toward the old stable and sheds of the opposite house. The neglected condition of the Chicago alleys makes this a serious situation. Dirt and dust or mud and filth are at the doorstep and under the windows in every season of the year. This is serious for small houses already shut out from adequate light and air.

TENEMENT ALLEYS

The alley is a characteristic feature of the Chicago tenement districts and, in fact, of the whole city. The "gridiron plan" calls for the bisecting of each block lengthwise by this narrow service street.[16] In the tenement districts the streets themselves are not kept even reasonably clean, and the alleys are not cleaned at all. Many of them were apparently paved at one time, but the paving is so buried under

[16] A former chief of the Chicago Sanitary Bureau, Mr. Charles B. Ball, once defined an alley as "a minor public thoroughfare not exceeding twenty feet in width, extending through a block in order to afford access of light and ventilation to the rear of the premises which abut upon it, as well as a suitable location for public service mains" (see Charles B. Ball, "The Alley Problem," *Housing Problems in America* [Fourth Annual Conference of the National Housing Association, 1915]). Mr. Ball thought that, although Chicago alleys were "at present a marked nuisance for lack of proper maintenance," they should be paved, lighted, and properly policed, and if properly cared for, they would be a beneficial feature in the problem of congestion. However, see the criticisms in the discussion following Mr. Ball's paper (*ibid.*, p. 141).

the dirt and refuse of years that there are no evidences of paving visible. In recent years the gradual disappearance of the horse has led to some improvement in the state of the alley streets. The manure heaps, which were such a menace not only to comfort but to health at the time of our first canvass, are much less frequent, though they still constitute a nuisance in some areas, especially in the neighborhoods where peddlers live. But everywhere the heaps of garbage, rubbish, and ashes remain. The whole question of the regularity of garbage collecting is involved here.[17]

The cleaning-up of the alleys is one of the cheapest and most practicable reforms possible in the tenement areas. Children only too frequently choose the alleys for playgrounds, which, after all, are relatively empty in contrast to the streets crowded in these districts with trucks and other vehicles. But the alleys could so easily be cleaned and kept clean. The garbage, and other forms of rubbish, could be removed. Paving could be kept clean as in well-to-do neighborhoods, and the present conditions of mud and filth could be done away with at a not prohibitive cost.

CHICAGO'S ONE- AND TWO-STORY TENEMENTS

Again, and this time in more favorable contrast with New York, the tenements in Chicago are for the most part low and small. There are relatively few tenements in Chicago that are more than three stories high. The results of the house-to-house canvass of 5,777 houses in different areas are shown in Table 13.

[17] *Revised Chicago Code, 1931*, secs. 4012, 4015, 4018, 4021, 4024. Section 4018 specifies that "garbage" and "miscellaneous waste" as defined in sec. 4012 shall be removed at such times and in such manner as the commissioner of public works may direct. However, it is the duty of the head of every household to place vessels containing "garbage" or "miscellaneous waste" upon the edge of the sidewalk adjoining his premises, or on the rear of the lot of his premises, in order that such garbage may be collected. Ashes are to be removed at the expense of the person, firm, or corporation occupying, operating, or controlling any building or portion thereof, at such times and in such manner as the commissioner of public works may direct. It is the duty of every person who has control of any place where horses, mules, cattle, or swine are kept or fed to provide a receptacle for manure and to remove from the premises at his own expense the contents of this receptacle at least once every seventy-two hours. It is unlawful to place garbage, waste, or vessels containing such in alleys. It is also the duty of the head of each household to maintain in good order and repair these vessels and receptacles for garbage, ashes, miscellaneous waste, or manure.

CHICAGO COTTAGES AND SMALL TENEMENTS

The typical Chicago two-story residence appears in this table which shows that only 2 per cent of the tenements in these districts were more than three stories high and only 16 per cent were even three-story buildings. Most of the buildings (58.9 per cent) were two-story houses with a very considerable percentage (22.8) only one-story houses. That is, approximately four-fifths of all the buildings in these areas were only one or two stories high. But in this, as in other respects, conditions varied, of course, in different sections of the city. Table 14 shows the percentage of buildings of the cottage type in each district and the percentage of higher buildings.

TABLE 13

BUILDINGS HAVING SPECIFIED NUMBER OF STORIES; ALL DISTRICTS

(Recanvass and Post-war Original Canvass Data)

Number of Stories	Number of Buildings	Per Cent Distribution
Total	5,777	100.0
One ("cottage type")	1,319*	22.8
Two	3,404†	58.9
Three	930‡	16.1
Four or more	124§	2.2

* Eighteen of these buildings are one-story and basement or cellar buildings because of the regrading of the street, and thirty-five are "one story and attic."

† Twelve of these buildings are "two stories and attic."

‡ Four of these buildings are "three stories and attic."

§ Only one building has five stories.

The two-story house was the predominant type in every district visited, except Burnside, where 57 per cent of the houses are of the cottage type, and the Lithuanian district in which one- and two-story houses are about equal in number and together constitute approximately 85 per cent of the total number. In the so-called "Bush" and "East Side" sections of South Chicago approximately one-third of the buildings were not tenements but were of the one-story cottage type. In the Slovak district on the West Side and in the Stock Yards district on the South Side approximately one-fifth of the dwellings were one-story cottages. In the St. Stanislaus district on the Northwest Side, crowded as it is, one-fifth of the houses were

TABLE 14

NUMBER AND PERCENTAGE OF TENEMENTS OF SPECIFIED NUMBER OF STORIES; BY DISTRICT

(Recanvass and Post-war Original Canvass Data)

District	Houses of Specified Number of Stories						
	Number				Percentage of Total*		
	All Houses	One Story	Two Stories	Three or More Stories	One Story	Two Stories	Three or More Stories
Total	5,777	1,319†	3,404‡	1,054§	22.8	58.9	18.3
West Side:							
The Old Ghetto	20	1	12	7	....	....	....
Pilsen	67	10	42	15	....	....	....
Lumber Yards	237	50	174	13	21.1	73.4	5.5
Hull-House	517	41	297	179	7.9	57.5	34.6
Polk Street	120	13	73	34	10.8	60.8	28.4
St. Stanislaus	666	136	388	142	20.4	58.3	21.3
Division Street	410	38	222	150	9.3	54.1	36.6
Ancona	135	10	71	54	7.4	52.6	40.0
South Side:							
Near South Side	325	65	194	66	20.0	59.7	20.3
Back of the Yards	575	141	392	42	24.5	68.2	7.3
Stock Yards, South	93	27	61	5	....	....	....
Southwest	411	176	174	61	42.8	42.4	14.8
South End:							
Burnside	305	174	126	5	57.1	41.3	1.6
South Chicago (East Side)	264	87	153	24	33.0	57.9	9.1
South Deering	119	44	73	2	37.0	61.3	1.7
Pullman	37	....	31	6	....	....	....
North Side:							
Lower North	340	24	187	129‖	7.1	55.0	37.9
Upper North	133	32	89	12	24.1	66.9	9.0
Olivet	223	30	154	39	13.5	69.1	17.4
Negro districts:							
Dearborn	190	41	120	29	21.6	63.2	15.2
La Salle	206	64	124	18	31.1	60.2	8.7
Upper Federal	297	98	190	9	33.0	64.0	3.0
Walnut Street	87	17	57	13	....	....	....

* Percentage not shown where base is less than 100

† Eighteen of these are one-story basement or cellar buildings because of regrading the streets; thirty-five are one-story and attic buildings.

‡ Twelve are two-story and attic buildings.

§ Four are three-story and attic buildings.

‖ Includes one building of five stories.

cottages. In twenty-one of the twenty-three original districts 50 per cent, or more than 50 per cent of all the houses were two stories. In Upper North, a mixed German, Magyar, and Italian district on the North Side, 91 per cent of the houses were one- or two-story dwellings. In South Chicago only 9 per cent of the buildings were three stories, and no building was more than three stories. In the two Stock Yards districts there were no tenements more than three stories high, and in one district 7 per cent and in another only 5 per cent of the buildings were as high as three stories. In the Slovak district only 6 per cent of the houses were three stories high, and there were no higher tenements in the district. The highest percentages of houses more than three stories high were found in the Bohemian district on the West Side (10 per cent), the Italian district on the Lower North Side (10 per cent), Ancona, a Polish district to the northwest (9 per cent), and the Ruthenian district on the Northwest Side (7 per cent). But everywhere from Halsted Street to South Chicago these one and two-story houses, a large proportion of tnem frame buildings, are in striking contrast to the high brick tenements of New York.

The Chicago tenements are likewise typically one, two, or three-family dwellings, as Tables 15 and 16 indicate. More than half (58 per cent) of the buildings used for dwellings in these districts contained apartments for only one or two families; and approximately three-fourths of all the buildings contained less than four apartments. There were four apartments in 11 per cent of the buildings; there were five or six apartments in another 11 per cent. Only 3.4 per cent contained seven or more apartments. Only three-tenths of 1 per cent contained fifteen or more. There were of course differences in the different districts, and these are shown in Table 16.

The numbers given in Table 16 show that the proportion of one-family houses varied from 67.5 per cent in Burnside to 5.9 per cent in the crowded district on the Northwest Side which is called "Ancona." There are in most of the districts a few very large apartment buildings. Usually these are on business streets—brick buildings with stores on the first floor and apartments massed solidly above. Such a building is the famous triangular building at the junction of Blue Island Avenue with Halsted and Harrison streets, where for more than a quarter of a century the marble elegance of the Greek bank occupied the first floor and four stories of Greek families and lodging groups lived above.

There are a few other large tenements in the Hull-House neighborhood. In sixteen blocks canvassed in this district there were six buildings each of which had more than ten apartments. These six buildings contained twelve, fifteen, twenty, twenty-five, thirty, and

TABLE 15

NUMBER OF APARTMENTS IN BUILDING USED FOR RESIDENCE IN ALL DISTRICTS

(Recanvass and Post-war Original Canvass Data)

Number of Apartments in Building	Buildings Used for Residence	
	Number	Per Cent Distribution
All buildings	5,777	100.0
One	1,462	25.3
Two	1,910	33.1
Three	932	16.1
Four	657	11.4
Five	270	4.7
Six	349	6.0
Seven	60	1.0
Eight	57	1.0
Nine	28	0.5
Ten or more	52	0.9

* A few of these tenements were very large. In all, twelve were found with seventeen, or more than seventeen, apartments.

forty-two apartments, respectively. But these were exceptional cases, and in the district as a whole only 4 per cent of the buildings contained seven or more apartments. There were three buildings in the La Salle district with twenty, thirty-five, and thirty-six apartments and four buildings in Pullman with twenty-three, thirty-four, thirty-six, and forty-eight apartments. But these, too, were exceptional.

In the Pilsen district on the Southwest Side, the average brick tenement is somewhat larger than in other sections. Here approximately one-half of the buildings had five or more apartments in comparison with 14 per cent for all the districts, and one-tenth had seven or more in comparison with 3.4 per cent for all districts.

TABLE 16

NUMBER OF BUILDINGS HAVING SPECIFIED NUMBER OF APARTMENTS; BY DISTRICT

(Recanvass and Post-war Original Canvass Data)

District	Number of Buildings Having Specified Number of Apartments										
	Total	1	2	3	4	5	6	7	8	9–11	12 or More
Total	5,777	1,462	1,910	932	657	270	349	60	57	47	33
West Side:											
The Old Ghetto	20	6	4	5	2	....	1	2	....	....	....
Pilsen	67	7	14	9	4	10	16	....	2	4	1
Lumber Yards	237	41	69	52	49	13	12	1	....	....	....
Hull-House	517	140	184	84	45	20	21	8	6	3	6
Polk Street	120	17	41	24	21	6	3	2	4	1	1
St. Stanislaus	666	100	175	83	83	55	127	13	10	15	5
Division Street	410	50	124	71	73	24	44	12	5	4	3
Ancona	135	8	43	33	13	11	15	3	5	3	1
South Side:											
Near South Side	325	70	96	53	51	28	24	....	2	1	....
Back of the Yards	575	152	144	113	110	32	14	6	1	2	1
Stock Yards, South	93	15	33	23	8	5	6	2	....	1	....
Southwest	411	129	122	74	46	17	17	2	2	1	1
South End:											
Burnside	305	206	92	5	2	....	....	....	....	....	....
South Chicago	264	97	85	42	31	3	5	....	1	....	....
South Deering	119	64	29	20	6	....	....	....	....	....	....
Pullman	37	2	17	4	8	....	....	....	....	....	6
North Side:											
Lower North	340	46	91	84	42	25	20	6	13	10	3
Upper North	133	34	57	19	9	6	6	1	1	....	....
Olivet	223	38	118	43	10	5	6	1	1	1	....
Negro districts:											
Dearborn Street	190	44	98	25	11	1	7	....	3	....	1
La Salle Street	206	54	100	25	13	5	3	1	1	1	3
Upper Federal Street	297	113	137	24	18	3	2	....	....	....	....
Walnut Street	87	29	37	17	2	1	....	....	....	....	1

In the South End districts, especially in Burnside and South Chicago, there seem to be a large proportion of one-family houses. Conditions in the Burnside triangle, which is an isolated district, may of course be exceptional, but there are many remote and isolated areas within the city limits that are not unlike Burnside. In many of the one-family houses, however, particularly in South Chicago, a large number of lodgers were found. There may be a larger number of families with lodgers occupying the single-family houses than in a larger tenement. Unfortunately, as has already been pointed out, these houses are technically classed as "private dwellings" and are governed only by the provisions of the building code relating to Class III houses instead of by the stricter regulations of the sections of the code dealing with Class VI or tenement houses. At the risk of repetition it must be emphasized that insanitary housing conditions, however, are just as bad for the single family in a so-called private dwelling as for two or more families in a house that is called a tenement, although the law may not be technically violated in the former case. Children who sleep in rooms crowded with lodgers or who are forced to use unfit toilet accommodations suffer, and should be protected by the standard which the community has set, whether the house is occupied by one, or more than one, family group.

CHAPTER VI

TENEMENT DWELLERS WITHOUT THE CONVENIENCES OF MODERN LIFE

Tenement Homes without Modern Conveniences; The Provision of Sinks; Objectionable Toilet Facilities; Basement, Hall, and Outside Toilets; Present Sanitary Conveniences Very Inadequate; Toilets under Sidewalks; Improvements in Newer Districts; Apartment Toilets; Hardships of Tenement Life.

SO ACCUSTOMED have we grown to modern sanitary conveniences that it is difficult to picture the homes of our grandfathers, when the water supply came from yard pumps in the case of the well-to-do or from longer distances in the case of the poor, when toilet accommodations were outside of the house, usually old-fashioned privy vaults, and when modern bath-tub arrangements were unknown. There is also the recollection of kerosene lamps, or even more recent memories of flickering and often leaking gas jets in place of electricity. In studying the modern housing problem, the question is at once raised whether modern municipalities have been successful in any attempt to require the landlords of families in the low wage-earning group to provide even the most important of these generally accepted conveniences of modern life. The proportion of the income of the unskilled city workman that goes for rent has increased enormously but his household comforts have not increased in the same measure. Are these modern conveniences necessities, or are they luxuries not to be expected by the poor? The answer depends, perhaps, upon how far they may be considered necessary for public health.

TENEMENT HOMES WITHOUT MODERN CONVENIENCES

These sanitary conveniences are, of course, such household necessities as a sink with running water, modern toilet facilities in every apartment, a bath tub, modern electric lighting, and a gas stove in the kitchen. There will probably be general agreement that the first two conveniences are necessities and that the bath tub and central heating are comforts urgently needed and not luxuries. Central heating by means of a modern furnace is another convenience that is accepted as necessary by all those above the poverty line; but the comfort of central heat is still not provided for families living below or on the margin. These families still live in the old tenements, many of them built before or soon after the Great Fire of 1871, and in the winter they huddle around the coal stoves with their children like the families of an earlier generation.

Dr. Leila Houghteling's very interesting study of the standards of living of unskilled laborers in Chicago contains some useful data for our purposes.[1] For example, with regard to the problem of the toilet, in 12 per cent of the 467 apartments investigated there were no decent toilet accommodations. The toilets were in the yard or under the porch or under the sidewalks instead of in the house. Worse than being merely outside of the house, many of these, as well as the inside toilets, were promiscuous and were not for the use of a single family. All told, approximately one-fourth of the families visited were using toilet accommodations which they shared with other families.

In the twenty cities visited by the cost-of-living investigators of the Bureau of Labor Statistics in 1918, nearly one-fifth of the families living in flats and nearly two-fifths of those in houses were still using outside toilets.[2]

With regard to bathrooms, Dr. Houghteling quoted the Chicago budget issued by the Council of Social Agencies, which suggests that a house with a bathroom should be found for every dependent family whenever possible.[3] But nearly half of the families visited by the investigators of the Bureau of Labor in 1918–19 were without baths. Dr. Houghteling found that 264, or 58 per cent of the 459 families for whom she had reports on this point, were without bathrooms. And these were not dependent families. She also found that among the 467 families visited by her investigators 71 per cent were using electricity. Most of the other families were using gas and 6 per cent fell back on old kerosene lamps.

[1] *The Income and Standard of Living of Unskilled Laborers in Chicago* (University of Chicago Press, 1927), pp. 109 ff.

[2] "Minimum Quantity Budget Necessary To Maintain a Worker's Family of Five in Health and Decency," *Monthly Labor Review*, June, 1920, p. 12.

[3] *Op. cit.*, p. 111.

A distinguished gentleman from New York, speaking a few years ago at a housing conference, recalled the conditions of his youth both in his New York home and in the residence halls of Yale University when he was a student. Well-to-do people at that time, he pointed out, were without the conveniences that people of small means now enjoy. It is quite true that the poor—even the very poor—are provided with many means of protecting and improving the health and comfort of their families which were unknown a half-century ago. Indoor toilets flushed with running water are considered as necessary for public health today as vaccination or the use of antitoxin. The question of wealth or poverty should not determine their availability. But in large sections of our metropolitan areas, many families still live under the old primitive conditions.

In this chapter, data are presented showing the conditions in Chicago tenements as we found them at the beginning and end of the last quarter of a century. In the letter of the law, Chicago has accepted the theory that the poor must be enabled to enjoy the benefits of modern sanitation; and in the tenement-house code very definite provisions have been made with regard to the sanitary accommodations of the tenement. Regulations regarding toilet facilities, sinks, and water-taps are carefully specified. But these provisions for the most part apply only to the tenements built since 1902. The primitive sanitary arrangements that still exist in most of the neighborhoods studied are, in large part, survivals of the period when modern plumbing was unknown. Changes in the tenement-house code that require the installation of adequate sanitary arrangements in old houses are avoided because of the heavy expense in proportion to the value of these dilapidated old buildings.

THE PROVISION OF SINKS

Looking first at the question of the sink with running water, the building code provides that in every tenement house built since 1910 every apartment shall have at least one kitchen sink with running water; and that in all other tenement houses there shall be a sink with running water easily accessible to every apartment that does not contain one.[4] This is a relatively easy provision to carry out, and canvassing returns indicated that it is, on the whole, very

[4] *Revised Chicago Code, 1931*, sec. 1444.

successfully in operation. The sink is much less expensive to instal than the modern toilet and much easier to keep in repair. Moreover, the need for a sink is more exigent than for the bath tub; and the sink does not require "room space" like the bath tub or the toilet. With the exception of certain houses in Pullman, only in a few rare cases were any hall sinks found, and in only one case a sink without running water. In one very exceptional case in a Ukrainian household in Burnside, a family was found without either sink, bath tub, or toilet, although they were hoping the landlord was going to "put in plumbing" before winter. In the meantime, they were using a neighbor's plumbing across the street.

Some cases were found of families temporarily without the sink because of frozen plumbing or repairs. Some of these conditions, especially when the landlord refuses to make prompt repairs, are extremely hard on the family. In some cases, for example, all water for use in second- and third-story flats was being carried up from the first floor of an adjoining house. The misery caused by such situations is very great indeed and should not be minimized. Particularly it is important to emphasize the needless hardship caused to large numbers of tenement families by delays in very necessary plumbing repairs in the winter. The attitude of some landlords in what promises to be a prolonged "cold spell" seems to be that of one West Side tenement owner who said, "It will only freeze again, so what's the use of fixing it?" In the so-called "block houses" of Pullman there is a very objectionable system of plumbing. Here, although each apartment has a separate toilet, it is not located within the apartment. These houses are built with two sets of apartments on each side of a central hall, usually with three apartments on each floor on each side. All three toilets and the only sink on each floor are grouped together at the end of the public entrance hall. There is, therefore, one sink for every three families, and this is in the space partitioned off in the hall in which the toilets are found.

Only one of the block houses visited by our investigator had been modernized. In this house, sinks have been installed in each of the twelve apartments and the house was the only one in the block with electricity. In these block houses, with the one exception noted, all the water for cooking, for scrubbing and cleaning, and for the family washing was being carried from the hall sink. And bathing, either for the children or for the tired worker from the shops, is obviously very difficult. On the whole, Pullman showed an extraordinary absence of modern household necessities and the people often seemed to be living under conditions of fifty years ago.

The problem of the sink used in common by all the tenants in the old houses now given over to the renting of furnished rooms was discussed in the report of one of our early investigations. The only requirement of the law for the old houses, built before 1901 and used as boarding-houses or lodging-houses, was that plumbing accommodations should be "adequate." Consequently, it was usual to find all of the tenants in a single house dependent upon a single sink for the water used for cooking, washing, and all other household purposes. As was to be expected, the condition of these sinks was in general bad. When there is only one sink for several families, someone is quite sure to use it, not only for dishwater but for general refuse. The effect on the standards of cleanliness provided by this absence of all facilities for decent living needs no comment.

OBJECTIONABLE TOILET FACILITIES

Going on to the question next in importance—the provision of toilet facilities—the situation is very much less satisfactory. It is important, however, that we look at the situation not only as it is but with regard to the very marked improvements in this respect that have been made since the first of these studies was undertaken.

In the first canvass a large number of vaults were found to be still in use in spite of the provisions of the tenement-house law. An ordinance passed in 1894[5] had made it illegal for privy vaults to be maintained on premises where sewer connections were possible, but during our first canvass, in 6 out of the 16 districts, 78 of the old insanitary vaults were found. The largest numbers were found back

[5] *Proceedings of the City Council, Chicago, for 1894–95*, p. 752 (June 18, 1894). And see *Report of the City Homes Association on Tenement Conditions in Chicago* (1901), p. 104, and the later health ordinance (Tolman, *Municipal Code, 1905*, sec. 1289): "It shall be unlawful for any person or corporation to maintain any privy vault or suffer the same to be and remain upon any premises abutting upon or adjoining any street, alley, court or public place, in which is located any public sewer. Any person or corporation violating the provisions of this section shall be fined not less than ten or more than two hundred dollars for each offense."

of the Yards and in South Chicago; but there were others in the Polish district on the Northwest Side, the Italian district on the Lower North Side, the Hull-House district, and the Negro district on the South Side. When the first district back of the Yards was canvassed, 44 vaults were found in the 13 blocks canvassed. The evil was greater than the number indicates, for 46 families and 248 persons were using these miserable toilet accommodations, which were so offensive and insanitary that they had been outlawed fifteen years before. At the time of our recanvass, however, every one of the 44 vaults had been removed.

Similar improvements have occurred in other sections of the city. For example, in South Chicago at the time of the pre-war canvass, 26 vaults were found in 2 of the 7 blocks canvassed. Although 15 of the vaults were said to be no longer in use, they had not been removed and almost uniformly remained as very offensive nuisances. In many cases no adequate substitute for them had been provided. For example, on one tenement lot 2 of these unused vaults were still standing open in a most shocking condition. There were 4 families with 14 children under twelve years of age and 5 lodgers living in this house, and the 2 filthy hall closets that were supposed to take the place of the old vaults were sources of demoralization. In another case where there was a saloon on the front of the lot there were 4 offensive vaults on the premises which, although they were in such condition that they could not be used, still constituted a public nuisance. A Hungarian saloonkeeper with his wife and 3 children lived on the first floor of a small tenement on the rear of the lot. There was neither cellar nor basement but in a low space under the house 30 chickens and 20 ducks were kept. The family on the floor above had 2 children and 8 lodgers. The only other sanitary accommodation, except for 4 noxious vaults, was a single hall closet, serving not only the family and the lodgers but also the patrons of the saloon.

The recent recanvass showed a wonderfully improved condition in South Chicago with every one of the old vaults removed. Not only were the old vaults gone, but the saloon and saloonkeeper, chickens, and ducks had all vanished. Progress had finally been made even if it had been made slowly.

The situation was very bad at the time of our first canvass in spite of the fact that marked progress was reported to have been made in removing the vault nuisance in the few years preceding. In 1901, at the time when the City Homes Association investigation was made, the South Chicago district was described as an area where "there is no sewerage, unless that name is given to a system of gutters by which a certain amount of sewerage is carried off. There is usually an odor from the foul waste matter which accumulates in these places. The land is undrained and in some cases the water stands for months under the houses and upon vacant lots. In certain places there was a green scum upon the water, which showed that it had been standing stagnant for some time. There are no water-closets and the outlawed privy vault is in general use. The yards, streets, and alleys are indiscriminately used for the disposal of all sorts of garbage and rubbish. Almost no garbage boxes were found. None of the streets are paved, and the whole district is filthy beyond description. The atmosphere of the neighborhood is clouded with smoke, and the district is extremely dreary, ugly, and unhealthful."[6]

The City Homes investigators also found the insanitary vault in very general use on the West Side in 1901 in spite of the fact that the privy had then been outlawed for seven years. The investigator reported, for example, that there were 1,581 privies in the 44 blocks east of Halsted Street near Hull-House, and these were used by 10,686 persons in 2,308 separate families; that is, in 1901, 45 per cent of all the families in this neighborhood were dependent upon these archaic, illegal, and dangerous toilet accommodations. The committee in 1901 also estimated that 20 per cent of all the families in the Polish district and 52 per cent of those in the Bohemian district were dependent on similar provisions.[7]

When our first canvass of these districts was made nearly a decade later, most of these offensive places had been removed. In the Polish district where, in 1901, it had been estimated that 20 per cent of the families were using these offensive vaults, only 7 were found in our pre-war canvass. In the Bohemian district a similar improvement had taken place, and there had been a drastic clearance all through the neighborhood. In 1901, the *City Homes Report* showed 71 out-

[6] See Hunter, *Tenement Conditions in Chicago*, p. 182.

[7] *Ibid.*, p. 104.

lawed vaults in a single Jewish block where not one was found in our first canvass.

One of the pioneer Hull-House neighborhood studies had dealt with the repeated cases of typhoid found in the nearby tenement district where vaults were still common and, with the ever present flies, were a serious menace to the health of the neighborhood. The activity of the Hull-House residents may have been responsible, in part at least, for the improvement in this area.

Although our later recanvass showed that four of the old vaults were still in existence, these cases were so exceptional that it is fair to say that this wretched type of toilet accommodation has finally been eliminated in all places in the city where sewer connections are possible.

BASEMENT, HALL, AND OUTSIDE TOILETS

In spite of this great improvement, sanitary provisions in the tenement districts are still far from satisfactory. In many places the old vaults have been replaced by yard closets located under the sidewalk, or near the alley, or in some other conspicuous place.

The modern standard for toilet accommodation set by the present code for new tenements requires private toilet facilities for each apartment, except in the case of very small apartments containing only one or two rooms.[8] Unfortunately, the same standard is not yet set for old houses, but considerations of decency require that in all houses, old as well as new, each family should have private toilet facilities within its own house. The number of yard, basement, and hall water closets which we found in sixteen of the districts first investigated and again canvassed in the post-war period showed

[8] *Revised Chicago Code, 1931*, sec. 1443, which provided that in every new tenement house there shall be a separate water-closet in a separate compartment within each apartment, accessible to each apartment, without passing through any other apartment, provided that where there are apartments, consisting of only one or two rooms, there shall be at least one water-closet for every two apartments. Every water-closet compartment in every new tenement house shall have a window opening upon a street, alley, yard, court, or vent shaft, and every water-closet compartment in every existing tenement house shall be ventilated by such a window, or else by a proper ventilating pipe running through the roof. Every water-closet compartment in every tenement house shall be provided with proper means of artificially lighting the same. If fixtures for gas or electricity are not provided in any such compartment, then the door thereof shall have ground glass or wire glass panels or transoms .

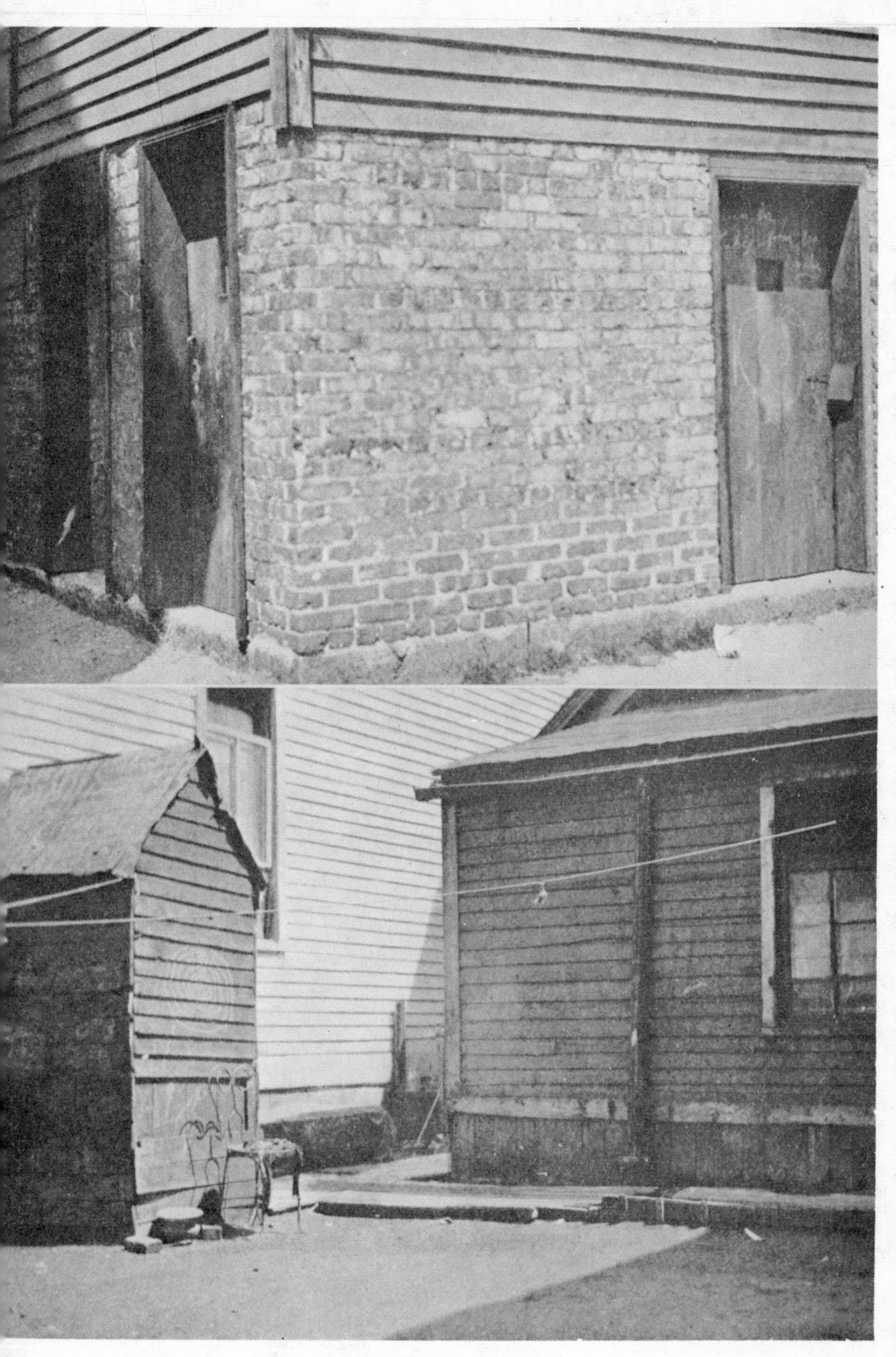

YARD AND BASEMENT TOILETS

how large an evil we still have in these public toilet facilities. That is, even the most recent canvass showed that 31 per cent of all the apartments visited had no toilet accommodations within the apartment as required by the tenement-house law of 1902. That is, more than twenty-five years after the law was passed requiring a private toilet within every apartment, nearly every third apartment was lacking the required convenience.

TABLE 17

TENEMENT TOILET ACCOMMODATIONS

(Data for Sixteen Districts)

Type of Accommodation*	Number of Toilets of Specified Type			
	Original Canvass		Recanvass	
	Number	Per Cent Distribution	Number	Per Cent Distribution†
Total	10,611	100.0	9,637	100.0
Yard	3,000	28.2	784	8.2
Vault	78	0.7	4	‡
Under sidewalk	108	1.0	242	2.5
Basement or cellar	959	9.0§	357	3.7‖
Hall	1,780	17.0§	1,618	16.8‖
Apartment	4,607	43.4§	6,563	68.1‖
Other	79	0.7	69	0.7

* Toilets on the porch and under the porch are included with "yard toilets"; those in a store are included with "other."

† The percentages in this table are based on the number reported.

‡ Less than one-tenth of 1 per cent.

§ All inside toilets, 69.4 per cent.

‖ All inside toilets, 88.5 per cent.

It is impossible to maintain standards of decency in a modern urban community without such sanitary provisions. The outside toilets freeze in winter and become filthy and indescribably offensive at all times. They are usually open, so that the family lacks the privacy necessary for decent living. They cannot be kept clean without great difficulty.

The type of toilet accommodations available in the sixteen districts originally canvassed and the situation in the same districts during the recent recanvass is shown in Table 17.

This summary table for sixteen of the districts first canvassed before 1920 and more recently recanvassed shows clearly that very considerable progress has been made in improving sanitary conditions in the homes of the poor. The miserable accommodations such as vaults, yard, and basement toilets had decreased from 37.9 to 11.9 per cent. The apartment toilet, which is the standard required for all houses built since 1902, still represents only 68 per cent of the total accommodations provided in these areas; but this is a substantial improvement as compared with the 43 per cent of the earlier canvass.

The situation still varies greatly from district to district as it did at the time of the original canvass, but in only three districts, Pilsen, Pullman, and the Lumber Yards, were less than 50 per cent of the toilets in apartments. In one block in the Pilsen (Bohemian) area only 15.5 per cent of the toilets were in the apartments; in Pullman the percentage was 32.7 and in the old Slovak area (Lumber Yards) the percentage was 47.6. The Polish district (St. Stanislaus) on the North West Side with 50.3 per cent, the Ruthenian district (Division St.) with 53.5 per cent, the old "Lower North" Italian district with 59.7 per cent, Ancona with 55.3 per cent were the four districts with between 50 and 60 per cent of the toilet accommodations in the apartments. In the Stock Yards district the percentages had increased since the original canvass from 34.4 to 69.1 per cent; in South Chicago from 32.4 to 72.3 per cent. The situation in all districts included in the post-war canvass and recanvass is shown in Table 18.

PRESENT SANITARY CONVENIENCES VERY INADEQUATE

In spite of the vast improvement resulting from the removal of the vault nuisance, it is important to emphasize the fact that sanitary provisions are still far from satisfactory. It has already been pointed out that the yard closet is frequently almost as great a nuisance as the old vault, but if properly placed it is illegal only in the case of the so-called new tenements. Many of the yard toilets are so situated that they exist in violation of the requirements of the building ordinances.

TABLE 18

NUMBER OF TOILETS OF SPECIFIED TYPE; BY DISTRICTS
(Recanvass and Post-war Original Canvass Data)

District	Number of Toilets of Specified Type									
	Total	Vault	Yard	Under Side-walk	On or under Porch	Base-ment	Hall	Apartment		Other
								Num-ber	Per-cent-age of Total	
All districts	12,168*	4	830	242	130	397	1,957	8,539	70.2†	69‡
West Side:										
Old Ghetto	42	....	2	....	....	2	16	22	§	....
Pilsen	155	....	17	32	2	6	62	24	15.5	12
Lumber Yards	483	....	44	54	5	102	33	230	47.6	15
Hull-House	1,207	2	49	....	9	9	214	923	76.5	1
Polk Street	352	....	18	....	....	....	26	308	87.5	....
St. Stanislaus	785	2	45	118	2	35	187	395	50.3	1
Division Street	1,035	....	60	....	9	87	313	554	53.5	12
Ancona	342	....	51	....	....	8	94	189	55.3	....
South Side:										
Near South Side	809	....	14	....	....	17	132	646	79.9	....
Back of the Yards	1,257	....	141	....	36	17	180	869	69.1	14
Stock Yards, South	216	....	17	....	1	4	27	163	75.5	4
Southwest (Lithuanian)	909	....	96	....	45	14	47	705	77.5	2
South End:										
Burnside	407	....	15	....	....	....	3	389	95.6	....
South Chicago (East Side)	491	....	95	....	1	12	25	355	72.3	3
South Deering	197	....	20	....	....	1	6	170	86.3	....
Pullman	245	....	....	....	....	....	165	80	32.7	....
North Side:										
Lower North	920	....	20	35	13	35	266	550	59.7	1
Upper North	270	....	13	3	3	9	39	200	74.1	3
Olivet district	473	....	32	....	....	17	34	390	82.4	....
Negro districts:										
Dearborn	401	....	15	....	2	2	24	357	89.0	1
La Salle	491	....	24	....	2	4	53	408	83.1	....
Upper Federal	515	....	40	....	....	14	11	450	87.4	....
Walnut (West Side)	166	....	2	....	....	2	....	162	97.6	....

* Type of toilet is not reported for 1,327 households, 1,280 of which are in St. Stanislaus district.

† Percentages are based on number reported.

‡ Twenty-one are under steps, 11 under back stairs, 5 under house, 5 in saloons, 1 in woodshed, 1 in lobby, 1 in public garage. The toilet for one rear building is in the cellar of the front building.

§ Not included because the total number of toilets, 42, is too small to serve as the basis of percentages.

Yard closets are permitted only in the case of buildings already existing at the time the ordinance was passed, and then they must be at least eight feet from any dwelling. In many of the neighborhoods it is difficult, if not impossible, to have the yard closet comply with the last regulation because so large a portion of the lot is already covered by buildings. In almost every instance yard closets are nearer than eight feet to one or both buildings.

In South Chicago, for example, at the time of the recanvass, 24.3 per cent of the families were dependent on yard closets, which had been the most inexpensive and convenient substitute for the old vaults. Although the improved yard toilet can supposedly be locked and is so constructed that it should flush easily, most of those inspected were nevertheless found unlocked, out of order, and situated in exposed locations. Everywhere it is the exception rather than the rule to find a lock either on the inside or on the outside of the door. Many of the doors hang on a single hinge and cannot be closed so as to afford any degree of privacy. The yard toilets are usually located in the spaces between the front and rear buildings. Often they are placed so as to offend all sense of decency. On one lot the yard toilet is directly beneath the kitchen window of a rear apartment on the first floor.

TOILETS UNDER THE SIDEWALKS

Most objectionable of all yard toilets are those located under the sidewalk. Here the conditions of sanitation are worst, partly because they are so easily accessible to passers-by from the streets. These offensive toilets are made possible by the raising of the street level, and their promiscuous use is to be attributed in part to the lack of "public comfort stations" in Chicago. Many of these toilets under the sidewalks are in such bad repair that they are in no condition to be used. The water supply in many of them is often out of order, and in some instances toilet seats are broken or entirely lacking. Frequently, too, the floors are broken and damaged by rat holes.

The yard toilets even of improved water-closet type were found to be out of repair or leaking. In the winter the leak sometimes becomes a sheet of solid ice covering the floor and preventing the door from being closed. No toilets can flush, of course, when they are frozen. In early winter investigators found the outdoor toilets already in bad repair. Toilets seen in this condition in winter were far more insanitary than the old privy vaults had been and could not be used at all when the water was frozen. The families visited often complained about their miserable situation. They said that it did no good to thaw out the toilets while the weather was cold; they would only freeze up again immediately. One family said that the landlord had been promising to have the toilet fixed ever since the preceding winter.

Toilets located on the back porch are somewhat more convenient than those in the yard and, in general, more private; but such toilets, like those out in the yard, are exposed and freeze easily. The porch toilets are moreover quite illegal and exist in violation of the building ordinances.[9]

Another evil to be noted is the inadequate number of the new toilets that have been installed in place of the old vaults. In South Chicago, for example, in the recent canvass, there were found to be only 491 toilets of all kinds for 570 apartments in which were living 1,018 children and 1,698 adults of whom 120 were lodgers in family households. This means that as many as 14, 15, 16, and in one case 17 people were found to be dependent upon a single toilet. In one case a toilet in an old saloon, supposedly now a soft-drink parlor, is used by the families in both the front and the rear houses, and this is only one of the many semi-public arrangements that must exist when there are more families and more apartments than there are toilets. Such lack of privacy and of decency cannot fail to have a demoralizing influence on family and neighborhood life.

The old Italian district in the Lower North area is conspicuous for the inadequate provision of toilet accommodations. In one block there are as many as 4 and 5 families using a single yard toilet and as many as 21 persons dependent on a single sidewalk toilet. In another block 6 families were using 1 sidewalk toilet. Worst of all is the situation—which, unfortunately, our tables do not picture—of an entire absence of toilet provisions upon some of the premises, leaving the tenants to make use of those in the next house or the

[9] *Revised Chicago Code, 1931*, sec. 1786.

next yard or a restaurant or soft-drink parlor. The difficulty of such a situation for families with small children need not be emphasized.

The hall toilets are, of course, distinctly better in some respects than the yard toilets. They are likely to be in better repair since they are less likely to freeze. In respect to privacy, however, they are extremely objectionable, and, being common property, they are often extremely dirty. Usually placed between a front and a rear apartment, they are used by the occupants of both. They are rarely locked and are accessible to agents and delivery boys coming into the buildings. In some instances where there is a store in the front of the building and an apartment in the rear, the hall toilet serves both store and family. Whether or not these cases are really illegal depends upon when they were built. The building ordinances provide that in all buildings used for both business and residence purposes, separate and sufficient water closets shall be provided for the use of families and patrons of the store, but this applies only to buildings constructed after 1902.[10] Few of these toilets can be locked from the inside. Such instances present not only serious problems in sanitation but, as the halls are invariably dark, also a moral problem, especially if there are young children living in the apartments. Such toilets are usually constructed without either a window or a ventilating shaft. This is also a violation of the building ordinances. Many have no means of artificial lighting except by lamps, candles, or matches, and absence of light usually means absence of cleanliness. When the responsibility for keeping these common toilets clean is divided between two, three, and sometimes four families, the problem is even more complicated.

IMPROVEMENTS IN NEWER DISTRICTS

In a newer district like South Deering better conditions were found. Whereas in South Chicago 24.3 per cent of the households are dependent upon the accommodations offered by yard toilets, in the South Deering district only 11.5 per cent of the households are still dependent upon this old type of toilet. It is important, however, to remember that South Chicago has gradually changed for the better since our first canvass. At that time 56 per cent of the families

[10] *Revised Municipal Code of Chicago, 1905*, sec. 1683.

were using yard toilets or vaults and the 24 per cent using yard toilets today must be compared with the earlier percentage. The measure of progress is, after all, an item not to be overlooked.

In one of the South Deering blocks over 98 per cent of the toilets were apartment toilets, and there were no yard toilets at all, no basement toilets, and only 1 hall toilet. Only 1 basement toilet was found in all four blocks and only 6 hall toilets. Over 80 per cent of the households had apartment toilets. Almost every household had a toilet that is not shared with any other family. In the four blocks there were 197 toilets and 200 households.

Even in South Deering, however, some very insanitary conditions were found at the time of the canvass. In one building, for example, which included a store and four apartments in which seven Mexican families including twenty persons were living, there were supposed to be toilets in the building, but when they were visited they had been out of order for a month, because of the bursting of a water pipe, and could not be used at all. The landlord had been notified more than once; he had done nothing about it and all seven of the families were using the toilet of the house next door. In this same house it was reported that the court was wet because of water dripping down from the second floor where the woman poured out her wash water because the drain pipe on that floor was also out of repair.

In the Burnside triangle, another of the newer districts, conditions were found to be, on the whole, very favorable. Ninety-five per cent of the families were in apartments having private toilets within the apartment. Some extremely bad cases, however, were found even here, for there were the twenty-two families using yard, hall, and basement closets. One family, for example, at the time our investigators called, had been for eight months without water in the house and without a toilet in the house that could be used. They had been using a yard toilet which was filthy and in bad repair. A contractor had undertaken to make some alterations on the house for the landlord but had not finished his work because of a disagreement. The woman had been going each morning to her sister's house one block away to bring home an inadequate water supply for the most urgent needs. Her washing she did at a neighbor's. She said she hated to have the children use the yard toilet, but it was the only way to avoid being a nuisance to the neighbors. She had reported her difficulties to a sanitary inspector, but without results.

Another extremely bad case in the triangle was found in a frame tenement where 5 families and 14 people were dependent upon two yard closets that were in poor repair and unspeakably filthy in the winter because of freezing. Repeated complaints to the landlord had been ignored. The seriousness of the situation is understood only

TABLE 19

NUMBER OF HOUSEHOLDS AND PERSONS USING SPECIFIED TYPE OF TOILET

(Recanvass and Post-war Original Canvass Data)

Type of Toilet	Number		Per Cent Distribution	
	Households	Persons	Households	Persons
Total	15,115	65,143	100.0	100.0
Not in the apartment:				
Yard	1,191	4,821	7.9	7.4
Under sidewalk	435	1,655	2.9	2.5
Porch	144	621	1.0	1.0
Basement	595	2,114	3.9	3.2
Hall	2,942	11,663	19.5	17.9
In the apartment	8,539	38,046	56.5	57.8
Others	130	496	0.8	0.8
No report	1,139	5,727	7.5	9.4

when one considers the large number of persons and families dependent upon these toilet accommodations that are so definitely below standard either in number or in type. For example, Table 19 shows the very large number of families and individuals affected. Thus, out of 15,115 households, only 56.5 per cent had the comfort of any kind of private toilet arrangements in their own apartment, while the other 45 per cent were still using miserable makeshift arrangements. Approximately 1,800 families (12 per cent) were using outside toilets in the yard, under the sidewalk, on the porch. Another 3,500 were using toilets in the basement or the public hall and many of these were used by other families.

APARTMENT TOILETS

But even the apartment toilets are also far from satisfactory. Many of them have been improvised from old pantry and closet space. This is indicated by the arrangements for entrance. Table 20 shows, for example, the number of apartment toilets that are off the kitchen, dining-room, and pantry. Approximately two-thirds of these toilets were entered from the pantry or kitchen—an arrangement that seems very objectionable. The explanation of this wholly undesirable arrangement lies in the fact that an attempt is first made

TABLE 20

TYPE OF ENTRANCE IN 8,539 APARTMENT TOILETS

Type of Entrance	Number	Per Cent Distribution
Total	8,539	100.0
Hall	1,694	20.0
Bedroom	369	4.3
Living-room	244	2.9
Kitchen or pantry	5,485	64.7
Dining-room	438	5.1
Basement	68	0.8
Porch	92	1.1
Other*	92	1.1
No report	57	†

* Other entrances include store, clothes closets, passageways, attics, etc.

† Percentages based on known cases.

to put into the apartments of these old houses modern plumbing facilities of some kind. The only place where space can be found is frequently off the kitchen in a former pantry or storeroom; it is also cheaper in most cases to put them close to the kitchen, which is already piped for water. Nearly two-thirds of the toilets in the apartments were, as Table 20 shows, off the kitchen, and another 5 per cent were off the dining-room. Toilet entrances from kitchen, pantry, and dining-room are too obviously objectionable to need discussing, especially when the toilet is also used as a place of storage for food, as actually happens in some cases.

Ventilation in these badly constructed apartment toilets is very poor. The law requires that new tenement houses shall have in every bathroom or toilet apartment "at least one window with a glass area of at least six square feet and a minimum width of one foot opening upon a street, alley, yard, court, or vent shaft."[11] Yard toilets are, of course, situated in shedlike compartments away from the house. Usually a little hole of some sort has been cut in the upper part of the door, but there is no through ventilation. It may be said, therefore, that although an increasing number and proportion of apartments have private toilet facilities and there is good cause for rejoicing over this improvement, nevertheless there are still many improvements to be made in the provisions for toilet facilities in these tenement neighborhoods.

Among modern home comforts that even the poor are expected to be able to enjoy are electric lights and gas stoves, possibly even furnace heat. The special study of the housing of dependent families showed many Chicago families living without these comforts.

Bad plumbing, lack of light and air, lack of modern conveniences for lighting and cooking, are common features in the housing of these families. Not infrequently the building has fallen into a serious condition of dilapidation. For example, a Negro bricklayer whose earning capacity had always been too low to support adequately his six children, was destitute after two weeks out of work. The family lived in an old apartment building which had been deserted by all the other tenants. There was no money for candles or a lamp. Some cooking was possible in a few huge kettles over the kitchen fireplace (there was no stove), but all the water had to be carried in from a neighbor's house, and it was easier on the whole to buy cooked meals or go without. The grate fire did little to dispel the cold. Fortunately, there was a fair amount of covering on the duofold and cot which served as beds. The toilet had been out of order ever since the family had lived there. The mother was very much depressed when her husband had been sent to the House of Correction for six months, and she was forced to move. "It goes from bad to worse," she said after they were in a shed at the rear of a lot near by. In this place she had the use of an old range in a room of the building in front. For this single room in a shed she was paying four dollars a week.

Not all these wretched homes are found in the central part of the

[11] *Revised Chicago Code, 1931*, sec. 1422.

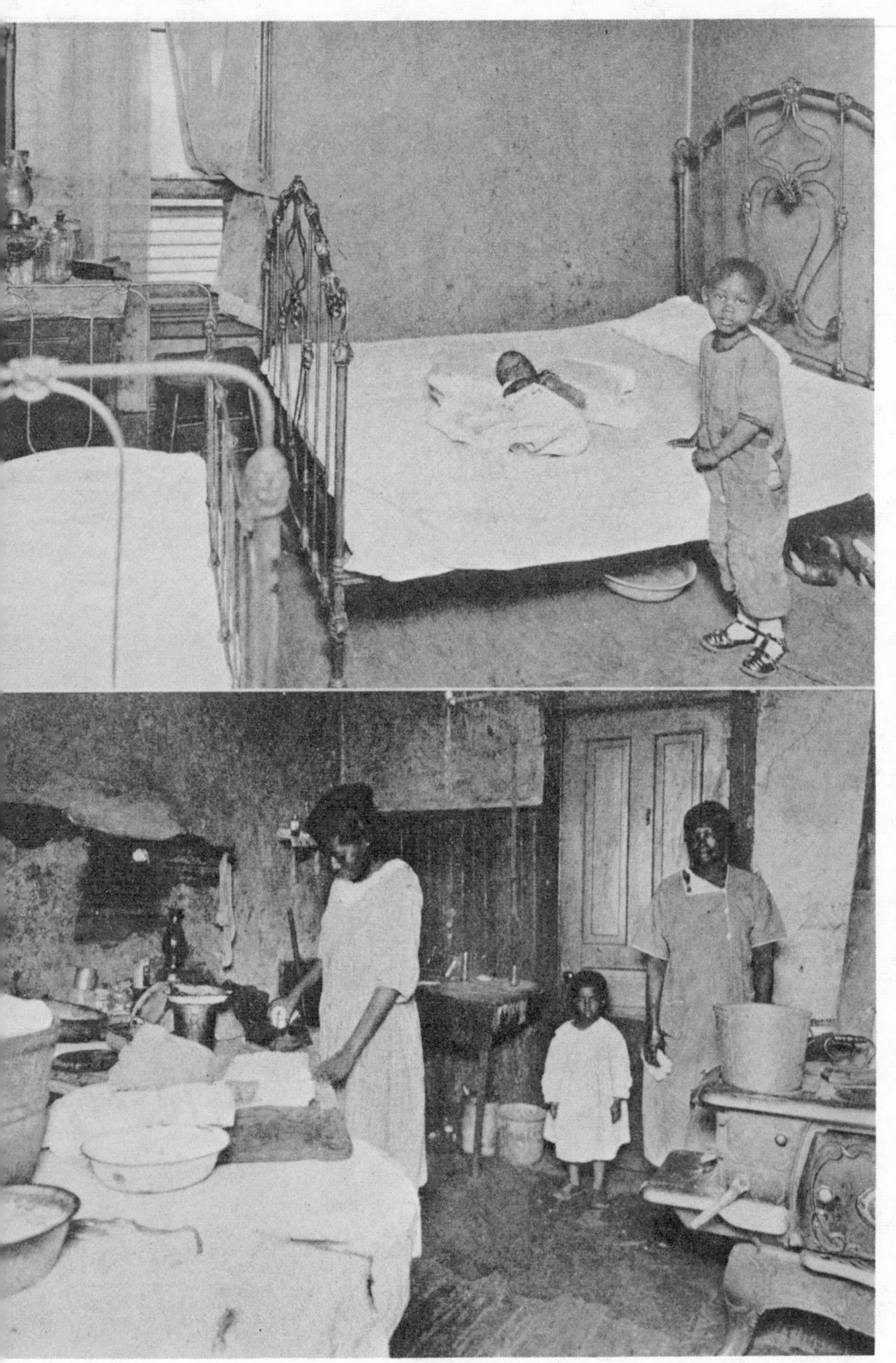

WITHOUT MODERN CONVENIENCES

city; some are found in the outlying districts. For example, in a three-room shanty renting for seventeen dollars a month the seven members of a Negro family were housed in the outer rim of the metropolitan area. The typical details of this dwelling were the blackened exterior, wide-board floors, loosely constructed and sagging walls—a most inadequate shelter, especially during the winter months. A brother and sister-in-law of the mother of this family had built their own shack quite near. It was one large room, 26 by 18 feet. One corner had a half-partition. A curtain, stretched from the end of this partition to the wall, completed the division from the rest of the room. This served as a kitchen. There was no plumbing in the building. Water was carried from the house next door. A part of the building had strips of tar paper tacked on with large spaces between the pieces. The whole structure was set up on posts—a strange home, indeed, to be found in a modern American city.

Many other reports showed the lack of the conveniences which families in better circumstances take for granted as necessities of modern life. For example, a German family with four children paid fourteen dollars rent for the rundown four-room cottage in which they lived in 1928. There was no sink in the kitchen, and the gas had been turned off so that the mother had to do her cooking in the basement on the garbage burner. As a result the family lived in the basement practically all the time. The children had colds and other ailments most of the winter, as might have been expected, because of the perpetual cold and dampness in the home.

In still another basement flat, perhaps one of the worst visited, other undesirable features were supplemented by an obsolete long-hopper toilet, poor plumbing in bad repair, windows mended with cardboard, and one of them entirely covered over with a tin sheet.

Day by day social workers are going in and out of the dilapidated tenements where they find families obliged to live under conditions of great privation and discomfort. They report that the tenement mothers not infrequently make efforts that are little short of heroic to keep their homes and their children clean and neat. That these women of the tenements so often succeed in making their miserable flats into real homes is evidence of their courage and their almost inexhaustible patience.

CHAPTER VII

TENEMENT DWELLERS WHO LIVE IN DARKNESS: THE PROBLEM OF LIGHT AND VENTILATION

Tenement Rooms below Legal Standard; Window Area and Outlook; Windowless Tenement Rooms; Dark and Gloomy Rooms; Windows on Narrow Passageways and Courts; The Objectionable "Shoestring" Lot; Tenement Courts.

THE effects of overcrowding cannot really be understood and appreciated without the facts regarding light and ventilation and certain other conditions regulated by the tenement-house code. With regard to the size of the room, for example, it is provided that in "new" tenement houses, i.e., houses built after 1902, all rooms used for living purposes must have not less than 70 square feet of floor area, that ceilings must be $8\frac{1}{2}$ feet high, that every habitable room must have windows opening directly upon a street, alley, yard, or court, and that the window area must be not less than one-tenth of the floor area. The code further provides that in all houses built after 1910 all rooms must contain at least 80 square feet of floor area.

These provisions do not apply to houses built before 1902, and in the old houses the small rooms may be legally occupied. But rooms that are small and dark or inadequately lighted and ventilated are quite as objectionable in old houses as in new ones. The dark-room evil, however, can be remedied only by expensive structural changes. The usual attitude of the landlord is that an old building is "not worth it" and so dark rooms continue to be dark.

TENEMENT ROOMS BELOW LEGAL STANDARD

In order to emphasize the necessity of giving some attention to the improvement of conditions in old houses, it seemed important to ascertain how far all houses, old as well as new, fell below the legal requirements. It proved to be impossible, however, to measure all the rooms in each apartment in each house. After the canvass of the first winter the plan was adopted of getting areas of sleeping-rooms only. In the first twenty districts canvassed, 13,586 of the rooms measured, about 26 per cent of the total number, were found to have areas below the legal minimum of 70 square feet; and 9,558 of the rooms measured, approximately 19 per cent of the total, were lower than $8\frac{1}{2}$ feet, the minimum height specified in the ordinance. The distribution of these rooms in the different districts canvassed will be found in Table 21. In the area on the West Side near the lumber yards 817 rooms, and 1,458 rooms in the Division Street area, in both cases 47 per cent of all the rooms measured, were below the legal requirement in area; and in the Upper North district 38.9 per cent of the rooms measured were illegal as to area and 27.9 per cent in the same area were illegal as to height. In the Upper Federal Street and La Salle Street districts approximately 35 per cent of all the rooms measured were illegal as to area.

WINDOW AREA AND OUTLOOK

Quite as important as the size of the rooms is the provision made for light and ventilation. In statements concerning light and air it is, of course, difficult to avoid the influence of the personal equation. A room that one person calls light another may call gloomy or even dark, and what is bad ventilation to some seems adequate to others. One objective test, however, is whether the rooms have windows and whether the windows can be opened to the outer air; that is, whether it is possible to let in light and air if the occupants can be convinced of their importance. The ordinance requires that all living-rooms (except alcove rooms) must have windows opening to the outer air.[1] A further objective test is found in the section of the code which provides, as a means of securing adequate light and ventilation, that in every new tenement house "every habitable room" must have its window area equal to one-tenth of its floor area and that all windows shall open directly to the outer air.[2] Although this provision, like so

[1] *Chicago Municipal Code, 1922*, sec. 650; *ibid., 1931*, sec. 1417.

[2] See *ibid., 1931*, secs. 1420–23; also secs. 1241–42. As early as 1905 the ordinance (*Revised Municipal Code of Chicago, 1905*, sec. 413) regulating windows was as follows: "In every new tenement house every habitable room, excepting water-closet compartments and bathrooms, shall have at least one window opening directly upon a street, alley, yard or court. The total area of the windows opening from any such room

many others, applies only to new-law houses, it seems important to apply this standard, which the community has set, to all the houses which were visited.

The returns for twenty districts canvassed[3] showed that in these districts 392 sleeping-rooms were entirely windowless or had only windows opening into another room; and that 2,456 other sleeping-rooms had windows with an area below the 10 per cent of floor area specified in the tenement-house ordinance. There were thus 2,848 sleeping-rooms in these districts which, measured by the present standards in the ordinance, would be illegal. While some of these cases are "pre-war," and overcrowding may have been slightly reduced since the war, the windowless rooms and the rooms with very small windows remain until the old buildings are pulled down, and they thus constitute a continuing menace to the health of large numbers of people in the poorer districts. Since the numbers in any one district are relatively small, the detailed table showing the distribution of these rooms in different sections of the city is not given. Some of the areas with very old houses—that is, the Hull House district, the Lower North district, and the Negro area on the South Side—had the largest proportion of such cases.

(other than water-closet compartments and bathrooms) upon a street, alley, yard or court, shall be at least one-tenth of the floor area of that room. . . ." The section (418) governing old houses is much more lax in its requirements: "No room in any now existing tenement house shall hereafter be constructed, altered, converted or occupied for living purposes unless it contains a window having a superficial area of not less than one-twelfth of the floor area of the room, which window shall open upon a street or alley or upon a yard or court having a superficial area of not less than 25 square feet; or unless such room adjoins another room in the same apartment, which other room shall have such a window opening upon such a street, alley, yard or court, and between which two adjoining rooms there shall be a sash window having at least 15 square feet of glazed surface the upper half of which shall be so made as to open easily." Even when the house was a private dwelling and not a tenement, the windowless room was supposed to be controlled. The corresponding section (285) for the private house was as follows: "In buildings of Class III, no room shall be considered habitable or used as a habitation unless it has at least one window of an area equal to one-tenth of the superficial area of such room opening into the external air."

[3] Fourteen of these districts were canvassed before the war, and six in the post-war period. As in the case of other structural conditions, data on this point were not secured in the recanvass.

TABLE 21

NUMBER OF VIOLATIONS OF ORDINANCE REGULATING AREA AND HEIGHT OF ROOMS; BY DISTRICTS

(Original Canvass Data)

District	Total Number of Rooms	Rooms with Violations of the Building Code			
		In Area*		In Height	
		Number	Percentage of Total	Number	Percentage of Total
All districts	51,423	13,586†	26.4	9,558	18.6
Pre-war canvass	46,266	12,012	26.0	8,716	18.8
Back of the Yards‡	6,656	1,459	21.9	935	14.0
Old Ghetto‡	771	194	25.2	253	32.8
Pilsen‡	1,042	287	27.5	119	11.4
St. Stanislaus‡	10,986	2,274	20.7	2,816	25.6
South Chicago‡	2,318	375	16.2	449	19.4
Walnut‡	1,284	193	15.0	306	23.8
Dearborn‡	2,390	578	24.2	455	19.0
Lower North‡	5,744	1,292	22.5	721	12.6
Downtown‡	330	17	5.2	4	1.2
Lumber Yards	1,746	817	46.8	638	36.5
Southwest	2,483	839	33.8	404	16.3
Hull-House	5,130	1,385	27.0	966	18.8
Division Street	3,113	1,458	46.8	405	13.0
Near South Side	2,273	844	37.1	245	10.8
Post-war canvass	5,157	1,574	30.5	842	16.3
Upper North	802	312	38.9	224	27.9
La Salle	1,001	353	35.3	121	12.1
Stockyards, South	524	147	28.1	73	13.9
Upper Federal	1,378	500	36.3	202	14.7
Burnside	878	140	15.9	154	17.5
South Deering	574	122	21.3	68	11.8

* Before December 5, 1910, the legal requirement was 70 square feet; since that date, the legal requirement has been 80 square feet.

† A total of 166 sleeping-rooms, having an area of 70 and less than 80 square feet in buildings erected since 1910, is included in this figure, distributed as follows: Southwest, 51; Hull-House, 34; Division Street, 6; Near South Side, 6; La Salle, 1; Stock Yards, South, 8; Burnside, 57; South Deering, 3. A total of 30 sleeping-rooms, having an area of 70 and less than 80 square feet in buildings whose date of erection was not reported, is excluded from this figure. These are distributed as follows: Lumber Yards, 3; Southwest, 13; Hull-House, 5; Burnside, 9.

‡ In these districts the figures represent the number of violations in all rooms and not those in sleeping-rooms alone. In the later stages of the canvass only sleeping-rooms were measured.

Even in the houses erected or rebuilt under the new law there are violations of the law. In one of the new-law houses in the Slovak (Lumber Yards) district, ten bedrooms visited during our canvass had less than 80 square feet of floor area, one room having an area of only 42 square feet. In another new-law house in the same district three bedrooms were found with illegally low ceilings.

WINDOWLESS TENEMENT ROOMS

The windowless rooms represent only 1 per cent of the total number of sleeping-rooms and the rooms with small-window areas 7 per cent of the total. But some of the rooms were very dark indeed. In some cases the window area was very much below the required 10 per cent of the floor area provided by the tenement code. In five rooms in the Slovak district the window area was less than 4 per cent; in two districts (Slovak and Stock Yards) there were sixty-two rooms in which it was less than 6 per cent of the floor area.

The evil is greater than these figures indicate for in many of these dark and airless rooms more than one person was sleeping. In one house, for example, six persons were sleeping in a windowless room. Data showing the number of persons sleeping in such rooms were not tabulated for all of the districts, but Table 22 shows the situation in three of the districts in the original canvass.

This table shows quite concretely how very bad a windowless room may at times become. In 7 cases, 5 persons were sleeping in rooms which had no windows, or windows which were useless; in 21 cases, 4 persons slept in similar rooms; in 42 cases, 3 persons occupied such rooms; in 81 cases, they were occupied by 2 persons. Summarizing, the table shows that, in these three districts, 2 or more persons occupied each of 152 rooms that were either windowless or windowless for all practical purposes.

The new districts canvassed, the Burnside and South Deering districts, are not yet sufficiently built over to make dark rooms a crying evil. In the Negro area recently canvassed in Upper Federal Street, 19 such rooms were found and 12 of them had 2 or more than 2 occupants. Five of these rooms had 2 occupants each, 1 had 3 occupants, and in 1 entirely windowless room 4 persons were sleeping. The number of persons sleeping in entirely windowless rooms was

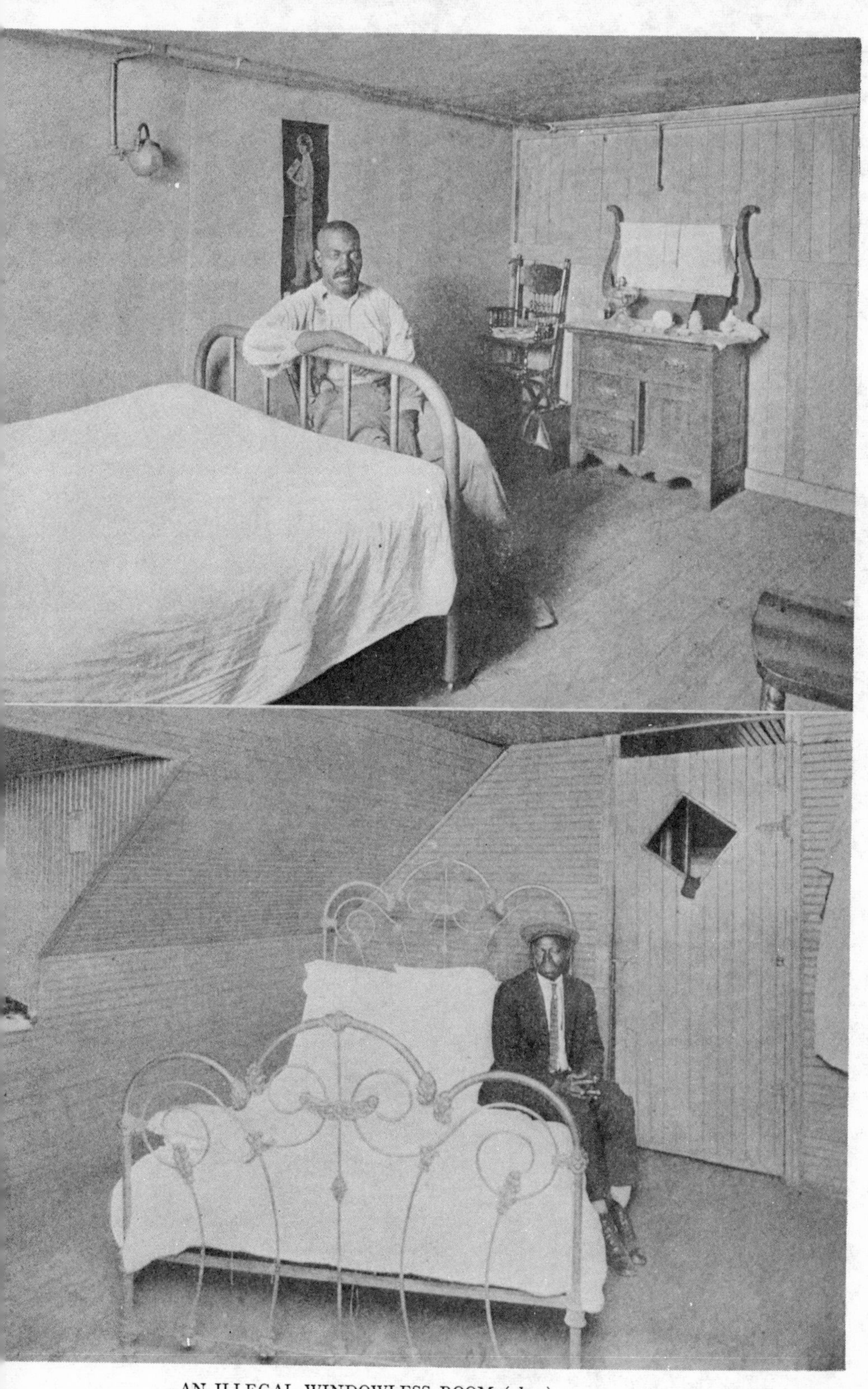

AN ILLEGAL WINDOWLESS ROOM (*above*)
A ROOM WITH INADEQUATE WINDOW SPACE (*below*)

74 per cent greater than the number of rooms. It would be safe to estimate that at least 5,000 persons were sleeping in the 2,848 rooms which were windowless or had windows with an area below 10 per cent of the floor space. Sometimes several of these bedrooms were found in a single apartment and several of these inadequately ventilated apartments in a single building. For example, 23 of the 119 windowless bedrooms in the Stock Yards district were in three buildings. In one two-room apartment occupied by 3 people, both

TABLE 22

NUMBER OF SLEEPING-ROOMS IN THREE DISTRICTS HAVING NO WINDOW, INTERIOR WINDOW, OR USELESS WINDOW

Number of Persons Occupying	Sleeping-Rooms in Three Districts Having	
	No Window or Interior Window	Outer Window Useless
Total	182	109
Unoccupied	30	30
One	56	23
Two	50	31
Three	27	15
Four	13	8
Five	5	2
Six	1	......

rooms were really without communication with the outer air because the windows were so obstructed; in another apartment three of the four rooms were for all practical purposes windowless. One twelve-room tenement in the Lithuanian district had five dark bedrooms so small that four were less than 500 cubic feet in content and so poorly equipped for ventilation that in no one of them was the window area more than 3 square feet and in no one of the five did these small windows open to the outer air. Four of the rooms opened into a hall and the fifth into a store.

But great emphasis must be laid on the fact that the 2,848 cases of windowless and illegally small-windowed sleeping-rooms are only a small percentage of the total number of rooms with inadequate light and ventilation. On the whole, the window area is a much less important factor in the problem of light and ventilation than the question of whether the window opens upon a yard or an open court of adequate size to give light and ventilation or whether it opens instead upon a passageway so narrow that the adjoining building can shut out all light and air.

DARK AND GLOOMY ROOMS

There is unfortunately no objective test of the amount of light in a room other than the one already mentioned of the window space in relation to the floor space. An experiment was made when the inquiry was first begun of asking for a report for each room as to whether or not it was so located that any sunshine was possible and as to the distance from the window in which reading was possible. These tests proved impossibly difficult and were given up. The following definitions were then adopted for use in the "Instructions to Investigators," and with the policy of having two investigators work together it was hoped that a reasonably satisfactory standard could be reached. A "dark" room was defined as a room in which you could read only when you were standing by the window, and a "gloomy" room as one in which you could read only a few feet away from the window. There are, of course, many complicating factors which make it difficult to secure a common standard of what is "light," "gloomy," or "dark." The hour of the day in which the room is visited, the condition of the weather, and even the curtaining which cannot always be disturbed have their effect. Some rooms were found in which the blinds were not only closed and difficult to open but were actually nailed shut. Sometimes, too, the window-panes are painted, especially on the ground floor, to insure some privacy to the occupants. Investigators were cautioned to make allowance for such conditions and to report conservatively on this as on other similar points.

The total number of rooms reported "light," "gloomy," or "dark" in the original canvass data is shown in Table 23. This table shows that 29 per cent of the rooms were dark or gloomy—were rooms that could not reasonably be described as "light rooms." The per-

LOT-LINE PASSAGEWAYS AND DARK ROOMS

centages in the districts canvassed before the war and after the war were approximately the same—71 per cent of the rooms in the pre-war canvass were light and 70 per cent in the post-war canvass. The percentages varied, of course, from district to district, as Table 24 indicates. Burnside, with its open spaces and vacant lots, had the highest percentage of light rooms, 83 per cent; the Stock Yards district, the old South Chicago district, and the Ruthenian district (Division St.) followed closely with approximately 80 per cent. At the other end of the scale was the Hull-House district with only 62.3 per cent of the rooms light and the Negro district in Upper Federal Street with only 63.4 per cent light.

TABLE 23

LIGHT, GLOOMY, AND DARK ROOMS IN TWENTY DISTRICTS

(Original Canvass Data)

	Number of Rooms	Per Cent Distribution
All rooms	51,221*	100.0
Light	36,321	71.0
Gloomy	11,942	23.3
Dark	2,958	5.7

* There were 202 cases of "no reports" omitted from the total.

WINDOWS ON NARROW PASSAGEWAYS AND COURTS

The outlook of the windows is also very important in determining whether a room shall be light, gloomy, or dark. A room with windows opening directly on a street, an open yard, or even an alley will probably be light and stands a good chance of being decently ventilated. Regarding outlook, the ordinances provide that the minimum of window space described above must open upon street, alley, yard, or court[4] and that 3 feet is the minimum width for an outer court belonging to a new tenement.[5] Table 25 shows many rooms with windows opening into airshafts, interior courts, other rooms, or halls, but the majority, 52 per cent, open on lot lines or passages. A lot-

[4] *Revised Municipal Code of Chicago, 1905*, sec. 413; *1931*, secs. 1241, 1406.

[5] *Ibid., 1931*, sec. 1416.

line window was for this investigation one opening within a foot of the lot line; a passage was the long, narrow, uncovered space left at one side of a tenement as the means of approach to the rear apartments. Such passages varied from 3 to 5 feet in width. The custom

TABLE 24

NUMBER OF LIGHT, GLOOMY, AND DARK ROOMS; BY DISTRICT

District	Number of Rooms			Percentage of Total Number	
	Total	Gloomy	Dark	Gloomy	Dark
All districts	51,221	11,942	2,958	23.3	5.7
Pre-war canvass	46,191	10,839	2,561	23.5	5.5
Back of the Yards*	6,631	1,410	206	21.3	3.1
Old Ghetto*	769	112	64	14.6	8.3
Pilsen*	1,042	190	66	18.3	6.3
St. Stanislaus*	10,972	3,015	456	27.5	4.1
South Chicago	2,317	436	26	18.8	1.1
Walnut*	1,284	219	59	17.1	4.6
Dearborn*	2,390	691	78	29.0	3.2
Lower North*	5,733	1,348	459	23.5	8.0
Downtown*	330	55	46	16.6	13.9
Lumber Yards	1,746	423	113	24.2	6.5
Southwest	2,483	501	105	20.2	4.2
Hull-House	5,124	1,354	576	26.4	11.3
Division Street	3,113	453	176	14.5	5.7
Near South Side	2,257†	632	131	28.0	5.8
Post-war canvass	5,030	1,103	397	22.0	7.9
Upper North	790	187	101	23.7	12.6
La Salle	977	223	97	22.8	9.7
Stock Yards, South	506	80	17	15.8	3.2
Upper Federal	1,355	370	127	27.3	9.3
Burnside	863	135	12	15.6	1.4
South Deering	539	108	43	20.0	7.5

* Number of rooms includes total number of rooms. In districts canvassed later, this information was secured only for rooms used as sleeping-rooms.

† Excludes nineteen rooms in a hotel.

in building is to make the lot-line wall of one house abut upon the passage of the adjoining tenement. Owing to this, lot-line windows of one house afford as much light and air as the passage windows of the one opposite. Not infrequently it happens, however, that a building will cover the full width of a lot. Particularly is this likely to be true along business streets. Here the effect is to deprive all rooms with lot-line openings of both light and air.

In any event such windows are not in accord with the regulation of the code, and the fact that a large percentage of gloomy and dark rooms have lot-line windows speaks strongly in favor of the rigid enforcement of the law.

Table 23 shows a total of 11,942 rooms reported "gloomy" and 2,958 reported "dark" in twenty districts canvassed. A careful study of the conditions in these 14,900 dark and gloomy rooms makes it clear that the area of the window is much less important than its outlook; that is, the determining factor is whether or not the window opens upon a narrow passage, airshaft, a covered porch, or a small court with another building so erected as to shut out all light and air. Table 25, therefore, offers an explanation of the inadequately lighted rooms in these districts.

TABLE 25

WINDOW OUTLOOK OF DARK AND GLOOMY ROOMS IN TWENTY DISTRICTS

	Number
Total	14,090*
No windows	402
Window opening upon:	
Another room or hall	578
Airshaft, porch, or interior court	4,657
Passage or lot line	7,370
Alley, yard, street, or roof	922
Two outlooks	161

* Outlook not reported for 810 rooms.

This table shows that approximately 52 per cent of the windows in these dark and gloomy rooms opened on the lot line with the building on the next lot so close that only a narrow passageway was left between the two houses.

THE OBJECTIONABLE "SHOESTRING LOT"

These dark rooms could not be avoided in the type of housing construction that resulted from the so-called "shoestring lot." In Chicago, as in so many other American cities laid out on the gridiron plan,[6] the back-yard service streets or alleys create serious housing difficulties. Some of these have been referred to in the discussion of

[6] See above, chap. iv, p. 171, and chap. v, pp. 190–97.

the rear house. People do not wish to live in houses fronting the alley. Only a house fronting on the street, therefore, is desirable enough to be a good renting property. The premises extend, however, all the way from street to alley. The typical city lot in Chicago is long and narrow, usually 25 feet wide and 125 feet long, and this has led to the practice of building houses close to the lot line on both sides. To leave adequate space on either side means a less economical use of the premises. Each lot-owner, therefore, constructs his house along the front of the lot and builds close to the lot line, going back to the rear of the lot as far as means will permit. Only the rooms that have front windows or rear windows have adequate light. The middle rooms are always dark. A study of these dark rooms makes clear the fact that adequate light and ventilation cannot be secured by regulating the window area; the controlling factor is the size of the yard or court upon which the window opens. Thus, although only a small proportion of the dark rooms could be explained by lack of window area, a very large percentage were clearly due to the fact that the windows opened on a court or upon a narrow passage between two houses, both of which were built close to the lot line. This evil of the shoestring lot is very serious because extremely difficult to control. In the new housing projects of the Marshall Field Estate and the Julius Rosenwald Fund, the elimination of the unsightly alley and the joint use of the rear portion of the lots for garden purposes offer a solution of the evil consequences of the narrow lot and no other building scheme avoids them. The new federal housing projects are also to be built on replanned neighborhood areas.[7] But Chicago has had few of the new housing developments of this kind.

A builder should be compelled to provide for light and air to come over his own lot or from a public street. If he builds close to the lot line and counts on some of his rooms getting sunlight, light, or air from the adjoining lot, his rooms may be light when the house is erected but will be dark as soon as his neighbor or neighbors exercise their right to build close to the lot line in their turn. The larger proportion of light rooms in districts like Burnside and South Deering may be explained by the considerable number of vacant lots still in these sections. In many of the houses, rooms are now airy and light

[7] See below, chap. xvi, p. 488, n. 18, and p. 492, n. 25.

that will be dark later. In such cases the lot-line windows are receiving air and light that are contributed by the adjoining landowner. So long as the benevolent neighbor delays building, or if he is accommodating enough to erect only a small building placed a good distance from the line, the lot-line windows of the first house will continue to receive and furnish an abundance of light and air. If, however, the next lot is covered by a house or a factory built to the boundary line, the side rooms in the buildings on both lots are effectually darkened.

A striking example of this is to be found in one of the worst tenements in the Hull-House district, a forty-apartment brick building built somewhat like the old dumb-bell tenements of New York. The house extends on both sides to the lot line. To the east is a vacant lot and the rooms on that side of the house are pleasant and bright. On the west, however, is a three-story brick building with its wall 6 inches from the wall of the first tenement. Not only is the new house dark, but all the middle apartments on that side of the older building, except the three on the top floor, are sunless and chilly though the window area of most of the rooms is theoretically adequate. Several of these middle apartments are so dark and damp that they cannot be occupied, and the front and rear apartments are gloomy and cheerless. It is, of course, only a question of time, too, until the apartments on the east side of the building will be reduced to the same wretched condition as those on the west.

TENEMENT COURTS

This same building furnishes a good example of the failure of a court to supply light and air. In the center is a long, narrow space, 9 feet wide by 67 feet deep. Upon this court, rooms open from every apartment. Except on the fourth floor, almost all of these rooms are gloomy, for the sun seldom reaches the bottom of the court, and strikes the second story for only a short time each day. The investigator says of this building: "Practically no apartments in this house, except the very small ones in the rear, which open on a narrow yard, are sure of light in every room." But the 114 members of 30 families were living in this cheerless place.

What has been said in the preceding paragraph as to the inadequacy of the court to furnish light and air is true of nearly all of the courts. This is, of course, a subject referred to before in the discussion of lot overcrowding. But the facts regarding lot-line windows show the close relation of lot overcrowding to the problems of light and ventilation. Of windows opening on passageways there is little to be said that has not already been included in the discussion of the lot-line window. The passage is, as a rule, a long, narrow opening between buildings both of which are too close to the lot line. Often it is covered and sometimes so filled with rubbish as to be offensive to the windows opening on it. There remains, however, the window opening on the shaft. Under the best of conditions this could not furnish much light, and even if it were open, it could not furnish much air. The situation in some of the tenements in the Hull-House district is described on some of the schedule cards. One of these speaks of the shaft in the house as "closed at the top all the time and at the bottom during the winter, so that there is no ventilation." One toilet on each floor had a window opening on the shaft so that the air was described as "sickening." In another house in this area the light shaft was reported to be "air tight above and below." One woman told the investigator that she had broken out the panes in the skylight in order to secure adequate ventilation, and to be free from the unbearable odors from a toilet opening on the shaft. In one very large building near Hull-House containing twenty-three apartments, there are four light shafts, which are supposed to ventilate inner rooms and toilets. All these were reported to be "tightly closed at the top by skylights." Air passages were reported to be closed, and the investigator was told that they would remain closed all winter.

These old tenements with shafts, most of them built in the nineties, are survivals of the worst period of New York tenement-house construction which some misguided architects and builders tried to transplant to the prairie metropolis. Fortunately, little progress with this type of large tenement was made in the Chicago area until the era of the modern fashionable skyscraper apartments. When these buildings cease to be fashionable and become the homes of the poor, a new and very serious housing problem will be left to the next generation.

CHAPTER VIII

THE PROBLEM OF CONGESTION[1]

High Population Density of West Side Tenement Areas; Overcrowding in the Tenements; High Rate of Occupancy per Room; Overcrowding Measured by Tenement-House Code; Illegally Occupied Sleeping-Rooms; Beds Everywhere; Bed Overcrowding.

DENSITY of population in a given area may be due to very different conditions: (1) to high buildings and the resulting density per acre caused by building into the air; (2) to overcrowding within the house, which even with small, low houses may lead to a high population density. And house and room overcrowding in Chicago tenement areas are often made worse by the presence of several buildings on one narrow lot.

HIGH POPULATION DENSITY OF WEST SIDE TENEMENT AREAS

The West Side wards, just beyond the river, have had the most densely populated sections of the city for a long period of time,[2] and here the density is caused by overcrowding on the lot and within the house. On the other hand, sections of the North Side have a population density caused by the erection of large numbers of new skyscraper apartments which, it is unnecessary to say, are very different indeed from the West Side tenements. In the tenement districts where, not infrequently, there are three houses to the lot and where the tenement-house regulations regarding cubic air-space cannot be enforced or, at any rate, have never been enforced, the problem of congestion is part of the problem of bad housing. And it is with this congestion in the tenement areas that the present chapter is concerned.

[1] With Mary Zahrobsky, research assistant, School of Social Service Administration.

[2] The population of Chicago, by wards, 1840–1920, compiled from reports of the United States Census and the area from the *Chicago Daily News Almanac*, and the computed density of population for corresponding census years will be found in Helen R. Jeter, *Trends of Population in the Chicago Region*, pp. 60–61.

Population density at the time of the two census enumerations 1910 and 1920 and also at the time of the special enumeration of 1934[3] is shown in Maps IV, V, and VI. The earlier map for 1910 was made before the period of census tracts and is based on the ward population of that census period. But this early map (Map IV) shows the extreme congestion in the river wards of the West Side at that time. While the South Side, Southwest, Far North Side, and Northwest were relatively sparsely settled with a density of less than 30 persons per acre, the West Side tenement districts, with few exceptions, had a density which was more than twice as great.

In 1910, when the average density of population for the entire city was 18 persons per acre, the ward which contained the poor district about the lumber yards had a density of 77 per acre; the ward including the Polish neighborhood around St. Stanislaus Church had an average density of 81 persons per acre; and the ward containing the Hull-House district was even more densely populated, with 91 persons per acre.

The density of the twelve most crowded wards in 1920, at the time of the census enumeration, which was midway between our earlier and later canvasses, is shown in Table 26. Six of these most densely populated wards were still to be found on the West Side, three were on the North Side, and three on the South Side. Each of these twelve wards had an average density of 50 or more persons per acre, and three of the West Side wards had more than 70 persons per acre, at a time when the average density for the city as a whole was only 21 persons per acre.

Population density for 1920 is also shown in Map V, where the West Side and the North Side are still seen to be heavily congested areas;[4] and the effect of continued migration of the Negroes into the

[3] The 1934 census enumeration was conducted under the auspices of a special Chicago Census Commission making use of emergency funds. Since the data for the regular 1930 enumeration differed verly slightly from the data collected in 1934, the maps prepared for 1930 and 1934 were almost identical, and only the 1934 map is therefore used in this volume. For the 1920 and 1934 maps we wish again to express our obligation to the Social Science Research Committee of the University of Chicago, and especially to Mr. Richard O. Lang, who has been in charge of this special branch of the Committee's work.

[4] The map for 1920 and the later maps of 1930 and 1934 are based on square-mile areas in place of the old method of ward divisions; i.e., population density for 1920, 1930, and 1934 is based on census tracts grouped into areas arranged without regard to the ward boundaries and showing density per square mile for these areas.

BLEM OF CONGESTION: A CROATION TENEMENT NEIGHBORHOOD ON THE WEST SIDE

Black Belt is seen in the development of a new area of concentration on the South Side.

At the time of the 1930 census, the West Side wards were still crowded areas, and Table 27 shows seven of them with an average density of more than 50 persons per acre. The area containing the St. Stanislaus district was almost as densely populated as in the pre-war period, but the old West Side river wards, the wards including Hull-House, the Ghetto, and the lumber yards district, have had a decrease in population density along with the development of the Lower West Side for business purposes. New areas of population concentration were beginning to make their appearance at the time of the census enumeration of 1930. The wards on the South Side which include the Black Belt and the North Side wards, where fashionable skyscraper apartments have risen, were becoming more congested.

TABLE 26

AVERAGE DENSITY OF POPULATION IN TWELVE WARDS OF GREATEST DENSITY IN CHICAGO, 1920

Average Number of Persons per Acre in 1920	Ward*	Division of City
89	Seventeenth	West
72	Sixteenth	West
71	Nineteenth	West
69	Fifteenth	West
63	Tenth	West
51	Twenty-eighth	West
62	Third	South
57	Second	South
53	Fourth	South
61	Twenty-third	North
50	Twenty-first	North
50	Twenty-second	North

* Ward numbers and boundaries have been changed for political purposes between census dates and therefore no comparisons can be made between ward statistics for two different census dates.

The thinly populated wards, of course, were those in the outlying districts on the Far South Side, Southwest, and Northwest. None of these wards had as many as 18 persons per acre, and two of them had fewer than 10. But the old river wards still appear as dark spots on the map showing density of population in the Chicago area.

At the time of the special census of 1934, as shown in Map VI, the density in the Negro district had spread over a wider area, while

TABLE 27

AVERAGE DENSITY OF POPULATION IN TWELVE WARDS OF GREATEST DENSITY IN CHICAGO, 1930

Average Number of Persons per Acre in 1930	Ward*	Division of City
85	Twenty-fourth	West
80	Thirty-fourth	West
60	Thirty-first	West
59	Twenty-ninth	West
58	Twenty-sixth	West
58	Thirty-second	West
56	Thirty-third	West
66	Third	South
63	Fourth	South
50	Sixth	South
55	Forty-fourth	North
53	Forty-third	North

* Ward numbers and boundaries were changed between 1920 and 1930 so that comparison with Table 26 cannot be made. Some of the same areas appear under different ward numbers in Tables 26 and 27. Although Vol. I of the 1930 *United States Census of Population* publishes population by wards in Chicago, Vol. III, Part I, does not. Population by so-called "community areas" is published for the first time. These areas are expected to be permanent statistical units and the boundaries will not be changed for political purposes. Each area is made up of a group of "census tracts," the boundaries of which will be subject to comparatively slight change from census to census.

in the once congested wards of the Lower West Side, especially along the south branch of the Chicago River, population density had declined in a noticeable degree. The Lower North was still densely crowded, as were also the relatively new apartment-house sections along the North Shore.

Although the density of population per square mile shows the centers of greatest concentration of population, it does not show the extremes of overcrowding in certain small sections. Some blocks, for example, are crowded far beyond the densities indicated in the

MAP IV

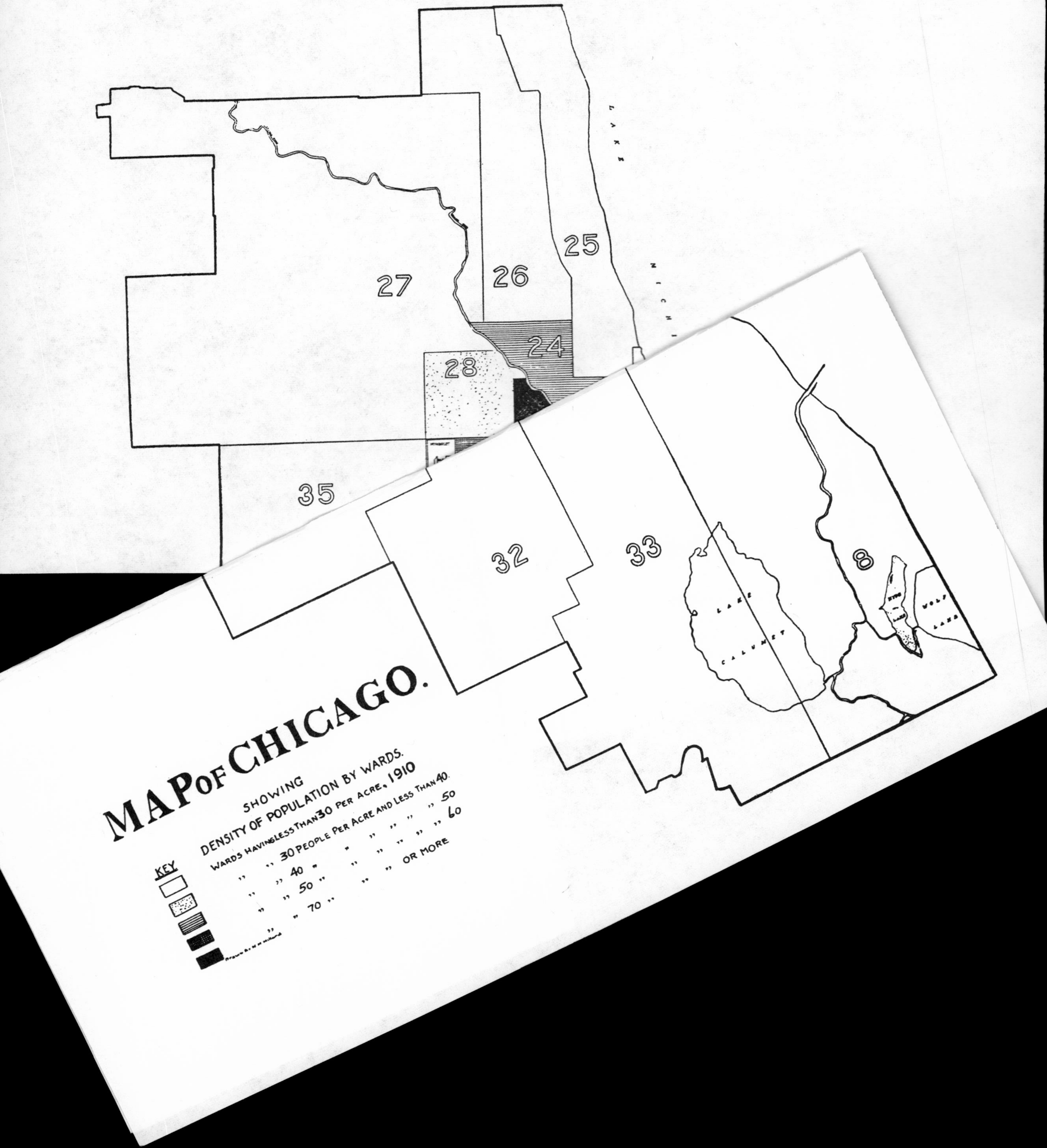

MAP OF CHICAGO.
SHOWING
DENSITY OF POPULATION BY WARDS.
1910
KEY
WARDS HAVING LESS THAN 30 PER ACRE.
" " 30 PEOPLE PER ACRE AND LESS THAN 40.
" " 40 " " " " " " 50
" " 50 " " " " " " 60
" " 70 " " " " OR MORE
LAKE MICHIGAN
LAKE CALUMET
WOLF LAKE
25
26
27
24
28
35
32
33
8

13
34
12
29

broader map areas. The most densely populated single block found in all the early canvasses was in the St. Stanislaus district where 1,520 persons lived, an average of 433 persons per acre. No other

TABLE 28

DENSITY OF POPULATION BY DISTRICTS

(Data Given for Sixteen Districts, Original Canvass and Recanvass)

District	Average Population per Acre	
	Original Canvass	Recanvass
All districts canvassed	205	155
West Side:		
Old Ghetto	357	84
Pilsen	374	291
Lumber Yards	265	175
Hull-House	187	99
St. Stanislaus	325	244
Division Street	254	229
South Side:		
Near South Side	209	185
Back of the Yards	189	149
Stock Yards, South	118	109
Southwest	157	120
South End:		
South Chicago	129	113
North Side:		
Lower North	334	222
Upper North	169	138
Negro Districts:		
Dearborn	141	137
La Salle	94	126
Walnut (West Side)	88	65

block had as many as 400 persons per acre, but 300 was not uncommon, and there were many blocks with a population density of between 200 and 300.

For the sixteen districts canvassed in both periods, shown in Table 28, the average density of population in the first period was 205 per acre. The district with the highest average density was Pilsen district,[5] with 374 per acre, but the Old Ghetto, Lower North, and St. Stanislaus were also found to average between 300 and 400 persons per acre.

Population in general had declined in these districts between the period of the pre-war inquiries and the period of the later studies. In the sixteen districts canvassed in both periods, 70,359 persons were found in the earlier period where only 53,062 persons lived in these same blocks in the later period. The average density for all districts fell from 205 persons per acre to 155. In each district, except La Salle, a Negro district, the average for the district had also fallen. In this district the density for every block was higher at the time of the post-war canvass than in the first inquiry. Moreover, the highest single-block density found in the recent period, higher in fact than any in the first period, including the one block in St. Stanislaus district, was a single block in another Negro district, Upper Federal, where our canvass in 1924 showed 576 persons per acre. The extreme congestion in these Negro districts is shown in Maps V and VI.

The chief reason for the falling-off in population in these tenement districts is undoubtedly the encroachment of business and industry and the decay and final disuse of some of the dwellings that seem no longer worth keeping up. Occasionally a new street cut through, or a new small park, may account for the disappearance of some of the buildings. The greatest change during the interval occurred in the one block of the Old Ghetto, but this has been described at another point.[6] In this block where there were 65 buildings with 200 apartments at the time of our first canvass, there were only 20 buildings with 57 apartments when the recanvass was made nearly fifteen years later. While this particular block had not been taken over for business or industrial purposes, any residential improvement had evidently been discouraged by commercial and industrial enterprise in adjacent blocks. Houses had been torn down but none had been built to take their places.

In other districts the same kinds of change are noted, chiefly the

[5] The Pilsen and Old Ghetto districts were single blocks. Although there were blocks in other districts that were more dense, the average for the larger districts is not so high.

[6] See chap. iii, pp. 85–92.

PROBLEMS OF CONGESTION

tearing-down of worn-out buildings in some cases to make way for factories or stores but more often simply to save taxes on so-called "improved" land. It is very rare in these districts to find new houses or apartment buildings replacing the old.

OVERCROWDING IN THE TENEMENTS

Overcrowding is the most serious aspect of the tenement-house problem, and although the depression led to extremely disastrous conditions of congestion, the problem is a serious one even in normal times. Overcrowding may, in fact, be looked upon as the crux of the whole tenement-house problem and at the same time the most difficult point to remedy. The plans for many of the new apartments do not help in this respect as they might. The new rooms are often exceedingly small, and the hallways are conspicuously small or lacking, so that in a household with children there is little privacy. If the dilapidated house and the dark rooms are used only by two people—a man and his wife, for example—the situation is dreary, but not exigent. It is the crowding-together of men, women, children, adolescent boys and girls, and lodgers and boarders in terribly insanitary rooms that leads to family discord and destroys not only the comforts but the ordinary decencies of life. Overcrowding—or household congestion, as it may be called—may be measured in two ways: (1) by the number of rooms in relation to the number, sex, and age of the occupants and (2) by the size of the rooms, particularly cubic air-space in relation to the number of occupants.[7]

[7] The English housing authority, Councilor Sir E. D. Simon, in *How to Abolish the Slums*, suggests three standards for measuring overcrowding. The first, he says, is in common usage but is too crude to be of much use; the other two, which are better, are not as yet much in use: (1) *The number of persons per room:* The standard used in the census is that a house is overcrowded if there are 2 or more persons per room, a child under ten being counted as equal to half an adult. This is called the "registrar-general's standard." Other standards on the persons-per-room basis to which attention is called include the Glasgow standard of 3 persons per room with a higher standard of 1½ persons per room sometimes used in less crowded districts. (2) *The number of persons per bedroom:* In Manchester, a standard of 2½ persons per bedroom is in use, which can, of course, be varied to 3, 3½, or any other desired figure. (3) *Provision for the separation of the sexes in sleeping-rooms:* On the third standard a house is held to be overcrowded unless the sleeping accommodation enables the parents to have one room, and boys and girls over ten years of age to be separated. This is called the "sex standard." This can be varied by taking a different age for separating the boys and girls. The Manchester

In discussing the problem of overcrowding, it is necessary to consider first the number of apartments having a specified number of rooms without regard to their size and without regard to the number of occupants. Data on this point are presented in Table 29, showing the number of apartments with one room to seven or more rooms in sixteen districts investigated in the pre-war canvass and in the recanvass carried on in the post-war period.

TABLE 29

NUMBER OF APARTMENTS HAVING A SPECIFIED NUMBER OF ROOMS (Data Given for Sixteen Districts; Original Canvass and Recanvass)

Size of Apartment	Apartments Canvassed*			
	Number		Per Cent Distribution	
	Canvass before 1920 (1)	Recanvass (2)	Canvass before 1920 (3)	Recanvass (4)
Total	15,137	12,822	100.0	100.0
One room	93	74	0.6	0.6
Two rooms	1,234	721	8.2	5.6
Three rooms	2,456	1,530	16.2	11.9
Four rooms	7,270	6,601	48.1	51.5
Five rooms	2,018	1,923	13.3	15.1
Six rooms	1,460	1,431	9.7	11.1
Seven rooms or more	606	542	3.9	4.2

* The apartments for which the number of rooms was not reported are omitted, 150 in the first canvass and 476 in the second.

Examining first the results of the earlier canvass, which are presented in columns 1 and 3, we find 7,270 four-room apartments, the predominant type, and only 93 small one-room apartments, and 606 exceptionally large ones of seven rooms or more. Not only the numbers but the percentages must be examined, for it is significant that the 93 one-room apartments were less than 1 per cent of the whole number investigated, while 48 per cent of the whole number had

Public Health Department adopted, in 1920, a system of applying both (2) and (3), and considered a house overcrowded if there are more than 2½ persons per bedroom, or if there were not adequate sleeping accommodations to separate the sexes. This was called the "Manchester standard."

four rooms, with the three-room and five-room apartments next in order of importance. Looking at the numbers cumulatively, 75 per cent, or approximately three-fourths of all the apartments, had four or more rooms.

The more recent canvass in the same districts of approximately 13,000 apartments brought similar results, set forth in columns 2 and 4 of the same table. That is, the later canvass showed very little change in the size of the apartments. The one-room apartments were still less than 1 per cent of the total number, and the four-room apartment remained the predominant type. But there were more five-room dwellings than three-room dwellings, and the proportion of six-room dwellings increased while the proportion of two-room dwellings decreased. Summarizing the findings briefly, it may be said that approximately one-half of all the tenements are four-room apartments. This was true in the old canvass and it is true today. In the more recent canvass approximately 82 per cent have four or more rooms today, and approximately 18 per cent less than four rooms—a slight improvement in the post-war as compared with the pre-war situation.

It is important to note, too, that the four-room apartment was common in nearly every district of the city that was visited by our investigators. Table 30 shows the size of the apartments occupied in the twenty-three different areas canvassed or recanvassed after 1923.

Looking at the returns for the twenty-three different districts as presented in Table 30, it appears that the four-room apartment was the predominant type in seventeen of the twenty-three districts. The exceptional cases were the Bohemian (Pilsen) district of the West Side, which had just as many three-room as four-room apartments; two of the Negro districts, in which five- and six-room apartments were more numerous than those with four rooms; Pullman, in which the three-room type was predominant; and Burnside, which had approximately as many apartments with five as with four rooms.

The Plymouth Court district, with its two-room apartments, that was overcrowded with Italian families in our early canvass was not recanvassed, for it had fortunately been taken over for business purposes. The number of houses left in the old Ghetto district was so small that percentages are not computed for this area. The numbers in the Pilsen district are small, but the housing in this district is

TABLE 30

PERCENTAGE OF APARTMENTS HAVING A SPECIFIED NUMBER OF ROOMS; BY DISTRICTS

(Recanvass and Post-war Original Canvass Data)

District	Total Number of Apartments	Percentage of Apartments Having a Specified Number of Rooms						
		1	2	3	4	5	6	7 or More
Total	15,556*	0.6	5.6	12.3	49.2	16.2	12.0	4.1
West Side:								
Old Ghetto	54	†	.....	.....	.....	.....	.....	.....
Pilsen	281	.....	5.0	42.3	42.3	5.7	3.2	1.5
Lumber Yards	639	1.0	9.7	20.8	40.0	14.2	9.1	5.2
Hull-House	1,328	0.2	6.0	19.1	36.9	20.6	11.0	6.2
Polk Street	360	.....	3.9	13.9	50.5	17.8	10.5	3.4
St. Stanislaus	2,332	0.7	4.6	8.2	73.2	7.0	4.7	1.6
Division Street	1,324	0.7	7.8	11.2	57.1	9.6	11.1	2.5
Ancona	470	0.6	9.2	18.5	48.5	14.9	7.5	0.8
South Side:								
Near South Side	924	0.2	3.1	13.7	44.0	16.2	14.6	8.2
Back of the Yards	1,508	0.7	7.7	9.4	62.1	10.9	6.4	2.8
Stock Yards, South	264	0.8	20.4	15.1	47.3	9.8	5.0	1.6
Southwest (Lithuanian)	993	0.2	3.7	7.1	50.3	22.1	12.1	4.5
South End:								
Burnside	406	0.2	2.0	7.4	35.2	35.5	16.0	3.7
South Chicago (East Side)	560	1.4	4.1	7.0	60.2	9.0	16.2	2.1
South Deering	205	0.5	2.4	9.8	35.1	18.0	22.4	11.8
Pullman	244	0.4	14.8	35.2	27.9	18.0	3.7	.....
North Side:								
Lower North	1,168	0.3	3.9	12.1	44.7	19.4	15.9	3.7
Upper North	314	.....	4.1	8.6	42.0	26.8	14.0	4.5
Olivet district	507	0.4	2.2	8.3	36.0	29.0	20.5	3.7
Negro districts:								
Dearborn	426	1.4	2.1	7.1	24.2	27.7	29.1	8.4
La Salle	534	1.3	3.8	9.8	30.1	26.6	20.0	8.4
Upper Federal	542	1.9	5.0	12.0	32.6	17.3	25.3	5.9
Walnut (West Side)	173	0.6	1.7	5.2	19.1	33.5	24.3	15.6

* Omitted from this total are 556 apartments for which the number of rooms was not reported.

† No percentages worked for base of less than 100.

quite uniform in character over a considerable area, and the small numbers probably constitute a representative sample. With regard to the Negro districts, it seems to be true, as later tables will show, that there is less overcrowding among the Negroes than among the immigrants. This is probably due to the fact that a superior class of Negroes were, until recently, obliged to live in the deteriorated areas of the city and that the standard of very poor white immigrants is being compared with the standard of a superior group of Negroes.

HIGH RATE OF OCCUPANCY PER ROOM

Passing on now to the number of rooms in relation to the number of occupants as a measure of household congestion, the standard set by the United States Bureau of Labor Statistics in an investigation carried on in 1918–19 should be examined. The Bureau of Labor found that

> for twenty cities selected at random, those living in houses averaged 1.007 rooms per person, and those in flats and apartments, 0.931 rooms per person. The standard health and decency budget must provide at the very least as many rooms per person as the average family was found to occupy. A housing standard of one room per person, exclusive of bath, has therefore been adopted as the minimum requirement consistent with health and decency.[8]

This is, of course, a statement based upon present conditions and more or less accepted standards. And it should, perhaps, be noted that most of the families included in the Bureau of Labor Statistics study were American. Non-English-speaking families, as well as families who had been in the United States less than five years, were excluded; so also were families with boarders or with more than three lodgers. This does not necessarily mean, however, that the standard is too high to apply in this study; the conditions of housing available for workingmen's families in Chicago, even in the lower-income groups, should not fall below the standard set for the working-class families in the country as a whole. Moreover, in setting such a standard it must be remembered that a separate room is not required for each member of the family, but only that the total number of rooms in the dwelling, including the general living-rooms, such as the parlor, dining-room, and kitchen, must be equal to the

[8] "Minimum Quantity Budget Necessary To Maintain a Worker's Family of Five in Health and Decency," *Monthly Labor Review*, X (June, 1920), 1317.

total number of persons in the family. Table 31 shows for the 16,112 dwellings investigated or recanvassed during the later period the number of rooms having a given number of occupants.

Using the standard of the Bureau of Labor Statistics, one room to one person, a zigzag line has been drawn in Table 31 so that

TABLE 31

NUMBER OF APARTMENTS OF SPECIFIED NUMBER OF ROOMS OCCUPIED BY A SPECIFIED NUMBER OF PERSONS

(Recanvass and Post-war Original Canvass Data)

Number of Rooms	Number of Apartments Occupied by a Specified Number of Persons													
	Total	1	2	3	4	5	6	7	8	9	10	11	12 or More	Vacant
Total	16,112*	941	2,531	2,716	2,570	2,319	1,630	1,107	653	357	165	77	49	997
1	92	58	15	5	5	5	......	1	....	1	...	...	....	2
2	865	307	272	118	60	35	18	2	4	......	..	...	....	49
3	1,910	234	499	393	285	203	90	54	36	12	3	1	....	100
4	7,654	253	1,192	1,353	1,369	1,245	844	557	284	145	58	21	5†	328
5	2,523	49	344	402	451	418	321	213	124	73	24	15‡	11§	78
6	1,865‡	24	158	246	316	315	246	190	134	80	55	24	14‖	63
7	347	5	23	33	43	55	54	53	24	23	12	5	10¶	7
8	216	3	11	11	28	25	39	28	32	14	8	9	5**	3
9	35	...	1	5	3‡	6	5	4	3	2	3	2	....	1
10	25	1	....	4	3	3	6‡	....	5‡	1	1	...	1††	....
11	8	...	....	......	1	....	2	2	2	1	...	...	....	....
12 or more	16	...	....	1‡‡	....	....	2§§	1	3‡‡	5‖‖	1	...	3¶¶	....
Not reported	556	7	16	145	6	9	3	2	2	......	...	...	....	366

* Downtown (Italian), with a total of 123 apartments, is not included because this district was not recanvassed.

† One apartment has 13, one 14, and one 15 persons.

‡ One family occupies two apartments counted as one in Tables 31 and 33

§ One apartment has 13, one 15, and two 16 persons.

‖ Three apartments have 13, one 14, and two 15 persons.

¶ Two apartments have 14, two 15, and one 20 persons.

** One apartment has 14, one 15 persons.

†† One apartment has 15 persons.

‡‡ One apartment has 13 rooms.

§§ One apartment has 16 rooms.

‖‖ One apartment has 14, one 18 rooms.

¶¶ Two apartments have 14 and 17 persons, and one apartment has 14 rooms and 16 persons.

all the cases above the line are below the standard and all the cases below the line are above the standard. This overcrowded or congested group above the line includes 5,506 apartments, or 36 per cent of the 15,115 occupied apartments for which information regarding occupancy was obtained. Using the Bureau of Labor Statistics standard, therefore, as a measure of overcrowding, more than one-third of our apartments fall into the overcrowded group.

MAP V

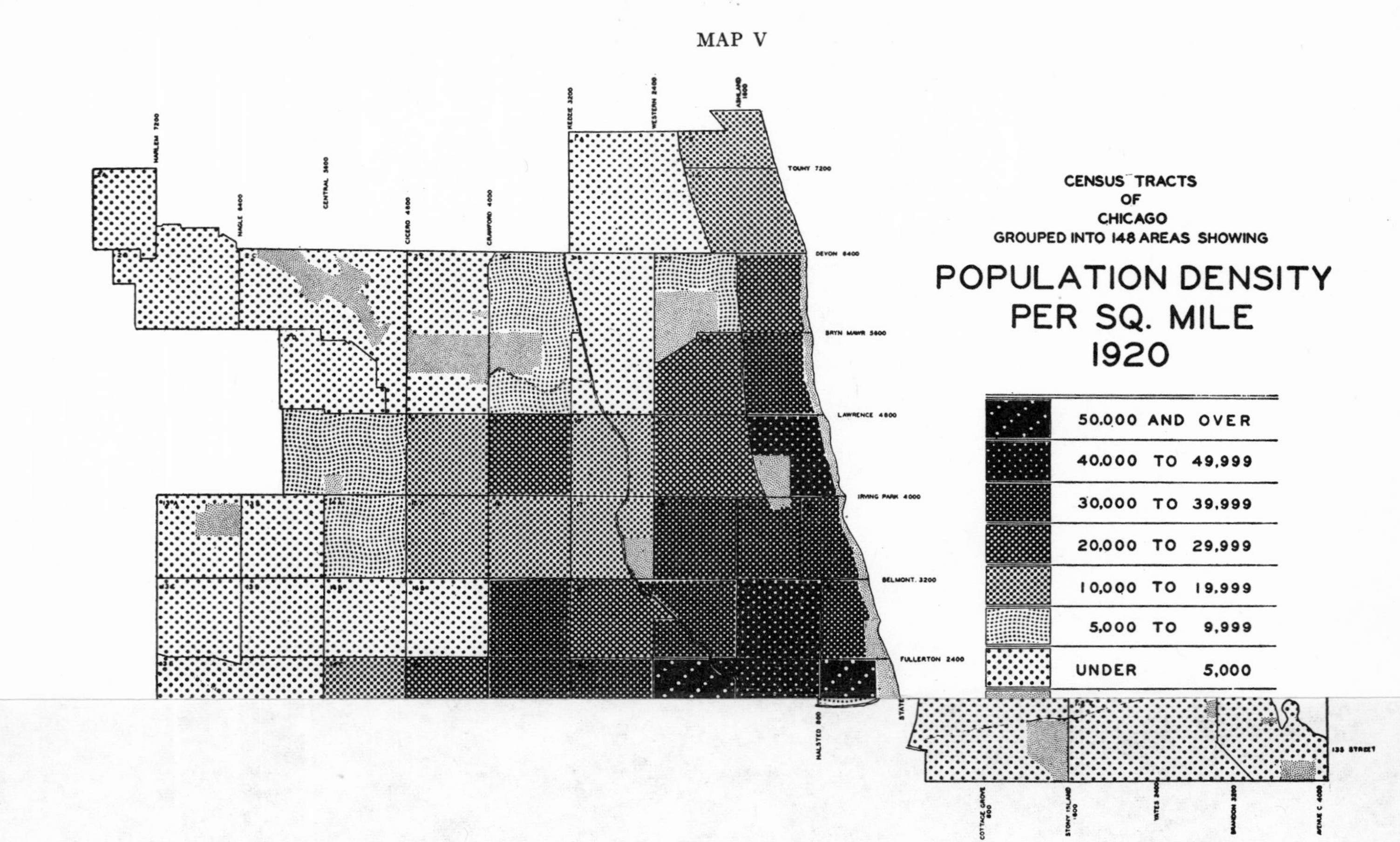

CENSUS TRACTS
OF
CHICAGO
GROUPED INTO 148 AREAS SHOWING
POPULATION DENSITY
PER SQ. MILE
1920
50,000 AND OVER
40,000 TO 49,999
30,000 TO 39,999
20,000 TO 29,999
10,000 TO 19,999
5,000 TO 9,999
UNDER 5,000
HARLEM 7200
NAGLE 6400
CENTRAL 5600
CICERO 4800
CRAWFORD 4000
KEDZIE 3200
WESTERN 2400
ASHLAND 1600
TOUHY 7200
DEVON 6400
BRYN MAWR 5600
LAWRENCE 4800
IRVING PARK 4000
BELMONT 3200
FULLERTON 2400
HALSTED 800
STATE
COTTAGE GROVE 800
STONY ISLAND 1600
YATES 2400
BRANDON 3200
AVENUE C 4000
135 STREET

This is, however, only an average based on approximately 15,000 apartments found in the twenty-three districts canvassed. The

TABLE 32

NUMBER AND PERCENTAGE OF APARTMENTS BELOW THE STANDARD OF ONE ROOM PER PERSON

(Recanvass and Post-war Original Canvass Data)

District	Total Number of Apartments Visited	Apartments† Overcrowded	Percentage of Apartments Overcrowded
Total	14,925*	5,509	36.9
West Side:			
Old Ghetto	54	22	40.7
Pilsen	280	75	26.8
Lumber Yards	628	202	32.2
Hull-House	1,228	431	35.1
Polk Street	353	142	40.2
St. Stanislaus	2,276	972	42.7
Division Street	1,322	569	43.0
Ancona	436	182	41.7
South Side:			
Near South Side	873	284	32.5
Back of the Yards	1,430	646	45.2
Stock Yards, South	251	116	46.2
Southwest (Lithuanian)	984	328	33.3
South End:			
Burnside	405	196	48.4
South Chicago (East Side)	533	267	50.0
South Deering	200	95	47.5
Pullman	222	65	29.2
North Side:			
Lower North	1,034	300	29.0
Upper North	300	67	22.3
Olivet district	493	113	23.0
Negro districts:			
Dearborn	405	104	25.8
La Salle	510	99	19.4
Upper Federal	540	205	38.0
Walnut (West Side)	168	29	17.3

* Omitted from the total are 997 vacant apartments and 190 other apartments for which the number of rooms was not reported.

† That is, overcrowded on the standard of one room per person.

percentages of overcrowded dwellings according to this standard vary greatly from one district to another. The total number of apartments investigated during the recent recanvass and the number and percentage of apartments in each district overcrowded by the Bureau of Labor standard is shown in Table 32.

The districts in the south end ranked highest in this form of overcrowding, the South Chicago district, known as "The Bush" leading with 50 per cent of the apartments overcrowded. The Burnside triangle came next with 48.4 per cent and South Deering third with 47.5 per cent overcrowded. It is strange to find these high percentages of overcrowding in the open spaces of Burnside and South Deering where crowding of any sort seems quite unnecessary.

The two Stock Yards districts ranked next with 46.2 per cent of apartments in one district, overcrowded according to this Bureau of Labor standard, and 45.2 per cent for another. The three districts on the Northwest Side—Division Street, St. Stanislaus, and Ancona—came next, with 43.0, 42.7, and 41.7 per cent of the apartments which fell below the standard of one room per person. At the other end of the scale were two Negro districts, one on the West Side (Walnut) with only 17.3 per cent and one on the South Side with only 19.4 per cent overcrowded. In eleven out of the twenty-three districts, overcrowding percentages were above the average.

Serious as this situation is, it represents an improvement over the condition found at the time of the first canvass. Comparable data are available for only eight of the original districts, but in these eight districts, as indicated in Table 33, there were 7,242 occupied apartments for which information regarding number of residents was obtained in the original canvass and 3,625, or 50 per cent, were overcrowded according to the Bureau of Labor Standard. The recanvass of these eight districts showed 6,085 occupied apartments, and of these, 2,074, or 34 per cent, were overcrowded according to the same standard.

The decline indicated in Tables 33 and 34 from 50 per cent to 34 per cent of overcrowding is extremely encouraging, but the fact that the more recent canvass of the same districts still shows 34 per cent of the apartments overcrowded according not to a liberal but a decent standard shows that household congestion remains one of the outstanding housing problems in Chicago.

Further evidence of overcrowding comes from the study made by Dr. Leila Houghteling[9] with regard to the housing of unskilled wage-earners in Chicago in 1926, from a study made by Elizabeth Hughes[10] for the Chicago Bureau of Public Welfare of the housing of Mexicans and Negroes in Chicago in 1925, and also from a

TABLE 33

NUMBER OF APARTMENTS OF SPECIFIED NUMBER OF ROOMS OCCUPIED BY A SPECIFIED NUMBER OF PERSONS

(Eight Selected Districts; Original Canvass Data before 1920)*

Number of Rooms	Total	Number of Apartments Occupied by a Specified Number of Persons										
		1	2	3	4	5	6	7	8	9	10 or More	Vacant or Not Reported
Total	7,672	232	919	1,137	1,315	1,185	1,001	657	419	210	167	430
1	39	12	11	6	5	3	....	2	....	....	....	....
2	730	91	224	169	107	56	34	8	3	1	1	36
3	1,348	53	216	252	252	214	148	68	30	11	3	101
4	3,298	45	308	437	604	582	518	344	185	84	41	150
5	1,084	19	92	139	164	182	146	107	94	40	43	58
6	782	8	47	96	135	101	110	92	68	51	42	32
7	214	1	15	24	33	32	26	23	27	14	15	4
8 or more	125	1	3	13	15	15	19	13	12	9	21	4
Not reported	52	2	3	1	....	....	....	....	....	....	1	45

* The districts included are Upper North, Division St., Lumber Yards, Hull-House, Near South Side Dearborn, Southwest Side, and Back of the Yards.

study made by Eleanor Goltz[11] of the housing of dependent families under the care of one of the family welfare agencies in Chicago.

Dr. Houghteling found that 67 per cent of the 467 families of unskilled wage-earners who were visited in 1926 were living under overcrowded conditions according to the Bureau of Labor Statistics

[9] *Op. cit.*, pp. 106 ff.

[10] *Living Conditions for Small Wage Earners in Chicago* (Department of Public Welfare, 1925).

[11] "Housing of Dependent Families in Chicago (School of Social Service, A.M. thesis, University of Chicago Library), pp. 27, 29; see below, chap. xiii.

standard of one room per person. Not only were many families below standard, but many were far below standard, as, for example, the households of three, four, or five persons living in one or two rooms; the households of seven or more persons living in four rooms; the households of ten or more persons living in four, five, and six rooms.

TABLE 34

NUMBER OF APARTMENTS OF SPECIFIED NUMBER OF ROOMS OCCUPIED BY A SPECIFIED NUMBER OF PERSONS

(Eight Selected Districts;* Recanvass)

Number of Rooms	Number of Apartments Occupied by a Specified Number of Persons												
	Total	1	2	3	4	5	6	7	8	9	10 or More	Vacant	Not Reported
Total	6,582*	426	1,078	1,033	1,040	934	652	436	246	122	118†	399	98
1	30	20	3	2	3	2	....	....	....	....	....	....	....
2	399	146	126	51	25	13	9	1	2	....	....	24	2
3	852	98	229	162	132	89	45	30	9	5	2	40	11
4	2,823	111	490	519	511	444	285	164	94	43	38	103	21
5	1,112	28	145	176	191	190	143	102	57	33	14	30	3
6	770	11	59	90	129	143	111	91	55	22	36	22	1
7	191	5	11	20	30	32	28	31	8	9	13	4	....
8 or more	143‡	2	4	8	16	19	30	17	20	10	15	1	1
Not reported	262	5	11	5	3	2	1	....	1	....	....	175	59

* The districts included in this table are Upper North, Division St., Lumber Yards, Hull-House, Near South Side, Dearborn, Southwest Side, and Back of the Yards.

† Thirty-two of these apartments have 11 persons; fourteen have 12; one has 13; and three have 15 persons.

‡ Seventeen of these apartments have 9 rooms; five have 10; one, 11; four, 12; one, 13, and one, 16 rooms.

In the study of Mexican and Negro housing published by the Chicago Department of Public Welfare, 47.5 per cent of all the families were found to be overcrowded according to the standard of one room per person.

The families selected for study by Miss Goltz were probably representative of the poorest in the city since they are those dependent upon charitable assistance. On the other hand, at the time of the study they were under the care and supervision of a family welfare

MAP IV

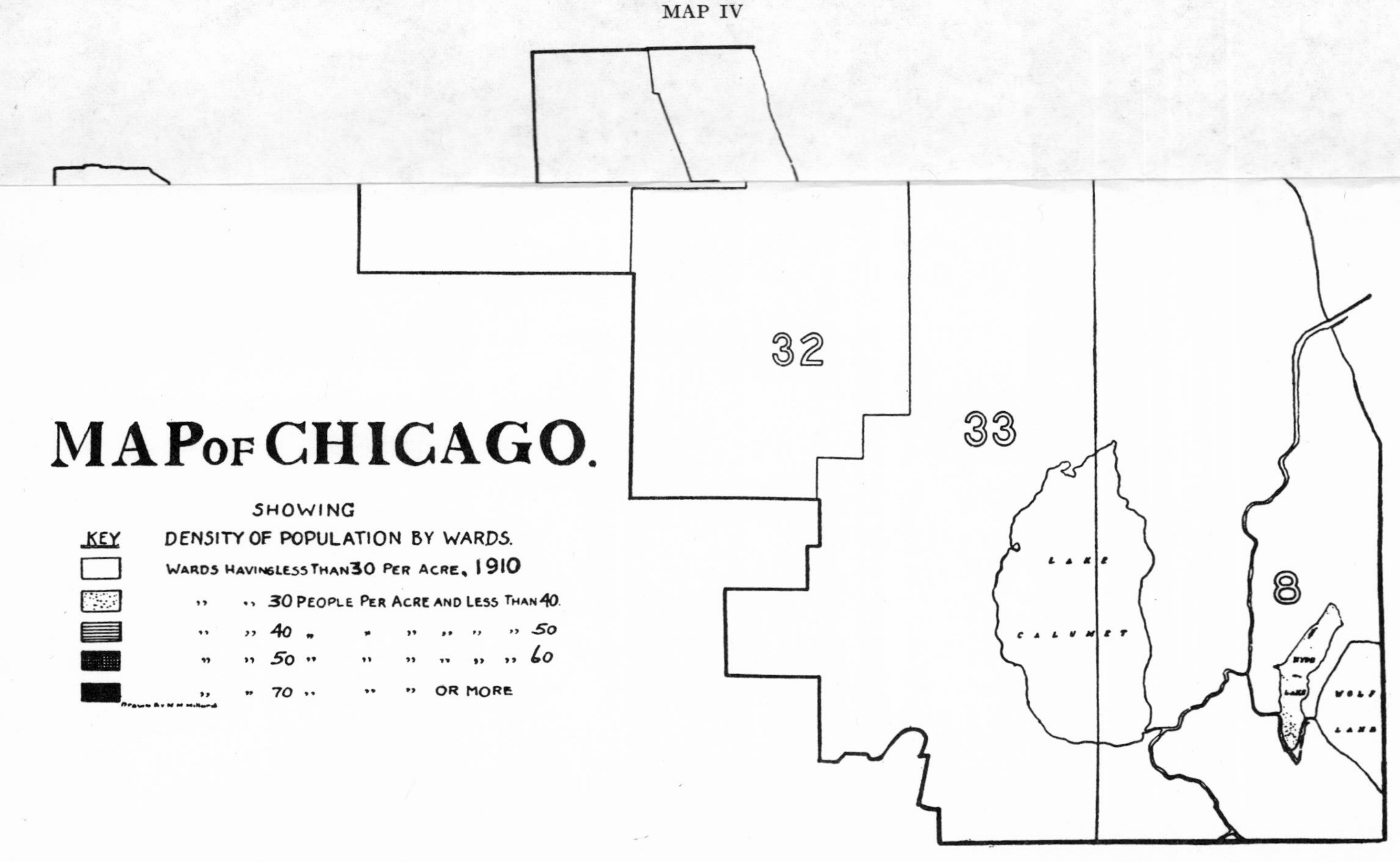
MAP OF CHICAGO.
SHOWING
DENSITY OF POPULATION BY WARDS.
KEY
WARDS HAVING LESS THAN 30 PER ACRE, 1910
" " 30 PEOPLE PER ACRE AND LESS THAN 40.
" " 40 " " " " " " 50
" " 50 " " " " " " 60
" " 70 " " " OR MORE
32
33
8
LAKE
CALUMET
WOLF
LAKE

agency and it may be supposed that the best possible quarters were found for them at the rent that the agency or the family was able to pay. Among the 2,226 families for whom it was possible to obtain information from the case records, 1,658, or 73 per cent, were living in apartments with less than one room per person. Only 30 per cent of the native-born white households, 26 per cent of the foreign-born white, and 18 per cent of the Negro households attained the Bureau of Labor Statistics standard. There were 421 cases in which the number of persons in the household was twice the number of rooms; 153 cases in which the number of persons was three or more times the number of rooms.

OVERCROWDING MEASURED BY TENEMENT-HOUSE CODE

The problem of overcrowding within the apartment is one of the outstanding housing problems in Chicago, and the evidence of overcrowding is ample. It is nevertheless one of the most difficult problems to deal with. The method of attacking it in the tenement-house ordinance is to relate the cubic contents of the room to the number of occupants. This method furnished a more accurate and scientific measure of overcrowding than is furnished by the Bureau of Labor Statistics method of correlating the number of persons and the number of rooms irrespective of the size of the rooms and irrespective also of whether the occupants are children or adults.

Our second measure of overcrowding, therefore, is furnished by the section of the Chicago tenement-house code which provides that every occupied room in a tenement house must have at least 400 cubic feet of air for each adult person "living and sleeping" in the room and 200 cubic feet of air for each child under twelve.[12]

To determine the number of persons "living" in a room as distinguished from the number "sleeping" in a room involves certain difficulties of definition, and data on this point were finally collected only for the rooms used as sleeping-rooms.[13] Even data on this point

[12] *Chicago Code, 1911*, sec. 1378; *Revised Chicago Code, 1931*, sec. 1421.

[13] After the experience of the first winter of field work, it was decided to secure cubic-feet returns only for sleeping-rooms, and new schedules called only for the measurement of sleeping-rooms. In determining the size of the rooms, accurate measurements were always taken by tape measures and rulers, and two investigators usually worked together in order to test as accurately as possible the enforcement of this important provision in the law.

could not always be regarded as accurate, since the head of the household sometimes understated the number of persons who actually slept in a room because of a suspicion that the investigator might

TABLE 35

NUMBER OF SLEEPING-ROOMS OF SPECIFIED NUMBER OF CUBIC FEET OF AIR-SPACE OCCUPIED BY SPECIFIED NUMBER OF PERSONS*
(Original Canvass Data before 1920)

Air-Space of Room in Cubic Feet	Number of Rooms Occupied By										
	Total	1 Child	1 Adult	1 Adult and 1 Child	2 Adults	2 Adults and 1 Child	3 Adults	3 Adults and 1 Child	4 Adults	4 Adults and 1 Child	5 Adults and More
Total.......	30,889	783	8,605	2,206	10,359	3,707	3,020	940	935	174	160
Less than 400....	890	22	337	97	291	91	37	4	9	2	.....
400 and less than 600...........	8,419	120	2,613	708	3,196	994	545	121	88	21	13
600 and less than 800..........	9,529	113	2,223	630	3,235	1,284	1,137	397	380	71	59
800 and less than 1,000.........	4,472	63	964	245	1,470	594	584	233	254	38	27
1,000 and less than 1,200....	2,064	78	592	114	660	242	236	60	57	13	12
1,200 and less than 1,400....	1,935	122	652	135	511	211	183	48	53	6	14
1,400 and less than 1,600....	1,657	129	563	129	483	141	125	30	40	11	6
1,600 and less than 1,800....	984	74	339	80	269	85	84	21	21	2	9
1,800 and less than 2,000....	519	40	188	40	128	37	43	14	15	5	9
2,000 and more..	420	22	134	28	116	28	46	12	18	5	11

* In this table "1 adult" means 1 adult or 2 children under twelve; i.e., the term "1 adult" is used whenever 400 cubic feet of air are required.

Number illegally occupied = 15,423 rooms, or 49.9 per cent of the total number of sleeping-rooms.

perhaps be an inspector. But although the returns on this point are not entirely accurate, it is clear that the error lies in an understatement of the facts.

Taking first the returns of the earlier canvass, Table 35 shows for the 30,889 sleeping-rooms in the seventeen districts investigated in the original canvass prior to 1920 the amount of air-space in relation to the number of occupants. In this table the zigzag line is so drawn that all cases of illegally occupied rooms—that is, rooms

TABLE 36

NUMBER OF SLEEPING-ROOMS OF SPECIFIED CUBIC FEET OF AIR-SPACE OCCUPIED BY A SPECIFIED NUMBER OF PERSONS*

(Original Canvass Data, 1923–26, for Three Districts Only)†

Air-Space of Room in Cubic Feet	Number of Rooms Occupied By										
	Total	1 Child	1 Adult	1 Adult and 1 Child	2 Adults	2 Adults and 1 Child	3 Adults	3 Adults and 1 Child	4 Adults	4 Adults and 1 Child	5 Adults or More
Total	2,687‡	83	849	296	934	309	125	56	25	4	6
Less than 400	37	1	15	4	13	4	....	....	....	....	....
400 and less than 600	475	12	194	51	169	37	10	2	....	....	....
600 and less than 800	878	15	281	98	325	102	34	17	5	1	....
800 and less than 1,000	591	15	140	71	203	95	43	17	5	1	1
1,000 and less than 1,200	256	7	72	23	95	34	15	2	4	2	2
1,200 and less than 1,400	164	14	48	21	48	16	7	7	3	....	....
1,400 and less than 1,600	142	15	44	19	37	9	7	7	2	....	2
1,600 and less than 1,800	82	3	31	6	21	10	5	3	2	....	1
1,800 and less than 2,000	37	1	11	1	19	1	2	....	2	....	....
2,000 and more	25	....	13	2	4	1	2	1	2	....	....

* In this table the term "1 adult" is used whenever 400 cubic feet of air are required, i.e., 1 adult means 1 adult or 2 children under twelve.

† Olivet, Ancona, Polk, and Pullman were canvassed with a new schedule which did not include this information. This table includes the other original canvasses, as follows: Upper Federal, Burnside, and South Deering.

‡ This total excludes 143 sleeping-rooms for which area was not reported, or in which the number of persons or occupancy was not reported.

not having 400 cubic feet of air for every adult and 200 for every child—are found above the line.

The total number of cases of illegal occupancy were found by adding the numbers above the zigzag line in Table 35. Altogether there are 15,423 such cases, or 49.9 per cent of the sleeping-rooms measured. That is, in these earlier canvasses practically half of the people were sleeping under conditions of overcrowding made illegal by the tenement-house code because the conditions are detrimental to health or morals or both.

It was impossible to secure comparable data during the recanvass because of the expense and difficulty of securing new measurements for all the rooms, but comparable information was gathered for three of the more recently canvassed districts—Upper Federal, Burnside, and South Deering. These data are presented in Table 36.

TABLE 37

SLEEPING-ROOMS ILLEGALLY OVERCROWDED IN THREE DISTRICTS*

(Original Canvass Data, 1923–26)†

District	Sleeping-Rooms		
	Total Number Occupied	Illegally Occupied	
		Number	Per Cent of Total
Total..........	2,687	990	36.9
Upper Federal.......	1,335	478	35.8
Burnside...........	857	337	39.3
South Deering.......	495	175	35.4

* The housing code requires a minimum of 400 cubic feet of air-space for each adult, and 200 cubic feet for each child under twelve years.

† Olivet, Ancona, Polk, and Pullman were canvassed with the new schedule, which did not include this information.

In these three more recently canvassed districts only 36.9 per cent of the rooms were illegally occupied. But each of these showed a high percentage of overcrowding according to the one-room standard. It is evident, therefore, that in these districts the rooms were large as regards cubic air-space, but the number of persons per room was excessive.

Table 37 summarizes the data about illegal occupancy for these three districts. Burnside, with 48.4 per cent of overcrowding according to the standard of one room per person, had only 39.3 per cent of the sleeping-rooms illegally occupied according to the Chicago tenement standard. Similarly, South Deering had 47.5 per cent of its apartments overcrowded according to the first method and only 35.4 per cent of illegal occupancy according to the second method.

No conclusions should be drawn with regard to improvements in conditions between the first and second canvass on the basis of these more recent figures since these three districts more recently canvassed were not at all representative of the crowded West Side districts in either period.

ILLEGALLY OCCUPIED SLEEPING ROOMS

It proved, of course, to be impossible in many cases for the investigator to ascertain the number of persons who actually slept in

TABLE 38

NUMBER OF APARTMENTS OVERCROWDED ACCORDING TO THE STANDARD OF ONE ROOM PER PERSON IN THREE DISTRICTS

(Original Canvass Data, 1923–26)

District	Total Apartments Reported	Apartments with Less than One Room per Person	
		Number	Percentage of Total
Upper Federal.......	540	205	38.0
Burnside............	405	196	48.4
South Deering.......	200	95	47.5

the apartment. The lady of the house usually insisted that mattresses rolled under the bed or piled one on top of the other, and the "sanitary couches" or cots were not in use although she might acknowledge that they had been used at some time before the investigator's visit. Frequently even the beds, when there was more than one bed in a room, were declared to be not in use. In many other cases where there were both day and night lodgers—a frequent occurrence, for example, near the Steel Mills in South Chicago—the investigator was told that the beds were occupied only by those seen there in the daytime. Here, as in other districts, the alarm almost inevitably was spread soon after the canvassing began that lodgers were to be prohibited, and the question as to the number of lodgers probably caused subterfuge and evasion of many kinds on the part of the foreign housewives, who were afraid that the visits of our investigators meant that the "City Hall" was going to interfere and prevent this important and often necessary method of increasing the family income. Investigators were instructed in all cases of doubt to err on the side of underestimating so that the number reported would be the minimum number of occupants. All tables relating to the number of persons sleeping in a room, therefore, are believed to include underestimates and to present the situation in an unduly favorable light. Even this method of underestimating revealed a very serious amount of illegal overcrowding in every district visited.

The percentages of overcrowding given in the tables represent, of course, only the average for all districts. The percentage for some districts was much higher and in others much lower than the average. Table 39 shows the percentages of illegally occupied sleeping-rooms for the twenty districts investigated in the original canvass.

The provision of the tenement-house code which attempts to prevent overcrowding by requiring for each person a definite minimum of cubic air-space is at once the most important and the most difficult to enforce of all the regulations which should control housing conditions. Among the twenty districts investigated, the number of rooms illegally overcrowded for sleeping purposes ran above 50 per cent of the total number occupied in nine different districts. In the thirteen blocks back of the Yards, 1,981 sleeping-rooms, 55 per cent of the entire number canvassed in that area, had less than the minimum amount of cubic air-space required by the ordinance; in the one block in the old Ghetto district there were 229 sleeping-rooms, 51 per cent of the total number, in which more people slept than the law allowed; in the Bohemian (Pilsen) block, 298 sleeping-rooms, 54 per cent of the entire number, were illegally crowded; in the ten Polish blocks (St. Stanislaus district) on the Northwest side, 3,328 sleeping-rooms, or 69 per cent, and in the seven South Chicago blocks, 60 per cent of the whole number were crowded beyond the legal limit. In the four Slovak blocks (Lumber Yards), in the ten Lithuanian blocks (Southwest), in the twelve blocks of the mixed Polish and Ruthenian district (Division St.), and the two additional Polish blocks, canvassed back of the Yards in 1919, the percentage of illegally occupied rooms varied from 50.5 to 53.9 per cent. In eleven districts the percentages of overcrowding fell below 50 per

TABLE 39

PERCENTAGE OF SLEEPING-ROOMS ILLEGALLY OCCUPIED; BY DISTRICTS

(Original Canvass Data, All Periods)

DISTRICTS	SLEEPING-ROOMS		
	Total Number Occupied	Illegally Occupied	
		Number	Percentage of Total Occupied
All districts*	33,576	16,413	48.9
West Side:			
Old Ghetto	446	229	51.3
Pilsen	546	298	54.4
Lumber Yards	1,721	912	52.9
Hull-House	4,564	1,636	35.8
St. Stanislaus	4,823	3,328	69.0
Division Street	2,863	1,544	53.9
South Side:			
Downtown	230	68	29.6
Near South Side	2,031	795	39.1
Back of the Yards	3,570	1,981	55.5
Stock Yards, South	467	236	50.5
Southwest	2,448	1,288	52.6
South End:			
Burnside	857	337	39.3
South Chicago	1,148	691	60.2
South Deering	495	175	35.4
North Side:			
Lower North	2,830	1,384	48.9
Upper North	692	327	47.3
Negro districts:			
Dearborn	1,145	305	26.6
La Salle	857	234	27.3
Upper Federal	1,335	478	35.8
Walnut	508	167	32.9

* This information was not obtained for Polk St., Ancona, Pullman, and Olivet.

cent, but in no district did the percentage fall as low as 25 per cent. Thus in the two South Side Negro districts canvassed before 1920 the percentages were 27.3 and 26.6 per cent, and these were the lowest percentages found in the investigation. When the Upper Federal Street district, another colored district, was canvassed in 1923, the percentage of overcrowding had risen to 36 per cent. The other districts with less than 50 per cent of illegal occupancy were the old downtown (Italian) district, 29.6 per cent; Walnut, 32.9 per cent; the Greek and Italian district near Hull-House, 35.8 per cent; the Serbian and Croatian in the South Deering area, 35.4 per cent; the Croatian district near St. Jerome's Croatian Church on the Near South Side, 39.1 per cent; the Magyar district in Burnside, 39.3 per cent; Lower North, 48.9 per cent; and the mixed German and Italian district on the Upper North Side with 47.3 per cent of illegal crowding.

These statistics of the total number of persons sleeping in rooms which do not contain the amount of cubic air-space required by the tenement-house law fail to give any adequate idea of the extremely insanitary conditions found in some cases. Taking first the cases from the pre-war canvass, it was found, for example, in the Jewish district, that one man occupied as a bedroom a windowless clothes closet containing only 18 square feet and 167 cubic feet, but large enough to hold a single bed. A case much worse than this in the same block was that of a household in which all the six members of the family slept not only in one room but in one bed, in order to make room for the ten lodgers who lived with them. Several other cases almost as bad as these were found in the same block. In one house two persons slept in a very dark room containing 34 square feet which contained only 265 cubic feet, and which was so close to the adjoining house that it had neither light nor ventilation; in another house four persons slept in a room containing 46 square feet which contained only 371 cubic feet, although 1,600 was the required legal minimum; three persons in another house slept in a room containing 53 square feet; and in still another case five persons slept in a room containing 65 square feet which contained 650 cubic feet instead of the 2,000 required by law. In the Bohemian district another man slept in a closet containing 22 square feet which contained 198 cubic feet, and six persons slept in a room 7 by 10 feet which contained only 625 cubic feet.

In the district back of the Yards, where 1,981 violations of the law against overcrowding were found at the time of the pre-war canvass,

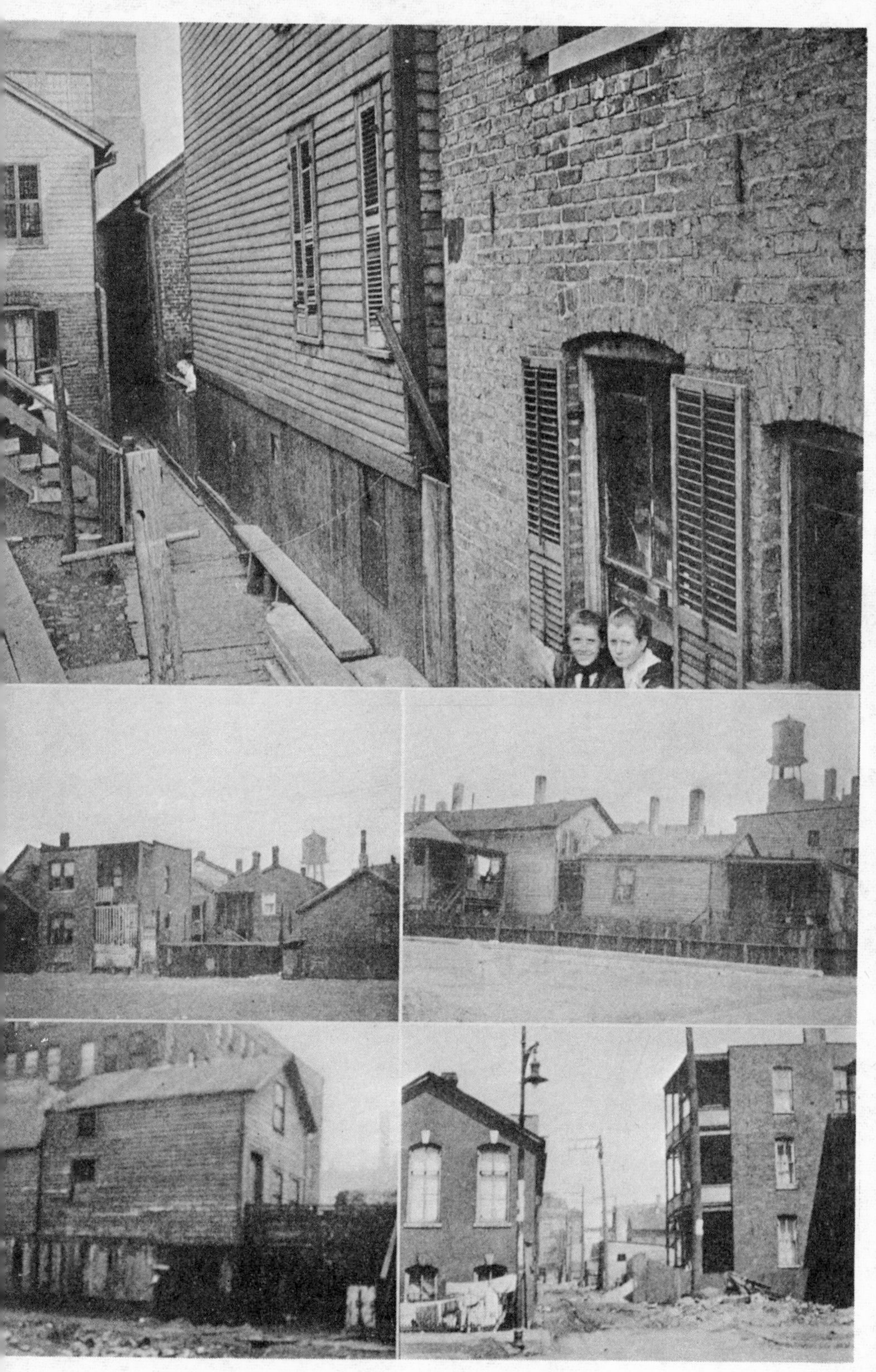

CONGESTION OF VARIOUS KINDS AND DEGREES

the number of cubic feet in the room was in many instances shockingly below the number of cubic feet required by law. Thus it appears that in nineteen cases when rooms of 350–400 cubic feet were being illegally occupied, in two cases 600 cubic feet, in ten cases 800, and in one case 1,000, and in another 1,400 were required by law. In 77 cases when 1,200 cubic feet of air were required, rooms containing less than 800 cubic feet were occupied. In one case four people slept in a room containing only 333 cubic feet—a room that could not have been legally occupied by even a single person over twelve years of age. In another case five people slept in a room containing 472 cubic feet—a room that could legally be occupied only by a single person. In another case seven people, for whom 2,800 cubic feet would have been the legal minimum, slept in a room containing only 657 cubic feet.

In South Chicago the universal practice of taking lodgers increased the overcrowding evil. In one South Chicago "home" a lodger slept with the father, mother, and two children in a room containing 800 cubic feet, although 1,600 cubic feet were required; in another case a room containing only 841 cubic feet was occupied at night by a man and his wife, their one child, and three lodgers, while four other lodgers occupied the same room during the day. In a small rear house in which there were two bedrooms containing 764 and 772 cubic feet, a man and his wife, a child under twelve, and a grown daughter occupied the one which contained 764 cubic feet, although the legal minimum was 1,400 cubic feet; two grown sons and two lodgers, who should have had 1,600 cubic feet of air, occupied the other bedroom, which contained only 772 cubic feet. In this case the man, who was a railroad laborer, was nominally the owner of the premises. He had, however, a large mortgage to pay; he therefore rented the front house and crowded his family into the rear apartment of the rear house. At the time the house was visited, during a cold week in December, the family was keeping two pigs and fifteen chickens in the basement. In another small apartment in a rear basement, where all the rooms were dark except the kitchen, a man, his wife, and child occupied a room containing 447 cubic feet, one lodger slept in the parlor, and three lodgers in the other dark bedroom, which contained only 611 cubic feet. The family had seven pigeons, which at that time they were keeping in the house. It is of interest to note that six families lived in this house and together they had twelve lodgers and six children under twelve years of age, but the only toilet accommodations for the entire house were two filthy yard closets.

In other districts similar cases of extreme overcrowding might be cited. Thus in a Slovak household (Lumber Yards) a sleeping-room containing 687 cubic feet, legally large enough for one adult and one child, was occupied by two adults and five children. A Polish butcher's family, consisting of three adults and four children, slept in a room containing but 536 cubic feet of air. The room had but one lot-line window, and this was never opened. The family of a Lithuanian laborer, two adults and five children, slept in a room having only 693 cubic feet of air-space instead of the required 1,800. Even worse was the case of another Lithuanian family, two adults and five children, sleeping in a room which contained just 423 cubic feet. This same room had but 65 square feet floor area, was only 6½ feet high, and had a total window area of but 4½ square feet. In another Lithuanian "home" the father, mother, and two children were sleeping in a room containing 500 cubic feet. Again in the household of a Polish laborer five adults were sleeping in a room with 763 cubic feet of air-space instead of the required 2,000.

In the Hull-House district four children were found sleeping in a room that had only 722 cubic feet of air-space. The room was windowless and quite dark, the only light and air coming from a small transom opening into an adjoining room. Five lodgers and a child were crowded into another room which could legally have been occupied by only three adults. Again, in a room large enough for only two adults slept three small children, an older boy and a girl, and their grandmother. The older girl and the grandmother occupied the only bed, and the others contented themselves with "shakedowns," which completely covered the floor of the small room. Perhaps the worst case of all in the Hull-House district was one in which a wide shelf over a basement stairway had been walled up until a tiny light-proof, air-proof room had been constructed. In this box, containing only 125 cubic feet of air-space, three men were sleeping.

In the more recent investigations many similar cases were found. In a home in South Chicago two adults and four children slept in a room containing 783 cubic feet, with a small window opening on a 16-inch passage. From this family one girl had been sent to the Parental School and one to Ridge Farm, a tuberculosis preventorium.

In the open space of the Burnside triangle there were similar cases of crowding within the house in spite of the air of spaciousness outside which comes from vacant blocks and lots. In one Russian-Polish household in "the triangle" a girl of thirteen, her father, and a younger brother were sleeping in one bed in a room containing only 637 cubic feet, but of course factors other than adequate air-space are involved here. In another household in "the triangle" an attic room containing only 657 cubic feet was occupied by two adults and four children. This room had only one small window measuring 24 by 55 inches, but the rear part of the attic was empty and an air current seemed to circulate.

In a house in the Upper Federal Street district two rooms were used for sleeping. One containing 1,743 cubic feet provided sleeping-room for four adults and four children. Two adults slept in the other room of 464 cubic feet—a dark, unfinished attic with a steeply sloping roof and the walls papered with newspapers.

In another house in Upper Federal Street one room used for light housekeeping contained 946 cubic feet. This room was occupied by two adults and three children for whom the legal requirement was not less than 1,400 cubic feet of air-space. This cruelly overcrowded room contained one double bed for the two adults, one single bed for the three children, in addition to one dresser, two chairs, and a small laundry stove, on which the cooking was done. A condition somewhat similar was found in a room of 729 cubic feet, containing three adults, one of whom slept on the floor, when the law required not less than 1,200 cubic feet of air for this group.

Much overcrowding was found among the few Italian residents in the Federal Street district. In one home an adult and four children were found sleeping in a room of 810 cubic feet. In another two children were found sleeping on the dining-room floor. In the latter case the cubic content—1,141 cubic feet—was adequate, but it serves as an illustration for the frequently recurring custom of using a family room, occupied during the day, as a bedroom at night. This is a regular and customary arrangement. Cots and davenports are found in the living- and dining-room, and sometimes even in the kitchen. The occupant is without even the scant privacy afforded by a bedroom shared with others, and goes to bed in a room that is usually disorderly and in serious need of ventilation after a day's use. There is an occasional instance of a bedroom which is used for some miscellaneous household purpose during the day. In some cases this was very undesirable, particularly because of the small size and frequently inadequate ventilation. In an Italian house, for example, a child's bedroom was heavily hung with drying herbs and vegetables which filled the room with strong and offensive odors.

Another very usual arrangement in the Federal Street area is for the same room to be slept in both by day and by night, so that the bed is rarely empty and the air is seldom fresh. When a man has night work, he uses a bedroom during the day and his wife sleeps there during the night. The pressing economic necessity that drives the Negroes to take in roomers multiplies this difficulty. Many of the men (the roomers are nearly all men) have night work, night shifts in the plants where they are employed, Pullman porters, taxi-drivers, and others. The householder makes extra money by renting during the day the rooms that would otherwise be unprofitable. Many room measurements had to be obtained with care, in order not to disturb the sleeping occupants. A woman living near Federal Street was very proud of the fact that her beds "were working twenty-three hours a day."

One of the worst features of this overcrowding is the demoralizing lack of privacy. Grown brothers and sisters, for example, often occupy the same room. Sometimes the crowding is unnecessary; the family prefers, especially in the winter, to huddle into the rooms near the kitchen and in this way save the expense of extra fuel and an extra stove. In one apartment a bedroom that was light and sunny was left vacant, although the family was sleeping in a dark room with only an interior window opening into a hall. The dark room was, of course, near the kitchen.

It is, however, not only in illegally overcrowded rooms that poor conditions exist. Many other rooms were found which, though satisfactory in the eyes of the law, are undesirable sleeping-places. For example, one investigator found a room made by partitioning off the rear part of a store and then used as a bedroom, living-room, and kitchen for the entire family. There is the combination storeroom and bedroom, such as that described in the following statement by one of our investigators: "This room contains, besides two lodgers, two barrels of wine and hundreds of quart bottles. The place is gloomy, and the whole apartment reeks with the smell of wine." There is also the room used by night as a sleeping-room and by day as a dining-room, living-room, or, most common of all, as a kitchen. The grave menace to health in such arrangements, the moral danger resulting from the total lack of privacy, especially where, as is too often the case here, there are lodgers in every available corner, need scarcely be pointed out.

BEDS EVERYWHERE

Further testimony on the subject of overcrowding is to be found in the very considerable number of cases in which every room in the house was used as a sleeping room. Table 40 shows for all the districts canvassed the number of apartments in which all the rooms were occupied as sleeping-rooms.

It appears from this table that in 728 of the homes visited even the kitchen was used as a bedroom at night. In 4,255 other households every room except the kitchen was used as a bedroom. Here, as in other evidences of overcrowding, the different districts varied considerably, and there were differences from block to block even in the same district. Most crowded of all in this respect was the old Italian district on Plymouth Court[13a] that happily disappeared during the war. The old Ghetto, the Slovak district near the Lumber Yards, the Stock Yards districts, and the Hull-House section were all seriously congested according to this standard of overcrowding.

Not only are the apartments crowded with respect to the number of rooms, with respect to the size of bedrooms, with respect to the proportion of the entire house used for sleeping arrangements, with respect to beds in use both day and night, but also with respect to

[13a] See above, pp. 110–11.

the number of beds in use at the same time. Cases of three or more persons sleeping in one bed have been cited above. Although our

TABLE 40

NUMBER OF HOUSEHOLDS USING SPECIFIED NUMBER OF ROOMS IN THE APARTMENT AS SLEEPING ROOMS
(Original Canvass Data, ALL PERIODS)

DISTRICT	TOTAL NUMBER OF HOUSE-HOLDS	HOUSEHOLDS USING SPECIFIED NUMBER OF ROOMS FOR SLEEPING PURPOSES					
		Households Using All Rooms for Sleeping		Using All but 1		Using All but 2	Using All but 3 or More
		Number	Percentage of Total	Number	Percentage of Total	Number	Number
Total	15,808*	728	4.6	4,255	26.9	6,406	4,419
Pre-war canvass	13,663	653	4.8	3,800	27.8	5,666	3,544
Lower North	1,394	77	5.5	399	28.6	561	357
St. Stanislaus	2,754	49	1.8	403	14.6	1,430	872
Division Street	1,416	53	3.7	352	24.9	630	381
Hull-House	1,963	135	6.9	783	39.9	593	452
Old Ghetto	191	21	11.0	75	39.3	61	34
Pilsen	272	7	2.6	119	43.8	104	42
Lumber Yards	852	82	9.6	329	38.6	297	144
Walnut Street	228	2	0.9	21	9.2	61	144
Near South Side	944	22	2.3	266	28.2	370	286
Dearborn	434	6	1.4	61	14.1	141	226
Downtown	118	42	35.6	58	49.2	13	5
Southwest	1,012	40	4.0	299	29.5	426	247
Back of the Yards	1,564	106	6.8	508	32.5	739	211
South Chicago	521	11	2.1	127	24.4	240	143
Post-war canvass	2,145	75	3.5	455	21.2	740	875
Upper North	366	3	0.8	48	13.1	143	172
La Salle	398	8	2.0	41	10.3	116	233
Upper Federal	533	37	6.9	148	27.8	164	184
Stock Yards, South	257	20	7.8	123	47.8	88	26
South Deering	194	5	2.6	41	21.1	66	82
Burnside	397	2	0.5	54	13.6	163	178

* Vacant apartments, 563; use of rooms not reported, 216.

schedule did not ask for this information in every case, it is probable that the conditions found in these districts would not vary greatly from that found by Dr. Houghteling in her study of the standard of living of unskilled wage-earners.

BED OVERCROWDING

In the Houghteling study already referred to, some valuable information regarding the sleeping arrangements of the independent wage-earning families was published. When Dr. Houghteling's schedules were taken, information was secured as to the number of

TABLE 41

NUMBER OF HOUSEHOLDS WITH SPECIFIED NUMBER OF PERSONS AND SPECIFIED NUMBER OF BEDS
(Houghteling Data)

Number of Persons in Household	Number of Households with Specified Number of Single Beds											
	Total	Total Not Reported	Total Not Reported	2	3	4	5	6	7	8	9	10 or More
Total	467	15	452	11	46	106	62	118	42	46	12	9
Not reported	2	....	2	....	....	....	....	1	....	....	....	1
Total reported	465	15	450	11	46	106	62	117	42	46	12	8
3	46	1	45	7	13	16	7	2	....	....	....	....
4	76	4	72	2	18	38	8	6	....	....	....	....
5	84	1	83	2	8	35	17	18	2	....	1	....
6	74	2	72	....	2	10	17	32	6	5	....	....
7	65	3	62	....	3	3	9	26	16	5	....	....
8	58	3	55	....	2	1	2	21	12	14	2	1
9	29	....	29	....	....	3	1	5	5	11	4	....
10	15	....	15	....	....	....	1	4	....	7	1	2
11	7	....	7	....	....	....	....	....	....	4	1	2
12	5	....	5	....	....	....	....	2	....	....	3	....
13	3	1	2	....	....	....	....	1	....	....	....	1
14 or over	3	....	3	....	....	....	....	....	1	....	....	2

double beds and the number of single beds in each household. In making Table 41, in order to obtain a unit of comparison, each double bed was considered as two single beds; and every cradle, cot, davenport, daybed, or any article of furniture on which an individual slept was considered a single bed. If a standard of one person to a single bed and two to a double bed be applied, this table shows that 235 of the families, or 52.2 per cent, were below, and 215 were at or above, the standard. Of those below the standard, many are far below it, as evidenced by the households of four or five persons having two single beds; the households of six or seven persons with three or four single beds; the households of eight or nine persons with five or six single beds. Further light is thrown on this question of overcrowding when it is recalled that in one hundred of these families there were boarders and roomers, most of whom were adults and not members of the family group.

Miss Goltz found nearly as great overcrowding with respect to the number of beds available in her study of the dependent families in one of the districts of a family welfare agency. In applying the standard each double or three quarter-width bed was counted as two single beds; each cot, sofa, or baby bed (always used for infants in this group of families) as one single bed; and each member of a household, regardless of age, was counted as a person.[14] Judged by this standard, the 113 households had 593 single beds available for 657 persons and 56 households, or 49 per cent of the total (all those beneath the heavy line in Table 42), were overcrowded.

Again it must be emphasized that the actual overcrowding in the districts canvassed is greater than the statistics indicate. This is due in part to the difficulty of securing accurate data regarding lodgers and to our uniform rule of underestimating in all doubtful cases. But at times, although there are rooms enough for comfortable or at least decent living, families crowd together because of the difficulty of keeping warm in winter.

In "the triangle," for example, one Russian mother told the investigator that, as soon as it got cold, she moved all the beds into the one room that had a stove in it (although there were two other bedrooms available) because that was the only way to keep warm. This meant that two adults and five children were sleeping in a room containing only 1,020 cubic feet of air space.

In some cases the mother knows that the family is occupying a

[14] Although it might well be argued that three young children could comfortably sleep in one double bed and that therefore a standard of one person to one single bed, as defined above, is too rigid, the rather frequent occurrence of three-quarter-width beds will balance this consideration. It is fair to assume, then, that more than one person to a single bed tends toward overcrowding.

house or a flat that is too crowded for decency or comfort, but inability to pay a higher rent or to sell the house or to find a larger place without moving too far from the old friends and neighbors prevents their moving into more adequate quarters. But, of course, they are sometimes so accustomed to living in cramped discomfort that they do not think of the situation as one that can be remedied.

TABLE 42*

NUMBER OF HOUSEHOLDS HAVING A SPECIFIED NUMBER OF PERSONS AND A SPECIFIED NUMBER OF SINGLE BEDS

(Charity Families Visited in Lower North District)

Number of Persons	Total	Number of Single Beds										
		1	2	3	4	5	6	7	8	9	10	11
Total	113	....	10	10	24	19	22	15	7	2	3	1
1	3	....	3	....	....	....	....	....	....	....	....	....
2	2	....	2	....	....	....	....	....	....	....	....	....
3	9	....	3	3	3	....	....	....	....	....	....	....
4	20	....	1	5	9	4	1	....	....	....	....	....
5	21	....	1	2	5	6	7	....	....	....	....	....
6	17	....	....	....	2	7	6	2	....	....	....	....
7	13	....	....	....	5	....	2	1	4	1	....	....
8	14	....	....	....	....	1	5	7	1	....	....	....
9	8	....	....	....	....	1	1	3	1	1	1	....
10	5	....	....	....	....	....	....	2	1	....	1	1
11	1	....	....	....	....	....	....	....	....	....	1	....

* Taken from Eleanor Goltz, *The Housing of Dependent Families in Chicago*, p. 36.

It may be questioned, in view of the widespread overcrowding and of the more significant fact that in certain areas thirty-seven out of every one hundred[15] sleeping-rooms are illegally occupied, whether the minimum set in the tenement-house code is too high. For more than twenty years the community has retained this minimum on its statute-books as a paper minimum enforced in no section of the city. But our minimum of 400 cubic feet of air for every per-

[15] See figures for three districts visited, p. 256.

son over 12, and 200 cubic feet of air for every person under twelve is not a high minimum. Professor Huxley, working among the East London tenement population, estimated that a minimum air-space of 800 cubic feet was necessary for an adult.

"Household congestion," as it may be called, is a result of many factors. High rents and scarcity of satisfactory apartments, lack of adequate heating facilities which make it necessary for the family to crowd into even less space than they seem to have; and the necessity of taking lodgers into an already overcrowded home in order to supplement the income—these are only a few of the causes of house and room congestion.

CHAPTER IX[1]

TENEMENT RENTS

Trends in Chicago Rent Levels; Changes in Rents in the Areas Canvassed; Size of Apartments; The Lack of Conveniences in Low-Rental Homes; Income and Expenditure for Rent; The Houghteling and Hughes Studies; What Does the Future Hold?

THE original data collected with regard to housing conditions during the years from 1909 to 1919 reflect the economic conditions of the relatively stable pre-war period. A rise in the general cost of living began to be appreciable in Chicago during 1917, the first year of the participation of the United States in the World War, and reached a maximum high level three years later, in June, 1920.[2] Rents in Chicago, however, remained practically unchanged until the end of 1919, and did not reach their peak until December, 1924.[3] Thus, while the first investigations of the districts were carried on in a period of comparatively stable rents, the canvasses of the second period may be expected to bring out the sharp contrasts of the post-war inflation years. These later years covered a period of accumulating profits, of climbing rents, of considerable building activity, and of a certain rise in the general standard of living of the wage-earning group. Preceding chapters have shown that in actual physical surroundings the conditions in certain districts were somewhat improved in the second period. Assuming that wages rose along with other factors in prosperity and that new

[1] By Helen Rankin Jeter, formerly of the Faculty of the School of Social Service Administration, University of Chicago, and now a member of the research staff of the federal Social Security Board. This chapter is published as it was written by Dr. Jeter three years ago except for minor editorial changes. Data have been added, for example, from the 1934 special Chicago census. These returns were added by Mary Zahrobsky, special research assistant, School of Social Service, from data made available through the courtesy of the University Social Science Research Committee.

[2] The cost of living index for Chicago in June, 1920, was 114.6 per cent above the 1913 level (see *Monthly Labor Review*, XXVIII [February, 1929], 378).

[3] Rents in December, 1924, were 105.8 per cent above the level for December, 1914 (*ibid.*, p. 181).

buildings were erected in accordance with demand, we should expect the undesirable dwellings of the 1908–19 period to have been abandoned by the families that dwelt in them in the earlier period and their places to have been taken, if at all, by groups of the newer immigrants and others whose wages lag behind those of the better-established groups.

TRENDS IN CHICAGO RENT LEVELS

An examination of the statistics provided by the Health Department shows that the number of building permits approved in Chicago had averaged about thirteen thousand per year during the six years preceding 1917. War industries attracted capital into more remunerative fields and the number of building permits in 1917 was only seven thousand. The next year the number fell to three thousand. Housing shortage together with an influx of population to Chicago during the war, was undoubtedly responsible for the beginning of an increase in rents during 1919, which reached at the end of that year a level 14 per cent above the level of 1914. In the same year (1919) there occurred a brief revival of building activity, but the number of buildings erected was still considerably below the yearly average for the pre-war period. Moreover, in 1920, along with the slight depression in business conditions, there occurred another drop in the number of building permits to only four thousand. Meantime, as shown in Table 43, rents had steadily risen since 1919 and were in 1924 and 1925 more than twice as high as they had been in 1914. Renewed activity in building during the years 1923, 1924, and 1925 finally compensated for the shortage of houses; rents began to drop in 1926, and have continued to drop during the major depression period. Since 1928 building activity has declined sharply but rents have continued to decline. In 1932 they were only 24.9 per cent above the 1914 level,[4] and in 1934 were actually 0.7 per cent lower than the 1914 level.

Housing shortage and rising rents may be assumed, therefore, to have prevented the entire abandonment of the old houses even by wage-earners whose standard of living had presumably risen during the prosperous years. Some degree of shifting in racial composition

[4] This represents a decline of 76.5 per cent between 1924 and 1932.

of the population of the districts investigated had taken place between the first and second investigations. This shift was, in general, a decrease in the proportion of foreign-born and an increase in the proportion of native-born in the districts canvassed. The chief increase in the number of American households was due to the migration of southern Negroes during the war.

TABLE 43

NUMBER OF BUILDING PERMITS APPROVED IN CHICAGO AND PERCENTAGE OF INCREASE IN RENTS, 1914–34; BY YEARS

Year	Number of Buildings for Which Permits Were Approved in Chicago*	Percentage of Increase in Rent over Level of December, 1914†
1914	13,937	....
1915	14,670	‡
1916	14,788	0.7
1917	6,959	1.4
1918	3,014	2.6
1919	9,026	14.0
1920	4,440	48.9
1921	10,309	83.9
1922	18,171	88.9
1923	22,195	95.4
1924	23,858	105.8
1925	18,665	104.4
1926	16,526	96.7
1927	13,494	90.0
1928	10,683	83.6
1929	7,411	77.2
1930	3,463	71.1
1931	1,947	56.5
1932	880	24.9
1933	866	2.1
1934	1,089	‡

* Figures from reports of the Department of Health of the city of Chicago.

† Figures from the U.S. Bureau of Labor Statistics, *Changes in Cost of Living* July 15, 1935, p. 13

‡ Decrease 0.1 per cent, December, 1915, and decrease 0.7 per cent, November, 1934.

CHANGES IN RENTS IN THE AREAS CANVASSED

Changes in rents in the areas canvassed were affected by the great Negro influx which occurred in these deteriorated areas. The Negroes were obliged to live in certain areas in which they were practically but not legally segregated. In many tenements a higher rental was charged to Negro tenants. An additional area, exclusively Negro, was included in the later canvass. Being the newest and economically the weakest group, and being handicapped, in addition, by existing social and economic barriers and discriminations of various kinds, the Negroes moved into some of the worst houses that had been formerly occupied by European immigrants. The decrease in the proportion of foreign-born, accounted for in part by the exodus to Europe during the war, was perhaps augmented by the increased prosperity of the older immigrant groups. The decrease is noted chiefly in the case of the Polish, the Bohemians, the Germans, and the Irish. Some of these undoubtedly returned to Europe while others probably moved to more prosperous neighborhoods in Chicago.

The shift in racial composition in several of the separate districts is more evident than that in the area as a whole. In the old Ghetto, for example, in the early canvass, 112 of the 195 households were Jewish while all the rest except one native white family were foreign-born of other European groups. When the district was recanvassed more than fifteen years later, of the 47 families left, 29 were American Negro, 11 Jewish, 5 Polish, and the other 2 German and Lithuanian respectively. When first visited, the Walnut Street district reported 64 per cent of its heads of households either native-born or foreign-born white and 36 per cent Negro. In the post-war canvass, 88 per cent were Negro. In these two West Side neighborhoods the change of tenants, and particularly the substitution of Negro for white tenants, was undoubtedly important in relation to the advance in rent.

In other districts, the proportions of certain smaller groups have increased even though the predominant national group remains the same. In the Lower North district, for example, which is predominantly Italian, the number of Negro households rose from 5 to 242, or 24 per cent of the total. In the Near South Side district, Croatians decreased from 20 per cent of the households to only 5 per cent, while Negroes and Mexicans, neither represented in the district in the pre-war canvass, came to form 10 per cent of the households in the post-war recanvass. In the Stock Yards, South, again the proportion of the Polish shrank from 77 per cent to 39 per cent while Mexicans, though not present in the neighborhood until after the war, became numerous enough to make nearly one-fifth of the population in the recanvass.

It thus seems probable that in spite of increased prosperity on the part of certain groups of wage-earners, and in spite of the building of new dwellings after 1920, there was still a demand for the old houses at the lowest possible rentals because there were new and relatively weak economic groups in the community. The amounts of rent paid by these new tenants and by the older groups probably depend primarily upon the relative bargaining power of tenant and landlord and only secondarily upon the size, convenience, condition, and location of the home.

Among the 15,410 apartments visited in the original canvass before 1920 and the 16,112 visited during the post-war canvass (following 1923) and the later recanvass a certain number were owned by the tenants,[5] others were occupied rent free because of kinship to the owner, or in return for services rendered. Moreover, a considerable number of the householders reported rents that included the rent of stores and were therefore not comparable to the rents of other dwellings. Finally, in spite of the fact that the amount of rent is a fact that is easily and precisely stated, there were apartments in both periods for which it was impossible to ascertain the amount of rent paid. Hence, as Table 44 indicates, the number of apartments for which the amount of rent is known for the earlier period is 12,300 and for the later period 11,751. The number of rented homes visited in the second period is approximately 2 per cent of all rented homes in Chicago[6] and is 46 per cent of the rented homes in the particular census tracts which include the housing districts.[7]

Among the 12,300 apartments for which information was available for the first canvass, as shown in Table 45, more than 85 per cent rented for amounts varying between $5.00 and $15 per month;

[5] For a discussion of ownership in these districts see below, chap. xii.

[6] The number of rented homes in Chicago reported by the U.S. census in 1930 was 572,234.

[7] Census tracts including the housing districts had 28,160 rented homes.

TABLE 44

TENURE OF APARTMENTS

(Original Canvass, Later Canvass, and Recanvass)

TENURE	NUMBER OF APARTMENTS VISITED	
	Original Canvass before 1920	Later Canvass and Recanvass
Total	15,410	16,112
Owned by tenant	2,023	2,721
Rent free	29	108
Rent includes store	225	430
Rented, amount of rent not reported	833	1,102
Rented, amount of rent reported	12,300	11,751

TABLE 45

APARTMENTS CLASSIFIED BY AMOUNT OF MONTHLY RENT; PER CENT DISTRIBUTION AND CUMULATIVE PERCENTAGES

MONTHLY RENT	APARTMENTS RENTED					
	Number		Per Cent Distribution		Cumulative Percentages	
	Original Canvass	Later Canvass and Recanvass	Original Canvass	Later Canvass and Recanvass	Original Canvass	Later Canvass and Recanvass
Total	12,300	11,751	100.0	100.0	....	....
Less than $5	404	28	3.3	0.2	3.3	0.2
$ 5 and less than $10	6,484	852	52.7	7.2	56.0	7.4
10 and less than 15	4,021	2,552	32.7	21.7	88.7	29.1
15 and less than 20	964	3,597	7.8	30.6	96.5	59.7
20 and less than 25	295	2,270	2.4	19.3	98.9	79.0
25 and less than 30	89	1,220	.7	10.4	99.6	89.4
30 and less than 35	27	513	.2	4.4	99.8	93.8
35 and less than 40	10	385	.1	3.3	99.9	97.1
40 and less than 45	2	150	*	1.3	99.9	98.4
45 and less than 50	....	97	....	0.8	99.9	99.2
50 and less than 55	2	55	(*)	0.5	99.9	99.7
55 and less than 60	1	10	(*)	0.1	99.9	99.8
60 and less than 75	1	22	(*)	0.2	100.0	100.0

* Less than one-tenth of 1 per cent.

99.6 per cent rented for less than $30. A considerable number rented for less than $5.00 and only one was as much as $60. The absolute amounts seem to be low, but the dwellings, described in earlier chapters, were crowded, cheerless, and uncomfortable.

TABLE 46

NUMBER OF RENTED APARTMENTS WITH SPECIFIED MONTHLY RENT; BY DISTRICTS

(Original Canvass Data)

District	Number of Rented Apartments with Specified Monthly Rent													
	Total Rent-ed	Less than $5	$5 and Less than $10	$10 and Less than $15	$15 and Less than $20	$20 and Less than $25	$25 and Less than $30	$30 and Less than $35	$35 and Less than $40	$40 and Less than $45	$45 and Less than $50	$50 and Less than $55	$55 and Less than $60	$60 and Over
All districts	12,300	404	6,484	4,021	964	295	89	27	10	2	....	2	1	1
West Side:														
Old Ghetto	157	4	84	49	18	2	....	....	....	....	....	....	....	....
Pilsen	223	11	196	15	1	....	....	....	....	....	....	....	....	....
Lumber Yards	673	42	438	177	14	1	1	....	....	....	....	....	....	....
Hull-House	1,768	12	609	775	232	109	17	12	1	....	....	....	....	1
Polk Street														
St. Stanislaus	2,297	148	1,883	229	35	2	....	....	....	....	....	....	....	....
Division Street	1,246	14	423	697	95	10	4	1	1	....	....	....	1	....
Ancona														
South Side:														
Downtown	112	12	76	24	....	....	....	....	....	....	....	....	....	....
Near South Side	821	17	386	324	80	10	2	2	....	....	....	....	....	....
Back of the Yards	1,154	34	813	287	15	3	2	....	....	....	....	....	....	....
Stock Yards, South	229	1	156	70	2	....	....	....	....	....	....	....	....	....
Southwest (Lithuanian)	736	13	251	400	41	10	10	4	6	....	....	1	....	....
South End:														
Burnside														
South Chicago (East Side)	398	7	234	154	3	....	....	....	....	....	....	....	....	....
South Deering														
Pullman														
North Side:														
Lower North	1,218	85	694	332	91	12	3	1	....	....	....	....	....	....
Upper North	312	1	132	157	17	3	1	1	....	....	....	....	....	....
Olivet														
Negro districts:														
Dearborn	397	....	32	122	153	68	19	2	....	....	....	1	....	....
La Salle	365	1	31	123	112	60	30	4	2	2	....	....	....	....
Upper Federal														
Walnut (West Side)	194	2	46	86	55	5	....	....	....	....	....	....	....	....

The circumstances in the second period, although mitigated by the addition of certain conveniences of modern life, were not much better. Nevertheless, the rents for the same districts and for the most part the same buildings, as shown in Table 45, had, in general, doubled. The rents covered practically the same range, that is, from less than $5.00 to not much above $60 but rents of less than

$5.00 had almost disappeared; 82.0 per cent of the apartments rented for amounts between $10 and $30, and 10.6 per cent rented for $30 or more. Although only four of the entire number of apart-

TABLE 47

NUMBER OF RENTED APARTMENTS WITH SPECIFIED MONTHLY RENT; BY DISTRICTS

(Later Canvass and Recanvass)

District	Number of Rented Apartments with Specified Monthly Rent													
	Total Rented	Less than $5	$5 and Less than $10	$10 and Less than $15	$15 and Less than $20	$20 and Less than $25	$25 and Less than $30	$30 and Less than $35	$35 and Less than $40	$40 and Less than $45	$45 and Less than $50	$50 and Less than $55	$55 and Less than $60	$60 and Over
All districts	11,751	28	852	2,552	3,597	2,270	1,220	513	385	150	97	55	10	22
West Side:														
Old Ghetto	49	....	8	5	5	15	12	3	1	....	....	....	....	....
Pilsen	230	....	49	120	51	8	1	1	....	....	....	....	....	....
Lumber Yards	441	5	130	155	101	26	16	4	3	....	....	1	....	....
Hull-House	1,005	....	52	174	252	225	107	54	39	42	40	11	2	7
Polk Street	255	....	3	28	81	87	43	4	9	....	....	....	....	....
St. Stanislaus	1,905	13	157	516	750	315	82	29	19	15	4	4	1	....
Division Street	1,061	....	45	168	295	326	142	36	35	5	3	3	2	1
Ancona	372	....	23	75	167	70	33	4	....	....	....	....	....	....
South Side:														
Downtown														
Near South Side	685	1	43	160	217	131	64	32	24	7	3	2	....	1
Back of the Yards	1,077	1	90	343	426	158	37	11	5	2	1	3	....	....
Stock-Yards, South	206	1	72	72	48	10	2	1	....	....	....	....	....	....
Southwest (Lithuanian)	647	1	27	114	201	102	118	36	20	5	9	7	....	7
South End:														
Burnside	156	....	5	27	44	34	26	15	5	....	....	....	....	....
South Chicago (East Side)	383	1	28	93	164	68	18	7	3	1	....	....	....	....
South Deering	118	....	2	18	35	29	20	7	4	1	1	....	....	1
Pullman	194	....	36	111	10	7	16	7	5	2	....	....	....	....
North Side:														
Lower North	970	4	54	205	323	198	114	51	19	1	1	....	....	....
Upper North	231	....	2	28	55	76	44	18	6	1	1	....	....	....
Olivet	352	....	2	29	88	94	57	38	33	7	1	3	....	....
Negro districts:														
Dearborn	375	1	3	21	67	91	91	41	36	14	8	1	....	1
La Salle	462	....	9	9	85	71	80	58	74	34	22	12	5	3
Upper Federal	427	....	8	70	104	100	68	41	26	3	1	6	....	....
Walnut (West Side)	150	....	4	11	28	29	29	15	19	10	2	2	....	1

ments rented for $50 or more during the period 1909–19, 87 ranged from $50 to $75 in the later period. The median rental for all apartments had increased from $9.00 to $18.

How far from typical these rents are of rented homes throughout the city of Chicago may be indicated by a comparison between Table 48 and Table 49. In Table 49 the United States census report

TABLE 48*

MONTHLY RENT, APRIL, 1930, OF NON-FARM RENTED HOMES IN CHICAGO "COMMUNITIES" WITH MEDIAN RENT BELOW $30

Rent	Area 31		24		28		30		34		37		47		50	
	Number Homes	Per Cent Distribution	Number Homes	Per Cent Distribution	Number Homes	Per Cent Distribution	Number Homes	Per Cent Distribution	Number Homes	Per Cent Distribution	Number Homes	Per Cent Distribution	Number Homes	Per Cent Distribution	Number Homes	Per Cent Distribution
Total	12,364	100.0	33,000	100.0	24,304	100.0	10,681	100.0	3,987	100.0	2,368	100.0	266	100.0	783	100.0
Under $10	1,302	10.5	1,043	3.2	526	2.2	118	1.1	147	3.7	25	1.1	1	0.4	10	1.3
$10–$14.99	3,131	25.3	3,246	9.8	1,961	8.1	488	4.6	497	12.5	195	8.2	12	4.5	95	12.1
15– 19.99	3,653	29.6	6,095	18.5	4,004	16.5	1,166	10.9	975	24.4	519	21.9	41	15.4	214	27.3
20– 29.99	2,727	22.1	10,193	30.9	8,211	33.8	3,769	35.3	1,592	39.9	1,059	44.7	121	45.5	252	32.2
30– 49.99	1,063	8.6	8,149	24.7	6,447	26.5	4,126	38.6	645	16.2	492	20.8	70	26.3	175	22.4
50– 74.99	285	2.3	3,312	10.0	1,912	7.9	704	6.6	75	1.9	56	2.4	11	4.1	27	3.5
75– 99.99	60	0.5	518	1.6	430	1.8	132	1.2	15	0.4	4	0.2	4	1.5	1	0.1
100–149.99	37	0.3	125	0.4	201	0.8	76	0.7	9	0.2	1	†	2	0.8	2	0.3
150–199.99	4	†	29	0.1	48	0.2	22	0.2	.....	.....	2	0.1	.....	.....	.....	.....
200 and over	4	†	16	†	29	0.1	6	0.1	.....	.....	1	†	.....	.....	.....	.....
Unknown	98	0.8	274	0.8	535	2.2	74	0.7	32	0.8	14	0.6	4	1.5	7	0.9
Median rent (dollars)	Under 20	.....	20–30	.....	20–30	.....	20–30	.....	20–30	.....	20–30	.....	20–30	.....	20–30	.....

* *Census Data of the City of Chicago* (1930), by E. W. Burgess and Charles Newcomb.

† Less than one-tenth of 1 per cent.

TABLE 48‡—*Continued*

Rent	Area 51		54		55		56		59		60		61		74		Total
	Number Homes	Per Cent Distribution	Number Homes	Per Cent Distribution	Number Homes	Per Cent Distribution	Number Homes	Per Cent Distribution	Number Homes	Per Cent Distribution	Number Homes	Per Cent Distribution	Number Homes	Per Cent Distribution	Number Homes	Per Cent Distribution	
Total	749	100.0	111	100.0	776	100.0	284	100.0	2,787	100.0	8,356	100.0	12,350	100.0	154	100.0	113,320
Under $10	16	2.1	8	7.2	15	1.9	3	1.1	55	2.0	304	3.6	492	4.0	2	1.3	4,067
10–$14.99	31	4.1	9	8.1	89	11.5	17	6.0	269	9.7	1,206	14.4	1,663	13.5	6	3.9	12,915
$15–19.99	62	8.3	12	10.8	153	19.7	55	19.4	526	18.9	2,470	29.6	2,969	24.0	16	10.4	22,930
20–29.99	284	37.9	45	40.5	301	38.8	115	40.5	802	28.8	2,752	32.9	3,795	30.7	53	34.4	36,071
30–49.99	303	40.5	27	24.3	172	22.2	77	27.1	850	30.5	1,299	15.6	2,327	18.8	69	44.8	26,291
50–74.99	34	4.5	2	1.8	35	4.5	12	4.2	220	7.9	222	2.7	765	6.2	2	1.3	7,674
75–99.99	4	0.5			3	0.4	2	0.7	31	1.1	40	0.5	124	1.0	1	0.6	1,369
100–149.99					2	0.3	1	0.4	14	0.5	14	0.2	73	0.6			557
150–199.99					1	0.1			7	0.2			15	0.1	1	0.6	129
200 and over	1	0.1							1	†	3	†	7	0.1	1	0.6	69
Unknown	14	1.9	8	7.2	5	0.6	2	0.7	12	0.4	46	0.5	120	1.0	3	2.0	1,248
Median rent (dollars)	20–30		20–30		20–30		20–30		20–30		20–30		20–30		20–30		

‡ Among the 75 census areas into which Chicago has been divided were a group of 16 in which rents of less than $30 a month were usually paid. The proportion of rented homes in these areas let for this amount ranged all the way from 50 to 88 per cent; and rents of less than $20 a month from 15 to 65 per cent. But, in order to appreciate how low these rents are, comparison with the city as a whole is necessary. Figures for the entire city, given in Table 49, show that only one-fourth rented for an amount less than $30 and just one-tenth of the rented homes were let for a sum less than $20. Not all our housing districts were located in these low rental areas, indicating that there are parts of the city where conditions equally as bad as those we found undoubtedly exist.

for April 1, 1930, shows that half of the 572,234 rented homes in Chicago are let for $50 or more per month.[8] Hence the entire group

TABLE 49*

RENTS IN CHICAGO, APRIL 1, 1930, AS REPORTED BY THE UNITED STATES CENSUS BUREAU

Monthly Rent	Rented Homes in Chicago Reported by the United States Census, April 1, 1930		
	Number	Per Cent Distribution	Cumulative Percentages
Total rented	572,234	100.0	....
Under $10	5,099	0.9	0.9
$ 10–$ 14.99	17,381	3.0	3.9
15– 19.99	33,804	5.9	9.8
20– 29.99	81,195	14.2	24.0
30– 49.99	146,256	25.6	49.6
50– 74.99	186,491	32.6	82.2
75– 99.99	60,495	10.6	92.8
100– 149.99	20,730	3.6	96.4
150– 199.99	4,820	0.8	97.2
200 and over	4,920	0.9	98.1
Unknown	11,043	1.9	100.0

* *Census Data of the City of Chicago* (1930), Table 10.

[8] [The data regarding rents from the 1934 special Chicago census were not available when Dr. Jeter completed this chapter. No attempt has been made to re-write her discussion on the basis of the more recent data. These data are, however, submitted in the accompanying table, since they indicate the probable decline in rents during the period from 1930 to 1934.]

RENTS IN CHICAGO, JANUARY 9, 1934, AS REPORTED BY THE CHICAGO CENSUS COMMISSION (SEE CENSUS DATA OF THE CITY OF CHICAGO, 1934, TABLE 1).

Monthly Rent	Rented Homes in Chicago		
	Number	Per Cent Distribution	Cumulative Percentages
Total reported	588,508	100 0	....
Under $10	16,957	2.9	2.9
$ 10–under $14.99	69,276	11.8	14.7
15–$19.99	73,499	12.5	27.2
20– 29.99	144,015	24.5	51.7
30– 49.99	212,565	36.1	87.8
50– 74.99	48,542	8.2	96.0
75– 99.99	8,774	1.5	97.5
100–149.99	4,651	0.8	98.3
150–199.99	1,383	0.2	98.5
200 and over	1,214	0.2	98.7
Unknown	7.632	1.3	100.0

of houses visited by our investigators fall within the lowest 25 per cent of all rented houses in the city. It seems safe to say that the conditions described in these pages are typical of a quarter of the rented homes in Chicago.

The rents paid in the several districts in the two periods are shown in Tables 46 and 47. In the earlier period more than half of the rents of less than $5.00 were to be found in the three districts known as St. Stanislaus, Lower North, and the Lumber Yards. No rents of as much as $25 per month were reported in the old Ghetto, in the Pilsen area, the St. Stanislaus area, the downtown district, or in the Stockyards (South), South Chicago (East Side), and Walnut Street (West Side). Occasional high rents were reported in the Hull-House district, in the Division Street area, and in the districts known as Southwest and Dearborn; but these districts were not necessarily the districts of the highest general level of rents. The median rentals shown in Table 50 indicate that in the Negro districts of Dearborn and La Salle the general level of rent throughout the period of the first investigation was twice as high as in many of the other districts, and in fact was nearly as high as the general level for the second period. The Dearborn rentals were reported for the year 1909 while the La Salle rentals were reported for 1919, the first year of transition from low to higher rents. In spite of the ten-year interval, both these medians are twice as high as the average for all districts. The next highest median was again in a Negro district, the Walnut Street area, and the rents in this case were 1911–12 rates.

In the second and post-war canvasses, the lower rents were still to be found in the St. Stanislaus district, in the Lower North canvass, and in the area near the Lumber Yards. The highest rents for this period were found in the areas influenced by the Negro migrations, in the Hull-House district, Division Street, and La Salle district. The median rentals, moreover, indicate the same marked differences in the general level for the several districts. The highest levels, which were again to be found in the Negro districts, were twice the general level of rents in Pullman, the Stock Yards (South), the Lumber Yards, and Pilsen.

These medians, shown for both periods in Table 50, vary for

the second period from $11 for the districts of the Stock Yards, South, and Pullman, to $26 for La Salle, five blocks of dwellings in-

TABLE 50

MEDIAN MONTHLY RENTS OF APARTMENTS VISITED DURING ORIGINAL CANVASS AND LATER CANVASS AND RECANVASS; AND OF CENSUS TRACTS CONTAINING THE HOUSING DISTRICTS, APRIL 1, 1930; BY DISTRICTS

(Districts Arranged in Order of Medians, 1923–27)

District	Median Monthly Rents of Apartments Visited		Median Monthly Rents in Census Tracts Containing Housing Districts (Original Census Data)	
	Original Canvass before 1920	Later Canvass and Recanvass	April 1, 1930	January 9, 1934
All districts	$ 9	$18	$20	$14
Pullman	......	$11	$22	$19
Stock Yards, South	$ 8	11	13	*
Lumber Yards	8	12	16	12
Pilsen	7	13	14	12
Back of the Yards	8	15	17	13
St. Stanislaus	8	16	17	12
South Chicago	10	16	19	14
Near South Side	10	18	19	13
Lower North	8	18	19	14
Ancona	......	18	19	13
Southwest	11	19	19	14
South Deering	......	20	27	14
Burnside	......	20	27	17
Hull-House	11	20	21	15
Polk Street	......	20	21	14
Upper Federal	......	21	29	18
Upper North	10	21	22	14
Old Ghetto	8	21	18	12
Division Street	11	21	20	13
Olivet	......	23	23	20
Dearborn	16	25	23	14
Walnut	13	25	32	18
La Salle	16	26	27	17

* Median was less than $10; exact amount could not be computed.

habited by Negroes. The increase in rents in the area known as the Stock Yards, South, was less, proportionately, than in any of the other districts. The median rental found in these two blocks adjoining the Stock Yards in the pre-war investigation was among the lowest medians of districts visited, but at that time six, if you leave out downtown, others of the sixteen districts included in the report had rentals as low or lower. While the rents in these six other districts have more than doubled, the Stock Yards, South, has increased less than one-half. The recent investigation of this district showed that in the blocks included there was great dilapidation in the buildings and a considerable number of saloons or "speakeasies" in the area. These two factors may account for slightly lower rentals in this district than in the other districts in the second period. The median rental for Pullman, however, is as low as the rent in Stock Yards, South. It is probable that this figure is not a very representative measure for all housing in the district, as two very distinct types of houses were included in the area visited. A study of three blocks included one block of 47 tenement apartments with a median rental of $12, one block of 118 tenement apartments with a $10 median rental, and one block of 80 apartments of a much better type whose median rental was $26. Thus, in Pullman the one large block comprised of a comparatively large number of poor dwellings with low rentals pulls the median for the community as a whole toward the lower end of the scale. This district is perhaps less homogeneous than other districts studied.

Table 50 also gives the medians for the census tracts containing the housing districts. The number of rented homes visited was 12,300 in the original canvass and 11,751 in 1923–27. The particular blocks visited are included in groups of blocks designated by the Bureau of the Census as "enumeration districts" and again grouped into larger areas called "census tracts." The census tracts in which the housing districts were located had 28,160 rented homes on April 1, 1930; and 26,616 on January 9, 1934. The median rentals for the tracts are given in the last column of Table 50. There is a close correspondence in order of district medians from lowest to highest between the housing districts of 1923–27 and the census tracts of 1930. The steady decline in rents during the depression period is evident in the median monthly rents of the 1934 survey. Decreases, some of them very sharp, had occurred in all the census tracts containing the housing districts in the four-year interval.

MAP VII

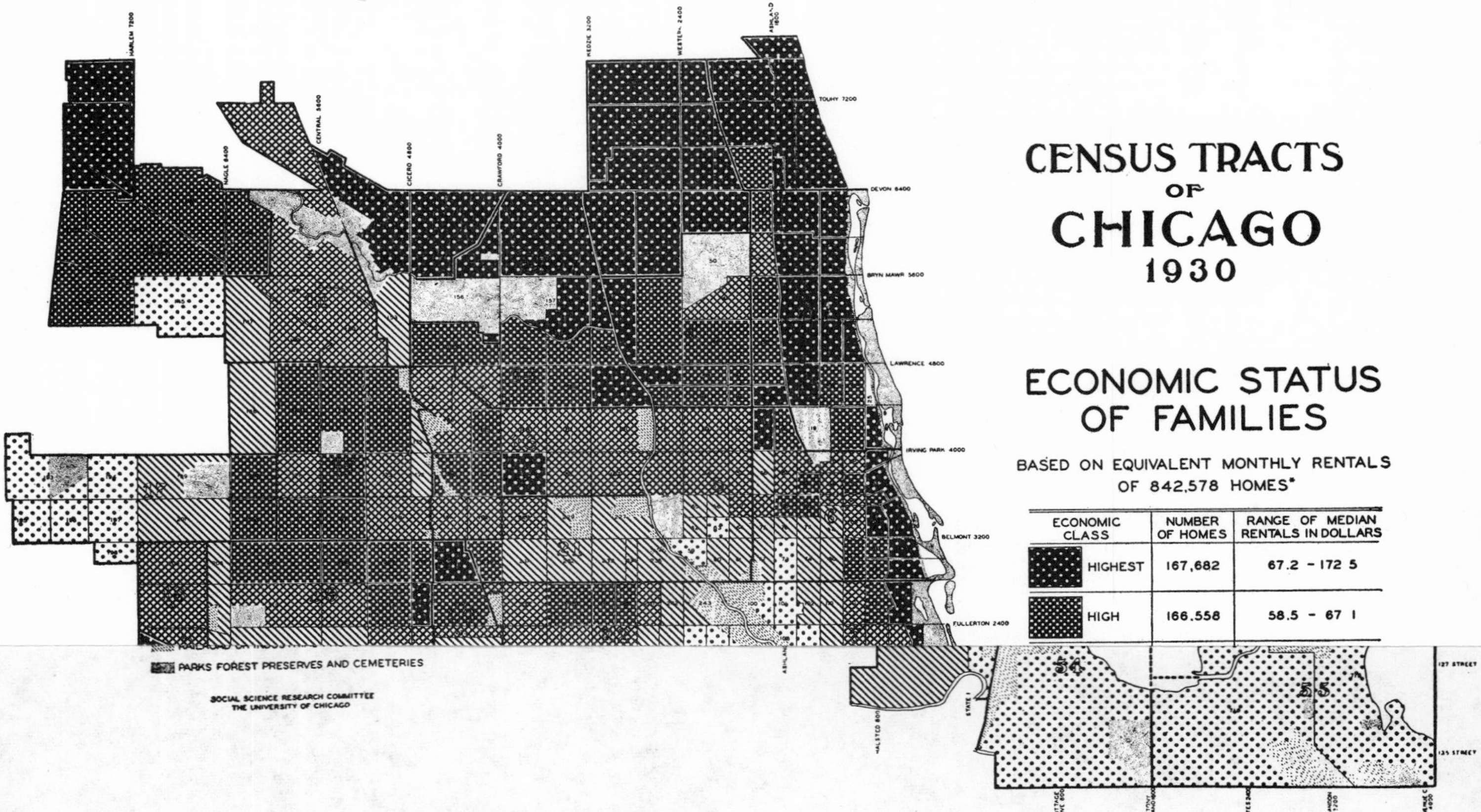

CENSUS TRACTS OF CHICAGO 1930

ECONOMIC STATUS OF FAMILIES

BASED ON EQUIVALENT MONTHLY RENTALS OF 842,578 HOMES*

ECONOMIC CLASS	NUMBER OF HOMES	RANGE OF MEDIAN RENTALS IN DOLLARS
HIGHEST	167,682	67.2 - 172 5
HIGH	166.558	58.5 - 67 1

PARKS FOREST PRESERVES AND CEMETERIES

SOCIAL SCIENCE RESEARCH COMMITTEE
THE UNIVERSITY OF CHICAGO

It is probable that the 46 per cent visited were fairly typical of the homes in the portions of the tracts not visited. In all the tracts there were undoubtedly blocks of houses not visited which were in general above the level of the blocks visited. Thus we should expect the median for each entire district to be somewhat above the median for the smaller area visited. This is actually the case, as is shown in Table 50. In only four districts—Pullman, South Deering, Burnside, Upper Federal and Walnut—was there any marked difference between the median for the selected area and the median for the census tract containing the area. The difference in Pullman has been explained above.[9] The size of the census tracts in Burnside and South Deering also allows for considerable variation in type of dwelling and consequent level of rent. In Upper Federal and Walnut we have census tracts which are almost entirely Negro and in which the rents are evidently higher for the tract as a whole than for the particular blocks visited.

If the data for the post-war period and the census data for 1930 covered exactly the same houses, we should expect the medians to be lower in 1930 because of generally decreasing rents. That they are not lower but slightly higher is probably due to the fact that the medians for the entire census tracts would have been slightly higher in the post-war period than the medians for the selected areas.

The rents paid in the districts under investigation may be further compared with the rents paid throughout the city in Map VII[10] prepared by the staff of the Social Science Research Committee of the University of Chicago. This map shows the distribution of homes throughout the city of Chicago, classified upon the basis of rents paid and approximate equivalents for homes owned in 1930.[11] The

[9] See p. 284.

[10] A second map, also made available by courtesy of the University's Social Science Research Committee, based on the 1934 special Chicago census, became available after Dr. Jeter had gone to Washington. However, the 1934 map was not used since the classified groups of rents had been completely changed. The general picture of the 1930 census map, showing "Homes by Rental Groups" (Map VII), corresponds closely to the 1934 map in showing the location of the low-rent groups in the same tenement areas that have already been described. The range of median rentals for 1934 is of course very much lower than for 1930 (see n. 8, above, p. 281).

[11] Values of homes owned have been converted into approximately equivalent monthly rentals.

map indicates approximately one-fifth of the homes and a very considerable proportion of the area of the city in the lowest economic group, that is, the group of median rentals from $14 to $33. All of the census tracts included in the housing investigation fall in this lowest economic group. The groups of families who pay the highest rents or live in owned homes whose equivalent rental value is highest live on the outskirts of the city—along the lake shore toward the north, a considerable area on the northern edge, patches directly west adjoining Oak Park, and finally a belt which extends upward toward the northeast, from Morgan Park, through Hyde Park, and ends at the lake shore between Seventy-ninth and Forty-second streets. The lowest rents and the lowest values are to be found in the central portion of the city extending along both branches of the Chicago River and in South Chicago, south of Ninety-fifth Street.

SIZE OF APARTMENTS

Certain differences in rents might be expected to follow differences in size of apartment. In both periods and in all districts the four-room apartment was by far the most common size. In fact, more than half the apartments visited were of four rooms. If the median rentals for these four-room apartments alone are considered, as in Table 51, it appears that the highest general levels of rents are still to be found in two of the Negro areas, the so-called La Salle Street district on the South Side and the Walnut Street district on the West Side. But the rents in a number of other districts closely approach these levels, and the differences between the highest and lowest district medians are less marked for the four-room apartments than for apartments of all sizes.

Even among the four-room apartments, however, there is a wide variation in rent, which may be due in part to location, in part to the condition of the apartments, and in part to the differences in bargaining power of the tenants. The monthly rentals in all districts combined, classified by the number of rooms in the apartment, are shown in Tables 52 and 53. Four-room apartments in the first period rented from less than $4.00 to $35 a month, in the second period, from less than $5.00 to $60 a month. For three-, five-, and six-room apartments, there is likewise a range from the lowest to nearly the highest rents. On the other hand, one- and two-room apartments in the districts canvassed are rarely more than $20 while

TABLE 51

MEDIAN MONTHLY RENTS OF FOUR-ROOM APARTMENTS, ORIGINAL CANVASS AND LATER POSTWAR CANVASS AND RECANVASS BY DISTRICTS

DISTRICT	MEDIAN MONTHLY RENTS OF FOUR-ROOM APARTMENTS	
	Original Canvass	Later Canvass
All districts	$ 9	$18
West Side:		
Old Ghetto	$10	$21
Pilsen	8	15
Lumber Yards	10	13
Hull-House	13	20
Polk Street	......	20
St. Stanislaus	8	16
Division Street	11	21
Ancona	......	18
South Side:		
Downtown	9	......
Near South Side	10	16
Back of the Yards	9	16
Stock Yards, South	11	15
Southwest (Lithuanian)	10	18
South End:		
Burnside	......	19
South Chicago (East Side)	9	16
South Deering	......	17
Pullman	......	13
North Side:		
Lower North	9	17
Upper North	10	20
Olivet	......	21
Negro districts:		
Dearborn	12	20
La Salle	14	23
Upper Federal	......	18
Walnut (West Side)	10	22

seven-, eight-, and nine-room apartments are seldom found for less than $20.

In Table 54 average rents per room for apartments of various size are shown for the 11,742 apartments for which the data are available. The vast majority of tenants whose homes were visited in the post-war period (after 1923) were paying $3.00, $4.00, or

TABLE 52

NUMBER OF APARTMENTS OF SPECIFIED NUMBER OF ROOMS RENTING FOR SPECIFIED MONTHLY RENT

(Original Canvass Data)

Monthly Rent	Number of Apartments of Specified Number of Rooms																
	Total	1	2	3	4	5	6	7	8	9	10	11	12	13	14	15 or More	Not Reported
Total...	12,300	51	1,135	2,186	6,209	1,483	971	176	61	13	2	4	1	1	0	3	4
Less than $4.00.....	131	25	74	20	11		1										
$ 4–$ 4.99..	273	9	173	66	24	1											
5– 5.99..	838	5	335	316	175	5	2										
6– 6.99..	1,198	4	306	423	440	23	1										1
7– 7.99..	1,511	2	169	444	838	50	7										1
8– 8.99..	1,695	2	37	362	1,179	92	22	1									
9– 9.99..	1,242		11	228	874	90	38										1
10– 10.99..	1,635		16	160	1,127	218	92	21	1								
11– 11.99..	727		1	58	489	134	38	5	1								1
12– 12.99..	922	2	5	54	503	232	113	10	3								
13– 13.99..	406			18	179	136	67	4	2								
14– 14.99..	331		1	10	122	107	83	8									
15– 15.99..	410		2	10	90	152	126	23	3	3				1			
16– 16.99..	237		1	4	37	68	106	14	6	1							
17– 17.99..	94		1		13	29	42	7	1	1							
18– 18.99..	185	1		4	30	50	70	18	11	1							
19– 19.99..	38				17	5	6	4	4	1	1						
20– 20.99..	167		1	6	31	36	69	14	8	1		1					
21– 21.99..	25				13	5	5	2									
22– 22.99..	67			1	5	17	25	13	3	2			1				
23– 23.99..	21			1	4	3	9	1	1	1		1					
24– 24.99..	15					4	8	1	2								
25– 25.99..	67		1		4	15	27	12	6		1					1*	
26– 26.99..	7					4	2	1									
27– 27.99..	8					1	1	3	2	1							
28– 28.99..	7					2	1	1	3								
29– 29.99..																	
30– 34.99..	27				4	3	7	7	3	1		1				1†	
35– 39.99..	10	1				1	3	4	1								
40– 44.99..	2		1					1									
45– 49.99..																	
50 and over.	4			1‡				1				1				1§	

* Seventeen rooms. † Sixteen rooms. ‡ $55 rent. § Twenty rooms; $70 rent.

$5.00 a room and most of this group were occupying three-, four-, or five-room apartments.

Before 1920 practically all these homes (99 per cent) had a monthly rental per room that was under $5.00. When recanvassed in the

TABLE 53
NUMBER OF APARTMENTS OF SPECIFIED NUMBER OF ROOMS RENTING FOR SPECIFIED MONTHLY RENT
(Post-war Canvass after 1923 and Recanvass)

Monthly Rent	Number of Apartments of Specified Number of Rooms													
	Total	1	2	3	4	5	6	7	8	9	10	11	12	Not reported
Total	11,751	58	718	1,577	6,201	1,765	1,154	171	80	8	4	0	6	9
Less than $5.00	28	10	12	4	2									
$ 5–$ 5.99	70	8	36	17	8	1								
6– 6.99	115	7	61	38	5	2	2							
7– 7.99	161	2	82	52	19	5	1							
8– 8.99	304	4	161	80	49	7	2							1
9– 9.99	202	2	58	81	54	5	1							1
10– 10.99	667	8	138	252	241	20	7							1
11– 11.99	252		42	84	118	8								
12– 12.99	704	5	51	236	374	26	11	1						
13– 13.99	423		19	92	279	26	6	1						
14– 14.99	506		13	85	375	26	3	2	1					1
15– 15.99	1,270	4	20	220	872	107*	37	4	5					1
16– 16.99	667	1	4	66	512	56	24	3						1
17– 17.99	511	1	3	71	364	47	17	7						1
18– 18.99	958		3	74	717	110	48	4	1					1
19– 19.99	191	4	1	3	153	21	7	2						
20– 20.99	1,369	2	7	64	869	278	134	6	7	1	1			
21– 21.99	121		1	3	84	24	9							
22– 22.99	447		2	9	320	77	35		4					
23– 23.99	237			7	152	54	20	4						
24– 24.99	96		1	1	49	25	20							
25– 25.99	883		2	25	312	313	199	20	11	1				
26– 26.99	70			1	26	28	14	1						
27– 27.99	110				31	52	22	3	1	1				
28– 28.99	141		1	3	34	66	35	2						
29– 29.99	16				4	9	3							
30– 34.99	513			6	67	169	222*	38	8	2	1			
35– 39.99	385			2	42	113	170	38	17	2				1
40– 44.99	150				31	37	57	9	15				1	
45– 49.99	97			1	34	30	23	5	2				2	
50– 54.99	55				3	17	16	10	7				2	
55– 59.99	10				1	5	2	2						
60– 64.99	14						4	7	1		1		1	
65– 69.99	4						3	1						
70– 74.99	2					1		1						
75 and over	2									1	1†			

* Two apartments occupied by one family counted as one apartment in this table and in Table LXXVI.
† Rent is $85.

years following 1923, rates had so advanced that less than two-thirds of the dwellings were to be secured at that price. The proportion available at less than $3.00 a room a month had fallen from 77 per cent before 1920 to 9 per cent in 1927. The second period showed 77 per cent between $3.00 and $6.00 as compared with only 22 per cent before 1920.

TABLE 54

NUMBER OF APARTMENTS OF SPECIFIED NUMBER OF ROOMS RENTING FOR SPECIFIED MONTHLY RENT PER ROOM; ALL DISTRICTS

(Post-war Canvass after 1923 and Recanvass)

Monthly Rent in Dollars per Room	Number of Apartments of Specified Number of Rooms												
	Total	1	2	3	4	5	6	7	8	9	10	11	12
Total	11,742*	58	718	1,577	6,201	1,765	1,154	171	80	8	4	...	6
$ 1–$ 1.99	95	...	...	21	33	20	13	2	6	...	...	...	...
2– 2.99	927	...	48	170	462	106	98	28	12	2	1	...	...
3– 3.99	3,112	2	143	417	1,900	341	253	28	19	5	1	...	3
4– 4.99	3,197	8	219	413	1,746	458	293	40	18	...	...	...	2
5– 5.99	2,862	8	180	357	1,425	468	359	47	17	...	...	...	1
6– 6.99	908	7	70	141	418	169	90	5	7	...	1	...	...
7– 7.99	300	2	33	19	97	113	23	12	1	...	...	...	...
8– 8.99	148	4	7	27	48	37	16	7	...	1	1	...	...
9– 9.99	44	2	4	3	2	30	2	1	...	...	...	...	...
10– 10.99	78	8	8	6	31	17	7	1	...	...	...	...	...
11– 11.99	39	...	2	2	30	5	...	...	...	...	...	...	...
12– 12.99	15	5	3	...	7	...	...	...	...	...	...	...	...
13– 13.99	1	...	...	...	1	...	...	...	...	...	...	...	...
14– 14.99	3	...	1	...	1	1	...	...	...	...	...	...	...
15– 15.99	5	4	...	1	...	...	...	...	...	...	...	...	...
16– 16.99	1	1	...	...	...	...	...	...	...	...	...	...	...
17– 17.99	1	1	...	...	...	...	...	...	...	...	...	...	...
18– 18.99	...	...	...	...	...	...	...	...	...	...	...	...	...
19– 19.99	4	4	...	...	...	...	...	...	...	...	...	...	...
20– 20.99	2	2	...	...	...	...	...	...	...	...	...	...	...

* Nine apartments for which the number of rooms was not reported are omitted.

Variations in rentals per room as between districts are rather extreme. The Lumber Yards, four Slovak blocks bounded by Sixteenth, Burlington, Eighteenth, and Union streets, in 1924 still had 78 per cent of its rentals under $4.00 per room per month. La Salle, the Negro district revisited in 1926, on the other hand, had only 10 per cent of its rentals so low. The high rentals per room were likewise to be found in only a few districts. Leading all districts in the proportion of monthly rentals at $10 or more per room is Hull-House, which had 73 apartments, 7 per cent of its total, in this classification in 1925. La Salle, a Negro district, ranked next with 13, or 3 per cent, of its apartments in 1926 costing the tenants at least $10 per room. Southwest followed with 2 per cent at $10 or more.

The rise in rents between the two periods under discussion was probably due largely to housing shortage and to increased demand in relation to inadequate supply of houses for rent. Another factor may have been present, however, i.e., increased land values due to anticipated future use of the land for commercial or industrial uses. Since assessed valuation and actual tax rates are based to a certain extent upon this anticipated use, the owner and landlord may be justified in asking higher rents; but higher rents in turn justify increased capitalization and consequently higher valuation of the building, which again justifies higher taxes. This circular effect of anticipated land value, taxation, income, and valuation of the building may conceivably go on without regard to the continuing decay of the building or the economic necessities of the renters; the land values might even increase without any tenants in the buildings. Since the owner's taxes are higher for so-called "improved" land than for vacant lots, he has a choice between razing the old buildings that he thinks he will eventually have to "throw in" with his sale for a factory site or a modern apartment building or getting out of them a little more than the extra taxes for "improved" land. In any case he will spend as little as possible upon the building since the building itself will add very little, if anything, to the sale price that he expects to be effective eventually. Rents, moreover, are slow to fall, even in the depression period, because the values of real property are based upon guesses into a somewhat distant future.

A few quotations from Olcott's *Land Values Blue Book of Chicago*[12] will illustrate the concrete ways in which the hope and philosophy of the real estate dealer are translated into reality. In its annual review of the real estate market in 1925 this statement appears:

[12] Issued annually. Published by George C. Olcott & Co., Inc., publishers and appraisers.

On the West Side there were several important developments. Principal among these were the New Produce Market at Blue Island Avenue and 15th Street and the Wieboldt department store building operations on Ashland Avenue and Monroe Street. Both of these improvements have been completed. The effect on values was to cause a widespread raising of asking prices on adjacent properties as well as much that was too remote to be affected at all.

And again in 1930:

If subways are to be installed station stops will advance in value rapidly. Many owners are quite optimistic that these events will cause a revival in the real estate market and are therefore hopeful of the future.

The general tone of the 1930 volume, however, is one of sadness. The annual review begins:

The real estate market during the past year was dull and featureless. Apparently the crest of the wave which had carried land values up each year for the past ten years had been reached in 1928. During 1929 values remained firm but weak. Owners refused to come down in their demands, only making concessions in price when forced to do so for financial reasons. During the first half of this year there was a distinct recession in prices, many holders being unable to carry the burden longer and therefore forced to sell. It is the history of real estate during a depression that it is the last to go down, as it is the last to go up with the return of good times.

Adequate statistics upon the subject of the possible dependence of rents upon land values are not available. For the particular districts under investigation land values seem to have increased somewhat less rapidly than rents. Although rents had in general doubled between the first and second periods of investigation, land values in the same blocks had increased less than 50 per cent. In three districts—Ancona, Southwest, and the old Ghetto—land values had declined although rents had nearly doubled. In two districts—the Near South Side and Walnut—both of which are Negro districts, land values had increased more than rents. In the remaining districts the increase in land values was in general less than the increase in rents.

THE LACK OF CONVENIENCES IN LOW-RENTAL HOMES

Interest attaches chiefly, of course, to the great number of rented apartments in each district which were available at the lower rentals. A few illustrations of what a certain rent obtained in comforts and conveniences in certain districts will be of service in interpreting

Table 54. In what in pre-prohibition days was known as "Whiskey Row" in the neighborhood of the Stock Yards stands an ancient and long worn-out frame cottage of five rooms. Windowpanes are broken, weather-boarding is loose in many places and gone altogether in some, steps and floors are warped and uneven from age, dampness, and long-continued use; not only paper but also plaster is missing in great patches from the walls. In 1923 a Mexican family was paying $18 a month for the doubtful privilege of living in this house. Near by is a similarly decrepit one-family cottage of six rooms which even in its most miserable days in 1923 was bringing in $21 a month. In another extremely dilapidated building in the same neighborhood a six-room rear flat cost its tenants $27 a month. Stairways in these old structures are "worn to the point of being dangerous and the inadequate plumbing presents a situation which contaminates the health of the tenants."[13] "The amount of rent paid for these inadequate, insanitary houses," the investigator felt compelled to add, "is all out of proportion to the value received."

The increase in rents, general throughout the neighborhood as it was, had no correspondingly general justification in improvements in the property. There were individual instances, to be sure, where genuine improvement in a house or an apartment warranted an advance in rent. But the influence of these increased rentals affected even the adjacent property, which not only had failed of any improvement but had even suffered an adverse change through more deterioration and further decline and decay.

A rental of $10 a month for three rooms in the Italian district on the Lower North Side seems low, but this is what a Negro family of father, mother, and two children received in return for this rent: In the first place, the rooms were so far below the street level that they must be called cellar-rooms. The bedroom had no window whatever and its walls were "wet from the overflow of a leaking toilet on the floor above." The kitchen lacked a flue for the kitchen stove (and there was no gas), so the mother did such cooking as she might at the home of her aunt a block distant and otherwise fed her family by the expensive and unsatisfactory "paper-bag" method.

[13] Alice Mae Miller, "Rents and Housing Conditions in the Stockyards District of Chicago" (unpublished Master's Thesis; School of Social Service Administration), p. 23.

Ten dollars a month was perhaps not so cheap, considering how little it purchased.[14]

With reference to these seemingly low rentals, the investigator of housing conditions in the Lithuanian district southwest of Halsted and Thirty-first streets comments that "almost invariably the lower rents, bad conditions and large families accompany one another," and that the thirty-four families in that district paying less than $10 a month in rent were living in the "poorest possible excuses for apartments." The correlation between "bad housing conditions and rents amounting to $10 or less" was high. Usually, too, the apartments that rented for less than $15 and many of them that brought less than $20 were "dark and dismal." Only stove heat was available, the floors were sometimes warped because of leaking roofs and continued dampness, and especially in basements and cellars was dampness present and seriously objectionable.[15]

In 1901 Robert Hunter said of South Chicago (East Side) that the blocks canvassed were the worst in that general area. The dwellings, then as at the time of our later canvass were "almost entirely made of wood." Some were dilapidated; all seemed neglected.[16] In the canvass in 1911 only 16 of the 263 buildings in the district were found to have been erected after the building code was adopted in 1902. The recanvass in 1925 found many of the same old buildings still doing service, since there had been comparatively little building activity in the district in the fourteen years which had elapsed between the two surveys. Probably the district is destined to use altogether by industry which already hems it in on all sides. Nevertheless, here as elsewhere rents have advanced. In 1911 all were under $4.00 per room per month; in 1925 half were $4.00 or more per month. Part of the increased rent may be due to a doubling in land values between 1911 and 1925. Higher taxes on the property afford the excuse or the necessity for asking higher rents for the building. The expenses incurred for necessary repairs or for im-

[14] Esther Quaintance, "Rents and Housing Conditions in the Italian District of the Lower North Side of Chicago" (unpublished Master's thesis; School of Social Service Administration), p. 39.

[15] J. S. Perry, "Rents and Housing Conditions among the Lithuanians in Chicago" (unpublished Master's thesis; in the School of Social Service Administration), pp. 43, 44.

[16] *Tenement Conditions in Chicago*, p. 181.

provements when they are made are likely to be recovered by advanced rents. Sometimes rents rise for no apparent reason except a change of tenants, which makes possible the establishment of a different rate.

In this South Chicago district during the long period between the canvass and the recanvass, a gradual change for the better took place in the provisions of toilets for these dwellings. The improvement in this respect in this district is also fairly representative for other districts where as great an interval intervened between surveys. In 1911 among the 543 families living in this block, 9 families were still dependent upon yard privies; 302 had yard water closets; 41 used basement or cellar toilets; 48 had a hall toilet; and only 135 had an apartment toilet. In 1925 the privy had completely disappeared and only 24 per cent of the homes were still dependent upon the yard water closet while 63 per cent had toilets within their dwellings.

Besides the very real improvement with respect to toilet provision, there have been other community improvements such as the substitution of gas for coal in cooking and of gas or electricity for oil in lighting. In some of these old buildings, then, living conditions are probably better in spite of the greater age of the buildings themselves. In others, greater age and more dilapidation are all that the years have brought.

In general, the Negro families pay higher rents than white families. The reason for this fact is to be found primarily in the restrictions that are imposed by real estate owners and others who desire to protect the white neighborhoods from encroachment.

The houses in the Negro districts are for the most part dilapidated; they are far too large for the average Negro family and are ill-suited in arrangement and design for more than one family. Moreover, the upkeep of such large, old-fashioned houses is far above that of simple and more modern houses and the landlords are loath to make frequent repairs. One of the inevitable results of houses too large, rents too high, and a newly migrant group, doubtless with an undue proportion of single men or men whose families are still in the South, is the practice of taking lodgers. These Negro districts contain a higher percentage of lodgers than any other one district investigated except the South Deering district, in which a large number of Mexicans live. In this district approximately 12 per cent of the persons are lodgers. For the four Negro districts combined, approximately 15 per cent of the total population is made up of lodgers; this is three times as high as the percentage of lodgers in all districts taken together.

In districts such as the Lower North District, where the Negroes are in the minority it appears that a Negro tenant may be asked to pay a higher rent than an Italian for a similar apartment in the same building. A five-room apartment on the first floor front cost a Negro family $50 a month. The second floor front with six rooms was at the same time rented to an Italian tenant for $35. In the same block, but in another building, six rooms on the second floor front were rented by an Italian family for $27 a month while the rear apartment containing four rooms cost a Negro family $25.

With regard to comparatively high rents and little choice in selecting a dwelling, the Mexican shares the disadvantage of the Negro. The Mexican, like the Negro, came to Chicago in response to a war-time demand for laborers. Very few Mexicans were found in the pre-war housing investigation; the more recent studies show a decided increase in their number, especially in certain districts. They are found grouped near each other, usually in the same block or in two or three adjacent blocks of a district. Two blocks in the Stock Yards district, one block in the South Chicago district, and one side of two blocks in the South Deering district show a predominance of Mexicans; groups of several families are found scattered throughout a number of districts.

In the South Chicago district the block farthest south has almost as many Negro dwellers as Mexican; thirteen Negro families, fourteen Mexican families, and five Mexican non-family groups live in this block. Neither Negroes nor Mexicans outnumber other groups in any but this one of the seven blocks making up the district. Land values were rated higher in this block than in the other six of the district but the houses themselves were more ramshackle in appearance. The proportion of vacancies was low in comparison with other blocks. The proportion of owners in the block was high (twenty-three out of seventy-six householders). The Mexicans and Negroes, however, were all renters. The median rental for a four-room home in this block was $22, $4.00 higher than in any other of the seven blocks and $7.00 higher than in four of them. Judged by the proportion of apartment toilets, this block ranks ahead of all the rest in the district, but it contains eleven of the forty-five rear houses found in the entire district and has the only cellar flat and four of the eight basement apartments in the district. It would seem that a portion of the difference in rental between this block and the others must be attributed to the presence of Negroes and Mexicans. The investigator making the recanvass in the district says "it is taken for granted among the landlords of the district that rents for Negroes and Mexicans should be higher than for other tenants" and considers that "it is almost an axiom that the latest immigrant finds access only to the poorest accommodations and must pay more for the scant comfort he receives."[17]

In the South Deering district the Mexicans are found mostly on one side of each of two blocks, namely, the side lying along Torrence Avenue; they do not, therefore, predominate in any one block. There is evidence, however, to show that higher rents are charged Mexican tenants and in some instances, at least, living conditions are less satisfactory than elsewhere in the district. In one case a Mexican had formerly paid a rental five dollars higher to a landlord of another nationality than he was at the time of the study paying for the same apartment to a compatriot from whom he was subrenting.

So, too, in the Stock Yards district the investigator sensed a definite hostility on the part of nationalities of longer residence toward the incoming Mexicans. They were admitted only into certain blocks and there was discrimination in the matter of rent. Two flats of the same size in the same building, identical in arrangement and conveniences, rented, one for $27 a month to a Mexican tenant and the other for $20 a month to an Irish tenant. Two cottages, similar except that one is in better condition than the other, rented for $10 and for $21, respectively, and it is the Polish tenant in the better house who pays $10 while the Mexican pays $21.

[17] Mary Faith Adams, "Present Housing Conditions in South Chicago, South Deering and Pullman" (unpublished Master's thesis; School of Social Service Administration), pp. 39 and 63.

The Mexicans are not the predominant nationality in any entire district, and no classification of lodgers according to the nationality of the householder has been made. A study made by the City Department of Public Welfare in 1925, however, including portions of some of the districts covered in the present study, found that 42 per cent of the Negro and 43 per cent of the Mexican one-family households contained lodgers while but 28 per cent of the native-white homes visited and but 17 per cent of the homes of other foreign-born nationalities had lodgers in them.[18]

There may be some connection between high rents and the keeping of lodgers. Lodgers may be taken in order to meet the high rental or, on the contrary, the rental may be advanced because lodgers are kept. However that may be, we are reasonably certain that rentals are higher for Negroes and Mexicans and that lodgers seem to be more numerous among the latest industrial recruits whether these are migrant or immigrant.

Almost four-fifths of all the rents for apartments in these districts even in the most recent canvass amounted to less than $25 per month (Table 53). Only a fourth of the rentals under $25 a month were paid for fewer than four rooms. Fifty-nine per cent of all rentals were under $25 a month and also secured living quarters with at least four rooms for the families paying them. Three-fifths paid less than $5.00 per room; nine-tenths paid less than $6.00 per room. As has been pointed out at some length, these rents did not include heat, nor did they provide dwellings with anything but a minimum of convenience; moreover, they were not likely to be found elsewhere than in the buildings of old construction, often situated in neighborhoods overshadowed by industry or invaded by commerce. As dwelling-places many of the buildings fall rather far below the standards set for tenements in Chicago both in structure and in sanitation.

INCOME AND EXPENDITURE FOR RENT

It would be interesting to know how great a strain is placed upon the incomes of these families in meeting the rents which prevail so generally throughout the older tenement districts of Chicago. The

[18] Elizabeth A. Hughes, *Living Conditions for Small-Wage Earners in Chicago* (Department of Public Welfare, City of Chicago, 1925), p. 13.

continued and uninterrupted use of these buildings from their erection down to their present decrepit old age indicates a steady demand for homes at the bottom of the rent scale. These investigations of housing conditions have made no attempt to gather data on income among renting families. Moreover, the available data concerning the relationship between rent and family incomes in the United States are meager. A committee of the President's Conference on Home Building and Home Ownership which recently brought together figures from all studies since 1922 makes the following statement:

> It is evident that the relationship between income and expenditure for housing is not a fixed percentage but a variable which depends upon housing facilities and housing costs in the community where the family is located, the size of the family, the family's present economic status and its probable economic future, whether the family is renting or buying its own home and, if it is buying, the basis on which the purchase is being made.[19]

Anthracite mine-workers devoted from 8 to 15 per cent of their total family expenditures to rent. Federal employees receiving not over $2,500 in five cities in 1928 spent from 16 to 22 per cent for housing. Expenditures for rent by members of the faculty of Yale University averaged from 19.0 to 23.5 per cent of their total income.

A recent study of the housing of salaried workers in Pittsburgh[20] shows that among 792 renters the percentage of the family income expended on rent declines from 28.1 per cent in the income group between $1,000 and $1,500 to 7.8 per cent in the salary group of $10,000 or more. The average for all income groups was 19.8 per cent of the income expended for rent.

THE HOUGHTELING AND HUGHES STUDIES

Two studies made in Chicago throw some light upon the proportion of their earnings that wage-earners must devote to the payment of rent. In *The Income and Standard of Living of Unskilled Laborers in Chicago*, Leila Houghteling discussed the cost of shelter in relation to the family budget. Her figures on rents were based

[19] *Home Ownership, Income and Types of Dwellings* ("Reports of the President's Conference on Home Building and Home Ownership," Vol. IV), p. 61.

[20] Theodore A. Veenstra, *Housing Status of Salaried Workers Employed in Pittsburgh* (University of Pittsburgh Bulletin, June 10, 1932), p. 16.

upon the reports of 337 families of unskilled wage-earners living in rented homes in Chicago in 1924–25. By far the greater proportion of these (85.6 per cent) were expending less than $400 per annum (or $33 per month) inrent. Nearly two-thirds were spending under $25 a month. Over half the families occupied four rooms or less. Rents are shown first in relation to the earnings of the chief wage-earner in each family, then in relation to the "family fund" or the joint income in the family. Somewhat less than one-fourth of the families were Negro, but this is a larger proportion than the percentage of Negroes found in all the districts of the housing studies. Well over half the families were spending less than 20 per cent of the chief wage-earner's wages for rent. Among the white families alone, however, 70 per cent spent less than 20 per cent of the chief wage-earner's income for rent. This shows again that rent plays a larger part in the budget of the Negro household. Practically 69 per cent of all the families in the Houghteling study were spending less than 20 per cent of the total family fund for shelter. If the Negro families are excluded the proportion expending less than a fifth of their joint earnings for rent rises to 80.7 per cent. Attention is called in the Houghteling study to the "diminution in the percentage expended for rent with the increase in financial resources" as evidenced by a decrease in the average expenditure for rent from "20.3 per cent in the group whose family funds are less than $1200 to 10.9 per cent among those whose family funds are $2400 or more."[21]

The houses and apartments in which the families included in the Houghteling study were living resembled in character and type the buildings and dwellings in the districts included in our canvass and recanvass. Almost 87 per cent were stove-heated, meaning that the rent did not include heat; about 94 per cent had gas or electricity for lighting and the rest were dependent upon oil lamps; 78 per cent had toilets of their own which did not have to be shared with any other family; 12 per cent were dependent upon toilets located outside the building in the yard, or under the porch or the sidewalk; 42.5 per cent had bathrooms.

The data on income in the Houghteling study were secured for the period of a year. The "unskilled laborers" were probably more

[21] *Op. cit.*, p. 114.

steadily employed than the men who were the heads of the households in the study made by Elizabeth Hughes for the City Department of Public Welfare. The two investigations were being carried on at the same time, but the second was briefer in duration and the information as to income was gathered in each family for only one month preceding the interview. Interviewing was begun in November, 1924, and concluded in April, 1925. Unemployment was rather severe throughout this period. Family incomes would doubtless be less affected by this than the earnings of the heads of the household taken alone. Data both on family income and on rental were secured for 886 households, 419, or 47 per cent, of which were Negro and 406, or 46 per cent, foreign-born. Almost 69 per cent of the foreign-born had expended less than a fifth, about 3 per cent exactly a fifth, and about 29 per cent over a fifth of their family earnings in a month for rent. Among the Negro families the proportions were as follows: under a fifth, 20 per cent of the families; precisely a fifth, 2 per cent; in excess of a fifth, 77 per cent. Miss Hughes comments:

> The higher rentals paid by Negro families affect the proportions in this table very noticeably. Partial explanation lies in the inclusion of more heat-furnished apartments of the better grade among the Negro homes visited. Possibly some further explanation may lie in a larger amount of unemployment among Negroes or in smaller earnings.[22]

With reference to family earnings and rentals, this report continues:

> Obviously the amount which can be apportioned to rent is affected by the size of the income as well as by the amount of the rental. It was possible to obtain statements of the aggregate earnings in one month in 1244 families. How representative these statements of earnings in the month preceding the visit from the Department's representative are of family earnings in the other eleven months of the year can only be conjectured. Doubtless for some families which earned more in the month inquired about there were others which endured special hardship and made less than their usual income. . . .[23]

Nine-tenths of the 1,244 families reported earnings of less than $200 a month, or $2,400 a year; 47 per cent, not much less than half, said their monthly earnings had been under $100; 10 per cent reported earnings of at least $200 a month, or $2,400 a year. To pay large

[22] *Op. cit.*, pp. 37, 38.

[23] *Ibid.*, p. 44.

rentals was clearly out of the question for the majority of these families in the month for which these statements of income were given. Miss Hughes commented: "Only one family in ten should afford a rental of $40 or more per month for an unheated apartment. One in three ought not to spend as much as $16 for rent without heat."[24]

The Houghteling figures are probably more representative of yearly earnings and are less affected by unemployment. Moreover, the Houghteling group contains a much smaller proportion of Negro families. Only 14 per cent of the 334 families reported a family fund of less than $1,200; 91 per cent reported less than $2,400; and only 9 per cent said they had had $2,400 or over to expend in a year. Approximately half of these unskilled laborers' families (49 per cent) had incomes of at least $1,600 per annum and by using one-fifth of their earnings to supply shelter could pay a rental of $24 a month for an unheated apartment.

The rents paid for the 11,751 apartments canvassed between 1923 and 1927 fall within the same general range as the rents paid by the 337 families of unskilled laborers in Chicago studied by Dr. Leila Houghteling in 1925. There is greater concentration in the low rent groups, however, than among Dr. Houghteling's families. While she found only two-thirds of the families paying less than $25 per month, we find four-fifths below that level. This difference is undoubtedly explained in part by the fact that the Houghteling sample contained a larger proportion of Negro families than the districts included in the housing investigation. In the canvassed districts that were predominantly Negro, the proportion paying rents of less than $25 ranged from two-thirds to less than one-half of the households.

The Houghteling figures with regard to the proportion spent for rent from the earnings of the chief wage-earner and from the family fund might throw some light on the economic level of the group of families whose apartments have been visited in the later canvass were it not for the fact that the proportion spent for rent seems to increase as the size of the income decreases. According to Dr. Houghteling, about three-fifths of the white families spent from 10

[24] *Ibid.*, p. 45.

to 20 per cent of the father's earnings for rent. Among those whose earnings were less than $2,000 a year, however, one-third spent 20 per cent or more for rent. In a few cases the rent was as much as 50 per cent of the earnings of the head of the family.

On the basis of the Houghteling figures it is a safe assumption that four-fifths of the 15,000 households whose apartments were visited between 1923 and 1927 had total family incomes of less than $2,000 per year. Many of these probably had still smaller incomes. These families were presumably those of unskilled wage-earners. That they were living, however, in the cheapest and least desirable of the dwellings in Chicago is indicated by a comparison of rents paid by 2,272 families known to the United Charities in 1928. Miss Eleanor Goltz found in her study of these charity families that the rental most frequently found was $5.00–$6.00 per room per month for all nativity groups except the Mexicans, for whom the most common rent was between $3.00 and $4.00. The median rental for the entire group of 2,272 charity families was $5.00 per room per month, the median rental for the 11,751 apartments visited in our investigation was between $4.00 and $5.00 per room. Evidently the case-workers who advise these charity families are unwilling for them to live in the very worst housing conditions and consequently they pay in some cases more than is paid by the "independent" wage-earner who has, to be sure, an income but so precarious an income that he must live in the cheapest house that he can find.

WHAT DOES THE FUTURE HOLD?

In conclusion, the rentals in these old buildings in Chicago's older tenement districts are low in comparison with rentals in buildings which can be erected in the city today. It seems now to be generally conceded that rents from three to five dollars per room, the rates paid in the vast majority of the 11,751 apartments, are too low to attract capital toward the building of homes for wage-earners. Cost of land, cost of material, and cost of construction are all higher than in the days when those old brick or frame buildings were erected. But though the majority of the buildings in these districts were built at much less cost and though many of them are so old that they should be abandoned, nevertheless in practically all of them rents have advanced to about the same extent as in newer buildings.

Between the earlier surveys and the later, improvements in some respects have been rather general. Toilet facilities are on the whole more adequate and of better type. In some buildings, however, living conditions in 1935 are as primitive as they were in 1908. The demand for these low-rental homes remains fairly steady in spite of a falling-off of population in certain districts and the general restrictions on immigration which mean fewer newcomers to the city from other countries. Such information as is available in Chicago upon the amount that families of unskilled laborers can expend for dwellings indicates an inability on the part of many to pay more than a very small rental. At least one-half cannot pay more than $18 per month, three-fourths cannot pay $25, and nine-tenths apparently should not undertake the payment of as much as $30 a month. In terms of rentals per room, the majority are unable to pay more than $4.50 per room per month for three-room apartments, more than $4.40 per room for four-room apartments, or more than $4.90 per room per month for five-room apartments.

Evidently the provision of modern housing at a rent within the grasp of the unskilled wage-earner is beyond possible attainment in the immediate future and the problem can scarcely be met by private ownership or private philanthropy in the tenement districts. It seems apparent that American cities, like certain European ones, must turn to public housing projects for the sake of health and decency.

[25] *Negro Housing* ("Reports of the President's Conference on Home Building and Home Ownership" Vol. VI), p. 106.

CHAPTER X[1]

THE PROBLEM OF FURNISHED ROOMS

Chicago Areas of Furnished Rooms; "Furnished Rooms" in Once Fashionable Homes; Post-war Changes in the Rooming-House Areas; Buildings Used for Light-Housekeeping; Social Workers Report Increase in Furnished Rooms; The South Side; The West and North Sides; Proximity of Vice; Rents; Overcrowding in Furnished Rooms; Insanitary Conditions Prevalent; Why Families Move to Furnished Rooms.

The use of "furnished rooms" in the poorer neighborhoods as a substitute for family life in a home has long been a serious problem in the deteriorated areas in all large cities[2] and in many countries.

Our first study of furnished rooms as one aspect of the housing problem in Chicago was published twenty-five years ago.[3] A recent recanvass, made on the eve of the present depression, showed that

[1] This chapter is largely based on the study by Mrs. Evelyn Heacox Wilson, whose unpublished Master's thesis on this subject may be found in the University of Chicago Library. Mrs. Wilson was a field-work supervisor and research assistant in the School of Social Service Administration and at one time an assistant superintendent of the United Charities of Chicago.

[2] See, e.g., Emily W. Dinwiddie, *Housing Conditions in Philadelphia*, in which, as early as 1904, she noted that the furnished rooming-house families formed "an objectionable class." "The tenants of the furnished apartments," she wrote, "as a rule belong to the lowest class. The houses are dirty and dilapidated, and often thoroughly disreputable. The furniture frequently consists of almost nothing except the beds and bedding, the latter often in a filthy condition."

Later, the Board of Public Welfare of Kansas City, in their *Report on Housing Conditions* in 1912, also dealt with "The Rooming House Evil." Here they reported (p. 28) that the furnished rooming-house district had been a desirable residence section of the city some twelve to fifteen years earlier. A house-to-house canvass of this district showed more than four hundred rooming-houses, many of which were boarding-houses as well as rooming-houses. "Light housekeeping" was frequently found, where the common practice was "to install a two-burner gas plate, with a rubber pipe from an ordinary gas fixture. A newspaper is pinned against the wall to keep the grease from the wall paper. . . . . A pail of water is upon the table; an improvised pantry, made of a large soap box, with cheap, dust-collecting curtains in front, is nearly always present."

[3] S. P. Breckinridge and Edith Abbott, "Chicago's Housing Problem: Families in Furnished Rooms," *American Journal of Sociology*, XVI (November, 1910), 289–308.

conditions had not changed greatly, and that our earlier analysis of the situation is still true. In the last five years, however, this problem has become greatly exaggerated as a result of the great need of family economies, of the loss of investments in homes, of evictions, and the fact that, temporarily, life in furnished rooms seemed to offer an immediate solution of certain pressing problems of destitution. Many families who were obliged to leave their old homes began by storing their furniture, and then later lost it entirely and found themselves unable to escape from rooming-house bondage.

CHICAGO AREAS OF FURNISHED ROOMS

A detailed recanvass has not been attempted since the depression, but in general the character of the problem seems to those in close touch with it not to be greatly changed. That is, the problem of furnished rooms remains, in part, a problem of the house, its structure and equipment; but it is not only a part of the housing problem; it is also a problem of family breakdown and demoralization, a problem of the degradation of family life; and it is also a problem of vice. The overlapping of the furnished rooming-house areas and the segregated vice districts was noted as a striking feature of the districts investigated more than twenty years ago. The segregated areas were abolished before the World War as a result of the report of the Chicago Vice Commission; but many survivals of the old districts are still to be found, and it is not far wrong today to repeat what we said before the days of "abolition"—that the "furnished rooms" territory is "honeycombed with vice," although vice is certainly less obvious, less flamboyant, than twenty-five years ago.

In the furnished rooming-house we have one housing problem that has never been charged to immigration. This fact emerged in our earlier study and it is still true today. Twenty-five years ago we found the rather shiftless American family occupying the furnished rooms of that period. Today, after more than two decades, the immigrant neighborhoods are still marked by the absence of furnished rooms; and the poor, thriftless, shiftless, and unfortunate Americans are the families who will probably be found in the rooming-house territory, on the North, South, or West sides of the city. The immigrant neighborhood is only too frequently congested and overcrowded with lodgers, but the immigrant family has a home, even if it is very poor. Perhaps there is more energy and ambition among those who were able to pull up their roots in the old world and make the long journey to the new. In any event, immigrant families with children did not so often drift into the makeshift, thriftless way of living that the furnished rooming-houses offered in normal times. It is interesting, for example, to know that the Jewish Social Service Bureau has so few furnished-room families that their social workers have said that this is not one of their problems. A recent inquiry indicated there were only a dozen cases of this type in the entire city under their care, and these were, for the most part, families that were American born, not immigrant. These were also said to be families with few children and in other respects not like the normal immigrant Jewish family.

At the time of the first canvass we found in each of the three divisions of the city—on the South, the West, and the North sides—an area that hung like a fringe on the business district and had gradually fallen into a neglected state. These districts are still to be found—districts in which family life has been transferred from normal homes to a wasteful existence in furnished rooms where they no longer have the responsibility of saving to pay a month's rent in advance, where they no longer have even the simplest bits of furniture of their own, where they live, families with children of all ages and both sexes, in one or two rooms, instead of a flat with at least three or four rooms to furnish and care for.

Revisiting these neighborhoods after twenty-five years, we found that the South Side had changed more than the furnished-room areas of the North Side or West Side, undoubtedly a result of the large Negro migrations. But in all the furnished-room areas, life was still going on in the same transient and irresponsible way, and people were still living under demoralizing conditions of crowding and lack of privacy. In general, the second canvass showed that the area in which rooming-houses are frequently found had greatly increased. This was especially true of the South Side area, which has at the same time become more predominantly Negro. The expansion on the North Side had followed the direction of elevated and surface lines. The West Side area was the most deteriorated and had the largest number of rooming-houses per unit of area, but this area had not had such an extensive growth in size as the other two.

Whether the rooming-house is a made-over one-family dwelling, or a single subdivided flat, or a small flat building, or a large tenement building, the housing conditions in all four types are very poor, and the rooms are used for purposes for which they were not designed. The buildings are always old. The upkeep and care of the premises are seldom satisfactory. It is usual for several families to share the bathroom, toilet, and hydrants. The individuals who use these accommodations feel no responsibility for taking care of them, since it would be the next user, rather than the one who exercised the care, who would be benefited.[4]

The rents charged for housekeeping rooms have increased substantially since the first study was made in 1909–10. In general, the rents charged for furnished rooms are very high for the kind of accommodation furnished. The rents are highest on the North Side and among the white families on the South Side. The rents on the West Side are slightly lower; but even there the rent for a furnished light-housekeeping apartment of one room is more than for an unfurnished flat of four rooms. An unfurnished four-room flat for a Negro family, however, would cost somewhere more than a furnished single room, partly because the Negroes pay higher rents in general for unfurnished apartments than white families would pay for the same quarters; and partly because the rents paid by the Negro families for furnished rooms tend to be lower than those that white families pay. This fact is explained by the less desirable arrangements among Negro rooming-houses of having several families use a single kitchen in common, instead of each family cooking on a gas plate in their own room.

[4] More than half a century ago the Health Department complained about the insanitary conditions in the old "one-family" homes that had degenerated into tenements. See *Chicago Health Department Report, 1881–1882*, in which attention is called to the "thousands of houses, which were originally occupied by one family according to the plan of the dwelling, now rented to and occupied by several families without any change in their interior arrangements; overcrowding is becoming general on account of an actual scarcity of houses within the city limits" (p. 47).

"FURNISHED ROOMS" IN ONCE FASHIONABLE HOMES

The West Side was to some extent unique in the old days because of the fine residences that had degenerated into low-grade rooming-houses. The once fashionable homes of the West Side—the one-time family mansions of Adams Street, of Washington Boulevard, of Aberdeen, and of Congress were still standing, although used for tenement purposes, when our first study was made. Most of these spacious old homes have now disappeared. One of the old landmarks of the inquiry of 1909–10 was a large, rambling brick house surrounded by a wide lawn that degenerated while our investigation was in progress into the "Palace Boarding Stable." At the time of the second investigation the old house had been destroyed and the spacious grounds taken over for factory purposes. A few blocks farther north a Scandinavian landlady, who told us of tenants "full to the eyes" and of her drastic methods of dealing with them, occupied a house that had once been the home of the Crane family. In another house near by, also taken over for furnished rooms, the widow of Abraham Lincoln is said to have made her home for some years.

In these houses the high ceilings, the "black-walnut" stairways, hardwood floors, marble fireplaces, and large rooms connected through "double doors" are evidences of their comfortable past. In front of a marble fireplace our investigators often found an air-tight cooking and heating stove with the stovepipe fitted into the old fireplace chimney. The "double doors" are now permanently closed, and since there are no closets in the room, clothes are hung against the "double doors," concealed sometimes by tawdry curtains. Not only the old marble fireplaces, but sometimes old pieces of furniture are left. In a fine old house on the West Side, in an attic apartment in which the paper was hanging in great pieces from the ceiling, and the stove stood propped on bricks, a large oil painting of some merit, an unmistakable relic of former prosperity, was hanging on the wall. In a basement apartment on Peoria Street, where the floors were warped and the furniture cheap and dilapidated, the present tenants were using the heavy old "black-walnut" bureau which obviously belonged to the period of mid-Victorian elegance.

Conditions found on the West Side at the time of our early survey have now been reproduced in other parts of the city. An illustration of the way that "furnished rooms" spell the downfall of neighborhoods as well as families is now to be found in certain areas on the South Side, where this particular stage of deterioration is most obvious at the present time. Along Prairie and Michigan avenues and other streets where well-known families once lived in spacious homes, and, later, along South Parkway after the Negro migration, once beautiful residences have been used for furnished rooming-houses when it has seemed uneconomical to tear them down.

That the degeneration of fine residences into furnished rooming-houses is a definite stage in the downfall of once fashionable neighborhoods was set out long ago by the late Charles Booth when he described such areas as characteristic of London life at the time when he was making his now historic studies of the "Life and Labour of the People in London." Mr. Booth wrote forty years ago:

> For such homes a well thought-out scheme of adaptation is essential, the sanitary and other difficulties being great. Moreover, the scheme ought to be of general application, as suited to the needs of the neighborhood . . . . and it is only by a successful alteration, so that the houses may be made into healthy and convenient homes for whatever class of occupant may be in view that the evils of non-adaptation and mal-adaptation may be obviated.[5]

[5] *Life and Labour of the People in London* (final volume), pp. 165–66. See also the discussion by Mrs. Bosanquet in the *Economic Journal*, XIII, 412. And for a more recent discussion of the English problem see also the report of the Housing Subcommittee of the Consultative Committee of Women's Organizations, *The Housing Problem—a Statement of the Present Position;* which has a section dealing with "Cast-Off Houses of the Middle Class." According to this report, it is quite usual in most English towns and especially in London, "to find that when a district ceases to be inhabited by the rich or moderately well-to-do, its homes are divided up among several working class families. Houses divided in this way have generally not been adapted for the use of several families, and in consequence they constitute almost the worst possible living conditions." What are called "made-down" houses are said to be "frequently not very large—from six to ten rooms. Decay in the character of the district has not meant a loss to the ground landlord or to the leaseholder. In many cases the rent extracted from the several families is more than the original rental of the house." Another English discussion of this subject is found in the *National Housing Manual* edited by Henry R. Aldridge (December, 1923), which also contains a section on this subject called "The Poor Dwellers in Furnished Lodgings," pp. 283–84. In this section attention is called to the fact that, as long ago as 1908, an officer, "acting on behalf of the National Housing and Town Planning Council, visited a number of towns to study the conditions pre-

POST-WAR CHANGES IN THE ROOMING-HOUSE AREAS

The field work for the first canvass of "furnished rooms" was part of the pre-war housing investigation. The recanvass was made a little more than a year before the beginning of the present depression, although some new data have been secured since that time. The old furnished-room districts on the North, the West, and the South sides were carefully studied again in the recanvass—this time by an experienced social worker who was interested both in housing and in family welfare problems. In each division of the city there was found to be a considerable increase in the areas devoted to furnished rooms. In general, the rooming-house areas for white tenants

---

vailing with regard to the housing of derelict families in so-called furnished rooms. His inquiries revealed the fact that the placing of a dirty truckle bed, a washstand, and a crazy chair in a squalid slum room was sufficient equipment in letting 'furnished' rooms." In 1923 it was said to be still possible to find conditions similar to those described fifteen years earlier, in spite of certain improvements by some local authorities. For example, a North of England town was said to contain "a block of two room, back to back houses, converted into single furnished rooms. The rooms on the ground floor are entered by separate doors from the front or back streets, and each have their own water tap and sink in the room. The rooms on the second floor are approached by a narrow flight of stairs at the end of the block, which leads into an unventilated and unlighted corridor. The corridor is about two feet wide and seven feet high. There are no windows at the end of the corridor, and when the doors of the respective rooms are closed, the corridor is in darkness even in the middle of the day. On each side of the corridor are the doors leading into these single rooms. None of these rooms have a water supply inside, or a soap stone sink, and contain no place for storing food. The rooms are without thorough ventilation, are damp, in bad repair, and overrun with vermin. The size of the room is about twelve feet by fourteen feet; the height seven feet six inches. In these rooms the people have to live, eat, sleep, and do every household task." Later improvements in methods of control were said to have been adopted by the local authorities, and the Public Health Act had also been amended so that by-laws for the regulation and supervision of "houses let in lodgings" included light-housekeeping rooms, and gave authority "(1) for fixing, and from time to time varying, the number of persons who may occupy a house, or part of a house, which is let in lodgings or occupied by members of more than one family, and for the separation of the sexes in a house so let or occupied; (2) for the registration of houses so let or occupied; (3) for the inspection of such houses; (4) for enforcing drainage and the provision of privy accommodations for such houses, and for promoting cleanliness and ventilation in such houses; (5) for the cleansing and lime washing at stated times of the premises, and for the paving of the courts and courtyards thereof; (6) for the giving of notice and taking of precautions in case of any infectious diseases." In England, however, the difficulty is not in any national law, but rather in the lack of vigorous administration by local authorities.

were found to be grouped together in distinct districts, whereas the furnished rooms and flats for Negro tenants were distributed irregularly over the whole Negro area. A large number of both white and Negro families from furnished rooms were found among the current records of the United Charities and these cases were carefully studied.[6]

During the period of approximately two decades between the first and second studies, the old problems had been aggravated and not removed. The problem remained essentially the same in character

[6] The social worker who made the recanvass (Evelyn Heacox Wilson) interviewed executives and case-workers in the Jewish Social Service Bureau, the Juvenile Court Pension Division, the Juvenile Court Investigation Division, the Cook County Hospital Social Service Department, the Central Charity Bureau, Chase Settlement House; and the following district offices of the United Charities of Chicago, where the furnished-room problem is of any importance: Northern, Lower North, Haymarket, Central, Stock Yards, Calumet, and Englewood. The various social agencies furnished family histories and case records, data regarding the growth of the problem, and their own experience with it. Chase House, a social settlement on the West Side, had recently made a canvass of six surrounding blocks and had secured the number and nationality of families in furnished rooms, lodgers, and flat-holders. The records of the United Charities furnished most of the family case histories. The records of 236 white rooming-house families known to the Charities for a period of six months, were used, together with 105 Negro family records known during a single month. In locating the white families the superintendents and case-workers in each of the seven districts involved gave assistance in determining first what streets and blocks contained rooming-houses. From the so-called "visible index cards" used by the social workers, and those filed as inactive during that fiscal year, the names of the families in those blocks were then taken and each of these family records was then examined to determine whether or not the family actually lived in furnished rooms. But this method could not be used in securing the names of the Negro families in furnished rooms because of the widely irregular distribution of negro rooming-houses and flats. It would have been necessary to examine the records of all the Negro families known to the United Charities in a given period, except for the fact that the district offices dealing with Negro families had recently made a study of the housing of their Negro clients for one month, so that the names of Negro furnished-room families during that month were available. Central District and Stock Yards District together had 105 such families during that month. The six months' period was used for the white rooming-house families, instead of the month of January alone, because the families of this type known to the United Charities in a single month would have constituted too small a sample to be helpful. In taking off data from the 341 records a simple schedule was used that called for such items as the number of rooms, rent per week, number of occupants (adults and children), and social status of the parents. Tables of rents were correlated with the numbers of rooms, and with the number of occupants. A spot map of the furnished-room addresses was prepared as a means of defining the districts.

and located in much the same areas on the West and the North sides, and everywhere the conditions that prevailed nearly twenty years ago had changed very little with regard to methods of living. But the South Side area had been greatly altered with regard to location, since the hurried migration of the fashionable residents of the South Side to the Lower North Side after the widening of Michigan Boulevard and the new apartment development that made the North Side seem a more attractive location for a fashionable home. The exodus of so many well-to-do and fashionable families and their friends from some of the old South Side boulevards meant the taking-over of a much larger area for rooming-house purposes used both by white and by Negro families.

In the old days we laid some stress on the fact that those deteriorated districts were on the fringe of the business district and were awaiting the business invasion. Some of them have been overtaken by the expansion of business activities of various kinds since that day. But with the South Side before us, it now appears that it is not always the business invasion but that elusive thing called "fashion" which spells the downfall of a neighborhood. This was perhaps first apparent in studying the history of the old South Side housing problem when parts of one street like Prairie Avenue were all fashion and corresponding parts of another street like Wabash or Federal, which was exactly parallel and approximately the same distance from the center of the city and the business district, were all squalor, furnished rooms, and vice. Writing twenty-five years ago, we pointed out that sharp contrasts were to be found in the South Side district and that black and dingy dwellings with dirty back yards, rickety sheds, and junk heaps were not far from Prairie Avenue, which was then one of the most beautiful and fashionable residence streets of the city. But, unfortunately, in 1935 Prairie Avenue is no longer either beautiful or fashionable.

The old homes of the wealthy—homes that were formerly spacious one-family dwellings—are usually expensive to heat, light, and keep in repair. No longer in demand as residences by the well-to-do, who alone can afford to live in them, they are used for various purposes and devoted to the easiest apparent method of bringing in money. Since good tenants are not attracted by what is no longer a very desirable neighborhood, the houses are adapted to the needs of the shifting birds of passage, who make up the down-and-out families or the tramp families looking for the kind of temporary and inexpensive dwelling-place to be found in furnished rooms.

The unstable, irresponsible, shiftless family is most likely to begin living in furnished rooms; and the influence of that type of living and of the neighborhoods in which rooming-houses are to be found is in the direction of increasing their instability and shiftlessness. The turnover of tenants in the light-housekeeping apartments is abnormally high. An unstable family which may desire to conceal itself for any reason finds this easy to accomplish by moving at frequent intervals from one neighborhood in which everybody is a recent comer and will soon be gone, to another neighborhood of the same type. Other families are attracted by the excitement and stimulation which they find in frequent changes.

The old one-family mansion can rarely be adapted properly to multiple dwelling purposes. Large rooms are, when possible, partitioned into two or three rooms, and the one-family dwelling becomes an improvised and not very comfortable tenement house. A single large room is often as large as an apartment of two, three, or more rooms in an ordinary tenement; and if the one large room is made into several, some of them will be windowless. The result is the one-room apartment which for a family with children is so devoid of the privacy required for decent living. Attempts have been made to remodel the old one-family dwelling into "multiple homes" for "light housekeepers," but the remodeling is usually hastily undertaken, without an architect's help and at the lowest possible cost. There is no attempt to make the house a suitable or convenient living-place for the new class of tenants. Hasty, makeshift alterations that turn the large rooms into smaller ones and make possible a larger monthly rental is all that is accomplished. In one house on the West Side, one end of a large hall has been made into an additional "housekeeping room" because it has a window, and all that remains for hallway purposes is a totally dark passage twenty inches wide. Through this hall one of the tenant families enjoys the only access to their one room and two other families were obliged to use it to get water from the common sink which had been placed in a dark corner at the end of the dark passage.

Windowless rooms are also sometimes found in these makeshift homes, usually the result of an attempt to subdivide a spacious room with all of the windows on one side. In one furnished rooming-house on the Lower North Side a family known to the United Charities had two front rooms in an ugly old brick rooming-house. The rooms were neatly but shabbily furnished. One of the rooms had no outside window, getting light and air by a large doorway opening into the large room. There were ten families on the same floor, all of whom shared the one toilet and bath.

BUILDINGS USED FOR LIGHT-HOUSEKEEPING

But many of the furnished rooming-houses are not large residences made over. There are said to be four types of buildings that have been adapted to light housekeeping use: (1) the old one-family home, already described as very objectionable as a made-over multiple family building; (2) the small apartment house subdivided into two or three "light-housekeeping apartments" with the one original bath now used by several families, all of whom have only one sink for cooking purposes; (3) the single large flat, which a tenant rents for the purpose of subletting one or two furnished rooms to each of several families all of whom have "kitchen privileges" in the same kitchen, use the same bath, as well as the single cooking stove, sink, and one set of dishes; (4) finally, there is also the large tenement, possibly sixty to a hundred apartments of one or two rooms each. Most of the buildings of this type were once ordinary flat buildings, and have been converted into furnished rooming-houses that are rather elegantly called "apartment hotels" by dividing each of the original apartments into two or three sets of "light-housekeeping" rooms. Others were originally hotels that have been fitted up for family use by the installation of a gas plate for cooking in each room.

"Light-housekeeping" families seem to move about from one type of furnished rooms to another, and the same family is found first in one and then in another. The smaller rooming-houses are usually better cared for than the larger ones, because in a smaller house or flat the owner usually lives there herself and is more concerned to keep the rooming-house clean and in good repair, whereas in a larger house a caretaker may be employed who is supposed to keep the bathrooms, toilets, and halls clean for the entire building but is often negligent.

But furnished-room houses of all types—whether stone, brick, or frame—are most of them extremely dilapidated and in bad repair, vermin-infested, with windows broken, doors and floor not solid—neglect everywhere! Many are without electricity, and some are even without gas, leaving the tenants to fall back on kerosene lamps.

Housing conditions in these made-over buildings are especially objectionable with regard to heat, light, and plumbing. For heat there are worn-out stoves with long pipes to a chimney at some distance, old heating-plants with leaking steam pipes in large buildings. But all attempts at heating are difficult because of the general bad repair. For example, a United Charities family of six on the West Side lived in a dilapidated rooming-house where the boards in the floor were thin and loose and some of the windowpanes were broken and stuffed with rags. It was impossible to keep the rooms warm in winter, and the social worker from the Charities found all of the six members of the family in bed at ten o'clock on a very cold morning because they could neither get warm nor keep warm in any other way.

Another West Side family was too warm because the steam pipes for the rest of the house passed through their two rooms for which they paid five dollars a week. Each of the rooms had one window opening on an alley where the entire neighborhood dumped their garbage. There was never any sunlight. The floor was two feet below the street level.

The last study showed the great extent of overcrowding in light-housekeeping rooms. Congestion and confusion are inevitable when a family, even of moderate size, attempts to carry on all its household activities in an apartment of one or two rooms. Sleeping conditions are likely to be particularly bad, especially in the larger families, of which there are a considerable number. Only about one-half of the white families studied had more than one room; and among the Negro families nearly nine-tenths of the families were living in a single room and only about one-tenth had two rooms or more.

SOCIAL WORKERS REPORT INCREASE IN FURNISHED ROOMS

Social workers who were interviewed during the recanvass, before the depression, thought that the old demoralizing furnished rooming-house life had increased substantially since pre-war days. It is interesting that this is one aspect of the housing problem that has been aggravated during the period since immigration has been practically suspended—an additional reason for thinking that this is a housing problem not due to immigration. Interviews with social workers are briefly summarized as follows: A probation officer who had been with the juvenile court for twenty-one years reported that families in furnished rooms were rare in 1908, and only people who were "down and out" would consider renting out their rooms in this fashion. In more recent years, however, she had found a great increase in the number of her clients living in furnished rooms. She felt that with the shortage of houses due to the World War had come a great increase in subletting of various kinds. The breakdown of the popular tradition against various abnormal and irregular methods of living had soon followed. Some younger married couples had known no other way of living, and now desired no other.

The superintendent of the Central District of the United Charities felt that in the last twelve or fifteen years there had been a marked increase in the number of families in furnished rooms on the South Side, and a remarkable growth of the areas devoted to furnished rooms for both white and Negro families. In 1915 Central District had few clients living in furnished rooms, and these were regarded as questionable families for whom little could be done. On the eve of the depression many white clients and nearly half the Negro clients of Central District were in rooming-houses.

The superintendents of the Haymarket District on the West Side, of Stock Yards District on the Southwest Side, and of Lower North District each told much the same story of the increase in the number of families in furnished rooms in their respective districts. The case-worker in Calumet District who covered the territory south of Hyde Park, along Sixty-third Street from South Park Avenue to the lake, thought that there had been a decided increase in rooming-house families during the three years that she had looked after that district. The case-worker who was assigned to the rooming-house area in

Englewood District, between Fifty-fifth and Sixty-third streets, from South Park Avenue west to Wentworth Avenue, felt that the number of families in furnished rooms had increased noticeably and very steadily. This increase may have been due to the gradual disappearance of old residents and a general neighborhood deterioration that seemed to be going on in that area. With the increase in the number of furnished-room clients there had clearly come a lowered standard of living and lack of stability.

The superintendent of the Cook County Hospital Social Service Department, who deals with clients from the whole city, reported an increasing number of clients from furnished rooms. A case supervisor of the Central (Catholic) Charity Bureau, also a city-wide organization, made a similar report. In fact, the six district superintendents of the Jewish Social Service Bureau were the only social workers interviewed who did not have a sufficiently large number of such clients to call furnished rooms one of their district problems and who did not think it was increasing. All social workers considered life in furnished rooms a harmful and demoralizing way of living; they all discouraged it when possible, and established such families in flats whenever this could safely be done.

The greatly increased area devoted to furnished rooms on the South Side has gone hand in hand with the swift deterioration of the once fashionable South Side streets—Michigan Avenue, South Parkway, Prairie Avenue, and other near-by streets. Along with the northward movement of the fashionable has come the great increase in the Negro population of the South Side. The story of the Negro migration has been told elsewhere. Here we are concerned only with its effect on the problem of furnished rooms. In the old days the South Side was divided into Negro and white areas stretching in parallel lines almost from the business district to Garfield Boulevard. Gradually the old "Black Belt" expanded in all available directions—to the south, to the west, to the east—everywhere except where it was checked by the pressure of business to the north. This movement went on simultaneously with the flight of the fashionable world to apartment-house life on the North Side. As Michigan and South Parkway ceased to be fashionable, the old mansions of the earlier day of wealth and fashion were left for make-shift uses.

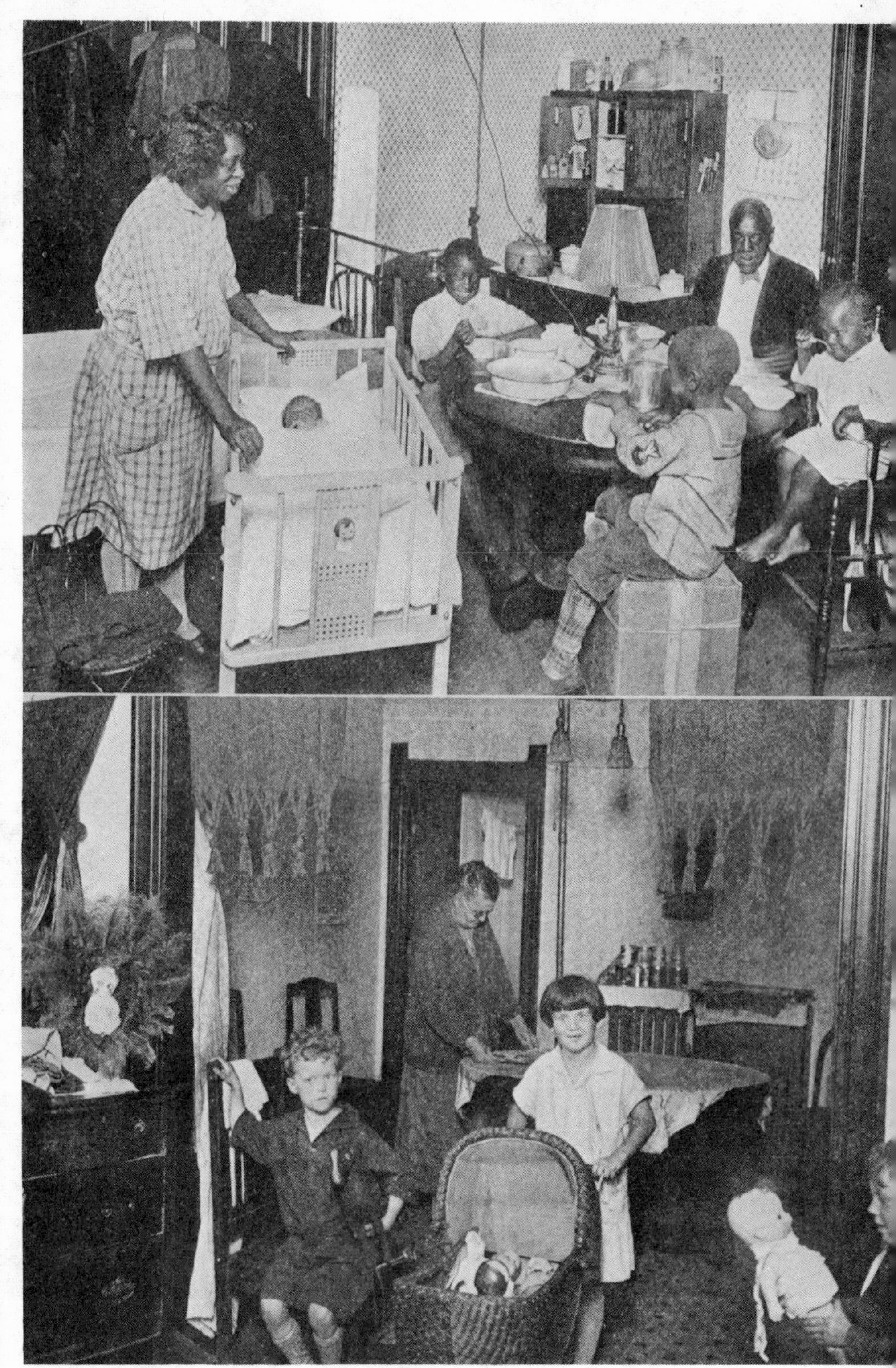

LIFE IN THE "FURNISHED ROOM" DISTRICTS

The history of the once fashionable West Side was repeated in certain areas of the South Side. The great homes built for the wealthy, often with spacious surrounding gardens, could not be used by tenants of small incomes. The downward movement soon led to the gradual increase of furnished-room territory. This was not due, and should not be attributed, to the increase in the Negro population. The same thing happened when fashion fled from the West Side and the once luxurious homes became furnished rooming-houses for poor white American families. On the South Side, the fact that the Negroes were close at hand and arriving in constantly increasing numbers meant that the new tenants of the areas in which deterioration had now begun were Negro. The Negro migrants were quick to yield to the apparently easy method of living offered by furnished rooms. Not only the old mansions of the wealthy, but flat buildings of all kinds have been turned into Negro furnished rooming-houses, and hundreds of tenements designed for one family, scattered all through the Negro residential areas, have been adapted for two or three families by the method of subletting furnished rooms in what used to be a one-family flat. Now all the families use the single kitchen and take their turn cooking at the one stove. The same families alternate between a furnished room in a flat and a furnished room in an old one-family house, but the method of living remains practically the same. Social agencies look upon the two methods of renting as identical unless the family is renting a room from relatives.[7]

Again the fact must be emphasized that while furnished rooming-house occupancy has been greatly aggravated by the depression, the tendency toward this mode of living has long been clearly marked.

THE SOUTH SIDE

Although the general location of the rooming-house areas has remained substantially the same as at the time of our first pre-war study, there have been some striking changes on the South Side and minor changes in the North Side and West Side areas. The pre-war South Side rooming-house area lay between Sixteenth and Thirty-third streets and between Prairie Avenue on the east and Clark

[7] No cases in which the landlord was a relative were used for the purpose of this study.

Street on the west. On Sixteenth Street and on Wabash Avenue northward toward Ninth Street, very dilapidated houses and the poorest families in the district were often found. The old district was in sharp contrast to the comfortable homes farther to the east. Dingy gray dwellings with dirty back yards, rickety sheds, and junk heaps were not far from some of the most beautiful and fashionable residence streets in the city. Today these once fashionable streets are likewise composed of dingy dwellings with dirty yards and a general air of dishevelment. Sixteenth Street probably remains as the northern boundary, except along Wabash Avenue, where rooming-houses stretch on almost to Roosevelt Road. The western boundary now extends beyond Clark Street toward Wentworth Avenue. On the east, the district reaches out rather irregularly and spasmodically toward the lake, and, west of Washington Park toward Sixty-fifth Street as the southern boundary. A remnant of the glorious Hyde Park of former days still survives in certain areas east of Cottage Grove and in the Midway district of pleasant homes and comfortable apartments surrounding the University. But toward the east of this section there are some areas in the vicinity of the Illinois Central tracks where furnished rooming-houses are found, some of them with families who are clients of the United Charities; from Sixtieth to Sixty-fifth streets, south of the Hyde Park district, there are also rooming-house families; while west and south of Washington Park there are Negro rooming-house families in large numbers.

There are now three quite distinct white rooming-house areas on the South Side. One of these occupies the once exclusive area along Calumet, Prairie and Michigan avenues, where the beautiful homes of the Pullmans, the Glessners, the Cranes, and other well-known Chicago families were once located. Michigan Avenue, once so fashionable, began falling under the encroaching automobile sales houses and other expanding commercial uses even in the days before the war. At that time the old "brown stone fronts" and other more pretentious houses had been taken over for "furnished rooms" north of Twenty-sixth Street, but everything now is business up to this point while furnished rooms are only too numerous along "the avenue" south of Twenty-sixth. Our earlier study showed that in this section the "light housekeeper" was gradually pushing farther and fárther toward the south, but we noted then that the northern end was poorer than the southern and this is still true; for the section nearest to the invading business houses is always more dilapidated and generally deteriorated as it is expected soon to go into the hands of the interloping business invaders. In this first South Side area, block after block is crowded with houses devoted to furnished rooms which are apparently more numerous here than in any other part of the South Side. South of Thirtieth Street the Negro rooming-houses gradually become more numerous, but with here and there a group of white rooming-houses still remaining, some of them with landlords who have been there for years. The Negro rooming-houses on Michigan Avenue stretch on and on through the "Thirties," "Forties," and even "Fifties" toward Garfield Boulevard.

The second white rooming-house district on the South Side lies along the streets near the Illinois Central Railroad embankment extending toward the south from approximately Twenty-ninth Street. And, finally, a third white rooming-house district lies south of the Midway where rooming-houses are scattered along, mixed with substantial apartment houses in the vicinity of Sixty-third Street.

THE WEST AND NORTH SIDES

On the West Side, at the time of our earlier study the furnished-rooms district was not only larger than those areas on the South and North Sides but its houses were older, with longer and more checkered histories. The recent study showed that this district had changed very little in the two intervening decades. The heart of the district still lies between Halsted Street and Ashland Boulevard, with Harrison Street as a southern boundary. The district has extended one block farther north (from Washington Boulevard to Randolph Street), and a half-mile west (from Ashland to Damen Avenue). Along the Madison Street surface-car line, the furnished-room signs are to be seen even farther along toward the west.[8]

[8] On the West Side there are more rooming-houses per block than on either the North or the South sides. Chase House, a social settlement near the corner of Adams

There are, however, many rooming-houses outside the limits of these boundaries. In this section the north-and-south streets are less important than those going east and west, with of course the single exception of Halsted Street, which serves as a noteworthy kind of boundary line, making a constant appeal to those living either east or west of it. Here are the great West Side theaters, the old saloons so drab and furtive in prohibition days, so gay and showy at the time of our earlier canvass, and now coming back to this earlier stage once more. Here also are the dance halls, the "movies," hotels, peddler's carts, the rush of "through cars," and the ever present possibility of excitement furnished by the city street on which life and business begin early and seemingly never cease. Traffic is apparently greater on the east-and-west streets and the houses are in general better than those on the north-and-south streets. On Washington Boulevard, for example, most of the buildings are either large stone-front blocks extending sometimes half the way from one street to another, or old and rather elegant residences, with imposing French windows, porches with iron railings, yards, and carriage sheds. Some of the houses are left much as they were in their better days, while others are patched and made over grotesquely. On the other hand, there are some houses, which were homes of comfort in the past, to be found on the north-and-south streets. Of these streets, Morgan and Sangamon perhaps rank first in the appearance of dingy, unrelieved poverty; Peoria and Green streets, which are parallel, are also dingy and forlorn, and here in the old days vice was mixed with poverty.

Madison is the great east-and-west street of the West Side. Passing as it does through the heart of the furnished-rooms district, it is more inviting even than Halsted Street to the people who live there. East of Halsted Street toward the river is the territory which is given over to "flops," drifting "hobos," and dejected unemployed men.

Street and Ashland Avenue, in the better part of the West Side furnished-room district, in their canvass of the six blocks surrounding the house referred to above (see p. 312, n. 6) reported that in these few blocks 499 light-housekeeping rooms were found, in addition to 1,299 lodging-rooms. Only 476 rooms were reserved for the exclusive use of the families who owned or had leased the buildings.

Here are the cheap lodging-houses and restaurants, the labor agencies, and the army recruiting stations which are all alike of interest to the homeless "casual." Many of these unfortunate men drift haplessly into the furnished-rooms territory and encourage the more vicious forms of amusement that sometimes seem to flourish there.

South of Madison, on the way toward Hull-House, the parallel east-and-west streets like Monroe, Adams, Van Buren, and Harrison have many stores in the region near Halsted, but westward toward Ashland and on to Damen they decrease in number. There are many types of houses here—frame cottages raised onto later brick basements and "first stories"—brick blocks designed for tenement use, and the old-fashioned residences that have degenerated into furnished rooms. This commercialization of the old and dignified, the unrelieved monotony of the tenement block, and the dilapidated houses of some of the north-and-south streets make the whole district extremely depressing.

The lodging-houses for single men and single women, many of them quasi-philanthropic, adjoining, and even scattered along the furnished-rooms territory, are a striking feature of the West Side, but one with which we are not here concerned. The purpose of this chapter is rather a discussion of the problems growing out of the fact that in all these districts large numbers of families with children make their homes in furnished rooms.

The North Side rooming-house district in 1909 lay in the area between the river on the south and Division Street on the north, and between Rush Street on the east and Wells on the west. The new canvass showed that this particular district had changed very little in two decades except that the northern boundary had moved another half-mile north—to North Avenue. This is in line with the tendency noted in the report on our first study when it was said that the district was then "steadily pushing north." But the district remains an area gridironed with noisy street cars. There are surface cars clanging north and south on Wells Street, on Clark Street, and on State Street; and there are other cars rushing east and west—on Grand Avenue, on Chicago Avenue, on Division Street, and on North Avenue. There are stores and city lights on many of these streets with light-housekeeping rooms above the stores and dilapidated houses with furnished rooms anywhere and everywhere.

There are now, however, two other North Side districts with furnished rooms in addition to the original district visited. The second rooming-house district which is on the North Side lies between Racine Avenue on the west and Sedgwick Street, a mile to the east; and between Center Avenue on the south and Fullerton Avenue, less than half a mile to the north. In this small area there are eight street-car lines on Racine Avenue, on Halsted Street, and on Larrabee Street, north and south; and, east and west, on Fullerton, Webster, and Center avenues; and not only these, but on Lincoln Avenue, which runs diagonally across this area, and on Clark Street, whose diagonal crosses the northeast end of the district. There is also the "elevated" between Sheffield and Bissell streets. This is a small business area, with old houses and tenements converted into houses with furnished rooms.

The third rooming-house district on the North Side lies in the neighborhood of 3800 north and 1000 west, where Sheridan Road, which is a business section at this point, turns to the west for a few blocks and is crossed by the "elevated."

PROXIMITY OF VICE

The problem of furnished rooms has long been connected with the city problems of vice and immorality. This situation is not peculiar to Chicago or to the present day. It is inevitably connected with any attempt to readapt the homes of the wealthy for cheap lodgings or tenements. In his classic account of *Life and Labour* at the close of the last century, Charles Booth pointed out that in the "city wilderness" the furnished room, especially when let by the day as well as by the week, afforded a convenient meeting place for people of unconventional and sometimes undesirable habits.

There can be no doubt that furnished rooms in this country are often put to the lowest uses, and one of the tragedies of these areas is the fact that order and disorder so often live side by side. Very near, often indeed adjoining, the houses used by men and women of immoral character are houses in which the rooms furnished with housekeeping necessities are let to poor but decent families. At the time of our first study, on the South Side a large section from Seventeenth to Twenty-fourth Street, and from State Street to the river, was segregated and devoted to the purposes of organized and commercialized vice. Similarly, on the West Side, from the river to Curtis Street, and between Lake and Van Buren streets, was another section of tolerated vice, a considerable part of which was included in the furnished-room district. Because this toleration did not amount to thorough segregation as on the South Side, respectability and vice in its worst forms were living, not only in the same streets, in the same blocks, but even in the same houses. Little children saw prostitutes and their so-called patrons coming and going through the common hallways. Immorality seemed to be scattered throughout the rooming-house districts—sometimes next door or just across the hall from a family who were doing their best to maintain decent standards and to rear the children without contacts of a degrading nature.

One Negro family, for example, who were known to a social agency had a two-room furnished apartment in an old brick building. They lived near a district in which moral conditions were very objectionable. The husband was intemperate, and after a short desertion was given a sentence of six months in the House of Correction, for non-support. The mother and the six children, all under fifteen years of age, moved into a house which apparently was owned by some kind of a vice syndicate, which was said to allow tenants to live there without paying any rent. This family occupied two large rooms which were partially furnished, containing a bed, dresser, three chairs, and a stove. There was only one window, which opened on a court. Three of the children slept on the floor. A report was current in the district that the vice syndicate owned a number of such houses which, when not in use for immoral purposes, were kept occupied by securing colored families from the neighborhood, who were allowed to live there free of rent until the house was to be used again, whereupon the free tenants would have to vacate without notice. In order to facilitate sudden shifts from one house to another in case of danger of arrest, the girls thus employed met, it was said, at an outside point, at an appointed time, and were transported to the houses to be used. While a house was being occupied by the temporary free tenants, it was supposed to be under observation, in order to prevent these tenants from soliciting trade away from the syndicate.

Another case of this type was that of a widow with three little girls aged fourteen, ten, and eight years, who applied to the United Charities for help. The family were living in one small, dark, basement room, in the center of a tenement building. The one window opened out on a high, narrow passageway, and there was practically no light or fresh air coming into the room. The only means of heating the room was by opening the door into a furnace room, which was used for a sleeping-room by several men. There was a kitchen in the basement for the use of all the roomers on that floor. The woman said that the young girls who occupied the room in front of hers were "sporting women," and that when their voices could be heard through the partition the language was often obscene. The family had been in furnished rooms for more than three years, ever since the house in which they had lived was burned, together with all their furniture. She finally moved away from her basement room about ten o'clock one night, giving as an excuse that the landlord would not let her stay there any longer because of the children. However, there was reason to think they were being irregularly provided for. The new landlord would give no definite information but hinted that if the truth were known it might not be necessary for the organization to "spend so much money." The children were exceedingly irregular in school and were reported to be running the streets while the mother worked.

The study of United Charities families in furnished rooms showed a close mingling of very different types of families—those of the lowest and most degraded sort along with some who still maintained decent standards of living. This proximity may easily lead to the spreading of infectious diseases by means of the common toilets and baths. The exchange of ideas and the lowering of standards by various contacts, are even more certain to take place. Observing a neighboring family "getting by" with a minimum of honest effort and responsibility may be the influence which persuades a previously "normal" family to adopt the easier method in its turn. In many rooming-house neighborhoods, also, the influence of commercialized vice is a large factor; and the ease with which unmarried couples can pose as married in a rooming-house apartment has its effect upon the moral standards in the midst of which all the families in furnished rooms must live.

The phenomenon of the "tramp family" is frequently found in furnished rooms. Such families exploit the landlord, the grocer, or anyone who will give them money or credit. They appeal to social agencies, churches, and private individuals. In a neighborhood where no one expects references or verification, they have no difficulty in securing listeners to their "hard-luck story," whether it be true or false. And in case they find their sources of supply cut off as a result of investigation, they can always move to another neighborhood or to another city.

Immigrant families, it has already been pointed out, do not make a practice of living in furnished rooms. This does not mean that they are not overcrowded, for the custom of renting rooms to lodgers often means that the family itself has almost no room left. But the rooms rented to outsiders are not for housekeeping purposes; and each family has its own house or flat and its own furniture, which is tenaciously preserved. Thus the immigrant families do not experience the disintegrating effects which are found in a light-housekeeping neighborhood. This conclusion is based particularly upon the Chase House Survey, which reported very few immigrant families in furnished rooms, and attention has already been called to the experience of the Jewish Social Service Bureau, whose occasional (but rare) rooming-house cases are invariably American-born Jews, and not recent immigrants.

The evidence seems to show that white families at the present time move into furnished rooms because of the ease of this type of living and because the desire not to be tied down is thus satisfied; and not because it is an inexpensive method of housing. Some Negro families, however, may choose to live in furnished rooms because they can save a little money in that way, when they would really prefer to have a flat.

RENTS

From the point of view of the rent paid, living in furnished rooms is still relatively expensive for poor people today—as it was at the time of our first canvass years ago. In pre-war days a four-room flat could be had unfurnished for $8.00–$10 a month, while a furnished room was usually $2.00 or $2.50 a week for a single room, or about $9.00 a month.[9] The rents during the recanvass are shown in Table 55. In general, an unfurnished flat of three or four rooms could be

TABLE 55

NUMBER OF FAMILIES LIVING IN FURNISHED ROOMS PAYING A SPECIFIED WEEKLY RENT FOR A SPECIFIED NUMBER OF FURNISHED ROOMS; ALL DISTRICTS COMBINED

(Recanvass Data)

Weekly Rent	Number of Families Occupying Specified Number of Furnished Rooms					
	Total	1	2	3	4	Not Reported
Total	341	195	90	25	4	27
$ 2.00– 2.99	1	1	....	....	....	....
3.00– 3.99	10	10	....	....	....	....
4.00– 4.99	13	13	....	....	....	....
5.00– 5.99	51	42	6	1	....	2
6.00– 6.99	38	31	4	1	....	2
7.00– 7.99	50	29	14	2	1	4
8.00– 8.99	29	10	15	....	....	4
9.00– 9.99	25	12	9	1	....	3
10.00–10.99	34	6	17	5	1	5
11.00–11.99	12	1	6	3	1	1
12.00–12.99	16	1	11	4	....	....
13.00–13.99	7	1	3	3	....	....
14.00–14.99	1	....	....	....	....	1
15.00–15.99	5	1	1	2	1	....
16.00–16.99	2	....	1	1	....	....
17.00–17.99	....	....	....	....	....	....
18.00–18.99	2	....	....	2	....	....
Not reported	45	37	3	....	....	5

rented before the depression for $15–$25 a month in a white neighborhood, or from $25 to $30 a month in a Negro district. One furnished room is usually rented from $5.00 to $7.00 a week, or from $22 to $30 a month. Rents in the several districts are shown in Table 56 and Table 57.

The rent charged for furnished rooms on the West Side is less than on the South or North sides. This may be due to the fact that the

[9] Breckinridge and Abbott, *op. cit.*, p. 306.

TABLE 56

NUMBER OF FAMILIES LIVING IN FURNISHED ROOMS PAYING A SPECIFIED WEEKLY RENT; BY DISTRICTS

(Recanvass Data)

WEEKLY RENT	FAMILIES LIVING IN FURNISHED ROOMS				
	Total	North Side	West Side	South Side	
				Negro	White
Total	341	96	70	105	70
$ 2.00–$ 2.99	1	....	....	1	....
3.00– 3.99	10	....	4	6	....
4.00– 4.99	13	1	2	10	....
5.00– 5.99	51	10	10	28	3
6.00– 6.99	38	7	10	18	3
7.00– 7.99	50	12	11	13	14
8.00– 8.99	29	13	6	3	7
9.00– 9.99	25	8	7	2	8
10.00– 10.99	34	15	4	3	12
11.00– 11.99	12	2	3	....	7
12.00– 12.99	16	9	2	....	5
13.00– 13.99	7	4	1	....	2
14.00– 14.99	1	1	....	....	....
15.00– 15.99	5	4	....	1	....
16.00– 16.99	2	2	....	....	....
17.00– 17.99	....	....	....	....	....
18.00– 18.99	2	1	....	....	1
Not reported	45	7	10	20	8

TABLE 57

MEDIAN RENT FOR FURNISHED APARTMENTS OF SPECIFIED NUMBER OF ROOMS; BY DISTRICTS

(Recanvass Data)

DISTRICT	MEDIAN WEEKLY RENT FOR FURNISHED APARTMENTS		
	All Sizes	One Room	Two Rooms
All districts	$8	$6	$ 9
Negro, South Side	$5	$5	$ 8
West Side	7	6	8
North Side	9	7	10
White, South Side	9	7	10

houses are older and more dilapidated. And it has already been pointed out that room rent for the Negro tenant is less than for the white, because the Negro roomers or rooming-house families usually are willing to accept "kitchen privileges" in a common kitchen.

Rooming-house landlords who lease unfurnished flats for the purpose of subletting furnished rooms in them make a high profit, because the rents they charge for the light-housekeeping rooms are so high in comparison with the rent they must pay for the unfurnished flats. On the Southeast Side, on West Sixty-fifth Street, there is a block in a residence district almost entirely given over to furnished rooms. A three-story building has been rented by a woman who has several similar buildings. Originally the building contained six five-room flats. Each flat has been subdivided and furnished, making out of each flat a three-room rear apartment renting for $12 a week, and a two-room front apartment renting for $11 a week. As one of the two-room apartments is occupied by the housekeeper and yields no rent, there are eleven apartments, yielding a total income of $550 a month. The monthly rental for the entire building was estimated by one of the tenants to be from $200 to $270 a month.

The apartments in this building are steam heated. They are furnished with old, dilapidated gas ranges for cooking, instead of the more usual gas plates. There is a bathroom on each floor, and the number of baths is not limited as is often the case. There is no check on the amount of gas used by each family, and it was said that the housekeeper is the worst one in the building for leaving her gas oven burning all day in cool weather. The hall lights are left burning all day long unless some tenant turns them off in the morning.

In a Negro rooming-house district on Wabash Avenue the landlord pays $65 a month for a three-story cement-block building. The English basement as well as the upper stories are sublet to families for $6.00 a room, including kitchen privileges. There is a small laundry stove in each room for heat, which can be used for cooking. There is a toilet and bath on each floor. At least eight rooms are rented in this way, bringing in an income of $48 a week, or over $200 a month, although the rent for the entire building unfurnished is only $65.

Although, as these figures show, the sum of the room rents may be double or treble the rent of the building unfurnished, there is a large loss to the landlords from vacant rooms, unpaid rents in many cases, and the neglect and abuse of the rooms by the tenants. The landlord of one family, known to the Central District of the United Charities, stated that to repair the damage the family had caused by their abuse of their room was going to cost more than the total rent they had paid.

OVERCROWDING IN FURNISHED ROOMS

From the standpoint of privacy as well as peace and quiet after the day's work the overcrowding in furnished rooms involves many hardships. In addition, the confusion of cooking, eating, dressing, and carrying on the daily household tasks in one or two rooms makes life difficult to keep above the lowest levels of bickering and degradation.

Many examples of overcrowding may be furnished by social agencies. One example is the United Charities family, who had two rooms for three adults and three children under twelve years of age. They were particularly crowded at night, as there was only one three-quarter-size bed and one sanitary couch for the six occupants.

A Negro family known to one district of the United Charities was found living in one small basement room, paying $5.50 a week. The father had been bitten by a dog, could not work, and had been evicted from his flat. In their single basement room there were two double beds for the seven members of the family. Four of the five children were girls, whose ages were fourteen, eight, five, and one. The boy was eleven. The family had colds most of the year, and the father finally came down with influenza. After living in this place for more than a year the family were re-established in a flat of their own.

Another district of the United Charities told of the X family of seven members, who had two small rooms for $10 a week. There was one double bed and a cot, on which all of them had to sleep. There were four girls, aged thirteen, eleven, nine, and five, and a boy aged seven.

Haymarket District, on the West Side, reported several instances of severe overcrowding. One family had only one double bed to accommodate the father and mother, two girls, thirteen and three, and a boy of nine. The two small basement rooms were examples of the worst housing conditions.

Another example of serious overcrowding known to the United Charities was the case of the V family. They had one double bed

TABLE 58

NUMBER OF FURNISHED ROOMS OCCUPIED BY A SPECIFIED NUMBER OF PERSONS; BY DISTRICTS; RECANVASS DATA

Districts	Number of Rooms	Number of Families of Specified Size, Expressed in "Equivalents of Adults"										
		1½	2	2½	3	3½	4	4½	5	5½	6	Total
Negro	1	11	20	20	18	14	5	1	....	1	1	91
	2	1	1	5	2	....	1	1	....	....	....	11
	3	....	....	....	1	....	....	....	....	....	....	1
	4	....	....	....	....	....	....	....	....	1	....	1
West Side	1	3	13	5	11	....	2	1	....	....	....	35
	2	3	1	3	5	2	2	....	2	....	....	18
	3	....	1	....	1	2	2	....	....	1	....	7
	4	....	....	....	....	....	....	....	....	....	....	....
North Side:	1	4	16	10	8	1	....	1	....	....	....	40
	2	3	5	3	8	7	6	1	2	....	1	36
	3	....	....	1	1	....	4	1	2	1	....	10
	4	....	....	....	....	....	....	....	1	....	....	1
South Side, White	1	....	10	10	3	3	2	....	....	....	....	28
	2	1	3	4	5	6	6	1	....	....	....	26
	3	....	....	2	1	....	2	....	....	....	1	6
	4	....	....	1	....	1	....	....	....	1	....	3
All districts	1	18	59	45	40	18	9	3	....	1	1	194
	2	8	10	15	20	15	15	3	4	....	1	91
	3	....	1	3	4	2	8	1	2	2	1	24
	4	....	....	1	....	1	....	....	1	2	....	5
	....	26	70	64	64	36	32	7	7	5	3	314

and a cot in their room for the parents and four children (twin boys of eleven, and a girl of eight, and a boy of five).

Examples of this kind could be given in great number. But Table 58 tells its own story of overcrowding, and the inevitable discomfort and demoralization need not be described.

Instances of extreme overcrowding are to be noted in each of the four districts shown in Table 58. For example, in the Negro group there are such cases as a family of seven living in a one-room apartment, while in another single room was a family of eight. However, there were no instances of seven or eight persons in single rooms in any of the white districts. A white family of seven was living in a three-room apartment on the South Side, and a family of eight (four adults and four children) living in two rooms on the North Side. Two other families with eight members (one with two adults and six children, and one with three adults and five children) were found on the North Side, with three rooms for each family.

Cases where six persons live in a single furnished room are not infrequent. There were six Negro families with that number of members in one room. These six families include two families consisting of two adults and four children each, three cases of one adult and five children, and one case where six "adults" (defined as persons over twelve years of age) occupied a single room.

There were two white families of six members (two adults and four children) each, living in one-room apartments on the South Side. One family of six (three adults and three children) was living in one room on the North Side. On the West Side, two families of this size (one with three adults and three children, and the other with two adults and four children) were living in one room.

Although many cases of extreme overcrowding among families in furnished rooms were found, it is nevertheless true that at least half of these families are small families with only one or two adults and only one or two children. However, since most of these small families live in only one furnished room, where all the activities of life must be carried on, with no possibility of peace or privacy, the fact that a large proportion of the families are small does not make this a desirable mode of life.

INSANITARY CONDITIONS PREVALENT

The plumbing in these houses is usually inadequate, old, and in poor repair. The water-tap, the sink, and the bathroom are in constant use and seldom clean. Landlords or caretakers frequently make regulations regarding the use of these common sanitary facilities. Sometimes tenants are allowed to take only one bath a week, or possibly two. They are also warned about the disposal of garbage and other waste, but the abuse of common plumbing facilities is very common and in all such cases privacy and even decency are almost impossible. Toilet accommodations are usually inadequate in all furnished rooming houses and flats[10] and the situation is sometimes dangerous. But the condition that prevails in most of these houses—a single toilet for the entire house, however large the number of tenant families—is not illegal because the houses were not built under the new law. The toilets are, however, almost invariably filthy or in bad repair, or both. The landlord is, of course, not always responsible for this condition, for when there is one toilet, and that one unlocked, in a public hall, in a house containing half-a-dozen families and often as many single roomers besides, there is every opportunity for abuse as well as neglect. In one house the toilet was out of repair because one tenant had emptied her garbage into it. The caretaker's only comment was, "You can't watch them all the time, you know!" Along with such limited toilet accommodations will be found a correspondingly limited water supply.[11] All the tenants in a single house, therefore, are frequently dependent upon a single sink for the water used for cooking, washing, and all other household purposes. As is to be expected, the condition of these

[10] The number of toilets is insufficient and does not meet the standard laid down in the city ordinance in which the following requirement is made: In new buildings, a separate water closet shall be provided within each apartment, except that, where there are apartments of only one or two rooms, there shall be at least one water closet for every two apartments (Busch-Hornstein, *Revised Chicago Code*, 1931, sec. 1443).

[11] In the first study remodeled houses were visited, and eleven of these had only a single toilet, which was either in the public hall or in the yard, for the use of the entire house. To understand what a difficult problem is involved it must be remembered that these are light-housekeeping rooms, and that water is needed for cooking and other household purposes. In three cases the one sink which furnished the whole water supply of the house and the one toilet were used by five families, numbering in one house more than forty persons. It must, of course, be remembered that plumbing accommodations are often very inadequate, not only in remodeled houses but in those built for tenement purposes. For example, a well-known furnished rooming-house on the West Side is a house containing twenty-eight furnished housekeeping apartments, and was, of course, built for a tenement, and not for the use of a single family. Here each family has two rooms, but although there is a sink in each apartment, the toilets are in the halls and there are only six for twenty-eight apartments. In the winter, when the investigators visited the house, they were all filthy, frozen, and vermin infested.

sinks is, in general, as bad as that of the toilets. When there is only one sink for several families, someone is quite sure to use it, not only for dishwater, but for general refuse. The effect on the standards of cleanliness provided by this absence of all facilities for decent living needs no comment.

Dark halls are another bad feature in houses used for furnished rooms. Some halls were so dark that one groped to find the way. These dark stairways in crowded houses not only involve well-known moral dangers, more especially since there is a constant danger of tenants of bad character, but they are almost invariably dirty and insanitary. There is also the possible danger of fire since most of the houses are old buildings, and many of them frame. And in some, of course, there is a stove in nearly every room, and in a large number of cases both gasoline and coal stoves were found in the same room. Such conditions in a house used by people of irregular habits make the danger from fire a serious one.

The great evil of the furnished rooming-house, however, is not that of inadequate or filthy sanitary arrangements, dark halls, or danger from fire, but the degradation that comes from a family living in one room with broken, dilapidated furniture, without responsibility or a sense of ownership. Parlor, bedroom, clothes closet, dining-room, kitchen, pantry, and even coal shed are here combined in one room where the cooking, eating, sleeping, washing, and all the family life go on.

The furniture which is found in light-housekeeping rooms is uniformly old and dilapidated, for the newly purchased is cheap and poor in quality, and soon goes to pieces. In many cases, where a landlady first "goes into the business," she makes her own old furniture, bought many years ago when she was first married, go as far as possible toward furnishing the house. Some secondhand furniture is perhaps bought and added to her own old furniture, but very little that is new ever goes into furnished rooms. Each apartment is usually supplied with a stove, a bed, a table, two chairs, a bureau, and a few dishes, two plates, two cups and saucers, and a few cooking utensils. Carpets are very rare, but occasionally there is a rug. Curtains fortunately are also rare. The bedding, which is always "furnished," is one of the most repulsive features of the room, for it is handed on uncleansed from tenant to tenant. Clean towels, sheets, and pillow cases are supposed to be furnished weekly to each tenant, and when this is done they are washed at a steam laundry and are reasonably clean. But only too often one finds sheets that are as dirty as the rest of the bedding. When tenants have "nothing of their own," the house is inevitably cheerless, and when the home is only a single room, it is necessarily disorderly and confused. In all families with hand-to-mouth methods, coal is bought by the basket or bushel, and little food is ever carried over from one meal to the next; but in light-housekeeping apartments such fuel and provisions as are on hand will probably be kept in the same room in which the family sleep.

The purpose of this chapter has been to set forth one of the less conspicuous aspects of the housing problem in Chicago, and one that is believed to be important because of its singularly demoralizing effect on family life. It should be pointed out again that this is something more than a local problem. In nearly every large city there are sections similar to those described in Chicago in which domestic life is driven out by business or industry or both, and during the period of transition, the houses which were once dignified and comfortable homes are crudely adapted for the use of the poor. Doubtless in many communities the problem described in this study assumes as serious aspects as in Chicago.[12] With reference to the treatment of such property by the city, nothing can be added to the conservative and yet far-seeing statement of the late Charles Booth.[13] While, however, a suitable scheme of adaptation is being elaborated, certain obvious requirements in administration may be noted. Reasonably frequent disinfections should be required without special evidence of contagion having spread in these sections. It may be too soon to look for a municipal ordinance which shall outlaw the one-room tenement for families with children, but in so far as the one-room tenement involves a violation of the ordinance requiring a minimum cubic air-space in rooms used for living and sleeping purposes, a rigid enforcement of the ordinance may be demanded. It has already been pointed out that nearly fifty per cent of the

[12] See, e.g., Dinwiddie, *op. cit.*, p. 23: "The filthiest living rooms were found in the furnished room houses." See also p. 19.

[13] Cited above, p. 310.

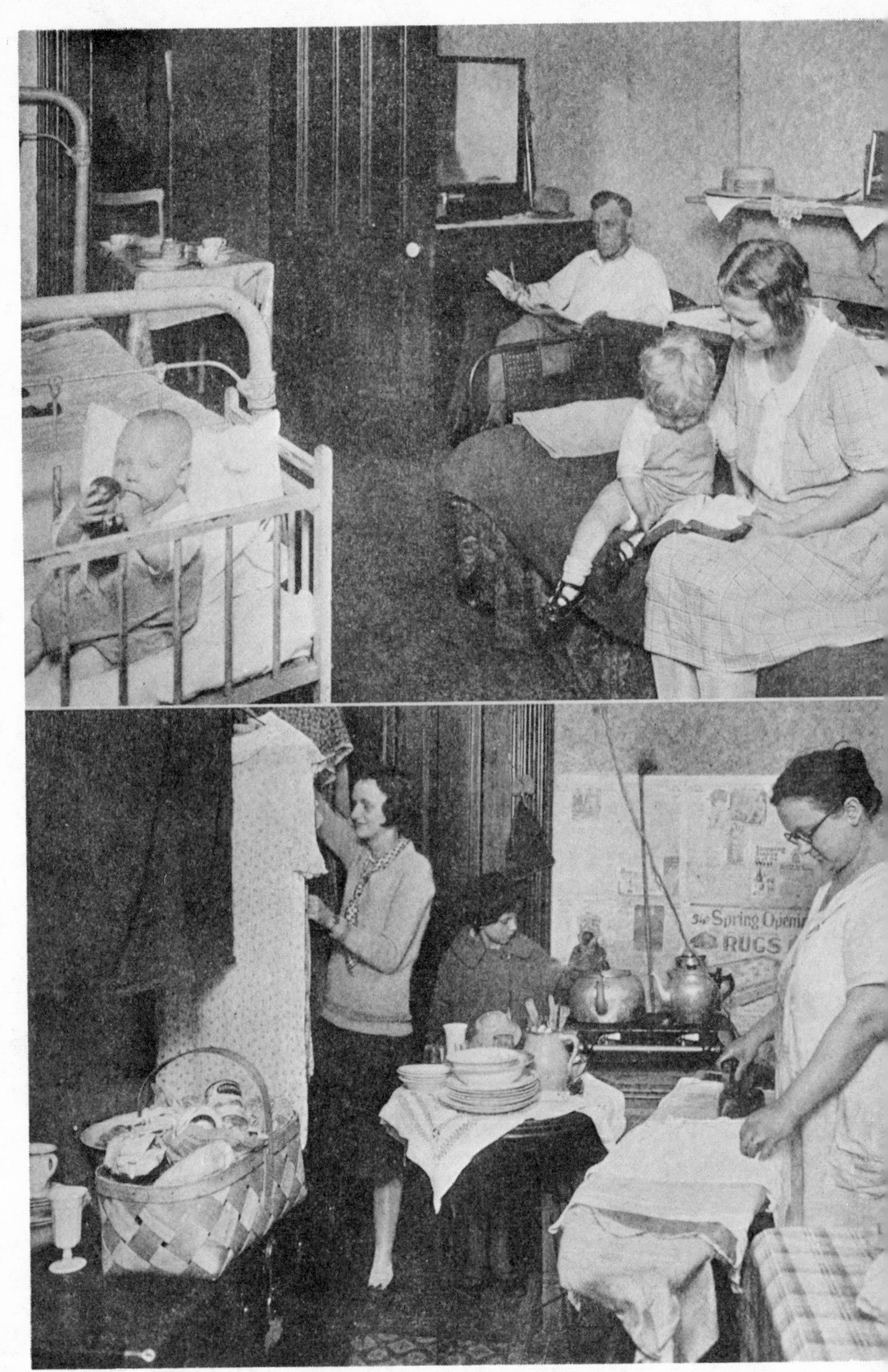

FAMILY GROUPS IN FURNISHED ROOMS

sleeping-rooms were illegally crowded as to cubic air-space, and nowhere is this overcrowding so harmful as in cases where a single room is used for all household purposes. The frequent inspection of such establishments for the purpose of enforcing this and other sections in the health code should be rendered possible by an adequate appropriation and a larger staff of inspectors.

WHY FAMILIES MOVE TO FURNISHED ROOMS

Social agencies often question why families move into furnished rooms. Usually the cause is complex. At the time of our first study we gave the following reasons: drink (in more than half of the families studied), gambling, illness, irregular employment, women working at night and wishing to leave the children near neighbors, and young married women who were employed and wished to avoid heavy home duties. Our conclusion was that "in general, uncertainty of employment, with bad management on the part of the wife, tends to promote a most disorderly manner of living, obviously demoralizing for the children in the family." In general, financial exigencies are the most compelling reason which leads a family to live in this manner.

Drink is undoubtedly less of a cause than it used to be for families to move into furnished rooms. Financial necessity, however, has become a more important factor than it was. A case-worker on the West Side said that in her opinion many of her families lived thus because they liked it. The desire for the excitement that can be found in many of the rooming-house neighborhoods, for change, anonymity, for drink and narcotics, and for easier housework, combine in influencing families to adopt this manner of life, even though, as we have pointed out, it is more expensive than renting an unfurnished flat. It involves very little responsibility and much freedom. "They say that they want their own flat, but they really don't," this worker said.

In the case of the Negro families, on the other hand, poverty is probably the greatest single reason for their living in furnished rooms. While for white families, in every section of the city, living in furnished rooms is more expensive than living in an unfurnished flat, for Negro families the opposite is true. It has already been pointed out that rooming-house rents for Negroes are proportionately lower than the cost of an unfurnished flat would be. This fact makes it apparent that many Negro families live in furnished rooms not because they prefer to do so but because they could really live more economically in that way.

Social agencies sometimes make an effort to rehabilitate a rooming-house family. If there is reasonable hope of success and permanence in the plan they will help a family to re-establish itself in a regular flat. Unfortunately, however, experience seems to indicate that most rooming-house families have become so accustomed to their easy method of living that they make little effort on their own part to make the rehabilitation a success. Even when they do succeed in getting a flat and furniture of their own for a time, a little trouble or difficulty of some kind will serve as an excuse for them to return to furnished rooms. The fact that living in furnished rooms requires no forethought and no saving of money to pay rent a month in advance seems to appeal to such families—even though it is more expensive in actual money.

Whenever it seems probable that a family will settle down, and when they are unable to do so alone or with the help of relatives, the United Charities makes an effort to get them out of furnished rooms and into a flat. This is clearly a move toward a more wholesome and normal family life.

The problem before the social agency is often exceedingly difficult and practically insurmountable. An unstable or transient family is likely to move before any solution can be worked out. For example, a white woman who lived in one of the oldest rooming-house districts on the South Side became known to the United Charities when a church from which she had been begging telephoned the Central District office. Neighbors had already called in the Humane Society and the Juvenile Protective Association because of her beating the children. Her husband had deserted, and she was living with her children, the oldest five years old and the youngest four months, in a large, scantily furnished basement room, untidy and very dirty, in a three-story rooming-house. The cooking was done on a gas plate in the room. The children were thin and pale and dirty, with the next to the youngest, fifteen months old, suffering from rickets and impetigo (a serious skin eruption). The oldest boy had ugly sores around his mouth. The family left the city the night after the situation became known to the United Charities. The train left at 11:00 P.M., but the mother with her children was at the station four hours before the time. The landlady and the case-worker did everything they could to persuade her to remain, but without effect. A year later it was learned that the children had all been burned to death in southern Illinois in a shack that caught fire and burned to the ground, with the children locked inside.

The United Charities established a wandering family with a bad record in a flat, and favorable results were soon apparent. Six years earlier the family had received aid from the Family Welfare Association of Minneapolis. Then for a period of nearly three years they roved about in Colorado, with their three children. They finally started for Chicago in an old Overland automobile. They were stranded twice on the way, once in Topeka and again in Kansas City, where they sold the car for six dollars. The Kansas City authorities sent them on to Chicago, as they had lived nowhere long enough to become legal residents. When they reached Chicago they found two furnished rooms, renting for $5.00 a week. The rooms were dark, damp, overheated, and below the street level. The family shared a toilet with two other families. The woman had a history of arrested pulmonary tuberculosis, and the living conditions seemed particularly dangerous for this reason. Her husband had syphilis and was incapacitated for work by paralysis of one side of his body. When contact was first made, both the husband and the wife were very antagonistic, refusing medical care, and telling false stories of their lives. With sympathetic treatment, however, they have become friendly, and reluctantly co-operative; and have seemed to enjoy the flat in which they were presently established, which rents for $22 a month.

It might be that social agencies could accomplish more toward the solution of the rooming-house problem than they are now doing. For the sake of the children so often found in these families, more effort might well be expended, and the ordinary furnished-room family be accepted for long-time care. Fifteen years ago the application of a furnished-room family to the United Charities was seldom accepted, but the tendency today is more and more toward adequate treatment.

Owing to the very frequent changes of address of such families, an efficient system of follow-up work is essential to good case work. Systematic and thorough use of the Social Service Exchange is very necessary, with special attention to changes of address, cross-references, and other identifying data. The ease with which families can move from city to city and the large number of "tramp families" are making the need for some nation-wide system of registering transient cases more and more keenly felt.

If the landlords should come to realize that they lose money in the end by accepting any tenant who applies, without asking for references or investigating them if secured, it is possible that there might be some amelioration of the present indiscriminate mixing of decent and degraded families. But probably there is needed, more than anything else (especially from the housing standpoint), some legislative enactment along the line of the present tenement-house code[14] applying to all furnished rooming-houses. Plumbing, heating arrangement, amount of light, cubic feet of air-space in sleeping-rooms, and certain standards of cleanliness, with provision for registration and systematic inspection, should all be included.

[14] Cf. Busch-Hornstein, *Revised Municipal Code, 1931*, secs. 1421, 1443, 2260.

CHAPTER XI

LODGERS, BOARDERS, AND NON-FAMILY GROUPS

Immigration and the Lodger Problem; Lodgers in the House-to-House Canvass; "Beds for All Who Come"; Lodgers and Tenement Rents; Non-family Groups of Immigrant Workers; Bulgarian, Croatian, and Serbian Groups; Italian and Greek Lodging Groups; Houses Rented by Non-family Groups; Recanvassing the Old Districts.

THE custom of taking lodgers or boarders has long been regarded as a neighborhood problem of great importance in connection with housing, and especially with overcrowding. At the time when our first housing studies were undertaken, twenty-five years ago, the taking of lodgers was looked upon as one of the most serious problems connected with immigration. When the United States Immigration Commission devoted two large volumes of its great immigration survey, prepared during the years 1908–11 at a cost of nearly a million dollars, to the subject "Immigrants in Cities," a great deal of space in all the studies of immigrant neighborhoods was devoted to the subject of lodgers.[1]

IMMIGRATION AND THE LODGER PROBLEM

But the taking of lodgers has not been primarily a problem of immigration but a problem of poverty in industrial neighborhoods. Lodgers and boarders have been a means of supplementing the husband's wage ever since the modern factory system began to call for "hands," and ever since men and women began to migrate to strange neighborhoods in search of work. The migrant worker must have a bed; and the wife of the workingman, eagerly looking for some way to make the inadequate wage of the husband and father more nearly equal to the family budget, has always welcomed the added income secured by providing beds for the homeless fellow-workers of her "man."

In the earlier discussions of this subject, however, housing re-

[1] See *U.S. Immigration Commission Reports* (1911), Vols. XXVI–XXVII. For criticism of these immigration and housing statistics see Edith Abbott, *Social Welfare and Professional Education*, chap. vi, "Social Statistics and Social Work," pp. 151–57.

formers treated the taking of lodgers as one of the besetting sins of the immigrant and not as one of the omnipresent problems of low wages and high rents in urban industrial neighborhoods. For example, one of the best known of the earlier advocates of housing reform was responsible for a typical statement of this sort[2] when he said "room over-crowding is bound up with another social problem, namely, the lodger evil. This prevails chiefly among the foreign elements of the population, more especially among the Italians and the Poles, and in some cities, the Hungarians and other Slavic races. It also prevails among the Jews in the larger cities. It is fraught with great danger to the social fabric of the country. It means the undermining of family life; often the breaking down of domestic standards. It frequently leads to the breaking up of homes and families, to the downfall and subsequent degraded career of young women, to grave immoralities—in a word, to the profanation of the home."

Many of the evil consequences of taking lodgers are accurately described in the foregoing statement; but the "lodger evil" existed among immigrants chiefly because they were our poorest workers, the lowest paid of the unskilled groups, with an inadequate wage to be supplemented, and with a group of homeless men among them whose labor was needed by the great industries but for whom no housing arrangements were provided. The immigrant lodgers were for the most part unmarried men or women employed in the adjacent industries, frequently *Landsleute*, friends from the old home in Europe from which the family had migrated.[2a]

The custom of taking lodgers became a common one in all the immigrant districts of our large cities, and the Chicago tenement districts, in so far as they suffered from this evil, were typical and not exceptional urban neighborhoods. In the days when the great tides of new immigrant workers were pouring into our industrial areas, the large number of immigrants, both men and women, especially when they first came to this country, wished to live near their work, and among people of the same nationality. The families who lived in the neighborhood were therefore constantly tempted to add to their incomes by taking in at least one more lodger.

[2] See the comment in Veiller, *Housing Reform* (1910), p. 33.

[2a] For lodgers in immigrant homes see S. P. Breckinridge, *New Homes for Old*, p. 39.

BULGARIAN NON-FAMILY GROUPS IN THE PRE-WAR PERIOD

LODGERS IN THE HOUSE-TO-HOUSE CANVASS

In the house-to-house canvasses before the war a great effort was made by our investigators to secure statistics showing the number of lodgers. But this was a subject on which the housewife was reluctant to give information, and the instructions to the investigators were always that they must "underestimate when in doubt." Not infrequently the taking of lodgers was denied in the presence of the unmade beds in which the lodgers had slept.

When the investigators had been in the district only a few days, a rumor frequently spread in the neighborhood to the effect that the inquiring visitors who were asking questions about the number of lodgers would make reports to the Health Department, and the Department would then order everyone to put all the lodgers out. The people therefore made every effort to conceal the fact that they took lodgers, or else they reported a much smaller number than the correct one. In some cases people said they did not take lodgers but their neighbors did, and when the neighbors were visited they made the same remark. All of our statistics regarding the extent of the lodger problem are believed to be underestimates, and yet the numbers are very large. In the Stock Yards district in the prewar canvass only 768 out of the 1,562 families visited said that they had no lodgers. That is, more than one-half of the families added to their incomes by filling up their rooms to the utmost capacity with the men and women who were too new to this country to realize that they could demand anything more than a place to sleep. They were sleeping on the floor both with and without mattresses and sleeping in beds with people who were total strangers.

Before the war, then, the problem of taking lodgers was identified with the immigration problem even if not caused by it. In more recent years there has been a marked tendency toward a wider use of the kitchenette apartment and toward "furnished rooms." More recently, as a result of the depression, the inability to pay rent led to a great deal of overcrowding and the taking-in of entire families as lodgers.

The importance of the "lodger evil" can best be understood by studying Table 59, which is based on the data collected during the first series of house-to-house canvasses and which shows the total number of lodgers in relation to the total number of people in each district.

This table shows that 10,578 men and women, about 15 per cent of the population in the blocks investigated, were lodgers. But in many districts the percentages were higher and, in all of them, the

TABLE 59

COMPOSITION OF HOUSEHOLDS (BY DISTRICTS) PRE-WAR CANVASS

District	Number in Household					Percentage of Lodgers* in Total Population
	Total (1)	Members of Family			Lodgers* (4)	
		Total (2)	Adults (3)	Children (3)		
All districts	71,442	60,864	38,791	22,073	10,578	14.8
Back of the Yards	8,731	6,348	3,899	2,449	2,383	27.3
Old Ghetto	1,033	813	419	394	220	21.3
Pilsen	1,239	1,183	810	373	56	4.5
St. Stanislaus	13,231	12,657	8,100†	4,557†	574	4.3
South Chicago	3,094	2,249	1,353	896	845	27.2
Dearborn and Walnut	2,673	2,009	1,620	389	664	24.9
Lower North	6,326	5,709	3,713	1,996	617	9.8
Downtown	628	559	309	250	69	11.0
Lumber Yards	3,778	3,294	2,099	1,195	484	12.8
Southwest	5,624	4,069	2,566	1,503	1,555	27.6
Hull-House	10,125	8,815	5,748	3,067	1,310	12.9
Division Street	6,562	5,796	3,499	2,297	766	11.7
Near South Side	4,378	3,720	2,203	1,517	658	15.0
Upper North	1,408	1,358	928	430	50	3.6
La Salle	1,419	1,247	984	263	172	12.1
Stock Yards, South	1,193	1,038	541	497	155	13.0

* Members of non-family groups are included with lodgers.

† Proportion of children estimated for this district on basis of reports from other districts.

numbers are believed to be seriously understated. In the Stock Yards district the lodgers constituted about one-fourth of the neighborhood population, and the accompanying data from the first canvass of this district are of special interest.

Population		Families	
Lodgers	2,383	Keeping lodgers	794
Persons in families	6,348	Not keeping lodgers	768
Total	8,731		1,562

It is clear from these figures that there was an average of three lodgers to each family. As was expected, more lodgers in proportion to the number of families were found along the section of Ashland Avenue that was then called "Whiskey Row"[3] than in the other districts. Instead of finding two or more families living above the saloon, the second floor was frequently provided with accommodations for lodgers, and in a few cases the apartments had been subdivided into very small rooms.

"BEDS FOR ALL WHO COME"

Several lodgers in a tenement family usually mean serious overcrowding in the small apartments in which the rooms are often below the legal area and under the legal height, as well as frequently dark and inadequately ventilated. Keeping lodgers means a great deal of additional work for the overburdened wife and mother, who has a constant excuse for not maintaining a satisfactory standard of cleanliness. But most serious of all the evil consequences, it also means a sacrifice of privacy, for in many cases the lodgers sleep in the same rooms with some member or members of the family. In the first canvass in the Stock Yards district there were 277 families in which the lodger shared a room, and frequently a bed, with some member of the family; in 181 cases there was one member of the family, in 60 cases two members of the family who were sleeping in the lodger's room and sometimes in the same bed; in 23 cases there were three members of the family, in 9 cases four, and in 3 cases five, sleeping in the same room, and in 1 case the lodger slept in the same room with a family of seven. These data are summarized below.

NUMBER OF CASES OF LODGERS SLEEPING IN ROOM

With 1 member of family.......	181	With 5 members of family......	3
With 2 members of family......	60	With 7 members of family......	1
With 3 members of family......	23		
With 4 members of family......	9	Total....................	277

In the pre-war days when we were first studying this problem, large numbers of men and women immigrants came to this country without their families. They crowded into the areas near the great

[3] See above, p. 133; see also below, pp. 348, 359–62.

industries—the women often wearing shawls over their heads, the men wearing equally queer European garments—and many homes opened to them. Unfortunately, many of them, both young women and young men, found places over the saloons, causing many very unfortunate situations to develop.

Sometimes men and women lodgers slept in the same room; and in other cases the men slept in a room which could only be reached by passing through a room in which the women slept. In other cases men lodgers slept in the same rooms with the young daughters of the household.[4]

Perhaps the worst feature of the mixed lodging arrangement, however, at the time of the earlier and later studies has always been the

[4] The early reports of the Immigrants' Protective League give many examples of such lodging groups. E.g., a young Polish girl is described as having come "to some man who is her brother or cousin. He lives in a three or four-room flat with a group of ten or twelve men, and because he is ignorant or careless of the danger to the girl he brings her to live with this group of men." The work of visiting immigrant girls often showed that living conditions were "dangerous both to her health and morals." About one-half of the Polish, Lithuanian, Slovak, and Russian Jewish girls who came to live with relatives found themselves "one more in a group of boarders. Sometimes all the other boarders are men, and the girl innocently does not see that because of the congestion and the consequent lack of privacy and other restraints which privacy exercises, she is quite unprotected against herself and the people with whom she lives." Some typical Polish cases were given: "A nineteen-year-old girl without relatives in Chicago is living with a man and his wife [a family of two], who have in a three-room flat four men and three women boarders. This girl pays two dollars a month for her part of a room, which is, among the Polish, the ordinary price. Each boarder selects and pays for his own food, which is usually cooked by the landlady. She is not paid for her work, but whatever is left belongs to her and this is usually all that the family need. Another 18 year old girl and a friend live with a family of four in a four room flat where there are six men and four women boarders. Occasionally a group of women rent rooms and live together. Five Polish girls, all under 20, were found living in two rooms. They all work in factories and each one does some part of their simple housekeeping.

"The Lithuanians often live in the same way. One girl was found living with a married cousin who had a four room flat in which she accommodated six men and two women boarders. The girl and the other boarders all worked at the Stock Yards. Another Lithuanian girl of 20 who cleans street cars at night boards in a four room flat which houses, in addition to the four members of the family, five men and one other woman boarder. These are not isolated cases. During the past year the League has found 173 Polish, 13 Lithuanian, and 17 Slovak girls living in families in which the only boarders were men, while 162 Polish, 20 Lithuanian, and 9 Slovak girls were found in families in which there were both men and women boarders" (Grace Abbott, *Second Annual Report of the Immigrants' Protective League*, Chicago, pp. 15–16).

common toilet-room. When there is an inside apartment toilet the entrance is very frequently from the kitchen which often serves at night as a bedroom.

LODGERS AND TENEMENT RENTS

The practice of taking lodgers is, of course, to be explained by the fact that the families are large, the earnings small, and the rents high. The lodger, however, is unfortunately in some measure the cause as well as the effect of high rents; the landlord finds it easy to excuse a high rental by pointing out that the families will surely take lodgers and earn enough to pay it.[5]

Landlords and agents are quick to see an opportunity to charge higher rents if the family can increase its ability to pay by "taking in lodgers." In South Chicago at the time of the first canvass the unique system of adding an extra fifty cents to the rent for every lodger taken was found to be a common practice among landlords.

A survey of living conditions among small wage-earners in Chicago which was made in 1925 showed that among Mexican and Negro households over 40 per cent had lodgers.[6] Among the native-born white households visited 28 per cent, and among the foreign born 17 per cent, had lodgers. It should be explained that more than half of the immigrant families visited during the 1925 investigation were Italians and the neighborhoods of this nationality have on the whole had fewer lodgers than many of the other national groups.

[5] See Mr. Veiller's very interesting comment in *Housing Reform*, p. 33: "Its economic consequences are also serious. To it may be charged, in large degree, the high rentals which prevail in many cities. Probably no more curious instance occurs of the peculiar intertwining of cause and effect. Often, the inadequate earnings of the poor immigrant make it necessary to supplement the family income by taking in boarders or lodgers. In many cases, such necessity does not exist, but the parsimonious habits of the people lead them to adopt this way of adding dollar to dollar. It is hard to tell to what extent the practice is due to necessity and to what extent avarice. The result is the same in both cases. The effect soon is to raise rents. Landlords are quick to realize that their tenants have augmented the family earnings by subletting a portion of their rooms. Thus, in a short time, the tenant is no better off than before; in fact, worse, because the practice has spread and standards of living have been readjusted. The total family income, though now greater, is still relatively where it was before, because of the increased cost of living."

[6] The figures were 42 per cent for Negroes and 43 per cent for Mexicans. See the report of a former research assistant, E. A. Hughes, *Living Conditions for Small Wage-Earners* (Chicago: Department of Public Welfare, 1925), p. 13 n.

During our first survey of housing conditions in South Chicago, in the district at the gates of the steel mills from Eighty-seventh to Eighty-ninth streets, we found as high a percentage of lodgers as we found in the earliest visit to the district back of the Yards. Very numerous in the steel-mills region were the cases of immigrant lodgers with "no place to go" who were "taken in" by some immigrant family usually of their own nationality. "They are *Landsleute*" was a common way the housewife had of describing the workingmen who lodged in her tiny home.

All the members of the strangely heterogeneous group seemed to feel the discomforts of their life when they tried to talk about it. But day by day they accepted the inconveniences of living as they had accepted those of the lonely journey and the steerage crossing from the old home to the new, as hardships that must inevitably be endured by those who wished to share the "promise of American life."

When our housing studies began twenty-five years ago, the immigrant man lodger, the immigrant girl lodger, and the co-operative non-family group were rather distinct problems of community interest. The Immigrants' Protective League shared our interest in what may be called three phases of the lodger problem and assisted in the first inquiries.

NON-FAMILY GROUPS OF IMMIGRANT WORKERS

In South Chicago, in the Stock Yards neighborhoods, and in other parts of the city near great industrial plants, there were also many non-family groups of workingmen—largely unmarried immigrants temporarily separated from their families—who apparently found the cheap American lodging-house expensive and uncomfortable and who attempted to solve their housing problem by organizing crude lodging groups of their own. These men suffer much needless discomfort, and the community loses by its failure to give its newly arrived immigrants an opportunity for decent living. Those who are familiar with those sections of the city have frequently suggested the necessity of simple and inexpensive lodging-houses near the great industrial plants.

The non-family groups of immigrant men were carefully studied at the time of the first canvass and one of these early inquiries[7] is briefly summarized here since the facts then discovered about the methods of housekeeping adopted are still true and non-family groups of men are still found in houses and flats planned for family use.

In addition to the great industrial neighborhoods of the city, Chicago had long been a center for the distribution of unskilled immigrant labor for various seasonal occupations. From Chicago men "shipped out" for construction work in the great railroad systems, for harvesting in the summer, for the cutting of timber or ice in the winter, and for road-building everywhere. Chicago has long been a winter resort for men who find work from early spring through the late fall. During the pre-war days the immigrant workingmen were many of them married, but they left their families at home when they came to this country to work and save money enough to bring over their wives and children. These men most often attached themselves to a family group as lodgers or boarders but frequently they established a non-family group of their own.

These groups were found organized either under a house-boss or

[7] This study by a former student, Milton B. Hunt, who helped in our early housing canvass, was "The Housing of Non-family Groups of Working Men in Chicago," *American Journal of Sociology*, XVI, 145–70. The purpose of the early study was described as follows: "To ascertain the methods of living among groups of immigrant men who had immigrated without their families, and to learn the types and condition of the houses in which they lived, the extent to which overcrowding was prevalent, the dimensions of their rooms, the rent, whether the men were a non-family group organized under a house boss or on a co-operative basis, or whether they were boarders or lodgers with a family group, and other facts which might give some insight into their living conditions. While the study was primarily one of housing conditions, additional facts of interest were gathered from the groups regarding their ages, social status, the length of their residence in the United States, their occupation, their wages, the length of their working hours, the method of payment prevailing in their industry, and the details of their group organization. An interpreter belonging to the nationality of the group visited was used in every case. Visits were usually made in the evening or on days when the men were most likely to be at home from their work so that as many of the men as possible might be seen in person. While the study was not extensive enough to cover all nationalities among which non-family groups were found, the groups selected were those which were most important and were also considered typical. Altogether, 99 groups, composed of 850 men, were visited, divided by nationality as follows: 24 groups of Bulgarians including 249 men; 33 groups of Croatians and Serbians including 326 men; 38 groups of Italians including 236 men; and 4 groups of Greeks with 39 men."

on a co-operative basis—the form of organization depending largely on whether that particular nationality belonged to the new or the old immigrant groups, for the non-family type of living was more often found among the more recent immigrants and is today found among the Mexicans.

By the lodger problem is usually meant the addition to a family group of men and women—more frequently men than women—who need a home of some sort in that neighborhood. There are, of course, the large numbers who live in cheap hotels, boarding-houses, and "flops"—the casuals who come and go in the "flophouses" near the Loop, particularly in the Madison Street district. No attempt will be made at this point to discuss the hotels or shelters for single men since our interest here lies largely in the housing of families and in the tenements where families live.

BULGARIAN, CROATIAN, AND SERBIAN GROUPS

Large numbers of non-family groups were found in our earlier study among (1) the Bulgarians, (2) the Serbs and Croats, (3) the Greeks, and (4) the Italians. Among the Poles practically no "non-family groups" of lodgers were found in our first study—probably because the Poles are an older immigrant group and lodgings with families have been easier to find. Many lodgers were found, and in some cases there were homes with more lodgers than members of the family, yet there was a family, usually with little children, giving a sense of a reasonably permanent dwelling-place. The lodgers, however, were always a temporary class, moving from colony to colony in response to the demand for labor or, more rarely, a move to more comfortable quarters as their own economic status changed.

At that time the Bulgarians were found grouped largely in two localities, one in the neighborhood of Adams Street where it crosses Peoria, Green, and Sangamon streets, just east of Halsted Street, and on some near-by streets parallel to Adams Street, the other at the gates of the steel mills in South Chicago. The first of these two was the center of interest to Bulgarians in Chicago. Here were the Bulgarian coffee-houses, the Macedonian bakeries, the Bulgarian grocers and butchers, the one-night lodging-houses, and the employment agencies. Here were found Bulgarian newspapers and friends from home. Here the men came in the spring from the smaller cities and towns to be shipped out by the employment agencies. Here they returned after finishing their work to wait for another job. From this center the men went back in large numbers to fight in the first Balkan War, which was a forerunner of the World War.

Another national center was in the midst of that mass of Slavic people, representing many nationalities, who had gathered in a crowded colony at the gates of the steel mills in South Chicago. Here were Bulgarians, Croatians, Serbians, Lithuanians, Poles, and men of many other nationalities. Sometimes several neighboring houses were inhabited by a single nationality, but more frequently one found representatives of different nationalities within the same group.

Household arrangements were varied and interesting. In the simple lodging-house, beds were let by the manager for a night. The men might get their meals with the owner in his restaurant and coffee-house, or they might shift for themselves. In other groups the men chose a "boss" who was responsible for the cooking, the washing, and the care of the rooms. Sometimes he did all this himself and received in return for his labor a fee in cash from each man. In case he did not wish to do all the work, he hired a cook or sent out the washing. Sometimes it was found that the boss had hired a Croatian woman to do the work for him. He usually owned the furnishings, paid the rent, and he bought the food for the men. At the end of the month there was a general reckoning, and the food expense was divided pro rata among the men. Again, it was found that a Bulgarian man and his wife had together assumed the position as boss. In that case the woman did the work and the man collected from the men their share of the expense. A monthly fee was usually paid by each man for lodging and cooking, and the food expense was divided equally among them so as to cover the cost of the woman's food as well as their own. Still another plan was that of the simple co-operative group, in which the total expense was shared equally by all the members of the group. A fourth plan seemed to be the most profitable of all to the landlord. According to this, each man was charged a weekly sum for the use of a room, where as many men as could be crowded together were lodged. The men thus herded together purchased each his own food and otherwise shifted for himself. There were 63 men found in simple co-operative groups, 167 were found living with a boss as manager, while 40 were found in the transient lodging-houses.

Croatians and Serbians are often referred to as Jugo-Slavs since the war, and even before the war they were often found in Chicago living in the same lodging-house groups. Non-family groups of men were found in the Croatian colony on the West Side near Eighteenth Street and Racine Avenue. In this neighborhood the men found the Croatian newspapers, a large Croatian church, Croatian lodge-halls, and stores of all varieties kept by the Croatians. In this section were many Serbians and Slovaks and a part of the large Bohemian colony which was already rapidly spreading to the westward when we first visited it.

Two large Serbian colonies had many non-family groups with men who had come from Dalmatia, Bosnia, or Herzegovina. The larger colony on Clybourn Avenue near Fullerton had a Serbian newspaper, Serbian restaurants, stores, saloons, and lodge-halls in the neighborhood. The small colony on Milwaukee Avenue near Wicker Park was less picturesque but obviously Serbian. Interviews were held with 33 Serbo-Croat non-family groups, including 185 Croatians and 141 Serbians, of whom 82 came from Austria and 59 from Dalmatia, in the early spring before the men had "shipped out" for the construction work that occupied them during the summer.

The size of the 99 non-family groups visited, including the few women and children living in them, varied greatly, as did the number of rooms in the apartments occupied by each group; but overcrowding was common in all but a very few of them.

In the smaller apartments of three rooms or less, there were 17 different groups with anywhere from two to six persons in the group. There were 49 groups varying from seven to thirteen persons, some of them occupying only two or three rooms, and there were 23 groups varying from thirteen to nineteen members. Some of these large groups lived in relatively small apartments—for example, a group of sixteen who occupied a four-room apartment, a group of eighteen living in a five-room apartment, a group of nineteen in a six-room apartment. The nationality of the groups visited and the numbers in each group are shown in Table 60.

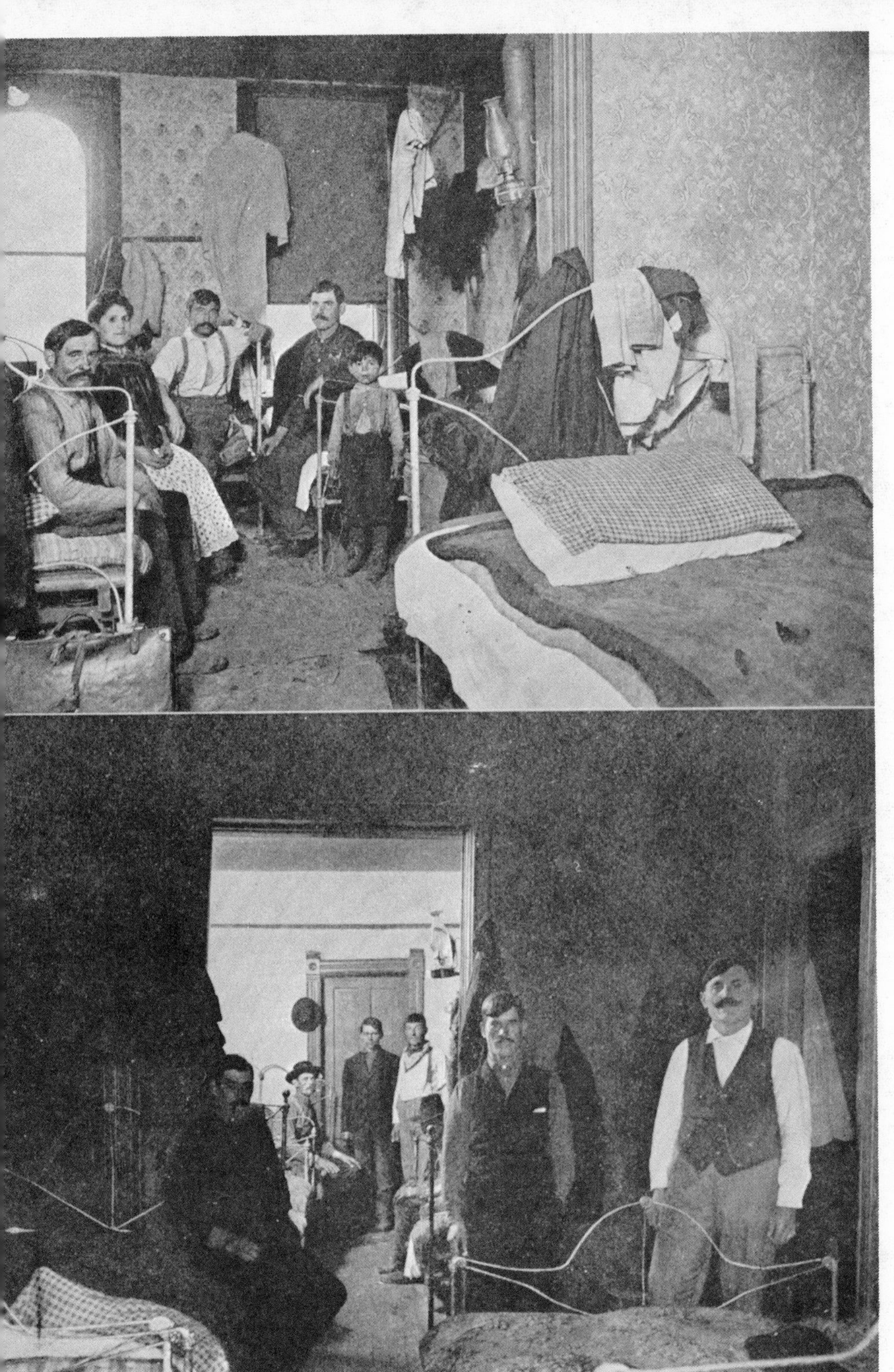

JUGO-SLAV LODGING GROUPS, PRE-WAR DAYS

Among the Bulgarian, Croatian, and Serbian groups the most common type of living arrangement was for a married couple to "own" a boarding-house. They paid the rent and owned the furniture and charged each man in the group a few dollars a month for his lodging, the preparation of his food, and his washing. The cost of food was divided proportionately each month among the men, the husband counting as one of the boarders. A cruder method of accounting was that of keeping a grocery book, in which the grocer or the butcher entered every day the cost of the food bought for each individual. This meant, in fact, a separate account with the grocer or the butcher for each boarder, and this he settled in person

TABLE 60

NATIONALITY OF NON-FAMILY GROUPS

Nationality of Groups	Number Of	
	Groups	Persons
All groups	99	939
Bulgarian	24	261
Serbian and Croatian	33	377
Italian	38	262
Greek	4	39

as often as necessary. The boarding mistress prepared and served separately the food for each man, who received exactly what he had paid for. There were, however, some groups in which the men paid a fixed sum each week. There were a few co-operative groups, some with and some without a "boss," but no one-night lodging-houses were discovered in these particular localities.

ITALIAN AND GREEK LODGING GROUPS

Some non-family groups were also found among the Italians, several of them living in basements. The groups visited were chosen from two colonies, one near Hull-House and one near Grand Avenue.

The organization of the Italian non-family group was unlike that of either the Bulgarian or the Croatian. There were lodging-houses where a small payment provided a cot and some blankets for the night, but each man provided his own food. There were the co-operative clubs, organized in two different ways: according to one plan the men paid the rent and the necessary group expenditures co-operatively, but each man bought and cooked his own food; in the other they paid collectively for all expenses, including food, and each man in turn cooked for the group, or the one who arrived home first prepared the simple meal. In cases where the men boarded in the family group they paid the usual three dollars a month for rent and cooking and washing, and they either paid collectively for the food at the end of the month, counting as their own the food consumed by the woman, or each man bought his own food and brought it to the woman to be cooked.

It has already been pointed out that during our canvassing among the Polish colonies no non-family groups were found. Table 61 shows the number of families having one or more lodgers at the time of our first canvass among the Polish groups in the Stock Yards and South Chicago districts. None of these, however, were organized as "non-family groups."

TABLE 61

LODGERS IN TWO POLISH DISTRICTS

District	Number of Families Having a Specified Number of Men as Lodgers											Number of Families without Lodgers
	1	2	3	4	5	6	7	8	9	10	Total Number with Lodgers	
Total......	148	157	76	77	24	25	10	4	1	1	523	279
Back of the Yards	122	121	60	56	20	17	9	4	1	1	411	213
South Chicago...	26	36	16	21	4	8	1	....	....	....	112	66

The taking of lodgers and boarders among these immigrants did not follow the American system. In many families the boarder paid a definite monthly rate for his room, his washing, and the preparation of his meals. He paid separately for the cost of his food. The housekeeper kept a special grocery book for each boarder, taking it to the grocer or the butcher, who kept a separate account with each man. The woman frequently cooked and served each man's food separately. This method was cumbersome and involved a great deal of work, but it insured to each man exactly the quality and quantity of food he paid for.

The non-family groups were found in houses of all kinds varying with the sections of the city in which they lived. A good many groups of Bulgarians and Italians were found in the once fashionable but deteriorated homes scattered in the old West Side near Hull-House.

Not infrequently they were to be discovered in a once fine mansion, with high front steps and hand rails, finished within with large, high rooms, great doors, large windows, and marble fireplaces, still furnished with old-fashioned walnut beds, bureaus, and tables, and often still retaining the old-fashioned "hanging lamp." Some groups of men were unexpectedly found in the "furnished rooms" district. They were found in the districts in which houses had been deserted by their former owners to make way for the industrial plants which were coming into the neighborhood—houses which suffered alike from neglect by the landlord and abuse by the tenant. Not infrequently they were found in the big brick block tenement houses, divided into monotonous apartments, insanitary in construction, and dark and dirty within.

The non-family groups among the Greeks found in the Hull-House neighborhood were all men engaged in the fruit and vegetable business. These early Greek colonies were found in the old frame houses and above the old stables in this area. Usually these groups rented the house, used the first floor of the stable for the horses and wagons used in those days, and were found living over the stable. These Greek "non-family" homes were, of course, invariably found to be in poor repair and they were always extremely insanitary because of the stables underneath, but they were uniformly clean and neat.

Some of these groups were organized on a co-operative basis, with all expenses equally divided at regular intervals; in one group, however, one of the men owned the entire building and the others rented rooms in which to sleep, and space in the stable for their horses, with the food provided and paid for on a co-operative plan.

HOUSES RENTED BY NON-FAMILY GROUPS

In general the non-family groups were found in every type of house from the modern brick apartment to the one-story frame cottage, now moved to the rear of the lot. These men were always eager to live at the lowest cost and save everything that could be saved to bring over their families or get a start toward their future business. They usually selected their apartments without regard to the type of building or its condition of cleanliness or repair, but solely because it was near their work or cheap. Groups were found in the rear frame buildings, hidden and darkened by more imposing buildings in the front, unpainted, and neglected by landlord and tenant alike. They were found in the poorly built frame buildings, now crowded, unpainted, and dingy, with outworn and inadequate sanitary arrangements—dwellings often ready for condemnation as "unfit for human habitation," some of them very old buildings hurriedly constructed long years ago after the Great Fire. Seven Italian groups were found in basements.

All these places were, however, supposed to be regulated at the time they were visited by the provision which applied alike to tenements and to lodging-houses—that every room occupied for living or sleeping purposes must contain not less than 400 cubic feet of air for every person sleeping in it. But more than two-thirds of the rooms were below the legal minimum. Table 62 shows the number of persons sleeping in rooms without the proper cubic air space.

This table shows that 658 men, or 70 per cent of the total number found, had less than the minimum requirement for air-space. As a matter of fact, this was an understatement, for these figures are based only on the number of men actually found there during the investigators' visits. In many cases there were more beds and couches in the rooms than were needed for the men who were seen at the time of the visit, and these beds were undoubtedly used from time to time, if not regularly.

More than half of the rooms were small and below the minimum size prescribed in the code, but some of the rooms were large and the lack of legal air-space was due to the fact that so many men were using a single room. Table 63 shows the number of men who enjoyed the luxury of individual rooms, only 39 out of 850 lodgers interviewed. The table also shows the number who shared their rooms used for sleeping purposes with one, two, three, four, five, or, in one case, six other men.

TABLE 62

NUMBER OF PERSONS IN NON-FAMILY GROUPS SLEEPING IN ROOMS WITH A SPECIFIED NUMBER OF CUBIC FEET OF AIR-SPACE PER PERSON

Nationality of Non-family Groups	Number of Persons Sleeping in Rooms with a Specified Number of Cubic Feet per Person							Total
	100 and below 150	150 and below 200	200 and below 250	250 and below 300	300 and below 350	350 and below 400	400 or Over	
Total	13	71	105	163	194	112	281	939*
Bulgarians	8	5	34	40	47	53	74	261
Croatians and Serbians	3	36	41	65	85	37	110	377
Italians	2	30	30	49	57	16	78	262
Greeks	....	....	....	9	5	6	19	39

* Includes 89 women and children.

TABLE 63

NUMBER OF ROOMS OCCUPIED BY NON-FAMILY GROUPS

Nationality of Non-family Group	Number of Rooms Occupied by Non-family Groups in Which Were Found							
	Total	1 Man	2 Men	3 Men	4 Men	5 Men	6 Men	7 Men
Total	283	39	107	42	49	12	33	1
Bulgarians	79	10	26	11	16	7	9	.....
Croatians and Serbians	97	4	36	11	26	3	17	.....
Italians	90	21	37	17	6	2	6	1
Greeks	17	4	8	3	1	.....	1	.....

Crowding and lack of cleanliness went hand in hand. Wherever a large group of workingmen were living alone, their rooms were inevitably dirty and ill kept. If the group boarded with a woman who "kept the house" and did the work, conditions were somewhat better, although in a large group the time required for cooking and the kitchen left a woman little time for cleaning. In general, the men worked where they could not be clean during the day, on the railroad, in the streets, or in the mills, and, coming to a cheerless home, their standard of cleanliness was lower than in a normal family group.

Their rooms were not only uncomfortably small and crowded but they were often very dark. Five were rooms with no windows, nine were rooms with no windows opening to the outer air, while in thirty-four the window-space was below the legal requirement.

Their occupations were extremely varied. The Croatians largely worked in the Harvester Works, for the Crane Company, and on the streets; the Bulgarians were a great unemployed group at that time though some were working on the railroads and on the streets—at paving, laying of pipes, work on the street railroads—and some were also doing heavy work in the factories; the Italians were nearly all at work on the railroads, the streets, or for building contractors, while some of them worked on their own account. The Greeks were largely working independently as peddlers though there were a few in railroad work. But although they did hard, heavy, and very dirty work[8] and came back to a home without a wife and children or any of the things men count most worth while in life, they were extremely friendly and seemed to welcome the call of the visitor and interpreter as a pleasant interlude in a dull evening. In some of the places there were musical instruments of some sort and occasional attempts to mitigate the dreariness of their monotonous way of living.

RECANVASSING THE OLD DISTRICTS

When the districts were recanvassed in the period from 1923 to 1927 and new districts were added to the investigation, a total of 663 non-family groups was reported in the twenty-three districts. The largest numbers of groups, shown in Table 64, were found

[8] At the time of our first inquiry there was a good deal of interest in questions relating to the employment—or unemployment—of these groups of men; the nature of the work they actually did; the number of hours worked a day and the arrangement for shifts; the rates of wages paid; and the time and medium of payment. An effort was made to secure certain information on these points but no attempt will be made now to present those early data since conditions have changed so much. See, on this point, the article by Hunt, *op. cit.*, pp. 167–68.

in the two Stock Yards districts and in the Greek and Italian neighborhood of Hull-House. In the 127 non-family groups near the Stock Yards were 21 groups of Lithuanians, 37 groups of Mexicans, 42 groups of Poles, and a few each of several other nationalities. In the Hull-House district were found 35 groups of Greeks, 39 groups of Italians, and 14 groups of Mexicans. The district next in importance was the Near South Side where the Croatian and Italian non-family groups were still to be found.

TABLE 64

NUMBER OF NON-FAMILY GROUPS FOUND IN THE DISTRICTS VISITED DURING THE RECANVASS

District	Number of Non-family Groups Found in Districts Visited during the Recanvass	District	Number of Non-family Groups Found in Districts Visited during the Recanvass
All districts	663		
West Side:		South End:	
Old Ghetto	7	Burnside	......
Pilsen	12	South Chicago (East Side)	16
Lumber Yards	40	South Deering	21
Hull-House	94	Pullman	45
Polk Street	19		
St. Stanislaus	35	North Side:	
Division Street	41	Lower North	33
Ancona	30	Upper North	14
		Olivet district	8
South Side:		Negro districts:	
Near South Side	66	Dearborn	17
Back of the Yards	81	La Salle	9
Stock Yards, South	46	Upper Federal	6
Southwest	15	Walnut (West Side)	8

The largest numbers of groups of any one nationality at this time, as shown in Table 65, were found among the Italians, and these Italian groups were found in ten of the different districts visited. The largest numbers were located in the Hull-House district, but there were 20 groups of Italians in Pullman, 17 in Polk district, 16 each in Lower North and Ancona, and 15 on the Near South Side.

Contrary to the reports at the time of the earlier investigation, the Polish groups figure largely among the non-family living arrangements during the more recent period. There were, in fact, 120 non-family groups of Polish men found in the recent canvass. Most of these were located in the Stock Yards district, in St. Stanislaus, Division Street, and Pullman.

Next in importance were the Mexican groups who had first come as a result of the war-time demand for labor; 71 of these groups were

TABLE 65

NATIONALITY OF NON-FAMILY GROUPS FOUND IN DISTRICTS VISITED DURING THE RECANVASS

Nationality of Non-family Group	Number of Non-family Groups Found in Districts Visited during the Recanvass	Nationality of Non-family Group	Number of Non-family Groups Found in Districts Visited during the Recanvass
All groups	663		
American, white	16	Magyar	11
American, Negro	42	Mexican	71
Bohemian	15	Polish	120
Chinese	10	Russian	15
Croatian	26	Scandinavian	18
German	12	Serbian	4
Greek	50	Slovak	28
Irish	4	Spanish	2
Italian	139	Ukrainian	1
Jewish	1	Other European	12
Lithuanian	55	Not reported	11

reported, chiefly in the Hull-House district, and the two Stock Yards districts.

Lithuanians, Greeks, Serbo-Croatians, and Slovaks were still found in fairly large numbers, but the non-family groups of Bulgarians had practically disappeared. A new group, again a group of recent migrants, was represented in the 42 groups of Negroes living for the most part on the South Side.

The problem of lodgers living with family groups was far less acute in the period of the second canvass than it had been before the war. In the early period we had found 10,578 lodgers, 14.8 per cent of the total population of the family households. In five districts

MIXED GROUPS OF POLISH LODGERS IN THE PRE-WAR DAYS

lodgers constituted more than 20 per cent of the family household population; these districts were Southwest, South Chicago, Back of the Yards, Dearborn, and the old Ghetto.

TABLE 66

COMPOSITION OF HOUSEHOLDS; BY DISTRICTS
(Recanvass and Post-war Original Canvass Data)

District	Number of Persons in Households					
	Total	Members of Families			Lodgers	Adults in Non-family Groups
		Total	Adults	Children		
All districts	65,143	59,938	36,062	23,876	3,167	1,934
West Side:						
Old Ghetto	237	193	131	62	17	27
Pilsen	965	920	660	260	16	29
Lumber Yards	2,503	2,340	1,431	909	74	89
Hull-House	5,371	4,907	2,989	1,918	195	269
Polk Street	1,604	1,541	759	782	12	51
St. Stanislaus	9,936	9,614	5,222	4,392	235	87
Division Street	5,914*	5,638	3,350	2,288	161	106
Ancona	1,870	1,717	780	937	72	81
South Side:						
Near South Side	3,876	3,579	2,326	1,253	97	200
Back of the Yards	6,521	5,856	3,351	2,505	382	283
Stock Yards, South	1,096	833	509	324	83	180
Southwest	4,274	3,906	2,429	1,477	323	45
South End:						
Burnside	2,122†	2,004	1,143	861	64	....
South Chicago	2,716	2,527	1,509	1,018	120	69
South Deering	1,124	893	512	381	133	98
Pullman	784	647	438	209	33	104
North Side:						
Lower North	4,211	4,034	2,394	1,640	104	73
Upper North	1,148	1,095	669	426	22	31
Olivet district	1,980	1,923	1,182	741	42	15
Negro districts:						
Dearborn	1,720	1,344	965	379	331	45
La Salle	1,911	1,588	1,270	318	291	32
Upper Federal	2,597‡	2,251	1,582	669	305	....
Walnut (West Side)	663	588	461	127	55	20

* Classification not reported for 9 persons included in total.
† Classification not reported for 54 persons included in total.
‡ Classification not reported for 41 persons included in total.

In the recanvass there were 3,167 lodgers living with families and 1,934 adults in non-family groups. Together these constitute only 8 per cent of the total population of family households. Table 66 shows the composition of households in the several districts.

In the Southwest district, where in 1914 the lodgers made up 28 per cent of the total population, a larger proportion than the children in this district, only 9 per cent of the population were lodgers in the more recent recanvass. The population of the district has declined not because the families are smaller but because there are fewer families and fewer lodgers. The nationality of the district has changed only slightly. It was predominantly Lithuanian in the period before the war and still remains predominantly Lithuanian.

In South Chicago and in the Stock Yards district a similar decrease in total population and in the number of lodgers was noted, while the proportion of children in the blocks canvassed had increased.

Without doubt the restriction of immigration since the war has reduced the number of men who are without families in Chicago and consequently has reduced the number of lodgers in the immigrant communities. In the Negro districts, on the other hand, the proportion of lodgers remains fairly high. The new problem since the depression has been the crowding of one family group with another to meet the difficulty of paying rent during a prolonged period of unemployment. However, the problems of housing and the depression will be discussed in a later chapter.

CHAPTER XII

HOME-OWNERSHIP AND THE PROBLEM OF THE TENEMENT LANDLORD

Chicago Home-Ownership Statistics, 1894; Census Statistics of Chicago Home-Ownership, 1890–1930; Immigration Commission Data, 1907–8; House-to-House Canvass; What Does "Home-Ownership" Mean?; Reasons for Tenement-House Buying; The Social Worker and the House-buying Family; The Children Help To Buy the Home; Home-Owners in the Depression.

IN MOST tenement neighborhoods in American cities, in normal times, a substantial number of families either own, or are in process of buying, the house in which they live. But in a metropolitan area like Chicago, home-ownership in the last generation has presented new problems that are very unlike those in the traditional picture of the workingman who is buying a home. The house he buys is no longer the workingman's cottage of an earlier generation, but a tenement with at least one flat that is available to rent.

"Home-ownership" has been an American tradition, and from very early days has been regarded as one of the characteristic features of American life. The familiar picture is that of the pleasant cottage home and garden of a sturdy artisan or mechanic who is on the thrifty road to independence and comfortable living. But the home-owners in the tenement districts are frequently the owners of multiple dwellings where they often live less comfortably than their own tenants. The tenement in which they are living has been purchased not so much because they want to "own a home" as because they have decided to "buy a building with an income," as a method of saving out of their meager earnings—a purchase made as an investment and not for the comforts of a "home and garden."

CHICAGO HOME-OWNERSHIP STATISTICS, 1894

The early report of the United States Bureau of Labor Statistics on the *Slums of Great Cities*,[1] which was one of the first studies of

[1] *Seventh Special Report of the United States Commissioner of Labor* (Washington, 1894).

housing conditions in Chicago, presented some interesting statistics regarding home-ownership forty years ago in the tenement district east and south of Hull-House.[2] For this district, the only one investigated at that time in Chicago, some interesting data which

TABLE 67

FAMILIES LIVING IN OWNED AND RENTED HOUSES
(Data from U.S. Bureau of Labor, 1894, for Area East of Hull-House)

Dwellings Occupied By	Families Living in Houses			Percentage Owned
	Total	Owned	Rented	
Total	3,881	397	3,484	10.2
A single family	370	77	293	20.8
Two families	626	73	553	11.7
Three families	481	68	413	14.1
Four families	620	51	569	8.2
Five families	492	48	444	9.8
Six families	638	48	590	7.5
Seven families	146	11	135	7.5
Eight families	221	13	208	5.9
Nine families	33	....	33	....
Ten families	19	1	18	*
Eleven families	29	3	26	*
Twelve families	48	....	48	....
Thirteen families	15	1	14	*
Fourteen families	27	2	25	*
Fifteen families	32	1	31	*
Eighteen families	18	....	18	....
Twenty-two families	24	....	24	....
Twenty-four families	42	....	42	....

* Percentages are not shown where basc is less than 100.

showed the number of home-owners as compared with renters, and showed also whether the home-owners lived in single-family houses or in tenements of various sizes, have been assembled in Table 67.

A generation ago, in the so-called "slum" district studied by the investigators, home-owners were already living in multiple dwellings. This early housing inquiry showed a very congested area on the east

[2] The district investigated extended from Halsted Street east to State Street, with Polk as its boundary on the north and Twelfth Street on the south, and between Taylor and Twelfth the district also extended west to Newberry Avenue. Colored maps of this district, showing nationalities and earnings, were afterward published in *Hull-House Maps and Papers* (1895).

as well as on the west side of the river stretching for nearly a mile east of Hull-House and just south of the "Loop." The river wards to the east and to the west were tenement districts even at that early date. Of the 3,881 families who were interviewed during the house-to-house canvass, 397 owned their own homes. In round numbers, 90 per cent were renters and only 10 per cent were home-owners. But the point of special interest in this early study is the fact that

TABLE 68

HOME-OWNERS IN TENEMENTS
(U.S. Bureau of Labor Data, 1894)

Home-Owners Living In	All Home-Owners in Single and Multiple Dwellings	
	Number	Per Cent Distribution
Total	397	100.0
Single-family dwellings	*77*	*19.4*
Tenements	*320*	*80.6*
For two families	73	18.4
For three families	68	17.1
For four families	51	12.8
For five families	48	12.1
For six families	48	12.1
For seven families	11	2.8
For eight families	13	3.3
For more than eight families	8	2.0

only one-fifth of the home-owners were living in one-family houses. Then, as now, the home-owners were really tenement landlords, and some of them were landlords on a relatively large scale. This may be seen more clearly in Table 68, which shows the number and percentage of owners living in single and multiple dwellings.

At that time only one out of every five home-owners lived in a single-family house. The other home-owners had invested in tenements. In eight of the dwellings canvassed, the home-owner was a tenement landlord for more than eight families; and one home-owner had purchased and was living in a building in which twelve families paid rent; two owners were landlords for thirteen families each, and one owner was landlord to fourteen families.

CENSUS STATISTICS OF CHICAGO HOME-OWNERSHIP, 1890–1930

Census statistics of home-ownership in Chicago (over a period of forty years) are interesting. In 1890 the census showed that 28.7 per cent of all the families were living in homes which they owned, whether incumbered or not. This was, as would be expected, a higher percentage of ownership in the city as a whole than in the region east of Hull-House, which the United States Bureau of Labor

TABLE 69

HOME-OWNERSHIP IN CHICAGO, 1890–1930

Census Year	Homes of Specified Tenure*	Rented	Owned	Percentage Owned
1890	219,690	156,566	63,124	28.7
1900	345,017	258,582	86,435	25.1
1910	463,919	342,472	121,447	26.2
1920	613,273	447,407	165,866	27.0
1930	833,984	572,234	261,750	31.4

* Compiled from U.S. Census, *Population*. This table includes only homes of known tenure; i.e., those homes for which there was no report as to whether the home was owned or rented are not included in this table.

selected for investigation as a "slum area." Looking at later census returns on this point which are assembled in Table 69, it is clear that home-ownership has not changed very greatly in Chicago over a period of forty years.

The census statistics showed a slight decline in the percentage of home-owning families between 1890 and 1900 (28.7 per cent to 25.1), perhaps the result of the "hard times" that followed the crisis of 1893. However, there was during the same period, as indicated in Table 70, also an increase in the percentage of incumbered homes. It seems reasonable, therefore, to say that there was little change in the proportion of home-owners in the city as a whole during the period from 1890, when the census first dealt with this subject, to 1930, when the last returns were published. The greatest change is apparently to be found in the percentage of incumbered homes. In

1900 and in 1910 this percentage was higher than in 1890, but substantially lower than in 1920, when the effect is seen of the buying of homes that accompanied the post-war housing shortage.

The special census in 1934 by the Chicago Census Commission showed a slight decrease in home-ownership. Of the 831,221 homes of specified tenure, 242,713, or 29.2 per cent, were owned.

IMMIGRATION COMMISSION DATA, 1907–8

In 1907–8 the federal Immigration Commission, a congressional investigating committee, also collected certain statistics regarding

TABLE 70

INCUMBERED HOMES IN CHICAGO, 1890–1920
(Data from U.S. Bureau of the Census)

Census Year	Total Number of Homes Owned	Total Number Reported as to Kind of Ownership	Number Reported Incumbered	Percentage Incumbered
1890	63,124	63,124	27,248	43.2
1900	86,435	82,981	43,735	52.7
1910	121,447	120,006	64,981	54.1
1920	165,866	161,101	102,719	63.8
1930	261,750	*	*	*

* No inquiry was made at the 1930 census concerning incumbrances on homes.

home-ownership in the tenement districts of Chicago in the course of its survey of *Immigrants in Cities*.[3] The number of resident home-owners was reported in each of the eleven different immigrant districts investigated in Chicago. Each district, however, consisted of only a single block, so the sample is a small one.

In these eleven widely scattered blocks, the Commission's investigators found 366 families, or 16.3 per cent of the total number, owning the homes in which they lived. The home-ownership data with the families classified as to father's birthplace are presented in Table 71.

The Commission's home-ownership data are clearly based on

[3] *Reports of the Immigration Commission*, Vols. XXVI–XXVII; see XXVI, 302: "Home-Ownership Statistics."

samples too small to allow any conclusions to be drawn regarding racial or national differences as to home-purchasing. There is, for example, no more reason, on the basis of these returns, for drawing the conclusion that the Swedes are more desirous of building homes than the South Italians, or more able to buy, than there is for holding the Germans or Irish superior to the native Americans.

TABLE 71

FAMILIES OWNING THEIR HOMES; BY GENERAL NATIVITY AND RACE OF HEAD OF FAMILY
(Data from *U.S. Immigration Commission Reports*)

General Nativity and Race of Head of Family	Number Reporting Complete Data	Owning Home	
		Number	Percentage of Total
Total: all heads of families	2,249	366	16.3
Total native-born	*131*	*22*	*16.8*
Total foreign-born	*2,118*	*344*	*16.2*
Bohemian and Moravian	232	41	17.7
German	178	82	46.1
Hebrew, Russian	214	23	10.7
Hebrew, Other	51	2	*
Irish	104	26	25.0
Italian, North	88	9	10.2
Italian, South	376	28	7.4
Lithuanian	166	19	11.4
Magyar	30	3	*
Polish	439	77	17.5
Serbian	13	....	*
Slovak	83	6	7.2
Swedish	144	28	19.4

* Percentage not computed, owing to small number involved.

It is interesting, however, to compare the total home-ownership percentage for the entire sample of eleven blocks, any one of which might well be called a "slum area," with the percentage of ownership in the slum area investigated by the United States Bureau of Labor approximately fifteen years earlier. This comparison shows 10.2 per cent in 1894 as compared with 16.3 per cent in 1907–8; that is, the later inquiry indicated an apparent increase in home-ownership. This difference, however, may well be due to the widely different choice of areas in the two samples.

1930

PERCENTAGE OF

BRYN MAWR 5600

LAWRENCE 4800

MAP VIII

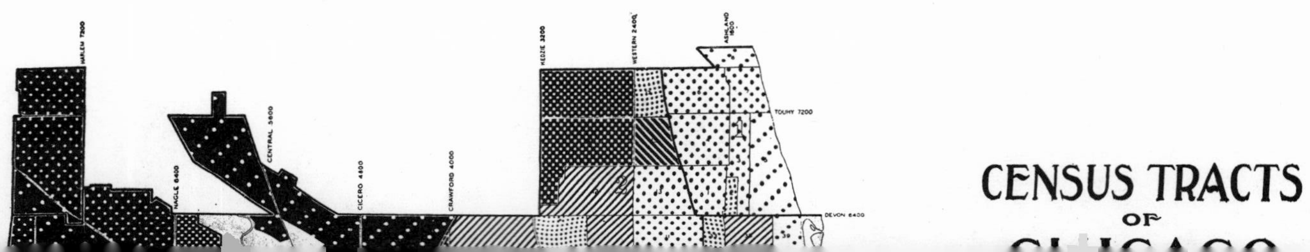
HARLEM 7200
NAGLE 6400
CENTRAL 5600
CICERO 4800
CRAWFORD 4000
KEDZIE 3200
WESTERN 2400
ASHLAND 1600
TOUHY 7200
DEVON 6400
CENSUS TRACTS
OF

The comparative distribution of owned homes among all the census tracts in Chicago in 1930 is shown in Map VIII. The tracts in which more than half the homes are owned by persons living in the building hang like a fringe on the outer edges of the city on the northwest, the southwest, and the south. In a few areas in the extreme northwest and southwest, from 80 to 90 per cent of the homes are occupied by the owners, while on the Near North Side, the Near West Side, and in the Negro area, less than 10 per cent of the homes are owned. An interesting comparison may be made between Map VIII showing percentages of owned homes and Map VII showing the distribution of rents. The areas of the very

TABLE 72

NUMBER AND PERCENTAGE OF OWNERS AMONG HEADS OF HOUSEHOLDS
(Original Canvass Data and Recanvass Data for Sixteen Districts)

Period of House-to-House Canvass	All Heads of Households	Heads of Households Who Are		Percentage of Owners
		Tenants	Owners	
Pre-war canvass, sixteen districts....	14,779	12,762	2,017	13.6
Recanvass, same districts, post-war..	12,424	10,378	2,046	16.5

highest rents are areas in which very few homes are owned, but the areas of the very lowest rents are also, in general, areas in which few homes are owned. The exceptions to this are the Morgan Park, Mount Greenwood, and Washington Heights neighborhoods where there are high percentages of home-ownership and where the few rented homes are to be had only for high rentals.

HOUSE-TO-HOUSE CANVASS

Coming now, finally, to our more recent inquiries, the housing cards used in our earlier house-to-house canvasses contained the items "Owned" and "Rented," and the schedule used both in the new canvasses and in the recanvasses also called for the same items. The data regarding the heads of households reported during these more recent canvasses as "tenants" or "owners" are presented in Table 72.

Although based on a much larger sample, our total home-ownership percentages (13.6 per cent "pre-war" and 16.5 per cent in the same areas during the decade following the war) are not greatly different from the Immigration Commission returns. Moreover, these returns may also be compared with the canvass of the Chicago Department of Public Welfare in 1925, which showed that 14 per cent of the 1,526 households studied, all in very deteriorated areas, were buying, or had bought, their homes. The percentage was reduced by the method of selection since the public welfare method was not a street or a house-to-house canvass but a study of selected families. It is important also to note that in the public welfare survey a special effort was made to secure data from Mexican families, who were, of course, the newest and poorest of the immigrant groups. Out of the 1,526 households, there were 668 Negro, 266 foreign-born Mexican, and 592 various native-born and foreign-born persons. But in no case was the Mexican head of a family the owner of his home. Among other foreign-born groups, the home ownership percentage was 23. The Negro ownership was 11 per cent compared with a 17 per cent of home-ownership among the native-white families.[4]

These later home-ownership percentages secured in the deteriorated areas which made up our housing sample may well be compared with those secured by the Bureau of Labor canvass in 1894 and the Immigration Commission of 1907–8. The total number of households canvassed in each sample and the percentage of home-ownership reported in these various inquiries which were carried on at different times in various deteriorated areas of Chicago will be found in Table 73. Data from the federal census for 1930 are also presented in this table, showing for the census tracts containing the housing districts canvassed a home-ownership percentage of 20.4. These home-ownership percentages, varying from 10.2 in 1894 to 18.0 in the decade of our post-war recanvass, are not strikingly dissimilar when the difference in the samples is taken into consideration. However, the differences in the percentage of home-ownership in the different parts of the city varied widely and were more striking than the differences in the same district at different periods. These variations in home-ownership from district to district are brought

[4] Elizabeth A. Hughes, *Living Conditions for Small Wage-Earners in Chicago* (City of Chicago Department of Public Welfare, 1925), pp. 6, 31.

together in Table 74, which shows the percentage of home-owners among the heads of households in all the districts canvassed together with the home-ownership percentage in the 1930 census enumeration tracts which included the districts canvassed. The tracts with a total population of 35,874 are, of course, very much larger areas than the districts canvassed, which had a total population of 15,115. These percentages for different districts are more important than a summary which presents only city totals.[5]

TABLE 73

NUMBER AND PERCENTAGE OF HOME-OWNERS AMONG HOUSEHOLDS CANVASSED IN SIX INVESTIGATIONS, 1894–1930

INVESTIGATIONS	Households in Chicago Canvassed	Home-Owners	Percentage of Home-Owners
U.S. Bureau of Labor, 1894	3,881	397	10.2
U.S. Immigration Commission, 1907–8	2,249	366	16.3
Chicago Department of Public Welfare, 1924	1,526	214	14.0
University of Chicago:			
Pre-war canvass	14,779	2,017	13.6
Post-war canvass and recanvass	15,115	2,720	18.0
U.S. Census, 1930:			
Census tracts including housing districts above	35,874	7,317	20.4

Both our earlier and later canvass showed a wide range in the home-ownership percentage in the different parts of the city—varying from 4.0 per cent in one of the poorest of the South Side Negro areas to 23.8 per cent in the Lithuanian district on South Halsted Street near St. George's Church. There were other districts with a high percentage of home-ownership. In the Polish-Lithuanian district back of the Yards, for example, 19.0 per cent of the families visited owned their homes; in the Polish district near the steel mills in South Chicago, 18.3 per cent were home-owners; in the small and mixed German-Hungarian district on the Upper North Side, 18.5 per cent were home-owners; and in the Slovak Lumber yard district, 17.3 per cent were home-owners.

[5] Attention should be called to the fact that the recanvass covered all the districts once included in the study, except the downtown Italian district, and seven new districts which were covered by the new canvass in the decade after the war.

The later canvass also showed striking differences between the districts studied at that time. Thus in the "Burnside triangle" 59.1

TABLE 74

PERCENTAGE OF HOME-OWNERS; BY DISTRICTS
(Pre-war Canvass Data, Recanvass and Post-war Canvass Data, Compared with U.S. Census Data, 1930)

Districts	Canvass before 1920			Canvass and Recanvass after 1923			Home Ownership in Census Tracts (1930)		
	All Heads of Households	Home-Owners	Percentage of Owners	All Heads of Households	Home-Owners	Percentage of Owners	Total	Home-Owners	Percentage Owned
All districts...	14,779	2,017	13.6	15,115	2,720	18.0	35,874	7,317	20.4
West Side:									
Old Ghetto......	200	17	8.5	54	2	3.7	141	13	9.2
Pilsen...........	295	35	11.9	281	33	11.7	2,934	519	17.7
Lumber Yards...	854	148	17.3	640	124	19.4	1,972	455	23.1
Hull-House......	1,984	208	10.5	1,255	171	13.6	1,709	241	14.1
Polk Street......	......	......	*	355	65	18.3	989	186	18.8
St. Stanislaus....	2,785	355	12.7	2,296	267	11.6	1,899	307	16.2
Division Street..	1,416	186	13.1	1,347	210	15.6	1,367	242	17.7
Ancona.........	......	......	......	439	55	12.5	2,769	455	16.4
South Side:									
Near South Side.	950	141	14.8	878	178	20.3	1,578	276	17.5
Back of the Yards	1,567	298	19.0	1,455	317	21.8	2,206	674	30.6
Stock Yards, South.........	273	29	10.6	254	47	18.5	370	65	17.6
Southwest......	1,013	241	23.8	992	272	27.4	3,039	934	30.7
South End:									
Burnside.......	......	......	*	411	243	59.1	709	432	60.9
South Chicago..	545	100	18.3	536	147	27.4	1,538	479	31.1
South Deering..	......	......	*	200	64	32.0	629	295	46.9
Pullman.......	......	......	*	222	48	21.6	965	423	43.8
North Side:									
Lower North....	1,438	116	8.1	1,036	138	13.3	2,893	317	11.0
Upper North....	372	69	18.5	306	53	17.3	1,392	262	18.8
Olivet district..	......	......	*	509	102	20.0	1,764	233	13.2
Negro districts:									
Dearborn.......	428	17	4.0	413	24	5.8	750	32	4.3
La Salle........	416	36	8.7	511	48	9.4	1,677	126	7.5
Upper Federal..	......	......	*	555	97	17.5	1,922	277	14.4
Walnut.........	243	21	8.6	170	15	8.8	662	74	11.2

* This district included only in the later canvass.

per cent of all the householders were home-owners (60.9 per cent in the census returns for 1930), while the poor Negro district on the South Side which had been covered in the earlier canvass again showed a home-ownership percentage of only 5.8 per cent and the census returns for the whole tract showed only a home-ownership percentage of 4.3. The old Jewish district on the West Side had been so largely depopulated in the period of twenty years between the first and second canvass that it is hardly fair to consider the returns of that area as sufficiently representative to justify quoting them.

It is very interesting to find that the great industrial neighborhoods showed high ownership percentages and substantial increases for the most part over the earlier canvass. South Chicago near the steel mills, for example, showed 27.4 per cent of the householders were home-owners—an increase from 18.3 per cent in the earlier canvass. South Deering showed 32 per cent and Pullman had 21.6 per cent—percentages which became 46.9 and 43.8 in the census-tract enumeration of 1930. And the two Stock Yards districts had increased from 19.0 and 10.6 per cent to 21.8 and 18.5, respectively, and these became 30.6 and 17.6 in the tract enumerations of 1930. But the increases were general in all parts of the city except those which were in a state approaching disintegration like the old Ghetto. While the Negro home-ownership percentages remained low in the old neighborhoods, in the Upper Federal Street district, which was very poor but nearer the new areas of Negro property, 17.5 per cent of the householders were home-owners at the time of our recanvass, but the federal-census enumeration of the tract including this area showed a slighter lower percentage—14.4. In general, the highest percentages of home-ownership were in the newer districts where more favorable opportunities for the purchase of property have been offered to workingmen.

The percentages based on the 1930 census also varied sharply from one district to another, with a home-ownership percentage of 60.9 in Burnside and coming down to 4.3 per cent in one of the poorest Negro areas. Percentages in the United States census are somewhat different from those of our housing canvass, for the census data come from very much larger areas and also represent a later point of time.

In the districts listed below the percentage of home-owning householders was above the average for all districts. The first six might be said to be newer industrial districts of the South End and the Stock Yards region. But four of these areas—Olivet, the Near South Side, the Slovak district near the Lumber Yards, and Polk Street—are all the areas of long-standing deterioration.

DISTRICTS WITH HOME-OWNERSHIP ABOVE THE AVERAGE, POST-WAR CANVASS

District	Percentage of Homes Owned	District	Percentage of Homes Owned
Burnside	59.1	Near South Side	20.3
South Deering	32.0	Olivet	20.0
Southwest	27.4	Lumber Yards	19.4
South Chicago	27.4	Stock Yards, South	18.5
Back of the Yards	21.8	Polk Street	18.3
Pullman	21.6		

Taking together the twenty-three districts studied most recently, 2,720 of the 15,115 householders, or 18 per cent, were at least nominal owners of the houses in which they were living. But the average alone is not so important here as is the wide range of home-ownership percentages, which, as we have already said, varied from district to district. In the twelve districts listed below, the percentage of

DISTRICTS WITH HOME-OWNERSHIP BELOW THE AVERAGE, POST-WAR CANVASS

District	Percentage of Homes Owned	District	Percentage of Homes Owned
Upper Federal Street	17.5	Pilsen	11.7
Upper North	17.3	St. Stanislaus	11.6
Division Street	15.6	La Salle Street	9.4
Hull-House	13.6	Walnut	8.8
Lower North	13.3	Dearborn Street	5.8
Ancona	12.5	Old Ghetto	3.7

owners fell below the average. It will be noted that four of these below-average percentages belong to the Negro districts and several of the others, notably Hull-House and Lower North, are areas that have long been on the fringe of the business area so that land values are high and houses so dilapidated that a prospective buyer is likely to find something more attractive.

Changes in home-ownership percentages between our earlier and later canvasses are interesting. Going back to Table 74 and comparing column 3 with column 6, some of the changes are quite striking. In South Chicago, for example, at the time the first study was made, there were 100 resident owners and 445 tenants in the seven blocks; that is, 18.3 per cent of the residents were owners. Fifteen years later, the recanvass showed such an increase of home-ownership that 27.4 per cent of the 536 resident households were then owning the houses in which they were living. As in other tenement districts of Chicago, some of these owners had purchased the old single-family cottages still to be found in such a neighborhood, but the majority were trying to pay for tenements a part of which could be rented, thus providing a helpful means of completing payments on the house.

Exceptional conditions as regards home-ownership existed in some of the neighborhoods. The condition in Burnside, for example, has already been discussed in the chapter in which the district itself is described.[6] In Pullman conditions are also exceptional,[7] and at the time of our recanvass, just before the depression, home-ownership varied greatly according to the block that happened to be chosen for investigation. One of the incidents in the history of Pullman was that the Pullman Company offered to sell houses to the occupants at a selling price equal to one hundred times the rent per month, and the company made liberal terms as to payments. In the three blocks in which our house-to-house canvass was made, it did not appear that more than half of the occupants had taken advantage of this offer. The number of home-owners in these three blocks was approximately 22 per cent of the total number of householders. However, two of the blocks were very unusual; there were only six houses, including 143 households, so that it would have been impossible to find a high percentage of ownership in these blocks unless the tenements were owned co-operatively. As it was, two of the three buildings in each block were really owned by persons living in them. One of these houses had recently been purchased by an American who was making plans for installing electricity and for re-

[6] See chap. iii, "The Tenement Areas," pp. 151–55.

[7] See Graham R. Taylor, *Satellite Cities*, pp. 28–67.

painting and in other ways modernizing his purchase. Another was owned by a Greek who took very great pride in his property.

The extent to which homes were owned in Pullman was ascertained more accurately from the returns from the third block, which was a block of row houses. Here forty-four out of seventy-nine houses were owned by the occupants; so that the number of home owners here was more than half of the total number of householders. In this block none of the separate dwellings had been divided and sublet as were some of those visited in the more northern districts. While ownership of the home seemed to be very desirable for many families in Pullman, it apparently was not invariably so. Some of the men who had not worked regularly since the steel cars had replaced the old woodwork processes were reluctant to seek new employment either in the districts to the north or downtown or farther out in the industrial section of the south end, because of the inconvenience and time-loss involved in living so far from work. But either they could not dispose of their homes in Pullman or they were unwilling to give them up. So they continued to live there and to accept part-time work, although, according to their wives, they found their employment unsatisfactory and their earnings precarious.

In South Deering 26.6 per cent of the houses were owned by resident landlords who had lived on the premises for less than two years. Nearly half the owners had been living in their houses less than four years. Nearly 19 per cent had lived in houses which they had owned for over ten years. One American owner had lived in the same house for forty years. A Croatian who had been living here for twenty years had finally become the owner not only of his own dwelling but also of the house next door, which, of course, he rents.

In the Negro districts conditions are also exceptional both because of the poverty of the people and because of the pressure for housing accommodations before the depression, owing to the migration from the South and the old policy of segregation. The Negroes, in fact, were for a time almost driven to buy homes on account of the substantial increases in rent, which at times were as much as 50 per cent. The Chicago Commission on Race Relations thought that high rents were the primary factor in the widespread buying of houses by Negroes during the years 1915–17,[8] although the high wages of the war period and the fact that many of the Negroes in the South had been accustomed to home-ownership also contributed to the desire to own their new homes in Chicago. The Negro home-owners who were interviewed in the special home-ownership study gave high rents as the first or second reason for buying, and all were buying by the contract or monthly payment plan.

The Commission on Race Relations thought that the tendency among the Negroes to buy according to this method had been economically unwise; with a maximum of the income going into monthly payments and with nothing allowed for repairs and up-keep, the home-owning families were often dependent in case of family emergency. It is also suggested that the Negro is handi-capped in the effort to buy a home by the low security rates given by the loan concerns to property tenanted by Negroes, by the fact that the Negro is required to pay higher prices for property, and by the combinations of property-owners in various districts to prevent the entrance of Negroes into their neighborhoods.

WHAT DOES "HOME-OWNERSHIP" MEAN?

The 1920 census returns showed that two-thirds of the purchased homes were not paid for, but were held with incumbrances of one kind or another. Even the 18 per cent of ownership which our last canvass showed for the twenty-three districts included in the survey (Table 74) is likely to give a false impression of prosperity, for many of these places which the people claim to own are heavily mort-gaged, and after a long struggle the house and all that has been paid slip away.

Attention has been called to the fact that the old idea of the prosperous workman owning "a home of his own"—usually pictured as a small cottage with a cheerful garden—is a false picture of home-ownership in tenement neighborhoods. These modern tenement homes are too often found along dingy, untidy streets, and almost invariably are entirely destitute of gardens, trees, shrubs, or flowers. The owners are only landlords renting out the apartments in the tenement building in which they have invested with the hope that

[8] *The Negro in Chicago* (University of Chicago Press, 1922), pp. 216–18.

the apartments can be rented for enough to pay the interest on the mortgage and something toward its redemption.

This urbanized form of home-ownership is far from being a sign of prosperity which indicates comfort. It has been pointed out already that the home-owning family not infrequently lives in the smallest and poorest apartment in the building, since this is the apartment that will be rented with difficulty, while the more desirable apartments are used to bring in the largest possible income and help to pay off what is due on the mortgage.

One "home" found at the time of our first canvass in the Stock Yards district can never be forgotten. A house on Paulina Street containing four apartments and an attic room was owned by a Lithuanian Stock-Yards laborer with five children. The four apartments were all rented, however, and the family was living in a very miserable attic room, which was shared by a very lively rooster. Similar cases were also found in the Lithuanian district near the Yards. There was, for example, a landlord who lived in three cellar rooms so low that no one more than 5 feet 8 inches tall could stand upright in any one of them. The kitchen, a fair-sized room with windows on the street, where sunlight crept in with difficulty, was merely gloomy; but the other two rooms were both small and dark with tiny lot-line windows only 4 feet square in area. In one of these rooms, 564 cubic feet in contents, the father and one child slept; the other, which contained only 443 cubic feet, was the bedroom of the mother and two children. A highly colored picture was an indistinguishable blur in the badly lighted room although it hung by the window. Another Stock Yards' employee occupied a very dilapidated frame cottage, its dirty bedrooms filled with lodgers, on the rear of the lot back of a good modern brick tenement which he had just erected and was trying to pay for. Only too often, then, ownership is not synonymous with prosperity, but means rather the effort to secure property and future welfare at the cost of present health, comfort, and decent living.

Data gathered in the recanvass confirmed our earlier reports on this point. One schedule after another showed that it was not uncommon to find the owner occupying the least desirable apartment in his tenement. These schedules showed an owner living in the rear house on a filthy alley, while he rented all the flats in the better tenement on the front of the lot. One owner occupied a third-floor rear apartment, while he rented all the more comfortable flats. Another occupied a third-floor middle apartment next to the attic used for drying clothes. More than one was found in rooms in the basement.

Both our first canvass and our recanvass showed that large numbers of families who were living in the deteriorated areas of the city and apparently in the very low income groups had bought tenement houses by making small down-payments; and, during the long period of completing the payments, they continued to live under conditions of hardship and discomfort. The purchase of a small cottage is easier to manage, but the purchase of a tenement house represents a relatively large investment and may absorb for years the joint savings of the family.

In one area on the Northwest Side in a Polish neighborhood, a particular type of home-owner is the "garage dweller." There was a time when this area was still largely made up of open spaces, and lots could be bought "for a song." The owners built homes when they could and in time the property became more valuable. Some of the prospective home-owners, however, who could buy only a lot and could not afford to build a house, solved the difficulty by putting up a portable garage on the rear of the lot, expecting to build a "real house" on the front of the lot at some future date. Sanitary conditions in these garage homes are very bad, and the heating of these garages in the winter is a real problem. Social workers reported that there had been almost continual illness in these garage-dwelling families. The children were always getting colds or "running ears," and occasionally pneumonia or more serious illness.

REASONS FOR TENEMENT-HOUSE BUYING[9]

What are the motives that lead some of the poorest men and women to invest in homes that can be paid for only with the greatest sacrifices and to put their hard-earned savings in worn-out property

[9] A special schedule study regarding the reasons for making such investments was made by a former social service student, Frances Bruton (now Mrs. Greene), and the results were first incorporated in her unpublished Master of Arts thesis on "Tenement

that they cannot hope to modernize, or even to repair, because of the heavy expenditures involved? One thinks first, perhaps, of what is often called the old "land hunger" and the belief in the superior social status of the man of property which brought many European peasants to the new world.[10]

Immigrant workingmen have frequently had some small property interest in Europe which they have cherished as a mark of distinction, and as soon as possible after their migration to America they are anxious to find a way to "become owners" again. One manager of a Lithuanian building and loan society said that his people had "all" been property-owners in Europe and expected as a matter of course to buy property in Chicago.

That is, home-ownership often places a man or a family in a superior social group—and such groups are found even among the poor. The social distinction is greater when a man becomes a tenement landlord and "boss" of the house as well as a home-owner. This is illustrated by the experiences of some of the settlements where it has sometimes been found that tenement-ownership in the

---

Ownership by Immigrant Workingmen in Chicago," now in the University of Chicago Library. The records of the United Charities and the Legal Aid Bureau were consulted, and tenement-owners interviewed whose names and addresses were found in their files. Securing further information by additional visits to families who had been found in our housing canvass was laborious and time-consuming. Several visits were frequently required to secure a single schedule. The man of the family was usually away at work, and the wife often had no idea of the arrangements for buying the house. When the man was seen, he was often hazy about the facts, and the papers were not in his immediate possession but at the bank. The reasons lying back of the purchase were not always clearly defined or easy to express. Most of those interviewed thought that they had bought the house because they "wanted a home," and they bought a tenement instead of a cottage because it was a better investment for one thing and because only multiple dwellings were to be found in the district where a home was wanted—usually in the immigrant colony where the people had been living.

The investigator also interviewed various types of real estate agents and the officers of various foreign building and loan associations experienced in the purchase of property by immigrant workingmen.

[10] Miss Addams discussed this point with her usual sympathy and breadth of view in several of her books. See, e.g., *Twenty Years at Hull-House*, in which she said, "The early immigrants [Bohemian] had been so stirred by the opportunity to own real estate, an appeal perhaps to the Slavic land hunger, and their energies had become so completely absorbed in money-making that all other interests had apparently dropped away" (p. 234).

neighborhood creates certain difficult relationships in the women's clubs and classes where a landlady and her tenant occasionally meet. One settlement resident, for example, told of the difficulties that arose in a cooking class because one member was the owner of the tenement in which some of the other members lived; the tenants felt their inferiority to the point of being so uncomfortable that they did not want to continue to come to the class. Social workers often say that the home-owners are a superior, thrifty, and resourceful group; and this may serve as an explanation of the social gulf that occasionally seems to exist in tenement districts between home-owners and renters or between tenement landlords and tenants.

A social worker told of one of her clients in the South Chicago district whose husband had died, leaving her with three children and about nine hundred dollars insurance. The widow had immediately invested the insurance in the poorly built frame house in which they had been renting an apartment. This was a rash investment, for she had absolutely no plan for completing the payments, and the rents would not even provide properly for the barest necessities for the children. But the widow so enjoyed her title of "boss" that she was very reluctant to part with her property even when necessary in order to receive a mother's pension.

With the old desire to own "a rood of land" has gone the traditional hope, stronger in America than in any other country in the world, of "owning a home." In the old days the immigrant thought that he was taking a step toward becoming an American when he made the initial payment on a house, and this was undoubtedly one of the motives that led him to buy. In the interviews with poor owners, several men told the investigator that owning a home made them "real Americans." One foreign householder said he "wanted a home" because it gave him a feeling of good citizenship. One immigrant Italian home-owner said he felt that he "belonged" to the United States more because he owned a house. This point was emphasized by representatives of some building and loan associations. For example, the manager of a Slavic organization said that his association existed to encourage the people of his nationality to own their homes and thereby "become better citizens."

Many people, when asked why they had bought a house even

when the purchase entailed grave hardships, thought it a foolish question. Some spoke of discomforts endured and others of exigent needs that could not be met, but all agreed with an Italian who had been paying on his house over a period of twelve years, and who said he had been "worried nearly crazy" most of the time, but nevertheless he would "do it again."

Wanting to own a home, the immigrant often found that the tenement offered a hope of payment. As the wife of a prosperous Hungarian who owned a good property said, "We want a home, and we wanted it to pay for itself." Owning a tenement home with a definite monthly income offers a very inviting prospect to a workingman who wants to own something in the way of property.

Perhaps a more important factor making for home-ownership is the difficulty a large family often has in finding a flat to rent. In the lowest-income groups, as among those in the higher-income levels, it is not easy for families with several children to find a decent home. Always, in every tenement neighborhood, there were some families with "so many kids" that a search for a house with a landlord who would rent to such undesirable tenants had been too nerve-racking to bear frequent repetition. As landlords put improvements in their buildings—such as electric lights, fresh wallpaper, or painting the woodwork—they are loath to rent to families having a number of young children. Both the real estate dealers and social workers regarded this as an important reason for tenement-purchasing by the poor.

A United Charities visitor told of an Italian widow who had twelve children and was forced to move because the house in which she lived had been sold. She could not find another flat of any kind—either desirable or undesirable—on account of the size of her family. In desperation she borrowed small sums from a number of her friends—ten dollars here, twenty-five dollars there, one-hundred dollars from another, and so on—and paid a deposit large enough to buy a house on contract.

Another widow was found sitting on the front step with the youngest of her thirteen children, weeping because she had been ordered to move the following week and she thought no "boss" would rent to her because of her "thirteen kids." An immigrant

Italian workingman with six children who had been making payments on his house over a period of seven years, and who had just bought his first entirely new suit of clothes since undertaking the purchase of the home, said he bought the home because he had a "big, big family," and he did not want any landlord to "boss the children when they're loud."

The purchase of homes among the poor as among the well-to-do was stimulated by the rent increases and the scarcity of apartments following the World War. Families were almost obliged to buy their homes as the only way to avoid the discomforts of moving because of higher rents and to escape the discouraging search for another home at a time when apartments were scarce. Sometimes the tenant was compelled to move because another house-hunter had bought the roof over his head by means of a small down-payment and had then given the tenant orders to move. "We just couldn't get caught that way again" was the explanation of an apparently unwise investment in a home that had been made after such an expulsion by a new owner.

The desire of an owner to have other flats in his building occupied by friends and relatives was sometimes another factor of some importance. That is, after a house has been sold, the new owner had not only wanted to move in at once, but frequently he wanted his brother to live on the second floor and perhaps his wife's cousin on the third; or he wanted the apartments for friends of his own nationality who could speak the same language and would live in a neighborly way. For this reason the sale of a tenement has often meant requesting all the old tenants to leave, some of whom, in turn, immediately set out to try to become owners themselves, even at too heavy risks. The necessity of frequent moving, whatever its cause, is undoubtedly one reason for buying homes. Many of the tenement-owners who were interviewed not only said that they had bought because they wished to own a home but added that they also wanted "to settle down." One Italian, for example, said, "In the old country families stay in one place."

In immigrant neighborhoods, particularly where there had been devastating bank failures or exploitation of immigrant savings, the purchase of any kind of house, an income-producing tenement or cottage, or even an empty lot in an undesirable neighborhood, is looked upon as a "safe" investment because there is, at least, an outward and visible evidence of the investment of the family reserve. In more than one family visited the tenement in process of being purchased was spoken of as a "safe" reserve for invalidity or old age. Frequently the purchaser knew little of the expense of upkeep and was ignorant of the important claims the house itself might have upon the tenement income which looked so large.

THE SOCIAL WORKER AND THE HOUSE-BUYING FAMILY

Cases not infrequently come to the attention of the United Charities in which families have been misled by the hopes of a regular monthly income and have made very unfortunate investments of their meager savings. A man who has successfully paid for one house which he bought in order "to have a home" sometimes regards the purchase of a second house as a good investment, and a number of the owners interviewed were found to have more than one house.

For the local storekeeper the investment often provides both a place for his business and a home for his family; but, as in many other cases of ownership, the investment in the business may mean a sacrifice of comfort in the home. The family too frequently live in the rather gloomy and crowded rear rooms behind the store, in order that all the more desirable apartments above may be rented. To save the expense of a clerk, the wife and mother frequently "helps" in the store and neglects her home and her children.

Home-ownership is so generally considered a sign of stability and thrift that it is sometimes difficult to condemn or even to question a home-ownership plan. Whether this purchase endangers the standard of living of the family group is, of course, the important question. Does "home-ownership" mean, for example, really living in poorer quarters, sending the mother out to work, or depriving the children of necessary opportunities for recreation and education, and making almost the last sacrifice to keep up the payments on the property? Social workers report that in the home-buying family "everything is at stake, for they have already sacrificed so much." Such families too often "live in the dark and sometimes damp basement flats or other undesirable apartments or rooms which they cannot rent;

their health is undermined by overwork, and the children are only too frequently underfed, and too poorly dressed, and taken out of school to go to work at the earliest legal working age." Although most of the home-owning families interviewed said they had made heavy sacrifices to become property-owners and landlords, many of them seemed unable to say what had been sacrificed. They only knew that they had "given up everything."

One of the social workers thinks that, in the Polish district which she knows, the women go out to work frequently as night scrub-women in order to help pay for the family investment in a tenement home. These women have an especially difficult task since they have their own housework to do during the day, to be followed by heavy, fatiguing work at night. After the depression began, many of these women went on working, but more recently they have been supporting the family rather than paying on a home. Many of them, she reports, have "deprived themselves of everything to own a home."

Representatives of immigrant groups and of building and loan associations would not, however, acknowledge that the children were put to work to pay for the home. Persons interviewed in different foreign colonies protested that the people of their own nationality were making every effort to keep their children in school, no matter what other consequences might be entailed by home-purchasing. One Lithuanian was emphatic in saying that his people were buying homes and sending their children to school at the same time, but he admitted that unusual efforts were sometimes necessary to promote this desirable end. For example, a widow was continuing the payments on the house and keeping a boy in high school and a girl in parochial school—by working during the day and "cooking moonshine by night"!

Nor did representatives of immigrant groups agree that the home-buying family lives in uncomfortable quarters. The president of one Polish organization even went so far as to say, "There is no housing problem among the Poles." And "building and loan" representatives thought that home-buying was likely to improve the landlord's own home conditions, for when a family was ready to put money into a home they wanted something better than the one they had been renting. Moreover, one settlement resident in a Polish neighborhood thought that too heavy family sacrifices were undoubtedly required in the early stages of the undertaking, but when they had "paid out," the family moved to the best flat in the house.

But many cases were found of home-owners living in basements that were certainly very undesirable. An elderly Italian and his wife, for example, were found living in the front basement of their house, which had two stories and a basement. The yard was six steps below the sidewalk and the front yard entirely covered by the porch of the first-floor flat. The front door of the Italian owner's apartment was under this porch. The old people had bought the house in 1912, making the first payment from savings, because they were getting too old for work and thought they could live on the income. The income at the time of the investigator's visit was thirty dollars a month from the first-floor flat; a son was living on the second floor and paying no rent. No payments had been made since the first one, but interest and taxes had been kept up. The owner, then bed-ridden with rheumatism and practically unable to work after buying the house, lived in the front basement flat, which was too dark to rent, while the rear basement flat, also dark, remained vacant. The wife said they knew that they would never be able to pay for the house when they bought it, but they thought they could keep up interest and taxes and have a home for their old age.

An officer of a building society reported another family living in a basement who dreamed they were owners of the large tenement in which they were living. The man had at one time bought stock in this co-operative venture and had paid a considerable sum. The building society's report was that this man would forfeit what he had paid because he had been foolish to think he could purchase an apartment worth $67,000! In addition to his very real sacrifice of money, he was living in the damp, poorly lighted basement of the building he had expected to own and was wondering what to do next.

A good many owners visited at some time during the housing canvass were found living in basement flats. During the last canvass in South Chicago several home-owners were found in third-floor rear apartments. One family was found living in the rear house on the premises which were being purchased; another owner was living in a third-floor middle apartment next to an attic used for drying clothes; the apartment of another home-buyer was in two undesirable sections, part of it being in the basement and the other portion on the second floor.

A family known to the Englewood District of the United Charities was living in the basement of the house they were buying in an apartment so dark and damp that the Board of Health had ordered them to move. The family came to the attention of the United Charities because the children were reported as not having enough to eat. But the family were paying $130 a month on their house. Another family in the Mary Crane District of the United Charities had been reported because the children were undernourished, but a visit showed that the father was buying his home. Hull-House was sending milk, because the children were so obviously in need, and at the same time trying to persuade the father that it was as necessary to feed his family properly as to provide them with a home of their own. In fact, social workers reported that in normal times when a case is referred to a social agency because children are underfed or underclothed, it is not unusual to find that the family is making regular monthly payments on a house.

Undernourishment and poor clothing are penalties paid by the father and mother as well as the children, who all suffer in health as a result of their privations, poor housing conditions, and the overwork and strain which come from their home-buying sacrifices. One district superintendent of the United Charities thought that the ownership of a house and tuberculosis "almost went hand in hand," so great were the household sacrifices required by home-buying.

The effort to buy homes may also send the mother out to work.[11] The records of the Vocational Guidance Bureau showed eighteen cases of working mothers from home-owning families. Occasionally the family buying a home asks for help from a relief society to help them over emergencies while they are paying on property. For in

[11] In discussing the wage-earning mother, Miss Breckinridge says, in *New Homes for Old*, p. 39: "Among the more recently arrived Bohemians, for example, it was said that mothers of small children were going to work as never before, because taking lodgers was not possible as single men have not been coming in such large numbers since the war. The old settlers felt that they must take advantage of the relatively high wages offered women to make payments on property."

order to complete the purchase, the family lives up to the margin of its income, and family emergencies such as illness, accident, death, divorce, and desertion either send the family to relief agencies or require other family sacrifices to keep them out of the dependent group. One very unusual case was that of an Italian woman who applied to the United Charities for relief, and gave the name of the woman who was her landlord and who bore out the story of the other's need. After receiving assistance for approximately a year, the woman dropped out of sight. Some years later she again came to the attention of the district, as a landlord who was evicting another of the agency's clients. She acknowledged that she had been buying the house during the time that she received relief and that the person who posed as the landlord was the one from whom she was buying on contract!

Does the resident landlord, who is usually as poor as his tenants, take better care of them than the well-to-do nonresident landlord, or the representatives of large estates or real estate companies that may be tenement-owners? This is another question for which adequate evidence is lacking. The resident owner is clearly in a very different position financially from the nonresident landlord, who is at least wealthy enough to live in a more desirable neighborhood. Certainly, the resident-tenement landlord, poor himself, is often slow about repairs, unable to improve the property, exacting about rents, and eager to increase rents. However, many varieties of resident landlords as of nonresident landlords were found, and while the local landlord frequently had less money to put out for repairs, he had a greater interest in his property and a stake in the neighborhood that made him eager to improve conditions. Frequently the resident landlord did a great deal of the work on the house himself, so that improvements were made at small cost.

As to rents, the old saying, "Only the poor are good to the poor, and those who have little, give to those who have less," was generally true. A careful study of rents charged by owners living in their buildings did not show that their rents were exorbitant as compared with the rents in other houses of the same type in the same neighborhood. On the other hand, many cases were found which indicated that frequently the resident landlord had a close personal relationship with the tenant and was more lenient in collecting rents and in increasing rents. The Hungarian housewife already spoken of said that the rent for a second-floor five-room apartment in her excellent house with electric light and hot-water heat was only twenty dollars. "Twenty dollars," she said in somewhat broken English, "is not much rent, but we don't want to soak 'em for more. They're a nice people and have been here a long time." The tenants are frequently relatives and friends, and in these cases such leniency is even greater.

THE CHILDREN HELP TO BUY THE HOME

The question whether a house is paid for at the cost of the education of the children is, of course, an important one. Although the families almost uniformly denied that they sacrificed the children's schooling to pay for the home, the records of the Vocational Guidance Bureau of the Chicago public schools threw light on this point.

The records of the Bureau showed that 516 children had come in for working certificates some time during the period of three months which was selected for study before the depression, and in the homes of more than one-third (196, or 38 per cent) of these children who were leaving school to go to work, the families were buying, or had bought, their homes; and nearly two-thirds (125) of these were either still paying a specified sum monthly or were carrying mortgages. The reason for taking the child out of school was shown on 174 records, and more than half of these (99) gave "economic reasons" to explain the request for working papers. Certain other reasons which were given are closely related. These include illness of the father or mother (5); "the child is fourteen and old enough to work" (3); "the child prefers to work" (4); "the child wants to learn a trade" (1); the family "did not think of high school" (1). Six children wanted jobs for after-school hours and holidays only.

On the records the explanatory term "economic reasons" is usually entered when a child is taken out of school to help pay for a house. For example, the records of the Bureau show the total family income, whether or not the home is owned, and, more important still, whether it is paid for or whether payments are still falling due with fatal regularity. The records also show the rentals secured from the house, the number of children at work in the family and their wages, whether or not the mother works, the nationality and occupation of the father, his wages, and, finally, the reason why the child is leaving school. Thus the records show that Augusta, a Slavic girl of fifteen who had finished the ninth grade, was taken out of school by her parents for "economic reasons." There were three younger children in the family. Her father, who was a molder in a foundry earning $38 a week, was buying a large tenement on which he was expected to pay $400 a month. The house brought in rentals of $1,000 a month. The family did not live in their own building where rents were high, but in another where their rent was $40 a month.

When it is remembered that payment on a house may cover a period of from six to twelve years or more, it becomes possible for a house to take its toll from the education of more than one child. Of the 196 home-owners who brought their children to get working papers at the earliest legal age for employment, more than half of them (56 per cent) had other children already working and contributing all or a part of their wages to the family income. Again, of those who gave "economic reasons" for taking the child out of school, more than half had other children working and contributing to the family income. The figures, like all the others from this source, may furnish an understatement, as the absence of an entry on the record may, of course, not mean the absence of that condition in the family, but that the interviewer at the Bureau was hurried and had time to ask only those questions essential to getting the children through the regular certification procedure. In any event, it is a matter of record that more than half of the home-owners whose children went to work instead of completing the elementary school or going on to high school gave the needs of the home as the reason for not permitting the child to complete his public-school education.

An interesting case in point was that of a little girl whose family wanted her to go to work to help pay for the house. The visiting teacher reported that several other children in the family were already working; and that an older brother who had also been taken out of school during the visiting teacher's experience to help pay for the house had already come to grief. He had secured a job as a bank messenger and a little later had been brought into the Juvenile

Court because another boy had persuaded him to forge a check on the bank. Following this trouble, he ran away and joined the navy; the visiting teacher hoped that the little girl might be better safeguarded and not go out to work too soon.

These figures from the Vocational Bureau are based on owners of houses—the kind of house is not specified except in 94 cases, where the entry of one or more rentals shows the house to be a tenement. Of the 94 families who receive rentals, 47 (50 per cent) had the wife or older children as well as the husband working.

Two of these 196 families thought that the break in their children's education would be only temporary and that when the immediate need for their earnings had passed they would return to school, but this probability diminished with every additional week that the child remained away.

An adequate discussion is not possible here of the various methods used by local tenement landlords in making payments on their investment. Most of these men have only small sums on hand for the initial payment, and such families often make their purchases through building and loan associations,[12] which thrive in the immi-

[12] If the purchaser is Bohemian (Czech), Slovak, Lithuanian, Polish, or Croatian, he probably goes to a building and loan association. For accounts of these organizations see Donald S. Tucker, *The Evolution of People's Banks* ("Columbia University Studies" [New York, 1922]), p. 246, and Henry S. Rosenthal, *Building, Loan and Savings Associations* (Cincinnati and Chicago, 1911), pp. 17–18. See *Illinois Revised Statutes, 1923*, chap. 32, secs. 213–14, for the definition of such an association: "Every association heretofore or hereinafter organized or incorporated under any law for the purpose of assisting their members to accumulate or invest their savings, by accumulating a fund from periodical payments on its stock or otherwise to be loaned among its members shall be known as Mutual Building and Loan or Homestead Associations."

The act contains further provisions designed to regulate domestic associations operating within the state, application to organize, the issuing of a license for the subscription of stock, the number of shares that must be subscribed before the meeting to organize and elect officers. The report of the organization must be submitted to the auditors. The directors and officers are regulated by law and must file bonds with the public auditor.

In *New Homes for Old*, Miss Breckinridge listed 681 foreign associations of this sort in Illinois, 255 of which were in Chicago. Each of the foreign building and loan representatives visited described his own particular nationality as having the largest proportion of home-owners. Many other people indorsed the claims of the Polish people to this distinction.

grant neighborhoods, by the "contract system," and by borrowing of friends. They rarely ask help from the banks, in part because the purchaser with the small amount of money he has in hand is not a "good risk" and would probably not be a favored borrower at the bank.

The co-operative character of these societies and their financial soundness explain their appeal to men who are inexperienced in real estate transactions. The fact that the purchaser must have one-third of the purchase price eliminates from their membership most of those who undertake the purchase of property without proper forethought, probably as the result of immediate urgent need.

The contract system of purchase has also been widely used—especially by the families who wish to buy homes and who are without the third of the purchase price required by the building and loan societies. Real estate dealers have a contract system by which a very small deposit will enable a man to "buy." In addition to the deposit, the contracts call for a stated weekly or monthly sum to be paid directly to the dealer while the title remains in the name of the dealer until final payment is made.

When the purchase of a home is undertaken, by whatever plan, the purchaser has undertaken a financial responsibility that remains with him for years. The time required for paying for the property might well cause a prospective purchaser to hesitate. One man who was interviewed had just paid the last indebtedness on a house he had bought on contract thirty-four years ago. "All my life I've been paying for it," he said.

HOME-OWNERS IN THE DEPRESSION

The difficulties of many home-owning families during the depression are shown by the large numbers of clients of the Legal Aid Bureau of the United Charities who have asked help in their real estate difficulties.

The following summary shows the number of real estate cases in the Legal Aid Bureau from 1925 to 1934, and since these are largely difficulties created by threatened foreclosures in the case of clients who could not pay for legal advice, they show the plight of the home-owner who lives near the margin.

Year	Number of Real Estate Cases Legal Aid	Year	Number of Real Estate Cases Legal Aid
1925*	294	1930	872
1926*	373	1931	1,383
1927	607	1932	2,544
1928	595	1933	2,581
1929	564	1934	2,715

* In 1927 the fiscal year was changed to the calendar year. Prior to that date the data are for the period from October 1 to September 30.

A substantial percentage of the families in certain districts who came to the large relief agencies during the depression either owned, or had owned, their homes. For example, in the Southwest District of the Cook County Bureau of Public Welfare, approximately one-fourth of the families on relief were still home-owners in 1935, with the number of home-owners going up to three-fourths of the relief families in some of the smaller sections of the district where there were unusually large numbers of workingmen's homes.

In another chapter attention has been called to the grave hardships endured by many landlords when the relief agencies adopted the policy of not paying rents for their clients.[13] Many landlords who became clients themselves would have found it unnecessary to apply for relief had the policy of paying rent for relief clients been adopted sooner. Since responsibility for rent has been assumed by public agencies, numerous landlords have been taken off the relief lists. One social worker told of a very interesting case of an aged man who in his earlier years had practiced medicine in the city, but whose life's savings had been swept away by business failures of various sorts during the depression. He had a large old home but could not dispose of it. When it was decided that rents could be paid out of public funds, the agency selected prospective tenants from their own list of relief clients, and by renting out rooms, the man who

[13] See chap. xv, "The Rent Moratorium of the Chicago Relief Agencies (1931–33) and Housing Deterioration."

would otherwise have been "on relief" himself was able to be self-supporting with the rents from his house.

In order to determine what was happening to the property of relief clients, as well as to discover whether or not the families themselves were any better off than those without property, a sample of fifty cases, in which it was known that a home had been or still was owned, were chosen at random for reading.

The application for relief in many of the home-owning families is of comparatively recent date. A large proportion of them did not ask for assistance until 1932 or later, and many of these cases seem to indicate that ownership of a home frequently put off temporarily the inevitable day of the relief application. Attention was called by the district superintendent to the case of a family who had at one time been comparatively well to do. An unfortunate business venture resulted in heavy losses, and soon afterward a serious illness, necessitating surgical treatment and prolonged hospital care, finally brought the family "on relief." After all possible resources were drawn upon, all insurance policies cashed, the home, including much of the furniture, had finally been sold before the family found it necessary to ask for help.

In the relief records tragic stories are found of the sacrifices which many of the families had undergone in order to buy their homes and the many more which they are now making to keep from losing them. The strain on the family's health, mental as well as physical, due to worry over arrears on interest payments and taxes, and the dread of foreclosure, has led in some cases to complete mental breakdown and in a few instances even to suicide.

The heavy burden carried by some families is illustrated by the case of a Croatian man and his wife who had come to the United States in 1884. They had both worked hard and very faithfully—he as an unskilled workman, she as a janitress. After years of saving they invested all they had, including a small sum secured from the sale of property in Jugo-Slavia, in an apartment building containing eleven flats, valued at $66,000. Then the man became ill and tenants no longer paid their rent regularly. Finally, when payments could no longer be met, the first mortgage-holder started a suit to foreclose, and in December, 1932, the building was sold and the family came to the relief agency. The family were allowed to remain on the premises for janitor work until very recently; but a real estate firm finally took over the management of the building, and the former owners were notified that their services were no longer required and that if a rental of $32.50 a month was not paid immediately, a five-day notice would be issued. The unfortunate, and now elderly, Croatians feel that they have been "robbed of their property."

In another case, a widow, aged sixty-one, a native of Chicago, was persuaded to trade her unincumbered "bungalow" for a two-story brick house. She was led to believe that she could pay off the first mortgage of $6,000 and a second mortgage of $500 with the income from her investment. Since the purchase in 1931 she has been unable to make any payments, has had to accept relief since December, 1932, and is now facing foreclosure.

Economies of various sorts have been resorted to by the home-owning families in order to meet the demands of the owner of the mortgage. Married sons and daughters or elderly parents have crowded into the home of one member of the group in order to "help out" financially; other families have moved into basement apartments in order to rent the more desirable quarters. Even after such sacrifices have been made, some families have had to face the loss of their property. One family, for example, purchased a two-flat building in 1919 for $12,200 and was dispossessed in 1933 for the non-payment of a $4,500 mortgage. The man, his wife, and two nieces are now occupying the basement room of a five-room cottage owned by a married son who has three young children of his own. This property also is heavily mortgaged; and although the son is employed, his wages have been paid so irregularly that he has scarcely been able to keep the family fed and clothed.

Family discord and strife frequently result from the amalgamation of different sections of the family who are brought together sometimes to "save the home" and sometimes to help some unfortunate member of the larger family group. When married children, especially those who are paying rent elsewhere, have been prevailed upon to come home to contribute toward the upkeep of the family homestead, this has often meant overcrowding and unpleasant family quarrels and differences. One native American family, for example, who purchased their five-room "bungalow" in 1924 for $9,000, paying part in cash and assuming a $3,800 mortgage, found it possible to pay only the interest without any reduction in the principal. In 1932 further financial burdens were assumed when the wife's parents came to share the home with the daughter, son-in-law, and two children, after a foreclosure on their own home. The husband greatly disliked this arrangement in his home and departed. For a time he continued to support his wife and his two children, but payments soon became more irregular. He lost his job, and a few months later he committed suicide. Although the relief agency has tried to persuade the holder of the mortgage to accept interest payments without pressing for payments on the principal, he is unwilling to do so, and foreclosure proceedings are being brought.

Many of the homes have been saved by the new government recovery agency, the Home Owners' Loan Corporation. One Lithuanian family with two children accumulated $7,000 out of the father's wages, which averaged $25 a week. In 1926 the man invested the $7,000 in a small two-flat building, taking out the remainder of the $11,900 in the form of a mortgage. Improvements on the property, together with special assessments, called for the expenditure of an additional $1,000, making it impossible to reduce the principal. In order to get out of debt, the family moved into the basement and rented the two upper apartments. Unemployment, however, made it necessary to use the "rent money" for living expenses. The house was already in the process of foreclosure when the family succeeded in negotiating an H.O.L.C. loan. However, this thrifty family is now worrying about the repayment of the loan, since their budget allows for only the payment of interest charges.

One family now "on relief" has gone to even greater extremes to protect the equity they still have in their home. The man, an educated German, purchased a two-story frame cottage in 1925, and hoped to pay off the mortgage from his wages. When he lost his work in 1930, his wife went out to scrub floors at night in order to help support the family. When they finally came to a relief agency for help, the man had "almost lost his mind over the mortgage." He has insisted upon spending money secured from work relief to pay the principal as well as the interest on the loan which he secured through the H.O.L.C. To make up for the deficiency in his budget, he was said to have encouraged his children to steal coal and to have himself stolen both meat and coal. In spite of the humiliation of his own arrest, he still sent out his children to steal, and only recently the relief agency found that he had paid a fine of $100 while on relief. Before securing the loan he had threatened to burn his house rather than see the mortgage foreclosed.

Worry over losing the home seems at times to have brought about actual mental breakdown. Several families were found where such worry had undoubtedly brought about conditions of "nervousness" and actual mental disturbance. One of the case-workers in a public relief office told of a Greek immigrant family in which the father, aged thirty-eight years, was unemployed. He worried so much about not having work and about not getting any regular income from the small second-floor apartment which he counted on renting to pay for his building that he had reached a condition of serious mental disturbance and had terrified his wife and children by his constant threats to "end it all."

In one family both husband and wife became so depressed and discouraged over the thought of losing the home that the wife was only prevented by neighbor's entreaties from carrying out a threat to jump out of the window. The husband also developed mental difficulties and secluded himself in the basement, refusing to meet anyone, even members of his own family.

In another family, while the man and his wife were at court trying to get through an order to forestall dispossession, the bailiff came out to the house with the master's deed and proceeded to carry out the order. Finding no one at home, he broke into the premises and had the furniture put out on the street. In the process of dispossession some of the family's most cherished household treasures disappeared. After the loss of his home the man became mentally deranged and is now a mental patient.

In a Lithuanian family known to the same relief office, the threat of suicide was actually carried out and the wife not only lost her husband but, after his death, also her home. This tragedy grew out of the fact that in 1926 the husband had invested $8,000 in a cottage home, assuming at that time a mortgage of $4,800. All went well until 1929, when he lost his work. Worry over his inability to "get a job" and the threatened loss of his home weighed so heavily upon him that he committed suicide in January, 1931. After his death the mortgage was foreclosed, and the new owner who took possession in 1933 allowed the Lithuanian widow and her seventeen-year-old daughter to live in an attic room in the cottage for which the relief agency pays $7.00 a month rent.

The mentally disturbed condition of another Lithuanian is directly traceable to his worry over the impending loss of his home. This man had immigrated in 1916, and out of his earnings of fifty-five cents an hour he had by 1929 saved enough to invest $3,500 in a frame cottage of four rooms. Two years later he was "laid off," but it was not until a year later that he came to the relief agency asking not for relief but for work. He said that unless he could get work and be relieved of his financial worries he would "go crazy." Less than a year later his anxieties overcame him and he was taken to one of the state hospitals, where he is still a patient. His wife, left with the care of three young children, has been given assistance regularly, but she is extremely fearful that the $3,500 invested in the home will be lost since carrying charges on the $2,300 loan secured through the H.O.L.C. are not being met.

Aged couples who have looked forward to security in a home of their own are especially helpless when threatened with the loss of the home. One such case is that of a Swedish man and his wife who have been in this country for more than forty years. In 1925, when both their children were grown up, they decided to buy a five-room brick "bungalow." Fifteen hundred dollars was paid down in cash; a first mortgage of $4,000 and a second one for $3,500 were assumed. The second mortgage had been paid off before 1931, when the man was retired from his work without a pension at the age of seventy years. The first mortgage on his home was still outstanding, and although arrangements have been made with the person who holds the mortgage to accept the current interest so that foreclosure is not imminent, both the man and his wife speak of their constant fear and dread of "old age without a house or provision for daily needs."

Another case of old people afraid of the future is that of a man who was born in Holland but came to the United States as a young man. This man was a well-trained accountant and held quite responsible positions until three years ago when at the age of sixty he was told he was "too old to work." Unfortunately, he had used all his savings to purchase a $7,500 five-room brick cottage in 1926. He had paid $1,500 in cash, had placed a mortgage of $3,500 in the new home, and had arranged to pay the balance on contract. Payments on the latter were completed in 1930, but $2,000 still remains unpaid on the mortgage. The man and his wife did not apply for relief until July, 1932, having lived on their savings as long as they could, but he is now beaten, "too old to work," and in fear of losing all his savings through foreclosure.

Another man and his wife in their early seventies came to this country from Germany when they were young. Although the man never earned more than $15 to $20 a week, he was able to bring up a family of five children and to save enough to buy a home. In 1924 he sold this home for $5,700 and bought a more modern building for $8,200, the amount of $3,200 being in the form of a mortgage. Nothing has been paid on the principal since the children now have families of their own and are themselves irregularly employed so that they can give but little assistance to their parents. The money invested in the home represents to this man and his wife their entire life-savings, and their only hope of saving their investment—temporarily, at least—is a loan from the Home Owners' Loan Corporation.

Not all families have been dispossessed after the mortgage has been foreclosed, but even though allowed to remain in the home, which they hoped some day would be their own, the families are kept in uncertainty as to how long the arrangement will be continued.

The ten-flat building which one man bought represents an investment of over $45,000. This man was born in Chicago and had been employed as a locomotive engineer. His earnings and a successful real estate investment made possible this large purchase. At the time he bought the flat building he took out a mortgage of $12,000 with a real estate company. This man died in 1931, leaving a considerable amount of the mortgage still unpaid, and the mortgage was foreclosed in July, 1933. In this case the new owner allowed the widow to remain in one of the apartments because she is in very poor health and has a young son to support.

Another American family with six children had been living in a bungalow in which they had an equity of $4,900. In 1930 the man, who "had always had a job" and was confident of regular employment, traded in his home for a three-flat building. He contracted to pay $9,700 in instalments in addition to a $9,500 mortgage. Early in 1934 he was discharged for drinking. In four years he had paid off $6,000, but very shortly after his discharge the instalments fell into arrears, the mortgage-holder foreclosed, but as yet has made no move to dispossess the former owners.

The President's Conference on Home Building and Home Ownership discussed the problem of making it possible for every thrifty, self-respecting American workman to own his home and brought together facts and opinions upon the obstacles to home-ownership.[14] The general consensus of opinion was that the buying of homes was made comparatively easy during periods of prosperity "where credit often comes altogether too easily," but that a considerable proportion of home loans are made for terms that are too short for the interest of the buyer. Hence the home-owner may face the necessity of refinancing at a time when his income has been reduced and credit is difficult to secure. The recent tragedy of thousands of foreclosures during the long period of economic depression bears witness once more to the fact that home-owning which absorbs the entire savings of the small wage-earner is a kind of thrift that may have unlooked-for consequences of disaster.

[14] See *Home Ownership, Income and Types of Dwellings*, Vol. IV of *Reports of the President's Conference on Home Building and Home Ownership*, ed. John M. Gries and James Ford (Washington, D.C., 1932).

CHAPTER XIII[1]

THE HOUSING OF DEPENDENT FAMILIES IN CHICAGO

Rear Tenements for Dependent Families; Basement Dwellings; Rear Apartments; General Deterioration; Dark Rooms; Sanitary Provisions; Rental and Ownership; Overcrowding; Life below the Margin.

ALTHOUGH housing conditions for the low paid wage-earner in Chicago are generally quite below standard in decency and comfort, they are much worse for the families who fall below the poverty line and become clients of a relief organization. The effect of the disastrous policy of not paying rents for dependent families is discussed in a later chapter,[2] but even in normal times, resourceful and intelligent case-workers are not able to find proper homes for their clients; and the rents for the families on the lowest economic stratum are very high in proportion to the quality of the shelter that is furnished.

Two inquiries into the housing of dependent families in Chicago were made in connection with these studies of Chicago housing conditions, the first in 1928–29 and the second in 1932. The first study included material from the records of 2,272 cases from all districts of the United Charities known to that agency during the year 1928, and a more detailed inquiry and field investigation of the homes of 113 clients of the Lower North District in 1929. It seemed important to know how the housing conditions for "relief families" had been affected by the economic depression, and for that reason a

[1] This chapter is largely the work of Eleanor D. Goltz, field-work instructor in the School of Social Service Administration, and is based on her study of "The Housing of Dependent Families," an A.M. thesis, in the University of Chicago Library. However, data for 1932 have been added to the earlier material.

[2] See below, chap. xv, p. 441, "The Rent Moratorium of the Chicago Relief Agencies."

second study was undertaken in 1932. At this time 2,515 families known to five South Side districts in May, 1932, were studied.[2a]

Among the 2,272 dependent families who were under the care of the largest private family welfare agency in Chicago in 1928, 113, or 5 per cent, were living in furnished rooms; in 1932, 17 per cent of the 2,515 dependent families studied were living in furnished rooms. Information is therefore available for 2,159 families living in unfurnished apartments in 1928 and for 2,115 families living in unfurnished apartments or flats in 1932.

REAR TENEMENTS FOR DEPENDENT FAMILIES

Very little information with regard to the buildings in which the apartments of relief families were located was found in the case records studied. Since 113 families were visited in the Lower North District in 1929, however, some information about the buildings has been collected which is probably representative of other districts of the United Charities. Although this agency does not encourage residence in rear dwellings, 11 of the 113 families visited in 1929 were housed in such buildings. Two of the rear dwellings were one-family houses of a single floor. One of these had four rooms, newly painted over crumbling plaster. In this little old frame cottage, renting for $16 a month to a family of four, there were a very old sink, an old-fashioned long-hopper toilet, and lighting by lamps since electricity had been turned off.

The second rear house was a very dilapidated five-room cottage —cold, and very "hard to heat"—located at two intersecting alleys and with only an alley entrance, but renting for $20 a month. Nine persons, five of them children under twelve, made up the household. The plaster was cracked, the floors worn, and there were cardboard-mended windows, an outworn iron sink, and, worst of all, an evil-smelling toilet in a dark closet off the kitchen.

Another rear home was a two-story building which was extremely dilapidated. This house was divided into two apartments, only one

[2a] It is perhaps unnecessary to explain that policies of the United Charities, like those of other family welfare agencies, have been undergoing reorganization as a result of depression changes. This study was undertaken not for the purpose of studying the policies of this one family welfare agency but only to call attention to the very great difficulties encountered in any attempt to provide decent homes for dependent families.

ALLEYS AND REAR TENEMENTS OF THE WEST SIDE

of which was occupied. The tenants paid a high rental of $13 a month for this weather-beaten house, crowded close to the building in front; and there was the familiar story of rickety steps, doors which had ceased to fit their casings years ago, oil lamps, broken windows, and fallen plaster. In the small, low-ceilinged rooms these sleeping arrangements had been worked out: a five-year old boy and a three-year old girl in a three-quarters bed in the living-room; the mother, father, and twenty-two month old daughter in a double bed in a tiny bedroom, the window of which opened onto the court between buildings; an aged dependent woman in a three-quarters bed in the back bedroom facing the alley.

In another shaky rear cottage of four rooms there were a native-born widow and her five children. She had paid for some repairs herself and brightened it with some paint and calcimine. The way to the toilet was down an outside stairway, across the court, in the first floor of the front building. Here one long-hopper toilet served five families in both front and rear buildings. But the place was far from comfortable, and the rent was high ($15) for the very unsatisfactory accommodations. "The Charities" had offered to help her find a new place; but she was reluctant to move because the house had a good deal of sunlight. Anywhere else, she said, "might be darker."

There were some other rear dwellings that were three-story buildings. One of these was a six-family tenement, backed up against the elevated tracks, and the family on the second floor had the elevated trains rumbling by their windows. "But where else can you go for $15?"

BASEMENT DWELLINGS

Among the 2,272 family records for 1928 which were studied, 251, about 11 per cent, were living in basement apartments. In 1932, only 159 families, 6 per cent of the 2,515 studied in the latter year, were found in basements. It is possible, of course, that the legal definition of a basement apartment was not followed by the case-workers, and that some of these so-called basement dwellings were, properly speaking, first-floor dwellings. On the other hand, it is probably safe to assume that all such apartments are considerably below street level.

Among the 113 cases visited in the Lower North District in 1929, 11 were classified as living in basements, and the usual report about these dwellings was that they were "damp and dark."

Only one of these basement dwellings seemed really dry and light enough to see to read in all the rooms. This was in the basement of an unusually well-kept apartment house with a little more space about it than was common in that neighborhood. Another brick building having six apartments looked fairly well kept from the outside in spite of its age. Inside, very dark, ill-smelling halls and stairs with worn treads led to the basement apartment that was noticeably damp and so dark that lights had to be used all day in two of the rooms. Negro families lived in both of these homes.

A native-born white family was preparing to move out of another basement dwelling, partly because of the dampness of the two bedrooms. Although the kitchen and living-room were light, having unobstructed window space, the bedrooms were dark all day. In another two-story brick building of substantial looking exterior, a family of six, with one man lodger, was found in a basement apartment. The entrance was dark and had a coal closet opening off from it. Ashes were kept in the vestibule, and coal dust and ashes easily worked into the living-room. The mother, a woman of American birth, said the children had colds all winter, but "the place shouldn't be damp, because there's a cellar under this basement." The lodger was given the best bed in the house, a "duofold" in the living-room where there were two windows facing upon the front street. The father and mother had a double bed in the bedroom, with one window opening a few feet from the next building. All the children slept in a single dark room which was just large enough to hold two double beds, in one of which a five-year-old son with an eleven-year-old daughter slept, and the two nine- and seven-year-old daughters in the other. Their dark room had only a window of half-size which opened into the kitchen over the sink and which was kept shut all the time.

In the rooming-house area on the Lower North Side one family was visited in a two-room furnished basement apartment at noon on a bright day, but even then the hall was very dark indeed. A light showed the hall opening into the furnace room one door away from the apartment. The house was very clean in spite of the heavy soot just outside the door. The pantry shelves were covered with clean paper, but the mother said it was necessary to change the paper every day because of the furnace grime. Both rooms had windows, but it was necessary to keep a light on all day in the kitchen because the next building is within a few feet of the window.

In May, 1932, for example, a family with seven children, six of whom were under twelve years, lived in three basement rooms, one of which was next to the furnace and could not be used because of the great heat. The rent, $14 a month, was paid out of the mother's earnings. It was impossible for the family to sit down together at the table, for the kitchen was too small. This family was neither immigrant nor Negro, but a native American white family.

A Negro family with four children under twelve lived rent free in a basement flat of two rooms which had originally been intended for storage purposes. Heavy cardboard replaced the windowpanes. The entire family slept in the front room on the two beds which constituted the whole of the furniture. Later the building was condemned, but the family remained in another section of it.

The stories of families living in great discomfort in crowded and miserable basement quarters cannot be too much emphasized. A series of summaries describing the basement homes of these dependent families, in normal times, before the depression is given below.

A Ukrainian family of five lived in a three-room basement, for which they paid $15. It was damp at times and three feet below street level. The father in this family had tuberculosis.

A Swedish painter and decorator with a wife and five children, one of whom was grown, lived in a three-room cellar (over half its height was below the finished grade)[3] renting for $15. The Health Department had ruled that this basement should never again be used for residence purposes. It was with considerable difficulty that the family could be persuaded to move. The three rooms were fairly light, not unusually damp, and were fitted almost luxuriously with mohair, an expensive radio, and lamps. The level of the flat and the overcrowding, which were the worst features, did not trouble the family enough to offset the advantages of the low rental.

[3] Sec. 651 of Building Ordinances prohibits dwellings in cellars, i.e., rooms with less than eight feet six inches height in the clear, or more than half that height below the finished grade of the premises of the building and four feet three inches above the street grade.

A Negro family of eight, six of them young children, were crowded into a two-room basement as dark and dirty as the worst. The alcove, lacking in provision for ventilation, too small to be called a room,[4] contained the one double bed, apparently the only sleeping space available.

Another Negro family of eight was housed in rooms intended for a furnace and storeroom. The mother and father occupied the front room, which had two small windows. All six children slept in the middle room, which had no ventilation at all, for the third room was too cold to use. The children were quarantined in this for a time with whooping cough.

Six people, Negroes, occupied a three-room basement apartment, paying $20 monthly rent. This family was composed of the mother, grandmother, and four children. The rooms were dark all day and overcrowded. There was one bed in the front room in which the mother and one of the older girls slept, and two beds in the second room with barely enough room between them in which to walk. The grandmother slept alone in one of these and the three children in the other. The kitchen was gray-looking and opened upon the remainder of the basement, where there were heaps of ashes and cinders.

An extreme case was found in a Negro family of nine, consisting of the mother and father and seven children, five of whom were under twelve years. They paid no rent and knew no landlord over the place, which had been condemned. The yards were full of paper, tin cans, and broken furniture. They lived in the basement of a one-story cottage where there had been a fire. All the windows, except those in the basement, and doors were out or off, and only the roof and walls remained. The basement flat consisted of two rooms, a small kitchen, and a tiny toilet without light or air. After the fire in the cottage above, the light and water had been turned off. The two front-room windows could not be opened, and since the basement was below street level, the dirt from the street drifted against the panes and in through the door.

Ten members of one Negro family in Central District lived in two basement rooms paying $18 a month. The basement was under a two-story frame house and was whitewashed and clean. Board partitions divided the space into rooms. There was a large furnace in the center of the basement and a coal bin which together took about one-half the room. In the front there was a tiny room, partitioned off with boards, in which there were two beds. Here the four boys slept with the father. In the rear there was a large double bed in which the four girls slept with their mother. The kitchen stove, a table, and four chairs were also in this room. A third room might have been used had not the broken window-panes allowed the rats to jump in from the yard.

[4] According to sec. 647, p. 133, of the Building Ordinances, a room must contain "at least eighty square feet of floor area; provided, however, that in case of a room having a window not less than eighteen feet in area opening upon a public street, the floor area need not be greater than seventy feet."

One family, after eviction, found shelter in a basement apartment which had never been intended for living quarters and had never been finished for this purpose. The seven members of the family, all of them over twelve except one child, lived in these rooms, forty-four and a half inches below the ground level, and forty-nine inches above the street, for several months. For the four girls, a sleeping-room was partitioned off, two sides being solid brick wall and the other two tightly boarded. Ventilation was through an eight-inch opening into the room in which the mother and father slept. A grown son and the parents were more fortunate with windows, having one each, two feet by two and a half, above their beds. The son's privacy from the other members of the family was secured partly by the furnace, behind which he slept, and partly by a sheet hung before his cot.

The data regarding the housing of dependent families in 1928 and 1932 are presented in Table 75 and give certain facts about the below-street-level flats in all districts of the United Charities.

TABLE 75

NUMBER AND PER CENT DISTRIBUTION OF DEPENDENT FAMILIES LIVING IN SPECIFIED LOCATION, 1928 AND 1932

Floor Location	Dependent Families			
	1928		1932	
	Number	Per Cent Distribution	Number	Per Cent Distribution
Total	2,272	100.0	2,515	100.0
Flats:				
Basement	251	11.0	159	6.3
First floor	848	37.3	750	29.8
Second floor	796	35.0	859	34.2
Third floor	206	9.1	262	10.4
Fourth floor	27	1.2	37	1.5
Fifth floor	4	0.2	2	0.1
Attic	10	0.5	......	......
Cottages	130	5.7	446	17.7

REAR APARTMENTS

Rear apartments are very unattractive in the tenement districts where there are no rear gardens and only a discouraging view over tenement stairs and roofs. In most of the buildings visited, the entrance to middle and rear apartments present difficulties that make such dwellings doubly undesirable. The entrance from the street was often through a narrow passageway, usually damp and dark, the "catchall" for the street litter. Sometimes it was necessary to climb a flight of ten wooden steps to reach a platform constructed for entrance into middle apartments and to descend again on the other side. Winter-time finds many of these stair-blocked passageways choked with drifts or black slush thawing into unwholesome pools. Ascending the back stairs (frequently exterior), one discovers that the only outlook from the windows is into the dark side-passageway or onto dingy steps or rear buildings or unkept yard space or alleys. In some cases the rear flats are neglected, while those in the front are kept fairly well cleaned and decorated.

A case in point was found in the Lower North District. In an attempt to find the United Charities family in the building, all the front apartments were visited. Halls and stairways, walls and woodwork, in the apartments were in good repair and freshly painted. A dark way between high buildings—really a wooden sidewalk platform built up to the street level—led to the decaying rear stairs and to the rear flat itself, which consisted of three neglected rooms. "The boss" did not expect to improve these rooms or to tear down the empty shell of a building in a bad state of disrepair outside the windows.

Some of these rear apartments were extremely uncomfortable. For example, a Polish-Austrian family with four children under twelve years of age rented a four-room rear apartment for $25. The front room was dark and damp, and the floor in the clothes closet was still wet from the previous rainstorm. The walls were damp, all the clothing was soaked, and there were dark, airless bedrooms and an outdoor toilet.

A Negro family with four children was paying $7 a month for two rear rooms with crude, board walls. The rooms were small and dark, and all the windows were shuttered except the kitchen window, which was too near the next building to admit any light. The family shared their toilet with another.

In both these cases later records showed that the United Charities had succeeded in moving both families into better apartments where the children could have a place that was more like a home.

Of the 113 households visited in the Lower North District, 24 were in rear apartments. Four of these were in rear basements, 7 were on the first floor, 7 on the second, 5 on the third, and 1 on the fourth. Conditions were comparable regardless of floor except in the case of rear basements, which were the worst of the lot, being damp and dark in all four instances.

GENERAL DETERIORATION

Bad plumbing, lack of light and air, were common features in the housing of the dependent families visited. It was only when a situation was very bad that it was singled out as unusual in a discussion of the conditions surrounding a dwelling. When a building has fallen into such a state of decay that all the modern conveniences are gone there can be no doubt of the injurious effects.

A Negro bricklayer, for example, whose earning-power had always been too low to support himself and his family of six children adequately, was destitute after being out of work two weeks. The family lived in an old apartment building which had been deserted by all the other tenants. There was no money for candles or a lamp. Some cooking was possible in the large kettles over the kitchen fireplace (there was no stove), but all the water had to be carried in from a neighbor's house; and it was easier on the whole to buy a little cooked food or go without. Very little heat came from the grate fire, but fortunately there was a fair amount of covering on the duofold and the cot which served as beds. The toilet had been out of repair ever since the family had lived there. The mother was very much depressed when her husband was sent to the House of Correction for six months and she was forced to move. "It goes from bad to worse," she said after they were in a shed at the rear of a lot near by. At this place she had the use of an old range in a room of the building in front. This single shed room cost $4 a week.

In some of the families in outlying districts the bad conditions were due to original structural deficiencies which resulted in inadequate protection from the weather. While these cases were not numerous, some of them were very bad.

For example, a three-room shanty renting for $17 a month housed the seven members of another Negro family in a loosely constructed building—a most inadequate shelter, especially during the cold season. A brother and sister-in-law of the mother of this family had built their own shack quite near. It was one large room, twenty-six by eighteen feet. One corner had a half-partition. A curtain, stretched from the end of this partition to the wall, completed the division from the rest of the room. This served as a kitchen. There was no plumbing in the building. Water was carried from the house next door. A part of the building had strips of tar paper tacked on with large spaces between the pieces. The whole structure was set up on posts.

A German family with four children paid $14 rent for the miserable four-room cottage in which they lived in 1928. There was no sink in the kitchen, and the gas had been turned off so that the mother had to do her cooking in the basement on the garbage burner. As a result the family lived in the basement practically all the time. The children were "ailing" most of the winter, as might have been expected because of the perpetual dampness and cold in their home.

Such housing conditions, of course, are worse when some members of the family are ill. For example, there was a Mexican family of eight, made up of grandmother, father, mother, and five children under twelve, living in four rooms renting for $20 a month. This clean but bare apartment was not separated from the three rooms of another Mexican family. Rent was pooled to pay the $35 rent for the seven rooms.

The grandmother, who had a tuberculous condition of the throat, slept with the eight-and ten-year-old children, both of whom had very bad tonsils. The physician considered this arrangement very dangerous. Both the father and the mother were patients at the Municipal Tuberculosis Sanitarium at various times during the contact of the family welfare organization with the family. Later a young man, also Mexican, who had been living with other friends, came to join this family. He was sick and in bed during most of his stay.

A list of uncomfortable homes for these families who had so little left with which to help themselves might be extended almost indefinitely. For example, in one room, rented at $5 a week, were a mother and four children under twelve years eating, cooking, and

INSANITARY ALLEYS AND REAR TENEMENTS

sleeping disorder and discomfort. In another building eight people were living in four rooms that were cold, dirty, unplastered, and with floors warped.

In a dilapidated building a mother, father, two children, and one adult relative lived in one dark, dingy rear room for which they paid $10 a month. In one inner rear basement room, unheated, with a rent of $4 a week, were a mother and three children under twelve years. In six rooms, which were cold, small, dirty, and in poor condition, and with only stove heat, but renting for $25 a month, were thirteen people: mother, father, five children under twelve years, and six adult relatives. In three rear rooms rented for $25 were a mother, father, four children, and one adult relative; this was in a poor, shabby, dirty, neglected neighborhood.

In one rear room, rented for $4 a week, in a house which had been condemned, were a mother, father, and three children. In three rear rooms rented for $10.50 a month were a mother, father, and two children under twelve, who were greatly inconvenienced because their rooms served as a thoroughfare to other flats. In five rooms renting for $30 a month were a mother, father, six children, and five adult relatives: thirteen people in a cold, poorly repaired, practically unfurnished place, with only a small grate fire. This story of miserable homes might be continued almost without end.

DARK ROOMS

For the 113 households visited in the Lower North District more complete information regarding light, heat, ventilation, and plumbing was obtained. Dark rooms were a great drawback here. For the purposes of this study, any room without a window opening onto a street, alley, yard, or court was considered a dark room. Nine families were living in the Lower North District who had one or two such rooms, i.e., rooms without any window opening to the outside air. Rooms with windows opening to the outside, but boarded up or nailed shut, were not considered dark, and were not included in the count. Of the twelve rooms in the nine houses, ten were used as bedrooms, one served as a combination living- and dining-room, and one was unused.

A few examples will illustrate these home conditions more clearly.

In one small, six-room house, two boys, aged sixteen and twelve, slept in a room the only window of which opened into the kitchen. There were twelve in the family, six of whom were adults. The mother shrugged her shoulders and remarked in resignation, "But what can you do? We can't pay more than $30 a month." In another house an unventilated dark room was the bedroom of three boys, aged five, twelve, and fifteen.

In a third house, the mother, about ready for confinement, was lying in a bed in a dark closet under the steps leading to the floor above. Properly speaking, this was not a room at all, but an alcove which had been pressed into service so that there would be sleeping space for the eight members of the family. An imitation window was a piece of glass near the ceiling, about six inches deep and the width of an ordinary window, which would have opened into the dark hall had it opened. It was necessary to turn on the light to see it.

Eleven rooms not technically dark rooms as defined above, but for all practical purposes as bad, were found. One of these, a small room with a window one foot from the next building and completely boarded over, served as bedroom for a father and mother and their fifteen-month-old baby. Two others had lot-line windows which could be opened to give a little air, but gave no light. Still another, where two boys, sixteen and fifteen years old, slept, had a window tightly nailed shut and useless for light because of the nearness of the building next door. Two kitchens had windows which were tightly boarded, and one bedroom had a tin sheet nailed over its window.

To classify rooms by the degree of gloom or light with anything like objectivity was impossible. The terms most used in the records to describe the sanitary condition were "light-airy" or "dark-damp." In the Lower North survey, the difficulty of windows shaded by the next building was very common. In addition to the households already mentioned, living where there were windowless rooms or rooms with windows covered over, thirteen apartments were found which had at least one room, and most of them more than one, noticeably dark because of the adjoining building.

Dark halls and stairways, though not so injurious to health as the lack of ventilation and sunlight in living-rooms, are nevertheless very objectionable. Dark halls were very common, but these were not included in the dark-room count. But dark halls were especially bad when steps were steep and winding, when the hand rail was useless or absent, or when the halls or landings were full of rubbish stacked high or full of pails of coal or ashes, or piles of wood. One family had a quarantine sign upon the door, but the landing was too dark for its presence to be noticed. A few halls had gaslights flickering feebly all day long, some had electric lights (useless to a stranger since the cord was almost impossible to find), and some were fairly well lighted by windows or skylights.

Unventilated toilets are another aspect of the dark-room evil. In some cases windowless toilets opened off the dark halls described above. Toilets within apartments were frequently as bad, some being located in small closets with no window at all, and others with small windows nailed or painted shut, or opening into another room.[5]

The problem of fresh air and ventilation is found not only in rooms with inadequate window space opening upon a street, court, or alley, but also where there are windows on only one or two sides of the apartment. In the "Standards Recommended for Permanent Industrial Housing Development" by the Bureau of Industrial Housing and Transportation, it is specified that (1) row or group houses are not to be more than two rooms deep so that (2) cross-ventilation as direct as possible can be provided for all rooms. But this arrangement was not often found in the old houses visited.

Proximity of other buildings at times practically destroys the usefulness of windows as a means of providing either light or air. The first-floor rear apartment of one four-story building which had equally high buildings within a foot of it on one side and approximately three feet on the other is a case in point. Only the kitchen was light enough so that artificial lights were not used during the day. A lot-line bedroom window had been boarded over since it was never opened because of the next building, and windows on the other side were almost as useless.

The lack of such conveniences as artificial lighting, heat, toilets,

[5] Revised Chicago Code (1931), sec. 1422, specifies that in new tenements every water closet shall have at least one window with a minimum area of six square feet opening upon a street, alley, yard, court, or vent shaft.

and baths, while of real importance in health and comfort, is not so difficult to meet as the problems of bad ventilation and light due to structural deficiencies. However, it is unusual to find one of these deteriorating buildings equipped with any of the modern conveniences beyond what is legally required, except perhaps in the matter of lighting, where electricity has supplanted gas just as, somewhat earlier, gas took the place of oil lamps.

Most of the 113 homes in the Lower North District, 86 per cent, were equipped with electricity. Five of the households using oil lamps were doing so because the electricity had been turned off upon failure to keep up with the payments. In 16 instances the cost of the electricity was paid by the landlords, 11 of these being the families living in one room.

In all cases where gas was still used for lighting purposes the houses were extremely old and dilapidated. Two of them had been condemned, and all of them had ceased to receive attention of any kind from the landlord.

Two other closely related factors are cooking and heating facilities. Cooking was done in all the homes except three of the furnished rooms. Three of the families living in one room did all their cooking on small gas plates in the room. Coal was used for cooking in 30 homes, coal and gas in 25, and gas alone in 55. Only a few of those who had both gas and coal equipment had had the gas turned off at that time.

One hundred and four of the homes were heated by coal stoves, and in 99 of these, or 95 per cent, fuel was furnished by the tenant. Only 9 households had furnace heat, and all these were rooming-house families.

SANITARY PROVISIONS

Of 113 households in the Lower North District, 67 had toilets within the apartment. Five households had toilets which had an entrance directly into their apartment but had another entrance into the next apartment also. The remaining 28 toilets were outside the apartment, 24 of them opening off an outside hall. Two opened from furnace rooms, one directly off the yard, and one, located under the street sidewalk, opened upon steps leading up to the sidewalk.

Most of those in common halls, in yards, or under sidewalks were unlocked and easily available to other persons in the building or even to chance passers-by. When a family reported, therefore, that they were the only household using the toilet, or that they were one of two or three, they could not be sure. In all, there were only thirteen shared toilets among those outside the apartments (this is exclusive of the furnished-room group) and six of these were known to be used at least occasionally by strangers from the street. One woman, who had good, light rooms, was looking for others because the toilet, supposed to be for her family's use exclusively, was used very commonly by anyone who happened into the store downstairs. Of the inside-apartment toilets, 40 opened directly upon the kitchen, 12 upon the living-room, and 9 upon inside hallways. Four opened from bedrooms, 1 directly from a pantry (used for food and dishes), and 1 from a rear storeroom.

Seventeen of the toilets had defective plumbing, the water in 7 of them ran constantly, 6 others were out of order because of freezing —a difficulty that lasted in each case as long as freezing weather remained—and 4 were "backed up" and clogged beyond use. Three old long-hopper toilets were found, and the one toilet under the sidewalk was in very bad condition. However, the Health Department inspector had visited the place recently, and the family was expecting some action. One evil-smelling old fixture had been moved from the basement up to a windowless closet off the kitchen.

The 13 rooming-house families all had toilets which were outside the apartment, and although none of the roomers knew how many persons used the toilet, they did know that the toilets were used only by the occupants of the house.

As indicated by the location of toilets, bathrooms were uncommon. There were 82 households with no baths at all, and 15 of the families with baths had only a cold-water tap, leaving only 6 (outside of furnished-room families) who had baths with hot-water taps. Hot water was usually provided by means of a tank in connection with the kitchen range. One old-type galvanized iron tub with a hot-water tap had been installed in a dark, windowless closet. The tub was not used for bathing because of its bad interior. However, it afforded a convenient receptable for used clothes until wash day—

a use not uncommon for the tubs with cold-water taps only. The other five hot-water tubs were in good condition and were used for the conventional purpose. The encouragement toward cleanliness which good, running hot-water facilities offer is not often available for these dependent families. The all-district survey provides no figures on the subject, but it is significant that the complete bathroom was rare enough, so that when it occurred the phrase "excellent—complete bath" was entered on the record as a detail worthy of special note when found in the home of a family known to the United Charities.

RENTAL AND OWNERSHIP

Obviously a prime consideration in finding a house for a dependent family is cheap rent. This factor lies behind almost all the unpleasant and undesirable conditions described above. In an American city which has left the housing entirely in private hands, as Chicago has done, rents for reasonably modern and well-kept houses or apartments are prohibitive not only for the dependent families but for the unskilled wage-earners. Such projects as the controlled building venture, or the limited dividend corporations, do not touch the poor man's housing problem. It is the handed-down, deteriorated building which must shelter these families. Health, conveniences, and aesthetic considerations must all be sacrificed before the small or insufficient income.

Among the 2,515 families studied in 1932 there are two important differences from the 2,272 families studied in 1928 in the matter of tenure: a larger proportion were living in furnished rooms and a larger proportion owned or were buying their homes. Whether these differences (shown in Table 76) are entirely due to the effects of the depression upon the economic status of hitherto independent families it is impossible to say, since the 1928 families lived in all districts of the city while the 1932 group lived only in the South Side districts. We have already noted considerable difference from district to district of the city in the matter of home-ownership. Whether or not these figures are representative of the entire city, it is nevertheless a matter of importance that 11 per cent of the families who were under the care of the five South Side districts of the United Charities in May, 1932, were home-owners.

The rents per room paid by 1,993 families who lived in houses and unfurnished apartments in 1928 and of 1,501 families [5a] who lived in similar fashion in 1932 are shown in Table 77.

The median rent paid for the relief families was between $5 and $6 per room in 1928 and between $4 and $5 in 1932. Approximately three-quarters paid less than $6 per room in both periods. Rents paid in 1932 were in general lower than in 1928, although a few high rents were paid in 1932 and the proportion paying $9 or more per room was larger than in 1928.

TABLE 76

TENURE OF HOME; DEPENDENT FAMILIES, 1928 AND 1932

TENURE OF HOME	DEPENDENT FAMILIES STUDIED			
	Number		Per Cent Distribution	
	1928	1932	1928	1932
All families studied....	2,272	2,515	100.0	100.0
Renting:	2,106	2,017	94.9	84.2
Houses and unfurnished apartments...........	*1,993*	*1,617*	*89.8*	*67.5*
Furnished rooms.........	*113*	*400*	*5.1*	*16.7*
Receiving rent free for service or other reasons......	32	118	1.4	4.9
Own or buying home.......	82	260	3.7	10.9
Type of tenure not reported.	52	120	*	*

* Percentages based on known cases.

Although these rents appear to be low, they are nevertheless somewhat above the rents paid per room by the 11,741 families whose homes were visited in the period from 1923 to 1926. The rents of the United Charities families were highest for the year 1928, although the rent index[6] published by the United States Bureau of Labor Statistics shows that rents in Chicago in 1928 were, in general, below rents for each year from 1923 to 1928. The two groups of

[5a] This total is 1,501 and not 1,617, as in Table 76, because in 116 schedules this information was not returned.

[6] See above, p. 273.

families are compared in Table 78. Although 62.4 per cent of the 11,751 families visited were paying less than $5 per room, only 48.6 per cent of the dependent families paid rents as low as these. Even in 1932 the rents paid by dependent families show a larger proportion

TABLE 77

NUMBER OF DEPENDENT HOUSEHOLDS PAYING SPECIFIED RENTAL PER ROOM PER MONTH FOR UNFURNISHED APARTMENTS, 1928 AND 1932

Rental Per Room per Month	Dependent Families			
	1928		1932	
	Number	Per Cent Distribution	Number	Per Cent Distribution
Total	1,993	100.0	1,501	100.0
Less than $1.00	....	....	3	0.2
$ 1–$ 1.99	9	0.5	17	1.1
2– 2.99	122	6.1	169	11.3
3– 3.99	394	19.8	434	28.9
4– 4.99	443	22.2	285	19.0
5– 5.99	500	25.1	256	17.1
6– 6.99	263	13.2	104	6.9
7– 7.99	101	5.1	56	3.7
8– 8.99	60	3.0	44	2.9
9– 9.99	23	1.1	13	0.9
10– 10.99	30	1.5	38	2.5
11– 11.99	14	0.7	6	0.4
12– 12.99	12	0.6	16	1.1
13– 13.99	6	0.3	9	0.6
14– 14.99	4	0.2	2	0.1
15– 15.99	6	0.3	12	0.8
16 and over	6	0.3	37	2.5

of rents of $5 or more than the families in the districts visited, although rents in general had fallen sharply between 1928 and 1932. This is partly explained by the fact that nearly one-half of the 1932 families were Negro and that rents are in general higher for Negro families.

Moreover, although rents appear to be higher per room, the dependent families lived in smaller apartments and under more crowded conditions. The proportion of one-, two-, and three-room apartments was considerably larger for this group of families than among the families in the districts visited from 1923 to 1926. Since rents per room are generally higher for the small apartments, the relief families are living in apartments which are relatively expensive considering their smallness and lack of conviences.

In some instances the families under the care of an agency are perhaps a little stronger in their housing position than are their neighbors. The possibilities of getting a landlord to make certain

TABLE 78

RENTS PAID BY DEPENDENT FAMILIES COMPARED WITH HOUSES CANVASSED

Rent per Room	Cumulative Percentages		
	11,751 Apartments Visited, 1923–27	Dependent Families	
		1,993 Records for 1928	1,501 Records for 1932
Less than $2	0.8	0.5	1.3
Less than 3	8.7	6.6	12.6
Less than 4	35.2	26.4	41.5
Less than 5	62.4	48.6	60.5
Less than 6	86.8	73.7	77.6
Less than 7	94.5	86.9	84.5
Less than 8	97.1	92.0	88.2
Less than 9	98.4	95.0	91.1

essential repairs are greater when the month's rent is fairly certain to be forthcoming. If he knows that the United Charities is standing behind a family where employment is irregular or impossible, he is more willing to spend a little energy and money to do the things that will hold the tenants.

On the other hand, the influence of the agency is limited by the policy adopted in relation to paying back rents. Rent arrears an agency cannot hope to pay. In many instances, then, it holds true that, although current rent is coming in regularly to a landlord, a large debt remains. This debt is used as a bargaining point by many a landlord. The situation of a woman who lived in a rear apartment in the Lower North District is an illustration. She was lying ill in the combination bedroom and living-room, watching two very large rats in a nest of feathers and paper they had dragged about the base of two pipes. An order from the Health Department induced the landlord to make a pretense of stopping the rat holes in this flat. When after a few hours the woman reported that the holes were again open, the landlord replied that when she paid the two weeks' rent which she owed him for the period before she knew the family agency he would repair the difficulty, not before.

TABLE 79

NUMBER OF HOUSEHOLDS WITH A SPECIFIED NUMBER OF PERSONS OCCUPYING A SPECIFIED NUMBER OF ROOMS; DEPENDENT FAMILIES, 1928

Number of Persons	All Households	Number of Households Occupying a Specified Number of Rooms								
		1	2	3	4	5	6	7	8 or Over	No Record
Total	2,272	141	134	313	983	380	221	42	14	44
1	36	14	2	8	5	3	1	....	....	3
2	99	25	15	14	33	6	3	2	....	1
3	168	20	21	34	67	11	11	2	....	2
4	361	40	35	69	154	44	6	4	1	8
5	383	19	33	60	189	48	25	3	....	6
6	410	14	15	57	189	87	33	5	3	7
7	336	6	7	40	153	73	41	6	2	8
8	217	3	3	17	101	45	33	6	3	6
9	145	....	2	5	54	40	33	7	3	1
10	68	....	....	7	26	12	19	1	1	2
11	24	....	1	2	4	5	9	2	1	....
12 or more	23	....	....	....	7	6	6	4	....	....
No record	2	....	....	....	1	....	1	....	....	....

OVERCROWDING

The condition of these homes of dependent families with respect to overcrowding has already been discussed.[7] There it was shown that 73 per cent of the United Charities families studied in 1928 were living in overcrowded homes with more than one person per room. Table 79 gives detailed figures for the 2,272 dependent

[7] See chap. viii, "The Problem of Congestion," pp. 251–53.

households. It is clear that these families were considerably worse off from the point of view of congestion than the families who were visited in the house-to-house canvass and who were presumably not dependent families but the families of independent wage-earners. In 1932, however, the dependent families were not living under as

TABLE 80

NUMBER OF HOUSEHOLDS OF A SPECIFIED NUMBER OF PERSONS OCCUPYING A SPECIFIED NUMBER OF ROOMS; DEPENDENT FAMILIES, 1932

Number of Persons	Total	Number of Dependent Households Occupying a Specified Number of Rooms, May, 1932								
		1	2	3	4	5	6	7	8 or Over	Not Reported
Total	2,115	89	123	217	617	449	301	77	29	213
1	16	4	....	2	4	4	1	....	....	1
2	168	27	20	25	52	21	11	4	....	8
3	344	25	36	63	123	54	15	....	4	24
4	406	15	28	43	135	88	39	8	3	47
5	356	7	15	36	113	84	50	13	2	36
6	275	3	11	23	74	63	57	10	2	32
7	179	3	1	10	47	47	40	14	3	14
8	140	....	5	8	26	39	37	5	3	17
9	90	1	2	1	24	23	22	7	3	7
10	43	....	1	3	7	9	9	7	4	3
11	26	....	1	2	6	3	5	5	....	4
12	34	....	....	....	3	9	12	3	5	2
Not reported	38	4	3	1	3	5	3	1	....	18

crowded conditions. They were better off in this respect than they had been in 1928, but they were still considerably worse off than the families visited in the house-to-house canvass. Table 80 shows that 964, or 52 per cent, of the unfurnished apartments in 1932 were overcrowded according to the Bureau of Labor Statistics Standard of at least one room per person. There were cases of nine persons living in one room and ten and eleven in two rooms.

The 400 dependent families living in furnished rooms were even more crowded. One case of fifteen persons living in one room is reported, while there were 21 cases of six, seven, eight, and nine persons in one room.

LIFE BELOW THE MARGIN

These statements in quantitative form convey only a limited idea of what overcrowding really means in the everyday life and comfort of a family.

One example of overcrowding was given by a Mexican family with two children living in one room. They kept two men lodgers and one woman in this one rear room in which they lived. Five cots for the seven persons occupied much of the floor space in this one-room home.

Sometimes temporary overcrowding, permitted in the face of emergency, stretches out into a long period of time, as in the case of a woman with three children who was living in three tiny rooms with her father, her brother and his wife, rent free. She had had an excellent standard of living until her husband deserted her. Then, penniless, she found herself dependent upon her brother, who had to take her into his own small quarters. The very best arrangements possible permitted her to have only one room and one double bed in which she and her three children might sleep.

A Negro family whose chief housing problem lay in overcrowding was a family made up of the mother, father, and four children. Their six rooms were extremely small. Like the woman in the previous case, they had had a much better way of life before the present emergency arose. They had owned a house in Savannah which they had held even after the husband and father became established in a good job in Chicago. At about the same time he became too sick to work, the renters in the South failed in their payments. The mother took in roomer after roomer to help make a living until there was little space left for her children. Three rooms were taken by the lodgers, leaving only a crowded living-room and a small bedroom for the six members of the immediate family. One sanitary cot and one double bed were available for them.

A Polish family of eleven was forced to move from a fairly large house to a four-room apartment, with a $20 rental which was within their reach. Only the front room was light in this old rear building, and in this room a woman relative slept with two little girls. One dark bedroom contained a double bed in which the father, mother, and two boys aged six months and two years, slept. Another double bed in the last bedroom was occupied by three girls and a six-year-old boy. All the children were under twelve years.

Another case record from the same district showed a family of a widowed mother, two boys, twelve and nine, and two girls, eleven and ten. The entire group slept in one room of their three. One room was closed off entirely because its extraordinary height, about twice that of the others, made it impossible to heat.

Examples might be multiplied showing the ever present difficulties to which overcrowding subjects these unfortunate families, but the following summaries must complete this unhappy picture.

A Sicilian family with four children under twelve and four older lived in a six-room flat, for which they paid $18. Two rooms were too dark to use since the windows were nine inches away from the neighboring building, and sleeping arrangements were particularly bad.

A Mexican family with ten children, only two of whom were over twelve, lived in an alley house of five rooms. It had no sun or air. When a relative suffered the same kind of fortune that the father had had, he brought his wife and two children to join the already overcrowded household. A little later in the year, the family moved into three dark rooms on the first floor of a large flat building. Here there were twelve people in three rooms. In one room were a cot, mattress, and gas plate. In another rags on which they slept were strewn around.

A native white family with three children had moved into a flat behind a saloon where the sleeping arrangements were so crowded that the nine-year-old boy and the seven-year-old girl slept in the crib with the baby.

A Negro couple with six children, one of whom was grown, had lived in an old frame building since 1925, paying $15 rent for three rooms. About a year after they moved in, the building was condemned, but they stayed on in their crowded rooms. Sleeping was especially difficult to arrange. A woman roomer had a bed with one of the children in the same small room in which the mother and two other children slept. The other three children, two young boys and a grown son, slept in the other bedroom.

A family who might easily have been more comfortable had they made the most of their resources were a Polish family with four children who occupied a four-room apartment in a small brick building. They used only two of those rooms, however, and only one bed, though a second had been given them. This bed that was occupied was used by the mother and the children. The father slept on rags on the floor.

The same family had previously occupied a house, a three-room apartment renting for $15, which was also overcrowded. Here, too, only two of the rooms were used and the entire family slept on one double bed.

Overcrowding was frequently found among the dependent families, especially among the Negroes, even in normal times; and long before the depression a family evicted for failure to pay rent was taken in by friends oftentimes as badly situated as themselves. The generosity of these people has been mentioned before, but the following families serve to illustrate further this neighborly kindness.

When a deserted Negro mother of five children was evicted from her three rear rooms, she was befriended by a man and his wife,.neither of whom she had known before the emergency. The two rooms were seriously overcrowded with eight people. In the one room available for them, the mother and one child slept on a sanitary cot and the other four children, all girls, shared the double bed.

Another deserted Negro mother with five children, all girls except a boy of twelve, was taken into a three-room basement apartment by a Negro widower. Her son slept with the landlord's boy in a dark inner room with no ventilation except the door. A rear bedroom had been fitted up with two double beds for the mother and the four daughters. Ventilation was through a single window, about one and a half by three feet, near the ceiling. It was never opened.

Another Negro widow, who could not earn her rent since two of her five children were newly born twins, was evicted. She was taken into a single tiny room between the apartments of other families. She had no stove, but kept the family warm by leaving open the doors to the other rooms. There was little space to move between the furniture, for the single bed, the couch, and the baby bed covered most of the floor space.

Finally, it is important to see more clearly the place which the housing of dependent families holds in the larger public problem. Economically and geographically a part of the low-wage-earning group, the dependent families share with this larger group the cheerlessness, discomfort, and hazards to health of deteriorated buildings.

In some respects their position is less satisfactory, as might be expected when a comparison in rents and congestion is made.

Further than the greater overcrowding, it is difficult to find much difference between the housing of dependent families and low-income groups. Dilapidation, lack of necessary sunshine and air and of sanitary conveniences, are common to all who live in old and dilapidated buildings in deteriorated neighborhoods. The solution of the problem of one group is closely related to that of the other. If the method of attack is direct, by building new houses at rentals within the reach of minimum incomes, the dependent group will share, with the outside help they now receive, the benefits of such building. That it is impossible to reduce rents of new houses to their level without public aid seems only too clear.

CHAPTER XIV[1]

EVICTIONS DURING THE DEPRESSION PERIOD

The Legal Process of Eviction; Increased Activity in the Renters' Court; Disorderly Conduct Cases: Evictions; Social Service in the Renters' Court.

THE eviction of families from their homes, by legal process, for the non-payment of rent became a not infrequent occurrence during the depression period in Chicago as in other large cities—the inevitable result of the loss of family resources and of the policy of the relief agencies regarding rents.

An action in forcible entry and detainer is one phase of the law regulating the relationship of landlord and tenant, and the legal procedure necessary to eviction is dealt with in Chicago in one of the specialized branches of the Municipal Court[2]—the Court of Forcible Entry and Detainer, or so-called "Renters' Court." This Court, being a civil rather than a criminal court, had not been regarded as especially in need of a social service department until the eviction difficulties that appeared in connection with the economic crisis. Social service problems arising in the Renters' Court seemed to be adequately cared for, in normal times, by the Legal Aid Society whenever the client was financially unable to procure other counsel.

[1] This chapter is largely based on a Master's thesis (June, 1933) in the School of Social Service Administration by Katherine F. Kiesling (see chap. xv, n. 1). Assistance given by Mrs. Ethel R. McDowell, the head of the Social Service Department of the Municipal Court, is acknowledged with warm appreciation. Miss Breckinridge, who supervised Miss Kiesling's thesis, has greatly helped regarding legal procedure.

[2] The Municipal Court of Chicago is a statutory court of limited and inferior jurisdiction. Among the classes of cases over which the Court has jurisdiction are the actions in forcible detainer, which are defined as follows: Cases of the fourth class—all civil actions, quasi-criminal actions excepted, for the recovery of money or personal property when the amount or value claimed by the plaintiff exclusive of costs does not exceed $1,000, and all proceedings for the trial of the right of property of which the value does not exceed $1,000 (Smith-Hurd, *Illinois Revised Statutes, 1935*, chap. 37, sec. 357. See also Cahill and Moore, 1935, chap. 37, sec. 390).

Either the client himself sought the services of this Society[3] before the case came up or he was referred there by the judge when it became evident during the hearing that a fair protection of his interests made such a course advisable.

With the great increase in unemployment in 1929 and the increase in the number of dependent families, the question of non-payment of rents, evictions, and rehousing became extremely acute and the problem of evictions assumed such distressing proportions[4] that a social service department was established in the Court in 1931.

THE LEGAL PROCESS OF EVICTION

Most of the cases in the Renters' Court are actions by landlords to evict tenants who are not paying their rents. Any time after the rent is due, the landlord or his agent may demand its payment, specifying the amount due, and notifying the tenant, in writing, that unless such payment is made within a time mentioned in the notice, which must be not less than five days after the service of the notice, the lease will be terminated.[5] This notice given the tenant by the landlord, demanding the payment of the rent within a certain length of time, is known as the "landlord's five-day notice," and is the first step in the legal process of eviction. In serving the five-day notice a written or printed copy is delivered to the tenant, or is left at the premises with someone above the age of twelve, or is posted on the premises if no one is in actual possession. If the tenant does

[3] The Legal Aid Society is supported by the United Charities of Chicago and the Chicago Bar Association. In some instances the United Charities may even pay the court costs of suits carried on under its direction. In landlord and tenant cases, the Legal Aid always represents the defendants, never the landlord. Even when some of the landlords themselves became recipients of charity, it has not varied its policy in this respect.

[4] In the summer of 1931 and again in the following winter and spring the School of Social Service Administration of the University of Chicago was asked to help in the emergency that had developed in the Renters' Court. Social service problems arising in the Renters' Court seemed to be adequately cared for in normal times, but the great expansion of the work led the School to assign two of the Leila Houghteling Fellows to the Court for field-work service in order to help some of the bewildered and frightened families until arrangements could be made for the expansion of the social service department of the Renters' Court.

[5] That is, if the advance rent is due on the first of the month, the landlord may serve notice on the second of the month.

not pay the rent due within the time limit set in the notice, the landlord may consider the lease ended and may sue for possession of the premises, in an action in forcible detainer. It is the appearance in court, not the service of the five-day notice, that actually breaks the lease. No further notice to the tenant is required before bringing suit. A claim for rent may be joined with the action, but as this requires payment of an additional court fee, it is seldom included when the landlord has reason to believe that his tenant would be incapable of paying the judgment even were it awarded.[6]

To bring an action in forcible detainer, the landlord first files his complaint in writing with the clerk of the court. This may be done any time within thirty days of the service of the landlord's five-day notice. The clerk then issues a summons, which is delivered by the bailiff to the tenant, who now becomes the defendant. This summons specifies the day and hour that the tenant shall appear in court for the hearing.[7]

[6] In the case of property that is being purchased on contract, in which the payments have become overdue, the law provides that notice that a proceeding for possession is to be instituted be given the purchaser at least thirty days prior to the institution of such proceeding, either by notifying him personally or by sending him notice by registered mail (Smith-Hurd, chap. 57, sec. 3).

[7] Prior to 1933 the time that was required by statute was not less than five days or more than fifteen days from the date of the summons (Smith-Hurd, *op. cit.*, *1931*, chap. 57, sec. 7. For change in statute, see *ibid.*, *1935*, chap. 57, sec. 6; chap. 110, sec. 226; and chap. 37, sec. 436; see also Cahill and Moore, chap. 57, sec. 6; chap. 110, sec. 259.4; chap. 37, sec. 475). In practice the time set was usually the minimum —five days. Either party to the suit might have the case tried by a jury if he wished, provided that he filed a written demand with the clerk at the time the suit was commenced (Smith-Hurd, chap. 110, sec. 188; Cahill and Moore, chap. 110, sec. 192). In any case relating to premises used for residence purposes, either party might demand the jury trial notwithstanding any waiver of jury trial contained in any lease or contract.

If the plaintiff fails to appear in court at the time set for the trial, or if neither party appears, the suit is dismissed. The plaintiff may, however, without extra cost, file a motion to set aside the order of dismissal and reopen the suit. The case is then heard on the next day, or whenever the plaintiff desires, in much the same manner as it would have been heard in the beginning. If only the defendant fails to appear, the suit proceeds *ex parti*. If the defendant desires to defend the suit, the case is usually continued two weeks. This is wholly at the discretion of the judge, but as the great majority of cases are not defended, and as the list is long and the number of people waiting large, it is considered more expeditious to defer until a set time those cases in which there is a contest. Also it gives both parties a greater opportunity to assemble their facts and arguments (Smith-Hurd, chap. 57, sec. 12).

In the great majority of the cases appearing before the Renters' Court during the depression period, the tenant admitted that he owed the rent and attempted no defense.[8] In such circumstances the judge had no choice but to give judgment for possession, his only power being to determine the number of days the defendant might have in which to move. Five days is the mimimum that may be allowed, and fifteen days, counting the day of the hearing, is the usual maximum, although occasionally twenty will be given, and in rare instances as many as thirty.

Each individual judge has, of course, his own system for determining the number of days to be allowed each defendant. A common practice is to give the minimum when the defendant does not appear in court at all, and to give ten days when the tenant does appear, and there are no children or any extenuating circumstances. If there is one child in the family, the judge usually allows eleven days; two children, twelve days; three children, thirteen days, etc., up to a maximum of fifteen days. Illness in the family may also be considered a legitimate reason for lengthening the time. The rule is not hard and fast, and is varied to meet the situation and special needs of the individual case, although the brief time devoted to each case prevents much individual consideration. One judge, for example, gave all cases five days regardless of any special circumstances.[9]

[8] The possible defenses are four: first, that no landlord's notice was served; second, that it was served before or on the same day that the rent was due, and when none was owing on the previous months; third, that the notice demanded more rent than was owed; and, fourth, that the rent was paid in full after the notice was served. Likewise, any money accepted by the landlord as advance rent after the notice was served vitiates the plaintiff's case. Undoubtedly, one skilled in the legal profession could find other technical defenses to bring forth in specific cases, but these are not important here.

[9] If, subsequent to the hearing, it appears that some facts pertinent to the case were omitted—facts that would have influenced the judgment—the party affected may come in on a motion, and have the case reheard. Blanks for such motions may be obtained in the clerk's office, and may be filled out and filed by the party himself. The clerks are supposed to render whatever assistance may be necessary, but they are usually rather busy and the client oftentimes finds the legal forms extremely confusing. A copy of any motion must be delivered to the opposing side before 4:00 P.M. of the day preceding the hearing, and his signature obtained, acknowledging that he has received it. If he refuses to sign it, the person delivering it must either go before a notary public or return to the clerk's office, and be sworn that he did deliver it. Or the copy may be mailed thirty-six hours before the time set for the hearing and the mailer then be sworn. In such case the recipient's signature is unnecessary. See *Rules of the Municipal Court* (available in Hiram T. Gilbert, *The Municipal Court of Chicago* [1928], p. 403), Rule 34.

The tenant has until midnight of the last day granted him by the court in which to move. If he has not moved within that time, eviction proceedings move rapidly. The tenant has not obeyed the order of the court; to enforce the court's order, the landlord may, therefore, procure from the clerk's office and file in the bailiff's office a writ of restitution, commonly referred to as "the twenty-four-hour notice," "the second court notice," or "the final notice." This writ is served by the bailiff on the tenant and informs him that he will be dispossessed within twenty-four hours. At any time following the service of this notice his furniture may be set on the street by the bailiffs.

To have the bailiffs evict a family after the writ has been served, the landlord must deposit a required sum of money in the bailiff's office, the exact amount being determined by the size and location of the flat to be vacated, the amount of furniture to be set out, and similar details. Often the landlord pays the money at the time he procures the writ. Frequently he waits a while, hoping that the mere service of the writ may lead the family to move so that it will not be necessary for him to go to any further expense.[10] Thus there may be a lapse of several days or even weeks after the service of the final writ before a family is actually evicted.[11]

This is, of course, a period of terrible uncertainty for the family. The unhappy tenant has no way of knowing when the eviction costs have been paid; the writ of restitution is the last notice of any kind that he receives. The bailiffs will not evict a family when a member is temporarily ill in bed, although when the illness is chronic, pro-

[10] The early attempts on the part of landlords to maintain payment of rents by means of eviction is undoubtedly due in part to the fact pointed out in the Philadelphia study, *No Money for Rent: A Study of the Rental Problem of Unemployment Relief Families and Their Landlords* (Joint Committee on Research of the Community Council of Philadelphia and Pennsylvania School of Social Work, 1933), that the landlord, in putting pressure on a family, is influenced in part "by the thought which seems to be widely held among real estate agents that the failure of one family to pay reacts upon other families which are perfectly able to do so" (p. 60).

[11] The money, however, must be paid within the same ninety days' time that is allowed for the service of the writ after it is filed. If a writ expires without service, another writ, a so-called "alias writ," may be served without additional cost and to the same purpose.

ceedings cannot be held up on that ground.[12] A quarantine for any contagious disease automatically stays an eviction until the quarantine is lifted, and tenants are sometimes accused of putting up old and discarded quarantine signs for this purpose. Nor will the bailiffs ordinarily evict a family in the rain. Occasionally an eviction may be delayed for a few days for some other cause that appears sufficiently urgent, though, strictly speaking, only the chief justice of the Municipal Court has the power to stay a writ once the eviction costs have been paid.[13]

The landlord may go to the Court of Small Claims and sue the former tenant for whatever the court and eviction proceedings have cost him, but this is seldom done, except in cases of landlord-tenant disputes. Under no circumstances can the landlord escape the eviction costs by swearing out a pauper's petition. Few of the defendants are represented by an attorney except in the contested cases, but many of the landlords are represented, particularly where the property is in the hands of a real estate agency.[14]

Special victims of the depression were those families who had lost their homes and gone, as they had supposed, temporarily, to furnished rooms. After the furniture had been mortgaged and lost, or stored and lost, and the family had descended more permanently into the furnished-room stratum, they were even more helpless than

[12] If illness persistently makes the eviction impracticable, the bailiffs may notify the landlord, who may have the sick person removed to the county hospital.

[13] There is no expense attached to the landlord's five-day notice so far as the landlord is concerned. Printed blanks for the notice may be secured free of charge at any Landlords' Bureau or real estate office, but the use of these forms is not necessary. The court action costs the landlord $3.00, of which $2.00 goes to the clerk's office for issuing the complaint in forcible detainer and $1.00 to the bailiff's office for delivering the summons. The fee for a joint action (forcible detainer and distress for rent combined) is $4.00. The landlord can escape the payment of the court costs by swearing out a pauper's petition, which petition must be approved by the chief justice. Originally, it was necessary only that it be signed by the presiding judge, but abuses grew up which necessitated a change of practice. For the writ of restitution the landlord pays $2.00. The actual eviction costs vary somewhat, but are based on the principle of $3.00 per room, with $1.00 added for "each flight up" that the flat is located. For a piano the charge is $10 extra if it is located on the first floor, $12 extra if on the second floor, and $15 if on the third.

[14] The average fee charged by lawyers for a case in forcible detainer is said to be approximately $15, out of which the court costs may or may not be paid.

tenement families since they were not protected by the legal eviction proceedings. Tenants living in furnished rooms and paying rent by the week can be quite easily "locked out" after a twenty-four-hour notice. Furnished room families are always afraid of being locked out by the landlord at any time, and when they go away they are always prepared to find themselves "locked out" when they return.

One woman, a widow, who lived in a furnished rooming-house with her children was afraid to go out to find work because she might be locked out. This woman came of good family, had two children, aged nine and eleven, and had her elderly mother to take care of. She ran a catering business in normal times, but she had been out of work and on relief, and the family lived in a single furnished room for which they were supposed to pay $7.00 a week. They were in arrears about $80 and were fearing to be locked out at any time; as tenants renting by the week in furnished rooms, they could be evicted without court process. The relief agency was giving this family food but refused to pay any rent for them. The woman had become terror-stricken at the thought of suddenly finding her children on the street with no place to go, and she had refused to leave the room for some time.

INCREASED ACTIVITY IN THE RENTERS' COURT

The increase in the volume of business in the Renters' Court is shown in Table 81. Until 1920 relatively minor and irregular fluctuations appeared from year to year. But beginning in 1921 there was an unmistakable increase which was maintained through the decade.[15] The high point of 17,351 suits filed in 1921 was looked upon as marking the beginning of the so-called post-war depression. For some unexplained reason, however, after the sudden and unprecedented increase of nearly 5,000 cases between 1920 and 1921, the figures never again went back to the former level and continued to rise slowly but fairly steadily until a new high point of 23,196 cases was reached in 1928. In 1929 there was a slight decrease in the number of suits filed, but in 1930 the effects of the depression following the financial collapse of the preceding year became obvious. In

[15] The population increased during this period from 2,196,238 in 1910 to 2,766,815 in 1920 and to 3,376,438 in 1930.

1930 there was an increase of approximately 31.8 per cent, and the number of suits filed continued to increase rapidly during the following year. But the spectacular rush of eviction cases came in the year 1932, and in that year the number of suits increased about 45 per cent. The policy of the relief agencies of withholding the payment of rents for relief clients[15a] began in December, 1931.

The increase in the number of writs filed, which is shown in Table 82, paralleled that of forcible detainer suits. The number of

TABLE 81

NUMBER OF FORCIBLE ENTRY AND DETAINER SUITS FILED, BY YEARS, FROM 1907 TO 1935

Year	Number of Suits Filed*	Year	Number of Suits Filed	Year	Number of Suits Filed
1907†	9,016	1917	12,922	1927	22,696
1908	12,241	1918	10,776	1928	23,196
1909	11,237	1919	11,912	1929	21,589
1910	11,238	1920	12,531	1930	28,462
1911	12,452	1921	17,351	1931	39,184
1912	13,324	1922	17,236	1932	56,246
1913	12,939	1923	17,549	1933	56,158
1914	15,580	1924	18,617	1934	38,603
1915	15,685	1925	18,399	1935	41,372
1916	12,656	1926	19,079		

* *Report of the Municipal Court for the Years 1931–1933*, p. 13.

† The fiscal year of the Municipal Court begins not on January 1 but on December 1 preceding. However, for convenience, the year is merely listed as a calendar year.

writs of restitution filed in the bailiff's office is usually much smaller than the number of original suits filed or even the number disposed of, as most of the tenants either move on the order of the court or effect some sort of a reconciliation with the landlord, or the landlord is financially unable to continue the proceedings.[15b]

There is also a great lag between the number of writs of restitution filed and the number of actual evictions taking place, but there seems to be no permanent record of the evictions themselves from which

[15a] See the following chapter for an account of the rent moratorium of the relief agencies of Chicago, 1931–33.

[15b] However, the year 1932 was unusual in this respect probably because the "no-rent" relief policy led to the filing of a very much larger number of suits in December, 1931. Many of these were received in the Bailiff's Office during the next year, which continued to be a very exceptional period. See the following chapter.

comparisons can be made over a period of time. Some interesting data are available,[15c] however, for the years 1932, 1934 and 1935. The total number of cases on which final eviction costs were paid in 1932 was 4,380, but only 3,947 actual evictions were carried through.[16] In the other cases, the family was found upon the bailiff's arrival to have moved, or the landlord called off the proceedings at the last moment. In 1934, when 38,603 suits were filed and there were 8,876 writs of

TABLE 82

NUMBER OF WRITS OF RESTITUTION RECEIVED IN THE BAILIFF'S OFFICE, BY YEARS, FROM 1908 TO 1935, INCLUSIVE

Year	Number of Writs	Year	Number of Writs	Year	Number of Writs
1908..........	1,614	1918.........	1,412	1927.........	4,363
1909..........	1,369	1919.........	1,371	1928.........	4,462
1910..........	1,323	1920.........	1,577	1929.........	3,993
1911..........	1,540	1921.........	2,545	1930.........	5,442
1912..........	1,745	1922.........	2,851	1931.........	7,215
1913..........	1,662	1923.........	3,225	1932.........	63,152
1914..........	2,292	1924.........	3,442	1933.........	46,411
1915..........	2,451	1925.........	3,280	1934.........	8,876
1916..........	1,810	1926.........	3,377	1935.........	3,463
1917..........	1,867				

* *Report of the Municipal Court of Chicago for the Years 1931–1933*, p. 28.

restitution, only 3,386 eviction orders were secured, and 2,103 cases in which the eviction proceedings finally went through and the families were literally "on the street." In 1935, with 41,372 suits filed, there were 3,463 writs ordered but only 1,912 actual evictions.

A family frequently moved into a flat, paying part of the first

[15c] Through the kindness of Mrs. Ethel McDowell, of the Municipal Court, see n. 1 at the beginning of this chapter.

[16] The figures do not include all the evictions that take place. Some cases, involving property in receivership, are made through the county sheriff's office. In the year 1931, e.g., there were 242 such "sheriff's evictions," statistics of which are not included in any of the statistics given above. When a bill of foreclosure is filed and a receiver appointed by the Circuit or Superior Court, the sheriff serves all the tenants as well as the owner of the building with a summons in chancery, and a writ of assistance may be issued to all delinquent tenants in behalf of the receiver. If the tenant does not then move and the receiver puts up the necessary fees, an eviction by the sheriff follows, unless the case is transferred (as is often done) to the Municipal Court of Forcible Retainer. Although relatively small in number, even these cases increased during the depression period.

month's rent, and then, having nothing more for several months, the landlord paid to get the family out. The costs paid by the landlords for a period of four years were as follows: $57,360 in 1929; $82,266 in 1930; $133,304 in 1931; and $183,500[17] in 1932. In the first seven months of 1932 the landlords expended a sum of $159,401 for the legal process necessary to dispossess tenants, exclusive of lawyers' fees.[18]

The clients in the Renters' Court came from homes of widely different types. These differences are shown by comparing the amount of rent and the number of rooms, which is done for 178 families in Table 83. Although four rooms for $12.50–$17.49 was of the most frequent occurrence, one family was renting four rooms for $6.00 a month and another was paying $65 a month for four rooms. One family paid $10 a month for seven rooms and another paid $50 a month for two rooms. One, a Negro family, who kept three roomers, was paying $130 a month for nine rooms.

17 Estimated on the basis of the first seven months.

18 Landlords or their agents in 1930 paid in $41,400 to the bailiff's office, and $56,500 in 1931 for forcible detainers and writs of restitution. The bailiff's office receives $1.00 on each forcible detainer for the service thereof, and $2.00 for each writ of restitution. There are no statistics published regarding the amount of money paid in eviction costs. Records of these payments are not generally available, but figures are presented from the files of the bailiff's office showing the following sums received in the bailiff's office for eviction costs: December, 1931, $1,013; January, 1932, $3,752; February, 1932, $4,219; March, 1932, $4,233; April, 1932, $8,306; May, 1932, $6,490; June, 1932, $6,498; July, 1932, $7,369; total for eight months, $41,880. The money paid the bailiff is for such costs of eviction as salaries of the professional movers who are hired to do this work. "Each of the five bailiffs assigned to evictions takes four union movers around with him. How much and under what arrangements these movers are paid seems to be a matter the Bailiff's Office prefers to regard as confidential. It is generally understood, however, that all money paid in eviction costs is turned over to the bailiff in charge of the particular district in which the eviction is to occur, and that whatever is left after all expenses have been paid remains with him. When the bailiffs and movers find upon arriving at an address that the tenant has already moved out, half the eviction costs are refunded to the landlord." Altogether a large sum of money has been spent by landlords in non-productive legal procedures, trying to get non-paying tenants out of their flats. During the seven months from December, 1931, to June, 1932, inclusive, the total amount spent in legal procedures by landlords, not counting lawyer's fees, amounted to $159,101, including $108,140 for forcible entries and detainers, $16,448 for writs of restitution, and $34,513 for eviction costs. A single complete eviction from a four-room, second-floor flat costs $20, or $32 if the tenant has a piano. And this figure takes no account of lawyer's fees.

When the "repeaters" were studied separately, it appeared that the median rent paid by the repeaters was $18.88. That almost none of the repeaters was paying over $20 is explained by the fact that $20, and in some districts $15, was the maximum rent that the relief agencies would pay, and virtually all the repeaters were dependent upon a relief agency.

TABLE 83*

AMOUNT OF RENT PAID, BY NUMBER OF ROOMS, OF 178 EVICTED FAMILIES

Amount of Rent	Number of Rooms									
	Total	1	2	3	4	5	6	7	8	9
Total	178†	2	9	22	77	21	28	12	5	2
$ 2.50–$ 7.49	2	....	1	....	1	....	....	....	....	....
7.50– 12.49	18	....	1	3	10	2	1	1	....	....
12.50– 17.49	44	1	1	9	27	3	3	....	....	....
17.50– 22.49	37	1	....	1	20	7	5	2	1	....
22.50– 27.49	12	....	2	1	3	1	3	1	1	....
27.50– 32.49	10	....	1	2	5	2	....	....	....	....
32.50– 37.49	7	....	....	1	2	....	1	2	1	....
37.50– 42.49	13	....	2	3	4	1	2	....	....	1
42.50– 47.49	9	....	....	1	2	2	3	1	....	....
47.50– 52.49	7	....	1	1	1	1	3	....	....	....
52.50– 57.49	6	....	....	....	1	2	1	2	....	....
57.50– 62.49	4	....	....	....	....	....	3	....	1	....
62.50– 67.49	3	....	....	....	1	....	2	....	....	....
67.50– 72.49	1	....	....	....	....	....	....	1	....	....
72.50– 77.49	1	....	....	....	....	....	....	....	1	....
77.50– 82.49	1	....	....	....	....	....	1	....	....	....
82.50 and over	3	....	....	....	....	....	....	2	....	1

* Twelve not reported; five buying on contract.

† One included in this total was $130 a month for nine rooms.

DISORDERLY CONDUCT CASES: EVICTIONS

Disorderly conduct charges which grew out of eviction cases attracted a good deal of notice during the depression. When an individual who has been evicted by the bailiff moves his belongings or any part of his belongings back into the premises from which he has been evicted, he is guilty of trespass. He may also be arrested by the landlord for disorderly conduct. He may also be charged with contempt of court for failing to obey the court order. No accurate statistics of such cases are available as they are not all heard in the same court and the records are scattered. However, in 1931 there were twelve warrants issued from the Municipal Court in the charge of disorderly conduct, and in the first six months of 1932 there were sixty-five issued. Not all of these were served. Most of the defendants were allowed to sign their own bond and were released. However, if the landlord said the tenant was stubborn, or likely to create an undue disturbance, a cash bond was required, with the result that the victim usually spent the night in jail. A few unfortunate persons who chanced to be served on a Saturday afternoon were forced to spend the entire week-end in jail. No record was kept of the number who thus passed a night in jail. The number was probably not large. It is important, however, to note that these people came out with a deep sense of injustice. A number of them seemed to be very quiet women from entirely feminine households.

If the case reached a hearing without having been dropped beforehand, and many cases were dropped, the usual procedure was for the judge to threaten the offending tenant with a jail sentence or fine, and then to give him two or three days in which to move, continuing the case through that time. Occasionally, if he were not out by the time specified, there would follow more severe threats and another continuance. Usually he moved after the first warning. So far as could be ascertained, such tenants all moved ultimately without the actual imposition of any of the threatened penalties. In at least one case a reconciliation was effected, the relief agency paid a month's rent, and the tenant resumed peaceful and legal occupancy of the premises.

Rarely if ever did any evicted family move back into the flat without help and stimulus from outside, usually from the Unemployed Council, a well-known radical organization. The common story told by the former tenants in court was that they did not move their possessions back, nor did they know the men who did the moving. And in a majority of cases this was undoubtedly true, although the court frequently refused to accept the statement as an excuse. Representatives of the Council, upon hearing that there was furniture on the street at a certain address, would assemble a group to resist the eviction process. The group often increased in number during the period of active resistance until a force of from fifty to one hundred men was assembled. Sometimes the owner of the furniture was swept along by the enthusiasm of the crowd to take an active part in the proceedings, but sometimes the owner was not even present and at other times he took little or no part in the rather disorderly proceedings. In one case the worker from the relief agency was with the family looking for a flat at the time the evicted furniture was moved back into the old flat. Frequently the family did not know the men who composed the resisting group, although the organization was usually recognized.

The proportion of Negro cases sent each month to the Social Service Department at the Renters' Court declined sharply and steadily month by month during the year. One worker suggested that the Negro landlords could no longer afford to bring their tenants to court and pay the necessary eviction expenses.

The number of "repeaters"—that is, persons brought into court a second time—fluctuated during the year. The number who were sent to the Social Service Department of the Renters' Court was as follows for the period indicated: December, 1931, 30 families; January, 1932, 91; February, 102; March, 122; April, 99; May, 101; June, 115; July, 120. The number of "repeaters" was 2 per cent of the total number of cases sent to the Social Service Department in December, 1931, and 13.9 per cent in July, 1932. While these numbers may not seem large, they represent very extreme discomforts and humiliations for the families involved.

SOCIAL SERVICE IN THE RENTERS' COURT

It was in the center of this client-agency-landlord triangle that the Social Service Department of the Renters' Court found itself when it was established in August, 1931. In the winter of 1929–30 it had been necessary for a woman clerk to spend a few hours a day in the Court taking down brief notations on the cases that appealed to the judge because of extreme poverty and distress. Card forms had been used, but little information was given aside from the date, the name of the tenant, and the number of children in the family, and sometimes the name of the opposing attorney.

No cases had been cleared with the Social Service Exchange. Cases on which any referrals at all were made were usually referred to the Illinois Humane Society,[19] frequently with the notation "Urgent." Occasionally, cases appear to have been referred to other agencies, even to several at a time, and without knowing whether someone might already be trying to care for the family. Even cases marked "Urgent" and referred to a special agency were sometimes cases in which the client admitted that he was receiving help from another organization.

Relief was sometimes provided promptly by the judge. One year the judge who sat in the Renters' Court collected from his friends the sum of $2,000 from which he himself paid the rent for some families. For others a "collection" was sometimes taken in the courtroom—if not enough for their rent, at least a few dollars "to help them out." The judge said that from five to fifteen dollars a day was raised by "passing the hat in the courtroom." One of the lawyers is reported to have said that it cost him more to go to Judge ———'s court than he got out of it. Both the bailiffs and the clerks maintained funds from which donations were frequently made, but these funds died a natural death when the city stopped paying its employees regularly.

[19] The Illinois Humane Society, to which these cases were referred for investigation, and to which the later skilled Social Service Department also referred some investigations, is an organization founded in 1869 as the Illinois Society for the Prevention of Cruelty to Animals. Owing to the large amount of work done for the protection of children, the name of the Society was changed in 1877 to the Illinois Humane Society. Its purpose is "the prevention of cruelty to children and animals." This organization receives complaints by telephone, in writing, or by personal call, and sends out officers to investigate and take whatever action seems expedient. At the present time the Society maintains three officers who work exclusively with cases involving animals, and four who work only with those involving children. The seven investigators are all men, as it was considered in the beginning that the work was much too rough for women, and the old tradition has been faithfully maintained.

During the year 1931 the Society investigated 1,583 complaints involving 4,155 children (see the *Humane Advocate: Sixty-third Annual Report* [February, 1932], pp. 12–13). Next to the "Court of Domestic Relations" and "Wives against Husbands," the "Renters' Court" was listed as the most fertile source of complaints received by the Humane Society in 1931, accounting for 531 of the 1,583 complaints received. As a favor to the Court, the Society investigated its cases to determine whether or not there were children involved, although, of course, there usually were children. No action was taken on these cases by the Society when the rather simple investigation had been completed. A typewritten report on each case investigated for the Court was given to the worker at the Court, but nothing was done with these reports except to file them neatly in a drawer.

Looking back over this period, it seems clear that the relief any individual received at the court depended in a large measure upon his emotional appeal. The arrangements were of the hit-and-miss variety, with babies in arms and weeping women determining to a large extent the aid given. This system, of course, placed a premium on emotional instability and dramatic "scenes," to the great disadvantage of the destitute families who endured their misery in dignified silence.

In August, 1931, the present Social Service Department was established, with two professional social workers sworn in as deputy clerks. One of the simplest and yet most valuable services that the Social Service Department was able to render the clients was that of explaining to them the meaning of the court procedure through which they had just passed. To many tenants the court notices, couched in legal terminology, mean very little, and the few moments devoted to the hearing of their cases before the judge leave them more baffled than before. In ordinary cases the explanation of the meaning of the court order and, when it seems advisable, a description of the events that may be expected to follow—that is, the writ of restitution and eviction, together with their time sequence—all help to give the unfortunate tenant a feeling of greater security and enable him to make his plans more intelligently.

The Social Service Department of the Renters' Court has been equally at the service of the landlords and tenants. The problems of the landlord are given as careful attention as those of their tenants. Sometimes when the landlord is so circumstanced that he must have a paying tenant in his flat in order to be self-supporting himself, and he cannot afford the eviction costs, a contact is made with the agency caring for his present tenant, and occasionally successful arrangements are made to move the family without further cost to the landlord.

CHAPTER XV

THE RENT MORATORIUM OF THE CHICAGO RELIEF AGENCIES, 1931–33, AND HOUSING DETERIORATION[1]

"Eviction Riots" in 1931; The Rent Moratorium for Relief Clients; The Plight of the Families; The Plight of the Landlords; Housing Deterioration; The Angelus; Rent in the Relief Budget.

THE evictions of the years following 1929 were, of course, a result of the period of prolonged unemployment and the loss of financial resources of all kinds; but along with these causes went the extraordinary policy of the family welfare agencies regarding rents. During the second summer after the depression,[2] the non-payment of rents in Chicago had become so widespread that landlords in all parts of the city were trying, by means of evictions and threatened evictions, to force their tenants to pay the accumulating arrears, or at least their current, if not their overdue, rents.

[1] This chapter is based, in part, on material furnished by Dr. Florence M. Warner, formerly superintendent of one of the Unemployment Relief Service stations in Chicago; in part on the thesis of Katherine F. Kiesling (see p. 426, n. 1). For nearly three months (April, May, and June 1–15, 1932) Miss Kiesling used a simple schedule in attempting to visit every family for whose eviction the court costs had been paid, and on whose record no relief agency was registered. Visits were also made to some of the families usually described as "repeaters" even if the eviction costs had not yet been paid. These were families who had been in the Renters' Court at least once before within the past year. An attempt was made to cover a random sample of the families in this group. About 300 visits were made in all, and 195 schedules were obtained. In visiting the families for whom no relief agency was registered it was learned that in many of the so-called "writ" cases (those in which the writ of restitution had been issued, and the eviction costs had been paid) there was a relief agency caring for the family, but that an error in the spelling of the name or in the address had prevented an identification when the list was cleared at the Social Service Exchange. The families visited, therefore, probably represented a fair cross-section of all families for whom the costs were paid, though with a somewhat higher proportion of non-relief families. A few families were visited after they had been evicted and had settled in new flats.

Acknowledgment is made again of the continued help of Miss Breckinridge and the generous assistance given by Mrs. Ethel McDowell, chief of social service in the Municipal Court.

[2] In the summer of 1931.

"EVICTION RIOTS" IN 1931

In the summer of 1931, the Renters' Court had become a center of new activity. The first series of what came to be called "rent riots" occurred in August, 1931. A crowd of something like two thousand people gathered in the center of a large Negro area on the South Side of the city to prevent the eviction of a destitute Negro family. When two Municipal Court bailiffs arrived, accompanied by a real estate agent, and moved the possessions of the evicted tenant into the street, the news spread rapidly, rioters gathered, and the household goods were moved back into the flat during disorderly proceedings in which three rioters were shot and killed, and three policemen and a fourth rioter seriously injured. The next day a Chicago newspaper announced that there would be a policy of "firmness in dealing with communistic eviction disorders." But the bailiff of the Municipal Court agreed to withhold further service of eviction warrants until the mayor of Chicago returned to the city and arrangements could be made for "every humane consideration to be given the hundreds of penniless families."[3] A Chicago newspaper announcement said that "promise of aid had been received from various charitable organizations"; and hope was expressed that some mysterious "fund" which the mayor was supposed to be able to produce from some mysterious source would in some mysterious way prevent further eviction difficulties.

At the so-called "Riot Inquest," a police lieutenant gave testimony which showed that evictions had been going on for some time, and that the recent riot had merely called public attention to the serious effect of the depression on the question of housing and the widespread inability to pay rents. It was as if a riot had been necessary before the unfortunate victims of the depression could get any promises of relief; and even these promises soon vanished. There had evidently been a good deal of unrest for some time. The lieutenant testified that "in the last few weeks bailiffs serving eviction notices had encountered hostility, but on the arrival of a few policemen the crowd had invariably dispersed quietly."[4]

[3] See the *Chicago Daily Tribune*, August 4–5, 1931. It was charged that this "riot" had its origin in a "communist" meeting which was reported to have been in progress in a nearby park at the time when the eviction proceedings began.

[4] See *ibid.*, August 6, 1931.

The non-payment of rents went from bad to worse because no amount of pressure by landlords could make destitute families pay their rents when they needed their small remaining savings to buy food for their children. Appeals to relief agencies for help of all kinds became continually more urgent. The relief rolls in Chicago had not shown the seasonal falling-off that had been expected during the summer months of 1931, and the number of new applicants for aid increased rapidly in the early autumn and still more rapidly as the cold weather came on. A large emergency relief fund had been raised by public subscription;[5] but the relief demands, which increased so alarmingly, represented such genuine need that the emergency fund was rapidly disappearing and there were grave fears that all relief funds might soon be exhausted.

THE RENT MORATORIUM FOR RELIEF CLIENTS

A temporary "no-rent" policy as a way of meeting the threatened emergency was formally adopted by the various relief agencies in Chicago before the end of December, 1931, since this seemed to them the only way of meeting the acute situation that seemed to be developing. This policy was of course dictated by the great increase in the number of families who were day by day forced to resort to the relief offices for such necessaries as food and fuel as well as rent. Very large additional relief funds were needed, and such funds could no longer be raised locally but could come only from the state government or the federal government. But the outlook for adequate state funds was not favorable; and there was at this time great reluctance on the part of the more conservative groups in the community to ask for federal funds. The federal administration then in Washington was known to be opposed to federal relief on the ground that a federal relief system would be the beginning, in America, of the English method of providing for the unemployed, which at that time was popularly miscalled "the dole."

Administration supporters and some very respected board members of the various agencies were alike reluctant to believe that a

[5] This was the second large "emergency fund" raised in Chicago by a public "drive." The first "drive" in 1930–31 had raised approximately $4,000,000, and the second $12,000,000. See *Social Service Review*, VI, 270–79, "Chicago Relief Statistics, 1928–31," by C. M. Brandenburg.

prolonged period of depression was in prospect which would make federal relief necessary. Faced with the almost bewildering rapidity with which relief funds were disappearing, it became clear in the early winter that rigorous methods of conserving relief funds must be adopted or the federal government must be asked to provide federal aid. The line of least resistance seemed to be a no-rent policy, with a vague hope that it might be only temporary.

Immediately after the Christmas holidays, news of the "rent moratorium" that had been decreed for the destitute tenement families, but not accepted by the tenement landlords, spread rapidly. New and conspicuous signs appeared on the walls of the widely scattered district offices of the relief agencies bearing the legends: "We Do Not Pay Rents." "Please Do Not Ask Us To Pay Rent."

Early in January, 1932, the judge sitting in the Renters' Court called a meeting of representatives of the relief agencies and of the landlords[6] in the hope that some acceptable compromise might be reached between the two groups. A representative of the landlords demanded that *some* rents be paid, explaining that when one month's rent was paid for a family, the landlord would try to carry the family along for three or four months. It was further urged by the landlords that shelter was as necessary as food in an emergency budget. But the relief agencies maintained their position on the ground that their funds were fast being depleted, that food and fuel were much more essential than rent, and that these most necessary budget items could be provided only if rents were not paid. The two sides could come to no agreement, and no definite action was taken. The judge urged the landlords to be as humane as possible, and the meeting came to a futile end.

Chicago was not alone in her adoption of the "rent moratorium" for relief families. Many of the leading "family welfare societies" in different cities began to pay rents only if eviction were imminent,[7] or if the need were not primarily caused by unemployment. In the

[6] In addition to the representatives of the two groups named above, there were also present at this meeting the chief justice of the Municipal Court, the clerk of the Court, the bailiff, and the director of social work in the Municipal Court.

[7] See the report of an investigation by the Department of Special Studies of the Family Welfare Association of America, Margaret Wead, "When the Rent Comes 'Round," *The Family*, XII (February, 1932), 313–17.

great cities, particularly in New York, Philadelphia, Detroit,[8] and Cleveland,[9] a no-rent or "eviction-rent" policy was finally

[8] A letter from the City of Detroit Bureau of Public Welfare (July 20, 1932) gave the following account of the rent policy of that organization:

"Our rent policy began to be modified in 1930 when we started to make arbitrary rent rates. These were accepted by the landlords and we accordingly lowered them each year with the general decline of all living costs. We paid rent in those cases where shelter was actually threatened and also on our long-time allowance cases. Such instances amounted to about 20 per cent of our load.

"Our budget expired on April 24, 1932, and we have been operating on a credit basis ever since then. We naturally do not feel able to commit the city to any item but food and, accordingly, since May 15 have not paid any rents. At first there was a terrific increase in evictions and about forty families were actually dispossessed every day. All sorts of makeshift adjustments were thought out and in fact three families lived in one of our district offices for two nights. We have recently found that the evictions have somewhat subsided and feel that this indicates that landlords have discovered that we really are not paying rent and that they therefore cannot force our hand in the usual manner.

"We are making plans for a temporary mass shelter for families and we are also requesting our Common Council to give us an appropriation of delinquent tax credits to the amount of $850,000 for one year, and with such tax credits, we can negotiate with landlords on a purely tax basis. At this point the above request has been refused on the grounds that all delinquent taxes are virtually collateral on past loans. It is argued that one department of the city cannot shrink the collateral that has been put up by the city as a whole."

The following news item from Detroit, which appeared in the *Chicago Tribune* August 7, 1932, gives further details regarding the extraordinary housing situation which developed there:

"Officials of the department of public welfare today planned the establishment of a tent city to house evicted welfare families.

"Three hundred tents have been loaned by the Michigan National Guard and members of the guard will be detailed to assist in erecting the tents.

"The first of the tent colonies at Clark Park now has twenty families.

"The mayor's unemployment committee is supplying blankets and cots for use in the tents. Each of the tents has room for eight persons. It is planned, however, to limit each tent to one family."

[9] A letter from the Associated Charities of Cleveland, Ohio (July 29, 1932), explained that prior to 1930 full rent was paid for the families for whom the organization was taking the responsibility. Later, this policy was modified, and up to March 1, 1932, the agency "paid 50 per cent of the rent for the unemployed family when any rent was paid." In the first quarter of 1932 there were 2,463 evictions as compared with 1,322 in the same months of the preceding year. And see also a Cleveland dispatch in the *New York Times*, September 8, 1933, reporting that the local Realty Owners' Association had decided to evict 2,500 indigent families occupying property owned by members of the Association. The dispatch also said: "The State Relief Commission today authorized liberalization of cash payments to landlords of charity tenants, in addition to tax rebates allowed by statute; but it was declared in behalf of the Realty Owners' Association that this would not check the eviction order."

adopted.[10] In Philadelphia, where great suffering was caused by the suspension of relief for nearly two months in the summer of 1932, because of the exhaustion of private and state relief funds, the State Emergency Relief Board did not include rent among the items that the County Relief Board was allowed to pay.[11]

Few rents were paid by relief agencies in Chicago during the months of January and February, 1932. Occasionally, when a family was actually evicted, it became necessary to make an exception; but such exceptions were rare. Beginning in March, when state funds became available, occasional rents were paid for certain families on relief; but the percentage of the relief funds that went for this item in the budget remained very small indeed. Although the State Relief Commission specifically named[12] shelter as one of the forms of relief that might be provided from Commission funds and added that, whenever possible, the home must be kept intact, as a matter of fact the payment of rents from state funds was allowed only in cases where eviction was imminent,[13] and the relief agencies, public

[10] Similar difficulties were apparently not unknown in England (see, e.g., Irene T. Barclay, "This Rent Question," *New Statesman and Nation*, December 5, 1931, pp. 707–8). In this case the chairman of the Public Assistance (relief) Committee censured an unemployed man because he had paid his rent while he was drawing "unemployment insurance benefit." The chairman is reported to have said: "You shouldn't pay rent when you are on the dole. The money is meant for food and clothing."

[11] See Philadelphia study (*No Money for Rent*), p. 5.

[12] In the "Rules for Local Administration of Unemployment Relief," put out by the Illinois Emergency Relief Commission.

[13] A communication dated April 18, 1932, directed to the secretary of the Joint Emergency Relief Fund of Cook County and the director of the Cook County Bureau of Public Welfare, and signed by the executive secretary of the Illinois Emergency Commission, approved the following suggestions for modifying the rent policy:

"(1) That in instances where there is no income that may be used for the payment of rents, there shall be no general policy of meeting the rentals but that individual decisions will govern each case, and consideration shall be given the various factors bearing upon a decision in the case, including such as (*a*) number of months of rent unpaid; (*b*) suitability of housing, and the amount of rent involved which would include a decision regarding the economy of moving or paying of rent in present quarters; (*c*) the efforts on the part of the case worker to obtain a postponement, concession, or rent reduction from the landlord, and upon the following conditions:

"*a*) That no publicity be given to any change of policy with respect to payment of rents.

"*b*) That in applying the above procedure to specific instances the greatest care shall be exercised in the treatment of each case to avoid abuses and to the end that the essential policy of not assuming rental obligations shall be maintained."

and private, continued to refuse to pay rents. The general policy was that no rent whatever was to be paid except when a family had been, or was to be, evicted. Then one month's rent[14] would be paid for a new flat. The purpose of this policy was plainly that of protecting relief funds from being too rapidly depleted.

The continued increase in the number of families on the relief rolls, and the very large funds required, led the emergency relief organizations and, in fact, all relief societies to continue their no-rent, delayed-rent, and occasional-rent policies through the year 1932 and the first half of the year 1933. In general, no rent was paid until a family received its writ of restitution.[15] Even then, the head of the family about to be evicted was not given any money with which to pay a deposit on any flat that might be found. Instead, he was told to find a new flat and to return to the relief office with the address of the new location and with the name of the landlord. Then, and then only, was the man given the money for a month's rent. The clients of the relief agencies complained very bitterly about this policy.

While every effort was made to avoid actual evictions, the relief offices,[16] under the pressure of relief needs, more and more frequently waited until the eviction costs had been paid before the family was given funds to move into a new flat, if and when one could be found. Relief families came into the social service office at the Renters' Court every day insisting that the workers at the relief agency with whom they dealt told them to wait until they were "on the street" and that not until then could the relief office do anything for them about paying any rent. In a number of these cases that were followed up afterward, the families were actually evicted. But these

[14] This amount, however, was not to exceed $20, and in some districts the maximum was $15. The United Charities, the great private relief society, was able for a time in the spring, when their private funds were being supplemented by state funds, to move some evicted families into new flats with the promise that they would pay half the regular rent (this half usually amounting to $15) for three months. After a month or two, however, when the end of the funds again approached, they were no longer able to continue this policy; and the end of the three-month period in some cases brought renewed complications.

[15] See the preceding chapter, p. 430.

[16] The private agencies were in some instances able to be a little more generous in their practice, if not in their policy, than the public agencies, although they would assume no obligations to pay rent.

evictions among the relief families were undoubtedly due to the difficulties under which the relief stations were working—the constantly recurring shortages of relief funds, the heavy "case loads" that made it impossible for the workers to know the dangers of impending evictions in all their families, the large number of untrained or inexperienced workers who were unable to act swiftly and wisely when evictions were threatened. Data assembled by the Renters' Court showed that in three months no fewer than one hundred and twenty-nine relief families had been "put on the street." This number was undoubtedly below the number of such families who were, in fact, evicted; for no reports regarding whether or not eviction actually occurred could be secured in a large number of other relief cases.

Because of the inadequate number of social workers on the staff, the relief agencies were unable to do anything to help families find new quarters except to pay the first month's rent when the new flat was found. In some cases in which the difficulties of finding a flat in a limited time were too great for a family, they moved back into their old flat after they had been evicted, and the head of the family was then brought into court on a disorderly conduct charge.

The relief agencies' "rent moratorium," which continued for approximately eighteen months, had some very serious consequences: (1) it was cruelly hard on the relief families, many of whom moved over and over again, with a growing discouragement that almost reached despair; (2) it was unfair to the landlords, who, with their incomes in many cases entirely cut off, were sometimes driven to the relief rolls themselves; (3) it led to such insanitary living arrangements that housing conditions became more and more deteriorated.

THE PLIGHT OF THE FAMILIES

First, the tenement "rent moratorium" led to almost incredible hardships among the unfortunate families on the relief rolls. The landlords were anxious to avoid the expense of evictions, but they felt that they could not continue to allow their buildings to be used indefinitely with no rents being paid while the buildings were steadily deteriorating under tenants without housekeeping resources. Their policy was to try to force the families who were in arrears to vacate the house voluntarily, so that a resort to the Renters' Court and the necessary eviction costs would not be necessary.[17] The landlords turned off the lights; they turned off the gas; and, if the house was furnace-heated, they turned off the heat in the winter; and, finally, they even turned off the water. Many cases of flats with the water shut off were reported from time to time.[18] The landlords became angry and terrified the miserable tenants by scolding and threatening. Some landlords finally adopted the drastic method of trying to freeze the tenants out by removing the window frames. In this way a landlord really could get the families who were unable to pay rent to leave without his having to resort to eviction and eviction costs.

When a family had been evicted or was clearly on the point of eviction, the relief agencies would, as has been said, help the family to move and pay one month's rent in advance. That is, the policy of the relief offices was to pay one month's rent in advance only as an emergency method of keeping the family "off the street," then the rent stopped again, and then the family was once more plunged into

[17] A worker in one relief station reported that some landlords took advantage of the ignorance of their tenants by using an imitation "five-day notice," i.e., they had some printed notices that looked enough like the court notices to convince the tenants that they would be evicted if they did not move. In some cases men were employed who posed as bailiffs and actually took charge of dispossessing the tenants.

[18] This was, of course, contrary to the regulations of the Health Department, and the Department took the position that turning off the water must not be used as a method of eviction. But in a single month in the spring of 1932 the Department investigated 135 cases in which the water had been shut off. Undoubtedly, there were many similar cases that did not come to their attention. This policy was said to have been "practically unheard of" before the rent moratorium.

Even as late as the summer of 1934 the following item appeared in the *Chicago Daily News* (June 25, 1934), with the head-line, "Water Supply Restored for Children's Sake." The item was as follows:

"Eleven families in a tenement at 1129 South Paulina street, including five children in one family sick with infectious diseases, had their water supply restored today by the city water department.

"The owner of the building, according to the water departments records, owes the city $344 for water consumed since July, 1931. The department has shut off the water several times, but each time it has been mysteriously reconnected.

"A few days ago, the department removed the meter and the pipe was cut off; but the connection was restored today, when it was learned that the children were sick. There are forty-five children in the building."

a state of rentless insecurity. No rent was to be paid unless the worker was convinced that the landlord really intended to proceed with eviction. A relief office might have two hundred and fifty families for whom eviction was imminent, and to keep "one jump ahead" of the bailiff and the landlord called for the ability to estimate, very shrewdly, the landlord's next move. Did he intend to pay the eviction expenses and put the family out or was he merely threatening? And if he did intend to evict, how soon would he act? By a policy of shrewd guesswork, the workers were supposed to save the relief funds from any unnecessary payment of rent, on the one hand; and, on the other hand, the office must act promptly enough to prevent an actual physical eviction.

Gradually, families facing eviction proceedings began to have great difficulties in finding new accommodations in the extremely short time that often elapsed between eviction and the serving of the writ of restitution, and particularly after the costs had been paid. The landlords became more cautious and refused to accept tenants whom they suspected of being on the relief rolls, and as a precautionary measure, many of the landlords began asking for evidence that the new tenant was working. And, as proof that he could be depended upon to continue to pay his rent after the first month, the landlords asked for three months' back-rent receipts from prospective tenants.

No landlord wanted to rent a flat to a tenant who was receiving relief from a social agency. A typical notation on the back of a case record at the Renters' Court reads: "Mrs. J. has been looking for a flat, but no one will let her have one because she has no money and they are afraid she is from the Charities and will pay only one month's rent." Another: "Mrs. L. says it is hard to get a flat now; the landlords ask lots of questions."

One family had a very unfortunate experience in this respect. The man had found a nice flat, and made definite arrangements with the landlady to take it. All the furniture was loaded on the truck and ready to start for the new flat when the new landlady appeared. She had just received the check for the rent from the relief agency and with it a receipt that she was to sign and return to them; it was the first intimation she had had that her future tenant was being cared for by a relief agency. She was quite pleasant and friendly, but she was also very determined that the prospective tenant should not have her flat, all agreements to the contrary notwithstanding. She said she already had three "charity tenants" and simply could not afford to take in another. The unhappy prospective tenant finally persuaded her to let him move his family into the flat on the basis of the original agreement, by impressing her with the fact that he was to be transferred to the Veterans' Bureau the next day, and that he had been informed that the Veterans' Bureau paid rents regularly (as the Bureau did, in fact, at that time). She let him move in on the condition that he bring her a signed statement from the Veterans' Bureau or from some responsible person, that she would get her rent regularly on the first of the month, or, in lieu of such a statement, that he would move out voluntarily on the first of the coming month. About three months later he was again in the Renters' Court.

Relief families hunting for new flats found it impossible to be straightforward and honorable in their dealings with their future landlords, and many of these families were greatly humiliated by their experiences, particularly because of the deceptions to which they thought it necessary to resort.[19] One woman, in great distress after a fruitless search for a flat, said bitterly, "They do not ask you *if* you are working; they ask you *where* you are working." This woman had moved on court order four times in a single year. Like many others, she also said that the landlords were suspicious when the prospective tenant did not have any money to pay down on the flat, and when he had to move in the same day he engaged it.

One woman, who had been in the Renters' Court, said very frankly that it had been necessary to lie to the landlord in order to get into the new flat. She had told the landlord that her husband was working, although he had had no regular work for nearly three years and had had none at all for the last six months. A man, who had also been in the Renters' Court, said he had rented his new flat in the

[19] A meeting of officials of the Chicago Church Federation, ministers, and resident workers from the church neighborhood houses was held April 4, 1932, to inquire "into the effect of the measures for relief upon the moral standards of the people and their communities." This group reported that the "resort to lying, deception, fraud, and stealing is manifest in many cases where no provision is made for payment of rent."

name of his sister, who was a nurse and working in a hospital. The man himself had been unemployed for two years, and he said that he knew the real estate company would not rent to anyone who was unemployed.[20]

One man, for example, who was at home alone with the children when the investigator called, explained that the first thing a man was asked when he was looking at a flat was: "Are you working?" Therefore his wife must do the flat-hunting, for as soon as he appeared in the middle of the day they immediately and quite properly suspected him of not working. In the few cases where the client had already selected a new flat, he rarely wished to confide the address to the investigator, for fear that in some roundabout way the knowledge might leak through to the new landlord that he was being put out for non-payment of rent. In one case, where the new flat was not to be ready for three or four days, the mother was in great anxiety lest they should be evicted before they could move. But she did not dare betray her anxiety to the new landlord; so she could do nothing to speed up the preparation of the new flat. "The landlords," she said, "now demand references, and they will not take people whose furniture has been set out on the street."

A family who had already moved from one home on court order found themselves again, only six months later, awaiting another writ of restitution in their new flat. The relief office had told the mother that only one month's rent would be paid for them when they got their writ; and the woman claimed that she had been told that when they found a new place they should not tell their prospective landlord that they were receiving relief. The woman was in despair about moving again and "inflicting" herself on another landlord. She told the investigator that she thought it was "positively underhanded" to move into a flat when you knew that you were not going to pay your rent but, on the contrary, you were "going to make the landlord pay to get you out."[21]

[20] The investigator who cleared the bailiff's eviction list from the Renters' Court with the Social Service Exchange thought that an increase in the number of "no records" returned seemed to indicate that more people were renting under false names or under the names of relatives whose employment would bear investigation.

[21] The testimony in the report of the Chicago Church Federation, which has already been referred to, said: "Both the agencies and the clients by their practice refuse to

The situation of the relief families was described by the superintendent of the United Charities, who said: "If some of the families give their new landlords the impression that the relief agency is to pay for their rent, you can hardly blame them, because they are desperate and will do anything to get shelter." He went on to explain that the relief agencies did not, in any manner, "aid, or abet unemployed families in deluding their landlords in this manner."[22] However, by refusing to pay more than the one month's rent, the clients often felt that the agency had placed them in a position where they could only find shelter by "deluding" their landlords.

The continued anxiety in the relief family recurrently face to face with the specter of eviction, the fear that they might be homeless, the dread of being "on the street," and the general family demoralization that inevitably followed the tenement "rent moratorium" can scarcely be exaggerated. Take, for example, the family of eleven children, ranging in age from twenty years down to a few months, who had been in court the middle of June. The family had been given fifteen days in which to move, and by the middle of July were still waiting, expecting to see the bailiffs arrive at any moment. The father was in the Bridewell, and the entire responsibility fell on the mother and the older girls, who seemed to have no idea what they were going to do when the fatal moment arrived. The family was receiving relief but knew that the agency did not pay rents; no one

---

recognize the obligation to pay rent regularly or to pay rent past due. The failure of relief agencies to provide some way for rent to be paid is destroying the sense of obligation that is essential to the maintenance of a society based on a business economy."

[22] Quoted in the *Chicago Daily Tribune*, October 6, 1932.

It is significant that the report of the Family Welfare Association of America, after the investigation of the rent situation which has already been referred to, felt that "the generally evasive attitude which some agencies have felt forced to adopt regarding rent is probably communicating itself to clients and may, if not safeguarded, seem to suggest that this is the only way the client also can meet the situation." It was recognized, of course, that the attitude of both client and agency was dictated by the exigencies of the emergency situation, but suggested that we probably "need to give more thought to the consequences of these attitudes." "Latent resentment," they observe, "toward those who are better off is always crystallized at a time of depression. Moreover, an irresponsible attitude toward the landlord by clients may easily extend itself to a more demanding attitude toward the agency and still further complicate the situation." There is also the influence of the practice on the attitude of the agency itself that cannot be overlooked (Margaret Wead in *The Family*).

had told them that they would receive another notice prior to their eviction. The landlord's lawyer had told them the week before that they had to be out by Sunday as another family was moving in; but no other family appeared on Sunday, nor had they as yet been "put on the street," as they had feared. One of the girls, however, finally was told to go down to the social service office at the Court to find out just what was going to happen to them and what they should do, when the tragic moment arrived and they were "on the street." She said, "You know you can't find flats for eleven children at a moment's notice."

In another family visited, the mother was not well. Her husband was in the penitentiary; and she had the care of her aged mother-in-law, and her two children, aged eleven and fourteen, who were at home. She was very anxious about her two younger children, whom she had sent to relatives in another state to be cared for. An older daughter, unable to bear the chaotic situation at home any longer, had left for parts unknown a month or so before. This family had already moved by court order twice in the preceding nine months and were, at the time of the visit, momentarily expecting a third eviction. This unhappy family appeared again in court for a fourth time, a few months later.

One family in the Renters' Court for a second time was waiting for their "writ" at the time of the investigator's visit. The situation had become so tense that the father had announced that if he did not get a job within the next week (he was a carpenter and had not had a job for over two years) he was going to "clear out"; he "couldn't stand it any longer." The mother, who was panic-stricken at the thought of his leaving her and the three children, said, "I just don't know what has come over him; he was never like that before—you just can't reason with him any more!"

In another family visited after they had been in the Renters' Court, the investigator talked with the distracted mother. Her husband was very ill, suffering from a prolonged and very serious malady; the boy of fourteen was seriously ill, probably dying; she had no light, she had no gas, she had no food; they were going to put her out on the street, and no one would help her; that was the burden of the lament that she repeated over and over again, bursting into uncontrolled weeping again and again. She threatened more than once to turn on the gas and kill the whole family; later in the interview she threatened to smother the baby.

An effort was made to visit families about to be evicted, first, in an effort to help them, because it was feared that many of them might be friendless, and, second, to make sure that no family did, actually, spend the night on the street. It was reassuring to find that this tragedy happened very rarely indeed, so incredibly kind were the relatives, friends, and neighbors about helping those who were literally homeless. Perhaps it was because an eviction was a peculiarly appealing form of distress that those who thought themselves utterly friendless and unknown found, in what seemed the last extremity of distress, neighbors who would take them in for a night or so. When a family was absolutely destitute, or when their relatives had reached the last down step, or when they were on the relief list and were going to be evicted again, then some family almost always appeared who could "take them in." There were many illustrations of the old saying that "only the poor are kind to the poor, and those who have little give to those who have less."

These makeshift arrangements were often extremely uncomfortable for the families, and not infrequently involved either dividing the family up into several sections, each going to a different place, or meant extreme overcrowding. For example, a family who had been receiving relief for about a year and a half were facing their second eviction in two and a half months. At the time of their previous eviction, their furniture had stood on the street two days; and the entire family, including four children, aged from four to eight, had stayed with friends. These friends had a five-room flat, and five children of their own, and were themselves receiving relief. This meant that thirteen human beings lived for those two days in five rooms. A widow who lived alone in a single room had offered to take the entire family of six into her one room for the night, should they need temporary shelter following the present impending eviction.

Another family was unfortunately evicted during the period of their transfer from one agency to another. When they were in process of being transferred, there was a nine-day interval during which the two children stayed with one neighbor, the mother with a second, and the husband with a third, as none of their friends had room enough for the entire family. Their furniture stood loaded on a truck in the street all this time.

The story is told of a family who were evicted on Saturday morning. They were strangers in the neighborhood and appeared to have no friends to whom they could turn. They were not receiving relief; and at nightfall the husband and wife with their children were still on the sidewalk, a very desolate group with no hope of beds for the night. A neighboring landlady, who had a vacant flat in her building, took pity on them and established them in the vacant flat for the night, with the understanding that early Monday morning they would get the relief needed and rent a flat somewhere. But on the following Monday morning the relief agency refused to help on the ground that the family were already established in satisfactory living quarters and could remain there!

Some of the families who appeared more than once in the Renters' Court were visibly shaken by their experiences[23] and attributed all the ills that befell them to the uncertainty of their housing problem. For example, one Renters' Court record was that of a man and his wife with six children under eight years of age, who were evicted in

[23] See the *Chicago Daily News* (June 1, 1932) for the following notes from a reporter who had been listening to eviction cases in the Renters' Court:

" 'My father is in jail and mama is sick,' says a 13-year-old boy, who answers to the next call. 'We can't pay the rent.'

"Records show that the boy is telling the truth and that this is the second time in the last few months that the family of four children and sick mother have been evicted.

" 'Twenty days to find a new place,' the judge rules, 'and see the social workers.'

"The next is a painter by trade. He is a cripple.

" 'How much do you owe?' the judge asks.

" 'Five months, and that's $50. But please don't put us out, your honor. My wife will have another baby in a few days. Please let us stay until after the baby is born, your honor."

LANDLORD POOR, TOO

"The judge turns to the landlord, who himself is in such bad financial condition he is almost on charity. The judge shakes his head in perplexity.

" 'Find another place in fifteen days," is the order.

"The next is a family of four children the youngest two weeks old, evicted four times since last September. The judge gives them ten days to find a new home.

" 'A new home!' the man says bitterly, 'a new eviction!' "

September, 1931, again in March, 1932, and were in court a third time in July, 1932. In the meantime, the children had had first measles and then scarlet fever, and the mother was convinced that their lowered vitality was due in part to their unstable life, although she admitted that in part the poor sanitary condition of their basement flat might also have been a factor in the family health situation.

When the visiting social-work investigator found a family facing eviction with no plans made, apparently without resources, and with no relief agency having any responsibility, an effort was made to connect the family at once with the proper relief station.[24] An occasional relief family was found who had failed to notify the social worker whom they knew at the relief station that the "five-day notice" had been received. Sometimes this happened because the family failed to realize the seriousness of the situation. They could not believe that they would really be "put on the street." Sometimes, however, the head of the family found it almost impossible to see the particular social worker who had charge of his relief because of the rush of work in some of the offices.

The general situation with regard to overcrowding grew very serious. Many families lived in conditions that were really demoralizing. For example, there was the case of a father, mother, and nine children who were occupying three rooms; of a woman sleeping in the same bed with a married couple who were friends, and with the twelve-year-old daughter sleeping on a cot in the same room; of a blind mother with a married daughter and her husband, who had gradually lost their possessions and were using one bed, a three-quarters bed, in a small room although the daughter was ill. In another case a mother was living with her friends, and her three

[24] The great congestion of work at the relief agencies meant that they were often a little slow about these situations that required immediate action. There was also the problem of visits made in the afternoon or on Saturdays; the relief office would be closed for the day, before the client could possibly reach it with his referral card. The best he could do was to go on the following morning; but the following morning was the time set for his eviction. The definite direction to go to a certain place, and the card of introduction, probably did something, however, toward adding to the family's feeling of security. If a relief agency were already responsible for the family, the court worker could only make certain that the agency was informed of the situation and sometimes give the client a card stating the facts for his social worker in the relief office.

boys were sleeping in cars in the garage; a man and his wife and three children were living with other relatives, so that there were nineteen people all living in four rooms.

THE PLIGHT OF THE LANDLORDS

With regard to the situation of the landlords, they were entirely right in thinking that shelter was one of the primary family needs and that if the grocery stores were to be paid, the gas company paid, the milk companies paid, the fuel companies paid, and the clothing and shoe companies paid, it was only fair that the landlords should also be paid. Certainly it was very unfair to the tenement landlords to compel them to furnish a free shelter for destitute families whose other necessities were met out of public funds.[25]

[25] The following extract from the "Brief" submitted by a Committee of the Landlord's Association for Rent Relief in connection with an emergency relief hearing at the city hall, October 9, 1933, shows the bitter resentment of the landlords to the relief rent policy:

"We have come to this hearing today to tell you of the plight of the landlord who has been housing clients of the Illinois Emergency Relief. We want to acquaint you with the serious injustice that has been perpetrated on us by the I.E.R. through their rent policy and the disastrous effect this policy has had upon the property owner in districts served by relief agencies.

"We also seek your aid in stopping this abuse in the future and also seek your counsel on how these inequities can in some measure be rectified.

"I. The rent policy of the I.E.R. has been in effect confiscation of Real Property perpetrated by subterfuge on the part of the relief worker against people of little means. The property owners in the poor districts were forced under the policy of the I.E.R. to house 200,000 families on relief rolls without compensation.

"1. 'Pay no rent except in case of emergency'; let the landlord carry the load. When he gets weary of carrying it put him to the expense of hiring lawyers and paying court costs and eviction fees. He may not have the money to carry on this expensive legal process and so you may retain his property indefinitely.

"2. Relief workers instructed clients to disregard Five Day Notices—clients taken to court and given time to vacate—still instructed to retain possession—even the Writ of Restitution was not regarded as emergency. At this point the worker might contact the landlord with a proposition that the landlord pay the cost of eviction to the client and the relief would advance the additional amount necessary to find new quarters.

"*a*) The Landlord has received $15.00 for one month's rent. He has spent $10.00 for court costs and attorney fees—lost about four months' rent and is faced with the choice of paying the Bailiff $20.00 for actual eviction or give his tenant $10.00 in order to regain possession of his property.

"*b*) The Charities endeavored to get as much time as possible from the court for their clients.

[Footnote continued on facing page]

When some of the tenement landlords became destitute and applied for aid, the agencies in some cases put them on the relief rolls instead of changing the rent policy. One woman who had owned some good flats that were either empty or had got relief tenants finally applied for relief herself when the bank in which she had a savings deposit had failed. "After all," she said, "I suppose I cannot eat brick and mortar, and if the relief agencies would rather give me relief food instead of paying the rents of the families they have in my houses, they can send in their rations."[26]

One landlord's representative who obtained writs of restitution against fifteen families in one building claimed that the families were all placed in his building by a relief society and were nearly a year in arrears. He said, "If the relief service would pay me every other month I would keep them all winter." "After these families are evicted," he said, "the Relief Commission will pay about $15 a family for rent in new quarters. Why not pay the $15 on what they owe in their present quarters so they need not be evicted?"[27] he asked.

Many cases were found, however, where both the landlord and the tenant were receiving relief,[28] and there are even cases to be found

---

"*c*) The Charities contacted the Courts and Bailiff's office to stay evictions and secure information when money for eviction was posted by landlord.

"3. Clients were given cash with which to rent flats so that their identity with Relief Agencies could be concealed. In this way a Great Sovereign State through its agency was taking advantage of poor property owners and hasten the time when the property would be taken away from them by Tax Forfeiture and Foreclosure.

"4. Property owners, deprived of income from their properties by this policy, were reduced to beg for charity from these same Relief Agencies."

[26] This woman owned three buildings, containing eleven flats. Four of them were vacant, and five of the seven tenants were receiving relief—three from the Unemployment Relief Service and two from the United Charities. The other two tenants were paying something like a dollar or so at very irregular intervals. The woman's husband was long since dead, and her grown son had been out of work for two years. Their little savings were lost when a bank closed. The woman's taxes were two years in arrears, her water tax was unpaid, and she herself was applying for relief.

[27] See *Chicago Daily News*, December 12, 1932.

[28] The files of one of the important private agencies to which the investigator had access contained cases of many landlords whose tenants were clients of Unemployment Relief Service. No cases were found where the landlord and tenant were both receiving relief from the same agency.

where one charity client evicted another for non-payment of rent. A well-known example is that of one agency representative who telephoned the Social Service of the Renters' Court to find out if it would not be possible for one of their clients to evict his tenant, and, under the circumstances, to escape the eviction costs by a pauper's writ. It developed that the tenant they wished to evict was a client of another relief agency in the city.

A representative of one of the large relief agencies, who did not attempt to justify the no-rent policy, said they did not pay rents because they could "get by" without paying the landlords and they did not have funds to pay for everything.[29] But the plight of the small landlords sometimes became very tragic. Their chief source of income—sometimes their entire income—was not only shut off but they were helpless to get the delinquent tenants out of their flat buildings without actually paying out more money than they could afford for the eviction costs.

The landlords became full of resentment against the relief agencies and the social workers. As a matter of fact, the hostility to social workers was not justified, for professional social workers were unanimous in their demand that more adequate relief funds must be made available and that rents must be paid.[30] But the landlords became convinced that the social workers were in league against them[31] and

[29] The Family Welfare Association report notes that the reason given for this attitude was that the client, by occupying a house, is not using up the landlord's capital, as he would be in consuming a commodity like food. "The more or less helpless condition of many landlords," it was pointed out, "makes it easy for both client and agency to drift into such practices" (Wead, *The Family*, XII, 315).

[30] The attitude of the social workers on the subject of rents is indicated by the following resolution passed unanimously by the Chicago Chapter of the American Association of Social Workers in the spring of 1933.

"The American Association of Social Workers earnestly request the Illinois Relief Commission to review again its policy with regard to the non-payment of rents. We believe that a serious condition is being created as a result of the great distress of the people who have been living so long in constant fear of eviction, the great over-crowding in many tenements, the very real suffering of the tenement landlords, the menace to public safety and public health as a result of the turning off of the water-supply and light in many tenements. The Relief Commission is urgently requested to make some plan for modifying the present situation."

[31] The following statement from the "Brief" submitted by the Committee of the Landlord's Association for Rent Relief, to which reference has already been made (see

were responsible for the fact that they could no longer even obtain what they called "justice in the courts." One landlord who represented a real estate company that sold houses on contract said that the landlords carried the home purchasers who were not keeping up their payments just as long as possible—gave them every "break" they could; finally, when they could no longer go on in this way and went to court, what happened? The judge, owing to pressure from the social agencies, continued the case, and then he continued it again, and then he extended the time, and extended it again and again. "All the landlords want," this representative of the group said emphatically, "is justice." As a result of this policy, he declared "from now on the landlords are not going to give the people any 'breaks'; the first month they cannot meet their payments we are going to 'clamp right down.' " He pictured the poor landlord, regarded as the "villain in the piece" at the time of the eviction, when he was in reality "just a poor man trying to earn an honest living." "We aren't the 'villyuns,' " he repeated over and over again. "We're doing good!" "You have to consider our part," he continued. "We pay our taxes, we have to pay the mortgages—when the mortgages come due; the person collecting doesn't wait if we can't pay it right then; when the persons in the house don't pay their gas and electric and water bills, it all falls back on the landlords." "We shouldn't be punished; we're doing good!" This landlord was particularly

---

n. 25), shows the attitude of the landlords to the social workers who were, inevitably perhaps, held responsible for this mistaken policy, although they were acting under orders:

"The prestige and standing of the Social Worker in the Community was reduced to a very low level as a result of this policy.

"1. They coached and encouraged their clients to deceive the landlords which in turn encouraged the client to deceive the Social Worker. 'Don't rent a flat from "A" because he can afford to bring suit if the rent isn't paid; rent from a small owner who won't have the money to spend for eviction.'

"2. The relief worker taught clients to disregard Private Property Rights upon which our American Institutions are based. (From free shelter against the will of the landlord to free food and clothing against the will of the owner of these commodities is but a logical step in the mental process of their clients.)

"3. By not co-operating with the landlord they missed a point of contact in the community that would have been valuable to them. (Landlords usually best qualified to give information of people in the community and had an interest to keep relief expenses down because of its effect on taxes.)"

eloquent on the subject because he had just paid $32 to get a tenant evicted; and there was a "good deal of justice" in his argument.

One landlord who was trying to evict a tenant became indignant when the judge, after several continuances, gave the family a rather long time in which to move; the landlord's lawyer in this case even threatened to mandamus the judge. When the court order was at last secured and it appeared that the relief agency involved would not move the family until the landlord had paid the eviction costs, he was still more angry and charged that an agency to which he had made large contributions for years was working against him.

As a matter of fact, many landlords were left to suffer indefinitely with large arrears in rent and all hope of collection receding day by day. Unable to meet the interest charges due on mortgages, foreclosures came and went, leaving the former landlord a tenant.[32]

Many of the victimized landlords belonged to the small-property

[32] No study of the special difficulties of landlords was made in Chicago, but they were undoubtedly very great. The Philadelphia study (*No Money for Rent*, p. 10) reports that in that city "about three in every five landlords were pursuing a policy of eviction. . . . . In the Spring of 1933 removals by compulsion were running at the rate of about 16 per cent per year, that is, one family in every six was being forced out of its home under pressure from the landlord."

This report showed that there were 60,000 families who were receiving relief from the Philadelphia County Relief Board during the month of February, 1933, and that this number increased to more than 70,000 in the following months. "Assuming that the February Relief Families were typical of these families, it is possible to make the following estimates: (1) 80 per cent of all families receiving relief in the spring of 1933 were renters (excluding owners and those living rent free), (2) the proportion of renting families actually in arrears was about 90 per cent, and (3) the average arrearage per family on relief was about $100. Applying these figures to the approximately 70,000 families on relief in the spring of 1933, we arrive at an estimate of more than $5,000,000. In other words, this figure would represent the amount owed the landlords for rent by families on relief at that time.

"Nor is this the whole story. The great majority of these families also owed money to previous landlords. It was found that families now receiving relief were moving about once a year. . . . . The indications are that this rate of movement has been greatly accentuated in the later stages of the depression, but there has undoubtedly been considerable movement ever since the depression began. Accordingly, it is obvious that the present indebtedness to present landlords is only a part of the total indebtedness which has been accumulated during the depression. The total figure owed by the families now receiving relief must, conservatively estimated, be several times $5,000,000.

"No account has been taken of the rent indebtedness of families not receiving relief. This phase of the problem is taken up in the present study in connection with the landlords' problems" (*ibid.*, pp. 33–34).

group to whom a few non-paying tenants meant not paying the interest on the mortgage and losing the property. The smaller landlords seemed to be "caught" more often with "relief tenants" than were the larger landlords, who seemed to know better how to guard against such tenants.[33] A representative of one of the large South Side real estate organizations said that his company kept out the "charity people" by making "every prospective tenant fill out an application blank, giving the places of his present and past employment and certain other data that the company verified before it would rent him a flat." Under no circumstances would this company rent a flat without investigating the prospective tenant's situation with regard to relief. This same representative said that he had found the number of people securing leases under false names increasing, and told of a number of cases where the work record of a prospective tenant had been verified and all seemed well, but after the rent payments had stopped, they found that the man employed and the tenant were two different persons.

The plight of some of the smaller landlords may be illustrated by the story of a woman who came into court about her tenants. Her husband had left her four flat buildings, believing he had provided an income for her for the rest of her life. Two of these buildings, which were located on one lot, included between them three flats, each of which normally rented at $15 a month, later reduced to $12. Except for one payment of $25 made two years ago, when a veteran occupying one of them received a bonus, the owner had not collected any rent from any one of these three flats for three years. On another nearby street she owned two other buildings, also on the same lot, each containing two flats. In normal times she collected $40 a month from the front flats, and $22.50 from the rear flats. One tenant had occupied a rear flat here a year and a half and paid, in all, $10. Another had lived there nearly two years, and paid a total of

[33] The investigator at the Renters' Court reported that a lawyer representing one of the landlords' bureaus made the statement that his cases, along with those of the other bureaus and associations, had increased only 10 or 15 per cent; that the rest of the increase in cases in court was due to non-lawyer cases. On the whole, the non-lawyer cases were those of the small property-holders; the larger landlords usually had lawyers, or had their property in the hands of real estate companies whose lawyers took care of the court work.

$30—and that at the beginning of his tenancy. Another paid $45 during the first three months of a two-year tenancy and had paid nothing since. Both of these last families were "relief clients" and, according to the woman landlord, were moved in by two relief agencies. She was very bitter toward the relief organizations which began paying rent for families and then stopped. The fourth family occupying these flats paid $16 for one month's rent when they moved in two years ago, and they had paid nothing since.

The woman said that she was positively ashamed of all of her buildings because they were in such poor repair, but that she could not afford to have them fixed. A few years ago she had spent $175 to repair a porch on one of them, and now one of the families had chopped it up for fuel.[34] This woman reported further that her taxes amounted to $150 a year, her insurance to $135 a year, and her water tax to $19 twice a year. The last year she had borrowed from a personal-loan company to pay the taxes and expected to have the loan repaid just in time to secure another loan for this year's taxes. Accustomed all her life to reasonably comfortable surroundings, her resources were exhausted, and she was then living from hand to mouth with the help of friends. However, she felt that she was more fortunate than many, for her property was not mortgaged.

HOUSING DETERIORATION

A third result of the no-rent policy was a lowering of housing standards. A great deal of illegal overcrowding was the result of the moving in with relatives or friends by families who had been evicted or who feared eviction. Flat buildings that used to have six families in them, three on each side, came to have two, three, and even four or five families in each flat; many normal six-family flat buildings had anywhere from twelve to twenty-four families as tenants or subtenants.

Great areas of kitchenettes seemed to spring up like mushrooms—flat buildings with once good, even fine, apartments made over into

[34] In illustration of some of the more remote effects of the non-payment of rent, a further observation of this woman landlord is of interest. The real estate agent who handled her property for her used to collect $50,000 a month in rents, of which he received a small percentage. At the time of her story he was collecting only $1,000 in a month at the same rate, and was not able then even to employ a stenographer.

furnished rooms and kitchenettes with a corresponding increase in the number of families in the building. There would be several families using the same kitchen, the same utensils, and the same bathroom, with the inevitable disorder and general lack of cleanliness. No one was responsible any longer for the cleanliness or repair of either the common bathroom, kitchen, or hall. No one was responsible for cleaning the halls or stairways or disposing of garbage. When a pipe burst or a window broke or a stairway railing was broken, the landlord would do nothing about it on the ground that he could not afford to keep things in repair when he was getting no income from the property; and the tenants of course had no money to pay for anything. It was almost as if no one cared any longer about the old decencies of life. When people were face to face with the need of such primary necessities as food and fuel, things like dishes or decent bathrooms seemed less important. There were flat buildings that were once very respectable indeed, where everything had become filthy and there were no funds to pay for any kind of upkeep. Conditions became insanitary and often degrading. The modern conveniences of life disappeared. Kerosene lamps were used for electric lights; garbage-burners were used for stoves.

Gradually the plumbing became unfit to use. Houses planned for central furnace heat were heated by stoves when there were no chimneys in the rooms where the stove was placed. Some families without even stoves burned a little coal in an old gas grate from which the fixture was removed. It was dangerous as well as uncomfortable because of smoke and lack of warmth. Stairways became dangerous, halls were no longer lighted and were filthy. Plastering fell off and was not replaced. Rats became a serious problem. Families living in basements hung their food on strings as the least expensive way to protect it from the rats.

The relief agencies paid very few gas and electric bills. In more than half of the dwellings visited, the gas and electricity had been cut off. How long the family had been without these necessities of life it was not easy to find out, as the person interviewed often did not know. When it was more than a matter of a few weeks, no one seemed to be able to remember. The schedule merely reported that the gas and electricity had been off "a long time," or "never on," or "since moved," and other similar expressions. These families had, of course, been accustomed to the use of gas and electricity, and it was interesting that some women said that they did not miss electricity so much for the lights as they did for the ironing, as they had no way to iron their children's dresses for school. Kerosene lamps were everywhere in use as a common substiturte for the once familiar electric lights.

The families who were without gas used various methods of cooking. About a third of the families had coal ranges; others had "coal heaters," garbage-burners, electric plates, charcoal; one used kerosene and one a gasoline stove. Two of those who used heaters had stoves without any flat surface on them at all to use for kettles; consequently, they were forced to set their cooking pans and kettles inside the stove, directly on the coals. Those who used charcoal got an old bucket from the grocer, punched some holes in it to make the proper drafts, put the charcoal inside, and laid a wire coat-hanger over the top to set the pans on. One of these buckets looked very strange, indeed, sitting on the top of a modern and expensive-looking gas range but with the gas shut off. Another was seen on the bare floor in the middle of a kitchen, with no other stove or cooking apparatus of any description. One family recorded as having no means of cooking had been accustomed to quite high standards of living, occupying a $40-a-month apartment. Their gas had been off a week, and in all that time they had not been able to prepare anything hot to eat.

The halls of once comfortable flat buildings were not only filthy and dark but they were also frigid because the furnaces were no longer used. The flats were cold, and the old gas grates were sometimes torn to pieces so that they could be used for coal, in spite of the fact that there were no proper chimneys. The rooms became incredibly smoked and dirty as a result. There was general deterioration and large numbers of houses gradually sank to the level of those "unfit for human habitation."

Attention should be called to the fact that a large proportion of the people of the tenements, even in normal times, live without the conveniences of modern life—without electricity, without bath rooms, without proper toilet facilities, without central or furnace heating.[35] Lack of proper sanitary arrangements and modern comforts was, of course, greatly aggravated during the depression years as an inevitable consequence of the no-rent or inadequate-rent policies set up for relief families. Landlords who were getting no rents would not make repairs. Plumbing that was out of order just remained out of order. Janitor service was withdrawn from what had once been very good flat buildings. The resentment of the landlords over what they considered very unfair treatment by the relief agencies was expressed in the general neglect of their buildings. Tenants who were visited during the Renters' Court study complained of water standing in the basements; and in one home the plumber who happened to arrive while the court worker was present said that a pipe must have burst somewhere, and that the water must be shut off from the entire building until all that was standing in the basement drained away. But the water had been standing there almost two feet deep for nearly two months. The mother in this family was in the Municipal Tuberculosis Sanitarium; one of the children was in the fresh-air room at school; and the other two children were very delicate. In this same flat, the drain to the kitchen sink had been stopped up for two months, and the waste water was caught in a tub on the floor. Something was also wrong with the plumbing in the toilet, so that the floor there was always damp.

Another Renters' Court family complained that the toilet had not flushed properly for more than a year; water was carried to the toilet from the sink, and the leaking condition of the toilet kept the floor of that room and the adjoining kitchen continually wet and disorderly. In still another Renters' Court flat, the toilet leaked so badly that all the floor boards around it were rotted and loose. In a Renters' Court flat in an old frame building not far from Hull-House, the door to the toilet was padlocked, and a sign on it read, "Do not use this toilet by order of the Board of Health." A representative of the Board of Health explained that the Board had not posted such a notice, and thought it had been put up by the landlord himself. The tenant, who had lived there five months, said the

[35] See *supra*, chap. vi, "Tenement Dwellers without the Conveniences of Modern Life."

sign had been there when she first moved in and that the landlord had promised to fix the toilet but had never done so. In general, there were many indications of the well-known fact that landlords were putting no money into repairs.

In one apartment building the janitor had not been giving any services whatsoever in the building for some time. The greater part of the basement was in an abominable condition. No floor—only the dirt, and there were small puddles of water in numerous places. The exterior of the furnace and its pipes showed need of repair and one of the tenants living in the building remarked that even though sufficient coal were placed there, satisfactory heat would not be given because of the condition of the furnace.

By 1933 an increasing number of property-owners were applying for relief. Some of them were glad to let clients use their flats if the agency would furnish heat, gas, and light in place of rent. The social workers made many ingenious arrangements by supplying coal and paying gas and light bills in exchange for the accommodation of clients—a kind of indirect payment of rent.

Another situation that developed was the use on a practically rent-free basis of certain buildings that had fallen into extremely bad repair. One of the best known of these buildings was the old hotel on the South Side that had come to be known as the "Angelus Building," a building regarded by many as a serious fire hazard, which became a popular shelter not only for relief families but for others who were partially self-sustaining but who were not able to pay rent.

THE ANGELUS

The so-called Angelus Building,[36] on the Near South Side in what is often referred to as the "Black Belt," served as an almost spectacular example of the depths to which Chicago's housing standards had fallen. Here, in a seven-story building, erected on the eve of the World's Fair of 1893 as the "Ozark Hotel" and operated during the Fair as one of the popular hotels in the part of the city where the Fair was located, were gathered, as if in honor of the second World's

[36] Obligations are acknowledged to Mrs. Sophia Boaz Pitts for many data about the families in this building. Mrs. Pitts, a former student and a veteran social worker, served as a secretary of the so-called "Angelus Guild."

Fair of 1933, the most forlorn and destitute of all of Chicago's great population of hungry and miserable people. Visiting this building in early June, going from floor to floor and through one dark hall after another, searchlight in hand, one could only think of Dickens and places like Tom-All-Alone's in London in the middle of the nineteenth century; and it became necessary to remind one's self often that this was the twentieth century in one of the greatest and wealthiest cities of the world.

In this seven-story Angelus there were 206 persons, 67 families with 118 children under sixteen years of age. No longer furnace-heated, during the Chicago winter of 1931–32 the families were for the most part trying to wring a little warmth out of the bits of relief fuel they were able to secure. On some days there was no heat in the building at all, and on all the winter days there was not enough heat to warm the poorly clad people who clung to it because they had no other shelter. Families getting coal from the Cook County Bureau of Public Welfare or the United Charities of Chicago were burning their coal in gas grates or in charcoal bucket-stoves. Electric lights were, for the most part, turned off and tenants were using kerosene lamps.

So miserable was the building that the people were most of them sheltered "rent-free" after being evicted from their old homes. Some families, however, still had "bits of jobs" and "bits of relief" and, anxious to preserve their self-respect, paid from two to four dollars a week—"whenever they had it to spare." Here, huddled in discomfort during the winter months of 1932–33, were 12 families carried on the relief lists of Cook County, 12 families carried on the Illinois Unemployment Relief Service, 11 carried by the United Charities of Chicago, and 3 by other organizations. Although so many of the families were assisted by what is called a "recognized social agency," no agency would take over the management of the wretched building and heat it properly. But coal was given to one Angelus family after another on the various relief lists; and the unfortunate unemployed man or woman carried the coal to his miserable quarters up one flight after another, put it under the kitchen sink or in the once usable bathroom, now useful as a coal shed, and then sparingly burned his allotment of warmth in an old gas grate or coal stove in the near darkness.

The bathrooms became coal sheds, not because poor Negro families did not want bath tubs or did not know how to use them, but because the flow of water in the old building was at first very slow and hot water was never available anywhere except for a short time when one enterprising Negro tenant collected twenty-five cents from various apartments to buy coal to operate the hot-water apparatus on Saturday night for weekly baths. But as the families could not go on paying twenty-five cents, this was soon discontinued. Worse than that, the water was finally shut off entirely and the visitor saw, one day, a tenant on his way to the fifth floor with a ten-gallon hogshead of water on his back. He had got the water nearly a block away.

But the old Angelus remained a shelter during the bitter "no rent" years of 1931–33 in spite of its dark and cheerless flats with windows only on the interior court, in spite of the extreme discomfort of being without water, in spite of kerosene lamps, and in spite of stoves that were only garbage-burners. The tenants were in danger of fire, but they were no longer in danger of eviction. The five-day notices they once dreaded and the more dreaded twenty-four-hour notices were no longer feared. Security of a kind was at last within reach, even if it was only security in semidarkness and cold.

Other old places were used, like the Angelus, rent free. Some clients of the relief agencies were very resourceful about reconditioning old garages, basement rooms, and attics that had long been unused which were sometimes offered on a rent-free basis if the prospective occupant would "fix them up." For example, what was formerly a carriage house, standing in the rear of a large lot, was used as a tenement. The woman who owned the premises permitted "unemployment relief families" to live in this carriage house for almost two years practically on rent-free terms. The walls in this apartment were typical of all the apartments, if they may be so described; there was no plaster or wallpaper; there were chinks in the wall through which daylight could be seen; and the floors had settled so that they had become uneven in places. There was no foundation, the wood floors resting merely on the ground. There was neither gas nor electricity in the building; all families were using kerosene for light; the running water was cold at all times. The entrance to the second floor was by a rickety outside stairway. During the winter the pipes froze and for several weeks the families who belonged to the Relief Station had to carry their water from the house in front.

A man and his wife, who were relief clients, lived with their two children and the wife's mother and brother in three rooms on the first floor. The windows, according to the wife, could not be raised and the only ventilation came from a door which opened into a hallway, on either end of which were doors opening to the outside. Another relief family with one child occupied the other half of the first floor.

One relief family with three children, aged nine, seven, and ten, were living on the second floor of a very old frame building in a queer kind of arrangement. There were five rooms, including two large and well-ventilated front bedrooms, one of which was used by the husband and wife in the relief family, and the other was used by the landlady and her children. In the same building behind these two rooms was the kitchen, with a large coal stove which constantly smoked; and the only ventilation in the room was by opening the door leading onto the second-floor hallway. Behind this kitchen were two tiny bedrooms, one occupied by three of the children and the other by another child of the landlady. Neither of these rooms had any ventilation at all.

One relief family consisting of a man and his wife, together with three sons, aged twenty-two, eighteen, and twelve, occupied the rear of a store in a very old frame building which was very cold in the winter. They had three rooms, including a large kitchen which had two windows that did not open and which was ventilated only by the kitchen door. The bedroom in which the three boys slept was walled off from the kitchen and had no windows at all. Back of the kitchen was a second large room where the mother slept and where again there was no ventilation. There was no gas or electricity, so they had an old coal stove and used kerosene lamps.

A relief family with two children was living on the first floor in a very old and ramshackle frame house. The water pipes froze in December and when the family were visited in May they said they had been carrying water from the second floor for five months. Their lights were off and they were using two kerosene lamps. In their living-room was a cot, occupied by the older child. There were no windows in the room. The bedroom, which was occupied by the man and his wife with a crib for the baby, also had no windows. The kitchen had two large windows, and the door leading from the kitchen to the living-room gave some ventilation to the latter room when either the kitchen windows or the kitchen door was open.

A very old five-story flat building was not unlike the Angelus in that it housed a large number of rentless relief families. In the winter of 1932–33 there were twenty-nine relief families living there. Owing to the fact that no rents had been paid by any of the families in the building for almost two years, it was in a very "run-down" condition. The majority of the families were using kerosene for lighting, and the social worker thought that there was grave danger of fire. The hallways up the five stories might almost be called "ramshackle," and they were very far from clean. Everyone said that if a fire started in the building the families living on the upper floors could probably not have escaped. Almost three-fourths of the families living there had children, the majority of them quite young.

One family lived in the rear of a grocery store where they had no rent to pay. The basement contained about two feet of water, and rats were a serious problem. A family of five lived in a dilapidated house located at the rear of an apartment building. There was almost no furniture. There were no electric lights and the water was cut off. Two families, one with five children and the other with two, were living in a flat located on the top floor of a rear building. The entrance was off an open stairway which was not very secure. The water was cut off by the landlord. The lights were off, the place was dark and gloomy, rats were around in the halls, and there was a general condition of decayed misery.

Another very wretched makeshift housing arrangement was that of a man and his wife with five small children and an aged mother, who lived in a three-room flat poorly furnished on the top floor of another ramshackle tenement. The only light on the stairway came through a cobwebbed skylight on the roof. Water had been shut off in the entire building and the family had to go two blocks for water. In spite of the living conditions, the family felt that they had a kind of security remaining there which they would not jeopardize by moving into a more sanitary place.

RENT IN THE RELIEF BUDGET

The percentage of the relief budget that went for rent decreased sharply in 1932. In the United Charities, the large private relief society, 27.7 per cent of the relief expenditures in the year 1928 were

TABLE 84

RELIEF EXPENDITURES BY THE UNITED CHARITIES, 1928–33
(Per Cent Distribution)

Type of Relief	1928	1929	1930	1931	1932	1933
Total: Amount expended	$265,905	$292,771	$514,235	$4,204,383	$3,813,617	$1,359,287
Total: Per cent	100.0	100.0	100.0	100.0	100.0	100.0
Food	29.2	27.4	30.9	55.3	73.9	54.8
Rent	27.7	28.0	28.5	19.9	7.6*	11.6
Fuel	11.1	10.0	13.4	8.0	7.8	9.1
Cash grants	21.7	23.6	19.4	10.6	2.0	7.3
Special work	1.4	1.1	1.6	3.4	3.5	7.0
Clothing and household furnishings	2.4	2.7	1.5	0.8	3.6	6.7
Miscellaneous	6.5	7.2	4.7	2.0	1.6	3.5

* The corresponding per cent distribution for the first three months of 1932 showed that the percentage spent for rent was only 3.4 per cent, a very sharp decline as compared with the preceding years. However, as the percentage based on the yearly totals indicates, the United Charities was able to begin some rent payments again, long before the public agencies were authorized to adopt such a policy.

for rent, but the percentage fell to 19.9 in 1931, and to 3.4 in the first three months of 1932. In the Jewish Social Service Bureau, which showed 28.1 per cent of its relief expenditures going for rent in 1928, the decline was less marked, with 19.5 per cent for rent in the first three months of 1932.[37]

Expenditures by type of relief are available for the entire period of

[37] See *The Social Service Year Book, 1932*, published by the Council of Social Agencies of Chicago, in which is given (p. 32) a brief statement regarding the payment of rent by the Chicago relief agencies, indicating that before the depression the Jewish Social Service Bureau, as well as the United Charities, devoted a little more than one-fourth of their relief expenditures to rent.

1928–33 for the United Charities, and the per cent distribution in Table 84 shows the proportionate expenditures for rent during these years.

The percentage of the relief expenditures that went for rent in the Unemployment Relief Service is shown in Table 85. Expenditures for rent almost disappeared, as Table 85 clearly shows, in the years 1932 and 1933. In view of the conflict that some observers

TABLE 85

RELIEF EXPENDITURES OF THE UNEMPLOYMENT RELIEF SERVICE, 1932–33

(Per Cent Distribution)

Type of Relief	December, 1931	1932*	1933
Total: Amount expended	$ 560,065	$20,646,662	$32,650,780
Total: Per cent	100.0	100.0	100.0
Food	52.5	89.2	77.3
Rent	27.9	1.1	1.6
Fuel	18.5	6.7	7.1
Cash grants	....	....	....
Special work	....	0.2	6.7
Clothing and household furnishings	0.6	2.4	5.2
Miscellaneous	0.5	0.4	2.1

* This Service, which was organized late in 1931, was carried under the name of the Joint Emergency Relief stations until March 31, 1932, when it was taken over as the Unemployment Relief Service of the Illinois Emergency Relief Commission and became entirely a public agency. The stations had been receiving state funds for some weeks before this change.

insist upon seeing between methods of work of public and private agencies, it is important to note that the Unemployment Relief Service was a private agency when the decision not to pay rent was first made, and the percentage of the relief expenditure that went for rent in this Service had fallen sharply from 27.9 in December to 1.1 in January, 1932, when this was still a private agency.

It is important in considering the problem of relief to understand that the great rent disaster visited on relief clients during the early period of the depression was not one of the consequences of the system of public relief. But this volume is a study of Chicago tenement conditions and, as far as the housing problem is concerned, the question whether public or private agencies were responsible for the "no rent" policy is a question of no importance.

We are concerned here with the disastrous results of this policy and not with the question as to which group of social agencies set it in motion. There can be no question of the serious consequences of this policy to the families, the injustice to the landlords, and the deterioration of the tenements which were, in many cases, virtually commandeered for the use of relief clients.

CHAPTER XVI

THE LONG FUTURE: SOME CONCLUSIONS AND SUGGESTIONS

Some Improvements in Chicago Tenement Neighborhoods; But Slums Remain Slums; Difficulties of Enforcing the Tenement-House Code; Low Wages and Low Incomes the Basic Difficulty; Demolition of Abandoned, Insanitary, and Condemned Houses; Bad Housing and the Demoralization of Family Life; Four Lines of Attack Necessary: (1) New Building on Vacant Land; (2) New Building To Accompany Slum Clearance; (3) Enforcement of Tenement-House Laws; (4) Repair and Reconditioning of Old Houses; Private Housing Programs Inadequate; Federal Aid.

TWENTY-FIVE years have passed since our School of Social Service began its first studies of housing conditions in Chicago. These studies were begun with enthusiasm in the hope that our new research department[1] might be able to help promote the cause of housing reform in Chicago by making public the facts about tenement homes. Publication was begun in serial form[2] of the findings of the house-to-house canvassing in tenement areas in different sections of the city. But gradually it became clear to our group of social investigators that the housing problem was almost as immovable as the Sphinx. The need for decent housing seemed at that time one of the first necessities of the vast numbers of men, women, and children crowded in airless, sunless rooms upon whom the serious consequences of insanitary, uncomfortable living conditions were visited. Difficulties of all kinds appeared in opposition to the enforcement of the tenement-house laws, and to any change in home construction or to plans for diminishing overcrowding in the poor streets. Those interested in city planning were apparently not interested in tenement areas. Housing reform, it appeared, was faced by questions of

[1] This early experiment in social research was supported by the Russell Sage Foundation of New York through one of the grants made to the three pioneer schools of social work in New York, Chicago, and Boston to encourage social research in the new professional schools.

[2] See above, chap. iii, pp. 73–77, for purpose and method of these studies.

speculative landownership and development, by the problem of "supporting insupportable land values." There was prolonged, persistent opposition on the part of tenement landlords and their friends to any vigorous regulation of tenement evils.

But during the years since these studies were first planned, which included the period of the war, some far-reaching changes, which have been part of the onward rush of life in a great city and a great nation, have brought some improvements in housing conditions, even in slum areas. And, in recent years, the development of new municipal, state, and, finally, federal housing authorities, have led to a new housing reform movement, and, more recently, to a few "isolated spots of improved dwellings."

SOME IMPROVEMENTS IN CHICAGO TENEMENT NEIGHBORHOODS

The improvements that have taken place in the tenement-house districts in Chicago in the last quarter of a century have not come as a result of the clearance of slum areas, nor can they be credited to any important changes, nor to any important improvements in the tenement ordinances of Chicago, nor to the enforcement of these ordinances. The most important change, which has already been mentioned, has come in the environment of the tenement areas as an incidental result of the substitution of motor vehicles for the old horse-drawn trucks, wagons, carts, and carriages, with the resulting improvements in the sanitary condition of streets and alleys.

The tenement areas have also benefited in some measure from the improvements which the general progress of invention has brought to the modern home—the use of gas, electric lights, better plumbing, central heat, and other household conveniences now regarded in areas of comfortable living as household necessities. While these benefits have been greatly retarded in reaching the neglected areas of Chicago, nevertheless some of these great improvements have been slowly extended to many of the tenement homes, even in the most deteriorated sections of the city.

Along with the disappearance of the horse from the Chicago streets went the filthy stables and the dreadful manure heaps that accumulated in the alleys of the tenement districts. "The alleys were unspeakably filthy and disgusting," wrote the investigator for

Dr. Theodore Sachs, the great Chicago physician who did such fine constructive work to provide proper care for tenement sufferers from tuberculosis. ". . . . Many little stables open on the alleys where manure heaps accumulate and piles of garbage, making them as noisome and insanitary as a city refuse heap."[3] While it is true that, even today, the alleys are still "disgusting" in many areas, it is also true that even the filthy alleys have been less filthy since the horses and stables have gone.

The disappearance of the stables not only meant an improvement of sanitary conditions through the disappearance of manure heaps from the alleys, but along with this change for the better has come a great improvement in the disgraceful condition of the streets, which are the playgrounds of the children in the tenement districts. Easily cleansed macadamized pavements have often been substituted for the old brick, cedar-block, and other kinds of paving less easy to keep in any reasonable state of cleanliness.

Another beneficial change came when the widespread use of the motor car led to the opening-up, widening, and repaving of many formerly little-used streets through dreary sections that were in an earlier day rarely seen or seldom used by the well-to-do. The result of the opening of these streets and of their more frequent use has been that the tenements seem less separate from, less apart from, the life of the city than they were before the development of new traffic arteries through relatively submerged districts. This has meant a great improvement in the general cleanliness of the streets as well as an improvement in the appearance of whole neighborhoods. There are better and cleaner sidewalks. Tenement areas have also been greatly improved during the present century by the opening of more and better parks and playgrounds. While this has not been as important as the changes in streets and alleys, the parks have nevertheless brought a new and cheerful atmosphere to some of these neglected sections.

Still another important change for the better has come, first through the suspension of immigration during the war and later through the enactment of the rigid exclusionist laws, the quota and per centum limitation acts. The changes in the immigration situa-

[3] See Dr. Theodore B. Sachs and Dr. Alice Hamilton, *Study of Tuberculosis in Chicago* (City Homes Association, 1905).

DILAPIDATED DWELLINGS

tion affected housing conditions by reducing the number of new residents who belonged to the non-English-speaking groups. These strange, bewildered, and usually friendless people felt the necessity, in the old days, of crowding into areas where their countrymen happened to live. The housing problem at the present day is much less complicated by the problem of lodgers than in the days when every industrial neighborhood was crowded with immigrants who had only just arrived and who were temporarily staying with *Landsleute*.[4]

BUT SLUMS REMAIN SLUMS

But in spite of the gradual improvements which the passing years have brought in the tenement areas, great masses of people still live in very miserable homes and in conditions of almost unbelievable discomfort for this modern period—without the accepted conveniences of modern life, without bathrooms, without a single private toilet for family use, with broken and frozen plumbing, occasionally without a sink, sometimes sleeping in windowless rooms, in dark rooms, in cellars and basements, in attics, in rooms many times illegally overcrowded.[5] And out of the housing investigations that have been made in Chicago, and there have been a number of those

[4] This is not meant to be an argument in support of immigration restriction. It is merely taking note of the fact that in the old days of "free immigration" when we had no adequate protective organization for recently arrived immigrants, these newcomers were one explanation of the important tenement-house problem of lodgers. The Chicago group who have been responsible for these studies were staunch supporters of a liberal immigration policy when the question of immigration restriction was still a public issue. But this group also wanted an active public immigration commission to mitigate the hardships of the new arrivals (see e.g., E. Abbott, "Immigration Legislation and the Problems of Assimilation," *Proceedings of the National Conference of Social Work, Toronto, 1924*, pp. 82–91).

[5] See the statement of the New York Court of Appeals in the recent decision, *New York City Housing Authority* v. *Muller et al.*, 1 North Eastern Reporter (2d) 153; 270 N.Y. 333 (1936), in which condemnation of certain slum property is upheld because the facts found were that "in certain areas of cities in the State there exist unsanitary and substandard housing conditions owing to overcrowding and concentration of population, improper planning, excessive land coverage, lack of proper light, air and space, unsanitary design and arrangement, or lack of proper sanitary facilities; that there is not an adequate supply of decent, safe, and sanitary dwelling accommodations for persons of low income; that these conditions cause an increase and spread of disease and crime and constitute a menace to the health, safety, morals, welfare, and comfort of the citizens of the State, and impair economic values; that these conditions cannot be remedied by the ordinary operation of private enterprise."

inquiries since the Civil War,[6] seem to come only further illustrations of the futility of such investigations.

The day-by-day misery which is often endured by the people in these homes is indescribable. In addition to the wretched structural inadequacies of the tenements and the lack of modern sanitary conveniences is the never ending struggle with house vermin. And rats in many places are really a terrible scourge.[7]

DIFFICULTIES OF ENFORCING THE TENEMENT-HOUSE CODE

For approximately thirty-five years the sanitary authorities have been trying to enforce the tenement-house law of 1902, and they have found it impossible to require expensive structural changes or to evict the unfortunate tenants for whom no better homes are available at rents they can probably afford. It is true that courageous housing reformers would have been more successful than our city officials in making the "new law" more effective, but apparently policies of this kind were long ago given up as "bad politics."

Minimum standards have been laid down in the tenement-house code regarding the size of rooms and the size of windows, but the

[6] See, e.g., *supra*, chap. i, pp. 30–33.

[7] The *Bulletin* of the Chicago Woman's City Club (March, 1934) announced that a rat-extermination program was at last in progress. From various districts of the United Charities had come so many complaints about areas being overrun with rats (in one family the baby had been bitten by a rat) that the commissioner of health secured special help from the Federal Emergency Relief Administration, which was then administering the Civil Works Program (C.W.A.). The first district selected in the campaign against rats was the area "back of the Yards," where a district of 130 blocks was selected for the beginning of the work.

"Each day 45 pounds of meat was used for rat bait. This was mixed with 5 pounds of red squill which the department has been informed is relatively harmless to children and pets. Ten men were supplied by the Civil Works Administration, Project 651, working under the supervision of the Board of Health. They were employed 32 days and placed about 102,000 pieces of this bait. Practically all premises within the above prescribed areas were baited and revisited for results. The relief obtained has been most gratifying, as is evidenced by the receipt of 95 letters from people living in this district.

"After the completion of the work in the district just mentioned, the ten men were continued in this activity by the Civil Works Administration in the vicinity of the Hull-House at 800 South Halsted Street, where they are now working. In addition, we have filed an application with the Civil Works Administration for 206 men for the purpose of continuing and enlarging the rat extermination campaign" (extract from a letter from the health commissioner published in the *Bulletin*). And see above, pp. 189–90.

Health Department seems to have found it impossible to apply these minimum standards to the dreary rows of old tenements that line one street after another in the deteriorated areas. Approximately one-fourth of the rooms visited by our investigators did not have the minimum area of 70 square feet prescribed by the ordinance, and 19 per cent did not have the minimum height of 8½ feet, with the percentage below the minimum running very much higher than this in some of the poorest housing areas. In 20 of the small districts canvassed by our investigators, 392 sleeping-rooms were entirely windowless, or had windows opening into another room and not into the outer air. There are also thousands of other rooms with inadequate light and ventilation, because the windows open upon a narrow court or passageway so small that both light and air are excluded. In the limited range of our studies, 14,090 dark and gloomy rooms were found; and of these, 980 were entirely windowless or had windows opening only into other rooms; 4,657 opened onto courts, shafts, or small porches that darkened the rooms; and 7,370 of these rooms opened onto the narrow passage or lot-line court that is the inevitable result of the old-fashioned shoestring lot.[8] Some of these buildings had shafts that could not be opened, and in others the shafts were never opened even if this were possible.

There has also been very great difficulty in enforcing the provisions of the tenement-house code regarding sanitary toilet accommodations. Since 1902 the ordinance has required a separate toilet "in a separate compartment within each apartment." Our investigators found large numbers of families without such sanitary conveniences. Approximately one-third of the families in the poorest areas do not have toilet accommodations in their apartments at all, but are still using old, insanitary yard toilets, sometimes under the sidewalks, sometimes in basements or cellars or public halls. Only a very small percentage of these families have bathrooms with running water that can be heated.

LOW WAGES AND LOW INCOMES THE BASIC DIFFICULTY

Regulations regarding the number of occupants per room are also flagrantly violated, and these miserable tenements are crowded and

[8] See *supra*, pp. 171–73, 233–35.

overcrowded far beyond the legal limit set in the tenement-house code. Of the one-room tenements in the sample areas canvassed, 5 were occupied by four persons each, and 5 others by five persons each, 1 by seven persons, and 1 by nine persons. Of the two-room apartments, 60 were occupied by four persons each; 35 by five persons each; 18 by six persons each; 2 by seven persons each; and 4 by eight persons each. There were 5,506 apartments, or 36 per cent of those canvassed, that were congested according to the Bureau of Labor Statistics standard. Using the Chicago tenement-law standard of 400 cubic feet of air for every person above twelve years of age, and 200 cubic feet of air for children under twelve, careful measurements made of 33,576 rooms used for sleeping purposes showed that 16,413, or 48.9 per cent of these rooms, were crowded beyond our legal minimum in Chicago. After the depression began and the dreadful period of "no money for rent" that was imposed upon the unemployed families on relief,[9] conditions became much worse.

In reciting these facts we are not indicting the present sanitary chiefs and Health Department officials any more than the long series of former occupants of these positions. Certainly no ordinary public official is likely to bring to the task enough "boldness and competence" to deal adequately with this difficult problem. No one of the sanitary officials has known what to tell these poor tenants to do. The people cannot pay the rents that are asked for better and larger homes. Household congestion, as we have said, is a condition that comes from scarcity of decent apartments at rents that are low enough to be within the purchasing range of the great mass of earners, and other low-income family groups.[10]

[9] See chap. xv, "The Rent Moratorium and Housing Deterioration."

[10] See the important statement by Senator Wagner of New York before the Senate Committee on Education and Labor, 74th Cong., 2d sess. (*Hearings*), on S. 4424, April 20–29, 1936, when the Housing Act for 1936 was under consideration. Senator Wagner pointed out that "at the present time, about 18,000,000 families in America, or 60 per cent of the nation, have incomes of not more than $1,000 a year. This means they can spend only $200 to $250 a year for rent. But taking the country as whole, at least $315 per year is necessary to provide a family of five with 3½ rooms of decent and sanitary quarters, at an average rate of $7.50 per room per month. The provision of safe and sanitary housing for low-income groups is thus a distinct and separate problem in its own right. By universal admission, it cannot be mixed, either administratively or substantively, with reorganizing the mortgage market, or stimulating the flow of credit into profit-seeking construction for the well-to-do. By universal admission, it requires partial public financial support to remedy a threatening social and economic evil."

MAP IX

PROPORTION OF POPULATION RECEIVING RELIEF IN CHICAGO BY SUB-COMMUNITIES OCTOBER, 1934

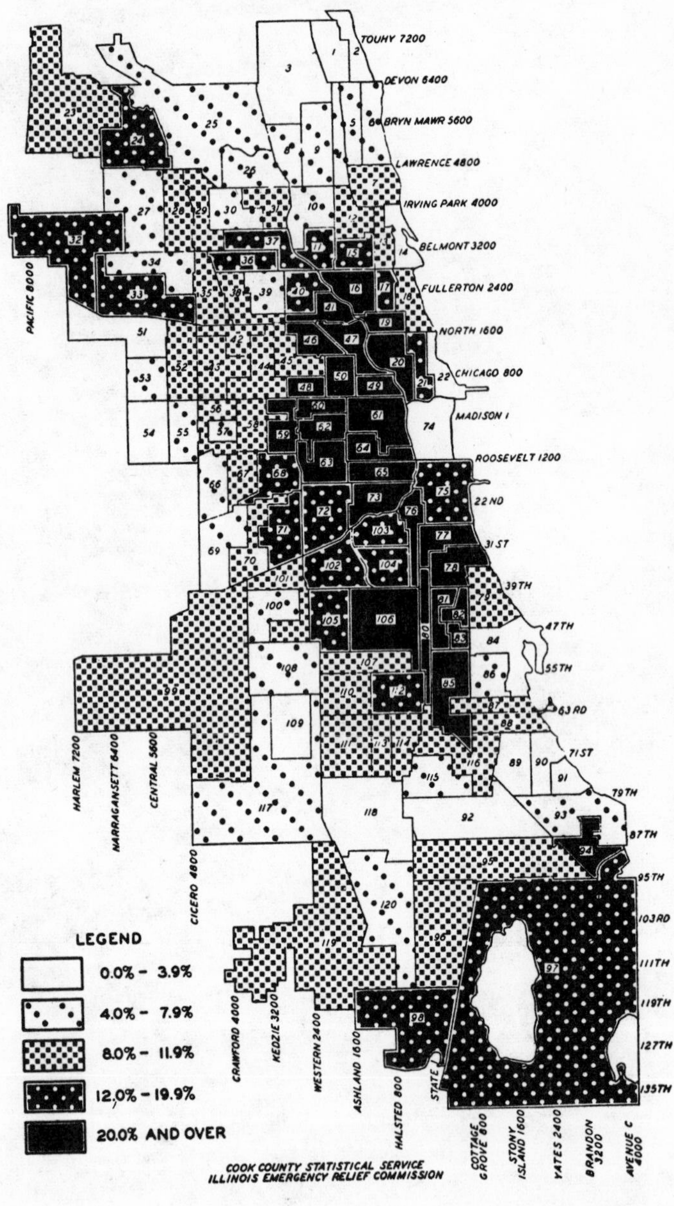

Bad housing and slums, therefore, remain together as one of the consequences of low wages, and it is difficult to see how, even if slums are abolished, they can be kept from reappearing unless people have adequate earnings to pay adequate rents. A permanent housing subsidy is probably the only alternative. Bad housing goes back to the same cause as poor and insufficient food. But bad housing is more obvious, a reproach to city pride, while underfed people can be more easily kept out of sight. The great poverty of the people in the tenement areas is shown in the Chicago relief map prepared by the Illinois Emergency Relief Commission (Map IX). Here the areas of relief are the old tenement districts—the old "river wards," the industrial areas which have been in recent years centers of the unemployed, the neglected Negro areas of the South Side, and other crowded neighborhoods, many of which have already been described.

DEMOLITION OF ABANDONED, INSANITARY, AND CONDEMNED HOUSES

The dilapidated condition of these old tenements has been described many times in the foregoing pages, and accounts have been given of people living in houses that are no longer fit for human habitation. Some of these houses have already been condemned and have even been vacated by official order. But only too often they are not torn down, and sooner or later even the most miserable places are reoccupied, sometimes by "squatters."[11] Renewed efforts to rid the city of vacant, dilapidated, and condemned buildings have been made in recent years, and progress in this new demolition program has been encouraging; but the great drawback to the program has

[11] See the very useful pamphlet, *Why Abandoned Buildings Should Be Demolished*, which was published recently by the Tenement House Committee of the New York Charity Organization Society. The general director of the Charity Organization Society, Mr. Stanley P. Davies, in his introductory note, describes these abandoned structures as "the moraine left in the wake of the building boom which ended in the late nineteen-twenties. They are usually located in deteriorated neighborhoods. Many of these buildings are in a deplorable condition, with electric wires, pipes, plaster and laths torn and hanging. The floors are frequently torn up and littered with rubbish and filth. Vagrants sleep in them at night. Fires which are made in them endanger adjacent buildings. Our study and follow-up of the condition of many of these abandoned structures has shown that, unless they are in a well supervised neighborhood, they cannot be effectively safeguarded from vandals. Their existence is a constant danger to the lives and morals of children who are attracted to them" (p. 2).

been its emergency and temporary character, when a long-time program is so greatly needed.

In the summer of 1929 the local newspapers announced that 538 buildings had been torn down in less than seven months.[12] This work was done by the building commissioner, who wished "to make Chicago a spotless town structurally" for the World's Fair of 1933, to celebrate Chicago's Century of Progress. The commissioner's program also called for the demolition of another 500 buildings before January 1, 1930.

In addition to the removal of the city's "dilapidated and vacant structures," the commissioner announced that he was "planning to remove thousands of occupied buildings which are unfit for use." At the same time the commissioner of health turned over to the building commissioner "a list of 200 tenements without plumbing or adequate sunlight, which, according to the bureau, are nests for tuberculosis, rickets, and other perils to children."

Efforts of the building commissioner to obtain an appropriation for this work had not been successful. Therefore, the 538 buildings that were "fire and health hazards" which were actually removed had been torn down with the consent of owners who were obliging enough to permit their removal on request, or the Fire Department had been able to co-operate in removing the old "two-story shacks."

But the most persistent efforts at demolition have come since the depression. In March, 1934, the new State Housing Board undertook as a "work-relief project" a survey of the buildings reported vacant by the recent Census Commission, and unemployed engineers were used for this survey. This corps of men visited all the buildings listed as vacant by the census, and these buildings were classified into those which should be demolished and those in need of major repairs, if they were to be again occupied. Unfit dwellings which were occupied in spite of their insanitary condition were not included in the survey. Altogether, some six thousand unoccupied buildings were put in these classes. After a building had been so classified, the title was traced and an attempt was made to get the owner's permission to tear down the building. At this time demolition was carried on as a "work-relief project," but actual supervision of the work was

[12] See, e.g., *Chicago Daily News*, August 17, 1929.

given to qualified wreckers who were willing to accept the salvage in payment for their services.

In addition to this work of the State Housing Board, the city has also been carrying on a demolition program. The mayor appointed a committee on substandard housing, with the health commissioner as chairman. This committee also set up a "work-relief project" to carry on the demolition of insanitary houses, along much the same lines as the program of the State Housing Board. Altogether, 2,232 buildings, no longer fit for use, housing approximately 6,066 family units, were demolished in a period of approximately fourteen months. However, there are grave difficulties in the way of securing the consent of the owners for the tearing-down of the dilapidated buildings which they own. As men become re-employed and vacant apartments tend to disappear, as the families who have been living with relatives under crowded conditions become able to move once more into homes of their own, new difficulties will be placed in the way of any demolition program. Abandoned buildings will once more be occupied unless large numbers of new houses are built; and landlords are usually not willing to wreck an income-producing building, whatever its sanitary or structural defects.

BAD HOUSING AND THE DEMORALIZATION OF FAMILY LIFE

What effect do bad living conditions actually have on the lives of the poor? It is impossible to say—so interwoven are all the difficulties of human beings whose lives are a constant struggle to maintain reasonably decent homes on the small earnings of the poor. Speaking recently at a congressional hearing on this subject, Senator Wagner said that attempting to discuss the housing problem comprehensively was like "tearing a seamless web." "There is hardly any phase of human endeavor," he said, "that is not affected by the conditions under which people live"; and he also reminded the Senate Committee that "bad housing leaves its permanent scars upon the minds and bodies of the young and this is transmitted as a social liability from generation to generation."[13]

In Chicago these "permanent scars" were illustrated not so long ago by the case of a man who was sentenced to our Illinois State

[13] U.S. Senate Hearings, *op. cit.*, p. 13.

Penitentiary.[14] He was the father of six children. The eldest child stayed with the grandparents, while the man and his wife slept with five other children in one room. A quarrel arose one night over the lighting of the kerosene lamp in the squalid home. The quarrel in which children and parents participated ended with the father violent. He shot his wife and a child, and the latter died. This was an exceptional situation, of course, and not a typical one, but every social worker who goes in and out of the poor homes on the mean streets of the city can furnish story after story of the demoralization of family life because of the misery of housing conditions.

Statistical tables portray very inadequately the discomforts and inconveniences of living in old frame tenements with old-fashioned coal stoves, with kerosene lamps, no bath, and an outside toilet. If the facts about the wretched tenements so many scores of thousands of our people call "home" could be adequately collected, tabulated, and published, these conditions could not be tolerated. The great mass of people want decent living conditions for all, fair play, and a fair chance even for the Negro and for the poorest Mexican immigrant. "There is no lack of sympathy or good will in the world." What has been lacking is a better understanding of what living conditions among the people really are and the ways in which they may be improved.[15]

The people who live in these dilapidated and insanitary houses more than do their part. With everything against them, in wretched buildings grimy and unpainted, there is usually a cheerful effort to maintain a wholesome cleanliness. Very often one finds fresh curtains at the windows, clean newspapers on the table, bits of carpet on worn floors. One of our investigators told of a very poor Greek

[14] See the *Chicago Tribune*, January 10 and 11, 1929.

[15] See the opinion of the New York Court of Appeals in the Muller case (*op. cit.*), where the court said that "the public evils, social and economic, of such conditions are unquestioned and unquestionable. Slum areas are the breeding places of disease which take toll not only from denizens but, by spread, from the inhabitants of the entire city and State.

"Juvenile delinquency, crime and immorality are there born, find protection and flourish.

"Enormous economic loss results directly from the necessary expenditure of public funds to maintain health and hospital services for afflicted slum dwellers and to war against crime and immorality.

"Indirectly, there is an equally heavy capital loss and a diminishing return in taxes because of the areas blighted by the existence of the slums."

painter who, in a crowded, deteriorated neighborhood, during a period of unemployment calcimined the walls of his rented apartment, and decorated them with elaborate stencilings, because he "liked to see things look nice." It is not easy to keep a house orderly when everything is so crowded and so poor. But where there are women and children, the old houses often become good homes, with a brave attempt to maintain decent conditions through the constant efforts put forth by the mothers in the tenements.

Nearly one hundred years ago the great novelist Charles Dickens who understood so well the joys, hopes, miseries, and defeats of the great masses of people, wrote in the Preface to one of the editions of *Oliver Twist* that he was "well convinced that nothing effectual" could be done to improve the lot of the poor until their homes were made "decent and wholesome." He added that he had long been convinced that "this reform must precede all other great reforms; that it must prepare the way for education, even for religion"; and that without removing this blot of bad housing, people "become so desperate," and are "made so miserable as to bear within themselves the certain seed of ruin of the whole community."

There has been great progress in providing new homes in England and in some of the Continental countries by various public authorities, especially since the war. But the problem is so vast that the task of properly rehousing the poor who still live under wretched housing conditions seems to remain almost insuperable.[16] To say that the problem is unsolvable is to listen to the counsel of despair. But it is true that the problem can be solved only in the long future, with the immediate steps piecemeal, and almost insignificant in results.

[16] See complaints by members of the Labour party in their numerous publications; and see Hugh Quigley and Ismay Goldie, *Housing and Slum Clearance in London* (London, 1934); and see Catherine Bauer's *Modern Housing*, in which as a result of her careful housing studies in Europe, she says that although "perhaps 30,000,000 people throughout Europe have been housed in a much better sort of environment than any but a very few of them could have hoped to find before the war, ... the slums still stand, many of them more crowded now than they were five years ago. Only a comparatively small portion of the new dwellings actually reaches the lowest income-group, and the matter of housing the unemployed has hardly been approached. In every country, moreover, there has been the difficulty that houses which average workers could pay for in 1930 are entirely beyond their means at present. The housing problem can never be solved by itself: in final analysis it depends on the distribution of purchasing power" (p. 135). See also the *Social Service Review* (University of Chicago Press), **X**, 135–36.

Here in Chicago our problem has both encouraging and very discouraging aspects—encouraging because we are finally to share with other cities in the federal public housing program, and areas have been selected in different parts of the city for at least three large housing projects.[17] These projects are largely on vacant lands with only a very small area from which old tenements are being cleared, so that condemnation difficulties have been avoided. Although these new housing projects have not helped to "clear the slums," any new tenement areas of this kind will give an impetus to better building and will set new and better standards before us as to what can be done in the way of improved housing plans. That is, although the new federal housing projects care for only a very small percentage,

[17] The most important of these projects which are being built in Chicago by the Housing Division of the Public Works Administration have been very fittingly called the "Jane Addams Houses" and the "Julia C. Lathrop Homes," in honor of Chicago's two great social pioneers. The Jane Addams Houses are located only a few blocks from Hull-House. This project, which is now in process of construction, will consist of three-story apartment buildings and two-story group houses. They will contain 304 family living units, of two, three, four, and five rooms. The buildings themselves will cover only about 25 per cent of the six-acre tract of land just south of Vernon Park that formerly belonged to the Jewish People's Institute. The rest of the area will be left open; a part of it will be planted with trees, shrubbery, and grass; and parts will be reserved for playgrounds and gardens. The buildings will be of the most modern construction, fireproof and sanitary. They will have ample light and air. All rooms will be outside rooms. Each living unit will have its separate bath and toilet facilities; kitchens and dining-rooms in the larger apartments, and in the smaller apartments, kitchens and dining-rooms combined. Each apartment will have running water, hot and cold. Heat will be furnished from a central heating plant. Gas stoves and electric refrigerators will be furnished.

In addition to this development on the vacant land of the old Institute grounds, the government purchased some fifteen acres of adjoining property to insure proper surroundings for the new project. Here the old buildings are being demolished and the land will be used for additional housing, similar to that of the Jane Addams Houses, except that there will be more open space for park and recreation purposes. The federal government has allotted $6,950,000 for this project, which will accommodate a total of 981 families, or, assuming an average of four to a family, nearly 4,000 persons.

The second of the federal housing developments is again very properly named after the other great Hull-House resident and will be called the "Julia C. Lathrop Homes," on the North Side, at Diversey Parkway and Clybourn Avenue, to house 975 families, for which $6,000,000 was allotted. The third will be called the "Trumbull Park Homes," for 462 families, at One Hundred and Third Street and Bensley Avenue, in South Chicago, estimated to cost $3,250,000. The sites of these two projects were selected with relation to centers of employment of large numbers of industrial workers.

Land is being acquired for a site for a fourth project on the South Side in a district occupied by Negroes.

Courtesy of Federal Emergency Administration of Public Works Housing Division

JANE ADDAMS HOUSES, CHICAGO

perhaps one-tenth of 1 per cent of the great numbers of people in need of new and decent homes, nevertheless the new projects, in spite of their inadequacy as regards number of families to be cared for, still have the great merit of furnishing "a visible object lesson" in modern housing reform at federal expense. A socially minded journalist has suggested that if the people in the slums have even a small object lesson like this before them, "one taste of genuine rehousing at low rentals," they will become politically articulate and "supply the political force" necessary for more adequate and more vigorous re-housing plans.[18]

Moreover, the beneficial results of caring for even a few families in new, low-cost homes is a substantial achievement in the right direction. But, in the meantime, the vast work of slum clearance still remains. Our studies have shown that in some of the tenement districts most of the houses are still the old frame tenements that belong to Chicago's early days of industrial pioneering. In several of the deteriorated areas canvassed by our investigators more than two-thirds of all the buildings were of old frame construction, and in a few areas from 80 to 90 per cent of the buildings were frame.

What is the way out? Certainly, there is no single path of reform and none that will serve as an easy road to slum abolition. There are various remedies proposed, but discussion now centers too exclusively on the provision of new buildings, in part because through new building it is hoped to revive the building industry and employ the unemployed.[19]

New buildings to replace the tenements of the slums are and have

[18] See one of the pamphlets published by the National Public Housing Conference entitled *Land Prices and the Courts* by Irving Brant.

[19] In the 1935 report of the National Association of Housing Officials, "A Housing Program for the United States," attention is called in the first paragraph to one of the outstanding difficulties of the present situation This is that "the building of houses for the lower income groups, and the clearing of slums, have been adopted by the United States government as means of providing work for the unemployed and stimulating the construction industries." No emergency program will meet the needs of a great housing program, and the most exigent demand today is for "a permanent and effective remedy for the slum evils, and for the deficiency of satisfactory housing accommodations for the lower income groups." That is, it is clear that, if it is to be effective, "the present emergency program must evolve into a more complete and permanent effort to deal with the whole problem of securing an adequate standard of housing for all."

long been imperatively needed. But they are needed on such a very grand scale and they have been so slow in coming that too much hope cannot be placed in this single plan of reform.[20]

A revolution in the building industry is also prophesied, with new and cheaper home-building—but revolutions of this kind also come slowly. And in the meantime, poor people continue to live as best they can in these obsolete buildings, sick people and old people are subjected to indescribable discomforts, and children are born in these dirty, crowded, insanitary quarters. Out of 58,000 births in Chicago, in a recent year, 20,739 were born in homes and not in hospitals or institutions. These were, many of them, the poorest of the poor whose children are born, and many of them die, in these crowded insanitary places.

FOUR LINES OF ATTACK NECESSARY

If we are to get rid of these old frame tenements, cheerless and uncomfortable alike in the fierce heat of summer and the bitter cold of winter, the attack should continue to be made along four different fronts:[21] (1) new building on vacant land where land values are cheap; (2) new building to accompany slum clearance even where land has a high speculative value. And this involves rent subsidies, for many of the slums are important in location for the workers; (3) better tenement-house laws and a continuous, vigorous drive for a vastly

[20] In his statement before the Senate Committee to which his Housing Bill of 1936 had been referred, Senator Wagner said that "when we consider the long-time deficit that has accumulated, the existence of unhealthful quarters that must be replaced, and normal growth in the future, it is very conservatively estimated that the country needs at least 10,000,000 new family units during the next 10 years."

[21] This volume has been necessarily limited to the conditions of the tenements of Chicago. No comprehensive study has been made of the large subject of modern housing plans and policies. There are now, fortunately, many new and some very excellent books on this subject. See, e.g., *Modern Housing*, by Catherine Bauer (1934); *Rehousing Urban America*, by Henry Wright (1935); *Housing America*, by the editors of *Fortune* (1932); *Housing Problems and Possibilities in the United States*, by Frank Watson (1935); *Rebuilding of Blighted Areas*, by Clarence Perry and Earl Morrow (1933), and other volumes in the magnificent series of the New York Regional Plan Association; and see the series of volumes published by the President's Conference on Home Building and Home Ownership (1931), and numerous other recent volumes published in recent years. Some of the excellent magazine articles should not be overlooked, such as the series of *New Republic* articles reprinted in the valuable small booklet, *New Homes for a New Deal*, by Albert Mayer, Henry Wright, and Lewis Mumford.

better enforcement of the tenement-house ordinances we have. Many old buildings would certainly be given up as too costly for maintenance if we had a vigorous, intelligent, fearless inspection system and a really enforceable order went forth that the old houses must be made to conform to legal standards supposedly required for new-law houses as long ago as 1902. A well-known housing expert once said that housing laws could not be regarded as self-operative. "Housing evils will not vanish of their own accord. The causes which have led to them are too deep-seated to permit anything so simple." When the community conscience has been sufficiently aroused to demand changes in the content of the law, it is little short of tragic not to make possible its enforcement. And finally (4) the old houses in which people must continue to live for a long time to come must be made more decently habitable by various methods of repair and reconditioning, since they will not all be abolished in any reasonably near future.[22]

PRIVATE HOUSING PROGRAMS INADEQUATE

One thing is clear: no real solution will come through private housing companies.[23] There is no desire here to minimize the importance of much of the work of the new housing companies and

[22] See e.g., the report of the Moyne Committee to the British Parliament (Cmd. 4397, London, 1933), which emphasizes the necessity of repairs and reconditioning, since even the most extensive slum-clearance plans still leave so much to be done.

Some housing reformers call the reconditioned homes "ancient tenements, cast-off hand-me-downs," but the social worker's point of view is that no possible method of improvement, however small, should be neglected, so long as it does not interfere with the more constructive large-scale improvements. While the latter are on the way, much can and should be done to make the old tenements more decent and livable.

[23] See, again, Senator Wagner's testimony (*op. cit.*, p. 18). "Experience indicates that these limited-profit companies cannot get rents down anywhere low enough to satisfy the needs of the lowest income groups."

See also the important statement made by the New York Court of Appeals in the Muller case already cited in this chapter. The Court said: "The menace of the slums in New York City has already been long recognized as serious enough to warrant public action. The session laws for nearly seventy years are sprinkled with acts applying the taxing power and the police power in attempts to cure or check it.

"The slums still stand. The menace still exists. What objections, then, can be urged to the application of the third power, least drastic, but, as here embodied, probably the most effective of all?

"It is said that private enterprise, curbed by restrictive legislation under the police

model housing estates of many kinds[24] in improving housing conditions for limited groups in the population, and providing new and useful experiments in replanning and rehousing. But the difficulty is that these private housing developments do not reach the poorest sections of the population. The low wage of the workers means that rents cannot be paid which will make building profitable for any association or for any individual who may try to house the low-income group. An English authority has said, and what he said applies also to us in America, "We have slums for the same reason that we have industrial depression, unemployment, and poverty. The enterprise of private owners cannot give us a new [metropolis] .... not because property-owners are wicked, but because, if private profit is the decisive test, those who own them cannot afford to rebuild the houses of the poor, and cannot afford to reopen workshops and factories, however much they may want to. The community can afford prosperity; the individual cannot."

The statement regarding "findings and policy" in the bill providing for the United States Housing Act[25] which was introduced by

---

power, is adequate and alone appropriate. There is some authority to that effect in other States. A sufficient answer should be the page of legislative history in this State and its result referred to above. Legislation merely restrictive in its nature has failed because the evil inheres not so much in this or that individual structure as in the character of a whole neighborhood of dilapidated and unsanitary structures. To eliminate the inherent evil and to provide housing facilities at low cost—the two things necessarily go together—require large-scale operations which can be carried out only where there is power to deal *in invitum* with the occasional greedy owner seeking excessive profit by holding out. The cure is to be wrought, not through the regulated ownership of the individual, but through the ownership and operation by or under the direct control of the public itself. Nor is there anything novel in that. The modern city functions in the public interest as proprietor and operator of many activities formerly, and in some instances still, carried on by private enterprise."

[24] E.g., in Chicago, the Julius Rosenwald Housing Development for Negroes on the South Side and the Marshall Field Houses on the North Side.

[25] Senate Bill 4424 (74th Cong. 2d sess. [April 3, 1936]), which is called a bill "to provide financial assistance to the States and political subdivisions thereof for the elimination of unsafe and insanitary housing conditions, for the development of decent, safe, and sanitary dwellings for families of low income, and for the reduction of unemploy-

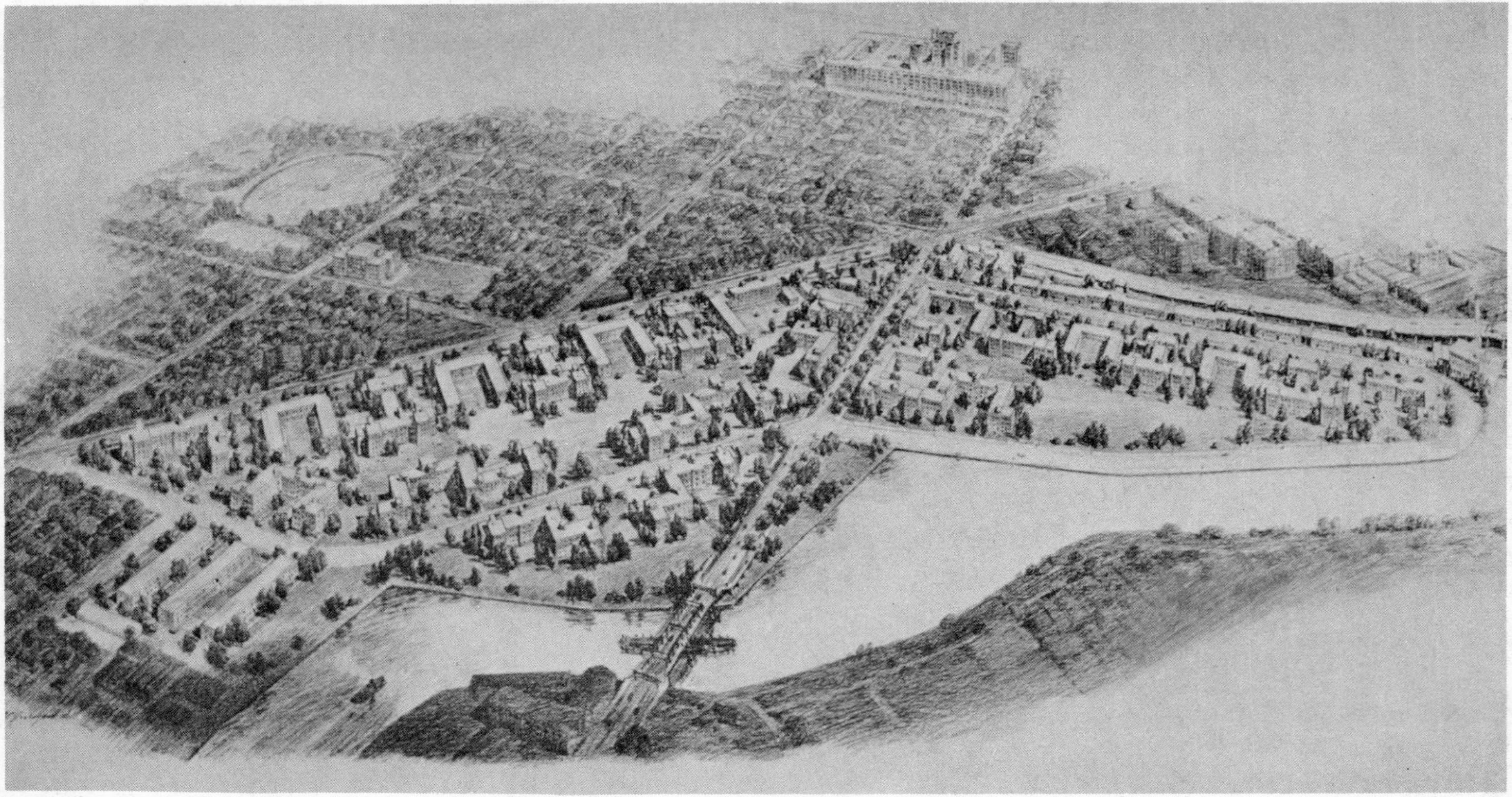

Courtesy of Federal Emergency Administration of Public Works Housing Division

JULIA C. LATHROP HOMES, CHICAGO

Senator Wagner in 1936 contains an authoritative paragraph stating briefly the case against the theory that it is possible to depend upon private housing companies and private enterprises of any kind to clear the slums.

The first section of this bill, introduced by one of the most influential men in the United States Senate, begins by pointing out that "there exist in urban and rural communities throughout the United States, slums, blighted areas, or unsafe, insanitary, or overcrowded dwellings, or a combination of these conditions, accompanied and aggravated by an acute shortage of decent, safe, and sanitary dwellings within the financial reach of families of low income."[26]

This important federal bill then clearly states that "private industry alone" has been and is now "unable to overcome the obstacles in the way of relieving the shortage of decent, safe, and sanitary dwellings for families of low income."

FEDERAL AID

The housing problem is not only too vast for private industry alone; it is also too vast for local authorities to deal with adequately and continuously. Senator Wagner's proposed housing act also stated clearly that "the several States and their political subdivi-

---

ment and the stimulation of business activity, to create a United States Housing Authority, and for other purposes."

And see also the earlier Senate Bill 2392 (74th Cong., 1st sess. [1935]). This bill, which, like the 1936 bill, failed of passage, was described in the title as "a bill to promote the public health, safety, and welfare by providing for the elimination of insanitary and dangerous housing conditions, to relieve congested areas, to aid in the construction and supervision of low-rental dwelling accommodations, and to further national industrial recovery through the employment of labor and materials."

[26] The bill further recites: "These conditions are inimical to the general welfare of the Nation, by encouraging the spread of disease and lowering the level of health, morale, and vitality of large portions of the American people; increasing the hazards of fires, accidents, and natural calamities; subjecting the moral standards of the young to bad influences; increasing the violation of the criminal laws of the United States and of the several States; impairing industrial and agricultural productive efficiency; lowering the standards of living of large portions of the American people; necessitating a vast and extraordinary expenditure of public funds, Federal, State, and local, for crime prevention, punishment and correction, fire prevention, public-health service, and relief."

sions have been and now are unable adequately to aid in remedying this condition without financial assistance." It is therefore declared to be the policy of the federal government to employ its funds and credit "to assist the several States and their political subdivisions to alleviate unemployment and to remedy the unsafe and insanitary housing conditions and the acute shortage of decent, safe, and sanitary dwellings for families of low income that are injurious to the health, safety, and morals of the citizens of the Nation."

It is necessary to face the fact that the housing problem is very difficult to solve and that even vigorous efforts to secure new and better homes bring small results. The New York figure which has been carefully worked out is that "even in so-called prosperous times two-thirds of the population of New York could not . . . . afford to rent decent, up-to-date quarters." Chicago is not unlike New York in the vast extent of the slum areas. Public housing—and public housing on a very large scale—will be necessary to meet the situation. More than that, this public housing policy must be a national policy, with federal funds available for a large-scale housing program. But even if public opinion were in favor of a large-scale housing program with federal aid, even then a very long period of time would be required to carry through the new program. The Wagner Bill of 1936 has failed like the similar Housing Bill of 1935, but the great need for decent homes for the workers will inevitably lead to the adoption of such a housing program in the not too distant future.

In spite of the fact that there has been a new interest in the housing problem in recent years and new leadership by national authorities, there is a long and discouraging way to go. President Roosevelt, in his social-security message to Congress, in January, 1935, said that security for the individual involved three factors, and the first of these was "decent homes to live in." But the question how to get these homes actually built for the poorest people who are now occupying the outlawed houses of the slum areas, remains an exigent social problem.

The final answer, if and when it comes, to the ever present housing question must come from the economic side. The unskilled workers even in periods of prosperity do not have the wages to pay for decent houses. The employer must pay higher wages, or very wide areas must be cleared and very great numbers of new houses must be furnished out of taxes. There is no other way. Shelter must be subsidized on a really vast scale if the slums are to be cleared and the workers are to have homes maintained on a modern basis. There may be a new day dawning on the darkness of the housing problem, but there is very little light visible as yet.

INDEX

PRINTED IN U.S.A.